Struggle and Survival
in Palestine/Israel

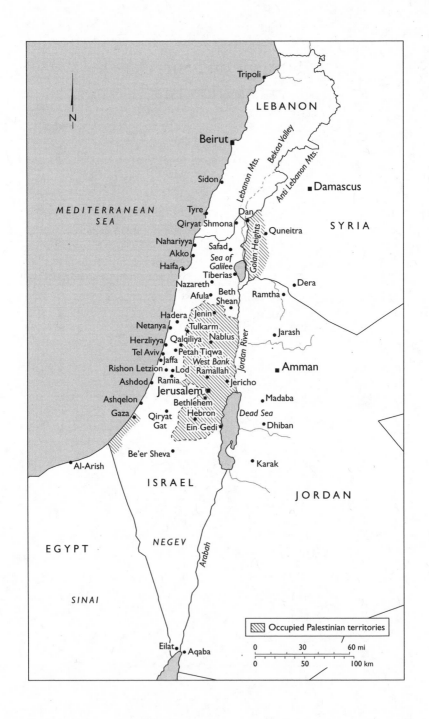

Struggle and Survival in Palestine/Israel

Edited by

Mark LeVine and Gershon Shafir

UNIVERSITY OF CALIFORNIA PRESS

Berkeley   Los Angeles   London

University of California Press, one of the most distinguished university presses in the United States, enriches lives around the world by advancing scholarship in the humanities, social sciences, and natural sciences. Its activities are supported by the UC Press Foundation and by philanthropic contributions from individuals and institutions. For more information, visit www.ucpress.edu.

University of California Press
Berkeley and Los Angeles, California

University of California Press, Ltd.
London, England

Library of Congress Cataloging-in-Publication Data

Struggle and survival in Palestine/Israel / edited by Mark LeVine and Gershon Shafir.
   p. cm.
Includes bibliographical references and index.
ISBN 978-0-520-26252-2 (cloth : alk. paper)
ISBN 978-0-520-26253-9 (pbk. : alk. paper)
   1. Palestine—History—1799–1917. 2. Palestine—History—1917-1948. 3. Palestine—Social conditions—19th century. 4. Palestine—Economic conditions—19th century. 5. Palestine—Social conditions—20th century. 6. Palestine—Economic conditions—20th century. 7. Cities and towns—Palestine—History. 8. Jews—Palestine—History—19th century. 9. Jews—Palestine—History—20th century. 10. Palestinian Arabs—History—19th century. 11. Palestinian Arabs—History—20th century. 12. Arab-Israeli conflict—Influence. I. LeVine, Mark Andrew, 1966– II. Shafir, Gershon.
   DS125.S77   2012
   956.94—dc23

2012006363

Manufactured in the United States of America

21 20 19 18 17 16 15 14 13 12
10 9 8 7 6 5 4 3 2 1

In keeping with a commitment to support environmentally responsible and sustainable printing practices, UC Press has printed this book on Rolland Enviro100, a 100% post-consumer fiber paper that is FSC certified, deinked, processed chlorine-free, and manufactured with renewable biogas energy. It is acid-free and EcoLogo certified.

To Alessandro, Francesca, Elliot, and Asher, for the stories they have yet to tell

CONTENTS

FOREWORD

It is with great pleasure that I welcome Mark LeVine and Gershon Shafir's *Struggle and Survival in Palestine/Israel* to the library of works in the emerging genre of social biography. At a time when many are frozen in place by fear of change and outdated ideologies, this book offers a wealth of portraits of individuals—Jews, Muslims, Christians, others—caught in the talons of history. The more we focus on individual lives, I believe, the less convincing the standard narratives of the Israel/Palestine drama become and the more the common humanity of all of the participants is evident. How and why people did things, as well as the often unforeseen consequences of their actions, are not readily explained by the standard toolbox of the social sciences. By plunging us into the biographies of ordinary (and not so ordinary) Israeli and Palestinian men and women, this book provides a salutary alternative to the limitations of structural approaches (the state, the economy, culture) to the tangled history of Israel/Palestine. LeVine and Shafir provide us with a varied canvas of human interactions that constitutes the backdrop of the present impasse.

Upon consideration, the choices individuals make under duress turn out to be far more imaginative, and their consequences more far reaching, than is generally appreciated. The individuals whose lives are recounted in this book pose a continual challenge to not just our historical but also our moral imaginations. Thus the sudden decision to resist authority (whether the colonial or the postcolonial state), like the rustling of butterfly wings that gives birth to a typhoon, can have enormous unforeseen historical consequences. The survivor who becomes an oppressor, the Palestinian peasant who undergoes multiple exiles—these are paradigmatic experiences too, even as they are individual destinies. So are the interconnections of individual Israeli and Palestinian lives through friendship and antagonism, dependency and superiority.

While the authors of the individual life stories contained in these pages are scrupulously aware of the deep ironies that often underlie their subjects, there is also no turning away from a recognition that the separate power spheres in which the lives of Israelis and Palestinians evolve and revolve have shaped different chances for all. In this sense, power, both political and personal, structures the lives of all of the protagonists. Even the least-advantaged Israelis have recourse to the authorities and the state in ways that have bestowed upon them options superior to those of the great majority of Palestinian men and women, just as some Palestinians have enjoyed more fortunate personal and political endowments than others.

Many of the biographies gathered here are haunted by the contrast between individuals' early expectations and how their lives actually unfolded after massive historical changes disrupted long-meditated calculations. Others provide examples of how disastrous events have given rise to stubborn refusals to bow down. In the process we learn that experiences of sociological marginalization cannot explain human outcomes, even though such experiences may exact a stiff price. Nor is being a member of a group a reliable predictor of behavior. A consideration of the human stories contained in this volume undermines the standard "who did what to whom first" narrative according to which different sides have sought to establish their position as superior. Rather than shaped by stable moral binaries, the protagonists are better understood as driven by different, often shifting subjectivities that can be (and often are) out of step with dominant ideologies and expectations. If readers emerge from these pages with a lively sense of the humanity of all sides, this book will have accomplished its mission.

Social biography, by introducing us to the intersubjectivity that underlies all human interactions, has the potential to help us to see what Foucault, in *The Birth of the Clinic* (1973), called the very conditions of possibility of the contemporary world. People trump politics every time.

Edmund Burke III

Introduction

Social Biographies in Making Sense of History

Gershon Shafir and Mark LeVine

Just as ordinary people live in the shadows, so their life stories commonly remain obscure. Yet their lives frequently reveal a great deal of humanity and wisdom, as well as the harshness and brutality of everyday life, which rarely take center stage within conventional historical narratives.

In the past few decades, the importance of life histories in the analysis and teaching of history has slowly grown. Still, it is unusual at the modern research university to teach and study social sciences through life histories or social biographies. These disciplines commonly focus on distant forces that shape individual lives; it is rare for social scientists to acknowledge ordinary men and women as actors in their own right.

But this emphasis on impersonal social forces periodically generates a profound unease, out of which emerge alternative approaches to studying human societies. These include oral history (Dunaway and Baum 1996; Portelli 1991), life course or cohort analysis (Barteaux 1981; Shanahan and Macmillan 2008; Weymann and Heinz 1996), greater reliance on ethnography (Burawoy 1991), and other methodologies aimed at getting to the details of human social interaction too often missed by the system-level analyses usually employed by scholars. Edmund Burke III's authoritative *Struggle and Survival in the Modern Middle East*, first published in 1993 and now in its second edition, has done more than most to bring the importance of life histories and social biographies to the attention of scholars, students, and

We would like to thank Sarah Farmer, Salim Tamari, Sandy Sufian, Erin F. Olsen, Roddey Reid, and Michael Shalev for their thoughtful comments, Niels Hooper for his steady support for this project, and Juliana Froggatt for her dedicated attention to the manuscript.

1

the educated public alike. In this volume, we offer an anthology of Palestinian and Israeli social biographies inspired by Burke's seminal collection.

MOVING BEYOND NOAH'S ARK

To anticipate a criticism that is likely to be leveled against this anthology, let us repeat Burke's forewarning in *Struggle and Survival in the Modern Middle East*: "Despite an energetic effort to cast the net as widely as possible, not all groups are represented within these pages." In fact, as he wittily concludes, given the diversity of the subject matter, "a kind of Noah's ark principle of coverage" is out of the question. Instead, like Burke before us, we have striven to assemble a "not entirely random selection of biographies [to] provide a set of core samples" (Burke 1993: 2) which highlight, in our view, the major social and historical processes at the heart of Palestinian-Israeli conflict and peacemaking, and the myriad ways in which they have been experienced.

These pages offer a broad range of individuals' stories, from as many groups, subgroups, and subgroups of subgroups for which we could find an author able and willing to write. But although our anthology is extensive enough to illustrate diversity, it is insufficient to document the full range. If we have learned anything from collecting these stories, it's that the work of documenting the past and present richness and complexity of the two societies is still in its infancy.

There is another reason not to become despondent over our failure to assemble a comprehensive Israeli and Palestinian Noah's ark. One of the intriguing findings that cut across many of the life histories in this anthology is that individuals are rarely typical representatives of their respective groups (more about this below). While creating a representative sample was unworkable, it also does not appear desirable.

With three exceptions, the chapters contained here were prepared specifically for this volume by noted historians, anthropologists, sociologists, political scientists, and other scholars of Israeli and/or Palestinian societies. The contributors variously relied on verbally transmitted tales that have withstood the ravages of time, letters exhumed from old boxes or family archives, interviews with their subjects, and diaries or published memoirs. They transformed personal narratives into social biographies by exploring how the protagonists were embedded in but also empowered by their immediate as well as broader social and historical context.

We asked our contributors to choose as their subject an individual whom they encountered as part of their fieldwork or research and who left a distinctive impression on them. Most of the chapters tell the stories of ordinary people, people not reported on the pages of history. Three authors wrote the biographies of close relatives. We have also included the biographies of several individuals, such as

S. Yizhar (see chapter 5), Tawfiq Canaan (see chapter 6), and Hillel Kook (see chapter 9), who at one point were well known but became less so as their convictions or the circumstances around them changed and their significance was forgotten.

In contrast to Burke's focus on individuals, several of our chapters are collective social biographies: the story of the village of Aylut in late Ottoman times (see chapter 1), the interlocking fates of the village of Burin and the Yitzhar settlement in the West Bank (see chapter 18), and the account of the Handala Cultural Center at the Beit Jibrin refugee camp (see chapter 25). Two of the chapters follow the protagonist through their engagement with specific media. We get to know Ruth Shapira, the owner of an erstwhile Palestinian house in the Abu Tur neighborhood of Eastern Jerusalem, via her entanglement with material possession and dispossession (see chapter 16), and Mais, a Palestinian teenager, through her relationship with the medium of language—Arabic and Hebrew, as well as the languages of conflict and reconciliation (see chapter 23). These social and material biographies provide enrichment and nuance to an already complex narrative while offering insights into an expanded palette of methodologies and domains of contestation.

REDEFINING *STRUGGLE AND SURVIVAL* IN A BROADER SOCIOCULTURAL ENVIRONMENT

Struggle and Survival in the Modern Middle East appeared just a few years after the publication of James Scott's seminal *Weapons of the Weak: Everyday Forms of Peasant Resistance.* Scott's book built on the pioneering work of subaltern studies scholars to explore previously unrecognized ways in which peasants and other subaltern social groups resisted exploitation and oppression by states and more powerful social and economic groups within a capitalist and/or colonial environment. Yet if Burke's title evokes the kind of resistance theorized by subaltern studies scholars, his approach is less bound by the specific theoretical paradigms that define the parameters of resistance for them (Scott 1985). Though almost three-quarters of Burke's twenty-five chapters explore working-class or peasant lives, he also focuses on wider fields of power that allow "individuals [to] navigate amidst social structures, processes and cultural interactions . . . in which terms are constantly shifting over time" (Burke 1993: 6).

Our volume extends Burke's field of vision ever wider beyond the "informal" and "hidden" modes of struggle that Scott explored. For a century in Israel/Palestine, struggle has been very much a public affair between the two national communities. Israeli Jews of either working or middle class, whether refugees, immigrants, or native-born, have been privileged by their citizenship rights in their state, whereas Palestinians, regardless of their socioeconomic status, have been marked out by the loss of their majority status in Palestine, by their group's dispersal, and by many forms of absence: the lack of citizenship for refugees even in the majority of Arab states, the curtailment of national life under military occupation in Gaza and the West Bank, and, in Israel, the relegation to second- or third-class citizens as non-Jews. For Palestinians, being defined by absence means that both survival and struggle have taken on distinct characteristics.

The fearful asymmetry in the relation of forces and in methods of struggle has powerfully inflected the life story and narrative of every Arab, Jewish, and other inhabitant of Palestine and Israel during the past century and a half.

And so, compared with Burke, we offer more life histories of middle-class individuals, all of whom are engaged in national affirmation and contestation. Life histories of struggle and survival neither need nor should be reduced exclusively to social class. Survival can mean mere physical endurance but can also encompass the persistence of identities and social relations in new contexts that are not always grounded in or defined by outright exploitation. In fact, focusing solely on the class dimension would obscure the fact that the survival of Palestinian national identity in the wake of exile and fragmentation is a central narrative thread of Palestinian history.

Similarly, the attempts to forge an Israeli nation with the immigrants of many continents is a key axis around which the Israeli narrative revolves. The literary, psychological, political, and other dimensions of both struggle and survival warrant equal attention as they play out against the larger narratives of national conflict and economic struggle and exploitation. Yet in pointing this out, we are again reminded that however broad the spectrum of struggle within and between the two communities, any possible calculus will place the threats to the survival of even the most well-off Palestinians at a higher level than those faced by marginalized groups within Israel's Jewish majority.

NARRATIVE AND AGENCY

Even with this volume's inevitably limited scope, its individual and collective biographies make at least four contributions to the study of Israeli and Palestinian nationalisms: (a) the emphasis on human agency and the humanization of history; (b) the introduction of marginal and subaltern voices that broaden the larger narrative; (c) the recognition that people are rarely typical representatives of their groups; and (d) the observation that people usually view—and sometimes conduct—their lives as narratives, requiring that distinct attention be paid to the literary aspects of their histories.

These contributions focus on two themes, *agency* and *imagination,* both of which are particularly valuable in approaching what is frequently portrayed as the intractable Israeli-Palestinian conflict. As the conflict has persisted, particular limitations of its study have rigidified into major analytic obstacles. The value of the four general contributions found in the study of life histories is that each matches up with and helps make visible one specific obstacle to a better understanding of the Israeli-Palestinian conflict. We have chosen to highlight the following four impediments to a nuanced, and therefore fuller and more satisfying, analysis of Israeli-Palestinian relations: (a) the often-repeated "myths of agency"—the assertion, on the one hand, that only in Israel have Jews recovered their sovereign and complete freedom of agency and, on the other hand, that Palestinians have lost their power and agency as a result of the *Nakba* and other scourges visited on them by Zionism; (b) the growing influence of those who seek to replace the view of the conflict as an interactive process with one that blames just one side or the other for its persistence; (c) the recurrent rigid sociological division of the contenders into two homogenous groups within a zero-sum conflict; and (d) the ongoing subjugation of personal narratives in order to legitimate public narrative plots.

Before proceeding to the presentation of each of these obstacles to analysis and understanding (in the next section), we wish to emphasize that while actors and researchers on both sides produce and reproduce them, it would be very unfortunate to think of Jewish Israelis and Palestinians as mirrors of each other. There are some oft-remarked parallels between them, and many more that are unexpected and therefore usefully explored. But at no time should we be oblivious to the fact that their vulnerabilities are of different types and magnitudes; for many decades Zionist and later Israeli Jews have had the upper hand in the conflict—an imbalance of power that began and was already exacerbated during the Mandate period—while Palestinians have suffered under the Mandatory regime, the State of Israel, and the devastating impact of the Zionist settlement enterprise during the long twentieth century and through to the present day. Indeed, the ever-widening inequality in power, life chances, and access to the tools of government between the two communities is the most important characteristic of their relationship and their "implicate" or "relational" histories during the past 130 years (Portugali 1993; Lockman 1996). Should our eyes wander for a minute, the life stories in this volume will remind us in no time of this profound disparity.

The asymmetry between Israelis and Palestinians is particularly pronounced in its interconnectedness: not only is their conflict presented as a zero-sum confrontation, but the stories of Israeli Jews by and large follow a redemptive arc, whereas most Palestinian lives traverse the same arc in reverse. Their repertoires of struggle and spans of survival clearly separate the antagonists, qua individuals, nations, and above all aspirants for an independent state. Having established a state, Israeli Jews possess both a wide range of options of struggle for their national goals and a tolerant international environment in which to achieve them. Palestinians, on the other hand, continue to find themselves in a political and legal limbo which has long constrained the tools of their struggle and the legitimation of these tools by the international community.

Our collection follows C. Wright Mills's dictum that "no social study that does not come back to the problem of biography, of history and of their intersection within a society has completed its intellectual journey" (Mills 1959: 6). We present this volume with the intention of telling good stories, and of helping to preserve them for posterity. At the same time, however, we hope to lighten the mythologization, homogenization, and essentialization of the contending sides which weigh so heavily on the understanding of the Palestinian-Israeli conflict. In fact, given the limited attention paid by Israeli Jews to Palestinian lives and by Palestinians to Israeli Jewish lives, reading this volume is among other things an exercise in empathy—or at least the beginning of such an exercise.

VALUE ADDED BY SOCIAL BIOGRAPHIES

What new explanatory value, then, does a study of life histories add to the understanding of the Israeli-Palestinian conflict? And how does a focus on biographies detour around the obstructions typically found in the historiography of this conflict?

The first contribution of social biographies is the restoration of human agency to history, in contrast to history written as the endeavors of countries, movements, parties, or organizations or as the unfolding of large-scale impersonal forces. Biographies are "the human heart of history" (Oates 1990: 7).

What does agency consist of? Scholars used to hold a notion of Enlightenment and post-Enlightenment subjectivity according to which the individual was a universal human subject who acts autonomously and is capable of making both ethically correct choices and rational political and economic decisions. We gave up on this sanguine view long ago. Anthony Giddens defines *agency* much more modestly, as the social actor's capacity to act or to "have acted differently" (Giddens 1984: 14), excluding a consideration of individual intentions. Even so, he does not provide a base line against which to measure the range of possibilities among which individuals make their choices or the capacities they can muster. Giddens's take, consequently, remains abstract and fails to inquire into what effective choice consists of, namely how much freedom individuals have when they engage with actual social forces.

The notion of agency in this volume builds on the recognition of the diversity and variation manifested in choices made by people over time. We will be well served by keeping in mind that even people in analogous conditions do not respond uniformly to large-scale social changes that throw their lives off kilter. Indeed, individuals commonly face painful dilemmas and embark on their course, sometimes under the immediate pressures of the moment and others times as part of self-conscious social movements, by choosing between alternatives. Manya Shochat started her political life as an advocate for Jewish social and cultural revival as part of a Russian revolution, only to become an early Zionist leader (see chapter 4). Majed al-Masri chose to forgo invitations to leave Palestine for safer shores and remained in the land of his birth (see chapter 19). Benni Gaon, who rose through the ranks of the Histadrut's cooperative socialist corporations, was a vocal and ideological champion of capitalist enterprise in Israel by the 1990s (see chapter 20). Each choice influences subsequent ones as individuals become who they are by making these very decisions.

The range of individuals' options is not fixed across time. By examining actual choices we will distinguish between historical eras when conformity is widespread and periods in which consensus ruptures, leading to greater variation across individual biographies (Burke 1993: 19). In focusing on the conundrum of agency we are asking not how individuals differ from some abstract notion of conformity but how they differ from other people in similar circumstances and how choices they make at one time differ from and potentially affect their subsequent decisions. Lest we forget, agency is also involved in attempts to reproduce familiar circumstances in the face of disruptive change.

Agency in this view consists not so much of freely determining one's life course through rational decision making guided by clear and unbroken preferences (see Frank 2006: 298) but of trying repeatedly to make the best of difficult situations in hard times. There is nothing left in this view of Max Weber's ideal of a life made well worth living through thick and thin by a value-driven vocation (Weber 1946a, 1946b). But although we view personalities as ambiguous, multiple, and fluid, our approach hardly means that people's choices are random and disconnected.

The very limited view of individual agency we encounter in studying Israeli-Palestinian relations originates in an equally circumscribed view of collective agency. The topic of agency occupies a particular place in the study of the Israeli-Palestinian conflict since the metahistorical narratives of both sides revolve around what we call the myth of agency. Nationalists everywhere appoint their histories with the ambition of overthrowing foreign powers to become autonomous actors, but over time Jews and Palestinians have vested this purpose with singular weight and intensity. A focal point of Zionist historiography has been the assertion that the movement was formed to recover for Jews the agency provided by the sovereignty that they lacked during two millennia of Diaspora life. In this foreshortened history, the era between the kingdoms of Judea and modern Israel is rendered well-nigh insignificant and irrelevant. But historians, most successfully David Biale, have demonstrated that far from being powerless, medieval Jewish communities wielded influence through cooperation or alliances with the political authority of the time (Biale 1986).

Of course, Diasporic agency was more limited than the sovereign kind, but agency is always relative (Biale 1986). Similarly, it is commonly argued that Palestinians labor within the "iron cage" of the overwhelming pressure exerted by

Zionism, the British Mandate, and later, pro-Israeli U.S. policies and, consequently, find themselves reduced to powerless objects. One of Rashid Khalidi's
explicit goals in writing *The Iron Cage: The Story of the Palestinian Struggle for
Statehood* was "to ascribe agency to the Palestinians[,] . . . [who] had many assets,
were far from helpless, and often faced a range of choices, some of which were better, or at least less bad, than others." By focusing on Palestinian decisions, Khalidi
identifies failures but also "put[s] the Palestinians at the center of a critical phase of
their history" (Khalidi 2006: xxx). Indeed, without agency there can be no choices,
and without choice there are no failures from which lessons can be learned, only
victims.

Agency, however, is never absolute—each side's agency constraints the freedom
of action and agency of the other, and it is their interconnection, embedded as it
is in asymmetrical power relations, that requires study. Preemption, displacement,
and oppression as well as thwarting, delay, and steadfastness are all aspects of the
continuum of agency. Biale and Khalidi's studies of agency examine broad historical events and potential turning points; our anthology of individual life histories
gives more teeth to their effort.

The second contribution of social biographies to making sense of history and
contemporary reality is in displacing, or at least limiting, the influence of easily
available and elite points of view with a wider range of perspectives. One of the
benefits of investigating the counternarratives of the marginalized voices of history is that they cast doubt on historical assertions that purport to be self-evident
and therefore beyond dispute. Not surprisingly, many social movements have
used storytelling to raise consciousness in people they wished to recruit. Slave
narratives were an important tool of the abolitionist movement, "an instrument
of liberation, when neither law nor society offered the same" (Blight 2007). The
feminist movement encouraged women to tell their life stories to one another and
the public to highlight their subjugation and their marginalization by mainstream
historiography. Even more explicitly, coming-out stories served as fundamental
catalysts in the rise of the gay rights movement. In all these cases, stories told as
memories of empowerment revealed personal and group autonomy (Davies and
Gannon 2006: 29).

The personal narratives told under such circumstances are usually forgotten
or massively rewritten stories—forgotten because they do not agree with officially
condoned political or academic truths and rewritten to fit into acceptable histories.
They fill in the silences, elisions, and falsifications of public narratives and thus,
side-by-side with real battles, produce a "battle of stories." Among such untold
or rarely told stories we number Henya Pekelman's tragic attempt to turn herself
into a female construction worker and, as such, a real-life pioneer of the Zionist
ideology, in the face of severe gender discrimination and the indifference of the
Labor Movement and labor unions (see chapter 7), and the story of generations of

Bedouin women whose black skin, prior to 1948, meant servitude and, indeed, de facto slavery (see chapter 15). Admittedly, a potential downside of such battles is to assume that all stories are equally valid and therefore matter equally. But before we dismiss embattled stories, let us remember that what is considered a deviant or marginal version at one time or place might not be so at another. As long as there is a range of narratives written or recounted by storytellers, professional and amateur, to chose from, other storytellers—including historians—have to be more honest and careful.

Marginality takes on an added meaning in this conflict since many if not most individual Palestinian life stories appear only in the peripheral vision of the majority of Israelis, and vice versa. In one of his letters from a Fascist prison to his wife, who all but stopped corresponding with him, Antonio Gramsci famously wrote, "Misfortune commonly has two effects: the first is the extinction of all feeling towards those who endure it, while the second—no less common—is the extinction in the latter of all feeling towards those who do not endure it" (Gramsci 1973). Indeed, under the pressure to circle the wagons and to declare "my tribe—right or wrong," nationalists and others pursuing exclusivist ethnic and/or religious identities forgo the ability to walk in the shoes of the adversary. In so doing they lose the imagination that is necessary to think creatively, transcend oppression, and prevent continued violence.

Among the many casualties of conflict is the sense of empathy for victims of the other side, and consequently, reading an anthology such as this offers an opportunity to experience a greater understanding of, and through it, empathy for, the other side. However, we remain acutely aware of Emmanuel Levinas's argument that empathy—literally being "in suffering" with someone else—can easily become a form of egoism, based on the problematic assumption that we can truly know or experience what someone else has undergone (Levinas 1998). The fact that Levinas, the philosopher of recognition par excellence, was famously unable fully to recognize Palestinian identity, rights, or suffering further clarifies the difficulty—and thus the necessity—of such a process (see Caro 2009). Empathy consists of sensitivity to others' vulnerability and need as well as, we believe, to the integrity of their biographies and to their sense of justice.

Looking at history from below also highlights the human cost associated with disruptive historical and social changes and "the ability of people to survive even under the most appalling conditions" (Burke 1993: 18). In this volume, the appalling loss of almost all of Yoshka Spronz's family members and his survival in Auschwitz are coupled with his desire to find a measure of closure by serving as a witness in the trial of one of the perpetrators, preserving the past by writing a memoir, and equally important, beginning life anew through the creation of a new family and emigration to Israel (see chapter 11). For their part, Palestinians are united by bearing the multiple burdens of displacement and suffering the profound insecurity of stateless refugees. The vulnerabilities of their shared situation, as so many of the chapters attest, led Palestinians from very different circumstances and through innumerable channels to become politicized. Their actions run the gamut from resistance, through petitions and search for legal recourse by the villagers of Aylut (see chapter 1), to armed resistance by Abdul Rahim Hajj Mohammad in the Arab revolt of 1936–39 (see chapter 8) and Majed al-Masri in the two intifadas (see chapter 19).

People not only survive but are also transformed by the conditions they endure—sometimes toward greater empathy, other times toward justifying appalling acts. Yitzhak Rabin's assassination by Yigael Amir, who hailed from Israel's ethnic periphery and at once sought to be accepted by the religious settler movement and to bring the Oslo peace process to an end, is one such example (see chapter 22). It is not our intention to romanticize or beautify such lives, Jewish or Palestinian; rather, we wish to show their richness and changeability, highlighting the issue of agency and spurring our imaginations to consider not solely lives and experiences we have heretofore ignored but solutions that presently have not penetrated our still-narrow consciousnesses.

Paying close attention to both sides and recognizing their internal diversity also allow us to put paid to stereotypes that proliferate in the literature on Israel/Palestine and give us what Burke termed "a misleading mastery" (Burke 1993: 8). This openness is particularly important now, when, strangely, the bilateral aspect of the conflict is being challenged. New schools of thought on the Israeli-Palestinian conflict seek to replace the view that is produced and reproduced by the interaction of the two sides with the notion that all the "historical responsibility" rests with one side. According to these approaches, Israelis and Palestinians are not responding to one another's behavior but acting out their unchanging "essence," and consequently, in place of the Israeli-Palestinian conflict there is only an "Israeli conflict" or a "Palestinian conflict." For example, acts of violence by Palestinians are commonly described without reference to the Israeli occupation under which they live, and the Israeli separation wall is equally frequently analyzed with little mention of prior Palestinian suicide attacks within the Green Line. In this volume, reporting on the Jewish victims of bomb attacks in Tel Aviv and elsewhere, the Russian-Jewish journalist Alexandra contends that Palestinians are insatiable in their territorial demands (see chapter 17).

So far we have examined the contributions of life stories to making sense of history; now we turn our telescope to the contribution of social biographies to the methods and metatheories deployed by other academic disciplines in analyzing their subject matter. Put differently, biographical narratives open the door to a renewed focus on human agency through an ant's-eye perspective, which also allows the rethinking of the methods used in the study of societies and their history.

The third contribution of social biographies is to suggest that the customary emphasis of social sciences on explaining individuals' behavior by their membership in groups is inflated and misplaced. In social science methodology, people appear primarily as representatives of the social categories from which they hail. The same holds even when the social sciences, among them most self-consciously survey research, sample individuals' opinions. The validity of their methodological individualism is predicated on the representative sampling of the population according to the membership of the individuals in broad social categories, and consequently, the findings of surveys are reported as correlations between clusters of variables such as class, race, ethnicity, religion, gender, and political affiliation with educational level, status, income, and so on. Variation between individuals within groups, according to this approach, is negligible, since when samples are large enough, individual differences cancel out. Methods that focus on intragroup and intergroup processes, such as prejudice, have an even stronger tendency to analyze individual conduct in terms of group behavior. Ironically, while most social science theories teach us that identities are neither fixed nor one-dimensional, actual research methods violate both of these premises.

One of the findings we anticipated in gathering the life stories included in this anthology but whose pervasiveness still surprised us is the extent to which no one turned out to be typical. No one was a "good" or "average" representative of his or her social group or category. Groups, it seems, are much more diverse than sociologists imagine them to be. In fact, one of the most effective ways to operationalize agency is to understand it as the extent to which individuals become who they are by differing from their putative group.

A particularly cogent example of individual-group mismatch is S. Yizhar, the unofficial spokesperson of the first sabra (native) generation, winner of the Israel Prize for literature, and a member of the Knesset, who focused some of his most potent stories on the internal struggle between the self-serving military exploits of his generation and universal norms of conduct (see chapter 5). Ruth Shapira (see chapter 16) gave up a comfortable and secure middle-class existence in the United States to pursue her aspirations toward an Israeli nationalist revival. Abu Ahmad broke away from political activism in the post-Oslo years to found a community center that offers new hope to the children of the Beit Jibrin refugee camp (see chapter 25), while Jonathan Pollak, inspired by anarchist ideas, regularly confronts Israeli soldiers in defense of Palestinian land even as he is viewed as a traitor by fellow Israeli Jews (see chapter 24).

Groups, for their part, spend a great deal of time, and have specialized functionaries for, homogenizing their members. The effectiveness of these efforts, as in the case of Palestinians and Israelis who are heavily mobilized to their nationalist causes, is telling. But even within these groups, one will be wise to listen to many voices and when confronted with unanimity, to question its depth.

The heterogeneity found in individual histories within groups and the variation in people's behavior over time also point to the potential for greater freedom in future choices.

Even when social scientists champion greater emphasis on individuals, as several well-known ones did in the middle of the twentieth century, they do not necessarily advocate the study of individual life histories. Dennis Wrong in "The Oversocialized Conception of Man in Modern Sociology" (1961), C. Wright Mills in the now iconic *The Sociological Imagination* (1959), and Herbert Marcuse in *One Dimensional Man* (1964) are united in taking the social sciences and humanities— and in Marcuse's case, even modern industrial society itself—to task for accepting and promoting conformity as natural. In their view, by accommodating the individualistic premises of the reigning American liberalism and formally democratic Western institutions, social science lost the potential to understand people's motivations and actions and could no longer enable individuals to comprehend the circumstances of their existence.

Mills suggested that to unsnare themselves from the trap of incomprehension, people need to learn the terrible but magnificent lessons of the "sociological imagination," which casts light on the circumstances of their unfreedom. Calling upon such imagination, individuals can understand the impersonal world-historical and socioeconomic forces that control their lives, putting them in a better position to "cope with their personal troubles in such ways as to control the structural transformations that usually lie behind them" (Mills 1959: 4). But while Mills sought "to define the meaning of the social sciences for the cultural tasks of our time" (Mills 1959: 18), he did not offer to study individual biographies. On the contrary, he sought to explain better the social causes of "personal troubles." Mills endorsed the sociological imagination to explain, in effect, how little the study of biography per se mattered.

In one of the best-known contemporary analyses, "Can the Subaltern Speak?," Gaytari Spivak similarly concludes that subalterns as a social category cannot express their collective experiences and aspirations, but she does not concern herself with individual voices (Spivak 1988). Like Mills, Wrong, and Marcuse, Spivak uses a method that falls within a fairly broad-based "social structure and personality" approach (Shanahan and Macmillan 2008: 21–41) but seeks to provide better social science explanations for the uniformity and conformity of individual behavior rather than analytic tools for differentiation between individuals.

Work with personal narratives requires epistemological and methodological assumptions that differ from those of the social sciences and consequently produce "a different type of knowledge." As selves and identities, people are unified and whole in ways in which they cannot be as members of groups, and the study of their life histories "provides evidence about individuals as whole persons." Studying whole persons and their history opens an important realm for us: the emotional tone of their accumulated experiences, among them overriding convictions and sentiments derived from feelings of humiliation and pride, revenge and justice, and a readiness to behave in ways and make sacrifices that, in other contexts, would be hard to account for. What we glean from individual life stories above all are their truth claims. These are different from other, let alone scientific, truth claims (Maynes et al. 2008: 10–11), but they teach us what individuals think is just or at least fair, what they experience as reasonable and acceptable.

Fourth, since the social biographies gathered in this volume are conventionally told as stories, they require us to consider the insights of literature for making sense of history. Whereas social scientists rarely report their findings in story form, narratives, as literary analysts such as Hayden White point out (1987), follow a plot, fall into particular genres, are told from a particular point of view, are held together and endowed with a moralizing significance, and address and interact with particular audiences. These requirements shape both life stories and lives and simultaneously empower and constrain their tellers or writers.

"Stories people tell about their lives," Mary Jo Maynes and her coauthors note in their magisterial *Telling Stories,* on the uses of narratives in the social sciences and history, "are never simply individual, but are told in historically specific times and settings and draw on the rules and models in circulation that govern how story elements link together in narrative logics" (Maynes et al. 2008: 3). To paraphrase Marx, individuals tell their life stories, but not in the way they wish. Enduring patterns of inequality in class, status, gender, and ethnic or race hierarchies constrain people's lives. These constraints frame and explain which biographic scripts are likely to be told and retold and thus endure. In addition, historical forces—in particular, radical or cataclysmic transformations—produce "critical moments," or "crossroads," which alter the social and personal resources on which people may draw to frame their biographies (Bagnoli and Ketokivi 2009: 318–19). In many Palestinian social biographies, 1948 serves as the marker which changed everything, especially for refugees like Matar 'Abdelrahim (see chapter 10)—as has immigration to Israel from Hungary by Yoshka Spronz (see chapter 11), from Morocco by Prosper Cohen (see chapter 13), and from Iraq by Rachel (see chapter 14).

While all social divides make their appearance in the life histories collected in this volume, the most self-conscious are the countervailing Israeli Jews' and Palestinians' nationalisms. One of the key questions in inquiring about nationalist narratives and their authority is just how wide a range of narratives they accept—in this case, for example, how much room they leave for the description of interaction between Jews and Palestinians. It is immediately noticeable that the range of narratives of interaction drops precipitously as we move from the Ottoman period to the Mandate to post-1948 Israel: with the growing importance of nationalist narratives, members of the adversarial national group are increasingly relegated to the background of individual life stories. Whereas the merchant Haim

Amzalak, from Ottoman Jaffa, had economic ties with Palestinian landowners (see chapter 2) and the musician Wasif Jawhariyyeh cultivated social bonds with individuals of varied backgrounds, including Jews, in Ottoman Jerusalem (see chapter 3), Mais, an Israeli-Palestinian and our contemporary, is likely to meet Jews either under duress, such as in checkpoints, or in deliberately created peace camp encounters (see chapter 23).

Events are linked in life histories not merely sequentially but as an ongoing narrative which "has as its latent or manifest purpose the desire to moralize the events of which it treats" (White 1987: 14). This is even more true of nationalist narratives aimed at a public audience. The genre of public narratives holds sway over the category of private ones among Israelis and Palestinians. Public narratives constrain private ones, but by providing a focus they contribute to making a life history appear whole or complete. In other words, the cultural and literary narratives which embed their subjects in broad nationalist narratives tie together in a meaningful and sympathetic way the subjects' disparate historical experiences. Nationalist frameworks have a clear teleological terminus for both Jews and Palestinians, but they appear to play a more significant role in Palestinian stories. Abdul Rahim's life, including his leadership of the Arab Revolt, as told in chapter 8, is a prime example of the uses of nationalist hagiography in establishing the tale of the unbroken continuity of Palestinian nationalist struggle.

Jewish Israelis take the State of Israel for granted as a central component of their identities and therefore are more likely to highlight their individual choices than are Palestinians, who rely on their nationalist narrative to produce and reproduce their interconnectedness in the absence of shared institutions. For example, in Rachel's life story, the agencies of the Israeli state provide resources for the assimilation of its Jewish citizens so they can realize the status aspirations deferred by their immigration—in her case, from Iraq (see chapter 14). Matar 'Abdelrahim, in contrast, as a refugee in Syria had to seek out and help construct a Palestinian community, which was able to provide moral support first for his and his family's survival and then for resistance to Israel (see chapter 10).

Palestinian foregrounding of a collective past and present is not altogether different from Jewish narratives of their Diasporic age. Heinrich Heine, the Jewish German Romantic poet, perceptively viewed the Bible as a portable homeland for Jews. Until the modern era almost no Jewish autobiographies were produced, and those that were written less told a life story than "construct[ed] the boundaries of [an] imaginary homeland" to locate themselves in history (Bar-Levav, 2002: 45). Nationalist tales of Palestinian *sumud* (steadfastness) emerged to meet a similar need.

Among the Jewish life stories in this collection there is a remarkable portion that are riven by internal doubts. Of course, immigration is a particularly taxing identity reformation, but the self-questioning found in, for example, the stories of

S. Yizhar (see chapter 5), Ruth Shapira (see chapter 16), and Jonathan Pollak (see chapter 24) is striking in its intensity and diversity. As newcomers, as trespassers, as colonizers they struggled with the legitimacy of their presence in Palestine. In addition, as the side that repeatedly had the upper hand in the conflict, Israeli Jews are much freer to construct genres of biographies describing conflict between their private and the Israeli public narratives. Among these is the famed "shooting and crying narrative," in which professed beliefs in humanism and actual behavior toward Palestinians clash. The search for legitimacy, however, is absent among more recent immigrants, like Alexandra from the former USSR (see chapter 17), and orthodox Jews such as Yigael Amir (see chapter 22) and David Ariel, a young settler from the militant Yitzhar settlement (see chapter 18), and it appeared in the thinking of Hillel Kook only after his return to Israel from a long sojourn in the United States (see chapter 9). By replacing nationalism, religious certainties close the gap between private and public narratives and reduce the space available for this self-conflictual genre.

It is sometimes argued that whereas European autobiographies are rich in interior dialogue and self-analysis, their non-Western counterparts by and large lack these elements. The "individualization" thesis of Anthony Giddens (1984) and Ulrich Beck (1992) emphasizes the prevalence of choice, commitment, and negotiations in modern Western societies at the expense of emphasis on stable institutions, customs, and norms. This thesis, certainly exaggerated for most people even in late-modern Western societies, represents one end of the continuum of choice and fate. European individualism, however, as Dipesh Chakrabarty points out, is one of the historical accomplishments that lie behind the public domain of citizenship. Where the latter is absent, the former will also be lacking, and in particular, there will be a dearth of "autobiographies in the confessional mode."

Without a sovereign political space—as the Palestinians have experienced—there is less room for private selves, and the limited availability of both encourages the writing of public autobiographies (Chakrabarty 2000: 35). Without national independence, there remains less room for subjectivities and genres of personal narratives, and authors pay more attention to nationalism as the force majeure of their life. As Palestinians are dispossessed of a nation-state, all their social biographies in this volume revolve in important ways around the axes of nationalism and national reconstruction.

THE HISTORY OF THE PRESENT AND THE POLITICS OF PRESENCE

Social biographies offer a particularly fruitful avenue for producing new knowledge about the historical and contemporary dynamics of the Israeli-Palestinian conflict in a way that reflects their deep complexity and implicate nature. Whether focused on individual life stories or sociospatial histories, they bring together the insights and methodologies of several disciplines: first, historical ethnography, which itself joins two disciplinary approaches that are often seen as incompatible (Haney and Horowitz 2006); second, historical sociology, which has a rich tradition of insightful macro-level analyses, as exemplified by the classic writings of Tönnies, Marx, and Weber, but whose component approaches separated with the institutionalization of sociology as a science and history as part of the humanities in the postwar era (see Orloff et al. 2005).

If the historical, anthropological, and sociological approaches are effectively triangulated, they may facilitate a more vivid presence for common or marginal and critical—in impact if not intent—individual and collective voices within the larger narratives of politics and identity in the Israeli-Palestinian context. The common denominator in these interactions is the historical dimension, or perhaps better, imagination, which when brought to sociological or anthropological analyses enables a more robust portrait of societies and the groups they comprise than can be achieved by the ethnographic gaze or sociological survey alone (see Comaroff and Comaroff 1992 for a seminal discussion of this trend, and MacFarlane 1977 for an example of the previously dominant trend of the more traditional use of history primarily to produce raw data for anthropological analysis).

To borrow a phrase from Nietzsche, like other actors in the Israeli-Palestinian conflict, historians "bear visibly the traces of those sufferings which . . . result [from] an excess of history" (Nietzsche 1997: 116). These scars are the product of not only the physical and psychic suffering of Palestinians and Israelis during more than a century of conflict but also the victimization of historiography, which has too often been reduced to an essentialist, teleological, and (for Israelis and the West more broadly) triumphalist view of Israel's and the world's history, in both their recent narratives and the *longue durée* of Palestine's modern history.

To write a better history of Israel and Palestine based on this understanding is to write a "history of the present." By this we mean not merely a history that covers the present day but rather one that is grounded in a comprehensive reading of the country's history during the past century and more, which will allow us to see the "very conditions of possibility" of contemporary Israeli and Palestinian experience (Foucault 1973). The problem, as we have already alluded, is that most histories of Israel/Palestine are histories not just of the present but *in* the present; that is, they are inseparable from the power relations and political struggles surrounding the country and its history, including those regarding the representation of the conflict within academia and the media. And if history is problematic in this manner, so equally are the other disciplines which it informs and engages.

The seminal French philosopher Michel Foucault well understood how easily history, and through it almost every analytical methodology, falls prey to ideological and political agendas. He believed that to overcome such tendencies, history at least must "uncover the past to rupture the present into a future that will leave the very function of history behind it" (Roth 1981: 44; Foucault 1977). He sought to establish a more critical relationship between the past and the present, which was the sine qua non for imagining scenarios for the future that transcended the uncritical and teleological narratives offered by states and competing nationalist ideologies alike.

We believe that a significant portion of the biographical narratives in this volume contribute to this endeavor, most importantly by complexifying the various discourses of modernity which are defined by the kind of exclusivist and hierarchical imaginations—grounded in ideologies, whether capitalism, colonialism, or nationalism—that make understanding how the present situation has been produced and might be transformed, and the empathy such knowledge can enable, impossible to achieve (LeVine 2009).

In order to transform, marginalized voices must attain a significant degree of presence—discursively, politically, and equally important, physically—within the systems of politics and power that have invested heavily in excluding them. Benedict Anderson famously discussed the importance of "imagined communities" in the formation and spread of national identities (Anderson 1991), but if identities broader than those of face-to-face interaction have always been a product of the imagination, their political valence and power have always been tied to the ability of individuals to come together collectively in the same spaces.

One trend within political science to address this dynamic is the concept of a politics of presence. Traditionally in the political and social science literature, the debate over presence has focused on the continued marginalization of minority or other subaltern groups within otherwise democratic societies; specifically, whether members of the dominant political group—white people or men, for example—can successfully represent the interests of African Americans or women, or whether regardless of how sympathetic the dominant group's stance is, members of marginalized groups need to be literally present in the halls of power to ensure their political needs and desires are at least considered (Phillips 1995: 5–6). But the contributions here point out that a very different politics of presence must be applied to nondemocratic societies or those riven by long-term ethnic or religious conflict. In such situations the struggle for presence is not just about guaranteeing formal rights and political participation but equally about entering into the larger imagination that undergirds them, without which political power will always remain out of reach. When these forms of presence are denied, groups often make their presence felt through various forms of violence, both within and between the two societies. This, however, merely serves to exacerbate the modalities of exclusion that govern their relations in most regards.

Our contributions, by moving beyond—but by no means attempting merely to dethrone—collective narratives and the explanatory power of group affiliation that social scientists and historians commonly emphasize, help to highlight the interpretive, and possibly political, price we pay for being too single-minded in our customary pursuits. They point to the power of social biographies to bring into the heart of history a greater consideration of human agency, as volatile as it is at times and as determined at others, and open the door to recognizing a wider variety of behaviors than social sciences and history customarily do, thus encouraging us to be more imaginative in reporting the past and conceiving of the future.

The stories that follow help to humanize, renew agency, and reimagine the basic premises of Israeli and Palestinian identity, history, politics, and, through them, conflict. In short, they allow for the presence of each people within the other's narratives in a manner that, while no doubt unsettling to partisans of the still dominant, narrow, and mutually exclusive forms of the two identities, is crucial to forging a shared narrative and politics in the future.

BIBLIOGRAPHY

Anderson, Benedict. *Imagined Communities: Reflections on the Origin and Spread of Nationalism.* London: Verso, 1991.

Bagnoli, Anne, and Kaisa Ketokivi. "At a Crossroads: Contemporary Lives between Fate and Choice." *European Societies,* Vol. 11, No. 3 (2009), pp. 315–324.

Bar-Levav, Avriel. "'When I was Alive': Jewish Ethical Wills as Egodocuments." In Rudolf Dekker, ed., *Egodocuments and History: Autobiographical Writing in Its Social Context Since the Middle Ages.* Rotterdam: Verloren Publishers, 2002, pp. 45–60.

Barteaux, Daniel, ed. *Biography and Society: The Life History Approach in the Social Sciences.* Beverly Hills: Sage, 1981.

Beck, Ulrich. *Risk Society: Towards a New Modernity.* London: Sage, 1992.

Biale, David. *Power and Powerlessness in Jewish History.* New York: Schocken, 1986.

Blight, David W. *A Slave No More.* Orlando: Harcourt, 2007.

Burawoy, Michael. *Ethnography Unbound: Power and Resistance in the Modern Metropolis.* Berkeley: University of California Press, 1991.

Burke, Edmund, III, ed. *Struggle and Survival in the Modern Middle East.* Berkeley: University of California Press, 1993.

Burke, Edmund, III, and David N. Yaghoubian, eds. *Struggle and Survival in the Modern Middle East.* Berkeley: University of California Press, 2006.

Caro, Jason. "Levinas and the Palestinians." *Philosophy and Social Criticism* 235 (2009), pp. 671–85.

Chakrabarty, Dipesh. *Provincializing Europe: Postcolonial Thought and Historical Difference.* Princeton: Princeton University Press, 2000.

Comaroff, John, and Jean Comaroff. *Ethnography and the Historical Imagination.* Boulder, CO: Westview Press, 1992.

Davies, Bronwyn, and Susanne Gannon. *Doing Collective Biography: Investigating the Production of Subjectivity.* Maidenhead, Berkshire, England: Open University Press, 2006.

Dunaway, David K., and Willa K. Baum, eds. *Oral History: An Interdisciplinary Anthology*, 2nd ed. Walnut Creek, CA: Altamira, 1996.

Fay, Mary Ann, ed. *Auto/biography and the Construction of Identity and Community in the Middle East*. New York: Palgrave, 2002.

Foucault, Michel. *The Birth of the Clinic: An Archaeology of Medical Perception*. Translated by A. M. Sheridan Smith. New York: Vintage, 1973.

———. Discipline and Punish: The Birth of the Prison. Translated by A. M. Sheridan. New York: Vintage, 1977.

———. "Foucault's 'History of the Present,'" edited and annotated by Michael S. Roth. *History and Theory*, Vol. 20, No. 1. (February 1981), pp. 32–46.

———. *Politics, Philosophy, Culture*. Translated by Alan Sheridan. London: Routledge, 1988.

Frank, Katherine. "Agency." *Anthropological Theory*, Vol. 6, No. 3 (2006), pp. 281–302.

Giddens, Anthony. *The Constitution of Society: Outline of the Theory of Structuration*. Berkeley: University of California Press, 1984.

Gramsci, Antonio. *Letters from Prison*. New York: Harper and Row, 1973.

Haney, Lynne, and Ruth Horowitz. "The Possibilities for History and Ethnography: Beyond the Revisit," paper presented at the Annual Meeting of the American Sociological Association, session on "Qualitative Methodology," Montreal, August 11–14, 2006.

Kelley, Robin D. G. *Race Rebels: Culture, Politics and the Black Working Class*. New York: Free Press, 1994.

Khalidi, Rashid. *The Iron Cage: The Story of the Palestinian Struggle for Statehood*. Boston: Beacon, 2006.

Levinas, Emanuel. *Entre Nous: On Thinking of the Other*. New York: Columbia University Press, 1998.

LeVine, Mark. *Impossible Peace: Israel/Palestine Since 1989*. London: Zed Books, 2009.

Lockman, Zachary. *Comrades and Enemies: Arab and Jewish Workers in Palestine, 1906–1948*. Berkeley: University of California Press, 1996.

MacFarlane, Alan. "Historical Anthropology." *Cambridge Anthropology*, Vol.3, No. 3 (1977). Available online at www.alanmacfarlane.com/TEXTS/frazerlecture.pdf.

Marcuse, Herbert. *One-Dimensional Man: Studies in the Ideology of Advanced Industrial Society*. Boston: Beacon, 1964.

Maynes, Mary Jo, Jennifer L. Pierce, and Barbara Laslett. *Telling Stories: The Use of Personal Narratives in the Social Sciences and History*. Ithaca: Cornell University Press, 2008.

Mills, C. Wright. *The Sociological Imagination*. Oxford: Oxford University Press, 1959.

Nietzsche, Friedrich. "On the Uses and Disadvantages of History for Life." In Nietzsche, *Untimely Meditations*. Cambridge: Cambridge University Press, 1997, p. 116.

Oates, Stephen B. *Biography as History*. Twelfth Charles Edmonson Historical Lectures. Waco, TX: Markham, 1990.

Orloff, Ann S., Julia Adams, and Elisabeth Clemens, eds. *Remaking Modernity: Politics, History, and Sociology*. Durham: Duke University Press, 2005.

Phillips, Anne. *The Politics of Presence*. Oxford: Oxford University Press, 1995.

Portelli, Alessandro. *The Death of Luigi Trastulli and Other Stories: Form and Meaning in Oral History*. New York: State University of New York Press, 1991.

Portugali, Juval. *Implicate Relations: Society and Space in the Israeli-Palestinian Conflict.* New York: Springer, 1993.

Scott, James C. *Weapons of the Weak: Everyday Forms of Peasant Resistance.* New Haven: Yale University Press, 1985.

Shanahan, Michael J., and Ross Macmillan. *Biography and the Sociological Imagination: Contexts and Contingencies.* New York: W. W. Norton, 2008.

Spivak, Gayatri Chakravorty. "Can the Subaltern Speak?" In Cary Nelson and Lawrence Grossberg, eds., *Marxism and the Interpretation of Culture.* Urbana: University of Illinois Press, 1988, pp. 271–313.

Weber, Max. "Politics as Vocation." In C. Wright Mills and Hans Gerth, eds., *From Max Weber: Essays in Sociology.* New York: Oxford University Press, 1946a, pp. 77–128.

———. "Science as Vocation." In C. Wright Mills and Hans Gerth, eds., *From Max Weber: Essays in Sociology.* New York: Oxford University Press, 1946b, pp. 129–56.

Weymann, Ansgar, and Walter R. Heinz, eds. *Society and Biography: Interrelationships between Social Structure, Institutions, and the Life Course.* Weinheim, Germany: Deutscher Studien Verlag, 1996.

White, Hayden V. *The Content of the Form: Narrative Discourse and Historical Representation.* Baltimore: Johns Hopkins University Press, 1987.

Wrong, Dennis H. "The Oversocialized Conception of Man in Modern Sociology." *American Sociological Review,* Vol. 26, No. 2 (April 1961), pp. 183–93.

PART ONE

Voices of the Ottoman Past

From the Mountains to the Sea

IT IS COMMONLY ARGUED THAT THE Israeli-Palestinian conflict has always been a dispute over territory—which community had the stronger historical claim to the land between the Jordan River and the Mediterranean Sea; who between them was better equipped physically, ideologically, politically, and financially to bring Palestine into the "modern world"; who, in the words of Israel's first prime minister, David Ben-Gurion, had the greater right to "rule the country." But the very notion of territoriality and understanding of land, its uses and value, changed greatly in the nineteenth century under the Ottoman Empire—not least in Palestine, among the country's indigenous Muslim and Christian populations, as well as among local and Diaspora Jews—and it would change even more as this region moved from empire to empire and then to statehood and occupation.

A primary motivation behind this volume is widening the number and type of voices that show how territory and identity have been intertwined within the larger discourses of Palestinian and Israeli national identities. Such a broad array of voices needs to be contextualized within the more nuanced and complex historical narrative that has emerged since the late 1980s in order to be fully appreciated. The new history produced by the generation of scholars who came of age in the 1980s opened many previously un- or underexplored avenues for studying Zionist/Israeli and Palestinian identities, the larger evolution of the two national movements, and the conflict between them. Chief among these avenues was the recognition that from the moment of Zionism's arrival on the soil of Palestine there was continual contact, intercourse, and of course conflict between Zionism and the emerging Palestinian nationalism.

The context for these relations was a significant increase in population in Palestine: from the 1880s till the outbreak of World War I, its non-Jewish Arab population increased from around five hundred thousand to a bit over seven hundred thousand, while its Jewish population rose from some twenty-five thousand to upward of eighty-five thousand. The area became more crowded, and conflicted, with each passing year. And in this environment, each of the two emerging nationalist movements naturally imagined itself as autonomously developing and independent of the other. Yet the reality was that from the start the two were implicately related—it is impossible to understand the emergence, dynamics, and history of either without the other. They were impacted not only by each other, however, but also by the larger forces operating in Palestine during the late Ottoman period.

To begin with, the modernization of political administration and economic relations in the Ottoman Empire, which intensified throughout the nineteenth century (as exemplified—but not initiated—by the Tanzimat reforms that began in 1839), set in motion a process of economic development and greater integration with the larger European economies that provided the grounding for the rise of the Israeli and Palestinian nationalist movements later on. Specifically, economic and political developments were inextricably linked as a weakening Ottoman state tried to modernize to keep pace with its European competitors, stem the tide of rising nationalism (epitomized by Greek independence in 1821), and respond to the challenge of Muhammad Ali. A key aspect of this process was the encouragement of the privatization of land, which later would enable Europeans to make large-scale land purchases, dispossessing thousands of Palestinian peasants.

While the Zionist movement is generally regarded as the most significant player in dispossessing the local peasantry, as Mahmoud Yazbak shows in chapter 1, on the collective biography of the village of Aylut, German religious settlers who self-styled themselves Templers preceded Zionism and engaged in similar practices. They dealt with the same non-Palestinian landowners from whom the Zionist movement would ultimately buy up to 20 percent of the land purchased before 1948. Yazbak's biography of territorial conflict in fin-de-siècle Palestine highlights the generative role played by the new capitalist relations in the subsequent nationalist-territorial conflict between Jews and Palestinian Arabs. Indeed, a new pattern was set during this period: the farther away the Ottoman authorities were from the place where land conflicts occurred, the more likely they were to enforce the authority of the Empire at the expense of the peasants. In Palestine this meant protecting the rights of the new European owners rather than those of the fellahin who had worked the land for generations.

The Ottoman rulers' modernizing Tanzimat reforms included a reorganization of the political geography of the eastern Mediterranean, which placed the Jerusalem region under the direct control of the central government. Increased trade with Europe and the wealth it generated helped encourage the urban-based notable class to garner increasing economic and political power in the emerging Palestinian polity. But this notable class was not limited to Muslims or even Palestinian Arabs more broadly. As Joseph B. Glass and Ruth Kark show in chapter 2, their biography of Haim Amzalak, segments of the local Arab Jewish (Sephardi) population also became part of the emerging "Palestinian" entrepreneur class during this period. Indeed, at least in the larger towns, such as Jaffa and Jerusalem, economic and social relations between members of all three religions were increasingly common during the last decades of Ottoman rule.

Amzalak represents a kind of liminal personality, a Jew who grew up at a moment—the second half of the nineteenth century—when the balance of power in the eastern Mediterranean between the Ottomans and Europe had yet to shift dramatically in the latter's favor. In the last decades of his long life, Amzalak became part of both Palestine's commercial elite and the still young Zionist movement. Yet he remained culturally part of his still largely Arab surroundings throughout his life and acted as a bridge between the two uneasily defined and relating communities.

The gradual (and never complete) turning of the Ottoman elite from a cosmopolitan Ottoman identity toward a more ethnically Turkish-focused one encouraged the stirrings of a specifically Palestinian nationalist identity as well. Part of this was no doubt in response to the increased suffering and exploitation of the Palestinian peasantry, as Yazbak's story recounts. Yet this negative trajectory of Palestinian identity formation—as a response to the Turkification of Ottoman identity—does not tell the whole story. Salim Tamari's fascinating portrait of the late Ottoman-era Greek Orthodox musician Wasif Jawhariyyeh, "A Musician's Lot" (chapter 3), shows that in the liminal period of the fin-de-siècle, a host of identities could interact with one another, sometimes within the same person, particularly in the space of the late Ottoman city. Jawhariyyeh was the beneficiary of the musical heritage of many parts of the Ottoman Empire and was on friendly terms with his Christian and Jewish neighbors in Jerusalem. His life story also reminds us of how exploring cultural production, performance, and circulation opens new insights into the complexity of identities beyond the boundaries of the hegemonic mono-ethnic/religious national ideology and how at a time of great economic transformation and political uncertainty, not only national and communal but also class identities were more fluid.

The centralizing Ottoman state generated greater inequality and indebtedness for the majority of Palestinians while offering more freedom of action for local elites who could take advantage of the expanding economic, political, and even cultural horizons to enjoy greater trade, wealth, and openness. These seemingly contradictory processes met yet another history-altering dynamic with the arrival of Zionism in the last decades of Ottoman rule, particularly with the second wave of immigration, or aliya, that began in 1904. Zionism's appearance in Palestine was, of course, the result as much of the push factor of increased anti-Semitism, including the large-scale violence of pogroms in the Russian Empire's Pale of Settlement beginning in the 1880s and intensifying in 1903–6, as of the pull factor of the religious importance of Palestine or the attractiveness of Zionism as a political ideology. But as Gershon Shafir's chapter 4, on the labor pioneer Manya Shochat, shows, even the most idealistic and socialist settlers were committed to policies of conquest—of jobs and territory—that made conflict with Palestinian Arabs inevitable, and increasingly dangerous. At the beginning, to succeed in their efforts, Jewish pioneers were willing to adopt Palestinian peasant living standards and emulate local mores, but they gradually formed a distinct society. When private Jewish enterprise failed them, the pioneers came to rely on the institutions of the Zionist movement and its pubic purse and adopted a more nationalist and separatist approach.

Jewish colonization of Palestine generated considerable conflict. Already by 1891 Ahad Haam had famously written his "Truth from Eretz Yisrael," which criticized settlers for "treat[ing] the Arabs . . . unjustly[,] . . . with hostility and cruelty." By 1909 the emerging labor Zionist leadership had committed itself to policies of conquering the land to conquer the labor market—that is, to secure work and European living standards for the increasing number of Jewish immigrants. This encouraged not only the creation by Israeli Jews of a militant nationalist movement but also the emergence of a similarly militant Palestinian nationalism.

As a Turkish-centered identity took hold among the Ottoman elite, the Ottoman state grew less willing to protect Palestinians, just when their position began to be threatened. The government's desire to see more land privatized, to gain revenue from its sale or development, also impacted its willingness to challenge technically illegal land sales to foreign Jews. Palestinians responded by shifting their allegiance from the empire and toward a more local, nationalist focus. The precise contours of their identity remained fluid and cosmopolitan until the British conquest in 1917 put an end to the thought of a broader pan-Arab nationalism.

"Left Naked on the Beach"

The Villagers of Aylut in the Grip of the New Templers

Mahmoud Yazbak

The village of Aylut is five kilometers to the northwest of the city of Nazareth. Most of the houses in the village are on a small hill and near the village *bayader* (threshing floors). Victor Guerin, who visited Aylut in 1876, estimated its population at two hundred people. In 1886, Gottlieb Schumacher put the figure at 350. The members of the British-based Palestine Exploration Fund described Aylut in 1881 as "a small village in the woods." Travelogues and journals penned by European pilgrims who toured Palestine in the nineteenth century, as part of a growing movement of interest in the Holy Land, on the whole lack references to Aylut, perhaps because no remnants of a possible Jewish or Christian history had ever come to light there. Guerin, though, in a passing remark, mentions five sections of limestone pillars lying close to the *walli's maqam,* which he thought could have belonged to an old church.

The *walli's maqam* to which Guerin referred still stands in Aylut. People call it the Shrine and Tomb of the Prophet Lot (Lut) and believe the name of the village to be derived from the name of the prophet. Others suggest that *Aylut* is Syriac in origin and means "summit." In reports by the Palestine Exploration Fund, the village's name is seen as a corruption of the Arabic word *Alit,* a species of tree.

The main landmark of the Shrine of the Prophet Lot is a tomb that was later incorporated into the village's small mosque compound. The tomb represented a holy site for the local people, who believed that the person buried there had special powers to fulfill their prayers and requests. Close to the shrine, there is a spring known as the Fountain of the Prophet Lot, whose waters flow copiously through the center of the village and border the *bayader.* The latter comprises a large, flat area of land, the village square, which, besides its agricultural function, acted as the main meeting point for the villagers throughout the year and was where they held their festivals, in particular wedding celebrations. As in other villages, a large oak tree stands in the middle for people to enjoy its shade on hot summer days. Over time the tree too became sacred, and local people placed lights in its branches twice a week, on Mondays and Thursdays, to drive evil spirits from the village.

In the nineteenth century, the Ottoman state granted families in Aylut the right to cultivate large areas of arable land extending some six to seven kilometers to the west of the village. The land included parts of the fertile plains of Marj Ibn 'Amir (the Jezreel Valley) and was divided into feddans (areas of about one acre each). In 1902, the area comprised eighteen such tracts, which the village's twenty-one families cultivated communally. The main crops they produced were wheat, barley, sesame, *kirsanna* (a kind of vetch), and various species of legumes, including beans, chickpeas, and lentils. Lands lying alongside the built-up area of the village were used for growing vegetables and irrigated with water from the village wells and fountains. The high-lying land surrounding the village was planted with several varieties of fruit trees, including some 250 dunams (a unit of land equal to one thousand square meters) of olive groves. The surrounding hills also provided the pasture for the village, which, like other Palestinian villages at the time, was bounded on all sides by *sabir* (cactus) that kept wild animals out.

In 1869, the Ottoman government allowed a family from Beirut by the name of Sursuq to purchase full ownership rights to twenty-two villages in Marj Ibn 'Amir, including several areas of agricultural land surrounding Nazareth. This followed the Ottoman Land Law of 1859, which freed state lands for sale to individual Ottoman citizens, partly in an effort to raise badly needed revenue for the state's treasury. In total, the Sursuq brothers—Niqula, Najib, and Iskandar—acquired 230,000 dunams of land in the area. The Sursuqs were a new breed of capitalists to this part of the world, for whom the land and the fellahin (the country's peasant farmers), who had cultivated it for centuries, were mere tools to make an easy profit. The new owners used the local fellahin, as well as fellahin they brought in from other areas, to cultivate the vast stretch of land, but now as hired farm laborers. The Sursuqs provided them with more modern agricultural implements and appointed urban merchants as agents to manage the villages. That they themselves held only usufruct but no ownership rights to the land made little difference in the minds of the local fellahin, since, as in time immemorial, they were allowed to remain on the land and continued to make a living from it. Thus they did not fully grasp the dramatic shift in their situation when proprietorship of the land passed from the state to the Sursuqs. However, once a capitalist landowner was no longer in need of the fellahin to work his land, their situation stood to deteriorate dramatically. Additionally, the 1859 Ottoman Land Law entitled the new owners to dispose of their land to whomever they pleased, and as their main interest was profit, they were not likely to show much regard for the plight of the peasants.

As was the case in many other Palestinian villages, the people of Aylut slowly became victims of the high-interest loans they had to take out from an expending stratum of moneylenders—in the case of Aylut, the Sursuqs themselves. The preferred form of collateral for the loans was land, and when the fellahin were no longer able to meet the repayments, they effectively became hostages of the moneylender, who would await an opportune moment to use his credit as a means of appropriating their land.

For the people of Aylut this moment came in 1902. From then onward, they found themselves forced into waging a protracted and desperate struggle against displacement. In 1902, without prior notice, the Sursuq brothers served a lawsuit against the people of Aylut in the Nazareth Commercial Court for allegedly defaulting on the payment of their accumulated debts. The Sursuq brothers' orderly records and standing in society convinced the court to rule in their favor against the fellahin. Indeed, the court not only ordered the fellahin to pay off the arrears immediately but also ruled that in case they failed to do so, the Sursuqs were entitled to confiscate from them a piece of arable land equal in value to the sum of their debts. In court, the people of Aylut vehemently protested that the loss of their land made them feel like they had been "left naked on the beach."

ENTER THE GERMAN TEMPLERS

The Ayluti fellahin could not fathom why the patience of Najib Sursuq had suddenly come to an end, or why he had refused to pay the *werko* (state land tax) on their behalf, as he had always done until now according to the provisions of an annually renewed loan. They were also at a loss to understand why he had insisted on confiscating their arable lands as repayment for his loans. Answers to these questions have surfaced a century later in the form of a file of documents discovered in the German consulate in Haifa and housed in the Israel State Archives. The file contains, among other papers, documents relating to the Aylut-Sursuq case that form part of a separate lawsuit filed against the people of Aylut in 1903 by a certain Hans Keller, a German merchant living in Haifa's German Colony, with the active intervention of his brother, Friedrich (Fritz) Keller, at the time the German vice-consul in Haifa and Acre. The two lawsuits, of Keller and the Sursuqs, throw into sharp relief European colonizing endeavors in Palestine and the displacement and dispossession these spelled for the indigenous population.

As early as 1870, the Sursuqs initiated a procedure to rent out the village of Sammuniyya, located on arable lands in Marj Ibn 'Amir, to German settlers from the newly established German Colony in Haifa. The Germans belonged to a millenarian movement called the Templers, who originated in Württemberg and began arriving in Palestine, the Holy Land, in the early 1860s. The German settlers wished to establish agricultural colonies in Palestine, and renting the land was a first step toward purchasing it outright. Notables from Nazareth—local landowners and cereal merchants—and the fellahin who lived off the land raised a protest and secured the intervention of the local authorities, the *qadi* (magistrate) and the *qa'imaqam* (district governor) of Nazareth, who ordered the immediate evacuation of the new settlers. The Sursuq brothers unsuccessfully appealed the decision to the higher authorities in Damascus, who ruled that "the German colonization is illegal." For now, the fellahin, with the help of notables from Nazareth, had retained their farming rights to the land.

From then on, the struggle over the land of Aylut played itself out between the same six groups of actors: the fellahin cultivators and their urban notable allies, who operated in the local markets; the absentee landowners like the Sursuqs, who were motivated by capitalist and international interests; the German Templers; the German diplomatic corps; the local representatives of the Ottoman state in Nazareth and Beirut; and the representative of the Imperial Ottoman state in faraway Istanbul. These actors fell roughly into two groups: local and foreign. The local powers (the notables and the nearby state agencies) by and large wished to protect the fellahin and the traditional order of village life, whereas the more distant powers—both Ottoman and European—which had set in motion the economic modernization and political centralization of the Ottoman Empire, viewed the fellahin as obstacles to their aims. While economic modernization and attempts to strengthen the control of state authorities over outlying regions have undermined the traditional lives of peasants in many societies, in Palestine these forces frequently came from the outside, in the form of the few thousand Templers and later the mass-based Zionist movement, and led to dispossession. The story of Aylut repeated in another dozen Palestinian villages in the vicinity of Marj Ibn 'Amir.

The background to the attempted centralization and modernization of the Ottoman Empire had been its shift toward a market economy through its integration into the European-dominated world economy in the mid-nineteenth century. The rise of the market economy in Palestine naturally prompted the merchants' interests in land ownership as an investment. The second half of the nineteenth century witnessed a gradual growth in the ranks of urban merchants who had become major agricultural landowners, and the higher taxes they paid strengthened the central authorities of the empire.

A stronger Ottoman Empire was now able to improve the security situation in the Palestinian countryside. Better public safety coupled with an increased demand for agricultural produce led to a gradual migration of the fellahin from Palestine's mountainous areas to the fertile plains. Even so, fluctuations in crop prices and the inability of the fellahin to track developments in the world economy only increased their financial dependence on urban merchants and moneylenders. With the passage of time, as the loans owed by the fellahin accrued ever higher interest, they found themselves ensnared in a vicious circle: forced to use their loans to pay off older debts and provide for their immediate needs, they were unable to put them to productive use to improve the yield of the land. The fellahin were therefore unable to stimulate the development of the village economy. In the case of the people of Aylut, their mounting debts pushed them into unfavorable contracts, first with Najib Sursuq and later with Hans Keller.

The fellahin typically paid the moneylenders high rates of interest, often in excess of 30 percent, as shown by the popular local saying "*Al-'ashara khamsta'ash*"— that is, a loan of ten pounds extended during the sowing season could mean a return of fifteen pounds at the end of the harvest. The peasantry's spiraling debts were to play a significant role in their dispossession and in the gradual creation of a narrow stratum of large landowners that by now sharply contrasted with the growing stratum of landless peasants who had become agricultural laborers. This would be the destiny awaiting the fellahin of Aylut if Hans Keller were to convince the authorities of his case.

The timing of Najib Sursuq's decision to call in the debts of the people of Aylut was not accidental. At the dawn of the twentieth century, the Templers of the German Colony in Haifa decided to revive their plans for a new agricultural colony in Marj Ibn 'Amir, preferably in Galilean Bethlehem. The German colonizers looked upon Bethlehem in the Galilee—and not, as all other Christian denominations believe, the town of Bethlehem near Jerusalem—as the true birthplace of Christ. The Templers' ambitions coincided with the business interests of the Sursuqs, much as they had when the former attempted to colonize the village of Sammuniyya in 1870.

The Sursuq brothers by now enjoyed long-standing economic ties with the German Colony and were well known to the German settlers. German merchants living in the Haifa colony, for example, had become the Sursuqs' agents for the export of their agricultural produce. In 1871 the Sursuqs commissioned Gottlieb Schumacher, a German engineer living in Haifa's German Colony, to conduct a topographic survey of Marj Ibn 'Amir and examine the options for constructing a road or a railway to connect the area to the Haifa harbor.

In early 1902, the heads of the colony, including Hans Keller, entered into negotiations with the Sursuq brothers for the purchase of thousands of dunams of land in the Palestinian villages of Galilean Bethlehem and Umm al-'Umad for their new agricultural colony. The two villages straddled Aylut's fertile land, which lay to its west. Negotiations over the sale of the land ended in the Sursuqs' agreement to sell the German Colony fourteen thousand dunam, which included the entire villages of Galilean Bethlehem and Umm al-'Umad. The land also included some two thousand dunams that the state had confiscated from the people of Aylut a short time before as payment for the villagers' debts to the Sursuqs.

To complete the transaction to the satisfaction of both parties, Najib Sursuq wanted to make sure that ownership of the land would transfer to the investors from the German Colony in Haifa with the land "cleansed" of its population. His solution was to further tighten his economic stranglehold on the residents of Aylut and so force them to abandon their lands.

Needless to say, the villagers lacked the resources and legal backing to stand up to the economic and political clout wielded by the Sursuq brothers. Despite their sympathy for the crisis Aylut faced, this time Nazareth's Muslim cereal merchants, the town's qadi, and its mufti could do nothing to stave off the Commercial Court's order. Thus they merely directed the villagers to pay the arrears they owned to the Sursuqs and to the state or else relinquish their inherited usufruct rights to a portion of their land equal to the said arrears, land that the Sursuqs had decided to sell to the German colonizers. The only way left for the fellahin to defend their land and safeguard their livelihoods was to forcibly resist the police and government officials who arrived to execute the ruling of the Nazareth Commercial Court by confiscating the land and evacuating its inhabitants.

When local government officials set out to Aylut to confiscate village property and evacuate land on behalf of Najib Sursuq, the villagers, who rejected the court's ruling as unjust, took up arms to defend their homes and possessions. During the clashes, local government officials arrested sixty-five men and imprisoned them in Nazareth and Acre. Fritz Keller recorded the clashes as follows: "The people of Aylut, who are well-known rebels, opposed the police forces with violence and arms. Men and women alike gathered to attack government officials while they were executing the government's orders. They opened fire on them and struck them, injuring a number of them, and then threw them out of the village." As on numerous other occasions, Keller was quick to blame the victims, portraying the fellahin as having brought their own downfall upon themselves.

With many of the menfolk of Aylut behind bars, their families pursued all possible means of securing their release. It was in this context that a certain Hanna Mansour offered his services to the people of Aylut to extricate them from the crisis. Mansour was a familiar figure to the people of Aylut as a wealthy Nazareth merchant to whom they had sold their produce and who on several occasions had provided some of them with small, short-term loans. However, they were unaware of his second role, as an agent of Najib Sursuq. In this latter capacity, Mansour stored the agricultural produce of a number of the villages in the Marj Ibn 'Amir area in his warehouses in Nazareth before sending it to the harbor in Haifa. Mansour was well aware of what had transpired between Najib Sursuq, the local government, and the people of Aylut, and of the designs of the German Colony on the village's land. His personal interests went hand in glove with those of the German Colony, whose plans had the blessing of the Sursuqs.

Ostensibly to help solve the crisis, Mansour called for a meeting between the mukhtars (village chiefs) of Aylut and Hans Keller. The result was a new contract between Keller and twenty-one villagers who represented all the families that still held usufruct rights of the village's remaining arable lands. Mansour was not an impartial mediator, as he portrayed himself to his clients in Aylut, but acted with duplicity from the outset against their interests.

THE CONTRACT CONTROVERSY

Though we no longer have a copy of the contract that Hans Keller and the people of Aylut signed in 1902 in the Nazareth Commercial Court, we are familiar with its main terms, as parts of it appeared in court discussions. The twenty-one families of Aylut rented back their ancestral land from Hans Keller for a period of three years for a payment of one-tenth of their crops and promised not sell any of their crops without his permission. In return, Keller agreed to pay the village's werko for three years. In case of breech of contract—if the fellahin did not cultivate all the arable land in the next three years, or if Keller did not pay the werko—the offending party was to owe the harmed party 180 Turkish pounds per annum.

After the contract was signed, local authorities in Nazareth released the sixty-five prisoners from the village, thus enabling them to cultivate their land in accordance with the contract. When the harvest season drew near, Hans Keller sent guards to the village to ensure that all the crops were collected and stored in the village barns. There the produce awaited the arrival of Hanna Mansour, Keller's agent, who was to divide it up in accordance with the contract. In the meantime, the people of Aylut were required to keep the guards at their own expense and house them in lodgings close to the barns, which they did.

Under the contract, the transfer of Keller's share of the produce was conditioned on delivery of official receipts from the local government in Nazareth for the werko paid by Keller on the fellahin's behalf. When they discovered that he had not fulfilled this requirement and seemed to have no intention of doing so, they concluded that Keller and his agents had duped them. On 5 September 1903, when Mansour sent pack animals to transport Keller's quota to his storerooms in Nazareth, the people of Aylut refused to comply and sent the unloaded animals back. They then took the decision to dismiss Keller's guards and sell their entire agricultural yield, including Keller's quota, to merchants from Nazareth.

Deprived of his tenth of the harvest, Keller sprang into action. He immediately contacted his brother, Fritz, the German vice–consul, and asked him to file an official complaint against the people of Aylut to the Ottoman authorities. Fritz Keller sent an urgent letter via Nakhleh Qashu', the consulate's dragoman, to the qadi of Nazareth, who was also the town's acting qa'imaqam. In the letter, Fritz Keller described his brother Hans as the *multazim* (tax farmer officially appointed by Istanbul) of Aylut. Of course, the vice-consul was fully aware that Hans had no official relation to the village but presented him this way to portray him as someone representing the interests of the Ottoman state. The German vice-consul claimed that "the people of Aylut have dared to expel the guards to allow themselves to steal the harvest, under the assumption that no one possesses the power to stop them." He finally added, "In the name of the Imperial German Government, I urgently request that you arrest all the aforementioned persons and subject them to legal sanctions."

The local government in Nazareth, which was sympathetic to the local fellahin, ignored Keller's wishes and instead ordered an investigation into Mansour's actions. It understood the grave nature of Aylut's economic situation and decided to step in to avert the villagers' dispossession. Besides considering traditional rural give-and-take, the court may have acted in this way because it otherwise risked creating another band of displaced, landless, and destitute fellahin with no source of livelihood who would add to the growing social and political unrest.

THE NOOSE TIGHTENS

Failing to receive satisfaction from the local authorities, the German vice-consul sent another complaint, this time to a higher office, the mutasarrif (district governor) of Acre, the qa'imaqamiyya (administrative district) of Nazareth. The farther away from Aylut the Ottoman authorities were, the more they wished to enforce the authority of the empire at the expense of the fellahin. In this letter, Fritz Keller sought to turn the mutasarrif against the qa'imaqam of Nazareth, alleging that "the people of Aylut have dared to disregard the rights of Hans, at the prompting of the qadi of Nazareth, who has assured them of his protection. Rather than ordering that the guards be redeployed to Aylut to safeguard Hans Keller's rights, he summoned the guards and then had them imprisoned. Following their release, he forbade them to return to Aylut." The letter was threatening in tone and demanded that the mutasarrif "inform us of all you have done with regard to this matter, as I intend to seek the involvement of our higher representatives [the consul-general] in Beirut."

On the very same day, the vice-consul sent a letter to the qadi of Nazareth bluntly accusing him of being "indifferent to our complaints and unwilling to act" and of "inciting the fellahin. . . . What emboldened them was your counsel not to allow the guards into the village without your written permission, and to allow them to remove cereals from the village. . . . Therefore, in the name of the German Imperial Government, I shall appeal to the higher authorities to hold you personally responsible for all losses suffered by Hans Keller." This letter reveals the extent of the fury of the dragoman Nakhleh Qashu' at having failed to "subject" the qadi to the will of the vice-consul and at the qadi's reluctance to "obey . . . a representative of the German Empire." It also leaves no doubt that Keller considered himself above the law of the land and of a higher status than local officials, since he was a foreigner and enjoyed the protection of the Capitulations (extraterritorial privileges granted to Europeans by the weak Ottoman government).

Thus even before the proper legal procedures had run their course, Keller urged the mutasarrif of Acre to bypass the local authorities in Nazareth and "order the administrative detention of the people of Aylut [he attached a list of names] pending their payment of the arrears owed to Hans Keller and the expenses he has sustained." Fritz Keller further requested that "the qadi of Nazareth be held in custody, and the notables who had incited the people of Aylut be punished according to the law." Again, he ended his letter with the threat that "if this matter is not concluded forthwith, I shall take the case to the highest quarters."

What is most striking in this letter is Keller's request for the administrative detention of the people of Aylut. It is clear that he was not interested in bringing the accused to justice before the courts but rather intended simply to have them thrown in jail without trial, as if his complaint were the equivalent of a judicial decision that needed only to be implemented by the Ottoman authorities. The case of Aylut also evidences the willingness of European authorities to run roughshod over the judicial rights of Ottoman subjects and the sense of condescension with which the representatives of the German consulate approached Ottoman subjects and local Ottoman authorities.

With his continuing pressures and threats, Vice-Consul Keller succeeded in intimidating the mutasarrif, who summoned the qa'imaqam of Nazareth and asked him to resolve the case to the satisfaction of the complainant. But three months after the case started, convinced that the local Ottoman authorities had disregarded his requests and failed to fulfill what he saw as their duties, the vice-consul decided to bring his complaint to the highest available authority. In his letter to the German consul-general in Beirut, Keller related his version of the case and urged intervention to protect the interests of a German citizen. The German consul-general wasted no time in getting involved and wrote to the wali, or provincial governor, in Beirut, asking him to look into the matter. However, the wali evidently decided not to take the matter seriously and returned the case to the mutasarrif, whom he asked to "deal with the matter as your wisdom dictates." This could hardly be to the satisfaction of Fritz Keller, who sent the mutasarrif a still harsher letter warning that "if you do not deal with the case with due diligence you will be held personally responsible." Keller further stipulated:

> Since correspondence on this matter has been needlessly drawn out, and in view of the fact that the fellahin of Aylut have confessed to stealing the harvest belonging to Hans[,] . . . *there is no need to investigate or to hear testimonies from witnesses* [my italics]. . . . Thus, I repeat my demand for the administrative detention of the peasants until such time as they repay the debt owed to Hans and his expenses. . . . I can allow no further delay or complacency in this matter. . . . German interests must be upheld. . . . I thereby demand that your Excellency execute my request posthaste; otherwise I shall be obliged to appeal once more to higher authorities. I await developments in this regard.

The local authorities in Nazareth seized Aylut's sesame harvest, as Fritz Keller had requested, but transported it to their own storehouses in Nazareth and not to those of Hanna Mansour. They did so because Hans Keller had not paid the werko for Aylut's fellahin, as his contract with them obliged him to, sending the villagers into arrears on the tax. Having obtained permission from the Nazareth Commercial Court beforehand, the authorities in Nazareth delivered the sesame to the town's requisition department, which declared its intention to sell the crop at auction in payment of the tax. Seeing that his repeated threats had fallen on deaf ears, Fritz Keller realized he had no option but to launch a lawsuit and asked his brother to submit a formal complaint.

THE KELLERS VS. THE PEOPLE OF AYLUT

Thus we find that on 13 April 1904, Adib Salem, a lawyer from Nazareth, filed a lawsuit to the Commercial Court in Nazareth on behalf of Hans Keller against twenty-one people from Aylut. In the complaint, which contained an elaboration of his charges against the people of Aylut, Hans Keller demanded "that the persons identified be arraigned in accordance with the law, and after their defense has been heard, that a summary judgment be issued against them, binding them to: (1) pay 180 Turkish pounds in lieu of a tenth of the harvest; (2) pay the expenses of the guards; (3) pay my own personal expenses and damages; and (4) pay all the expenses of this court." Around two months later, with the defendants unrepresented, the court ruled in favor of the plaintiff and ordered the defendants to pay Keller the sum of 180 Turkish pounds, in addition to other losses he had incurred and the full court expenses.

Rather than appealing the ruling to the judicial authorities, the mukhtars of Aylut traveled to see the German consul-general in Beirut, hoping to persuade him to protect them against Keller. The fellahin were used to seeking protection from powerful patrons, in this case the representative of a foreign government, instead of working through institutional channels. They submitted a letter of grievance explaining the details of their case, starting with the actions of the Sursuqs, and listing the injustices that they believed Keller had visited upon them. Significantly, the people of Aylut addressed the consul-general as if he were a judicial authority with the power to annul the court's ruling. They underlined their inability to pay the sums demanded of them and pleaded, "Unless your Excellency saves us from the clutches of this despot [Keller], who has almost brought us to ruin, then we will surely be destroyed." The villagers concluded the letter with the following entreaty: "We trust that your Excellency will fulfill our wishes without delay.... Right is on our side, and in the name of justice we reiterate our appeal that you not turn us away empty-handed."

The consul-general handed the mukhtars a letter addressed to Keller, which asked him to receive them and try to reach a compromise acceptable to all parties. However, while the mukhtars were in Beirut, Fritz Keller pressured the qa'imaqam of Nazareth into executing the court ruling. Backed into a corner, the qa'imaqam relented and appointed a special committee to confiscate a section of arable land in Aylut equal to the debt owed to Hans Keller.

Armed with the consul-general's letter, the mukhtars meanwhile went to meet Hans Keller at his offices. Keller refused to make any concessions, even small ones, and insisted on the full application of the court's ruling. Alarmed by the very real threat of losing their lands, the people of Aylut offered to sign another three-year contract, as part of which they would repay Keller 400 pounds, which he demanded immediately, plus 140 pounds in interest over the course of three harvests because they couldn't pay the base sum right away. It was obvious from the outset to all involved that the fellahin of Aylut would have no way of fulfilling this commitment.

At the end of the harvest of 1906, the crisis of Aylut inevitably flared up again. As expected, the villagers were simply unable to raise the sums they had committed themselves to pay. Hans and Fritz Keller sent an urgent request via the qa'imaqam for the immediate implementation of the court's decision that the villagers' property be confiscated in payment for part of the debts owed to Hans. Officials from Nazareth's requisitions department set off to Aylut to execute the confiscation on 2 October 1906. The German vice-consulate in Haifa provided the officials with an inventory of all the possessions to be impounded, which Fritz Keller had personally compiled. The inventory tellingly illustrates how deeply the villagers had sunk into poverty: their possessions amounted to no more than seven hundred goats and sheep and a small number of horses and donkeys. Fritz Keller again was quick to pen his version of the developments that followed. He claimed that as soon as the head of the requisitions department arrived at the village, accompanied by the consulate dragoman Nakhleh Qashu' and several police officers, "the villagers, men, women, and children alike, assaulted them with weapons and cudgels and battered them with sticks and stones, forcibly preventing them from carrying out the confiscation and threatening to kill them. Had they not retreated, their very lives would have been in danger. Hence they turned back to Nazareth empty handed." The moment they had left, the villagers smuggled their animals to neighboring villages in the area, waiting for the immediate danger to pass.

THE LIMITS OF RESISTANCE AT THE DUSK
OF THE OTTOMAN ERA

The fellahin of Aylut were unable to protect their land in the modernizing Ottoman Empire, which was forced to placate European interests even when these undermined its sovereignty. But once more the fellahin were spared total destitution thanks to personal patronage—this time the intervention of the Nazareth merchant Arafat Abbas. Encouraged by the local government, Abbas lent them the sums they owed and provided them with working animals to plow and cultivate the land in return for a contract in which they committed to sell the local government all of the village's produce for the following three years, exempt of all taxes and duties. While Aylut's economic hardships continued unabatedly, its villagers had forestalled the confiscation of their lands and saved themselves from being uprooted, if only temporarily. Ultimately, in their struggle against the German Hans Keller, what enabled them to remain on their land and in their homes was the traditional convergence of their long-standing interests with those of the merchants from nearby Nazareth.

SUGGESTIONS FOR FURTHER READING

Conder, C. R. *The Survey of Western Palestine: Memoirs of the Topography, Orthography, Hydrography, and Archaeology.* London: Committee of the Palestine Exploration Fund, 1882, 1889.

Doumani, Beshara. *Rediscovering Palestine: Merchants and Peasants in Jabal Nablus, 1700–1900.* Berkeley: University of California Press, 1995.

Guerin, Victor. *Description géographique, historique et archéologique de la Palestine.* 7 vols. Paris: Imprimerie impériale, 1868–80.

Israel State Archives. Files of the German Consulate in Haifa, P\552\1737.

Khalidi, Rashid. *Palestinian Identity: The Construction of Modern National Consciousness.* New York: Columbia University Press, 1997.

Schölch, Alexander. *Palestine in Transformation, 1856–1882: Studies in Social, Economic and Political Development.* Translated by William C. Young and Michael C. Gerrity. Washington, D.C.: Institute for Palestine Studies, 1993.

Shumacher, G. "The Population of the Liva of 'Akka." *Palestine Exploration Fund Quarterly Statement,* 1887.

2

The Sephardi Entrepreneur and British Vice-Consul Haim Amzalak

Joseph B. Glass and Ruth Kark

Haim Amzalak awoke on the morning of December 12, 1916, in a villa in Alexandria and prepared for his audience with the Egyptian sultan Hussein Kamel, the son of the khedive Ismail Pasha. This was an important honor for him. Before he got out of bed that morning, his thoughts roamed through different events of his lifetime spent in Palestine. For the past two years, he had lived in exile after the Ottomans had deported subjects of enemy nations from their territory. Haim and his family, subjects of the British crown, had found refuge in British-controlled Egypt.

Amzalak's life may be viewed in the frameworks of the Middle Eastern entrepreneur class, the Sephardi Jewish elite, and political developments in the Ottoman Empire and Palestine in the nineteenth and the beginning of the twentieth centuries.

GROWING UP IN JERUSALEM

Haim Amzalak was born in the holy city of Jerusalem in 1828 to one of the most prominent Sephardic Jewish families of the city, who were part of the larger, cross-cultural Middle Eastern entrepreneurial class. Jerusalem at that time was a small city with no more than ten thousand inhabitants. They lived in an area of less than one square kilometer, enclosed by impressive walls which had been built on the order of Sultan Suleiman the Magnificent in the sixteenth century. However, by the early nineteenth century Jerusalem had become a backwater of the Ottoman Empire.

Haim was the middle child. He had a stepsister, Esther, from his father's first marriage. She married Eliyahu Navon, the son of one of Jerusalem's prominent rabbis. Haim had an older brother, Yitzhak David (b. 1825) who like Haim was born to his father's second wife, and two younger brothers, Solomon (b. 1832) and Raphael (b. 1835) from his father's third wife, Rachel. He and his siblings all dressed in the best clothing and wanted for nothing. Servants attended to the cooking, cleaning, and other domestic chores in their household. This was in contrast to most of Jerusalem's Jewish population who dwelled in squalid poverty, often in dilapidated structures. Many of the city's Jews were supported by contributions sent from Jews in the Diaspora.

His mother died when Haim was just a toddler. His stepmother Rachel, stepsister Esther, and the family servants raised him. He studied with private tutors who ensured that he was well versed in the Bible, the Talmud, and various rabbinical commentaries. Haim also learned Hebrew, Arabic, Ladino, English, and French.

His father, Joseph Amzalak, was a unique character in Jerusalem. He dressed in the Middle Eastern style and wore, in addition, a light blue pelisse faced with furs. He spoke English at a time when very few of the local inhabitants knew the language. Joseph was extremely proud of his English citizenship, which he received because of his birth in the British colony of Gibraltar. Joseph had been a merchant, plying his ships between Africa and the West Indies. He had twice visited London. Starting with little, he had become a very wealthy man. He had come to Jerusalem to spend his last days in acts of charity and awaiting his eventual death in order to be buried in Jerusalem in the cemetery on the Mount of Olives.

Haim knew his father to be a man of sincere beliefs. Joseph said that he had come to Jerusalem on the counsel of a rabbi whom he had met in Malta in 1813. At that time, Malta was suffering from a devastating plague, which took the lives of more than five thousand people. The rabbi warned Joseph that if he did not change his ways and make his home in the land of his forefathers, he too would fall prey to this plague. Joseph took heed and uprooted his family to Acre and then to Jerusalem. In 1816, Joseph received a *firman* (imperial edict) from Sultan Mahmoud II allowing him safe passage to Jerusalem. This firman was kept in the family home, cased in a special silver box inscribed with a large letter *A,* for *Amzalak.*

English-speaking residents and visitors of the city called on Haim's father. His home welcomed guests from many nations and faiths with coffee and sweets served by servants. From what Haim understood as a child, their conversations dabbled in religion, Christian missionary activities, politics, finance, and current events.

When Haim was eleven an English gentleman towering to the height of six feet three inches and his wife came to the Amzalak home. This was not the couple's first visit. Joseph told Haim of an earlier call in 1827, the year before Haim was born. This gentleman was none other than the famous English Jewish philanthropist Sir Moses Montefiore. Haim remembered the silver box that Sir Moses and his wife Lady Judith had bestowed upon his father after their second visit to the Holy Land in 1839. Haim knew the Hebrew inscription by heart: "A memento of affection and a token of gratitude, to a distinguished friend, who does acts of charity at all times, to Joseph Amzalak forever in the holy city of Jerusalem, that will be rebuilt in our lifetimes, in order that my memory will never forget it, Moses Montefiore, here in London, the capital, a great day in the year 5600 [1839/1840] to the creation of the world."

And then there was the Danish Christian missionary John Nicolayson, who headed the first British mission post in Jerusalem. He and his family frequently visited the Amzalak house. The Jewish community was suspicious of Nicolayson because his purpose for being in Jerusalem was essentially to convert Jews to Christianity. The rabbis cautioned the community to stay away from Nicolayson and the other missionaries, but Joseph did not pay any attention to these warnings. Haim often heard his father and Nicolayson discussing commentaries of the Bible at great length. It seemed that their discussion would always end up with each trying to convince the other with regard to the Messiah, and they would both quote different biblical passages and commentaries to prove their respective opinions.

The Amzalak house, within the walled Old City of Jerusalem, was a lively one, with five children and a number of servants. It was large, roomy, and filled with expensive furniture, a rare sight in Jerusalem at that time. On one occasion, a British gentleman, William Henry Bartlett, called on Haim's father. Bartlett was an artist. After a lengthy conversation, he received permission to spend time in their home sketching the family. A few years later, this sketch and a detailed written description of the family appeared in Bartlett's book *Walks about the City and Environs of Jerusalem.*

Haim grew up during trying times. When he was three, Muhammad 'Ali's Egyptian army took over the city with almost no resistance from the local Ottoman governor or his soldiers. This resulted in change and turmoil for the inhabitants of Jerusalem. Palestine was placed under the command of Ibrahim Pasha from 1831 to 1841.

In 1834 the rural population revolted against the repressive Egyptian policy of conscription and taxation. That May, hundreds of rebellious peasants from villages in the Nablus and Jerusalem areas, including the leading clan from the village of Abu Ghosh, near Jerusalem, stormed the city. On the 16th the city gates were closed and the siege of the city began. On the night of the 22nd the rebels took control of every part of the city except the citadel, where the soldiers had barricaded themselves in. The onslaught of hundreds of men struck terror into the hearts of the city's residents. Some houses were broken into, but by morning the rebel leaders had ordered their followers not to harm the Muslim, Christian, or Jewish inhabitants. For more than a week the rebels tried to take the citadel, but without artillery they were unable to penetrate its formidable fortifications. The besieged garrison fired back with canons. The Amzalaks lived close by, and during this battle they could hear the cannonballs that flew low over their house.

In the middle of the battles, on May 26, 1834, the windows of the Amzalak house began to shake, the house tottered, and stones fell everywhere. Jerusalem was experiencing an earthquake. Cries and shrieks could be heard throughout the neighborhood. The Amzalak family rushed out of their house after the first shock, fearing additional tremors. Like many others, they sought an open area to in which wait out the tremors and congregated in the Nicolaysons' large garden. Here there was not the threat of being crushed under a building. A second quake, stronger than the first, hit the city. Throughout the night the aftershocks continued.

The situation in Jerusalem was unbearable. There was a lack of supplies to the city. The rebels had looted some houses, and the earthquake had damaged some. The city was in turmoil, and the battle was still going on between the garrison held up in the citadel and the rebels. On the 28th the situation changed. Ibrahim Pasha and his forces landed in Jaffa and headed to Jerusalem. Upon hearing this news, the rebels quietly disappeared from the city, fearing the wrath of the Egyptian leader.

Under Muhammad 'Ali, edicts of discrimination against non-Muslims were partially annulled. Jews were allowed to pray at the Western Wall without obtaining prior permission and to build and renovate their prayer houses. In 1835 and 1836 Haim witnessed the renovation of the four Sephardic synagogues in the Jewish Quarter, in one of which his family prayed. The ashkenazim of the city built a new synagogue called Menahem Zion on the Hurva site, in 1837.

On January 1, 1837, another earthquake shook Jerusalem. It was not as intense a quake as the one in 1834, but within a couple of days news came that Safad and Tiberias had been devastated by the seismic disturbance, which was centered in the Galilee. The city walls of Tiberias toppled; most of houses there and in Safad lay in ruins. More than two thousand Jews from Safad and Tiberias perished in the earthquake or died of famine and disease following it. Some of those in the Galilee who survived the earthquake fled the area and took up residence in Jerusalem. This changed the Jerusalem's demographic composition, as many of the refugees were ashkenazim, while before the Sephardim had been the dominant Jewish group. Many refugees were malnourished, sick, and without any earthly possessions.

In addition to earthquakes, Jerusalem suffered from the ravages of epidemics again and again. These were times of fear, since no one knew who would fall prey to the plagues. In mid-May 1838, the city was placed under quarantine, which lasted more than two months. All direct communication with the rest of the country was cut off. Few fresh provisions passed through the gates. On July 6, Haim's older brother, Yitzhak David, died, but not from the plague. The quarantine authorities declared this, thus saving the family from special isolation. Quarantine officers escorted the family to bury him on the Mount of Olives. Joseph was inconsolable and Rachel, who was hysterical, wanted to flee the country. Haim's father was in tears when he called on Nicolayson, whom he implored to intervene on his behalf to obtain permission to take the family to Jaffa and if need be embark for another country.

In 1839, William Tanner Young, the first British vice-consul in Jerusalem, arrived. The Egyptian regime had given Britain permission to establish consular representation in the city. This would have a profound effect on the Amzalak family. As British subjects, they were extended special protection under the Capitulation agreements. Shortly after Young's arrival, an *euz bashi* (captain) of the Egyptian army beat Haim's father outside the citadel. Dr. Georgio Grasso and Haim's brother-in-law witnessed this outrage. Immediately Nicolayson complained to the commander of the garrison, but nothing was done. The matter was then brought to the attention of the vice-consul, who complained to Ibrahim Pasha that one of his subjects had been mistreated. Young demanded satisfaction. He insisted that the perpetrator be beaten on the same spot where he had beaten Joseph Amzalak. In the meantime, the *euz bashi* had been transferred to Damascus and, when questioned, denied that he had beaten Joseph Amzalak, and thus was not punished. Despite the lack of reparation, the Amzalaks were glad to be under the protection of the British consulate, and the immediate response to the incident, which had been a grave offence against Joseph Amzalak, would serve as a future warning against the abuse of any British subject in the city. For his part, Haim, like his father, was always proud to be a British subject.

Adulthood for Haim started with his bar mitzvah in 1841. One Saturday morning, his family congregated at the Yochanan Ben-Zakai Synagogue. The women were in a separate gallery, where they peered through wooden trelliswork. Haim was called up to the Sefer (Torah scrolls), recited the benedictions, and chanted a passage from the Prophets. From this point onward, he could be counted among the quorum of Jewish men needed for prayers.

Haim's teenage years were occupied with study. He trained in the Jewish tradition and also prepared for a career in business. He studied a number of languages, including Hebrew, English, and Arabic. He was a headstrong youth and at one point decided to quit his studies. This upset his stepmother Rachel to no end. She was unable to sleep at nights. She appealed to Chief Rabbi Yehuda Navon to intervene and speak to Haim in the hope that Haim would either study with his brother-in-law Eliyahu Navon or take on another tutor.

PUBLIC AND ENTREPRENEURIAL CAREER

In 1845, when Haim was seventeen, his father passed away. Joseph Amzalak's death at the age of seventy-seven was a great loss to the Jewish community of Jerusalem. Throughout his years in Jerusalem, he had been a pillar of the community and had been known for his philanthropy. He was buried in the Jewish cemetery on the Mount of Olives with all the pomp and ceremony befitting his elevated status. In fact, Joseph had originally settled in Jerusalem so that when the time came he would be laid to rest in the place that would allow him to be among the first resurrected when the Messiah arrived.

Prior to his death, Joseph had arranged for Haim's engagement to Esther, the daughter of a prominent rabbi, Joseph Levi of Hebron. Haim had no say in the matter, as was the tradition at the time. His father's selection of a bride for his son took into account social and financial connections that would best position Haim within the Jewish community. The couple's married life started out in Jerusalem in the 1850s. They would have five children together.

During Haim's early twenties, he gained some notoriety in Jerusalem. In 1851, he was imprisoned overnight in the British Consulate as a means of keeping the public peace. Haim was accused of committing an act of violence against someone in Jerusalem. He was taken before the British consul, James Finn, and vehemently denied the allegation. Nonetheless, Haim was detained for the night and required to deposit bonds as securities against his keeping the public peace. His wife was also accused of gross cruelty. The following year, Haim called on the British Consul to intervene when a fellah (peasant) insulted him in the street. The consul, representing the interests of a British subject, brought this incident to the attention of the Pasha of Jerusalem, and the fellah was punished. Haim also had a long-standing quarrel with his wife's brother. After three years, the British Consul in Jerusalem intervened to make peace between the two.

Whatever his local problems, Haim needed to travel abroad to secure new business connections, which he did in 1852. This was a lengthy journey that included stops in Lombardy (today in northern Italy), the Venetian states, and the Austrian territories. On his return trip he stopped in Trieste, Corfu, Smyrna (Izmir), and Beirut before landing in Jaffa. The relationships forged during this trip would become part of the foundation of his business as an international trader.

Haim moved from Jerusalem to Jaffa to further his business activities, as Jaffa was developing as the main port for goods entering and leaving Palestine. By permanently residing there, Haim could keep track of the market and develop connections with local and foreign merchants. He could also oversee the cargoes entering and leaving the port. Some fifty years later, Haim was amused by the fact that his decision to move merited mention in the *Jewish Encyclopedia*. Under the entry for Jaffa, he found the following: "Jews even from Jerusalem went to Jaffa and established themselves there for commercial purposes. Among these may be cited Amzaleg [sic], the present English consul in the city."

When Haim and his family settled in Jaffa, the city had a population of some five thousand people. The majority were Muslim, but they were of mixed origins. Some families settled in Jaffa in the eighteenth century, while others had migrated from other parts of Palestine in the nineteenth century. As in many port cities, one could find a mix of immigrants. They had come from Egypt, North Africa, Lebanon, and as far away as Afghanistan. Close to a third of the city's inhabitants were Christian. This population was also diverse, with Greek Orthodox, Catholics, Maronites, Armenians, and Copts. In the mid nineteenth century, the Jewish community did not exceed 350 people (out of a total of about 5,000). It was predominantly Sephardim and Maghrebi Jews (North Africans). There were only three ashkenazi families. Over the sixty-some years that Haim lived in the city, its population increased tenfold, and the number of Jews reached around fifteen thousand (out of a total of forty thousand). Haim watched the city undergo a rapid transition and changes in its demographic composition. By 1890, there were more ashkenazi than Sephardi Jews. There was also a secularizing trend among the Jewish population, particularly the ashkenazi immigrants. More Christian immigrants arrived, including a group of American Protestants who came and left in the 1860s and the German Templers, who began to arrive at the end of the 1860s.

In Jaffa, Haim established Haim Amzalak and Company, a trading firm that exported local grains, oranges, and other agricultural produce and imported British manufactured goods. In 1875 he became the local representative of the British insurance underwriting company Lloyd's. For a number of years, he worked in partnership with the first Jewish bank in Jerusalem, Jacob Valero and Company. His business transactions extended into investment in real estate. He and his wife owned oranges groves in the vicinity of Jaffa, and he also purchased land with other wealthy Jews in Jaffa—Aharon Chlouche and Joseph Moyal—with the intention of developing or reselling it. Some of this land was parceled into building plots in what became new Jewish neighborhoods in Jaffa and later part of the new city of Tel Aviv. Haim rose to be one of the most prominent businessmen in Jaffa and also a community leader.

Haim and Esther raised their family in Jaffa. They had five children, Joseph (b. 1860 and named in memory of Haim's father), Bolissa (b. 1862), Abraham (b. 1864), Rosa, and Sultana. Haim also took it upon himself to raise his nephew Ben-Zion following the early death of his brother Solomon in Jaffa in 1876.

The family lived in an impressive three-story house close to the port, where one could hear the hustle and bustle of porters, traders, peasants, pilgrims, and city residents. During the hot and humid summers, the family would often stay in their estate (*bayara*) outside the city. It was a relaxing and comfortable place to stay, with an irrigated garden filled with various fruit trees and vines, and on one occasion they entertained Sir Moses Montefiore there. The only drawback was the mosquitoes that infested the area.

The couple provided their children with a traditional Jewish education, which was supplemented with a well-rounded general education and the study of different local and European languages. The children were raised in a wealthy milieu and taught manners befitting their status and English tradition. In 1875, on his fifth visit to the Holy Land, Sir Moses Montefiore described them as "most amiable." He took a special liking to Bolissa and arranged for the shipment of a piano from England to the family in Jaffa.

After Esther passed away, Haim remarried and fathered four more daughters— the twins Rachel and Rozina (b. 1896), Gamila (b. 1900), and Fortuni (b. 1902). Haim had these children when he was in his late sixties and early seventies.

As tradition dictated, Haim groomed his eldest son to take over the family business. Joseph apprenticed at his father's side in the field of international trade and for twenty-five years served as the surveyor of the Lloyd's agency under his father. When Haim retired from his position with Lloyd's in 1911, his son took over. Haim also enlisted his nephew Joseph Navon in some of his business dealings. Navon acted as Haim's business representative in Jerusalem for a number of years.

CONSULAR ACTIVITY

As Haim became more established in Jaffa and better known as a businessman and community leader, Portugal—from which the Amzalak family had originated and where it still had relatives—recognized him and appointed him its consul in Jerusalem in 1871. This title carried great status, as the representative of a foreign country in Palestine. Haim was responsible for Portuguese interests in the region, which were quite limited, as there was no direct trade between Portugal and Palestine and very few Portuguese visitors to the Holy Land. He held this position for twenty-one years.

In 1872, Haim received a more prestigious appointment, the British vice-consulship for Jaffa. The British had strong interests in the region, their trade connections with Jaffa were expanding, and numerous British citizens passed through the port city on route to Jerusalem. According to some of his rivals, Haim received this position because he was the only eligible British subject in Jaffa. But Haim knew that the British consul in Jerusalem, Noel Temple Moore, held him in high esteem as a loyal and capable British subject.

Following his appointment as vice-consul, Haim raised the Union Jack over his house in Jaffa. Afghani guards were stationed outside his home, and when he walked through the city on official business, two *kawasses* (consular guards) would escort him, striking their metal-tipped batons on the ground to let all know that the British vice-consul was just steps behind them. Haim also often wore a special uniform that displayed his position. It consisted of the levee dress of a British vice-consul and was adorned with embroidered cuffs, epaulettes, and bullion fringes as well as a sword. He would wear this uniform for formal occasions when greeting important British guests and when he met with Ottoman officials. Haim saw this position as one of honor and would not accept a salary for his work.

The local Jewish community was very proud of Haim's achievement. The Hebrew newspaper the *Habazeleth* reported on his appointment: "Today is a happy day for Israel, today a royal decree was read appointing Haim Amzalak to the position of vice-consul of Great Britain." He also received congratulatory notes and greeted Sir Moses Montefiore when the latter came on his last visit to Palestine in 1875. Haim, in his capacity as vice-consul, sailed out to Montefiore's ship, which was anchored just outside the port, with his two kawasses furnishing their official batons. Montefiore could not contain his joy. He wrote in his diary: "It was a source of high gratification to me to see one of my brethren, a native of the Holy Land, filling so high and honorable an office. I knew his father well. He was one of the most worthy and charitable of our brethren in Jerusalem, and I am now much pleased to have the opportunity of evincing my regard for his son, whose abilities and high character had been so honorably acknowledged by the consular functions entrusted him."

This consular duty was quite demanding. Haim represented the interests of the British government and British subjects either visiting or residing in the Jaffa area. Since Jaffa was a commercial port, he had the added task of reporting on trade activities. His reports provided detailed statistics on the annual volume of imports and exports, recounting type and quantity of goods and the national flags of the ships engaged in this trade. His reports also described trends and incidents affecting trade in the region: the annual harvests, changes in agricultural production, public works projects, plagues, and a disproportionately large amount of information about the development of the new Jewish and German Templers' agricultural settlements.

Haim was concerned about the port's situation. The ships arriving at Jaffa anchored off the coast. Small rowboats went from the port to the ships to load the oceangoing vessels. When weather conditions were bad, the sea was rough, and on occasion the anchored ships broke free and were dashed to pieces on the reefs of rocks near the landing place, sometimes killing passengers and losing cargo. This was almost the case with the Russian ship *Chihchov*, which in 1891 hit rocks two hundred meters off the coast and started to break up. Many of the passengers were on deck, panic stricken and awaiting assistance. The *qa'imaqam* (governor) of Jaffa ordered soldiers along the shore to keep everyone away from the ship until the Russian consul reached the scene. Haim, who was informed of the imminent danger to the ship's passengers, pressured the Russian consul to act immediately. He, the Russian consul, and the *qa'imaqam* successfully coordinated the rescue operation.

Haim imbued his children with a love of and loyalty for England. When the HMS *Bacchante* called at the port of Jaffa, Haim's son Joseph greeted Prince George and Prince Albert Victor of England and accompanied them on part of their ride toward Jerusalem. In 1882, Joseph went on a special mission for his father. The British government had sent the Oxford professor Edward H. Palmer to the Sinai Peninsula to persuade the Bedouin to remain neutral during the British occupation of Egypt. Following the British bombardment of Alexandria, Haim sent his son to warn Palmer of a potential anti-British Arab backlash. Joseph, disguised as a Bedouin, rode from Jaffa to Gaza. There he warned Palmer of the local populace's hostility toward the British. Palmer slipped out of Gaza under the cloak of darkness and safely crossed the Sinai into British-controlled Egypt. The qa'imaqam of Gaza sent soldiers to arrest Joseph, but he successfully evaded his pursuers by leaving the main road and quickly riding to Jaffa along the coast. The English government wanted to reward him with the large sum of five hundred pounds for his services. He flatly refused to accept it. Eventually, the Earl of Granville, on behalf of the British government, presented him with a gold medal, which was inscribed, "Presented to Mr. J. Amzalak by H. M. Government, 1884." Haim was extremely proud of his son on this occasion.

Joseph was also among the founders and served as president of the Anglo Jewish Club. Haim was most gratified on the occasion of the club's celebration of the coronation of King George V and Queen Mary in 1911 when his son gave a speech declaring how everyone present felt the same patriotism, devotion, and loyalty, and how their hearts went out to their sovereigns with the same sincerity as that of their friends in England.

ASSISTING JEWISH ORGANIZATIONS AND SETTLERS

Haim had an important role in the Jewish community. He was involved in acts of charity and the leadership of different groups. He served as president of the local branch of the Alliance Israélite Universelle, an organization established in France in 1860 to promote modern education among Jewish communities in North Africa and the Middle East. He was a leader of the Sephardi community of Jaffa and was part of an effort to create a united community council of Sephardi, ashkenazi, and North African Jews in 1890.

Haim took particular interest in the efforts of Jews in Palestine to return to the soil. The Mikveh Israel agricultural school was set up on the outskirts of Jaffa in 1870. Haim supported this project to educate young Jews in agricultural productivity but at the same time was critical of the school's achievements. He believed that the funds invested in it could have been used to reap greater benefits.

Groups of Jewish settlers called on Haim in the early 1880s to help acquire land for new agricultural projects. Through his business connections, Haim knew certain Arab landowners and was aware of the market value of different tracts of land. He was also well versed in the customs of negotiations with Arab owners, and he had the status and legal protection of a British vice-consul. Haim was involved in purchases for two of the first Jewish colonies near Jaffa—Petach Tikvah and Rishon Letzion.

Haim's involvement in the fledgling Jewish movement to return to the soil extended to financial contributions and his role as honorary president of Va'ad Halutzei Yesod HaMa'ala (the avant-garde committee for the colonization of Palestine). In this capacity, he set sail for Constantinople in May 1882 to meet with Laurence Oliphant. This prominent British proto-Zionist hoped to obtain a lease of the northern half of Palestine from the Ottoman sultan, with a view to settling large numbers of Jews there. Haim was to advise him on possible lands for future Jewish settlement. However, the timing for the realization of this plan was wrong. The British invasion of Egypt later that year curtailed these efforts.

THE FIRST WORLD WAR AND DEPORTATION TO EGYPT

Haim's life in Palestine came to an end in 1914. World War I broke out on August 1 that year. The Ottoman Empire on September 8 annulled the Capitulation agreements that it had made with foreign governments, including Great Britain. Subjects of Britain were considered enemies of the empire and were under the threat of internment or expulsion. The Ottoman regime offered the Jews of Palestine who were subjects of foreign governments the opportunity to renounce their foreign citizenship and take up Ottoman citizenship. For Haim and his family this was not a viable solution. They had been loyal subjects of the British crown for decades. Haim had been the British vice-consul in Jaffa for more than thirty years. It was unthinkable for him to relinquish his British citizenship.

On December 17, 1914, the expulsion of citizens of enemy states (Britain, France, and Russia) from Palestine began. Beha ed-din Effendi, the new qa'imaqam of Jaffa, issued orders that non-Ottomanized belligerents be deported that afternoon at four o'clock. That day, the police started to round up foreign Jewish inhabitants of Jaffa from the streets and their houses. Many of these people were dragged to the port without being allowed to collect their belongings. As Jaffa still only offered offshore anchorage, rowboats transported the deportees to an American ship, the USS *Tennessee* (the United States was neutral at this point in the war). Some of the Arab boatmen took advantage of this situation by beating and robbing the refugees. There was absolute pandemonium. Many families were separated.

In fleeing Jaffa, Haim and his family abandoned most of their possessions and property to plunder and destruction, but they managed to smuggle out some jewels and gold. Haim had believed that the war would last only three or four months, but as it dragged on they rented a villa in Alexandria, where they had fled. Fortunately, Haim's son Abraham had already been living in Egypt, where he enjoyed a position of authority and importance in the colonial administration. He was able to facilitate his family's relocation.

Haim's grandsons also made him proud during the war. Maurice joined the Jewish military unit in the British Army, the Zion Mule Corps. This 650-man supply unit served in Gallipoli. Three sons of his nephew Ben-Zion Amzalak, James, Edward, and Daniel, also enlisted in the British Army during their exile in Egypt. Daniel was a sergeant-major in charge of rationing at the Suez Canal town of Kantara. Edward, a medical doctor, was stationed in Cairo and reached the rank of captain. James, also called Jimmy, served in the British medical corps. These members of the Amzalak family exhibited the same loyalty to Britain as their parents and their grandfather Haim.

HAIM'S END

As Haim was getting ready for his audience with the Egyptian sultan Hussein Kamel in December 1916, his thoughts were on his achievements and his family. He felt proud to be a loyal British subject. He finished dressing and preparing for the visit. Haim asked for a glass of water and then collapsed. His family gathered around him, and within moments, he had stopped breathing. He passed away at the age of eighty-eight in exile from the land of his birth but under the flag that he had held so dear. He was buried in the Shatbi Sephardi Jewish cemetery in Alexandria.

SUGGESTIONS FOR FURTHER READING

This narrative is based on material from Joseph B. Glass and Ruth Kark, *Sephardi Entrepreneurs in Eretz Israel: The Amzalak Family, 1816–1918* (Jerusalem: Magnes Press, 1991). For more on another prominent family, see Glass and Kark, *Sephardi Entrepreneurs in Jerusalem: The Valero Family, 1800–1948* (Jerusalem and New York: Gefen Publishing House, 2007).

On the history of Jaffa in the late Ottoman period, see Kark, *Jaffa—A City in Evolution, 1799–1917* (Jerusalem: Yad Izhak Ben-Zvi, 1990). On the history of Jerusalem in the late Ottoman period, see Kark and Michal Nordheim Oren, *Jerusalem and Its Environs—Quarters, Neighborhoods and Villages, 1800–1948* (Detroit: Wayne State University Press, 2001).

On the history of Sephardi Jews in Palestine, see Kark and Glass, "Sephardi and Oriental Jews in Eretz-Israel/Palestine, 1800–1948," in Reeva Simon, Michael Laskier, and Sara Reager, eds., *Jews in the Middle East and North Africa* (New York: Columbia University Press, 2003), pp. 335–46.

3

A Musician's Lot

Wasif Jawhariyyeh's Old Jerusalem

Salim Tamari

Conventional narratives about the modernity of Jerusalem regard the city in the late nineteenth century as a provincial capital in the Ottoman hinterland whose social fabric was basically communitarian and confessional. Ethnicity and sectarian identities were identical, as confessional consciousness was defined in ethnic-religious terms, and the boundaries of these identities were physically delineated by habitat in the confines of the Old City quarters. The quartered city corresponded, in these narratives, to the ethno-confessional divisions of the four communities: Muslim, Christian, Armenian, and Jewish. In these quarters social nodes were more or less exclusive, physically defined, and reinforced by mechanisms of mutual aid, craft specialization, ritual celebrations, internal school systems, and, above all, the rules of confessional endogamy. Although there was a substantial degree of interconfessional interaction in the city, it was confined mainly to the marketplace and ritual social visitations. The modernity of the city is seen as the product of the breakup of the Ottoman system under the triple impact of European penetration, Zionist immigration, and the modernizing schemes of the British Mandate.

Although on the eve of the First World War Jerusalem had a strong communitarian makeup and religious identity was very pronounced, the communal boundaries were nevertheless primarily defined not by confession or ethnicity but by the *mahallat,* the neighborhood unit. (An exception is the case of the Armenians, who congregated around the Armenian Patriarchate.) The British Mandate dropped this neighborhood unit from usage as an administrative unit in favor of the quarter system (*hay* or *harat*), which was based on distinctly religious sectarian identity.

The bonds of patronage and clientelism superseded and supplemented communal bonds of confessional affiliation.

In this chapter I will use my reading of the memoirs of a Jerusalem musician, Wasif Jawhariyyeh, to point to substantial weaknesses in this conventional narrative. I suggest that Jerusalem's modernity was a feature of the internal dynamics within the Ottoman city and propose that the social structure of the walled city was much more fluid than is generally believed. Furthermore, I will argue that the quarter system dividing the Old City into bounded confessional domains was introduced and retroactively imposed on the city by British colonial regulations.

THE OUD PLAYER AND HIS FAMILY

"I was born on Wednesday morning, the 14th of January 1897, according to the Western calendar, which happened to be the eve of the Orthodox New Year. At the moment my father was preparing a tray of *knafeh,* as was customary then in Eastern Orthodox households. I was named Wasif after the Damascene Wasif bey al-'Adhem, who was then my father's close friend and the sitting judge in Jerusalem's Criminal Court."

Thus opens the memoirs of Wasif Jawhariyyeh, one of Jerusalem's most illustrious citizens: composer, oud player, poet, and chronicler. They cover a period of forty-four years of Jerusalem's turbulent modern history (1904–48), spanning four regimes and five wars. More significantly, they mark the transition of Palestinian society into modernity and the breaking out of its Arab population beyond the ghettoized confines of the walled city.

Wasif's father, Jiryis (Girgis), was the mukhtar of the Eastern Orthodox Christian community in the Old City (1884) and a member of Jerusalem's municipal council under the mayoralty of Salim al-Husseini and Faidy al-Alami. Trained as a lawyer, he was well versed in Muslim shari'a law and spoke several languages, including Greek, Turkish, and Arabic. He worked briefly as a government tax assessor but later turned to private business as a silk farmer and café proprietor. He was also a skilled icon maker and amateur musician, and he encouraged his son's musical talents. Wasif's mother, Hilaneh Barakat, descended from a leading Orthodox family from what later became known as the Christian Quarter.

Wasif's father and grandfather both occupied important public positions, but the men of the family also held a number of more modest occupations. Wasif's elder brother Khalil was a carpenter's apprentice before being conscripted into the Ottoman army, and Wasif himself held a number of odd jobs before he became an itinerant oud player and began singing at wedding parties. The family's fortunes improved significantly when Jiryis became a prominent lawyer and bailiff, Khalil opened a successful café near Jaffa Gate, and Wasif entered government service. We can say with some certainty that the family members inhabited that precarious space between artisanal workers and the middle ranks of the civil service. However, it is impossible to understand the Jawhariyyehs' social position in pre-Mandate Palestine without relating it to their critical bonds as protégés of the Husseini family, feudal landlords and patricians in Jerusalem's inner circle of a'yan (notables). Jiryis spent part of his early career looking after the Husseini estates in Jerusalem's western villages, and after his death Wasif was "adopted" by Hussein Effendi, who later became mayor of Jerusalem. Hussein Effendi arranged a number of jobs in the city for Wasif and ensured that he was treated well in the Ottoman army. The family was on such intimate terms with their patrons that Wasif was entrusted with the welfare of Hussein Effendi's mistress, Persephone, when she became ill.

Wasif's musical career occupies a substantial part of his memoirs. We are fortunate to have his unpublished "Musical Notebook," which he began just prior to World War I. It reflects the progression of Wasif's interests from classical *andalusiat* and Aleppo *muwashshahat* to choral music (which he performed at weddings and family celebrations), love songs, melodies based on classical poetry, and finally *taqatiq* and erotic songs. Untrained in musical notation, Wasif invented his own system. He also wrote a chapter on the adaptation of the Western notation system for the oud.

Using a method of marking time that is typical in semiliterate cultures, Wasif traces the beginning of his musical career to the "year of the seven snowstorms," which he later figures was either 1906 or 1907, when he was nine years old. During the festival of Saint Dimitri that year the Jawhariyyeh household was celebrating the saint's birthday when their neighbor and friend, Mitri Abdallah Khalil, then an apprentice carpenter, constructed for Wasif his first tambourine.

> Qustandi al-Sus was one of the most famous singers in the mahallat. He sang for Sheikh Salameh Hijazi on his renowned oud most of the evening, and then they allowed me to perform. I danced the *dabkeh*, then I sang a piece of "Romeo and Juliet" to the melodies composed by Sheik Salameh and the accompaniment of Qustandi's oud. When the latter heard me he was so pleased that he handed me his precious oud—which drove me into a frenzy—and I began to play it and sing to the tune of "Zeina . . . Zeina." The next day my father took a barber's blade and forged me a beautiful handle for my tambourine. . . . Thus began my musical career at the age of nine.

The Jawhariyyeh house was the perfect location for developing his musical talents. All the family members—with the exception of Tawfiq, who was tone deaf—either played instruments or sang, or at least enjoyed good music. Jiryis was one of the few Jerusalemites who owned a Master's Voice phonograph (as he called it), and he had a number of early recordings by leading Egyptian singers, such as

Sheikh Minyalawi and Salameh Hijazi. He encouraged his children to lip-synch along with these records and was particularly severe with Wasif when he made mistakes. Jiryis was also keen to host prominent singers and musicians who visited Jerusalem. One of these, the Egyptian oud player Qaftanji, spent a week with the Jawhariyyehs, and from him Wasif learned a number of melodies that he used to sing on summer nights on the roof or in the outhouse.

Jiryis was sufficiently moved by his son's desire that he allowed him to accompany a number of well-known performers in Mahallat as-Sa'diyyeh to learn their art. They included Hanna Fasheh, who crafted his own instruments, and Sabri Abed Rabbo, who sold Wasif his first oud when he was eleven years old. Jiryis was so impressed with Wasif's persistence that he even hired one of Jerusalem's best-known oud tutors, Abdul Hamid Quttaineh, to give him lessons twice a week.

Contrary to the impression conveyed by Wasif's comments about his truancy and rebelliousness, he had a substantial amount of formal schooling in addition to his musical training. This education is reflected in his polished language, rich poetic imagination, and elegant handwriting. References abound in his diaries to classical poetry and contemporary literature by figures such as Khalil Sakakini, Ahmad Shawqi, and Khalil Gibran. Wasif and Tawfiq first attended the Dabbaghah School, which was governed by the Lutheran Church next to the Holy Sepulcher. At school Wasif learned basic Arabic grammar, dictation, reading, and arithmetic. He also studied German and Bible recitation. His school uniform was the *qumbaz* and the Damascene red leather shoes known as *balaghat.* In 1909, when Wasif was twelve years old, the brothers were taken out of the Dabbaghah School after the mathematics teacher savagely beat them for mocking him. For several years thereafter, Wasif accompanied his father while he worked as overseer of the Husseini estates; he also occasionally performed as a singer (and later an oud player) in the neighborhood.

When Khalil Sakakini established his progressive Dusturiyyeh National School in Musrara, Jiryis intervened with the mayor to have Wasif admitted as a day student. Sakakini had acquired a reputation for using radical methods of pedagogy in his school and for strictly banning physical punishment and written exams. In addition to advanced grammar, literature, and mathematics, the curriculum included English, French, and Turkish. Sakakini was a pioneer in introducing two disciplines unique to his school at the time: physical education and Qur'anic studies for Christians. His study of the Qur'an strongly influenced Wasif. He writes:

> I received my copy of the Qur'an from al-Hajjeh Um Musa Kadhem Pasha al-Husseini . . . who taught me how to treat it with respect and maintain its cleanliness. My Qur'anic teacher was Sheikh Amin Al-Ansari, a well-known faqih in Jerusalem. Sakakini's idea was that the essence of learning Arabic lies in mastering the Qur'an, both reading and incantation. My Muslim classmates and I would start with Surat al-Baqara and continue. . . . I can say in all frankness today that my mastery of Arabic

music and singing is attributed to these lessons—especially my ability to render classical poetry and *muwashshahat* in musical form.

Sakakini was a music lover who had a special fondness for the oud and the
violin. Some of the Dusturiyyeh students had seen Wasif performing in local weddings and taunted him for being a "paid street singer" (*ajeer*), but Sakakini defended him and taught the students to enjoy Wasif's music. Eventually, despite
his love for the Dusturiyyeh National School's liberal environment, Wasif was
compelled by his patron, Hussein al-Husseini, to enroll in al-Mutran School (St.
George's) in Sheikh Jarrah, "to gain knowledge of the English language and build
a solid base for my future." At al-Mutran Wasif excelled in acting in school plays,
in which he was also able to develop his musical talents. He remained there for
two years (1912—14), until the school was closed at the beginning of the war. Wasif
finished the fourth secondary class (his tenth year of studies) and ended his formal
schooling without a secondary school certificate.

After the termination of his formal schooling, Wasif continued his musical
education in the company of Jerusalem's foremost oud players and composers, including his first tutor, Abdul Hamid Quttaineh; Muhammad al-Sibasi; and Hama-
deh al-Afifi, who taught him the art of *muwashshahat* in the Turkish tradition.
But Wasif's most important mentor was the master oud player Omar al-Batsh. In
the spring of 1915, after his father's death, Wasif accompanied Hussein Effendi and
several Turkish officers to a party at which a division of the army military band
known as the Izmir Group was performing Andalusian *muwashshahat*. Wasif
was mesmerized by the performance of a young oud player wearing a military
uniform, who was introduced to him as Omar al-Batsh. Omar became Wasif's
constant companion for the duration of the war. Wasif prevailed upon Hussein
Effendi, now his official patron, to hire Omar to give him four oud lessons a week
at the headquarters of the army orchestra in Mascobiyyeh.

From Omar, Wasif learned how to read musical notation and considerably expanded his repertoire of classical Arabic music. Omar began to bring Wasif to his
performances to sing and accompany him on the oud, but above all he taught him
to be a discriminating listener and instructed him in the performance of the classical *muwashshahat*. Throughout his diaries Wasif refers to Omar as "my teacher"
and "my master."

Throughout his adult years, Wasif saw himself as a musician and oud player
above all else. Nevertheless, he held a number of different jobs during his adolescence and afterward. These ranged from apprenticeships held in his youth to government positions arranged by his patrons. When Wasif sought employment in
various government and municipal agencies, it was only to provide the resources
he needed to dedicate himself to his passionate obsession: the oud and the company of men and women who shared his vision.

As was customary in the Old City, Wasif held a number of apprenticeships during his boyhood. These assignments supplemented his formal schooling and often
furthered his evolving musical career. In the summer of 1907, at the age of nine,
Wasif became an apprentice in the barbershop of Mattia al-Hallaq (Abu ʿAbdal-
lah). A barber in Ottoman Jerusalem was much more than a hairstylist: he was also
an herbalist, was trained to apply leeches for bloodletting and suction cups for the
relief of congestion, and in general performed the function of a local doctor. It is
possible that Jiryis wanted one of his sons to follow such a vocation, but Wasif had
other ambitions.

> I would hold the customer by the neck while Abu ʿAbdallah was washing his hair
> so that the water would not drip down his shirt. Water was poured from a brass pot
> and would flow directly from his head to another brass container that was clasped
> around the customer's neck. [Initially] I was delighted with this first job. In the eve-
> ning my brother Khalil would pass by in the company of Muhammad al-Maddah,
> a *qabadayy* [tough guy] and grocer from Mahallat Bab al Amud. Muhammad was
> initiating Khalil into the arts of manhood, and both of them would take me to their
> odah (garçonnière), where we would play the tambourine and sing.

Wasif learned creative truancy at this time. He would escape his master's shop
to listen to the oud played by Hussein Nashashibi at another barbershop—that of a
certain Abu Manuel, whose shop the Nashashibi family owned. It was also during
this period that Wasif's obsession with oud performance began and he started to
seek out musical instruction.

Hussein Effendi, Wasif's patron, arranged his first paid job, as a clerk in the municipality of Jerusalem in charge of recording contributions for the Ottoman war
effort. After a short bout of service in the Ottoman navy, Wasif resumed his career
in the municipality at the end of the war, when he was promoted to the position
of court clerk in the Ministry of Justice, serving under Judge Ali bey Jarallah in
Mascobiyyeh. After the death of Hussein Effendi (whom Wasif called "my second
father"), Wasif resigned from his job at the court in order to help Hussein's widow,
Um Salim, with the administration of the Husseini estates in Deir Amr.

Hussein Effendi, who had served as mayor from 1920 to 1934, was succeeded
by Ragheb Bey al-Nashashibi, after Ismaʿil al-Hussaini and Musa Kazim al Husseini briefly filled the position. Ragheb was an amateur oud player and socialite
who hired Wasif to give oud and singing lessons to him and his mistress, Um
Mansour. As compensation, Wasif was added to the payroll of the Tax Bureau
with a monthly salary of twenty Egyptian pounds. At the end of each month,
Wasif would go to the Regie (tobacco state monopoly) Department and collect
his salary, without being required to perform any further duties. His relationships
with the Husseini family and later the Nashashibis (who became ascendant under
British rule) helped him to pursue his career as a musician while maintaining a

steady income from public coffers. Here is how he describes one of those many jobs:

> Musa Kazim Pasha, then mayor of Jerusalem, sent for me through Sergeant Aref al-Nammari. I went to meet him in city hall, then located at Jaffa Gate. He rebuked me for staying out of touch since the death of the late Hussein Effendi and asked about my family, especially about the health of my mother. Then he appointed me assistant inspector [*mufatish baj*] with a temporary income of twenty-four Egyptian pounds per month, until the position was institutionalized. I kissed his hands and signed for the new position working under the late Abdel Qader al Afifi Effendi. My job consisted of the following: I had to inspect all animals sold in Jerusalem at the animal suq [Al-Jum'a] every Friday near the Sultan's Pool area. I was to work under the supervision of the late Mustafa al-Kurd, known as Abu Darwish, a top expert in this fine art. Abu Darwish would say to me, "Do not burden yourself! Sit there, drink your coffee, and smoke the *arghileh*. I will do all the inspection and will hand you the receipts on a daily basis." This suited me very well. I would start my day at the Ma'aref Café with friends smoking the *arghileh* until ten or eleven in the morning, when Abu Darwish would arrive and order his first smoke, then his second, and then his third. Then he would pull five pounds from his *'ajami* belt: "Here, Wasif Effendi, this is your spending money for the day," he would say, and then he would pay me another sum against a signed receipt, which I would hand over to the municipality.

Wasif was entering adulthood, but he had not quite reached the age of reason. He was overwhelmed by what he called this "period of total anarchy in my life." He lived like a vagabond, sleeping all day and partying all night. "I only went home to change my clothes, sleeping in a different house every day. My body was totally exhausted from drinking and merrymaking. One moment I am in Mahallat Bab Hatta[,] . . . in the morning I am picnicking with members of Jerusalem's a'yan families, the next day I am holding an orgy with thugs and gangsters in the alleys of the Old City. My only source of livelihood was my salary from the Regie Department arranged by Ragheb Bey." When his mother complained that he came home late at night, if at all, he retorted with the famous line "He who seeks glory must toil the nights" (*Man talaba al-'ula sahar al-layali*). Wasif thus became involved in a libertine popular culture and café scene, an aspect of Jerusalem life hidden in previous accounts of the city's history. His account of his childhood and adult life in the city tell us about the advent of modernity in this urban context and hint at the complex nature of the interactions between Jerusalem's communities.

URBAN LIFE AND COMMUNAL BOUNDARIES

Wasif Jawhariyyeh's vivid depiction of daily life in Mahallat as-Sa'diyyeh (situated between Bab es-Sahira and the Via Dolorosa) during the first decades of the twentieth century is one of the most valuable records of Palestinian urban life that exists anywhere. He periodizes and describes in detail, for example, the bourgeoi-sification of domestic living arrangements:

> During the summer months [of 1904] we would sit around the lowered table for the main meal. Food was served in enameled zinc plates. That year we stopped eating with wooden spoons imported from Anatolia and Greece and replaced them with brass ones that were oxidized periodically. We replaced the common drinking *taseh* tied to the pottery jar with individual crystal glasses. In 1906 my father acquired single iron beds for each of my siblings, thus ending the habit of sleeping on the floor. What a delight it was to be relieved of the burden of having to place our mattresses into the wall alcoves every night.

For the social historian, Jawhariyyeh's diaries also provide a contemporaneous record of the growth of the city outside the city walls. Although Sheikh Jarrah, Yemin Moshe, and Wa'riyyeh were established before his time, Wasif describes the growth of Musrara and the Mascobiyyeh neighborhoods along Jaffa Road during his boyhood, followed by Talbieh and Katamon in the 1930s. These expansions—and the similar one that preceded them in Baq'a—saw hundreds of families move to modern tiled buildings built of mortar fortified by iron railings. It was in these neighborhoods that the implements of modernity were introduced: electricity, first in the Notre Dame compound just opposite the new gate; the automobile, on Jaffa Road; the motion picture projector; and above all the phonograph, which introduced Jawhariyyeh to the world of Salameh Hijazi and Sayyid Darwish.

Jawhariyyeh's cognitive map of Jerusalem's neighborhoods and his identifica-tion of communal boundaries prevalent in his youth clearly suggest that the divi-sion of the city into four confessional quarters was a late development. The British demarcated the new boundaries to preserve an equilibrium between the city's four ancient communities. The basis of this balance was the preservation of the status quo in the administration of Jerusalem's holy sites, which was carefully negotiated during the late Ottoman period and elaborated and codified during early Mandate rule.

However, the diaries implicitly challenge the notion of regulating relations between Jerusalemites by dividing them into four different religious and ethnic habitats. Jawhariyyeh's recollection of daily life in the alleys of the Old City shows the weakness of this concept in two respects. First, it suggests that there was no clear correspondence between neighborhood and religion but instead a substan-tial intermixing of religious groups in each quarter. Second, the primary admin-istrative unit of habitation was the mahallat, the basic unit of social demarcation, within which a substantial amount of communal solidarity was exhibited. Such cohesiveness was clearly articulated in periodic social visitations and by the shar-ing of ceremonies, including weddings and funerals, but also by the inhabitants' active participation in religious festivities. These solidarities undermined the fixity of the confessional system with a premodern (perhaps even primordial) network of affinities.

The confessional boundaries were also being undermined by the rise of the nationalist movement in Palestine—initially in the context of the constitutional Ottoman movement at the turn of the century; then after the 1908 coup, which received a lot of support among intellectual circles in Jerusalem; and later by the anti-Turkish trends within greater Syrian nationalism. Jawhariyyeh's memoirs depict such shifts in a haphazard and selective manner. Jawhariyyeh—who was not involved in any political party but was an Ottoman patriot and later a Palestinian nationalist—clearly believed that the move toward modernity (and presumably post-Ottoman nationalism) was linked to the rising middle classes' migration to the outskirts of the city. Already by the mid-nineteenth century, members of the notable clans had established bases in Sheikh Jarrah to the north and Wa'riyyeh to the south. Within the Jewish population, there was a similar move originating with the construction of the new neighborhoods of Mea Shi'arim and Yemin Moshe—signaling a separation of ways between modern Palestinian Arab nationalism and Jewish communal consciousness even before the entrenchment of Zionism among the city's Jewish population.

Jawhariyyeh's relationship with the Jewish community of Jerusalem is complex. Memories of clashes between Palestinian Arabs and the Zionist movement during the 1920s and 1936–39 no doubt color his narrative, and the events of 1948 mediate his perspective. But he also recalls a different era, when as a teenager he participated in the events of Purim (which he describes in great detail, including the costumes he used to wear with his brother Khalil) and took part in family picnics in the spring at the shrine of Shimon as-Siddiq (Simon the Just) in Wadi al-Joz. He also mentions a number of Sephardim with whom his family was on intimate terms, including the Eliashar, Hazzan, Anteibi, Mani (from Hebron), and Navon families.

Deeply involved in the affairs of the Arab Orthodox community, Jawhariyyeh nevertheless exhibits a unique affinity for the Muslim culture of his city. His narrative compels us to rethink the received wisdom about Jerusalem's communal and confessional structure in Ottoman times. For example, endless stories—many scandalous and satirical—draw a picture of the profound coexistence of Christian and Jewish families in the heart of what came to be known as the Muslim Quarter. This was not merely the tolerant cohabitation of protected dhimmi minorities but rather a positive engagement in the affairs of neighbors whose religion was coincidental to their wider urban heritage. There is no doubt that the Jawhariyyeh family, though deeply conscious of its Orthodox heritage, was immersed in Muslim culture. Jiryis made his sons read and memorize the Qur'an at an early age. When he died, in September of 1914, he was eulogized by Khalil Sakakini ("With the death of Jawhariyyeh, the era of wit has come to an end") and by Sheikh Ali Rimawi, who lamented, "I cannot believe that Jawhariyyeh's soul will remain in Zion [Cemetery,] . . . for tonight surely it will move to Mamillah [the Muslim cemetery]." This attitude clearly transcended the normative rules of coexistence at the time.

Many of Jawhariyyeh's anecdotes challenge social and religious taboos and would seem unthinkable in today's puritanical atmosphere. An example is the one titled "A Dog's Religion":

> My father was strolling with his intimate companion Salih al-Jamal, who died a bachelor. They passed several elderly gentlemen who were sitting by the wooden niche built by the municipality opposite the special opening constructed at Jaffa Gate to receive the German emperor. After they saluted the men, a dog happened to pass by. One of the notables asked my father, "Ya Abu Khalil, would you say this dog is Muslim or Christian?" This question was an obvious provocation, since the enquirer was a well-known Muslim, and my father was clearly a Christian. But his quick wit saved him from aggravating the situation further: "It should be easy to find out, my dear sir. Today, Friday, is our [i.e., the Orthodox] fasting day. You can throw him a bone. If he picks it up, then he is definitely not a Christian."

CULTURAL HYBRIDITY: A CHRISTIAN RAMADAN AND A MUSLIM PURIM

The Jawhariyyeh diaries invite the reader into a world of religious syncretism and cultural hybridity that is difficult to imagine in today's atmosphere of ethnic exclusivity and religious fundamentalism. They come from a prenationalist era when religious groups incorporated the Other in their festivals and rituals. Jawhariyyeh describes the feast of Easter/Pesach as an occasion for joint Muslim, Christian, and Jewish celebrations. He details the Muslim processions of Palm Sunday, which proceeded from the Abrahamic Mosque in Hebron toward Jerusalem. Jawhariyyeh recalls the festival of Nebi Musa as a Muslim popular celebration that merged with the Christian Orthodox Easter. The fantasia of Sabt enNour (Fire Saturday, commemorating the resurrection of Christ) was the greatest popular Christian celebration in Palestine and was closely coordinated with Muslim folk festivals. Christian and Muslim youths in Jewish neighborhoods celebrated Purim. Twice a year Muslim and Christian families—including the Jawhariyyehs—joined the Jewish celebrations at the shrine of Simon the Just in Sheikh Jarrah (an event known as Shat'hat al-Yahudiyya, or the Jewish Outing), where "Haim the oud player and Zaki the tambourine player would sing to the accompaniment of Andalusian melodies."

But the greatest celebrations of all happened during Ramadan. Jawhariyyeh devotes a substantial section of his diaries to the street festivals, the foods, and the dramatic displays of qara qoz (shadow plays) and sanduq al 'ajab (magic lantern shows). Many of the shadow plays were performed in a mixture of Ottoman

Turkish and Aleppo dialects, and some included daring social satire and veiled political criticism of the regime, although Jawhariyyeh does not explicitly mention these displays of dissent. Several goods manufacturers and sweets shops (such as Zalatimo) used the performances to enhance their sales by introducing commercial presentations sung by the shadow players.

The city also celebrated seasonal events that were not tied to religious feasts. Jawhariyyeh identifies two such secular occasions: the summer outings (*shat'hat*) of Sa'ed wa Sa'eed, and the spring visits to Bir Ayyub. In the pre–World War I era, Sa'ed wa Sa'eed became the choice location for the Old City's Christian and Muslim families to picnic on hot summer afternoons. The growth of new mansions around Musrara and the American Colony area especially encouraged these excursions. The picnickers consumed large quantities of arrack and food during these outings, which usually lasted until late in the evening, when revelers had to return before the city gates were closed. In the spring, similar parties were held at Bir Ayyub, at the springs of Lower Silwan, where Jerusalem families found a reprieve from the severe winters of the Old City.

With the implementation of the terms of the Balfour Declaration during the British Mandate, this era of religious syncretism came to a close. Palestinian nationalism—previously a secular movement—started to become infused with religious fervor. The new colonial authority interpreted the protocols regarding religious control and access in terms of confessional exclusivity. Military edict banned Christians from entering Islamic holy places and excluded Muslims from Christian churches and monasteries. It had been customary for young Jerusalemites of all religions to picnic in the green meadows in the Haram area, but now the area was off limits. Jawhariyyeh describes an adventure on an April day in 1919, during the early days of the British military government, when he passed as a "Musilman" to the Indian guards of the Haram area while his blue-eyed companion Muhammad Marzuqa was barred because Jawhariyyeh explained to them that he was Jewish.

The complexity of Jerusalem's Ottoman identity is also shown in Jawhariyyeh's account of his involvement with the Red Crescent Society, which was founded in 1915, ostensibly to garner support in Palestine for the Ottoman armed forces against the Allies. Through public music events and direct solicitations, the Red Crescent Society raised substantial funds for the war effort. Jawhariyyeh believed that the group could create a bridge between the interests of the Jewish community in Palestine and the Ottoman government (this was before Zionism appeared as an active force). Both Ibrahim Antaibi, the director of the Alliance Israelite school system in Jerusalem, and a Miss Landau—described as "the liaison between the Jewish community in Jerusalem and the Ottoman military leadership"—were pivotal in cementing those ties. With this objective, they mobilized a large number of young Jerusalem women, who wore ceremonial Ottoman military uniforms with a red crescent insignia, to solicit contributions for the army. Jawhariyyeh describes several of them as "attractive ladies" who developed intimate relations with high-ranking Ottoman officials: Miss Tenanbaum ("one of the most beautiful Jewish women in Palestine") became the mistress of Jamal Pasha, the commander of the Fourth Army (after the war she married Michael Abcarius, the famous Jerusalem attorney); Miss Sima al-Maghribiyyah became the mistress of Sa'd Allah Bey, the commander of the Jerusalem garrison; and Miss Cobb became the mistress of Majid Bey, the mutasarrif (governor) of the city. During the war years, personal as well as political links thus played a part in the complex interactions of Jerusalem's communities. Through his literary and enormously entertaining narrative of the events, Wasif Jawhariyyeh reveals the radical transformations that were encompassing Palestinian and Syrian society in that period: the emergence of secular Arab nationalism, the separation of Palestinian national identity from its Syrian context, and the enhancement of Jerusalem as a capital city.

SUGGESTIONS FOR FURTHER READING

Jawharīyah, Wāṣif, Salīm Tamārī, and Issam Nassar. *Al-Quds al-'Uthmānīyah fī al-mudhakkirāt al-Jawharīyah: Al-kitāb al-awwal min mudhakkirāt al-mūsīqī Wāṣif Jawharīyah, 1904–1917.* Al-Quds: Mu'assasat al-Dirāsāt al-Maqdisīyah, 2003.

Tamari, Salim. *Mountain against the Sea: Essays on Palestinian Society and Culture.* Berkeley: University of California Press, 2009.

4

Revolutionary Pioneer

Manya Shochat and Her Commune

Gershon Shafir

The opening sentence written by her main biographer states that "among the founding fathers of the Jewish Labor Movement in Palestine during the Second Aliya a special place is reserved for Manya Wilbushewitz-Shochat," who, as he continues, "was undoubtedly one of the most famous, and maybe the most famous, women of that era." Such gender confusion would be laughable if it were not so indicative of the limited range of roles available to women during the most formative era of Zionist settlement in Palestine—the period of the Second Aliya (wave of immigration)—and for long afterward.

INTO THE VORTEX OF THE REVOLUTION IN THE PALE OF SETTLEMENT

Manya Wilbushewitz was shaped by the ideological and political struggle over the future of the large, crisis-ridden Jewish community in tsarist Russia. During the last decades of the nineteenth century the belated arrival of modernization undermined the traditional Jewish middleman minority roles in the manorial economy of the Russian Pale of Settlement and Central Europe and plunged Jews into an existential crisis. Though prior to the First World War a significant portion of the Jewish population was able to use its commercial skills and urban traditions to attain remarkably swift upward social mobility, and frequently assimilate culturally, the majority now was made redundant or displaced. Rapid demographic expansion further fueled the immiseration of the Jewish masses. At the same time, fear of competition on the part of the middle and lower-middle classes led to waves of pogroms in southern Russia, squashing Jewish hopes of emancipation. In response to this climactic sequence of changes, Eastern European Jews, displaying a remarkable outburst of creativity, experimented with a variety of alternatives: assimilation, socialism, Jewish socialism, cultural nationalism and autonomy, territorial nationalism, and retreat behind the walls of a revivalist and fundamentalist orthodoxy. Masses of Jews chose to emigrate from Eastern to Western Europe and the New World. And some, but relatively few, went to Palestine.

Manya grew up near the estate of her grandparents near Grodno, in what is today Belarus. As a supplier to the Russian military, her grandfather enjoyed the lifestyle of a Russian landowner and was free to travel throughout the Russian Empire, unlike Jews who remained confined to the Pale of Settlement on its eastern end. Her father owned a grain mill on the banks of the Neman River. While he was deeply religious, her mother was a committed secularist, a child of the Jewish Haskalah movement—which sought to integrate Jews into the modernizing Russian society—who spoke Polish, Russian, and German equally well. Notwithstanding their profound differences, they had ten children, of whom Manya, born in 1879, was the eighth.

At first Manya took after her father and became religious, but she soon developed an interest in the lives of the Russian peasants who worked on the estate. While still a teenager, she moved to the nearby town of Minsk to apprentice in the carpentry shop of her brother Gedaliah. After turning nineteen, she went for four months with a small group of young volunteers to help starving Tatar villagers in central Russia. There she witnessed the Russian rural communal system, which inspired the early Russian socialist movement and stirred Manya to set up and be part of a series of short-lived communal living arrangements in the next two decades.

Diminutive of stature, Manya looked like typical Russian revolutionary women with her wired-rimmed glasses and short-cropped hair. Her friend Rachel Yanait Ben-Zvi spoke of "the surrealist quality of her adventures" and of "the extravagance with which she pursued her goals, however implausible they seemed."

Back in Minsk, a medium-size industrial town, she received her introduction to both Russian and Jewish revolutionary groups. Among the latter were the Bund— the largest Jewish party in the Pale, which sought equal rights and, later, cultural autonomy for Jews within a future revolutionary Russia—and Po'alei Zion (Workers of Zion), which supported emigration to and the creation of a Jewish socialist homeland in Palestine. With time Manya grew closer to Po'alei Zion, although she also maintained her ties with the Bund.

At the end of 1899, the nineteen-year-old Manya was arrested for her political activities. First she was kept in the local jail in Grodno and then sent to a Moscow prison. Her year-and-a-half long imprisonment gave rise to a most extraordinary period, which she described as the most bitter and tumultuous chapter in her life.

During her interrogation by the Russian police, she was offered the cruel choice to turn in a few of her colleagues in return for a promise to save many others, including her first love. While struggling with her conscience, she encountered among her interrogators a seemingly unattached civilian who claimed to have been a past revolutionary. This was no other than Sergei Zubatov, the head of the Okhrana, the tsarist secret police. Zubatov "confessed" to Manya his distaste for the tsarist government and engaged her in a vigorous and soul-searching discussion lasting many months on the future of the Russian working class. Zubatov was well versed in the internal debates of the Russian revolutionary movement and sought to turn its captured members into his epigones. His ultimate goal was to create a so-called yellow union—a nonrevolutionary workers' union that would procure benefits for the workers without endangering the tsarist regime. Manya portrayed him as a character larger than life who resembled Dostoevsky's Grand Inquisitor, and she admitted to having been hypnotized by his enthusiasm and sincerity. Zubatov himself trusted Manya to the extent of sending her as his personal emissary to meet with such luminaries as Minister of the Interior von Plehve and Father Gapon, who later became famous for leading the Bloody Sunday demonstration that sparked the 1905 Revolution. Though she seemed to have developed a love-hate relationship with Zubatov, ultimately Manya helped establish the Jewish Independent Labor Party, which, following Zubatov's vision, engaged in bread-and-butter struggle with employers while shying away from revolutionary agitation. Starting in July 1901, party members engaged in successful strike activity under Zubatov's protection, but when he fell out with von Plehve, in 1903 the party found itself in the throes of a deep crisis.

The most controversial part of Manya's biography concerns her collaboration with Zubatov. After the Russian Revolution of 1917, the new regime found in the Okhrana's archives her extensive correspondence with him. Manya appears to have been fully devoted to Zubatov and his methods. She not only informed on members of the revolutionary movement—from both the Bund and Russian secret societies, even turning in her first love, Gregory Gershuni—but implored Zubatov to arrest them so he could reeducate them and bring them under his influence. Her breathless letters, in which she professed her dedication to his vision, provided the chief of the Okhrana with ongoing analysis of the activities of various chapters of the Bund, evaluated the dedication and importance of their leaders, gave their code names, and reported on the location of their meetings with the intention of bringing its activities to an end. Not surprisingly, Vladimir Medem, a prominent Bundist leader, denounced her as an agent of the Okhrana.

When Medem published some of her letters in the United States in 1922, Manya's colleagues from Palestine would not rally to her defense. Even though there was no love lost between the Bund and its archenemy Po'alei Zion, Berl Katznelson, one of the Zionist leaders, held Manya responsible for bringing these accusations on her with "that absolute, childish, naïve and stupid self-confidence of hers." Some of her biographers put her collaboration with Zubatov down to the impetuosity of an impressionable nineteen-year-old. While Manya certainly was not a paid police agent, the results of her actions in undermining the Bund were just as devastating.

In 1903, the Haskalah movement was shaken to the core by the outbreak of a pogrom in the town of Kishinev (now Chisinau in present-day Moldova). Jewish, in part Zionist, self-defense organizations sprung up. The Jewish Independent Labor Party collapsed, and Manya joined a terrorist organization seeking to assassinate von Plehve and was sent to Berlin to raise funds to finance the operation. While she was away, the plot was betrayed. She went to Paris, where she successfully raised funds, purchased weapons from an armament factory in Liège, Belgium, and transported several crates of Browning guns and ammunition to Jewish self-defense organizations. While she was waiting to deliver a shipment in Odessa, a young man used a subterfuge to gain admittance to the house where she was hiding the weapons. Suspecting him of being a police agent, Manya shot him with a small gun equipped with a silencer, stuffed his body in a trunk, and mailed it to a distant destination.

SUDDENLY IN PALESTINE

A new venue opened up for Manya after the 1903 pogrom wave and the failure of her terrorist band. The brother she was closest to, Nachum, an engineer, wished to remove her from Russia and invited her to join his exploratory tour of Palestine on both sides of the Jordan River and in the Houran mountains in southern Syria. She arrived on January 2, 1904, one of the first immigrants of the Second Aliya. During the six-week horseback tour through Palestine, Manya converted to Zionism.

Manya was one of the few immigrants of the Second Aliya to hail from a non-Zionist revolutionary movement. She arrived in Palestine with a storied revolutionary record, whereas her contemporaries who later became the leaders of Labor Zionism were younger and unknown and acquired their prominent status only after their immigration. She also came from a wealthier stratum than most other contemporary immigrants, who arrived penniless. Befitting her prior experience, Manya soon found herself in the midst of, and sometimes leading, feverish activity among the new immigrants, many of whom were seeking livelihood as agricultural workers while also debating the proper strategy for a Jewish future in Palestine. Communal living and self-defense, that most male sphere of activity, were the two issues that inspired her in Russia and became her chosen fields of activity after her settlement in Palestine.

The Second Aliya was the formative period of Zionist immigration and settlement in Palestine, the generation of the founding fathers and mothers of the

Zionist community in Palestine. It followed on the heels of the twenty thousand immigrants of the First Aliya, who arrived there between 1882 and 1904 and founded about twenty agricultural *moshavot* (the plural of *moshava*, literally "colony"). The Second Aliya lasted about a decade, from 1904 to 1914, and brought into the country between thirty-five thousand and forty thousand Jews. Among them were David Ben-Gurion and Yitzhak Ben-Zvi, who became the leaders of the labor settlement movement (*hityashvut ovedet*) and later the State of Israel.

Most of the immigrants of the Second Aliya were young men and women from urban backgrounds who understood that to sink roots in Palestine they would have to engage in agriculture. But the new arrivals faced a dilemma. Though they had left Europe behind, Europe did not leave them; they arrived in Palestine accustomed to an Eastern European urban standard of living but had to compete for work with Palestinian Arab fellahin. The latter only needed work when they were not cultivating their own land, were accustomed to lower living standards, and were paid accordingly. The new Jewish immigrants, in short, discovered that they were priced out of the Palestinian agricultural labor market. The consequence was that the vineyards of the First Aliya employed a large, unskilled, and seasonal Palestinian Arab labor force mixed with only a small number of Jews. As a result of repeated experimentation, the immigrants of the Second Aliya came up with innovative types of social organization and colonization, in particular the kibbutz, but the early social innovations with which Manya was associated proved abortive.

A few of the Jewish immigrants tried to make themselves competitive by adopting the living standards of the fellahin and accepting downward wage equalization. Living in tents and eating frugally, these workers sought employment in the vineyards and farms of First Aliya members. In some cases, Manya reported, Jewish workers even refused positive discrimination on the part of the vineyard owners since they were concerned that by accepting charity or philanthropic help they would become dependent and vulnerable to displacement. These attempts, however, petered out in a few months because the agricultural workers were unable to lower their living standards permanently. By 1905, members of the newly formed Hapo'el Hatzair (Young Worker) party tried to force the farmers to hire only Jews to do both skilled and unskilled work. They called their strategy "conquest of labor," but the farmers of the First Aliya, who now became their nemeses, followed the economic logic of preferring low-paid Arabs. In general, many of the immigrants recollected that as young men and women they were able to remain idealists in one way of another for no more than five years. Once they were ready to form families, their imported customary economic needs asserted themselves.

One approach that grew in importance was collective or cooperative living. Jewish agricultural life in Palestine was fertile ground for a variety of cooperative lifestyles, most of which were temporary. Jewish cooperation was rooted mostly in the immediate need to make up for the low wages that resulted from the downward pressure of competition with Palestinian Arab workers in the moshavot. By pooling their resources, the workers were better able to survive on the same individual wage. Similar backgrounds, the workers' youth, and the fact that their wages did not usually suffice to support a family made sharing easier and more attractive. Most widespread was the commune (*kvutza*)—that is, a communal living and cooking arrangement among workers employed on different farms or vineyards at the same moshava. Manya observed that when immigrants suffered from malaria in these novel and difficult circumstances, they were able to hold out because of the communal treasury.

It is likely that the communal organization of life in Palestine had been modeled on the Russian *artel* with which Manya was familiar before emigrating to Palestine. Originally a medieval association of farmers, artisans, or workers to carry out joint projects, with industrialization the artel came to be used by seasonal migrant workers as a tool of transition to the conditions of city life. These artels served as a surrogate families that formed and disbanded according to the needs of the casual labor market. The artel was a temporary, ad hoc labor association, not a permanent cooperative or collective settlement.

Manya's approach was more ambitious—she was one of the few immigrants actively promoting not just communal living but communal settlement. She advocated the formation of economically viable permanent Jewish agricultural collectives. She read profusely about secular and religious collective utopias and visited some in Russia and later in the United States. She was particularly eager to establish such a commune in the Houran mountains of southern Syria, where Baron Edmund de Rothschild owned an extensive undeveloped plot. Whereas many of the immigrants of the Second Aliya spoke disparagingly of the dependence of the First Aliya's farmers on Jewish philanthropy, which blunted their nationalist desires, Manya traveled to Paris to gain such financial aid. However, all her hoped-for sources of support—the Jewish Colonization Association (JCA, a non-Zionist worldwide colonization body founded in 1891 by the Baron Maurice de Hirsch); Baron Edmund de Rothschild, who supported many of the First Aliya's moshavot; and Max Nordau, a leader of the World Zionist Organization (WZO)—rejected her requests. In the meantime, a new opportunity arose in the Galilee.

THE BIG EXPERIMENT: IN THE SEDJRA COLLECTIVE

The agricultural economy of the Galilee differed from the one Manya found in the First Aliya settlements of Petach Tikvah and Rishon Letzion in the southern coastal zone. Instead of irrigating vineyards and orange orchards that required considerable initial investment and a large-scale unskilled and low-paid labor force, the Galilee Arabs practiced tenant farming, better known as sharecropping.

In return for a plot of land, seeds, animals, and living expenses, the sharecropper owed the property owner two-thirds of his yield. Such a model obviated the need for an initial investment, but the income from rain-fed grain farming, mostly of wheat and barley, fell below European standards of living.

The JCA established several agricultural training farms for Jewish workers in the Galilee. One of them was in an old walled Arab *han,* or caravanserai, next to the tiny settlement of Sedjra in the mountains ridges between Nazareth and Tiberias. The training farm ended every year in the red, with no relief in sight. With the backing of Yehoshua Hankin, the well-known purchaser of Arab-owned land (known to Zionists as "the redeemer of land"), Manya prevailed on Eliahu Krause, the farm's manager, to hire a group of Jewish workers as tenant farmers in the hope that they would end the year without a loss. Manya now had her own two hundred acres, along with mules, teams of oxen, seed, and a loan to cover living expenses, but she still needed to assemble a group of collectively minded agricultural workers to cultivate it. She contacted Yisrael Shochat, with whom she was already falling in love, and he brought her a group of workers, among them Israel Giladi, Alexander Zeid, and Yitzhak Ben-Zvi. With a few late arrivals the collective came to number twelve men and six women. The newcomers to Sedjra turned themselves into a collective by pooling their wages and establishing committees to prepare work assignments, settle internal disputes, and so on. In the evenings they gathered to study, learning about modern agriculture from Krause, socialism from Manya, Hebrew from Ben-Gurion (who was in Sedjra at the time but not a member of the collective), and Arabic from a local Arab teacher, while Shochat discussed the affairs of the day. Thus, in autumn 1907 the Sedjra collective was born.

What Shochat did not share with Manya at the time was that the workers who came with him and made up the collective's core had already established, in September 1907, the clandestine society or order Bar Giora (named after the last leader of the Jewish revolt against the Roman Empire). Shochat, Ben-Zvi, and other Second Aliya immigrants were involved in the self-defense organizations that were set up to protect Jewish townships from pogroms in Russia and now sought to impart to the Zionist settlers their quasi-military knowledge. Bar Giora members joined Manya's initiative because they "wanted to concentrate in the Galilee . . . in order to prepare . . . for their roles in the order." Though this might not have been the sole reason for their membership in the collective, Manya subsequently conceded that only a few joined because they were "interested in the experiment of collective life and work itself." A lesser-known facet of the Second Aliya is that the cooperative tendency among the agricultural workers had to contend with a strong individualist current. One contemporary observer wrote that the pioneers were "developed" people who could not tolerate collective discipline in the long run. For some years, then, it remained an open question whether the Jewish workers could subordinate their individualism to the group and learn to live collectively or whether they would find the demands of cooperation too trying.

Krause, convinced that agricultural settlement was impossible without the involvement of wives, agreed to include women as full members of the agricultural collective. Though Manya was employed as the collective's bookkeeper, the other female members plowed the farm's fields with oxen, wearing the kaffiyeh (Arab headdress) and baggy gray pants that became the fashion for the Jewish women in the Galilee. They also tended the kitchen, baked bread, and prepared bulgur in the communal oven.

Manya and Shochat became lovers in Sedjra and married in May 1908. Lore has it that Ben-Gurion had a crush on her, but she chose the tall and dashing Shochat, who was nine years her junior, a rejection that Ben-Gurion never forgave. Bar Giora employed Ben-Gurion as a guard, but he was not allowed to become a member in spite of his demonstrated courage. He became a devoted husband to Paula, the woman he married; Manya's marriage was repeatedly punctured by Shochat's infidelities. Her son, Geda, who was born in the Galilee, grew up to become a pilot and later committed suicide. Her daughter, Anna, described having been effectively an orphan with parents who devoted their lives to the cause of Zionism.

The Sedjra experiment lasted for the full agricultural season of 1907–8, and for the first time field crops were cultivated there without deficit. Krause invited the collective to continue its work, hoping that other Jews would follow suit and become tenant farmers, but the group turned him down and disbanded. The historical accounts and memoirs of the Sedjra experiment end abruptly at this point, merely stating that upon successfully completing its task, the collective broke up.

The most likely reason for the discontinuation of the Sedjra collective was not excessive individualism but rather that the experiment revealed the limits of equalizing the workers' living standards with those of the fellahin. Rain-fed grain farming did not support a European standard of living, and the JCA did not take the decisive step of offering the members of the collective land to settle on and thus become the kind of farmers found in the moshavot. Lack of funds to buy land and limited financial support by the JCA made sharecropping a dead-end strategy for Jewish colonization. Sedjra remained an inspirational event in the history of collectivism in Palestine, but it was not the basis of a model. It did not lead to the kibbutz, that most famous invention of the Second Aliya and hallmark of Zionist colonization in Palestine.

Degania, the first kibbutz, was formed on the southern tip of Lake Tiberias in 1909. The success of this collective was due to the willingness of the WZO's newly formed Palestine Office to use land purchased by the Jewish National Fund for the settlement of Jewish agricultural workers. The WZO and the JNF were founded on nationalist and not business principles. According to the JNF's charter, its land could only be leased, not sold, and only to Jews. Those cultivating its land, consequently, were shielded from the labor market. Degania solved, as Sedjra could not, the problem of unequal competition with Palestinian Arabs and made it possible to attain a European standard of living, a living wage, in Palestine. In the kibbutz, the agricultural workers were settlers who came to think of themselves not as workers but as laborers and members of the labor settlement movement. Manya, on her part, therefore was not, as later historians sought to designate her, "the mother of collective settlement in Palestine," since the kibbutz movement developed separately from the Sedjra experiment.

AMONG THE HASHOMER GUARDS

As the workers' collective in Sedjra coalesced, its members transformed Bar Giora into Hashomer (The Guard). By 1909, Shochat and Bar Giora's goal was to set up a Jewish guard organization that would seek openly "to conquer" the work of protecting Jewish settlements from their Arab guards. Hashomer (as Bar Giora before it) was a self-designated elite of carefully selected individuals. After a year-long trial period they were sworn to secrecy and loyalty in a midnight ceremony. Incidentally, the strong emphasis on individual qualifications and suitability led Hashomer to recruit a small number of Yemenite and Sephardi Jews. Women too, among them Manya, were accepted as full members. At the same time, women were not assigned regular guard duty and were less likely to be in possession of arms, though stories abound about occasions on which Manya and others assumed guard duties voluntarily. Ironically, many members of Bar Giora and Hashomer were simultaneously members of the Marxist Po'alei Zion, whose ideology should have inspired them to join ranks with the members of the Arab "working class." In fact, political differences between the Jewish parties mattered little since their members acted similarly, and ideological convictions played scanty role in the behavior of the Second Aliya members.

Manya was described as possessing enormous powers of persuasion and being the center of Hashomer's social life, energizing and captivating everyone. She "approached everyone as a sister, as a mother." Manya always carried her sewing kit with her, like a first aid kit, and would patch her male comrades' clothing. One of her friends recollected that during a discussion on the eve of Hashomer's second convention, in 1910, in Manya and Shochat's new home in the German colony of Haifa, "Manya spent the whole time in the kitchen, bringing tea and food to the members, while continuing to participate actively in the dialogue." Manya's own summary of women's role, "the power of the women of Hashomer—the women who, despite remaining in the background, knew how to bear the burdens of wandering, the suffering and the illnesses that were an integral part of their lives, and to exude strength at the same time," clearly demonstrates the dominance of traditional female roles over pioneering ones in Palestine. Though Manya was considered by both Hashomer members and contemporaneous Jewish organizations as a central figure of the organization, was involved in planning its course, and acted on its behalf as a chief negotiator, fund-raiser, weapons procurer, and dedicated human relations authority, she was never offered a leadership role. The Second Aliya paid tribute to women's pioneering and rights but never lived up to its promises.

Jewish moshavot were guarded at night by Arabs or members of the Druze and Circassian minorities known for their martial qualities. Circassians from an adjacent village, for example, guarded Krause's training farm in Sedjra. Having noticed that one of the guards repaired to his village every night instead of staying at his post, a group of Bar Giora members hid Krause's horse and then woke him up. Krause paced around, all upset, and immediately fired the surprised guard when he returned in the morning. Krause also agreed to replace the Circassian guards with Bar Giora members. Though the Jewish guards were ambushed several times by the disgruntled Circassians, they successfully persisted in their new task.

At the same time, to carry out their role effectively, Hashomer members had to learn to behave like the Arab guards they replaced—that is, to learn Arabic and seek to comprehend their manners, sense of honor, and ethics. In imitation of Palestinian villages, Hashomer established hospitality rooms (madfia) to entertain passersby. Contemporary photographs invariably show Hashomer members in Arab clothing and headdresses. Hashomer not only imitated the Bedouin outwardly but also derived its idea of heroism from them and the Circassians. In the Second Aliya, to be an upright Jew meant to carry oneself like a mounted Bedouin! Some of the workers, in fact, accused members of Hashomer of assimilation into the Palestinian environment. But as Manya, who became one of the organization's chroniclers, remarked, "Experience taught them that if courage is required in the moment of a clash, much more important is the daily contact, which alone can create an atmosphere of good relations and security in the vicinity." Such close contact also ensured the relatively free flow of information about local thieves and potential assaults.

The Arab custom of blood feud, as Manya observed, made both sides cautious in their interactions and paradoxically cut down on casualties. The killing of a Palestinian, Bedouin, or Circassian villager demanded, according to this code, vengeance through the killing of a person from the assailer's kin group, and by extension, if the act was committed by a Jew, that meant anyone from his moshava. Hashomer did on rare occasions carry out retaliatory actions against Arab attackers but tried to avoid entanglement in blood feuds, deciding on two occasions to revenge the death of its members by locating and killing the murderer himself and not one of his kin.

Even so, Hashomer took a militant position vis-à-vis the Arab villagers when it came to employment. Hashomer members viewed their role as a vanguard in the service of the conquest of labor strategy and demanded that the moshavot that sought to employ them expand their number of Jewish workers. (After the Jewish guards passed the test in Sedjra, other Jewish colonies wanted to hire them.) Confrontations between Jewish farmers and their Arab guards led to the swift expansion of Hashomer, which reached its zenith by 1912, when it guarded all the Jewish settlements in the lower Galilee and all the large plantation moshavot of the southern coastal zone except three. At its peak, Hashomer consisted of forty members and fifty to sixty candidates for membership and for the harvest season was able to deploy about three hundred guards.

The group's militant defense of exclusive Jewish labor and guarding led to its decline. In Rechovot, a conflict erupted between the organization and the planters when the latter refused Hashomer's demand that they fire all Palestinian workers from Zarnuga, the village of the murderers of one of the Jewish guards. Hashomer also withdraw from Hedera because it refused to acquiesce in the reintroduction of a combined Jewish-Arab guard force. In Rishon Letzion, Hashomer demanded the fining and firing of all Palestinian workers who snatched the gun of one of its guards; the colony's board decided only to warn the workers and to pay them damages for loss of workdays and bodily harm sustained during the clash. Ultimately, even had Hashomer adopted a less contentious attitude toward Arabs, it could not have accepted the presence of the Palestinian worker or coguard in the moshavot. It was not a professional guard organization but was established to obtain and ensure exclusive Jewish access to land and labor markets. Hashomer, like the Second Aliya's agricultural workers, threw its support behind a colonization method based on exclusive Jewish employment. Its members were willing to learn Arab methods and culture but not to abandon their goals of conquest.

CONQUEST GROUPS AND THE FIRST WORLD WAR

Hashomer was called into the service of the WZO's new Palestine Office to create yet another type of collective—the conquest group. Its aim was to establish Jewish presence on and prepare land newly purchased by the WZO until it was handed to its permanent Jewish settlers. In 1910, a Greek Orthodox Lebanese banker by the name of Elias Sursuq agreed to sell the lands of the village of Fulla in the Jezreel Valley, or Marj Ibn 'Amir, to the WZO and evict its Arab tenants. Arthur Ruppin, the director of the WZO's Palestine Office, planned to use the site for his first major settlement, to be called Merchavia. When the news leaked out, the Palestinian political and religious elite tried to convince the Ottoman government to prevent the plan from going forward, and Ruppin was convinced that Fulla would be a major test case over the future of Zionist colonization.

Against this volatile background, Hashomer agreed to take possession of Fulla and begin cultivating its land. While Manya and Shochat remained in Haifa, Hashomer members began plowing the land with twelve donkey teams. The relations between the Jewish collective and the adjacent Arab villages remained tense, since the latter were displeased with the settlement, which took away their land and would not, unlike First Aliya moshavot, employ them. As a wagon left Merchavia on its way to another Jewish settlement, Yechezkel Nissanov, one of the two guards present, refused to surrender his mules to attacking Palestinians, who shot and killed him. His wife Rivkale was at the time in the hospital giving birth. Manya volunteered to visit her. She sat by Rivkale's bedside for long hours, talking to her about the dreams and dangers of Hashomer, until Rivkale finally understood that she was being told her husband was dead. A *Yizkor* (Remember) memorial volume that was devoted to Hashomer casualties such as Nissanov extolled the virtues of military prowess and served as an instrument for mobilizing Jewish youths in the Diaspora for Zionism.

Hashomer also discovered Manya's skills as a bookkeeper and a fund-raiser. We can garner fascinating details from her correspondence with the Hovevei Zion (Lovers of Zion) Federation in Odessa, a main supporter of the immigrants. While Hashomer raised almost forty thousand francs in 1911, at the end of the year its treasury held only fifty-three hundred, and Manya implored Menachem Ussishkin, the head of Hovevei Zion, to wire her two thousand francs immediately. Hashomer's main expenses were surety bonds paid to the colonies that hired its guards, an assistance fund for sick members, weapons and ammunition, and horses. The last item was the costliest. About half of Hashomer guards, all of whom started on foot, were now mounted. Manya was cognizant of the difficulties of raising money in Russia, whose regime was hostile to Jewish causes, but pleaded that "just as a young, healthy child cannot stop growing simply because his parents cannot afford bigger shoes to replace the old ones that no longer fit," so Hashomer could not stop its growth. Finally, she called on Ussishkin to remember that Hashomer was the protector of Jewish national existence and national honor, and therefore he had to find the money to support its activities.

The members of the guard organization who refused Krause's offer to stay in Sedjra as tenant farmers were now eager to accept the WZO offer of land for settlement. At first Hashomer served as a conquest group for Tel Adash, a new Jewish settlement a short distance from Merchavia, and in 1913 provided its permanent settlers. A second Hashomer settlement, Kfar Giladi, was set up at the junction of the Lebanese and Syrian borders at the northern tip of Palestine during the First World War.

In 1912, Ben-Gurion and Ben-Zvi decided that to protect the cause of Zionism in Palestine and, in particular, represent Jewish interests in land conflicts in court, they should become lawyers. They therefore traveled to Istanbul to study law. The two already harbored political ambitions, so Shochat, their potential rival, decided to follow suit and acquire similar education and standing. Hashomer was left without two of its most important leaders. Manya, on her part, joined her husband abroad and financed his education with an inheritance from her parents. In less than two years the First World War broke out, and all four returned to Palestine. The Ottoman state, fighting against Russia and many of the Western powers, was freer to express its hostility toward Zionists in Palestine. It closed down the important Zionist bodies, forbade the public use of Hebrew, and conducted searches for Jewish valuables, money, and weapons.

Manya, as a prominent Hashomer leader, was arrested on suspicion of concealing the organization's weapons. It turned out that a Jew from Rishon Letzion had informed on her, arguing that he had done so to save the rest of the organization—invoking, in a bizarre turn of fate, Manya's yet publicly unknown dilemma from her revolutionary past in Russia. Her interrogator was the recently appointed regional governor of Jaffa, Baha-Al-Din, from the Young Turks Party, which sought to unify all nationalities and minorities living in the Ottoman Empire in loyalty to the Turkish state. He now, in Zubatov style, feigned interest in Zionism. Manya was taken in by his alleged sympathy and told him of her and Hashomer's goals until Baha-Al-Din, exploding with rage, shouted, "What? A nation within the nation?" Manya grabbed a dagger from his desk and threw it at his feet, denouncing him as a bigot and a weakling. The authorities decided to banish her, Shochat, and other Zionist leaders. Manya and her family were sent to Bursa, several hours from Istanbul, and spent three years there. At the end of the war, the Shochats returned to a Palestine conquered by the United Kingdom.

During the British Mandatory period, Manya and Shochat were gradually eased to the margins of the labor settlement movement. Their chosen path, self-defense, was taken up by a new political party, Achdut Ha'avoda (United Labor), and the new Jewish trade union, the Histadrut. The latter gathered under its aegis all of the effective organizational innovations of the Second Aliya, namely collective settlement, cooperative organizations, conquest of labor, and security. There was no room left for the kind of semiautonomous self-defense organization Shochat was keen on. In May 1920, Hashomer was abolished, and for a decade and a half the Jewish community paid relatively little attention to the cultivation of Jewish defense forces since by and large it preferred to rely on the protection of the British Mandatory authorities. Shochat retired from public life in the early 1930s, and though Manya continued her involvement with various causes, she was no longer elected to the main Zionist decision-making bodies. When Jewish safety became a central concern with the outbreak of the Arab Revolt in 1936, Jewish self-defense was led by a new cadre.

Manya lived to see the establishment of the State of Israel. She died in 1962 and was buried at the Hashomer cemetery in Kfar Giladi.

SUGGESTIONS FOR FURTHER READING

Ben-Zvi, Rachel Yanait. *Before Golda: Manya Shochat.* New York: Biblio, 1989.
Goldstein, Yaacov. "Heroine or Traitor? The Controversy over Manya Vilbushevich-Shohat and Her Links with Zubatov." *Studies in Contemporary Jewry,* Vol. 6 (1990), pp. 284–305.
Reinharz, Shulamit. "Manya Wilbushewitz-Shochat and the Winding Road to Sejera." In Deborah S. Bernstein, ed., *Pioneers and Homemakers: Jewish Women in Pre-State Israel.* Albany: State University of New York Press, 1992, pp. 95–118.

PART TWO

From Empire to Empire

Palestine under British Rule

IF THE ROUGHLY FOUR-DECADE PERIOD from the 1870s through World War I in Palestine witnessed the planting of the seeds of national identities and the conflict between them, the region's subsequent three decades under British rule saw the struggle over territory and identity erupt into full bloom, culminating in a war that resulted in the division of Palestine into three units, the creation of a Jewish state, the exile of upward of three-quarters of a million Palestinians, who were effectively replaced as the majority population of the new Jewish state by an influx of hundreds of thousands of Jews from Europe and the Muslim world.

It is easy, given the intense drama of the 1948 war, to read the history of Palestine under British rule as inevitably leading to the all-out conflict whose resulting dynamics continue to this day. But the reality of this period was much more complex and less preordained than might be imagined by viewing it through the lens of subsequent history.

To be sure, the transition from one empire to another—from Ottoman to British rule—brought about far-reaching changes. But in the everyday life of Palestinian Arabs and Jews, including the tens of thousands of European Jews who immigrated to the country during the Mandate period, the currents of change and conflict were often subordinated by the weight of mundane concerns, the desire for personal and communal advancement, and the political and economic struggles that pitted zero-sum goals against the need at different levels to cooperate across communal divisions to address more immediate problems.

David De Vries and Talia Pfeffermann's account of Henya Pekelman (chapter 7), a female construction worker in Mandate Palestine, well illustrates the discrepancy in the historiography of the Jewish community in Palestine between the

Zionist rhetoric of social reform and the continued inequality between the sexes. Particularly relevant here are the struggles and conflicts between the need to fulfill nationalist visions and ideologies that have one specific view of women and their role in society, and the personal desires and need for survival and advancement that meet with deep disappointment when they are not realized. Pekelman's story serves as a reminder that gender, power, and nationalism in this period rarely intersected in ways that allowed women to fulfill the various components of their core identities.

Beyond the particularities of daily life and its myriad struggles, there were several broader factors during the Mandate period that contributed significantly to the development of Palestinian Arab and Zionist identities and the conflict between them. First was the continued process of political, economic, and technological modernization that began during the late Ottoman period and gained steam under British rule. Both communities sought to maximize the increasing incorporation of Palestine into European and even global markets and to adopt technologies that would further this end, especially in the agricultural sphere. Here, however, the large influx of Jewish capital from abroad gave the burgeoning Zionist community a strong edge over its Palestinian counterpart, a gap that was exacerbated by the British view of the modernization of the Palestinian Arab sector as a direct threat to its mandated commitment to foster the development of a Jewish national home.

Yet it would be wrong to assume that Palestinian Arab economic and social modernization stagnated during the Mandate. Quite the opposite. However structurally disadvantaged, this community's economy and, as important, intellectual life continued to develop, particularly for the middle and upper classes. The life of Dr. Tawfiq Canaan, as Philippe Bourmaud recounts in "'A Son of the Country'" (chapter 6), well evidences this process.

Considered "the father of Palestinian ethnography," Canaan was one of the better-known figures in Mandate Palestine, a famed physician and an opinionated man of significant political activity. Aside from being one of the driving forces behind the modernization of Palestinian Arab medicine, Canaan was instrumental in promoting the writing down of Palestinian Arab folklore and through this, creating a heritage that became the core of the post-1948 Palestinian nationalism. As important, Bourmaud eloquently explores, Canaan understood the contradictory nature of modernization—it was desirable on its face yet changed the landscape and erased practices and beliefs that he viewed as quite as ancient as the Bible. What's more, he understood that Jewish immigration not only accelerated the pace of transformation but by this very process made Palestinian Arabs, who were not as modernized, feel alien to the new community that was growing next to them.

The entire Palestinian Arab leadership, of course, shared Canaan's concern about Jewish immigration, which rapidly increased, along with land purchases, under British rule. Indeed, the intensity of the policies of "conquering" labor and land was proportional to the country's Jewish population. During this period, the number of Jews in Palestine grew almost tenfold, from approximately 57,000 to 555,000 between 1917 and 1945. By contrast, the Palestinian Arab population roughly doubled, from 660,000 to 1.2 million people. Jews increased their percentage of the population from about 9 to 31 percent.

While Jewish land purchases did not increase nearly as significantly as the Jewish percentage of the population—even at the end of the Mandate, Jews owned only about 7 percent of Palestine's land—it is impossible to overstate their political importance. The number of Jewish settlements grew from about 29 in 1920 to more than 270 at the end of the Mandate, encompassing enough territory to enable Jews to create a socially, politically, and ultimately militarily viable presence along the coastal, Galilee, and Negev regions of Palestine.

Territorial conflict was intimately connected to the political conflicts that surrounded it. Indeed, the doomed intercommunal politics of the period are another crucial element in the failure to achieve compromise or reconciliation. The most important dynamic was that while the onset of British rule allowed for the rapid development of a public and officially accountable Jewish political establishment that was part of the Mandate's structure, Palestinian Arab political life was severely curtailed, specifically because the development of a robust and accountable political system and governing class would by definition allow for more successful resistance to Zionist colonization and development.

The British need to stunt the evolution of Palestinian politics had two primary effects. First, as in other colonial situations, it encouraged a level of corruption, discord, and incompetence among Palestinian political and economic elites that ultimately proved disastrous to the national cause. Second, violent resistance became a crucial if episodic means of Palestinian resistance to the increasingly powerful Zionist presence in the country. Yet each of these outbreaks during the Mandate led to major victories for the Zionist movement.

Yet although the Palestinian Arab elite ultimately failed to secure a state for its people, away from the often compromised political and economic leadership a growing cadre of well-educated bourgeois and upper-class members became central to Palestinian national life during the Mandate, laying the groundwork for the organizations that would provide the backbone for communal solidarity and resistance after the Catastrophe, or *Nakba,* of 1948.

The zero-sum territorial conflict between Palestinian Arabs and Jews impacted almost every aspect of life in Mandate Palestine and profoundly shaped relations not merely between but within the two communities. Palestinian Arab society in particular fractured along class lines over conflict with the Zionist movement and competing economic and political interests between elites and the majority of the population. The best evidence of this dynamic was the Great Revolt of 1936 to 1939, among whose primary causes was the deep and growing frustration of the Palestinian Arab peasantry and working class with both the inefficacy and the corruption of their leadership. Yet this narrative of subaltern rebellion against the native elites and colonizers alike is simplistic if not provided with appropriate nuance.

Sonia Nimr's portrait of Abdul Rahim Hajj Mohammad, one of the revolt's leaders, in "'A Nation in a Hero'" (chapter 8), sheds important light on how ordinary Palestinians saw the revolt as a way not merely to resist increasing Zionist territorial encroachment but to take control of their own destinies. Abdul Rahim was from a land-owning family, and his early exposure to the impact of Zionism on Palestinian peasants led him to become one of the organizers of the general strike in 1936 in the Tulkarm region. He used existing social networks to form alliances with the urban middle class, especially the well-educated political figures who were not content with the policies adopted by the elite national leadership. At the same time, he used the complicated web of clan loyalties—based on marriage, mutual interest, or business—to help strengthen and solidify the power of the resistance. These alliances were crucial to what success the revolt managed to achieve, and they have served as a model for resistance and solidarity to the present day.

The rapidly increasing Jewish population in Palestine simultaneously enhanced the conflict with the Palestinian population and presented valuable opportunities for advancing Jewish national interests. These dynamics grew even more pronounced during World War II as the scale of the destruction of European Jewry became clear. Traditionally, scholars have rather sharply differentiated the various strands of Jewish, and particularly Zionist, ideology and experience in pre-1948 Palestine. But the reality, as is so often the case, was much more that of a spectrum on which many people went back and forth depending on the situation. Rebecca Kook's biographical essay about her father, Hillel Kook, offers a powerful case in point (see chapter 9). The elder Kook, a member of one of the important rabbinical families in Palestine, whose uncle was considered the spiritual godfather of Revisionist Zionism, defies any simplistic political characterizations, as he transversed the boundaries of set identities on the left and the right alike.

Kook was born in Ukrainian Russia and immigrated to Palestine in 1925 in the wake of two decades of pogroms. He began his political life as a founding member of the militant/terrorist organization the Irgun. Yet at the height of its power, he called for the establishment of a secular democratic republic in Palestine and the dismantling of the World Zionist Organization after the achievement of independence. His family was part of the religious elite, yet he strove for the separation of religious from national identity and demanded that Israel recognize all of its population, Palestinian Arabs as well as Jews, as constituting a single nation. Kook *fille* demonstrates through her father's life that while most histories of the Mandate tell a story of conflicting claims and promises, there were and still remain many paths not chosen that can instruct us about the broader history, present, and future of the country and its two national communities.

Similarly, Nitsa Ben-Ari's recollection of the life of S. Yizhar (the pen name of Yizhar Smilansky), the most important novelist to write in modern, sabra Hebrew, reveals the dichotomies that can exist between the public persona and the private life and sentiments of even the most ardent supporters of an ideology or cause (see chapter 5). In this case, the well-known writer and commentator has long been imagined as deeply rooted in the establishment, fully identifying with its policies, rhetoric, and dreams. Indeed, Yizhar was among its political representatives, yet a very different picture emerges from his writings, whose strong subversive streak regarding Zionist ideology is central to his self-identified position as the "outsider-insider" who focused much of his attention on the minority view(s) within the Jewish community.

Comparing the lives of the people described in part 2 reveals not only the many paths never taken in Mandate Palestine—and with them, possibilities for rapprochement never explored or even imagined—but also the richness of the experiences that did define the period, and it provides new insight into why the two national movements collided in open warfare in 1948.

5

Hero or Antihero?

S. Yizhar's Ambivalent Zionism and the First Sabra Generation

Nitsa Ben-Ari

Since his first story in 1938, "Ephraim Goes Back to Alfalfa," Yizhar Smilansky has been considered the first Israeli writer, indeed the first sabra (Israeli-born) Hebrew writer to use modern, sabra Hebrew as a literary language. From him onward, a Hebrew writer was almost by definition Israeli. Not that there had not been other sabra writers, but this was how Yizhar was acknowledged by his contemporaries, be they younger writers, some of whom adopted him as a model, or young readers who admired him for speaking their language and expressing their innermost feelings. For them he was the new Brenner, the new Bialik. In fact, this sense of a pioneering breakthrough in literature accompanied Yizhar from the start as a sense of creation, one might say genesis. For him it meant creating from nix, using all the senses, molding words, literally feeling them, tasting them, listening to them, watching how they connected, even how they appeared on paper—all this with the utmost wonder and exhilaration, which permeated him to the last word he wrote.

He was a symbol of the New Hebrew in more than the literary aspect. He was a Haganah commander, an officer in the Israeli Defense Forces, a participant in the War of Independence who never failed to volunteer for the Army Reserve, even when not required to do so by law. He was a distinguished member of the Knesset (Israel's parliament), part of its Committee for Security and Foreign Affairs. He was a devoted and admired teacher, both in secondary schools and in the university, and he was a famous speaker, well known for his rhetoric—in fact, his extraordinary Hebrew, his wit, his wisdom, and his insightful, unorthodox thinking made him a favorite with the media, which, especially in times of crisis, sought interviews with him. At the age of forty-two he had already written his incontestable masterpiece. By forty-three he had won the Israel Prize for literature, and he later won every important Israeli prize, both literary and other. He was a brilliant emissary of the Jewish Agency, repeatedly sent abroad to convince Jewish youths to make aliya. All this seems to depict a person well rooted in the establishment, fully identifying with its policies, rhetoric, and dreams.

Yet a very different picture emerges from his writings. They always had a subversive streak, especially regarding Zionist ideology. In that respect, Yizhar took up Brenner's position of the "outsider-insider"—in fact, Brenner, though preceding Yizhar's generation, was a constant and almost tangible presence in his intellectual life. Far from being monolithic, Zionism had a strongly romantic streak and various—often clashing—factions, and Yizhar identified more often than not with the minority. His identification with the literary and cultural scene was never wholehearted either. Like Brenner, he reserved "the right of outcry." There was always a controversy around his writing, always ambivalence to it, and always innate sadness in the man. This is how he described himself, in an interview with Eilat Negev: "I was born with some genetic flaw . . . some sadness in my heart. Such a person—no matter where he goes, will be a poet, for it is in him, something is flawed in him. The experience is just an opportunity, the biography is just the materials you talk through, otherwise you'll scream like a mute person."

This "flaw"—an integral part of his life and his writing—was an almost existential trait, obvious in his work and his career alike. It may have accounted for his poetic formation, but it was also responsible for his ambivalent views on some of the most critical issues of Israeli culture. It certainly accounts for the feeling of belonging and not belonging that he so keenly expressed, a characteristic of many more Israelis than is formally believed.

Yizhar was born into the Weitzes and the Smilanskys, both families of early pioneers, the very core of Zionism. His father, Ze'ev, immigrated in 1890, before the publication of Theodor Herzl's *Jewish State*. His mother, Miriam, immigrated in 1908 and adopted this year as her birthdate, insisting that her tombstone should read 1908–79. His parents spoke only Hebrew, refusing any other language. They gave their son the education deemed best for the New Hebrew, based on an ideological infrastructure established by a small group of culture shapers who sought to break away from the feeble, effeminate, nonproductive, Diaspora Jew. The New Jew, virile, muscular, suntanned, rough, and productive, would work the land of the Forefathers with his own hands. He would skip millennia of Diaspora to establish a direct link with the biblical Hebrews of yore. Yizhar was indeed a product of this education, even if he later criticized some of its aspects. He was profoundly influenced by the methodology advocated by teachers such as Simcha Chaim Vilkomitz and Dr. Yitzhak Epstein, who taught all about the history, geography, fauna, and flora of the land of Israel with unprecedented fervor, preferably on the spot, amid nature.

Till the age of thirty-two Yizhar categorically refused to travel outside the country, and no conversation of his with any member of the family staying abroad did not end with the questions: When are you coming back? What are you doing there, anyway?! On the other hand, many of his stories express a longing for the far away, the not-here, an ambivalence that came to typify him no less than did his loving descriptions of the local landscape.

The Smilanskys came from the Kharson province of Ukraine, where their business was managing or leasing estates for the local gentry. The founder of the line, Shmaya Smilansky, had eight children, the most charismatic being Moshe, one of the youngest. At sixteen, Moshe Smilansky was the first of the youngsters to immigrate to Eretz Yisrael, his brother Meir, his sister Shifra, and his nephews Zeev and David following a few months later. According to the family legend, he carried the Bible in one pocket and Tolstoy in another. They planned to earn a living in agriculture, and Shmaya Smilansky, mistaking the green, luscious landscape for fertile land, bought a lot for them in Hadera, at the time a malaria-ridden tract of land. As a result, they all fell ill. Shifra eventually succumbed to the repeated attacks of malaria and yellow fever and died a few years later. With the exception of Shifra and Moshe, the others were persuaded by their parents to return to Europe to recuperate and learn a profession which would be of greater use than agriculture. Zeev, Yizhar's father, taught Hebrew and worked in factories as a locksmith (and may have picked up statistics) in Odessa, and though he dreamed of becoming a pioneer in a commune, he believed the redemption of the land would come through industry rather than agriculture.

Moshe, later known to Yizhar as Uncle Moshe even though he was Yizhar's great-uncle, dedicated himself to orchards and fruit plantations, eventually becoming the avowed father of the Jewish citrus groves. Having become an expert on the subject, he published books, magazines, and manuals on his beloved citrus and organized and chaired the Citrus Growers Association, serving in this capacity for many years. With the help of funds raised abroad, especially in the United States and England, he bought land from Arab owners, many of whom lived in Lebanon. Like many of his relatives, Moshe had literary talent, and he became famous for his stories about life in Eretz Yisrael. Especially popular were his romantic stories about Bedouin sheikhs, first published in Central European organs and captivating the imagination of youths there. Symbolically, he wrote the stories under the pseudonym Hawaja Musa, his name among his Arab acquaintances. Compared to most pioneer settlers, Moshe Smilansky was a man of the world, a capitalist. It was in his house that Yizhar first encountered a gramophone and classical music, though his uncle's records were mostly cantor favorites. Moshe differed from most of his contemporaries in his attitude toward the Arab population: he was peace-seeking, a supporter of the Brit Shalom movement, founded by intellectuals such as Martin Buber, Judah Leon Magnes, Hugo Bergman, and Gershom Sholem. At a time when mainstream Zionism hoped to establish a Hebrew state, Brit Shalom opted for binational autonomy for Jews and Arabs under British Mandatory rule, with each group enjoying equal rights. Famous for opposing the demands of Hebrew laborers to exclude Arab workers, Moshe was unpopular with the socialist parties, yet he was a central figure in the country, respected by Jews and Arabs alike. Yizhar described his intriguing personality in *Preliminaries:* "[So] taciturn that people shun him, yet capable as orator of expressing the innermost feelings of all . . . concealing his true feelings, yet weeping suddenly among his brothers like Joseph in his day." The citrus-growing industry eventually became a main national source of income, and Moshe's role in developing it was not contested. Although he never held any official public office, a hundred thousand people showed up for his funeral in 1953.

Yizhar's father, Ze'ev Smilansky, one of the founders of the socialist journal *Hapo'el Hatza'ir,* was even more of an introvert. His writing was mostly polemical and scientific: he published hundreds of papers and essays, never signing them with his name, out of modesty, as was customary at the time. A confirmed socialist, he opposed any kind of exploitation. Sadly though, at the age of fifty-five, during a world economic crisis, he was fired from his job in the Statistics Department of the Tel Aviv municipality and, having no other alternative, turned to his uncle Moshe (who was younger than him) for work. Moshe made him the foreman in one of the citrus groves, a job Ze'ev hated passionately: for him it represented a betrayal of his ideals and was a symbol of his failure. The figure of his father as a broken man, a failed pioneer, haunted Yizhar throughout his life.

The Weitzes came from Poland. Yosef Weitz (1890–1972), known as Uncle Yosef, was born in the Wohlin district to a family of lumber merchants. He grew up surrounded by forests. When he was seventeen he went to Odessa and witnessed a pogrom, a trauma that shook him to the point of severe illness. He had planned to study in Odessa, but due to his fragile psychological state his family sent him to Eretz Yisrael to recover, with his elder sister Miriam to take care of him. Yosef describes this in his *My Diaries and Letters to My Sons,* at the same time depicting himself as a fervent pioneer come to Eretz Yisrael for purely ideological motives. The alternative aliya stories did not seem mutually exclusive to him. He settled in Rechovot, where he worked as a night watchman and a laborer. One of Yizhar's short stories for youths, "Hashomer Bakramim" (Night watchman in the vineyard, in *Shisha Sipurei Kaitz,* 1951), hilariously describes his "heroic" uncle trembling on a night shift, mistaking a cow for a fierce robber. Yosef immediately distinguished himself politically and was among the founders of the Hapo'el Hatza'ir party.

Yosef's days as a laborer were not to last long. Both he and his sister were good looking and had many suitors; Yosef soon married Ruhama, a rich farmer's daughter, betraying, so to speak, his socialist ideology. The couple moved to the Galilee, where Yosef's new job, in the Keren Kayemet (Jewish National Fund), sent him.

His third son, Yechiam, later to become Yizhar's best friend, was born there, in Sedjra. Ruhama and Yosef were to be among the first Jewish settlers in the new neighborhood of Beit Hakerem in Jerusalem.

Between 1932 and 1948, Yosef Weitz was the powerful director of both the Land Settlement Purchase and the Forestation Departments of the Jewish National Fund. In this capacity he did his utmost to change the local landscape, attempting to make it as similar to Poland as possible, as swiftly as possible. He continuously advocated the "transfer" of the local Arab population to neighboring Arab countries, a policy internationally practiced at the time. In his *Diaries* and his letters to Yechiam, he openly discussed the option of transfer, and according to Benny Morris, Weitz was the head of a transfer committee, though others claim his role was secondary.

The duality within the family vis-à-vis Palestine's Arabs was no doubt a formative feature in Yizhar's life. At a conference in honor of Martin Buber, Yizhar presented a paper titled "About Arabs and Uncles," in which he refers to the way the Arabs were conceived of in the early Yishuv days: "When the pioneers entered the Land . . . the Arabs were part of the ancient scene, part of the eastern reality. . . . Nothing that had to be considered seriously, nothing that could be helpful or harmful . . . just part of an ancient and backward scene . . . part of the backwardness and the desolation forlorn of change. . . . So here before you are two uncles and two paths, and between them the whole history of the Palestinian Question during these one hundred years."

Miriam Weitz's self-image was no less problematic than her brother's. Realizing that she could not wed a certain young man with whom she had been in love, she consented to marry Ze'ev Smilansky, fifteen years her senior. The couple first lived in Jaffa, where Ze'ev worked in a factory that produced irrigation pumps and motors, a pioneering enterprise established at about the same time that Henry Ford started his endeavor. Their firstborn, Yisrael, was born in Jaffa. He was the apex of their life and hopes: handsome, strong, and full of confidence, the very image of the New Hebrew. This was an image Yizhar felt he could never live up to. They soon moved to Chulda, where Ze'ev planted trees as part of early forestation experiments, dreaming all the while of joining his friends in the future commune of Nahalal. It was in Chulda that their second son, Yizhar, was born, on September 21, 1916, in the midst of World War I, when the country was broken and starving. He was sickly and thin; his mother nicknamed him *Ma'us* ("repelling") and never hid her preference for his older brother. In 1918 she insisted they move to town, and her admiring husband acquiesced, giving up the dream of Nahalal. This did not prevent Miriam from seeing herself as a brave Zionist pioneer. The family lived for a while in Jaffa. Then, in 1922, again spurred by his wife, Ze'ev had his brother David arrange for him to work in the Tel Aviv municipality, and the family moved to Mendele Street in Tel Aviv.

Yizhar was eleven years old when, in 1927, during the world recession crisis, his father lost his job and the family was obliged to move back to Rechovot and depend on Uncle Moshe. In Rechovot Yizhar had no friends, but he had taught himself to read (from the age of three, according to him) and read everything he could lay his hands on. As a boy, he was especially influenced by world classics published by Omanut and Mizpeh, translated in a mixed biblical and talmudic, high stylistic register of what was then considered (by Jewish Enlightenment norms) proper literary Hebrew. Somewhat paradoxically, the books, published to fill the gaps in the developing New Hebrew culture, resonated with longing for "there," elsewhere, so that regardless of how well rooted Yizhar was "here," his imagination carried him to the vast territories opened by world literature. Imitating the old-fashioned language of translated novels provided him with a rich and stratified language and hours of fun with his cousins when they met: they would enact scenes from adventure stories in that mock-heroic literary style, with the distinct feeling of belonging to an elite club, impenetrable to passersby innocently walking in the citrus groves.

TEACHING AND THE URGE TO WRITE

When Yizhar graduated from elementary school, his father had no money to pay for further studies. Uncle Moshe meanwhile decided to send his own son, who did not show any particular talent, to take an entrance examination at the teachers' seminary in Beit Hakerem, Jerusalem. Yizhar happened to go along and took the examination too, though he had not prepared for it. He passed with flying colors and was admitted with a scholarship. David Yelin, the founder of the seminary and a central figure in the revival of the Hebrew language, was then headmaster, and together with an outstanding staff of teachers, such as Ben-Zion Dinaburg (later to become a Knesset member and the third minister of education), he zealously applied the new ideological principles. More than any other teacher, Dinaburg was responsible for transferring Yizhar from the moshava to the intellectual world. In an article Yizhar wrote about Dinaburg, he called the latter "a teacher to his bone marrow, a storm wind, who caught a silent boy from the sleepy moshava and threw him from the top of the cliff into the sea, swim if you want to live." In a new and exciting way, Dinaburg taught the Bible, history, literature, Zionist history, and education, sometimes all at once, and "went straight into the boy's bones, into his soul, into the rest of his life." Yizhar loved his Bible lessons, in which he excelled. Proficiency in the fauna and flora of his native land, taught by Professor Avizohar, in Hebrew, followed as naturally. For Yizhar, whose parents brandished the flag of secularity to the point of categorically refusing to celebrate any of the old Jewish holidays, the New Hebrew education system provided a substitute for religion and faith. Celebrating the beauty of nature soon became part of it. Throughout his life he would exult in the daily wonder of sunset, for example, which would provide him with extraordinary moments of elation of a deeply religious character.

But the New Hebrew education system left something to be desired: although sabra patriotism instilled by the educators covered so many aspects of life, it fell short where music was concerned. In Beit Hakerem, Yizhar made friends with Yedidya Havkin, later described in the novella "Havakuk," who taught the boy all he wanted to know about music. Beethoven's music is present in the lives of the protagonists of this novella as a purifying and exulting force with tremendous impact. The encounter with European music would add its weight to the here-there dichotomy: stories such as "Havakuk" express a longing the new ideology failed to satisfy, reverberating throughout Yizhar's work. Faced with the scorned shtetl's rhythm of "ya-ba-bam" on the one hand and the limited first vestiges of so-called Hebrew native songs on the other, Yizhar's soul now yearned for the elation of "other" music.

While in Beit Hakerem, he became even closer to Uncle Yosef's son Yechiam, and the bond between the cousins became exceptionally strong. He graduated at eighteen, in 1934, and reluctantly looked for a job as teacher. By then, however, he had made a few literary attempts (mostly poetry, surprisingly or not surprisingly enough) and knew all he wanted to do in life was write.

Yizhar's first job as a teacher was in the moshava Yavne'el. He taught in what was practically a one-room school. From day one he charmed the pupils with his informal attitude, playing with them during the breaks and performing gymnastic feats on the parallel bars. He taught all subjects, including arithmetic, of which he knew very little, and apparently future teachers had to spend a while uprooting the mistakes and misconceptions he instilled in his pupils. Daytime teaching and nighttime guard duty prevented him from writing, and he refused to continue in this way. His brother offered to pay for a year of schooling at the University of Jerusalem, and Yizhar took him up on this, studying biology, but the money soon ran out, and his parents needed his help. Reluctantly, he found another teaching job, in kibbutz Geva, but he gave it up after a week or two, when the kibbutz failed to provide him with his own room, and returned home to work as a simple laborer in the citrus groves in Rechovot. In the evenings he wrote "Ephraim Goes Back to Alfalfa," set in a Geva-like narrow-minded kibbutz. The story reflects both his experience of dull and excruciating physical work and his brief encounter with kibbutz norms. "In its provincial self-absorption and high moral standards, the kibbutz, as Yizhar describes it, seems at times almost an extension of the shtetl from which the chalutzim longed to escape," a reviewer commented. Yizhar sent "Ephraim" to Yitzhak Lamdan, the editor of Gilionot. The choice was not self-evident, as Gilionot was a privately owned literary review. Other periodicals—in the somewhat limited supply of the time—were unacceptable: Hapo'el Hatza'ir was a party organ his father had participated in founding and later left, brokenhearted, on the basis of political disagreement; the monthly *Moznaim* did not encourage young, unknown talents and did not accept a previous attempt of Yizhar's at a short story. Lamdan was quick to recognize the young sabra's talent. He was the one who gave him his pen name, to differentiate him from the other Smilansky writers: S. Yizhar, a Hebrew-sounding name, holding so much promise. Lamdan coached Yizhar and published all of his early stories.

The story was a great success, and critics refused to believe its writer was so young and inexperienced. Writing, however, was a luxury. His parents still needed financial support, and Yizhar was compelled to go back to teaching. His family on the Weitz side in Ben-Shemen arranged for him to teach Bible and Literature in the Ben-Shemen Youth Village. Ben-Shemen, run by the legendary headmaster Dr. Lehman, was the haven for Youth Aliya children, who had been separated from their families in Europe before the war. It was known for its German (Yekke) orientation and its outstanding faculty. In a normal world, the Ben-Shemen teachers would have populated faculties in European universities. Yet when it came to dealing with the psychological problems of these young refugees, the learned educators fell short. Nobody knew how best to approach the problem of the sorrow and loss these youngsters had suffered—so the policy adopted was silence, avoiding the past and starting anew. In Ben-Shemen, as elsewhere, Yizhar gained his students' affection by his informal and unpatronizing ways. Though he was but a poor teacher from the periphery who walked around in shorts and sandals, for them he was the role model of the sabra, a prince of sorts. Youthful as he was, his authority was natural and never challenged. He used the same revolutionary methods imbued in the seminary, teaching Hebrew in Hebrew, taking lessons out of the classroom, striving to instill the love of the homeland in newcomers and turn them into locals. His story "Poretz Gader Yishchehu Nachash" (One who breaks through a fence may find himself bitten by a snake), in which he turns the meaning of the biblical verse that gives the work its title upside down, is perhaps the best portrayal of his unorthodox way of teaching. For someone who abhorred teaching, he always excelled at it. His Bible lessons were an inspiration: he would teach with a closed book in hand, reciting whole chapters dramatically, almost ecstatically, by heart. Yizhar would also insist on calling each living creature, each plant or herb, however insignificant, by its exact Hebrew name:

> As if it were your duty to say it right, and precisely, till it hurts and even till you bleed, without plastering or beguiling, the whole truth, with all the undertones of light and shade, and not just in empty words, so as to get it over with. . . . For sometimes this blessed blindness is good, in which people see every day, and that lets them off easily, and they are content with the "generally speaking" and that's it, and let them remain unidentified, all the sorts of grass and thorns and goat dung, without any private names, for even if they do have a name, it will soon be erased and all of them will evaporate into this general "what the heck" that awaits all in the end. . . . But here

comes this twitter, that flew over innocently, and you don't know what it is and what its name is, and how it flies and whether it will come down and how it will walk—jump on two legs at a time or put one foot after another, and the weed will not rest and you will not rest until you know that it is indeed wheat and barley, even when they all sway equally in the light wind now, with, among them, you don't even have to check, the false-corn species. (*Beautiful Malcolmia*)

In 1941 Yizhar married Noemi Wollman, his friend from the seminary, and their first son, Yisrael, was born in Jerusalem in April 1942. He was named after Yizhar's elder brother, who had been killed in a motorcycle accident three months earlier. (Hilla, Yizhar's daughter, would be born in 1944, and Ze'ev, the youngest, in 1954, both in Rechovot.) At the same time Yizhar resumed his studies at the Hebrew University in Jerusalem. Once a week he would walk to Lydda, take the crowded bus to Ramleh, and from there catch an equally crowded bus to Jerusalem, where he would scramble on foot to the University on Mount Scopus. As a faithful follower of the New Hebrew ideology, he now studied geology, attempting, as it were, to know the country inside out.

During World War II, in the face of oncoming military danger and economic difficulties, Yizhar was obliged to join the Haganah and stop his studies for lack of time and funds. He became a commanding officer and often let his students participate in operational missions.

His father's death in 1944 left his mother alone in their house at 14 Moskowitz Street, Rechovot. A family council ruled that Yizhar and his family should move in with her, and they lived in the house until 1991. A small secondary school for workers' children was then established in Rechovot, and Yizhar taught there for a year, then spent another year as its headmaster. This did not stop him from continuing his activity in the Haganah, until in 1948, with the founding of the state and the outbreak of the War of Independence, he joined the army. Writing was now even more of a luxury than before.

THE TRAUMA

Yizhar's innate sadness was reinforced by a trauma that was to leave a mark on the lives of so many of his generation. Many of his beloved students joined the Palmach (the name is an abbreviation of the Hebrew *Plugot Mahatz*), which was the elite striking force of the Haganah—the underground military organization of prestate Israel. Some fell in fierce battles—a loss that Yizhar would never wholly overcome. The greatest shock was the death of his beloved cousin Yechiam, who insisted upon joining the notorious Palmach mission Night of the Bridges, in June 1946, and died a violent death. From then on, Yizhar seemed to have lost his naïve faith in the wisdom and sound judgment of political leaders. The fact that the topics of his writing almost never went beyond his youth may be attributed to the 1946 trauma. In the interview with Eilat Negev, he described his cousin's death thus:

> His death was an earthquake for me, from which I haven't recovered until today. What I had with him, I never had with anybody else. A possibility of speaking taken away. I feel emptiness, and now I have to build him inside me, so that we can go on talking. Part of my second ego is Yechiam's image. Not that we were alike. As you see, he was handsome, full of humor, a personality. Since his death in a stupid mission, aimed "to show" the British, I began to have serious doubts about the righteousness of Zionism, and war, and land. Until then I was whole. It strengthened my feeling that no stone is worth dying for.

In 1945, Yizhar started publishing short stories for youths in the weekly *Davar Liyladim* journal, the bulk of them appearing between 1945 and 1947. Many were written from the point of view of a native Israeli, humorous and Dickens-like, describing trifles in everyday life. The clash between the trivial event and the mock-epic tone was obviously adopted from his favorite *Pickwick Papers,* one of the earliest novels Yizhar had read, in the old-fashioned translation. The style gave him ample opportunity to use the mixed maskilim language, with its rare biblical words, that he had acquired from his early readings. Not many have noticed or referred to the humor—always present, though subtle—in Yizhar's writing, which especially characterized his stories for youths written before 1948.

The tone and themes changed after the war. In 1947 he published *Hachorsha Bagiva,* describing the battle when the Chulda agricultural farm, which he knew and loved, fell to the Arabs. By then he was established as a promising Israeli writer, and Chayim Ben-Dor wrote him the famous letter expressing the expectations of a whole generation to read his next book. Written on February 12, 1944, it said:

> Every youth in the world has its own author standing high above him—and in him. We only had two—Bialik and Brenner. A third has not yet arisen. . . . In you there is that something that characterized Brenner[:] . . . the truth, to the end, without concession, without illusion. Eyes that see through all the shells and hit the root. In that certain place where life's marrow is sucked. And your truth is a "sabra" truth, it grew among . . . citrus groves and sand dunes, in the khamsins and in the fields of Emek Yizre'el. It is Israeli.

(The letter was not sent, and Yizhar first read it when it appeared in a volume commemorating Ben-Dor's death in the War of Independence.)

Critics such as Baruch Kurtzweil commended his literary style, yet not all critics were as appreciative. Especially suspicious of the new sabra writer was the Polish-born writer and critic Shlomo Zemach, who in 1952 summed up *Midnight Convoy* as paving the way for a convoy that would start in the middle of the night to go to a certain settlement beyond enemy lines. All the rest is but the air surrounding this act.

People may have, or rather must have, grown up in places where the language was different. So that you cannot criticize these hesitant steps into the riches and secrets of the language, and it is good to wake up the sleeping and restore their vitality . . . though the diligence of these youngsters of our camp is a great bore. My profession makes it necessary for me to know the various end-of-summer weeds, and I know the field flowers . . . stem, flower, and fruit. So I do not complain. I see great efforts and enormous seriousness as well as grammar and meticulousness, strict with itself. I see abstention and asceticism in the wastefulness, and in the bounty—a closed miserly hand.

Zemach was deaf to the need of the New Hebrews to know their surroundings by name. But he was right in claiming that the profusion of words in Yizhar's writing did not amplify the action. Yizhar's writing never centered on a story. One of his most typical narratives was "Sipur shelo Hitchil" (A story that did not start), in which he flatly refuses to surrender to a plot. The infatuation with words and with the old-new language was a theme of its own. His love affair with the language was perhaps more intimate and erotic than any of his descriptions of budding love. The idea of a woman, the elaborate struggle with writing it, was to him more fascinating than any woman of flesh and blood. Zemach also accused Yizhar's writing of being devoid of eroticism—and indeed, as a true sabra, Yizhar could not bring himself to write about sex and intimacy explicitly. Implicitly, though, and when it referred to "the birds and the bees," his writing was charged with erotic power.

Having been a captain in the Haganah Field Force and served as an intelligence officer in the 1948 war, Yizhar was exposed to prisoners' interrogations; he also accompanied convoys beyond the Egyptian lines and witnessed the expulsion of Arab villagers. After the war, these painful experiences found an outlet in stories and novellas such as "Hashavui" (The prisoner) and "Khirbet Khiz'e," published together in 1949 by Sifryat Poalim, and in Shayara shel Hatzot (Midnight Convoy). "Khirbet Khiz'e," perhaps the most famous of Yizhar's stories, shows the moral compunction and thorough unease of a soldier whose unit is charged with the evacuation of an Arab village. Most of the inhabitants still in the village are old people and children, who represent no immediate threat, and the soldier watches their faces with doubt and dismay as they are lead to the trucks. Except for him, no one seems uneasy about the "transfer," and when he raises some questions, he is "comforted" with the words that soon the village will be inhabited with new Jewish immigrants and will flourish. "Hashavui" depicts another painful scene: an Arab shepherd is caught during a skirmish and questioned by Israeli soldiers. There seems to be no doubt as to his innocence, and the storyteller hopes his commander will let the man go, yet "security" has the upper hand, and at the end of the day the shepherd is taken away. There is no big drama in the stories; they are but a glimpse into the reflections of a single soldier who sees things differently. They should not be taken as political stories either, for Yizhar was not an engaged, mobilized writer. More than anything else they depict the human condition that makes it possible for an oppressed people to gain power and be transformed into an oppressor. Yet the painful questions these stories brought forth have been reverberating in Israeli society ever since.

POLITICS, AMBIVALENCE, WRITING

Yizhar's reputation as a writer drew the interest of those politicians who felt that adding intellectuals to the ranks would benefit their party. Approached by Zalman Aran—one of Mapai's prominent party activists and later the influential education minister who followed Dinaburg—Yizhar reluctantly agreed to join the party's list of nominees, and toward the end of the war he was elected to the Knesset. The moderate Mapai was not popular among the youths and writers of the time, who were mostly drawn to personalities such as Meir Ya'ari and Yitzhak Tabenkin in the leftist Mapam party. Yizhar consented—as his wife had advised—primarily with the hope that the job would allow him time to write. *Yemey Ziklag* (Days of Ziklag) was already burning in his bones.

His greatest contribution to legislation was the National Gardens and Parks Law, which ensured nature reserves and defended local flora and fauna. His brilliant 1962 speech in the House reflected his strong feeling about conserving the delicate balance between nature and civilization in the tiny country and his objection to "improving" the age-old landscape. Other laws he tried to promote, such as one encouraging the industry known today as high-tech, were rudely waved off by Pinchas Sapir, then the minister of industry and commerce, who reacted to Yizhar's speech sarcastically: "Your Hebrew is fabulous, but you understand nothing in economics." Yizhar was the first to bring up legislation in favor of public health care for all (1965), paving the way for what would later be implemented in Israel. Politics also involved agreeing to decisions not in accordance with his moral code. Against his better judgment he was forced to vote for the renewal of the Military Government (Memshal Tzvai) over the Arab population. The matter was hanging on one single voice, and David Ben-Gurion, then the prime minister, personally explained to Yizhar that if the Military Government were to be abolished, he would quit, with the result that Menachem Begin would gain power.

With the 1948 war over, Yizhar met many of his former pupils, Palmachniks who had taken part in fierce fighting and told him about their experiences. Why he chose to write about Khirbet Maachaz of all places is not clear; it was not a particularly strategic spot, nor was it one of the mythic battlegrounds, though it had changed hands a number of times, resulting in great losses. To him, these very characteristics, combined with the biblical resonance, must have seemed symbolic of the whole war. Although well acquainted with some of the combatants, who had spent hours confiding in him, he made a thorough investigation of his own, studying the weather, the topography, even the map of the sky as it was at the time and the hours of sunrise and sunset. He worked on *Yemey Ziklag* over a period of seven years, from 1951 to 1958. He wrote most of it on small notepaper, in barely decipherable handwriting, some in the bus on his way to Jerusalem, some in Knesset sessions: it just poured out of him. He then copied it into a notebook, which he gave to a typist. When she had finished transcribing it, he sent her a florist's whole stock of flowers.

His earlier works had earned him the praise of the critics, but not so "Khirbet Khiz'e" and "Hashavui," which aroused public scandal. There were voices that claimed he was serving the enemy's interest and helping their cause. An even greater scandal erupted when *Yemey Ziklag* was published. It contained some of the most virulent antiwar passages in his writing. Especially controversial was the famous *Akeda* symbol:

> I hate Avraham Avinu who is going to sacrifice Yitzhak. What right does he have over Yitzhak. Let him sacrifice himself. I hate God that sent him to sacrifice Yitzhak, barring all other ways, leaving only the way of the *akeda* open. I hate the thought that Yitzhak is nothing but a test-case between Avraham and his God. This proof of love. This demand for a proof of love. This sanctification of God through the binding of Yitzhak. Murdering the sons as a test of love! Using force and intervening and taking life to settle a quarrel. And that the world was silent and did not rise and shout: Rascals, why should the sons die?

So far, Yizhar had depicted Palmach youths as a group, a bunch of idealists, afraid of no one and ready to give their all to the motherland. *Yemey Ziklag* described them as individuals, each with his own weaknesses, from a personal, not a national, point of view. Critics of the old school claimed it was a distortion of the true spirit of the 1948 heroic fighters, in fact of the image of the whole generation. They found the novel too long, repetitive, difficult. What both readers and critics apparently missed was the new nature of the writing; it was an attempt to recapture in full, minute by minute, seven days and seven nights in a certain space, through the eyes of a group of young soldiers occupying this space. Moreover, *Yemey Ziklag* is where Yizhar categorically split with the establishment: he wanted to portray young individuals, regardless of the values of Zionism. This was a challenge he had wanted to face, and it passed unnoticed. Some readers, like Yosef Oren, even saw a Mapai conspiracy in the novel. A jury headed by Baruch Kurtzweil, the most influential literary critic of the time, rejected the book's candidacy for the Bialik Prize for the above reasons. Yizhar received two awards for *Yemey Ziklag,* the Brenner Prize and the Israel Prize, but the early rejection had been painful.

By 1960 Yizhar was becoming critical of the contemporary young generation. In an essay published in 1960, "Al Pney Hano'ar" he expressed his disappointment with shallow youngsters. He quoted Arthur Koestler, who derisively dubbed modern youths the "espresso generation" for seeking quick, sharp, and cheap pleasures. A young avant-garde writer named Dan Omer then fiercely counterattacked in his book *On the Way,* a subversive novel banned for its pornography and antireligious vehemence: "And in Ziklag there are factories producing espresso machines, not far from the alfalfa fields, and the children that will be born tomorrow, for children will always be born tomorrow, will also die in street-fighting on the Arab front. Senseless battles, sunset-less battles, against 8 million others. Battles we shall all die in. We are all future-casualties of these 80 million battles." If young bohemians rejected Yizhar as an institutionalized writer, mainstream poets did not accept him either. On December 9, 1967, Nathan Alterman, one of the group that Yizhar called "annexation poets," responded pugnaciously to this charge in an article in *Haaretz.*

The feeling of emptiness following the gigantic feat of *Yemey Ziklag,* topped by the disappointment with the reviews and his estrangement from contemporary youths, was a shattering experience for Yizhar. His self-esteem was wounded; he felt hurt and alone. Moreover, the country in which he had been born was disappearing under his very eyes. It was emptied of Arab inhabitants, filled with new immigrants who didn't share his ideals, who saw the land as "impaired," "defective" (*mekulkelet*), and did their utmost to "repair" it. To him the land was in no need of repair. The open spaces of his childhood, sparsely populated, with Arab villages strewn here and there, seemed perfect. In 1990 he recalled how his world was shattered when a new generation of Jews arrived in the massive aliya of 1948–53, refugees who brought their own world with its own norms. The old world—Yizhar's world—was done with by force, abruptly, rudely, not because it was not beautiful but because its time was up. Particularly hateful to him were the *shikunim,* housing projects built during these years to quickly accommodate the new immigrants, who otherwise lived in tents. They blemished Yizhar's beloved empty landscape, the "perfect plane" that had taken a million years to form, never to be again.

He wrote some more stories for youths for *Davar Li'yladim,* of a different nature than the prewar ones. They were no longer about the present, which had lost its appeal, but about the past, his boyhood country as he remembered it, his lost Eden. He felt torn between the knowledge, on the one hand, that the newcomers had to be integrated and housed, that the land had to change to accommodate the growing population, and the penetrating sense, on the other, that he was being robbed of his homeland. "Tarazinot" and *Hakirkara shel Hadod Moshe* were among the stories for youths that he wrote in this period, and they abound with longing for the lost land of citrus groves. This is how he described the sense of loss, of indifferent temporariness, later, in *Preliminaries:* "Suddenly he knows that soon, almost imperceptibly, none of this will remain, neither this vineyard nor this sandy path, none of this will remain . . . because everything here is provisional, with no necessity to exist like this particularly, the vineyard that will be replaced by an orange grove, and the building plots that will replace the orange grove, and the houses that will be built on the plots . . . because everything here is provisional, and the ancient cycle of the year has no binding force here."

No less aggravating for him was the lot of the Arab population hinted at in these stories. Yizhar grew up within sight of the neighboring Arab villages Zarnuga and Kubeba, they were part of his childhood landscape. They appeared in many of the stories, such as, for instance, "Hatznicha min Hatzameret" (Fall from the treetop) from 1959, in which a sad note accompanies the description of Abdul Aziz, Uncle Moshe's loyal helper: "But Abdul Aziz was there. Not a young man. But straight-backed. Silent. Mustache whitening. . . . Very solemn, and his demeanor marked with a streak of sadness (for things that were? For things to come?)—and he was strong, and meticulous, and clean."

The bitter tone accompanying his writing at the time is perhaps more noticeable in the stories for adults: "But one word, if need be, about the ugly housing projects and the shriveled souls that created them. Ugly housing projects will give birth to ugly people, ugly people will give birth to ugly women, ugly women will give birth to ugly children, and ugly children will give birth to an ugly world. And an ugly world will not give birth to anything any more, it will just be filled up and clogged and suffocated and that's all." Although his quarrel was with the people who built the shikunim, he did not hide his ambivalent feelings toward what he called *hayehudim hamekulkalim* (the defective Jews)—ambivalent because theoretically, of course, they were his brothers, part of him:

> What do I want from them? Want? Not from them. Would perhaps like to be able to say "what are they to me." Yet they are me and I am them. No, just want to run away. That's all. Something in me struggles to flee, get away. Burning in me not to give in . . . not to be swept and swollen by all this general superficiality . . . to give my heart to another, belong to another rather than that here, more to any there than any here, more to any impossible than all the possibles possible here. Oh God, all the possibles possible here!

Both critics and readers ignored the stories for children, such as *Beraglaim Yechefot*, while *Sipurey Mishor* received some, mostly negative, reviews. Far from being best-sellers, the books did not sell at all. Years later, major critics like Dan Miron and Gershon Shaked changed their minds and lauded the stories, but in the 1960s the verdict was not favorable, and their value went unrecognized.

In a radio interview in 1989 with Zisi Stavi for Galey Zahal when *Yemey Ziklag* was republished, Yizhar claimed that he didn't care how many readers he had and that he would not write in any other way to please anyone: if only seven readers remained, let there be only seven. In the 1960s, refusing to adapt to public taste and feeling, perhaps, that there was not even one reader left, he stopped writing.

THIRTY YEARS OF SILENCE

Yizhar never talked about the reasons why he had stopped writing fiction. Directly asked, he would say he had had other projects in mind, such as writing about education issues. But it was no coincidence that he stopped short after what he took as a rejection from his readers. Justifiably or not, he felt that he had no one to "talk to." One can say that, after realizing his masterpiece had been misread, or rather that most readers (and especially famous literati such as Prof. Kurtzweil) did not know *how* to read it, he may have decided to dedicate himself to teaching readers how to read. His nonfiction book *Likro Sipur* (Reading a story), an adaptation of his PhD in education, may have been a product of this state of mind.

He now traveled a lot, sent by the Jewish Agency to meet Jewish youths, promoting youth aliyas from England, Holland, Switzerland, and Argentina. However, this period ended in 1977, when the right-wing Likud party came to power. Yizhar, strongly opposed to it, was no longer sent abroad to do the job he excelled at. Neither did he hide his views. True to his beliefs, he started writing vehement political articles against the new regime. His anger focused on the settlers of Gush Emunim, and in a continuous outpour of polemic essays he took on the role of a Whip. His articles were later collected in a small, relatively unknown booklet called *Dapey Riv* (Quarrel pages), in which, under the full name Yizhar Smilansky, he addressed the settlers:

> If you come in the name of Judaism—Judaism is a shame; and if you come in the name of Zionism—Zionism is a shame. I know nothing will prove it to you. I know nothing will open your eyes to see that Arabs are like you. And that they are not dung to be trodden upon and swept out. And you cannot get rid of the Arab as you get rid of rocks, bushes, and goats that stand in your way. This Arab who, according to you, not only is his land free to take but his blood as well, and you are free to do with him whatever Jewish history shouted against.
>
> I know that biblical verses will not prove it to you . . . nor Jewish tradition or heritage—since you are the proof that one can keep all the mitzvoth—and not be a Jew.

A turning point occurred when, around 1988, Ohad Zmora wrote to him, asking his permission to republish *Yemey Ziklag*. Yizhar hesitated, pondering whether he had better revise it, perhaps shorten it (it is more than one thousand pages long), then reconsidered, content with the slightest revisions. Zmora published several other of his books too, also slightly revised by Yizhar. Suddenly Yizhar felt he had a public again. Revising his books and seeing them on sale again must have triggered a desire to write that had been dormant all those years, although it took ten more years and the forthcoming inevitable demolition of 14 Moskowitz Street (where he had lived for about sixty-three years) to drive him to break the thirty years' silence.

THE RETURN

The house at 14 Moskowitz had to be torn down. The town, Rechovot, grew around it, strangling it with tall buildings; the municipality refused to consider it a conservation site, and Yizhar's family had to sell and move. This meant a physical rupture with the past, which could only be recaptured by writing its story. The journalist Ariana Melamed, then the literary editor of *Hadashot*, which had just begun to appear in 1989, turned to writers with an invitation to write about a place they deemed special. Yizhar sent the first two passages of *Miqdamot* (*Preliminaries*), considered a masterpiece by many, for this special issue. He called it "The First Place." The full novel *Miqdamot* followed, written in one flow, in a few months, and published by Zmora-Bitan in 1990. As if the public had been holding its breath and awaiting Yizhar's comeback, the novel was immediately and unanimously praised. Letters and phone calls flooded the house. For the first time in years, critics and readers alike acclaimed Yizhar, praising his insight, his love affair with the Hebrew language, and the special qualities of his style.

The book aroused great emotion. Old-timers who remembered the 1920s reacted with particular enthusiasm. It took some time for the message to come through, though: it was a penetrating reckoning with Zionism, which had gradually and consistently destroyed Yizhar's beloved home. *Zalhavim* followed in 1993. In biographical terms, it was a follow-up, depicting Yizhar's teens in the 1930s, with special focus on the dilemmas that youths had been preoccupied with at the time. It quotes Yechiam, his best friend, deliberating on whether youths should not follow their personal dreams rather than the communal interest: "And he has no idea what he is going to become, or who will want to listen to his wishes, when everyone unanimously comes to him with one single claim, get up you lazy fellow and get yourself mobilized to help your people, help your people, yes, one with all our jubilant brothers, and when, says Yechiam rather quietly, when do you look for God?" Thematically, though, *Zalhavim* was a continuation of the lament for old Eretz Yisrael. But now Yizhar's ambivalent feelings about Zionist ideologies and practices were no longer considered subversive. Although he would never personally identify with what came to be known as the post-Zionist trend in historical research, this school of new historiography did legitimize a critical approach to the old ideals. Moreover, the sense of being torn between here and anywhere-but-here had become a dilemma shared by many.

An incredibly fruitful period followed. The Zmora-Bitan publishing house celebrated Yizhar's eightieth birthday with a luxurious edition of his collected works

and the Festschrift *Dvarim L'Yizhar*, to which major Israeli personalities contributed. (As the editor of the Festschrift, I cannot but express my amazement at how
eagerly people contributed to it.) The flow of books, astonishing for an octogenar-
ian, did not stop. Four were the result of Yizhar's last outbreak of creativity, all
masterpieces of their various genres: *Zdadiyim* (Asides, 1996), *Etzel Hayam* (By
the sea, 1996), *Malcolmia Yefehfia* (*Beautiful Malcolmia*, 1998), and *Giluy Eliyahu*
(Discovering Elijah, 1999). The last, a virulent attack on wars of all kind, is the only
novel in which, as the narrator, Yizhar appears as an adult, although one must note
that his war novels and novellas were often written from a grown-up's perspective.

His late writing presented metaliterary thoughts, providing a clue to his aims as
an author. It tackled the binary opposition between plot in the conservative sense
of the word and in the Yizharic sense, so obvious in "Sipur shelo Hitchil." Rina
Ben-Shahar claimed, and rightly so, that Yizhar's plot or narrative was the language itself. I suggested refining this explanation somewhat, emphasizing that the
"plot" was the exhilaration of creating in language, even the invitation to share the
exhilaration with the reader. Translating Yizhar would have been an impossible
task if all the text wanted to convey was the exhilaration of writing Hebrew. Yisrael
Asael took this issue even further, arguing that Yizhar's aim was inviting the reader
to participate in existential moments of vision, of revelation, in words. Asael cited
Paul Valéry's claim that if poetry were dance, then words, just as music or dance,
should transport the reader into a poetic state. This is very close to Yizhar's sense
of the elation that prose should provide. He invited the reader to participate in
such moments of trance, of cosmic transcendental experience, which his writing
abounded in, what he called *hedvat hanefesh hamitpaeelet*, the joy of the exhilarated soul.

After the outpour of the six late books, Yizhar did not write any more. He basked
in the warmth of recognition, almost adoration, of young and old. Though he had
never expected to, he enjoyed his new home in the moshav Meishar, near Gedera,
where he devoted most of his time to reading. The trauma, the genetic sadness had
been somewhat appeased. Or so it seemed. No major literary or political media
supplement appeared, in festive or tragic occasions, without an interview with "the
greatest Israeli writer," now usually much more benevolent and optimistic. His
heart finally failed him on August 21, 2006, when he was a month short of ninety
years old. Besides a few that echoed bitter conflicts, a deluge of favorable obituaries
followed. Ceremonies, conferences, and reading sessions in his memory are held
every year. S. Yizhar has finally become part of the consensus.

SUGGESTIONS FOR FURTHER READING

For a complete list of Yizhar's work, see http://library.osu.edu/sites/users/galron.1/00113 .php.

Translations of Yizhar's works into English

"About Arabs and Uncles." Translated by Steven Bowman. *Hebrew Studies,* Volume 47 (2006), pp. 321–26. Originally in Hebrew, in K. Yaron and P. Mendes Flohr, eds., *Mordechai Martin Buber Bemivchan Hazman.* Jerusalem: Magnes Press, 1993, pp. 11–15.

Khirbet Khizeh. Translated by Nicholas de Lange and Yaacob Dweck. Jerusalem: Ibis Press, 2008.

Preliminaries. Translated by Nicholas de Lange. Jerusalem: Toby Press, 2007.

Analyses of Yizhar's writings

Aberbach, David. "S. Yizhar (1916–2006)." *Jewish Quarterly,* Volume 203 (Autumn 2006), pp. 28–32.

Ben-Ari, Nitsa. *Suppression of the Erotic in Modern Hebrew Literature.* Ottawa: Ottawa University Press, 2006, pp. 111–20, 346–48.

Ben-Shahar, Rina. "S. Yizhar: Meafyenim leshonyim-signoniyim bisefarav ha'acharonim" (Language-style characteristics of his latest works). In Elit Olstein, Shoshana Kulka, and Ora Schwarzwald, eds., *Sefer Raphael: Papers in Communication, Linguistics, and Language Teaching.* Jerusalem: Carmel, 2000, pp. 103–24.

Miron, Dan. "A Late New Beginning." Preface to S. Yizhar, *Preliminaries,* translated by Nicholas de Lange. Jerusalem: Toby Press, 2007, pp. 1–28.

6

"A Son of the Country"

Dr. Tawfiq Canaan, Modernist Physician and Palestinian Ethnographer

Philippe Bourmaud

Just a few months before the death of the Beit Jala–born physician Dr. Tawfiq Canaan, on January 15, 1964, the German journal *Zeitschrift des Deutschen Palästina-Vereins* paid homage to its many-times contributor by publishing an extensive, if incomplete, list of his writings. The bibliography of about a hundred books and articles, short and long, published in European languages, was an appropriate tribute to the book-loving Canaan. For thirty years or so, he would remain hardly more than a footnote in Palestinian history, in spite of Palestinian ethnographers' acknowledged indebtedness to his works. Yet from the 1970s onward, he would be called the father of Palestinian ethnography, and in the 1990s his work would inspire festivals in the cities under Palestinian autonomy. In turn, this led to a reassessment of his biography by Palestinian and other researchers, who gave greater importance to his medical work and his political activity while also showing that Palestinian ethnography had had many a midwife. Out of a footnote, a conflict of interpretations has grown.

During his lifetime, Canaan was a man of some eminence in Palestinian society under the Mandate, a famed physician and an opinionated man of significant political activity. He promoted the writing down of Palestinian Arab folklore and thus provided a later generation with the wherewithal to assert a different kind of Palestinian cultural nationalism, one based on core elements of Palestinian heritage such as the kaffiyeh, the *dabkeh,* and the Palestinian peasant experience.

Canaan's concern for the peasants and Bedouins of the country appears to have been sincere and motivated by his sense of the great cultural loss happening under his very eyes. Modernization, as he saw it, was most desirable; still, it was changing the landscape and erasing practices and beliefs which he viewed as quite as ancient as the Bible, if not more. Jewish immigration not only accelerated the pace of transformation but—Canaan argued—made Palestinian Arabs feel alien to the new community that was evolving next to them. These ideas were not uncommon among the Palestinian Arab educated class. But Canaan's upbringing made him feel them especially acutely, and he nurtured a desire to salvage through ethnography what he saw as a specifically national cultural heritage. His background, medical training, and early professional experience drew the guidelines of an intellectual project which he adhered to throughout his life.

THE SON OF THE PASTOR

Tawfiq Canaan was born in the Christian village of Beit Jala, a few miles south of Jerusalem, on September 24, 1882, the son of a Protestant Christian family. His father, Bishara Canaan, was one of the first Arab Protestant pastors in the country. He was a Lutheranist and as such a member of a very small and recent community: the bulk of Protestant missionary activity in Palestine had been accomplished from 1841 onward by diverse societies within the framework of the Anglo-Protestant Bishopric of Jerusalem, which was the result of a compromise between the Church of England and the Lutheran Church of Prussia. When Bishop Barclay, the last man to hold the bishopric, died in 1881, Anglican missionaries and their Lutheranist counterparts parted ways, and small Lutheran communities began to emerge under the protection of imperial Germany.

In Beit Jala, there was a competition for the hearts and souls of the Arab parishioners between Greek Orthodoxy, promoted by tsarist Russia; Roman Catholicism, supported by France; and Protestantism, mostly in the form of German-supported Lutheranism. Most of Tawfiq Canaan's career bore the seal of his proximity and loyalty to German institutions. His intellectual training in these institutions, especially his high school years at Jerusalem's Syrian Orphanage, contributed to his modernist views, since Protestantism had been introduced in the Middle East as a modern, more rational form of religion than Eastern or Roman Christianity, both viewed as decadent and far too lax ethically. Protestants also considered their practice superior to Islam, which they commonly dismissed as a form of superstition, full of empty ritualism, plagued with a stifling sense of social and religious authority, and hostile to any spirit of personal inquiry.

In the second half of the nineteenth century, the Bethlehem area was changing at a rapid pace. In Beit Jala, a village that used to be overwhelmingly Greek Orthodox, the arrival of Western missionaries and church institutions started a real estate bonanza. The increase in religious tourism in the same years spurred a small local industry of olive-wood carvings and religious artifacts in the mostly Christian villages of Bethlehem, Beit Sahour, and Beit Jala. As local business expanded, so did the population. In spite of extensive emigration, the village began to resemble a small town. The people of nearby Jerusalem still identified its population as fellahin, but this category was more a matter of social status than lifestyle.

Indeed, Canaan was raised somewhere between the countryside of neighboring villages where his father would take him on a horse on apostolic or proselytizing tours, and a quasi-urban bourgeois way of life, which came along with the connection with European institutions. In that period, he developed a lifelong attachment to Palestinian peasants, though he was never one of them.

BRILLIANT STUDENT OF THE AMERICAN MISSIONARIES

Canaan had been sent to high school in Jerusalem and was set for a modernistic college education at the Syrian Orphanage of Jerusalem, owned and operated by the Schneller family, yet in 1899, shortly after he finished high school, his father died, leaving his family impoverished. Canaan was able to rely on the solidarity network of Protestant institutions and so attend the Syrian Protestant College in Beirut (SPC; today's American University of Beirut), run by American Presbyterian missionaries. The college was even in the habit of halving registration fees for impoverished students, and Canaan took to giving private lessons to pay for his daily expenses and to support his family in Beit Jala.

The loss of family income did not rush Canaan into a profession. Instead, before entering the Medical Department, he chose first to get a BA from the Collegiate Department, which was a way to catch up with either humanities or science studies. Such a course of study was common at the SPC, which recruited most of its students among the former pupils of missionary or public high schools in the Levant and Eastern Anatolia. Those institutions usually gave instruction that was strong in literature and in one foreign language but insufficient in science. Canaan also needed to reach the required level in English, the language in which all medical courses were taught. As a result, he didn't start his four-year-long medical studies until October 1901. Canaan's lengthy stay at the SPC, from 1898 to 1905, is proof of the institution's efficacy in avoiding dropouts on account of economic hardship.

Canaan turned out to be an outstanding student, getting a prize in most medical classes during his third and fourth years of medical studies. He was further selected as the class valedictorian, and on receiving his MD in July 1905, he gave the speech on graduation day on behalf of his fellow students in front of the whole teaching body at the SPC, the American consul, the three delegates of the (military) Imperial Medical School (IMS) at Istanbul, many notables from Beirut, and his fellow students' parents. Canaan's speech was a modernist profession of faith and probably made quite an impression; at any rate, he had the rather unusual honor of seeing it printed in Arabic in the Egypt-based newspaper *Al-Muqtataf* a few days later, under the title "Modern Therapeutics."

Higher education in Beirut was all about getting a position. Students were sent to the SPC or its Catholic rival, the Jesuit-run Faculté Française de Médecine (FFM), first and foremost so that they could enter the skilled-job market that was expanding throughout the eastern Mediterranean. With an MD, graduates could get positions as military physicians in the Anglo-Egyptian military corps in Sudan, in the Ottoman civilian medical administration established in 1869, or in one of the many foreign hospitals and dispensaries scattered throughout the Levant and Anatolia. Yet at the moment when Canaan embarked on studying medicine, there was a glitch: the MD he would get from the SPC would not allow him to practice. The Medical Department had been founded in 1867 without the authorization of the Ottoman government, which refused to recognize it as a fully fledged medical faculty. The medical diplomas given by the American missionaries were of no value in its eyes, although a number of former students often managed to get a verbal authorization to practice from local officials. Since an agreement dating back to 1876, the IMS, acting as the highest jurisdiction for medical matters in the empire, had only agreed to recognize the SPC as a preparatory school of medicine. This meant that students with an MD from the college were recognized in Istanbul to have gone through a medical training and were therefore allowed to travel to Istanbul and take, in one single session, all the examinations of the IMS's curriculum. Provided they passed, they would get an IMS diploma, which alone would serve as a license to practise medicine in the sultan's realms. This lengthy and costly process deterred many SPC graduates from becoming official MDs.

Three years before Canaan started his medical curriculum in 1901, the government had fully recognized the SPC's French rival. For Canaan, the son of a pastor, going over to the Catholic enemy as many of his classmates had done was plainly out of the question, but there was a high risk that getting an MD from the SPC would prove a hindrance in his career; indeed, the lack of recognition for this degree would prevent him from getting a job in any of the hospitals or dispensaries of the Ottoman Empire. But by 1903 an agreement was found, by which a delegation of medical professors would come every year from Istanbul to supervise the examinations and have the new doctors pronounce the Ottoman Hippocratic oath, which explains the presence of the three Ottoman delegates in front of Canaan when he delivered his speech.

JERUSALEM, 1905: A MEDICAL BABEL

When Canaan started working in Jerusalem after graduating in 1905, the great European powers had largely divided the city's medical field along lines of protection. This protection went beyond the defense by a state of its nationals abroad against unfair treatment by local powers; in the Ottoman Empire, special rules, known as the Capitulations, applied to foreign citizens and Ottoman citizens and institutions under formal foreign protection and were officially designed to ensure fairness of judicial treatments for non-Muslim Europeans. In practice, in the nineteenth century, the Capitulation system had become a form of privilege for individuals and a kind of extraterritoriality for institutions. Most of the latter were of a religious nature, as the Ottoman state granted tax discounts for foreign religious foundations. After the empire made foreign property ownership and building activity legal in 1867, this system allowed religious protected institutions, hospitals among them, to mushroom and expand.

Jerusalem, home to somewhere between eighty and a hundred thousand inhabitants, counted as many as eleven hospitals and an even greater number of dispensaries, and this did not include three additional hospitals on the way to or inside Bethlehem. All of these, except the Municipal Hospital of Jerusalem, fell under the protection of European countries, be it Germany, Britain, France, Russia, Greece, or Austria-Hungary. These institutions were waging a war of popularity, which hopefully would translate into influence for the protecting nation. Thus, hospitals became showrooms of medical progress. Yet the personality of the physician was more decisive in the success of the institution.

Canaan first got a job as a deputy physician at the (German Lutheran) Hospital of the Deaconesses of Kaiserwerth. The institution, renovated for the ostentatious visit of Kaiser Wilhelm II in 1898 to Jerusalem, was quickly getting an edge in the medical competition between European nations just then, largely due to the reputation of the head physician, Dr. Samuel Grussendorf, who swiftly got a good reputation and was a sound scientist by all accounts.

Under Grussendorf's direction, Canaan acknowledged, he got a prolonged medical training and especially a deeper knowledge of infectious diseases. He also got access to a bacteriological laboratory and an X-ray apparatus, which were hallmarks of innovation in the Jerusalem medical landscape. The relation between the two men was quite hierarchical, since it was a matter of fact that European institutions in Jerusalem could only be headed by European physicians, as Arab physicians would not be trusted by these hospitals' patients and would be especially disdained by the European practitioners in town.

But things were changing rapidly on that account. Since the late 1890s, Ottoman physicians had been appointed as heads of the French hospitals in Bethlehem, Jaffa, and Nazareth. Canaan too made good use of his opportunities to work as head physician of the German hospital: when he replaced Grussendorf, gone for a few months on a furlough to Europe in 1906, he was able to establish his popular standing in Jerusalem. The attendance at the outpatient consultation jumped from around five thousand to more than ten thousand per month. In 1910, the head physician of the Jewish hospital Shaare Tzedeq, Dr. Moritz Wallach, entrusted him with the interim direction of this hospital, which signalled Canaan's rising fame. Also in 1910, he was appointed physician of the municipality, and by

1913 he opened his own clinic in the Musrara neighborhood, just north of the Old City. This was the first medical institution in Palestine opened by a locally born physician. He would live there with his German wife, Margot (née Eilender); his sister Badra; his sister-in-law Nora; his three daughters, Yesma, Nada, and Leila; and his son, Theo, until 1948.

There is no point in looking for community borders in the emerging medical profession of Jerusalem prior to World War I. Instead, in spite of national rivalries and the nascent Arab-Zionist confrontation, international cooperation took place in the name of public health and the fight against infectious diseases. Such cooperation was visible during an epidemic of meningitis in Jerusalem in 1910, when Drs. Wallach and Canaan coordinated the gathering of data about patients afflicted with that disease from such institutions as the municipal hospital, then headed by the Jewish physician of Algerian origins Dr. Abraham Albert Abu Chédid. After reporting the following year on the epidemic in the SPC alumni journal, *Al-Kulliyeh,* Canaan worked in medical-cooperation projects on a much larger scale. When the German epidemiologist Professor Mühlens came to Jerusalem in 1912, he invited Canaan to join his project of an epidemiological survey of Palestine focusing on malaria. Soon the country became a focus for coordinated actions against infectious diseases, with competing projects from Germany and the United States merging in 1913 into an International Health Bureau. Canaan headed the bureau, as well as the antituberculosis team there, for a few months in 1913–14. At the time, tuberculosis was becoming an epidemiological priority, with areas of endemicity such as Nablus. Medical mobilization became a noticeable feature in Jerusalem, and Jurji Zaydan, the founder of the Egyptian newspaper *Al-Hilal,* noted in 1914 how advanced the Holy City was in that regard compared to the rest of the Middle East.

Much as the medical sector in Jerusalem was international, so was its tiny intellectual world. Canaan, who is reported to have met his German wife, Margot Eilender, at Esperanto classes, was an active member of that community. The institutional pattern in the humanities was similar to that in the medical sector, with domination by a few Western research institutes, often of one denomination or another, such as the German Evangelical Palestine Institute, headed by the theologian Gustaf Dalman, or the École Biblique et Archéologique Française (EBAF) of the Dominicans.

Canaan, who was well versed in textual knowledge of the Bible, was especially influenced by Dalman, with whom he remained connected at least until the end of the 1930s. Indeed, the physician developed a growing interest in the ethnography of Palestine as his medical practice led him to hold itinerating consultations in the villages around Jerusalem, much as he had watched his father do in his childhood. At the same time, Canaan was catching up on the relevant bibliography. He started reading the works of Ignaz Goldziher, one of the founders of Islamic studies in Europe, and those on Palestinian Islam by Dr. Paul Kahle, whose articles on religious sanctuaries in Palestine, published between 1909 and 1911, can be seen as forerunners of Canaan's major book, *Mohammedan Saints and Sanctuaries,* and of Dalman's series of encyclopedic proportions on work and customs in Palestine. Around the time of the Ottoman revolution of 1908, Jerusalem was also turning into a town of conferences, their proceedings often printed in the local press or by one of the several small publishing houses that were sprouting alongside the research institutes. This enabled Canaan to start publishing, first on medical issues, with the pamphlet *Death Or Life* (1908), and then in 1911 on ethnography, with the printed version of his 1909 conference on Palestinian peasantry. The SPC publication *Al-Kulliyeh* was also a ready outlet for his works, yet all of this was of a very local scope. Canaan's cooperation with Mühlens was decisive in his career as both a physician and an ethnographer, as it connected him with European medical research centers and enabled him to be publish with the Colonial Institute of Hamburg, the main German institution for colonial science.

SUPERSTITION AND POPULAR MEDICINE IN THE LAND OF THE BIBLE

Canaan's first book, *Aberglaube und Volksmedizin im Lande der Bibel* (Superstition and popular medicine in the land of the Bible, 1914), is seminal in his ethnographical career. Yet its posterity in Palestinian ethnography was very limited, inasmuch as it was virtually ignored by later Palestinian researchers for want of an Arabic or an English version. Published by the Colonial Institute of Hamburg, it was a bold step in a specialty which was not his own. It was also an ambitious scientific project for which he lacked access to up-to-date materials. The noted scholar on Islam and politician Carl Heinrich Becker, who was a professor of the history and culture of the Orient at the institute and wrote the preface to the book, noted this but saw a redeeming grace in Canaan's ignorance of Edmond Doutté's important work dealing with similar issues, *Magie et religion dans l'Afrique du Nord* (1909). The many correspondances between the two independently written books was proof of the depth of the common stock of practices and representations of magic and healing throughout the Arab world. In his later works, Canaan would multiply his references to Doutté's opus.

The two projects differ in conception. Ethnographical research—and France's precolonial policy—motivated Doutté's presence in Morocco. Yet Canaan was brought to popular medicine and magic through his professional concerns, which overlapped with his early experience of Palestinian peasantry. The preface of his book singles out the difficulties entailed by the medical pluralism amid which young practitioners with an MD started working. Canaan in his foreword is not quite as direct and states his pride as "a son of the country" to be able to present his work, the research for which had been facilitated by his constant contact with patients. Indeed, soon after his return to Jerusalem after graduating in 1905, he had developed a curiosity about the artifacts his patients used to protect themselves against disease. Word spread that the young physician was interested in such objects, and he accumulated a collection of amulets, talismans, cups, and so forth that numbered more than fourteen hundred items at the end of his life and is now hosted by the Birzeit University Library and the Pitt-Rivers Museum in Oxford.

Handling this material, Canaan was less interested in the objects themselves than in their meaning, the representations of well-being and illness in their connection to the supernatural. This translated in the way he wrote, mostly in the dry, objectivist, descriptive style of much of the ethnographical production concerning Palestine up to the 1920s. Canaan was taught in the Kantian tradition, and his interest in the representations of magic stemmed partly from a phenomenological desire to go from clear consciousness into the depths of collective folk imagination and national psyche. This forbade him, "a son of the country," from displaying any form of subjectivity in his prose. When Canaan used the first-person singular, it was to refer to the conditions of his research or to place his arguments within an ongoing specialist debate. His ethnographical writing would not vary much from that norm in later works, except for recurring mentions of his own collection as a source.

Canaan's book covered a great variety of topics around the notion of popular medicine: talismans and magic squares, "fear cups" used in the popular healing of diseases consecutive to fits of fright, swearing, tombs of saints famous for curing the sick, and so on. He would develop all of these themes at greater length after World War I.

A PHYSICIAN AT WAR

With the Ottoman Empire entering the First World War on November 5, 1914, Canaan was mobilized for service in the military medical service. Given the concentration of military corps—Ottoman, German, and Austrian—in Palestine, the physician was able to stay in the region for most of the war, first in Nazareth, then mostly between Bir al-Sabʿ and Gaza, and finally between Nablus and Damascus by the end of the conflict.

While these circumstances proved fruitful from an ethnographical point of view, with Canaan collecting around two hundred artifacts of popular medicine in less than four years, the period was not as productive for his medical research. Canaan's one medical article in those years shows that the military medical services in Palestine were doing epidemiological work, but less about endemic typhus than less-dangerous diseases. The article dealt with the Jericho boil, a form of leishmaniasis prevalent in the Jordan Valley. Both the German military medical service, with which Canaan kept contact, and its Austrian counterpart were doing research on that usually benign disease, which apparently grew more and more infectious in those years. Canaan's wartime work on leishmaniasis would prove to be a significant turn in his medical career: it was the beginning of his lifelong specialization in skin diseases.

THE MORAVIAN LEPROSARIUM AT TALBIYEH

Canaan's medical career and his interest in Palestinian ethnography often intersected. Among his circle of acquaintances were Dr. Adolph Einszler and his wife Lydia, née Schick. Dr. Einszler, a Catholic Austrian citizen by birth, had settled in Jerusalem, where he had converted to Protestantism and begun working in the early 1880s at the leprosarium of the Moravian Brothers in Talbiyeh (today in West Jerusalem). Canaan had known him since their days at the German hospital, when the two men had shared responsibilities during Dr. Grussendorf's leave. Einszler's wife, the daughter of the architect of the German consulate, was interested in popular culture and beliefs, on which she started writing ethnographic articles in the 1890s. She collected artifacts of popular material culture and popular magical medicine, which she at times lent to Canaan or exchanged for pieces from his collection.

Einszler died on April 27, 1919, and Canaan succeeded him in supervising the leprosarium; this represented continuity in its service and a logical continuation of Canaan's professional interests. At the leprosarium, he welcomed visitors and friends, such as Dalman, who stayed there when he sojourned again in Jerusalem in 1921 and 1925, yet Canaan's position there was especially important in raising his professional standing and scientific reputation.

In the job, Canaan had an unusual field of study. Leprosy was a disease of limited prevalence and feeble contagiosity, especially in the West, which meant that most specialists of the disease around the world would have met it only occasionally. Yet Canaan had a permanent population of patients under his care, as the Ottoman administration had made it compulsory for lepers in the region to live in Jerusalem, Ramleh, Nablus, or Damascus. After World War I, the British authority chose the leprosarium to host all the lepers of Palestine. Jewish immigration also brought a number of lepers, who were also housed there. Over the years, Canaan published several accounts of leprosy, as both a domestic and an immigrant's disease. With a reasonable number and variety of patients, he was able to work on therapeutical means to reduce the progression of the disease, such as tincture of iodine or an age-old remedy, chaulmoogra.

Canaan's specialization required frequent updating and relations with a world of specialists. Fortunately, the Charter of the League of Nations obliged mandatory powers to enable development in all its forms in their territories. British authorities were to facilitate competence building for the population of Palestine and enable its professionals to improve their training. The number of physicians who took postgraduate courses or went abroad for an upgrade in their specialty in Europe or the United States boomed after 1918. Canaan took advantage of the new opportunities and went abroad for two postgraduate courses, including one in internal medicine in Berlin during the first semester of the academic year 1922–23. Afterward, he took the directorship of the Internal Medicine Division at the reopened German hospital in Jerusalem and held it until the hospital closed in 1940.

Canaan's network among Jerusalem-based physicians of Germanic origin was extensive: it included Drs. Grussendorf, Einszler, and Mühlens, of course, and after World War I the German leishmaniologist Dr. Huntermueller and the surgeon of the German hospital Eberhard Gmelin, Canaan's close friend until the latter, close to the Nazi Party, left for Germany in 1939. His scientific connections also included Jewish scientists who had settled in Palestine, such as the lifelong anti-Zionist Dr. Wallach and, among Zionists, the German researcher Saul Adler, who isolated leishmaniasis from sand flies in Jericho in 1929, the noted Czech ophthalmologist Dr. Albert Ticho, and Judah Magnes, the president of the Hebrew University of Jerusalem. Part and parcel of Canaan's academic notoriety was his address book.

To what extent did this translate into researching with Jewish physicians, as Canaan had engaged in prior to World War I? That is not clear. He was not working in a binational environment, as would have been the case had he been a civil servant of the Palestine government. Furthermore, he complained in 1936 that the notion of using only "Hebrew labor" had extended to Jewish hospitals, where not one employee, be they physician, matron, or nurse, was non-Jewish.

It seems that some of Canaan's work was of a freelance kind, which did not prevent him from contributing to the research in infectious tropical diseases that were becoming hot public health concerns. There was, for instance, a definite momentum in leishmaniasis research around the years 1929–31, due to the fact that the disease was discovered outside the Jericho region where it had long been known. Canaan found cases of visceral leishmaniasis (kala-azar), a more severe form of the disease, in Jerusalem and the neighboring villages during those years, while another scientist, Arye Dostrovsky, found it in Haifa in 1930. While Canaan had been convinced during World War I that leishmaniasis was endemic only to Jericho, he now came around to the idea that it had been present, though not epidemic, in other regions of Palestine before the late 1920s. By 1945, he had reported on visceral leishmaniasis in Jaffa, Yazur (near Ramleh), Birzeit, Haifa, Beit Iksa, Nablus, Tulkarm, Al-Lydd (later Lod), and Halhul (near Hebron). In the same period, he discovered that cutaneous leishmaniasis, similar in its symptoms to the

Jericho boil, could be found in Bethlehem and the nearby villages, including his native Beit Jala. The disease was now present in both the plains and the hills of Palestine, which Canaan attributed to contamination from Jericho, the Egyptian army, and Jewish immigrants. This earned him a degree of bibliometric notoriety in his field, and his name was included in 1932 on the list of famous doctors in tropical medicine compiled by Dr. Gottlieb Olpp, the head of an important medical center for tropical medicine in Germany and himself a researcher into the use of chaulmoogra against leprosy. Among Palestinian Arab physicians, though, this aspect of Canaan's work did not have much influence. Palestinian epidemiologists mostly ignored leishmaniasis until the 1970s.

Another way to get standing in a specialty was to take part in academies, such as the British-inspired Medical Academy of Jerusalem, of which Canaan was appointed secretary in July 1923. International surveys were also a boost to scientific reputation, such as the world inquiry on leprosy undertaken under the direction of the prominent Brazilian bacteriologist and later World Health Organization leprosy expert Heráclides César de Souza-Araújo between 1924 and 1927, for which Canaan wrote the report about Palestine. By the end of the 1920s he had become an international authority on the disease.

Canaan occupied the post of director of the leprosarium until the military occupation of the premises during the war of 1948, when the Zionist forces decided to expel the Arab personnel and patients while keeping their Jewish counterparts on the spot. He then helped to orgazine a new leprosarium in the West Bank village of Surda.

WITH THE PALESTINE ORIENTAL SOCIETY
(1920–1936)

Canaan was also engaged in the main venture devised by the British authorities to bring together representatives of the Arab and the Jewish communities in the humanities, the Palestine Oriental Society, which existed from 1920 to 1948. In the columns of the society's periodical, the *Journal of the Palestine Oriental Society* (*JPOS*), Canaan's articles appeared alongside those of English writers and a couple of Jewish Zionist writers, most notably the linguist Eliezer Ben-Yehuda and the ethnographer and Labor Zionist activist Yitzhak Ben-Zvi. It is hard to say to what extent Canaan's inclusion reflected a political choice, giving credit to the occupation authorities for their cultural policy, or a philosophical stance that science ought to remain above the political fray.

Canaan politicized neither his "nativist ethnography" nor its objects of study. Even his studies of pilgrimages to local shrines, which had become occasions of mobilization and protest since the beginning of the Mandate, were the continuation of a long trend of ethnographic research. His writing was focused on beliefs and the practices translating such beliefs and did not touch upon the possible political use of pilgrimages. Moreover, his belief in the survival of ancient ethnographical features up to the present was not guided by a desire to give legitimacy to the presence of Palestinian Arabs by right of antiquity, as would be the case with Palestinian folklorists a few generations later. It was a standard assumption shared by all researchers on Palestine at the time, deriving from the preoccupation in biblical studies with trying to explain sacred texts by present practices.

Among the authors for the *JPOS*, there were of course differences of approach: while Ben-Zvi would go looking specifically for traces of Jewish presence, Canaan was bent on underlining continuities, the mingling and the stratification of religious influences. His main referential corpus was the Bible, but he also compared practices in the Qur'an and the Sunnah. Canaan influenced a group of Palestinian Arab intellectuals who strengthened his approach and became part of his intellectual circle. Of those men—Khalil Totah, Omar Saleh al-Barghouty, Elias Haddad, and Stephan Stephan—the last three were also members of the Palestine Oriental Society. The relationship between them and Canaan was not one-directional: they also facilitated his work, as shown by the references in his writings to fieldwork in Dayr Ghassana, Barghouty's native village.

During the Mandate years, Canaan found another scientific interlocutor in the Finnish ethnographist Hilma Granqvist. She had settled in the village of Artas, near Bethlehem, which had been a spot of ethnographic interest since the beginning of the twentieth century. Hers was probably the first local example of an ethnological project based on immersion, which enabled her to acquire more of an insider's understanding than Canaan, with his urban fashion, ever could. Granqvist influenced Canaan's ethnographic style, and from the 1920s onward his ethnography tended to move away from the systematic form of description of *Aberglaube und Volksmedizin im Lande der Bibel* and toward more interpretive writing.

These contacts enabled Canaan to cover more ground, literally, as he embarked on what remains his best-known project, a survey of pilgrimage places and sanctuaries in the newly territorialized Palestine. This work was published in the *JPOS* from 1924 to 1927 and then as the book *Mohammedan Saints and Sanctuaries in Palestine* in 1927 by the Palestine Oriental Society. It established his academic credit in ethnography, and in 1928 he was appointed chief editor of the *JPOS*.

The late 1920s were a period of great productivity for Canaan, as reflected by the quick succession of articles, medical as well as and ethnographical, that followed the publication of *Mohammedan Saints and Sanctuaries*. In particular, he developed an interest in Bedouin tribes in Transjordan. This led him to take part, in 1929, in the Petra Exploration Commission of the (British) Palestine Exploration Fund, an institution similar to the Palestine Oriental Society. He presented the results of that mission in a series of articles for the *JPOS*, "Studies in the Topography and Folklore of Petra."

Canaan's cooperation with the Palestine Oriental Society came to an end when he sided clearly with the Arab Revolt of 1936. By taking a more militant profile, he lost not only academic connections but also part of his social status.

PORTRAIT OF THE PHYSICIAN AS A SOCIALITE

Canaan was active in Jerusalem society under the Mandate. This was something that the SPC encouraged and trained its students to do: social life in the college, with plays, clubs, concerts, and conferences, was part and parcel of their studies. After its students graduated, the Medical Department kept in touch with them through a medical congress every other year, which Canaan attended on several occasions. Former students also met in local alumni associations. The one at Jerusalem, established in 1911, had Canaan among its founders and regular members. In 1927, he became its president. These structures of sociability were places for future professionals to facilitate their installation in society and earn a fair reputation. This Canaan managed to do in his clinic at Musrara, where he welcomed some of the most famed physicians in Jerusalem.

Already prior to World War I, the Protestant members of the alumni association were also invited to take part in the life of the Jerusalem YMCA. During the Mandate years, the club of the YMCA became the zenith of Jerusalem society life. This was a milieu with which Canaan, as an alumni of the SPC and a famed physician, was well familiar. Over the course of his life, he presided over the YMCA during three years.

Canaan also had a religion-based social network. In 1912, because he had married a German citizen, he was admitted as a member of the congregation of the Church of the Redeemer, in the Old City of Jerusalem. The German government had erected this church on the former Hospital of the Crusader Order of St. John of Jerusalem, and its status limited membership to native German speakers or to nationals of countries whose language was of German origin. It was, therefore, not one of the missionary congregations, which were conceived as part of an Arab national church, with a degree of autonomy which was meant to facilitate conversions to Protestantism of disgruntled Arab Orthodox Christians, whose church was in the hands of Greek prelates. His membership in the Church of the Redeemer of course singled out Canaan among Arab Protestants, though it did not make him any bit alien to Palestinian Arab national concerns. After 1912, he became a pillar of the German Lutheran congregation in Jerusalem, which kept him in touch with German interests and after the war of 1948 offered him responsibilities for relief work among the refugees.

His networking skills took the form of regularity and loyalty in social matters, proof of which are his regular donations to the alumni associations. Yet his social status also derived from his visibility through conferences and especially through his articles in the press. Taking part in the debates of the hour, he became the image of a committed and opinionated man.

"HEALTH, FOUNDATION OF NATIONAL LIFE": A PHYSICIAN IN POLITICS

Canaan's biographers underline his nationalism and the connection between his ethnography and his political involvement during the Mandate, linking his interest in popular culture with a desire to defend Palestine against the political, demographic, and cultural challenge of Zionism. Yet his ethnographical program was certainly not one of mere conservation, and he seemed more interested in expanding the political struggle in the medical field.

Although Nassib Boulos speaks of Canaan's son, the architect Theo Canaan, as having inherited socialist views from his parents, I have not found anything to support the notion that Canaan Sr. had socialistic inclinations. He was a modernist nationalist attached to traditional values. On the one hand, Canaan expressed nostalgia about the presumed progressive disappearance of an ancient popular culture overwhelmed by modernity. On the other hand, as a professional he remained a staunch supporter of modern medicine against all sorts of popular practices that he saw as superstitious and antihygienic. These views also informed his ethnographic writing.

This stood out clearly on June 27, 1923, when Canaan again made a speech for the graduation ceremonies of his alma mater, which had become the American University of Beirut. It was published in Arabic in July 1923 under the title "Health, Foundation of National Life." *National* is a rendition of *qawmī*, which refers to an ethnocultural definition of a nation, here Arabness. The issues which he described through his observations in Jerusalem he indeed assumed to be relevant throughout the Levant. Yet the political situation in Palestine and the issue of the demographic ratio there between Jews and Arabs was a hidden concern in his speech.

Canaan saw the Arab nation threatened by sanitary dangers coming from within the household. They caused high infant mortality in the poorer classes and a risk of degeneration, he said, akin to what caused the decline of the Roman Empire. Focusing on cultural causes and the family level, the physician put most of the responsibility on the shoulders of Arab mothers, "the pillars of the success of nations."

Entrusted with the education of their children and the transmission of culture, mothers were in fact endangering the next generation and thus the Arab national collective with their lack of education. Canaan blamed the great distrust of academically trained physicians among his compatriots. Mothers would only visit trained physicians when the health of their children had deteriorated beyond cure. Furthermore, they could not be brought to trust Western medicine or to give up the belief that disease came from jinns, the evil eye, or the similar idea of the evil soul projecting ailments over people. Canaan presented his audience with a clear indictment of those artifacts—small eyelike pieces of blue glass, amulets and talismans, and pieces of alum to be placed under the tongue or on other parts of the body—which made up most of his ethnographic collection. Like the rest of the medical profession in Palestine, Canaan kept making the modernist case for Western medicine against popular medicine beyond purely scientific interest.

In the rest of his speech, Canaan criticized family structures—arranged marriages within the family, marriage of girls under fifteen—and made a much shorter indictment of male behaviors and their public health consequences. In very chaste and chosen words, he blamed male philandering for the post–World War I spread of syphilis, which he never called by name. His most explicit reference to the disease was a mention of *Les Avariés* (1902), a play by the French playwright Eugène Brieux that analyzes its moral and family consequences. Ailments looking like syphilis had been found for decades in Palestine, but the Mandate Charter had made it compulsory for the Department of Health of the Palestine Government to pay special attention to syphilis. This led to a systemic exaggeration of the prevalence of the disease in official reports and explains Canaan's retrospective reading of the history of the disease in his country. The measures he advocated to fight syphilis were eugenic, such as forbidding marriage unless both spouses presented a medical certificate stating their good health on that account.

He concluded his speech by saying that immigration seemed responsible for the growing prevalence of tuberculosis in Palestine, as medical authorities had noted its quasi-absence there during the nineteenth century. In this instance, the goal of the regeneration of the Palestinian people met with immediate politics and the issue of Jewish immigration to Palestine, but it was never stated in so many words.

Canaan's concern for family health and infant mortality was a lasting one: he published the article "Infant Mortality among the Arab Population of Palestine" in 1932, "Children's Disease and Infant Mortality among the Arab Population of Palestine" in 1935, and "Arab Fertility and Child Mortality" in 1946. These reflect a nationalism that was not based on the idea that national Arab Palestinian culture ought to be preserved—as a heritage, as an authentic, autochthonous answer to Western modernity, or as a resource in the face of projects to supersede national Arab identity. Such views were representative of the generation of Palestinian folklorists who unearthed Canaan's writings in the 1970s. Rather, like other Arab writers of the Mandate period, he believed that the survival of the Palestinian people would depend not on cultural forms but on "the high moral standard of the Palestinians," which alone could help them overcome the double threat of westernization and Zionism. Indeed, Canaan concluded one article, "The Child in Palestinian Arab Superstition," by balancing the results to be expected from the development policy of the Mandate against their moral consequences: "The European civilization which is bringing to Palestine many a blessing is eradicating at the same time many a beautiful and sound moral principle."

His nationalism also took more direct political forms. As already mentioned, he took a strong position in the Arab Revolt of 1936, supporting the use of arms against British forces. In this he was not alone in his family, as one of his sisters, Badra, who was active in one of Palestine's women's organizations, also called for mobilization. Yet he gave his views a more international range: *The Palestine Arab Cause* (1936) was a short opus and the first of two books he devoted to the revolt, and it was translated into Arabic and French (from English). In it he addressed world opinion and called on British people of good faith to denounce the effects of the mandatory power's policies, especially those concerning immigration and nationality. He furthermore signed a petition in support of the general strike that Palestinian Arab personalities sent to the Arab Higher Committee on August 6, 1936, clearly demanding self-determination for Palestinian Arabs and the end of the Mandate. Following sharp criticisms from the Zionists and hostile reactions on the part of the British authorities, Canaan published a second, longer book, *Conflict in the Land of Peace* (1936), following which the mandatory power severed its connections with him.

The Palestine Arab Cause was attacked on the basis of the accuracy of its information and the sources its author used, which the anonymous writer of *Comments on Dr. Canaan's Pamphlet* claimed Canaan had simply made up. In *Conflict in the Land of Peace*, the physician-turned-pamphleteer presents a more developed case for the Palestinian Arab cause, mostly based on a compilation of quotations. His meticulously referenced prose shows a learning curve in the Arab-Zionist debate. First, Canaan expresses enthusiasm for cold facts and especially statistics: "Facts and statistics, the truth of which has been shown independently by others, were adduced to give further support to the arguments and assertions put forward here. Unbiased information of this sort cannot fail to throw a revealing light on this unnecessarily complicated subject in some of its aspects." Statistics were inherent to mandatory governance. Reporting on the development of the countries under mandate to the Mandate Commission of the League of Nations required a specific kind of intellectual apparatus. Tools had to be devised to show that the Mandate's objectives were being met and progress was being made: for this task, figures had the look of indisputable, nonpartisan truths. As a result, starting with *Conflict in the Land of Peace*, Canaan would insist on producing statistical proof of Palestinian Arab contributions to progress, especially in the epidemiological realm.

Two other aspects of *Conflict in the Land of Peace* are of particular interest: the question of land sales, and the extent to which Palestine and Palestinian Arabs benefited from Jewish immigration. As for the former, Canaan noted the systemic conditions that linked Jewish takeover of significant parts of the best agricultural lands and rural joblessness among Palestinian Arabs. He therefore defended an official prohibition of land sales, which were destablizing the country and feeding the anger at the root of the Arab Revolt. Yet he did not consider the circumstances that led to land sales, other than the shrinking of available good land and growing rural poverty. In particular, he did not tackle the issue of massive land sales by absentee landlords, except indirectly through a comment by Theodor Herzl on their willingness to exaggerate the value of their plots and sell all the same.

Now this is where the plot thickens. Kenneth W. Stein, for his study of land sales during the British Mandate, consulted a list compiled by Zionists and held at the Central Zionist Archives. The list includes the names of national activists reported to have sold land to Zionist organizations, along with a brief outline of their roles in the Palestinian Arab national movement. Among the names is *Canaan*, misspelled as *Cannan* yet recognizable beyond doubt, as belonging to an "exponent of Palestine Arab cause in articles and pamphlets." This document reports Canaan to have sold a piece of land of undetermined dimension in the Beisan area, apparently in a joint arrangement with the politician and representative of the Mandate government Musa al-Alami.

What should we make of such a document? On the one hand, there is some room for suspicion about the accuracy of the information, inasmuch as the sale is not much detailed, which makes it look a bit like a rumor and not a fact based on a definite contract. Indeed, Stein's reference to this document has drawn criticism on his book. In a number of cases, the land-sale list seems to record mere rumor.

On the other hand, massive land sales to the Zionist camp had already been the object of growing, wall-to-wall reprobation among Palestinian Arabs before World War I. Land was definitely being sold, and someone was selling it: rich absentee landlords did, and so did impoverished peasants, especially in the 1930s. Did Canaan do it? Standing on its own, unsupported by other sources, the document Stein produced gives us no room to establish the veracity of its contents. All we can say is that it clashes with the image of integrity that surrounds Canaan in his biographies and with his increasingly radical nationalist commitments.

The Arab Revolt of 1936 was a turning point for him as for many other Palestinians. While he openly waged the battle on the public opinion front, Canaan secretly provided weaponry to the rebels, according to oral testimony collected by the Palestinian academic Khaled Nashef. Whether one pictures Canaan selling land to Zionist organizations or trafficking in guns and grenades, the polished image of the author of *The Palestine Arab Cause* appears to be shattered. In any case, the book gives an idea of the end game to the Palestine question that he stood for.

Canaan advocated a form of binational state, which he thought possible if the ratio between the Arab and Jewish communities stopped changing—that is to say, if Jewish immigration were frozen. He opposed the partition of Palestine along the lines of the Peel plan, since a small Jewish state, he argued, would have been a primary and easy target for states with an anti-Semitic policy. If anything, his opinions seem to betray a reading of Ahad Ha'am, when he says that "Jews should . . . continue to work scientifically and spiritually, thus making Palestine the spiritual and religious center for Jewry." Could it be that he had revamped his views to match what a Western audience would expect to read? That seems unlikely, in a time when the goal of establishing a Jewish national home was far from being prevalently accepted in Western public opinion.

More significant than his possible pandering to Western opinion is the fact that *The Palestine Arab Cause* and *Conflict in the Land of Peace* were written in English: American University of Beirut–trained Palestinian Arab politicians and professionals were used to representing their cause on the international plane, acting as spokespeople, as was the case with Canaan, or as diplomatic go-betweens, as did Dr. Izzat Tannous, whom Canaan must have known in the early 1920s at the latest, when they were both active members of the Jerusalem branch of the AUB alumni association. While Canaan also published articles in the Palestinian Arab press, he was in no way a political leader among his people (nor was he even formally affiliated with any party, for that matter); he was more of a visible face representing the Palestinian Arabs to the Western world. And so it makes sense to presume that the end game Canaan favors in *The Palestine Arab Cause* does not simply reflect his individual views but matches the image of the Palestinian Arab national movement that his political friends wanted to convey to the world.

Indeed, from 1936 until 1948, Canaan's medical writings were also counterargumentative, conceived to provide Palestinian Arab nationalists with the necessary material to face up to Zionist representatives on the international level. As Sandra M. Sufian has argued, Canaan was the first Palestinian Arab author who tried to counter the dominant Zionist narrative linking Jewish agricultural colonization with the decrease in the prevalence of malaria over the Mandate years, using geographical and statistical data to prove the effectiveness of Palestinian Arab antimalarial measures. All through the 1940s, Canaan would provide facts and figures about the Palestinian Arab commitment to improving health while criticizing in detail Zionist claims in the medical field.

Yet Canaan's role was not simply that of an expert, even if a partisan one. Though he was not formally involved in the politics of the revolt or in the negotiations that surrounded it, he did enter the game of factional politics. In those years, he was known to be connected with the Arab Higher Council. He kept in touch with the mufti of Jerusalem, Hajj Amin al-Husseini, as did one of his close relations within the Lutheran community of Jerusalem, Dawud Haddad, who was then the head professor of the Schneller Syrian Orphanage and would write, as the Lutheran bishop of Jerusalem, Canaan's official obituary. They kept the mufti well informed about the situation of the German institutions in Jerusalem, as he showed in his conversations with Lutheran bishops during his stay in Berlin during World War II.

Neither Canaan's falling-out with the British mandatory government nor his German ties made him neglect the British public. He addressed it, for instance, through a memorandum on the Arab-Zionist conflict which he sent, on July 29, 1938, to the Scottish Presbyterian church through its Jerusalem branch. However, Canaan's strong stance in 1936 had irretrievably damaged his image in the eyes of the British authorities. The resentment of the mandatory powers toward Canaan paved the way for his being jailed at the outbreak of World War II.

With the declaration of war, hostility to British rule became a dangerous game for a man identified with German interests. Canaan was arrested on September 3, 1939, and after a court hearing he was imprisoned in Acre for nine weeks without being officially charged. His wife, as a German citizen, and his sister Badra were also arrested and imprisoned in Bethlehem before being transferred to Wilhelma, a former German Templer colony built in the late nineteenth century near Jaffa. In 1943, the women's freedom of movement was restored. Canaan, who defined himself as both a Germanophile and an Anglophile, was very much disappointed by being jailed and stopped expressing himself on directly political issues. He moved for good from direct political involvement to professional activism with a political agenda.

THE PALESTINE ARAB MEDICAL ASSOCIATION
(1944–1948)

From 1944 to 1948, Canaan's main field of activity was the professional realm, as president of the Palestine Arab Medical Association. Founded on August 4, 1944, the association was a nationalistic venture, though not a narrowly ethnonationalistic one: the vice-president, the Jerusalem-based cardiologist Vahan Kalbian, originated from Cilicia. In the increasingly polarized world of the Mandate, he fell on the Arab side, as the association had been conceived in the face of Jewish immigration.

The association was a long-delayed outcome of the Arab Medical Conference held in 1934 in Haifa. The original priority of its participants had been the professional protection of Palestinian Arab physicians against the growing competition of Jewish physicians. The latter's number exploded between 1933 and 1936 as hundreds arrived from Nazi Germany. Among the immigrant physicians were a number of outstanding practitioners ready to work at any rate, which amounted to unfair competition for Palestinian Arab physicians in the main cities of Jerusalem, Jaffa, and Haifa.

By 1944, the Palestinian medical profession had changed significantly. Over the years 1937–39, control of the practice of medicine had been tightened, with the establishment of quotas for the licensing of physicians. Jewish immigration had vastly decreased following the adoption the 1939 White Paper. Yet Zionist organizations were boasting about their involvement in public health, be it the drying of marshes to fight malaria, the setting-up of a network of mother-and-child health care centers, the training of nurses, or the development of a system of sick funds for Jewish workers.

In response, Canaan's association and its outlet, the *Journal of the Palestine Arab Medical Association* (*JPAMA*), aimed less at waging a battle on the front of the control of medical practice than at counterpropaganda. As Canaan had done during the Arab Revolt, the *JPAMA* reported on the extent of Arab participation in drying the marshes. In its columns, Canaan published frequently on his favorite medical subjects: leishmaniasis, amoebiasis, leprosy, and hygiene. For most of his four years as president, the association worked as something between a professional union and a scientific institution.

With the war of 1948, its role expanded. On December 28, 1947, Palestinian Arab irregulars shot and killed Dr. Hugo Lehrs, the Jewish head physician of the government clinic in Beit Safafa, just south of Jerusalem. A couple of days later, a Palestinian Arab physician in one of the government clinics in Jaffa was also killed. This prompted the division of the government health care system between Jewish and Arab areas. The Higher Arab Relief Committee was founded to take over the hospitals and clinics on the Arab side, which were progressively handed over to the Palestine Arab Medical Association. At least two important Palestinian Arab physicians and nationalist activists, Canaan and Tannous, were among the committee's founding members.

In May 1948, the association took over government hospitals in Jerusalem, and Canaan took charge of the Austrian hospice, in the Old City, which had been hastily transformed into a hospital early that year. Continuous shelling forced the medical staff to abandon the premises.

Meanwhile, Jerusalem was being progressively divided into east and west, and Canaan had to relocate: Talbiyeh and the leprosarium were on the western side of the city, while the Musrara neighborhood was on the seam line that would become a no-man's-land. Early in 1948, he had been able to entrust an international organization with his collection of artifacts of popular culture, but looters and Israeli institutions seized his library after he left his house.

Canaan's family took provisional lodgings in the Greek Orthodox convent in the Christian quarter of the Old City. The Lutheran World Federation set up clinics for refugees, where the physician started working, and in 1950 it and the United Nations Relief and Works Agency for Palestine Refugees in the Near East took over the Augusta Victoria compound and transformed it into a hospital. Canaan was appointed director, a position he held until his retirement in 1955. He then started writing again, ethnographic pieces about a folklore which, under Jordanian rule, he kept calling Palestinian. He continued to reside in the hospital until his death in 1964.

SUGGESTIONS FOR FURTHER READING

Aubin-Boltanski, Emma. *Pèlerinages et Nationalisme en Palestine: Prophètes, Héros et Ancêtres.* Paris: Éditions de l'EHESS, 2008.

Boulos, Nassib D. *A Palestinian Landscape.* Beirut: Arab Institute for Research and Publishing, 1998.

Canaan, Tawfiq. "The Child in Palestinian Arab Superstition." *Journal of the Palestine Oriental Society,* Vol. 7 (1927), pp. 159–86.

———. *Mohammedan Saints and Sanctuaries in Palestine.* Jerusalem: Palestine Oriental Society, 1927.

Nashef, Khaled. "Tawfiq Canaan: His Life and Works." *Jerusalem Quarterly File,* Vol. 16 (November 2002). Available online at www.jerusalemquarterly.org/ViewArticle. aspx?id=162 (retrieved December 18, 2011).

Sufian, Sandra M. *Healing the Land and the Nation: Malaria and the Zionist Project in Mandatory Palestine, 1920–1947.* Chicago: University of Chicago Press, 2007.

Stein, Kenneth W. *The Land Question in Palestine, 1917–1939.* Chapel Hill and London: University of North Carolina Press, 1987.

Tamari, Salim. "Lepers, Lunatics and Saints—The Nativist Ethnography of Tawfiq Canaan and His Jerusalem Circle." *Jerusalem Quarterly File,* Vol. 20 (January 2004). Available online at www.jerusalemquarterly.org/ViewArticle.aspx?id=129 (retrieved December 18, 2011).

7

The Ordeal of Henya Pekelman, a Female Construction Worker

David De Vries and Talia Pfeffermann

Henya Pekelman was born in 1903 to a Jewish lower-middle-class family in the small town of Marculesti, Bessarabia (today part of Moldova). Most of the Jewish residents in Marculesti were farmers who lived off the land, but Henya's large family engaged mainly in minor commerce. Henya studied in a cheder, a Jewish religious preschool, finishing her schooling at the age of eleven on the eve of the First World War. She was a mischievous and inquisitive child, beloved by her warm and supportive father. But relations between her parents were poor, and family quarrels, slanderous exchanges, and ugly gossip were part of daily life.

During World War I Henya's brother was conscripted into the Russian army, forcing her to help support the family from her teenage years. She borrowed money to sustain her parents, traded in flour and tobacco in the town's market, and was quickly absorbed in the local petty and collusive business culture.

Her background as a tobacco trader and an independent knitting worker and her experience of living among farmers in a small community encouraged Henya's identification with socialist ideas and notions of solidarity. They also attracted her to the burgeoning Zionist movement in Bessarabia. Henya associated herself with a local branch of the Zionist youth organization at seventeen and quickly became enchanted with the notion of immigrating to Palestine.

When the war was over in 1918, Henya's brother came home, but he was largely alienated from his family. Shortly after, Henya's father fell ill and on his deathbed crowned Henya "the man of the house." After her father's death she became the sole provider for the family. The stream of Zionist pioneers who passed through town on their way from Russia to Palestine cemented her decision to immigrate.

Despite the family's objections, she persuaded her mother to join her, sold the family property, and joined the local Zionist network, the first step for those intending to immigrate to Palestine. After a long journey which she and her mother began in the fall of 1920, through eastern Romania, Turkey, and Lebanon, they arrived in Palestine in September 1922.

In the next two years Henya roamed Palestine looking for work in simple construction jobs, flooring, and tobacco agriculture. She joined labor recruiting groups in Tel Aviv and Jerusalem, was part of cooperative communities of workers in Jerusalem and in the north, and even attempted a small-scale venture in tobacco growing. Often unemployed and poor, she also had to support her mother, who found occasional work as a seamstress. In autumn 1924 Henya was raped by a worker in Tel Aviv named Yeruham Mirkin, who was once her business partner. The violation upon her was extreme.

The worker denied the act and renounced fatherhood of the resulting daughter. Henya's pregnancy led some of her socialist Zionist peers to ostracize her. This reaction stands in contradiction to the perception some people have of the Jewish pioneers in Palestine, who propounded sexual liberation yet in fact followed a fairly strict sexual code.

The child, named Tikvah, died a few weeks old, and the British police incarcerated Henya on suspicion of poisoning the baby. In late 1925 she was freed from jail. A year or so later she married Moshe Ba'al-Taksa, an immigrant from Russia, and in 1928 she gave birth to another daughter. In 1935 Henya published part of her Hebrew-language autobiography. The press, as well as the leaders of the women workers in the Jewish community, ignored the book.

In January 1940, Henya threw herself off the balcony of the movie theater in Dizengoff square in Tel Aviv where she worked as an usher. She was buried in Wahalat Yitzhak cemetery.

HOW TO BE A ZIONIST WORKER?

While largely ignored during and after her life, Henya's autobiography, *Chayei po'elet ba'aretz* (The life of a woman worker in her homeland), offers dramatic testimony to the struggles and sentiments of young immigrant women like her as they participated in the construction of a Zionist identity that simultaneously was inconceivable without them and largely marginalized them from the official narrative. As she wrote, "Lacking paint and paintbrush, I thus wrote of my life. Innocent things, without frills, unadorned" (all translations are ours). Her book reveals not just the many ways that nationalism and gender inflect each other but how women attempt to carve out their futures in situations where their power of action is severely constrained by their marginalized position within society at large.

Zionism for Henya meant the entire process of preparing to immigrate, the experience of the journey and of landing in Palestine, and the initial absorption into the work force. Working-class identity and Zionism were closely intertwined for her, as for so many other immigrants of the late Ottoman and early Mandate periods, with socialist Zionist rhetoric celebrating "the national destiny of the working class" and "constructive socialism." When the kibbutz became a central image of Zionism, the notion of the "urban workers' community" emerged to ensure that industrial and proletarian workers in the Jewish towns of Palestine maintained a socialist and Zionist identity. The tendency to behave as a worker and be part of a social stratum whose way of life is labor-oriented was inseparable from the actual immigration to Palestine, from the effort to speak Hebrew, and from the daily participation in Zionist recreational activities and lifestyles. Few of the Jewish workers in the 1920s made a distinction between their identity as workers and their Zionist identity, and Henya was no different. Her consciousness was formed by the political changes in Eastern Europe during her youth, during meetings and lectures at the Zionist youth movements, and while living on the training farm in her home country—a nationalism from the bottom up, developed by a woman who lived a life of action and work and did not constantly trouble her mind with various ideological articulations. In that sense Henya was like so many other female workers in the 1920s and 1930s, whose stories were published in bulletins and in *Dvar Hapoelet*, the women workers' magazine of the labor movement.

Henya's memories of her early years in Palestine also reveal a class difference in Jewish society that was rarely discussed, either at the time or in scholarship on the Yishuv. As she describes one Friday evening, she went to a "ball" wearing a "burlap dress that my mother had embroidered and sandals without socks." She couldn't help comparing her outfit to those of the other attendees, the men "all smartly dressed," the "young women clothed with silk dressed and red lipsticks. Everybody in the room stared at me in bewilderment."

Henya frequently declared that the significance of individuals was their ability to contribute to the collective and to national objectives. "If there is a need for sacrifice," she writes in her book, "I will be happy to be sacrificed on the altar of my homeland." Her thoughts dwelt on the construction of the country: "The suffering of the individual is nothing compared to the suffering of the entire nation. Hoping that people shall no longer suffer exile—I have forgotten my own suffering." Even in retrospect, as she writes her story a few years after the events, she calls herself "the working woman whose foremost thought was the homeland." The order of priorities, which positioned the homeland first and foremost and required the formation of a "new person" who was worthy of living in this society, necessitated in her mind the cultivation of a sense of difference and distance from the Arabs—the majority in Palestine, of whom her book makes no mention.

A JEWISH PROLETARIAT

Turning from an immigrant into a worker was the key economic and social trans-formation that shaped Henya's life in Palestine. But her narrated experiences did not fit the idealized imagining of that experience as portrayed by the labor move-ment. Instead, her life was defined by chronic unemployment, poverty, roaming from one place to another seeking work, and frequent job changes, mostly in con-struction and agriculture.

Part of the problem was that the urban and rural economies in Palestine during the early 1920s were in a profound crisis, and their ability to absorb the increasing flow of job-seeking immigrants was limited. The immigrants entered a reality of stiff competition for jobs with both Arab and veteran Jewish workers, and many experienced long periods of unemployment. Social and political mechanisms reg-ulated supply and demand in the labor market. The relevant institutions were the Histadrut, the umbrella group of the local labor organizations; Achdut Ha'avoda, labor's leading political party; and the labor exchanges, which constituted the local labor councils of the Histadrut. They acted both on the supply side, by referring workers to jobs, and on the demand side, through Histadrut companies, as an employer. These institutions were perceived as resources for job seekers, although they did not always promise success. Moreover, to support the working public through economic hardship, party institutions provided vocational training in critical professions and offered other forms of assistance—the workers' kitchens, informal justice systems for resolving disputes, and others.

The Jewish workers in 1920s Palestine gradually learned that they could to a certain extent acquire job skills, find employment, eat, and manage their work disputes through the nascent Histadrut institutions. This reliance mirrored the de-pendence of these institutions on political organs and economic resources outside Palestine, such as the Zionist movement's leadership, the Zionist Congress, and their fund-raising apparatuses.

Upon arriving in Palestine, the female immigrant worker had to adjust to this reality. For women—Henya tells us—competition for jobs was doubly harsh, since Jewish employers preferred not only Arab laborers who worked for lower pay but also a male workforce, particularly in the central fields of the Jewish economy in the midtwenties: agriculture, construction, and transportation infrastructure. The apparatuses of the political parties often collaborated with this discrimination and referred women to domestic work or jobs in factories with harsh conditions and low pay that did not enable subsistence. Letters sent by women to the unions of female workers reveal voices of protest against the discrimination, and many requests for help.

In this context Henya was notable for her independence, characterized by her personal initiative, resourcefulness, and unwillingness to compromise with the dictates of social norms or institutional difficulties that confronted her. "I always found work for myself, and the contractors liked my work," she wrote. In fact, she noted that other workers "saw how persistently I find work independently, not through the Histadrut's labor exchange." Driven by her determination to work and make a living, between 1922 and 1924 she wandered from place to place, changed jobs, and challenged the cycle of dependence on institutional mechanisms when they did not meet her expectations and needs. She enlisted her local knowledge and improvisation skills to make ends meet, bypassed the bureaucracies of the labor exchanges, and broadened her job search circles by using personal acquaintances within the apparatus, workers in different workplaces, and people from her hometown. Through these circles, based on networks of people from the same home countries and on networks of labor-recruiting groups, she often found help. However, in conditions of chronic unemployment, the constant process of finding work, losing work, and searching once again became a blur and, often, frustratingly futile. "In 1923 the economic downturn was increasingly felt. All branches saw more and more unemployed, me included. Most of the workers were bachelors and didn't care much for their condition, but I had to provide not only for myself but for my mother as well. . . . I roamed about all day long hoping to find some work. I came home tired after many futile searches and sat in our tent endlessly worried."

Henya's story reveals the extent to which the immigrants' experience of urban work was one of exhausting intraworker competition and struggle without any shelter of protective legislation from the British authorities. But she created opportunities for herself and worked the system, all the while challenging the official rhetoric of the Histadrut and larger labor movement through her experiences and willingness to record them.

In an attempt to escape the cycle of dependency in which male and female workers were trapped, in 1924 Henya joined a tobacco-growing initiative in Petach Tikvah (a few kilometers east of Tel Aviv) as a business partner, ostensibly crossing the lines of class affiliation which she had proudly declared her whole life. However, she noted that even as a partner in the business (which began to flourish that year) she was treated by the local farmers as an employed worker, and when the initiative failed she went back to work as an agricultural laborer.

The shift from searching for work to being an entrepreneur and employer was no trivial matter, creating tensions with the social, labor, and national language that prevailed in Henya's social stratum. The labor leaders frequently slandered those who tended toward economic individualism, referring to "the embourgeoisement of the worker." But for Henya these were natural strategies for economic survival, and so she did not indicate a conflict of any kind between the material reality that dictated such transitions and her ideological commitment to the collective. This was the case, for example when she "contacted Yeruham Mirkin and his relative regarding growing tobacco. Ben Shamir [the relative] had to attain the money for the work and I had to manage it. The profits we shared equally." When the work was completed, Henya reverted to her position as an ordinary wage worker.

HENYA AND THE ZIONIST LABOR MOVEMENT

The immigrants' increasing disposition to think and act like workers was a marked attribute of the creation of a working class. The aspiration to be a pioneer expressed their desire to be at the forefront of the realization of the ethos to perform physical labor, preferably agricultural, and be part of a productive collective. The fulfillment of this aspiration required many immigrants to reinvent themselves and undergo a type of self-redemption by adopting a new value system, adapting themselves physically, receiving appropriate vocational training, ascetically settling for less, and acquiring a new language. The process demanded the individual's total dedication and was riddled with doubts and difficulties, documented in many protocols, diaries, and autobiographies of the period.

Henya's world was delimited by work scarcity and the numerous vulnerabilities of the nascent laboring community. She was determined to make a living through productive work, was proud of her ability to do so, and kept her self-esteem through myriad difficulties by means of her working-class consciousness. As she explained it to her mother, who lamented not being able to support her daughter: "I aspire to always be a worker, and to earn my bread through labor. . . . I belong to a class, I belong to people, who have laws, to the society of workers, the proletarians. . . . A worker with a consciousness would never want to be bourgeois; his aspiration is to improve his living conditions."

The importance she attributed to her life as a worker also influenced her romantic choices. She rejected the courtship of a physician only because his profession seemed less productive than that of a builder or an agricultural worker: "When I met him in Istanbul as a carpenter," she wrote, "I liked him very much. Later, when I met him in Tel Aviv as a physician, I felt very distant from him."

Despite her enthusiastic laborite consciousness she was not uncritical of the class aspect of her identity. Henya saw through the weakness of the system that was limited in the support it could offer her, writing about the bureaucrats whose behavior did not correspond to their declared ethical codes. In one episode, officials of one of the labor parties in Tel Aviv created an inequitable division of labor, giving preference to a particular woman worker: "Since the labor union considered her a party activist, she and her group were given one construction project after the other." Henya, who was not a member of the party apparatus, found it difficult to make a living in construction, despite her training.

The writings of other workers also criticize the conduct of the labor movement. These memoirs and autobiographies frequently voice doubts as to the correct ideological way, and their writers often express criticism, though their perspective is still that of one who is an integral part of the movement, a dedicated and loyal member of the collective. This was not the case with Henya. Although she was close to organizational actions led by the Histadrut and the political parties, she positions herself as an outsider. Moreover, her probing of her ideological surroundings, doubts, and reservations is written from the perspective of one standing on the threshold as a welcome guest.

This duality is exemplified by Henya's descriptions of her contact with Gdud Ha'avoda, the early 1920s socialist and communitarian labor battalion. Henya's ascetic and high work ethic led members of the battalion with whom she worked in Jerusalem to suggest that she join them; in an unusual move, they were also willing to accept her elderly mother. Aware of the honor bestowed upon her, Henya examined the ways of the battalion and found that they did not meet the high moral standards she had set for herself: "In the battalion there were at the time many lazy and egotistical comrades, who exploited the good ones, and this held me back from joining." This unwillingness to compromise her private, stringent standards and those of her environment characterized her broader attitude toward life: in any clash between practice and ideology, ideology won out, even when this meant she had to implement it alone.

WOMEN WORKERS

Henya's writings provide a comprehensive and detailed description of the daily practices women employed to overcome the imbalanced opportunity structure and gender discrimination in the job market and to construct their identity as equal members of the emerging society, as well as the responses they garnered. Her testimony surveys experiences in a broad variety of realms, starting with politics, where women's attempts to organize met with patronizing responses from party leaders, and continuing through the social arena, the workers' lifestyle, and the prevalent tension, both hidden and open, around the question of women's social roles.

Women's struggle was unique. Some employed a strategy of gender blurring, representing themselves in the labor market as having a vague feminine identity and increasing their involvement with workers' organizations, party politics, and the labor movement's cultural institutions. Henya recounts women's attempts to enter market segments that were occupied solely by men, such as construction and carpentry. These attempts originated in the idea that by proving their economic efficiency, women would be accepted into the community of laborers as equals and reject traditional Diaspora-associated perceptions. Henya describes her Sisyphean experience in a training group for women pavers. The graduates of the program organized in an independent work group, similar to the ones set up by men, which acted as contractors in the construction industry. She dwells on the foremen's skepticism of the women's professional skills.

The descriptions of working life also depict Henya's strategy of behaving like her male co-workers as a mechanism for fending on her own when the paving group fell apart. She found work by taunting a group of male workers, claiming they were taking the best jobs. "I once passed by a building where cement was molded on the roof," Henya wrote. "I knew all the workers there, and they asked me why I roam about without work. I answered that since they seize all available jobs, a girl is left only with housekeeping—which I haven't yet agreed to do." When they replied that she was welcome to work with them as long as she could keep up, she climbed up the scaffolding and went to work, saying they were the ones causing her to slow down. Instead of waiting for approval, she set facts on the ground and continued to show up for work on the site until the construction job was finished.

Equally as interesting, Henya's words and actions suggest that many female workers preferred Oriental and masculine clothing, which, along with their male patterns of behavior, led to the creation of a new culture of the body, one that blurred physical differences into an androgyny of sorts. This was further emphasized by what Henya describes as lively, carnivalesque folk dancing during which the young men shouted, "We don't need women."

At the Friday-evening ball described earlier in this chapter, it was not merely Henya's outfit that left the bourgeois partygoers bewildered. Beyond diverging from their dress code, she initiated lively folk dances. The most interesting aspect of her description is the responses of the other guests to her appearance and conduct, and their unspoken condemnation, of which Henya was fully aware, concealed in the praise they showered on her.

Henya constantly examined the expected male and female roles and consistently offers a different interpretation of the binary distinctions that prevailed in her society. Describing her affair with a co-worker, she dreams, "We can both move to a settlement; we will plough together, sow together, and together reap the crops. We shall live together in a little house that we ourselves shall build. I will help him outside in all his work, and he will help me with all the household work. We will both have one outlook, and together we can fight the obstacles that arise in our path."

Unfortunately, the blurring of gender identity which Henya largely embodied was usually a lost cause. To get jobs that were mostly taken by men and keep them or advance to better ones, women had to enter into networks of connections and pressure, which men had to do to a lesser degree. In fact, the blurring of gender identity served as a means for women's integration into only a small part of the labor market. Henya's transitions from job to job and place to place evince a deepening void between her hopes for work and the employers' attitude toward her, between her expectations of belonging to a community and her loneliness.

Henya thus enables us to observe how in the process of becoming a worker, different identities are at work simultaneously—national, class, and gender. These identities served as tools for understanding and coping. Henya's Zionism colored her experiences as a worker and provided them with justification and logic. "Were it not for the stomach occasionally reminding us the duty of eating," she wrote, "we would forget that altogether. Each and everyone cared mostly for building the land." Her material suffering, which was such a deep-seated part of her identity as a worker, gave meaning to her loneliness in Zionist society as long as she could perceive (and justify) it in terms of a necessary sacrifice for a common goal. Her gender identity, in particular the part that blurred gender distinctions, pointed to a partial and alternative way of surviving. "In the streets of Haifa," she wrote, "women workers were seen in simple cotton dresses and without shoes. Their faces were suntanned, and a unique smile spread all over them. These workers did not crave to attract the men; they had a human aspiration, they had a battle from within and without, against the sentiments of deference that were imprinted in their souls for generations. This battle gave them more grace than silk dresses and cosmetics."

At the same time, Henya notes that excruciating inner conflicts troubled the women around her, who could only resolve them by giving up their gender battle and taking upon themselves the image of woman as shaped by the social environment—namely, by sufficing with traditional female roles in the home and in child rearing without adequate representation or participation in the social and political centers of power. Henya's recognition of women's conditions disillusioned her and distanced her from her original desire to be an active partner in the construction of nation and society: "I have changed; I have come to know life very clearly, and people as well."

GENDER INEQUALITY AMONG THE PIONEERS

Henya's story also underscores a political dimension that was an integral part of working women's experience in this formative period of British rule in Palestine. First and foremost, she exposes the priorities of the labor movement, which positioned nation and state building at the top, and far below, equality between men and women. The difficulty in translating the ideology of gender equality in agricultural society to an urban reality often attested to passivity and neglect.

Henya emphasizes the labor movement's institutional indifference toward women workers, its failure to persuade Jewish employers in the towns to hire women, and its refraining from positioning women in key roles in the local labor organizations.

Working women increasingly expected that the institutions of the labor movement would provide them with organizational representation. However, Henya claimed that this was not merely an abstract hope of help from remote institutions but a search for actual representation on the ground, in the workplaces themselves, and in the community where the power relations encountered by female immigrant workers required collective representation. In the last instance, she argued, "the woman worker remained empty handed."

Nevertheless, party and bureaucratic conflicts and, no less significantly, tensions between national and local interests marginalized the concern for women workers' interests. The labor movement's leadership rejected the frequent criticism against this marginalization with the argument that preference must be given to building social and cultural institutions, to organizing in the workplace, and to taking control of the labor market, justifications Henya never accepted.

The growing distance between the institutions of the labor movement—particularly the Women Workers' Council—and the female worker as an individual is no rarity in the history of labor movements or in the bureaucratic institutionalization of workers' communities and professional unions. But with Henya this is illuminated in a more complex manner, stemming not only from the embourgeoisement of party and Histadrut leadership. The distance originated in this case from overemphasizing the national aspect of Zionist identity as a sacrifice that individuals were expected to make. "We, the pioneers," Henya wrote, "came to our homeland, to build our new lives and to sacrifice ourselves for our country." By representing an agenda dictated by the labor leadership, female labor leaders grew alienated from people like Henya whose experiences demanded a more personal treatment in finding employment and providing for material needs.

In fact, Henya's book discloses the problem of representation as it developed in the initial stages of the labor movement. It also undermines the party-political elite's argument that the labor movement, and particularly the women workers' movement, faithfully represented women workers both physically—in the job market and in the workplace—and politically. The separate organization of women workers within the Histadrut was unable to compensate for this political deficiency because there were very few women in the leadership of the two main workers' political parties that led the labor movement (Achdut Ha'avoda and Hapo'el Hatza'ir).

Henya's criticism emerges clearly from the way she portrays the female leaders, conveying a vague sense of revulsion at the political development of the Yishuv. Describing one of the leaders of the female workers, Henya held that she "was among those women whose main power was but in their mouth . . . and all her doings were the opposite to what she said, and truthfully she cared only for herself." Indeed, Henya's words provide historians with an important sign: in the labor movement there was a gap, even at its inception, between its growing political power in the Yishuv and its ability to represent workers, male and female.

Henya was deeply aware of her gender identity and of its political and social implications. Moreover, her language and style meant to embody the new Zionist woman she and her co-workers drew for themselves. The active, enterprising personality was the basis for the very act of writing and self-representation, while the direct and precise language exemplifies the traits of a new femininity—direct, open, devoid of adornment and embellishment. As she declares in the poem with which she begins the book,

> I have not diminished the shadows. I have not augmented the light.
> Without paint or brush I have written of my life,
> Simple words without mascara or decoration
> For which the worker's heart yearns . . .

HENYA'S TRAGEDY

In autumn 1924 Henya experienced what she refers to as "her tragedy." Yeruham Mirkin, whose advances she had rejected, lured her into his rented room, locked the door on the pretense of not wanting the landlady to see them together, and raped her. The word *rape* is never explicitly used in the book, only *sexual assault.* In fact, in the book Henya cannot bear to describe the act, so it appears as two blank lines, with her first memory afterward being her stumbling on the beach "like a madwoman."

According to her narrative, Henya tried to abort the child with a hot bath, and when this failed, thought to commit suicide by drowning herself at the beach. But, according to her account, a higher power "suddenly seized me [and] pulled me by my hair." The power, or inner voice, gave her the will to live through the suffering and overcome the intense guilt for her violated honor: "Why should you kill yourself? Because a contemptible man abused you? Your death will place the blame on you alone, but if you live—you can still take revenge on him. You need to go on living just for the revenge."

However courageous her willingness to stand against her assailant, the reality was that in 1920s Jewish Palestine, as in most places, rape was not frequently discussed; it was a biblical term that was seldom used in spoken Hebrew in a sexual context. When the book was republished in 2007 and the press mentioned Henya's rape, the family of the alleged rapist adamantly denied it. Regardless, the suspect denied his paternity and refused to take responsibility for his act, and Henya, who felt that she could not remain where people knew her, went away to cope with her "personal tragedy" alone.

Her journey was now paved with hardships and loneliness. Since she would have been ostracized for being unmarried and pregnant, she tried to hide her unusual circumstances by changing her name and inventing an imaginary husband

and went back to work at flooring in Tel Aviv. Difficulties earning a living and many conflicts with other workers reduced her to an emotional state she described as "torments of death," filled with vengefulness and suicidal thoughts.

In May 1925 Henya gave birth to a daughter and named her Tikvah ("hope"). A few weeks later the baby died from unclear causes. The police arrested Henya on suspicion of poisoning the child (she was supposedly motivated by worries that she would not be able to sustain Tikvah). Henya suspected that the real culprit was the father. She was released in early 1927, feeling like a social outcast, isolated and persecuted. "And from that day when I was released, my emotional tragedy began," she wrote at the end of her book. A few months later she married, then had another daughter (Zipporah, meaning "a female bird," alluding to the sense of freedom Henya was seeking). The family lived in Tel Aviv, in harsh economic circumstances. Freedom was, as she later wrote, worse than hell.

In the coming years Henya divided her life between work, family, and writing the autobiography which is the only source for the story unraveled above. The small book (published in 1935) is in fact the first volume and covers her story only up to 1928. The drafts for the second volume were apparently lost, and whatever happened to Henya in the early 1930s is unknown, even to her family and the workers she associated with in the passing decade.

The incompleteness and partiality of Henya's life story as retold in the book is quite telling. The book opens with a poetic eulogy on secrecy, openness, individuality, and nationalism and ends twice: first with Henya's final note on the tragic life she has had following the rape, the death of her child, and incarceration, and secondly with a feminist tractate written by her husband. Throughout the book there is an attempt to write the private story as an integral, yet different, component of the collective story. It sheds light on the experiences of a single woman in the city who must construct her life within the confined opportunities available to her, reorganize her world after immigration, integrate into her new environment, and manage the tension between a desire to meet the collective needs and the personal interest of economic subsistence.

Especially prominent is Henya's need to balance her desire to belong with her need to define herself according to her own conceptions. This gives rise to her resistance to what she calls "the demands and taste of society," to which, she explains openly, "I cannot surrender." For Henya, writing—and self-publishing—her book, which conveyed the multidimensionality of the Jewish female worker's identity, was a clear expression of her unwillingness to surrender to the mainstream notions of Jewish society in pre-1948 Palestine. Writing also clearly provided her with support to cope with social loneliness and, above all, the violence of men.

Henya's opposition to the status quo in which she found herself had many manifestations: her gender-crossing dress, her strategy of gender blurring to enter the labor market by adopting masculine behavioral patterns, her constant speaking out against and open defiance of the establishment and social frameworks. The culmination of this defiance was her decision to write openly and explicitly about the occurrence of a rape in the community, about pregnancy and childbirth out of wedlock. Although other such cases were known, topics such as intimacy and sexuality were concealed and suppressed in the discourse of the pioneering settlement society, and in this respect Henya's voice is unparalleled. Not only does she raise these topics for public debate, but her story contains harsh criticism of society's conduct and its attitude toward those who have suffered these calamities.

Henya's continuous denunciation positions her as patroller of her community's borders: ideological borders (reconciling her belonging to a socialist movement with her role as an entrepreneur), borders that shape gender behavior, ethical borders (justifying the social and Zionist priorities and exposing the problems of achieving them). She constantly examines the limits of these expanses and of her own power, of what is allowed and what is forbidden, while offering her own interpretations and possibilities for a different life.

Moreover, her insistent objections are extremely charged. They hover between silence and direct and even callous words on topics she perceives as interpersonal or social distortions. Her silence contains many tones—awkwardness, shame, insult, concealment—and alongside these are thunderous silences, giving rise to a cumulative and powerful anger. "A strong desire for revenge began to flood all the chambers of my heart," she writes. "A revenge against all those who abuse woman's honor. Many generations blame only the young girl, and it is she who suffers; and no wonder that she herself almost ceases to believe that others would testify to her integrity." But more than rebelling, in her writing Henya created a space for herself, a space for liberty, a realm of self-respect and self-importance and sometimes of absolute justice. Her anger depicts secreted opposition as an active mode. Such opposition is not part of an organized collective militancy but rather reflects a series of behaviors and acts that workers may implement within the confines and dependencies dictated to them in the absence of organized collective militancy.

It is not surprising that the literature that deals with workers, social-democratic parties, and labor movements often downgrades the capacity of small, weak groups and individuals to stand against the power of institutions and male leaders. Accustomed to the organizational passivity of urban women workers and to their embourgeoisement as they achieved higher economic status, society mostly perceived working women as anomalies, existing on the so-called margins of society, and sometimes considered them a threat to the collective.

For this reason, Labor's silent reception of the book must have been frustrating. The Histadrut's leaders aspired to represent women's interests, to protect female workers, and to help them in their struggle in the labor market. But they clearly prioritized nationalism and Zionism and subjugated all social actions to these causes. In a system in which Zionism and politics took precedence over representation, equal opportunity, and social justice, the woman worker was abandoned. However, while Henya speaks out in anger against the establishment, she does not deny the ideology it represents. Even when she pays a heavy personal price and feels that the community has turned its back on her after her rape and pregnancy, her writing refrains from any measure of rebellion against Zionism or socialism. Her book was thus a cry for attention, a sort of therapeutic act by a working woman who had lost all illusions but had allowed herself to write in opposition and make her voice heard without practically challenging the social ethos or the conformity it required.

EPILOGUE

Five years lapsed between the appearance of the book in Jerusalem and Tel Aviv in 1935 and Henya's death. Not much is known about her life in these years. The book did not receive any press, not even from the Histadrut's women workers' councils that knew Henya well from her requests for jobs. The costs of the publication were probably burdensome, and Henya had to support her ailing husband and seven-year-old daughter. Women workers in the Yishuv suffered more than men from the economic slowdown of the mid-decade. This slowdown followed the financial uncertainty in the wake of Italy's war with Ethiopia, the outbreak of the Arab rebellion in Palestine in 1936, and the arrival in November of that year of the Peel Commission. The contraction of immigration to Palestine in 1937–38 and the consequent reduction in the import of capital brought about a surge in unemployment. This was only partially alleviated by the withdrawal of Palestinian Arab workers from the Jewish economy during the rebellion.

For Henya it meant that she had to find extra work, and in 1938 the labor exchange of the Women Workers' Council assigned her to be an evening usher in the newly built cinema on Dizengoff Square in Tel Aviv. The feminization of the service sector accelerated during these harsh times, mostly because of the reduction of labor costs by private capital, and Henya could now probably boast that there was hardly an unskilled occupation in the Tel Aviv economy that she had not experienced. However, the new employment arrangement could have been unstable as well, and Henya's material insecurity was probably far from dissipating. In January 1940, at the age of thirty-eight, Henya committed suicide by jumping off a rooftop of the cinema. The press published a death notice reminding the public that she had written *Chayei po'elet ba'aretz*. It failed, however, to note the doubling of the number of suicides in the Yishuv in 1935–40 compared with the previous five years and the tripling of the number of women therein over the same period, which was probably associated with the grim economic climate of the prewar years.

After its emergence in 1935, Henya's book sank into obscurity. It is all the more ironic that the reception of its republication in 2007 (followed by its staging as a play in 2009) completely contrasts with the frail resonance of the original edition. In 1935 the labor movement was in the early phase of its hegemony in the Yishuv and the Zionist movement, and its leaders and the press completely ignored the book's revealing aspects on the state of women workers in the Yishuv and particularly in the labor movement itself. Now, when the concept of a labor movement has almost totally disappeared from the Israeli political scene and the organizational power of workers is nothing but a shadow of its state and ambitions during the Mandate period, the book has been well received—demonstrating, perhaps, a growing openness in Israeli society to a critical historiography of its past.

A NOTE ON SOURCES

This essay is based on Henya M. Pekelman, *Chayei po'elet ba'aretz* (The life of a worker in her homeland; Or Yehuda: Kineret, Zmora Bitan, Dvir Publishing House, 2007; in Hebrew). The book was originally published in Tel Aviv in 1935. Information on Pekelman's hometown was gathered from Leib Koperstein and Meir Kotik, *Marculesti, Memorial of a Jewish Town in Bessarabia* (Tel Aviv: Irgun Yotzei Marculesti Beisrael, 1977; in Hebrew). See also Tamar Hess, "Henya Pekelman: An Injured Witness of Socialist Zionist Settlement in Mandatory Palestine," *Women's Studies Quarterly*, Vol. 36, Nos. 1–2 (Spring/Summer 2008), pp. 208–13. For women workers in early Mandate Palestine, we consulted Rachel Katzenelson Shazar, *Words of Women Workers* (Tel Aviv: Histadrut, 1930; in Hebrew); see also Deborah Bernstein, *The Struggle for Equality: Urban Women Workers in Prestate Israeli Society* (New York: Praeger, 1987). Additional information on the perspective of the leadership of the women workers' movement was found in Ada Maimon, *Fifty Years of the Women Workers' Movement* (Tel Aviv: Am Oved, 1955; in Hebrew).

SUGGESTIONS FOR FURTHER READING

For the social history of workers in 1920s Palestine, see David De Vries, *Idealism and Bureaucracy: The Origins of "Red Haifa"* (Tel Aviv: Hakibbutz Hameuchad, 1999; in Hebrew). For women and the question of equality in the Yishuv, see Deborah Bernstein, *Pioneers and Homemakers: Jewish Women in Pre-state Israel* (Albany: State University of New York Press, 1992), and Bernstein, "Daughters of the Nation: Between the Public and Private Sphere in Pre-state Israel," in Judith R. Baskin, ed., *Jewish Women in Historical Perspective* (Detroit: Wayne State University Press, 1998), pp. 287–311. Among the works on gender and Zionism, see Eyal Kafkafi, "The Psycho-intellectual Aspect of Gender Inequality in Israel's Labor Movement," *Israel Studies*, Vol. 4, No. 1 (1999), pp. 188–211. For the movement of women workers in the Zionist-socialist labor movement, see Bat-Sheva

Margalit-Stern, *Redemption in Bondage: The Women Workers Movement in Palestine, 1920–1939* (Jerusalem: Yad Ben Zviv and Schechter Institute, 2006; in Hebrew), and Margalit-Stern, "'They Have Wings but No Strength to Fly': The Women's Workers Movement between Feminine Control and Masculine Dominance," in Ruth Kark, Margalit Shilo, and Galit Hasan-Rokem, eds., *Jewish Women in Pre-state Israel: Life History, Politics, and Culture* (Boston: Brandeis University Press, 2008), pp. 202–16. On Pekelman and her book, see Orna Ben-Meir, "The Israeli Shoe: Biblical Sandals and Native Israeli Identity," in Edna Nahshon, ed., *Jews and Shoes* (Oxford, U.K.: Berg, 2008), pp. 77–90, and Talia Pfefferman, "Women's Silence in 'The Life of a Worker in Her Homeland' (1935) by Henya Pekelman," in Margalit Shilo and Gideon Kats, eds., *Gender in Israel* (Beersheba: Ben-Gurion University, 2011; in Hebrew), pp. 23–49.

8

"A Nation in a Hero"

Abdul Rahim Hajj Mohammad
and the Arab Revolt

Sonia Nimr

When the First Intifada against the Israeli occupation started in the occupied Palestinian territories, in 1987, one could hear the older generation of Palestinians drawing comparisons with the Great Revolt of 1936–39. "It is the same," said those who were old enough to witness the revolt, which saw the Mandate period's biggest challenge to British rule, Zionist colonization, and the Palestinians' own increasingly feckless elite. "The people defied the authorities and took matters into their own hands." More comparisons were made between the national committees of the thirties and the popular committees of the late eighties, tactics of civil disobedience, the role of rebel courts and the *shabab* (young men), and the involvement of all sectors of the society in the uprising.

However, when the Second Intifada broke out, in September 2000, only one comparison was made with the 1936–39 revolt, in connection with a shooting incident in an area known as Wadi al Haramiya—the Valley of Thieves—which lies on the road between Ramallah and Nablus. Since the valley is strategically located between two mountains, it has been known throughout history as a weak point in the defenses of all occupiers. Rebels (especially during 1936–39 revolt) used the high mountains around it as a vantage point for attacks. During the second year of the Second Intifada, Israeli army soldiers had erected a checkpoint in the Valley of Thieves. Such is the valley's mythical identity that a story began to circulate in which a lone Palestinian sniper stationed on one of the mountains killed ten soldiers using only fourteen bullets, and then vanished. According to the narrative, the Israeli military could not find the shooter, but in the spot where he had lain in ambush, a Second World War–era M1 rifle was found.

As people heard the news about the incident and the old rifle, they started to make stories about the man and began to compare his style with that of the rebels of 1936–39, further enhancing the story's mythical character. "He is one of the old rebels, for this is their style," they said, and "He is an old fighter who has stayed in hiding since 1939." The older people nodded their heads in agreement, and stories of that old 1936–39 revolt started circulating again. It was still alive in people's memory.

When a young man from Silwad (near Jerusalem) was arrested two years later for activities supposedly connected to this incident, people (especially the older generation) continued to prefer the story about the old fighter. They needed heroes, and the only ones they could think of were those rebels of the 1936–39 revolt.

EMERGENCE OF GRASSROOTS ARMED STRUGGLE

From the outset of Zionist colonization, Palestinian Arabs resisted the movement's attempts to gain control over the country and establish a Jewish national home there. For the most part, the traditional urban elite families led this resistance, which was mainly verbal but also consisted of sending numerous delegations to London and organizing periodic demonstrations. Intracommunal rivalries, the predominance of factional over class relations, and the concerted efforts of both the Zionist movement and British authorities to prevent the emergence of a strong Palestinian leadership that could challenge the terms of the Mandate (which, as enshrined in the Balfour Declaration, centered on developing a "National Home" for Jews while merely protecting the "civil and religious rights of existing non-Jewish communities in Palestine") all ensured that this resistance could not protect Palestinians from Zionism's steady territorial and political advance.

Without a strong and cohesive national leadership, Palestinians engaged in a series of uprisings in the 1920s and early 1930s (particularly in 1921, 1929, and 1933) that consisted of protests and attacks against Jews and occasionally British forces. But the first significant organized grassroots opposition was the al Qassam movement that began in 1935 and combined religious and national ideologies as a grounding for armed struggle against Zionism and, even more, British rule. Izz ad-Din al-Qassam (1871–1935) was a Syrian religious scholar who joined the jihad movement in Syria against the French. He was sentenced to death and in 1921 fled to Palestine, where he started a resistance movement with a group of devoted men (almost his entire group consisted of workers and peasants).

Al-Qassam believed that the struggle should be directed mainly against the British Mandate. He died in a clash with the British police in the woods of Yaabad, near Jenin, in 1935. His death would soon prompt a countrywide revolt against British rule, Zionist colonization, and the fecklessness of the existing Palestinian leadership.

The revolt of 1936–39, or the Great Arab Revolt in Palestine, as some historians describe it, started with a spark: a Qassamite group attacked a Jewish car traveling on the Nablus–Tulkarm road on 15 April 1936, killing one passenger and injuring two. In reprisal, Jews murdered two Palestinian Arab workers the following night on the main road to the Petach Tikvah settlement. The cycle escalated, with more violent incidents between Palestinian Arabs and Jews in different areas of the country.

On 19 April, following these clashes and the seeming deterioration of the situation, a number of Palestinian nationalists, many of whom were members of the dissolved Istiqlal Party, met in Nablus to decide how to take stronger and more organized action. They agreed to form a national committee and start a general strike until the demands of the Arabs were conceded. Soon, national committees formed in other towns and villages, to supervise the strike and lead the people.

The strike lasted for six months. This was a declaration of civil disobedience; a boycott of all official bodies, such as courts; and a refusal to pay taxes. The village heads gave their collective resignations to the authorities, as did the workers in the municipalities, except for those who were responsible for water, electricity, and garbage collection. This was the climax of an economic, political, and social conflict between the Palestinian Arabs, on one hand, and the British and the Zionists on the other. The Mandate government reacted by imposing emergency law, arresting activists, and engaging in collective punishments, including demolishing houses in towns and villages and destroying a substantial part of the old town of Jaffa, which itself resulted in the demolition of 250 houses. This aggravated the situation even further. The rebel forces, which consisted overwhelmingly of peasants, launched guerrilla warfare against the British forces and installations as well as Zionist settlements.

As the revolt quickly picked up steam, the rebels developed their tactical, administrative, and logistical organization. Having common national, political, and economic objectives, the revolt succeeded in mobilizing public support and was aided by the exiled political leadership of the national movement.

The revolt reached the peak of its power in the summer of 1938, when the rebels were practically in control of all the countryside and managed to free a number of towns, including Jerusalem, from British forces. Some towns were freed for a few hours as a display of strength and control by the rebels, such as Hebron, which they held for only three hours. Others, like the Old City of Jerusalem, were liberated for as long as five days. So successful was the revolt at one point that a British police inspector, Robin Martin from the Palestine Police Force, noted that "the British had to practically reoccupy Palestine from the hands of the rebels."

In the spring of 1939, the British forces comprised a large number of reinforcements, including four battalions, a battery of artillery, and armored cars. The formerly underground Haganah, or Zionist defense forces, also began to work directly with the British; together the government and Haganah managed to crush the revolt.

But the changing international conditions with the onset of World War II meant that the British had to offer the Palestinians an incentive to give up the revolt or risk losing the propaganda battle with Germany in one of the most strategically important territories in their empire. As a result, they promised the Palestinians their independence within ten years, as well as the limitation of Jewish immigration and land sales. The Palestinians interpreted this as the British conceding to their demands. However, these promises were never realized.

The Great Arab Revolt in Palestine came to an end as the Second World War started. The number of casualties was especially high among Palestinians: an estimated total of 5,000 were killed, 15,000 injured, and 5,600 imprisoned, and 112 were hanged by the Mandate authorities. On the Jewish side, casualties were 2,344, out of which 415 were killed. The British casualties were 620 dead and injured.

Despite the fact that the revolt of 1936–39 did not succeed in stopping the building of the Jewish state in Palestine nor in stopping the British from supporting it, it is regarded by the Palestinians as the first organized armed resistance in their modern history and is still remembered for being their first grassroots movement, which achieved the longest commercial strike in the history of the Middle East, succeeded in involving the majority of the Palestinian people, and forced the British to retake most of Palestine from the hands of the rebels.

The revolt had such an effect on people that some of its symbols, such as the gun and the horse, were embroidered on women's dresses. It was honored by popular poets of the period and in popular songs. Today, folk songs and dances still celebrate the revolt; perhaps the most famous is the song/dance "Rej'at el Baroudeh" (The gun has returned) by the well-known Fonoun dance troupe. Even some British police who served in Palestine during that time wrote a song about the rebels.

A KNIGHT ON HORSEBACK

Apart from Izz ad-Din al-Qassam, whose killing by the British helped spark the revolt, Abdul Rahim Hajj Mohammad (hereafter Abdul Rahim or Abu Kamal), who was killed by the British in 1939, four years after al-Qassam, was the most respected leader of the Great Revolt. Abdul Rahim was born in 1892 in the small village of Dhinnabah, near Tulkarm, to a wealthy landowning family that had a long history of resisting invading powers: one of his great-grandfathers fought against Napoleon's invasion of Palestine in 1798 and was sentenced to death by hanging, while another great-grandfather joined the resistance against Ibrahim Pasha's occupation in 1831. When his father died, likely while serving in the Ottoman army, Abdul Rahim took over the work in the family's lands.

Few sources exist to describe Abdul Rahim's life, but from what some of his companions and fellow rebels said about him, we can piece together much of his actions and beliefs. Like other young Palestinians of his social class and region, from his childhood Abdul Rahim routinely helped his father in the fields, sometimes accompanying him to towns and other villages to sell his produce. When free from studying, he would play with friends, childhood games like *Askar wa Haramiyah* (like cops and robbers), which was one of the favorite games at the time, or practicing with a slingshot. His first official education was in the village *kuttab* (the village mosque, where the sheikh taught children reading and writing and the Qur'an). This was followed by schooling in Tulkarm, probably starting when he was seven or eight. At a relatively young age, he was drafted into the Ottoman army, since service was compulsory for young males in the Arab countries under Ottoman rule. While in the army, he served in Beirut and Tripoli in Lebanon. When the First World War ended in 1918 with the defeat of the Ottoman Empire, Abdul Rahim returned to his village and worked as a grain merchant in Tulkarm.

Abdul Rahim became aware at a still young age of the dangers of the Zionist project in Palestine and the British Mandate's commitment to support it. Jewish colonies were built on the coastal plains not far from his lands. He saw peasants evicted from sold lands becoming homeless and unskilled laborers in towns. According to his friend and personal assistant Shaker Milhim, this made him sad and angry. He also witnessed the uprisings of 1921, 1923, and 1929, which spread in almost every town, including Tulkarm, and the brutal force the British used to suppress the Palestinian protesters.

His companions described Abdul Rahim as a quiet person, well dressed and a good horseman. Given his early exposure to the impact of Zionism on Palestinian peasants, it's not surprising that he was one of the organizers of the general strike in 1936 in his village, Dhinnabah, and in the nearby town of Tulkarm as well. During this period he started to recruit a number of young men from the area to raid Jewish orange orchards in the settlements near Tulkarm, especially those that were built in the area of Wadi al Hawarith, which were owned by absentee landlords and from which peasants had been evicted.

In the midthirties he started to train these recruits to use arms, hiring ex-soldiers from the Ottoman army to help him. The training was conducted in the mountainous area of Tulkarm. His base was in the hills of the village of Bala'a. He was able to train a good number of dedicated men using knowledge from his own experience in the Ottoman army. His connections as a well-known grain merchant in the areas of Tulkarm, Jenin, and Nablus helped to recruit people under his banner. During this period his groups started small-scale military operations against British troops and Zionist colonies.

Abdul Rahim used existing networks in his favor. He formed alliances with the urban middle class, especially the well-educated political figures who were not content with the policies adopted by the elite national leadership. Some of these later became members of the Central Committee for Jihad, such as Akram Zuaiter. He also used clan alliances toward political ends. Abdul Rahim belonged to the Samara clan, which is tied to other clans in a complicated web of alliances through marriage, mutual interests, and business. These alliances provided him with men, supplies, and to some extent arms. But more important, they ensured him a base of political support.

The 1935 killing of Izz ad-Din al-Qassam had a powerful effect on Palestinians. They began to realize that sending delegations to London and engaging in other forms of negotiation aimed at convincing the British to revoke the Balfour Declaration and stop the Zionist project, which was the policy the traditional Palestinian leadership preferred, were not bearing any fruits. Increasingly, it seemed, the only way to gain their rights was through armed struggle.

At this pivotal political moment, Abdul Rahim suffered a personal loss, as his wife Badia'a died in 1934, leaving him with four boys. When he took to the mountains with a group of rebels and started military actions against both the British police and the Jewish colonies, he left his sister to take care of and raise his four children. His oldest son, Kamal, remembers this period: "When my mother died we moved to live with our aunt Halima, who was a widow. She took care of us. She had a powerful personality. She was a trader, traded with grains. Later she traded with textiles and paid for our needs and education. Our father didn't give us money. . . . When he wanted to see us he sent one of his men to take us to the mountains, where we would spend a night or two and come back. Every time we visited him he was in a different location." As his life became more subsumed into the resistance, Abdul Rahim took practical steps to ensure his continued freedom of action: he sold his shop in Tulkarm and dedicated his money and time to the revolt.

Milhim recalls how the group began to form and operate: "First there was the strike. Everybody joined in the strike. Then we began to hear of some people who had obtained guns, and then some of them went to the road and ambushed the army convoy on its way to Jenin. After that, the British who knew who the attackers were started to look for them. They came to my house many times looking for Abdul Rahim, and since then he never slept in his house in Dhinnabah. People started to gather around him, joining the revolt, and little by little they became a large group."

During the general strike of April–October 1936, Abdul Rahim and his guerrilla fighters continued with wider-scale operations against the British army and police convoys on the road between Nablus and Tulkarm. Perhaps the most important engagement was the battle of Bala'a on 21 June 1936, when the rebels ambushed a Jewish convoy protected by a British force. The fighting was on a large enough scale that the British had to call for reinforcements; three planes were sent there in addition to the regular forces. The battle lasted for seven hours; the fighting was mainly between the rebel forces and the British force. According to the British sources, three of the rebels were killed and twenty-one injured, and the British casualties were one dead and two injured.

Abdul Rahim became a wanted man, and a reward was set for his arrest. The rebel groups considered the British convoys, military bases, and installations as fair targets. They also attacked Jewish convoys carrying supplies to Jewish colonies, so Jewish and British armed personnel protected these shipments after the beginning of the strike. The rebels distributed leaflets in the towns and villages asking people to join the revolt. People flocked to join the rebels, whose numbers swelled with ten to fifteen recruits from each village, for a total of two to four hundred regular recruits in each district, and many more could be called when needed. The skirmishing between the rebel forces and the British police and Jewish settlements continued during the summer and fall of 1936.

In August 1936, the Arab insurgent leader Fawzi al-Qawuqji arrived in Palestine with a group of Arab and Druze volunteers to lead and organize the revolt. He was a Syrian and worked as an instructor at the military academy in Baghdad in Iraq. The volunteers who came with him were well-seasoned revolutionaries from Syria, Iraq, and Lebanon who had participated in the Syrian revolt. With his military experience, al-Qawuqji organized and trained the rebel forces, mainly in the areas of Jenin-Nablus and Tulkarm. In the latter area there was another operating rebel group, led by Arif Abdul Raziq, who would later compete with Abdul Rahim for the title of general commander of the revolt. In the Jenin area a few other groups were formed. Each of these rebel groups worked separately, but al-Qawuqji tried to unite and coordinate them. He signed all communiqués under the title "the General Commander of the great revolt in Southern Syria, Palestine."

Abdul Rahim joined al-Qawuqji's forces and fought alongside him in the famous second battle of Bala'a in September 1936. According to al-Qawuqji's memoirs, Abdu Rahim "proved himself to be a good leader and a worthy commander." The battle was a success: it lasted more than six hours, and the rebels showed better organization and more advanced military skills than they had before. According to the British authorities' official announcement, the British casualties were three killed, including the pilot of one plane shot down by the rebels, and four injured; on the rebel side, ten were killed and six injured.

Although al-Qawuqji led the battles and military actions with a high degree of professionalism, he was less skilled in his relations with the local Palestinian leaders. The leadership of the Arab Higher Committee, especially Mufti Hajj Amin al-Hussaini, mistrusted him because of his close relationship with some of the families of the opposition who were affiliated with the Jordanian prince Abdullah.

Nor did the rebel fighters trust him fully either, first, because in all his communiqués he mentioned Palestine as Southern Syria—which wasn't to their liking, as they were fighting for independence and their own government—and second, because he put most of his fighting units under Arabs who came with him rather than Palestinian commanders.

The rebels' attacks officially stopped in October 1936 after the Arab kings and princes of Jordan, Iraq, and Saudi Arabia requested that the Palestinians stop the strike and the fighting, promising to ask the British to find a peaceful and just solution to the increasingly zero-sum conflict between Palestinian Arabs and Jews.

The Palestinians acceded to the Arab leaders' request, and al-Qawuqji left Palestine for Transjordan and then Iraq with most of his volunteer troops. Abdul Rahim left in October 1936 for Damascus, evading arrest after the British police had announced a sizable reward (five hundred pounds) for his capture. He met with Syrian and Lebanese nationalists and organized collaborations for arms smuggling to Palestine. He also collected donations and bought arms for the revolt. Then he moved to the village of Qarnayel in Lebanon, where he was in close contact with his men in Palestine.

FULL SPEED AHEAD

The British government announced in November 1936 that it would send a royal commission, the Peel Commission, to Palestine to investigate "the violent incidents" and to study the situation more broadly. It also stated that a limitation on Jewish immigration to Palestine was not justified. This led Palestinian Arabs to boycott the royal commission's investigation at the beginning of its investigation. Disappointed by the results of the Peel Commission, and particularly the partition plan it was clearly going to recommend, they resumed their revolt with more force and impetus.

The Central Committee for Jihad, in Damascus, and particularly Hajj Amin al-Hussaini, the grand mufti who was still in Jerusalem, asked the rebel leaders who were not in Palestine, including Abdul Rahim, to return and resume their actions to pressure the Peel Commission to change its recommendations, which were supposed to be published in July 1937 (the commission's main proposal was indeed to partition the country into Jewish and Arab states, with Jaffa and Jerusalem remaining under a more constricted British mandatory rule).

There was a general readiness among the Palestinians to continue the armed struggle, even as a measure unconnected with the increasingly sporadic and unorganized general strike. It soon became apparent to the British authorities that the revolt was spreading to all parts of the country and that the rebels' organization, fighting skills, and operations had improved considerably. As Elias Sanbar described it in his book *Palestine 1948*, "It was a giant Ant Colony of men and equipment, in which the relations were invested, and no time was lost or dead, in using the arms. When a group of men relaxed, the arms were used by another group in another area."

Abdul Rahim returned to Palestine in April 1937 to lead his platoons in the Tulkarm- Jenin-Nablus area, which became known as the triangle of terror, where the rebel military operations were most concentrated. The last three months of the year witnessed a series of violent attacks against Jewish buses, telephone wires, the Iraqi Petroleum Company pipeline, and military posts and targets. These months also witnessed some big battles between rebel forces and British troops. By the end of 1937 the revolt was organized and coordinated at a national level. In every area there were rebel forces with a semimilitary hierarchy. There were general, regional, and platoon commanders, and under each general and regional commander were committees for administrative, financial, and media affairs. One of the rebels recalls the development in the organization of the *fasail* (rebel platoons) in the Tulkarm area: "In the beginning we were with Abdul Rahim himself. But when the number of rebels grew bigger, the fasail were formed. . . . There were four fasail, led by four commanders. Each had a separate budget, but all were responsible to Ahmad Massad, who commanded a fasail, and in turn he was responsible to Abdul Rahim."

In December 1937, Abdul Rahim was injured in the battle of Nazlah al Sharkiya, near Jenin. Four rebels were killed in the attack, but he escaped arrest despite his injury when the head of the village hid him in a cave until the British forces withdrew. Abdul Rahim was treated locally for a month, then went to Damascus for better treatment. He came back to Palestine in January 1938.

During this period a grudging respect developed between the British officers and one of their most elusive prey. Sir John Hackett, the former commander of the Transjordan Frontier Force, explained that Abdul Rahim was one of the best rebel leaders in Nablus.

> I tried to make contact with him; had I made that contact with him, I would have shot him. I sent a message to him with my local Arab officer, Rashid Abdul Fattah, who was a first cousin to Abdul Rahim, telling him that it is beneath the dignity of a regular British carry officer to be shot at with bent *banduks* [rifles] and bad ammunition—if he would send a cadre on for instructing, in the hope that the match could be resumed on level terms later on. He sent a message back saying that he sympathized with my predicament and he would take advantage of my offer to send his best cadre, but unfortunately they were very busy and he couldn't spare any.

UP THE MOUNTAIN AND DOWN AGAIN

In the first few months of 1938, the rebels continued their guerrilla warfare, and the revolt reached its peak that summer. With the rebels extending their control over most of the roads and almost all of the countryside, most rural areas were no-go zones for the British. According to the British police inspector Robin Martin, during 1938

> the whole country was in rebellion, the Arab rebel forces had an awful lot of control, they were very strong indeed. I don't know how many forces the Arabs may have had, but the British had at least 20,000 troops and I think the Arabs must have had with various irregulars and village volunteers and things like that, twice the number up and down. They held the whole of the country apart from the main towns. Palestine's government together with the British forces then held the main towns and their various camps in which they were stationed, but the outside was really rebel armies.

All the railway stations between Jerusalem and Lydda and most of the stations between Lydda and the Egyptian border were destroyed. Rebels raided police stations, taking their arms and ammunition. Most of the police stations were closed, except for those in Gaza and Hebron, which the army held. One of the most daring attacks was carried out against the Jenin police station on 24 August 1938, when Assistant District Commissioner W. S. S. Moffat was killed in his guarded office.

With the growing numbers of the rebels joining the revolt, it was necessary to centralize its command, to coordinate the different groups, and to solve administrative and logistical problems. There was also a need for constant contact with the central committee in Damascus, which consisted of Palestinian leaders whom the British had exiled. The committee was the political and logistic leadership of the revolt; it provided the rebels with financial support, arms, and supplies. France, the mandatory power in Syria, considered this a British issue, especially as the central committee didn't commit any acts against the French. Moreover, the Syrian public supported the Palestinian revolt, and the French did not want to antagonize them by cracking down on the Palestinian presence.

All was not smooth, however, within the ranks of the rebels. There was growing tension over authority between some of the revolt commanders, especially Abdul Rahim and Arif Abdul Raziq, as both were general commanders in the Tulkarm area and both wanted to be named general commander of the revolt. This was exacerbated by the fact that the competition for social and political power between their families—Abdul Rahim's Samara and Arif Abdul Raziq's Hajj Ibrahim—had heated up, souring their relations.

A conference was held in September 1938 in the village of Dayr Ghassana, near Ramallah, for all rebel leaders, in part to heal the rift between the two commanders. They agreed to form the Bureau of the Arab Revolt in Palestine, and Abdul Rahim and Arif Abdul Raziq would rotate as general commander of the rebel forces. Abdul Rahim began signing his communiqués under the name "Al Mujahid Al Sagheir [the small fighter], the Bureau of the great Arab revolt, Southern

Syria." When the British authorities heard of this meeting, they deployed a large force aided by fighter planes and attacked the village to kill or arrest the rebel leaders. The rebels fought back, and during this battle another of the main leaders, Mohammad al Salih (also known by his nom de guerre, Abu Khalid), was killed.

ATTEMPTING TO BUILD A CIVIL RESISTANCE

Civil disobedience was an important part of the revolt since its earliest days, after having been declared a national policy at a conference of national committees in Jerusalem on 7 May 1936. At the beginning of the strike, the national committees replaced the Mandate civil courts in solving the problems of the public. One of Abdul Rahim's first commands was in fact a communiqué establishing popular, or rebel, courts. Throughout the revolt, local fasail in every part of the country set up a rebel court in their area of command. The judgment of a fasail leader usually ended a dispute, but if one of the parties was not satisfied, he could appeal to the regional commander or area leader.

The rebel leaders were very strict and declared anyone who dealt with the British to be a collaborator—this was the ultimate sin against the people and the revolt, and the sentence was usually death by shooting. Some rebel leaders, like Abu Durra in the Jenin area, were known to kill anyone suspected of collaboration even without a trial. But not everyone was so severe. Raji al Khatib, a fasail commander from Galilee, was visiting Abdul Rahim and witnessed one of his courts:

> Once I went with Sheikh Ahmad to a village called Burqa to meet Abdul Rahim Hajj Mohammad. When we were there, a leader named Fawzi Jarrar came to him with a collaborator in order to set a trial for him. After the hearing in the court which was set by Hajj Mohammad, after listening to all parties, he told the collaborator, "Aren't you ashamed of yourself? Your life now is in our hands, but I am not going to kill you, I am going to pardon you." He gave him seventeen Palestinian pounds, olive oil, and a sack of flour for his family and let him go. A few days later the same man came back to Abdul Rahim; he had given the oil and flour to his family and bought a rifle with the money and asked Abdul Rahim [if he could] join the revolt.

But the case which was most talked about happened in August 1938, after a group of rebels captured a Jewish engineer. The fasail court decided to execute him by shooting but gave him the right to appeal to the revolt's higher court, which was headed by Abdul Rahim. After listening to the engineer and some witnesses, the higher court decided to free the prisoner, and Abdul Rahim issued a communiqué in which he stated, "As many Arab witnesses have testified on his behalf, and as he did not confess to believing in Zionism [that is, he was not a collaborator], and as the court believes in the famous Arab saying 'Forgive when you can,' and as we consider him a prisoner of war and he should not be harmed, the court has decided to set him free . . . and give him five pounds from the revolt treasury and Arabic clothes and send him back to his home in peace."

For Abdul Rahim the revolt was national in its goals and scope, but as in other anticolonial movements, nationalist ideology masked social differences and the peasant character of the revolt. This was clear during the summer of 1938, when the rebels gained control over the countryside and most of the towns. Although the peasants, who were the vast majority of the rebels, did not have an articulated social or political program during the revolt, they did have common political, national, and social objectives which allowed them to form a broad alliance with workers and urban middle-class radical elements. They depended on their society's existing social structure: family-clan relations and alliances which provided them with supplies, men, and protection. But they also depended on precapitalist patron-client relations with the notable classes, which were leading the national movement. Ahmad Nazzal, a fasail leader in the Jenin area, explained his views on the class difference: "Those rich people were not going straight, and we never considered them or took their opinions. They were collaborators and did not want the revolt. No one from them gave money to the revolt. The peasants were the ones who made the revolt."

The peasants' social and even political power manifested itself in some orders that Abdul Rahim issued. Although they had practical purposes—ordering townspeople to wear the peasant kaffiyeh instead of the Turkish tarbush (fez) meant the British couldn't distinguish between peasants and townsfolk—they also had social implications and displayed the peasants' dominance.

One order that reflected underlying class differences within the revolt was the moratorium on debt, which was obviously to the benefit of the lower classes and against the interest of the wealthier classes. Another order canceled rents on flats, clearly identifying the rebels with the lower urban classes and urban workers. Abdul Rahim also banned creditors from collecting their debts from villagers. According to one of his communiqués, released on 20 September 1938:

> In view of the economic crises in the present position of the fellah during this agricultural season and the heavy burden lying on their shoulders, certain creditors in towns who look after their own personal interests only have begun to visit the villages, pressing the debtors to settle their accounts. Due to these reasons attention is drawn to the following points:
>
> 1. Creditors are warned not to visit villages or send their agents to ask for settlement of debts.
> 2. Any person who takes legal steps against his debtor will be held responsible for his actions. . . .

Abdul Rahim remained against political assassination, and he refused to perform assassinations for any political faction, even the Central Committee for Jihad in Syria, headed by the exiled Mufti Hajj Amin al-Hussaini. It was a widely known fact that during the revolt, the Hussaini faction and others got some rebel leaders and rebels of lower ranks to assassinate their traditional rivals. Among those killed on behalf of Hussaini were Hassan Sidqi al Adjani from Jerusalem and Anwar al Shuqairi from Acre, both members of prominent opposition families. However, Abdul Rahim's refusal to participate in internecine political violence seems not to have hurt his relationship with Hussaini or the Central Committee for Jihad. In fact, he often visited Damascus to obtain fresh supplies of arms and discuss the progress of the revolt with the Higher Arab Committee.

Abdul Rahim's personal assistant Shakir Milhim recalls an incident when a member of the Hussaini faction brought Abdul Rahim a letter. It contained a list of people whom the writer wished to be assassinated, all rivals of the Hussaini faction. When Abdul Rahim had read the list, he told the messenger to tell the people in Damascus that he did not carry out assassinations and that he was "fighting for Palestine and not for the Hussainis." The messenger threatened that Abdul Rahim's supplies and financial aid would be cut off should he fail to carry out the assassinations. According to Milhim, supplies were indeed cut off from Damascus for a while, and Abdul Rahim had to ask the Chamber of Commerce in Jerusalem and the municipality of Ramallah for financial aid.

In February 1939, Abdul Rahim went to Damascus to discuss the situation with the Central Committee for Jihad, which promised to continue supporting him—at this stage it could not afford to be seen as withdrawing support for the revolt. More important, the exiled leadership needed him in that critical time, when so-called peace bands—formed in 1939 by anti-Hussaini opposition groups with the support and collaboration of both the British authorities and the Zionist movement—were launching counterattacks against the rebels. These bands created confusion by terrorizing supporters of the rebellion while helping convince rebels to surrender to the British.

FROM DEATH TO MEMORY

The intensification of attacks by the British on rebel forces at the beginning of 1939 further complicated matters for Abdul Rahim and the resistance. Alarmed by the increasing tension and the possibility of war in Europe, the British set out to finish the revolt by both military and diplomatic means. They conducted their military operations aided by two army divisions, squadrons of airplanes, the Palestine police (which consisted of mainly of British, Jewish, and a small number of Palestinian members), the Transjordan Frontier Force, six thousand Jewish forces, and the local peace bands, which comprised close to one thousand armed men.

While the British were conducting a heated military campaign against the remaining rebels in Palestine, the government in London called for a conference in

February 1939 between Palestinians, Jews, and representatives from Arab countries. In the course of discussions it became clear that the conference could not offer a solution to the problems in Palestine. The Palestinians presented their demands of recognition of their right to independence, the abandonment of the Jewish national home, the immediate cessation of Jewish immigration and land sales, and the cancellation of the Mandate. The Jewish delegation wanted the continuation of the Mandate and the implementation of the Balfour Declaration and refused to accept minority status for Jews in Palestine. The conference failed. But the fighting back home continued.

The failure of attempts toward a negotiated solution of the Palestinian-Jewish conflict served as the backdrop for Abdul Rahim's return to Palestine in March 1939. He stopped to spend the night at the village of Sanur, near Jenin, with two of his regional commanders, close associates, and a small force of rebels. The British were informed of his arrival and dispatched a large military force, which cordoned the village. The villagers begged Abdul Rahim to leave in disguise. But he refused, went out with his rebels, and clashed with the British force in the plains of Sanur. In the battle, he and one of his regional commanders were killed.

He was buried in Sanur without much ceremony, but two weeks later a group of his rebels came at night and secretly took his body to be buried in his own village of Dhinnabah with the honor and dignity befitting his stature in the revolt. News of his death prompted a spontaneous, multiday general strike in recognition of his contribution to the resistance against both British rule and Zionism. Some eyewitnesses to his killing said that the British colonel who led the operation had stood near the body of the dead leader and took his hat off in salute. Indeed, the officer in charge of apprehending the rebels at Sanur, Jeffrey Motrin, explained in his memoirs that "Abdul Rahim had a special respect among his people, and among us, he was a man of good manners." Said Abu Laimoun, one of the rebels with Abdul Rahim when he was killed, explained that

> Abu Smadi's wife was the first to see the English coming. She told us. Fawzi Jarrar told the rebels to spread south of the village. Abdul Rahim and Said Beit Iba went down the mountain; he [Abdul Rahim] left his horse and went on foot down the mountain. When he reached the school . . . I heard three shots. I was only a few meters away from him. I saw him lying on the ground; beside him was Abu Khalifa, also dead. The English came. I saw with my own eyes a big officer taking his handkerchief out of his pocket and cover Abdul Rahim's face with it. The English respected him. After that we went to the place where he died and carried him on a ladder to the Jarrar house.

Abdul Rahim's death made the headlines in local newspapers in Palestine and throughout the Arab world.

His killing dealt the revolt a severe blow. It had more setbacks with the sur-render of Arif Abdul Raziq and sixteen of his men to the French authorities on the Syrian border and the arrest of Abu Durra, the Jenin area commander, at the border with Transjordan. The Central Committee for Jihad tried to boost morale by announcing that Ahmad al-Hasan had taken command of the revolt, but this had little effect. Al-Hasan lacked Abdul Rahim's charismatic personality and con-nections and so failed to keep the momentum Abdul Rahim had generated.

The situation in Palestine changed drastically with the outbreak of war in the summer of 1939. Soon thereafter, most of the rebels who were not arrested went back to their villages. Many surrendered their arms, and rebel operations ceased. By winter 1939 the revolt had ended.

Although Palestinians themselves do not agree on whether the revolt of 1936–39 was a failure or a success, and despite the disagreement among historians and academics on whether to call it a revolt, a rebellion, a revolution, or even a bandits' war, it remains a landmark in the history of the Palestinian people: the first sus-tained, organized, grassroots armed struggle against Zionism—a struggle which continues today. The memory of those who fought and died in that revolt is still fresh in the collective memory of the Palestinian people, and it came alive again when a sniper shot ten Israeli soldiers in 2000 in the Valley of Thieves, during the second year of the Al-Aqsa Intifada. It continues to inspire people in folk songs and poems.

And the name Abdul Rahim Hajj Mohammad is still alive, passing from one generation to the next. In Amman, Jordan, a major street in a predominantly Palestinian neighborhood was named after him in May 2007. A boys' school was named after him in his native village of Dhinnabah (now in the West Bank), which organizes an event in March every year to commemorate the anniversary of his death. Most recently, in March 2009 the Palestine technical college Khadouri, in Tulkarm, organized a major commemoration of the seventieth anniversary of Abdul Rahim's death.

Younger Palestinians may have adopted new heroes, depending on their po-litical beliefs and affiliations. But in the Tulkarm area, older men and women still recite songs to praise his character and mourn his death. In the cemetery of the small village of Dhinnabah, near Tulkarm, the visitor will find numerous graves of martyrs from the past century of conflict. Among them stands a humble stone engraved with these words:

The Martyr for his country—Abdul Rahim Hajj Mohammad
29/3/1939
Mercy be on his soul, He was a Nation in a Hero

A NOTE ON SOURCES

Both interviews and Arabic written sources were used in the writing of this chapter. The following are the written sources.

Allush, Naji. *The Arab Resistance in Palestine, 1917–1948*. Beirut: Palestine Research Center, 1967.

Abduh, Ziyad. *Abdul Rahim Hajj Mohammad, Hero and Revolution*. Al Zarqa, Jordan: Arab Agency for Publishing and Distribution, 1984.

Darwaza, Mohammad Izzat. *The Palestinian Leadership at Its Different Stages*. Sidon, Lebanon: al Maktaba al Assriya, 1959.

Al-Hout, Bayan. *Leaders and Political Institutions in Palestine, 1917–1948*. Beirut: Institute for Palestine Studies, 1981.

Qasmiya, Kairya, ed. *Palestine in the Memoirs of al Qawuqji,1936–1948*. Beirut: Palestine Liberation Organization Research Center and Dar Al-Quds, 1975.

Sanbar, Elias. *Palestine 1948*. Beirut: Arab Society for Studies and Publishing, 1987.

Sirhan, Nimr, and Mustafa Kabaha. *Abdul Raheem Haj Mohammad, General Commander of the Palestinian Revolt, 1936–1939*. Ramallah: N. Sarhan, 2000.

SUGGESTIONS FOR FURTHER READING

Bowden, Tom. *The Breakdown of Public Security: The Case of Ireland, 1916–1921, and Palestine, 1936–1939*. London: Sage Publications, 1979.

Clark, David. "The Colonial Police and Anti-terrorism: Bengal 1930–36, Palestine 1937–47, and Cyprus 1955–59." DPhil thesis, Oxford University, 1978.

Lesch, Ann Mosely. *Arab Politics in Palestine, 1917–1939: The Frustration of a Nationalist Movement*. Ithaca, NY: Cornell University Press, 1979.

Marlowe, John. *Rebellion in Palestine*. London: Crescent Press, 1948.

9

Hillel Kook

Revisionism and Rescue

Rebecca Kook

Hillel Kook's life defies easy political categorization. He transversed the boundaries of set political identities, opting for Left at some points, Right at others, and more often than not rejecting such labels and categories altogether. He began his political life as a founding member of the Irgun (from the Hebrew *Irgun Zvai Leumi*), the underground military organization that fought the Arabs of Palestine and led the military campaign to drive the British out of that region. During the Second World War, he lobbied the Roosevelt administration to pursue rescue plans for the Jews of Europe in the face of opposition from the American Zionist establishment. In 1945 he published an article in the *International Herald Tribune* titled "Post Zionism" in which he called for the establishment of a secular democratic republic in Palestine and the dismantling of the World Zionist Organization after the achievement of independence for this state. In 1949 he was elected to the Israeli parliament on the Herut list (headed by Menachem Begin), only to resign after two years. He later emerged as a lone voice calling for the separation of religious from national identity and demanding that Israel recognize all of its population as constituting a single nation.

To examine the life story of Hillel Kook is to consider those who helped to construct Israel's political identities but in the end were excluded by the very state they helped to build. Considering Hillel's life, like those of many others during this period, reminds us of the many paths not chosen and the ability of individuals at critical historical junctures to defy conventional boundaries and opt for alternative paths. His crossing of colonial and national boundaries, from Palestine to Poland (months before the Nazi invasion), to Switzerland and New York (armed with a British colonial laissez-passer), is mirrored in his crossing of political boundaries and identities. From this vista, the Mandate in Palestine can also be seen as a period of pluralism and multiplicity.

CHILDHOOD IN UKRAINE AND JERUSALEM

Hillel Kook was born in 1915, in Ukraine, where his family had moved to escape the widespread pogroms conducted against Lithuanian Jewry at the turn of the century. His parents made do in a small town called Yelizavetgrad until 1925, when they joined his uncle, Rabbi Abraham Isaac Kook, in Palestine. Though not officially affiliated with any of the Zionist organizations, the Kook family was openly, and actively, Zionist. Hence, Hillel's early memories of anti-Semitism and violence were quickly overshadowed by later memories of a childhood spent in Jerusalem, amid different sounds and cultures, and enveloped by a family rooted firmly in its beliefs in the importance of a Jewish homeland and the important role the Jewish people played in world history. The Kook clan settled in a quarter established by immigrants from Bukhara (now in Uzbekistan). Hillel's father was the principal of a Talmud Torah (a primary school for religious studies), and the family, which had eight children, lived in the school's top-floor apartment. Down the street was the home of Hillel's uncle, then the chief rabbi of Jerusalem and later the first chief rabbi of Palestine.

It is difficult to reconstruct the atmosphere of Hillel's youth, since none of his family members wrote memoirs. It is possible, however, to draw a picture based on different scraps of memory—photographs, anecdotes, and letters. The photographs are particularly revealing. Those that have survived show the siblings in the yard, on the terrace, on the winding stairway to the front door, the girls wearing knee-length skirts and fashionable hats, a far cry from contemporary Orthodox female garb. An especially beautiful photo shows one of the sisters lounging in a bedroom, her beautiful light long hair spread out freely on the sofa as a cousin reclines nearby.

Hillel's father, Rabbi Dov Kook, would never decline an invitation to share a meal in the home of any of his children—even those who did not keep the strict halachic rule—because he believed that the laws guiding relations between people and their fellows trumped those regarding relations between people and God. In a story told by Hillel's siblings, their mother would say that she had eight children, four girls and four boys. Of the four boys, two were destined to serve humankind and two to serve the Lord. In fact, all of her children became educated. Two of the brothers became doctors, one became a distinguished rabbi, and one—the youngest, Hillel, considered an *ilui* (prodigy)—was destined to follow in the family's rabbinical tradition. Of the sisters, two became scientists and the other two educated and working women. As glimpses in the photographs suggested, all of the siblings seemed to carve out their own destinies—women and men alike.

The adolescent Hillel spent much time in his uncle's house. Rabbi Abraham Isaac Kook was a central figure in the Yishuv (the Jewish community in Palestine) and maintained close relationships with many of the leading figures of Zionist Palestine, in both the arts and politics. His household was known to be a meeting place of members of Jewish Palestinian society with widely different world views, and he was seen as a bridge between them, with his empathy for and cooperation with nonreligious Zionists. Rabbi Kook was also known for his dialectical merging of notions of the profane and the sacred, seeing roots of the sacred in the profane and thus embracing the Zionist project as a step toward fulfilling the messianic promise. He believed that both religious and nonreligious Jews played an important role in rebuilding the Jewish homeland; the Merkaz Harav Yeshiva that he established in 1923 reflected this dialectic and proposed to serve as a center for integrated learning, including science and religion, sacred and profane philosophy, although it eventually came to offer only sacred studies. It was the first center of Torah learning to employ Hebrew as the language of instruction, and as such the first openly Zionist one. The Hebrew language, in fact, conveyed an identity which proved to be defining for Hillel and many of his generation. Thus, while Yiddish was his mother tongue and the language of the long jokes told around the table, Hebrew was the language of politics, education, and everyday life.

The modernist and rationalist dimensions of Rabbi Kook's theology had deep allure for Hillel and many others who searched for a way to negotiate between their religious background and the secularism and openness of the developing Zionist society around them. The story Hillel told of his secular awakening is particularly revealing. "Every day, on my way to the yeshiva, I passed a kiosk that sold ham sandwiches to the British soldiers. I believed in God, I still do. But I wondered—why does he care what sandwich I eat? One day, I crossed the street. I bought a sandwich and ate it. Nothing happened." Most probably something of an urban legend, this tale reflects the deep belief of many youths of similar class and religious background in their ability to maintain a rational dialogue with their faith, as well as their temptation to always "cross the street," to traverse the religious and the secular, the sacred and the profane.

THE EARLY YEARS IN THE IRGUN

The Yishuv of the 1920s was a vibrant yet highly contentious political arena. The main fault lines of Israeli society were already set in place, as were the bases for the defining political categories—the Left, consisting of the different groups within the labor movement; the religious Zionists; and the Revisionist Right, followers of Ze'ev Jabotinsky. There were also many smaller political and religious groups, ranging from the Communists to the Haredim (the Orthodox). The most contentious dividing line was between Labor and the Revisionists. Their conflict was one of ideology, political rivalry, and world view. It was also personal. The rivalry between David Ben-Gurion and Jabotinsky was deep and virulent. Fierce allegations permeated the local party press, which nicknamed Jabotinsky "Vladimir Hitler" and Ben-Gurion "The Bolshevik Tyrant."

Jabotinsky was a well-known figure in Zionist politics. The founder of the Jewish Legion of the First World War, he quickly became known for his oppositional, military, and often provocative positions. During the early 1920s, he vociferously opposed the policies and positions of the moderate Chaim Weizmann, the president of the World Zionist Organization (WZO), whom he described as too compliant toward and appeasing of the Mandate authority. Though himself an Anglophile and a staunch supporter of cooperation with the British, Jabotinsky advocated a far more blunt approach, demanding the right of the Jews to self-defense and self-rule. The conflict with Weizmann led Jabotinsky to resign from the Executive of the WZO in 1923. He then founded Beitar, a Zionist activist youth movement emphasizing self-defense, and two years later he established the Revisionist Party.

Whereas the labor movement equivocated over the ultimate aim of the Zionist movement, Jabotinsky was the first Zionist leader to define political independence as its final goal. The labor movement accepted Winston Churchill's 1921 White Paper, which detached the east bank of the Jordan from the Palestine Mandate, while the Revisionists sought a Jewish state on both banks. The labor movement accepted the British program which allocated spots to potential Jewish immigrants on the basis of Palestine's "absorptive capacity," whereas the Revisionists demanded unrestricted immigration for the Jews of Eastern Europe. The Revisionists also highlighted self-defense as a critical element of the nationalist project, while the labor movement was slow to accept its importance. Supported mostly by middle- and lower-middle-class Jews, the Revisionists emphasized the role of capital in enabling the absorption of masses of immigrants, while the labor movement put its trust in a collective economy. Finally, the labor movement prided itself on its pragmatism, while the Revisionists aimed for doctrinal clarity and frequently acted in an in-your-face fashion.

The Revisionist challenge to Labor Zionism was beginning to gain momentum when Hillel entered his uncle's Merkaz Harav Yeshiva in 1929. Political sentiments were at a high, and his transition from the small, sheltered atmosphere of the Talmud Torah to the newly established yeshiva was a mark of passage from childhood to adulthood in more ways than one. It was also in 1929 that extensive anti-Jewish riots broke out across Palestine. The meaning and implications of the riots emerged as a central source of contention between the two main movements of the Yishuv, and they proved to be a seminal event in Hillel's political coming-of-age.

Set off by a conflict over religious rights of worship at the Western Wall in the Old City of Jerusalem, where a large assembly of Revisionists and the Beitar youth movement during the Tisha B'Av Jewish fast brought tensions to boiling point, the riots spread to settlements outside Jerusalem, most notably Hebron. The violence of the Palestinians fed off the frustration and anger they had against the settlement of Jews. All in all, more than two hundred Jews and Arabs—including many elderly and children—were killed. The labor movement saw the riots as an expression of mainly religious sentiments, while the Revisionists viewed them as nationalist and political, constituting further proof of the conflicting goals of the Jews and Arabs. According to Jabotinsky, it was incumbent upon the Jews to make it clear to the Arabs that they were there to stay and able and willing to defend themselves against any aggression. Both sides, Labor and Revisionist alike, saw the riots as evidence of the British officials' powerlessness to contain and respond to such violence.

The Revisionist response was clear cut: more defense was needed, and if the British could not provide it, the Jews would provide it themselves. The Labor response was more strategically minded; wary of losing British support, they rallied their energies toward lobbying the British for enhanced policing forces and defense for the Jewish settlements. The Revisionist response resonated with youths like Hillel, who, because of his middle-class and religious background, was alienated from the socialist ideology of the labor movement and hence less open to its arguments.

Thus, when a young commander established Haganah Bet (or the Second Haganah) two years later as a more offense-oriented breakaway from the labor movement's defense organization Haganah, Hillel was quick to join. Haganah Bet attracted many members of the Revisionist movement because of its more militant approach, and until 1937, when it became the Irgun Zvai Leumi, it included both Revisionist and Labor sympathizers. In fact, neither Hillel nor David Raziel, whom he met in Merkaz Harav and who had a deep and lasting impact on him, were members of the Revisionist movement when they joined Haganah Bet. Thus, while the political rivalry described above was deep and pervasive, it provided only a generalized context and not a detailed accounting of the different arenas of political action.

The small group of militants who joined Haganah Bet and later stayed on to form the Irgun and constitute its command had similar social biographies—they were young, intellectual individualists, many of whom came from an Orthodox background, and many were from Jerusalem. One of their favorite books was *The Grey Wolf,* the autobiography of Kemal Atatürk. They fashioned themselves after other young nationalists, embodying the new national Jew. They adopted European mannerisms and pursuits, such as boxing and philosophy, were good dressers, and maintained a delicate dialogue with their Jewish background, in the cases of Hillel and Raziel, negotiating between sacred and profane studies. They established a secret society called the Sohba ("fraternity" in Arabic), which had long meetings for reading, arguing, discussing. The choice of an Arabic name most probably reflects their feeling of belonging to the land and their rejection of their immigrant origins. Indeed, they all went by the label *Palestinian* and saw themselves as deserving it perhaps even more—and belonging to the land more—than the region's Arabs. They considered themselves a vanguard, possessing in insight, intellect, and valor what they lacked in authority and material resources, and indeed, this group of students later played key roles the Revisionist movement. In a later interview Hillel recollected:

> We were a group of young commanders for whom the Irgun was an evolutionary process; we were looking for some path, most likely because we needed a clear justification for our existence, not to be just some group waiting for riots to justify ourselves and defend Jewish settlements. We had unconscious thoughts and desires that gradually we succeeded in articulating. And from this came the name—the military national organization [Irgun Zvai Leumi] and from here the initial thoughts of a Hebrew army, and finally came the Hebrew national liberation movement with the Irgun as its formal instrument. It was a gradual process, however—with a lot of talk, discussion, and searching.

While officially Hillel spent the next few years studying—first at Merkaz Harav and then at the Hebrew University in Jerusalem—in fact he spent most of his time training with the Irgun. He participated in the first course for lieutenants that the group organized, along with Raziel and Yair Stern. They would patrol Jerusalem and occasionally Jewish villages and towns outside the city. Often Hillel would accompany Raziel to the hills outside Jerusalem, in the Judean desert, where they would walk, talk, practice boxing, and train with weapons.

The years in Palestine and in the Irgun were formative in Hillel's political development and the evolution of his nationalist consciousness. As he says in the quote above, these years contain an empowering and a nationalizing process. The twin notions of nationalism and sovereignty were embodied in what he perceived as the spirit of the Irgun, with its emphasis on self-defense and national identity. What started as self-defense, though, quickly took on an offensive character.

In 1936, the Arab Revolt, which was to last for three years, broke out in Palestine. The split in the Yishuv that first appeared in the aftermath of the 1929 riots, between those who supported a moderate response and those who favored a combative response to Arab militancy, hardened during this period, and with it the identity of the Irgun as a militant organization reflecting a radical alternative to the official bodies of the Yishuv. After a general strike protesting Jewish immigration and land sales, intermittent Arab actions against both British and Jewish targets and fierce reprisals by the British and, to a lesser extent, the Jewish underground—the Irgun—characterized the years from 1936 to 1939. In 1937, Arab attacks targeted

Jewish civilians in mixed towns, in the fields, and on the roads. The Irgun began retaliating in March 1937, with the killing of two Arabs on the beach in Bat Yam, but greatly escalated its responses in 1938 and 1939—that is, for the remainder of the revolt. Its attacks took the form of shooting at traveling cars and placing bombs in crowded places, killing dozens of Arab shoppers in marketplaces in Haifa, Jerusalem, and Jaffa. On occasion, the Irgun targeted British police as well.

RESCUE WORK DURING THE SECOND WORLD WAR

At the end of 1937, Raziel, then the commander of the Irgun, decided to send Hillel to Europe to meet with Jabotinsky to discuss issues relating to the direction and leadership of the group. Hillel, by now wanted by the British because of his prominent role in the Irgun, remained in Europe to oversee the immigration of Jews to Palestine and to supervise Irgun training camps set up in Poland. He also took on a nom de guerre: Peter Bergson.

Hillel spent the next three years scuttling between European capitals, between political salons in Warsaw, Jabotinsky's offices in London and Paris, and Zionist meetings in Geneva. This budding cosmopolitanism was not, apparently, unusual for the young Zionist cadres from Palestine. In the memoirs of many individuals—both Labor and Revisionist—this sense of ease of travel between Europe and Palestine is common. This seemingly borderless Europe must have felt particularly at odds with the growing sense of imminent crisis that Hillel and his comrades encountered in their meetings with Jewish communities in Poland and elsewhere. The Nazi Party had been in power for more than four years, and anti-Jewish policy and legislation were rampant in Germany, Poland, Hungary, and elsewhere on the continent. In a surviving letter that Hillel sent to his brother in Palestine, there is a hint of this dissonance: much talk about the efforts to organize the immigration of Jews to Palestine alongside stories of his travels and romantic escapades in Paris and London.

Neither Hillel's travels nor his embroilment in inter-Zionist politics and rivalries ended in Europe; rather, they only began. In the summer of 1940, Jabotinsky summoned Hillel to New York, to breathe life into the campaign for a Jewish army which had been conducted in the United States since 1939. Hillel arrived with very little money and even less of an understanding of America and its Jewish community. He moved into a small apartment on the East Side, which he shared with a young Revisionist from Poland. The continuing war and the news from Europe kept Hillel in the United States for the next eight years. Cut off from the Irgun in Palestine, he and a small group of other members considered themselves the Irgun delegation in the United States and were, for all intents and purposes, its only active branch until 1943. During these years, the Irgun delegation, led by Hillel, established a series of political action committees focused on Jewish and Zionist issues. The most notable, from 1942 to 1945, was the Emergency Committee to Save the Jewish People of Europe.

When Hillel, now Peter Bergson, arrived in New York, he was twenty-five years old and unprepared for the reality of American pluralism. In later years he would often recollect that he had expected American Jewry to be simply *one more* Jewish community, not significantly different from those he had encountered in Warsaw, Poland, Paris, and London. What he encountered, however, was a Jewish community of a vastly different type. From the vantage point of a young man born in an Eastern European shtetl and raised in Palestine on the rhetoric of Jewish unity, the Jews of America appeared more American than Jewish. For the majority of non-Orthodox Jews, no matter what schul they attended, their political and civic identity was American.

The American Jewish community at the outbreak of World War II numbered close to five million, with numerous competing and rival organizations. The conventional thinking among American Jews was that their ability to integrate into American society was contingent upon downplaying their Jewish identity. This was difficult for an outsider like Hillel to understand or accept. With a significant Jewish presence in the media, the entertainment industry, the arts, and other arenas, the status of Jews as Americans seemed unthreatened. Clearly, however, for American Jews, their status felt much more tenuous. Numerous studies of the time emphasize the anti-Semitic attitudes and the limitations placed on Jews in various sectors. Many American Jews, therefore, still considered themselves outsiders to American society and as such were quick to conclude that Jewish issues would interest no one but other Jews.

Official news of the mass extermination of European Jewry reached the American press in November 1942. While the Roosevelt administration had known of their plight for months, it did not define their rescue as an official war aim, nor did it consider plans aimed solely at rescuing or even easing the situation of the threatened Jewish communities. The official policy of the administration toward the extermination of the Jews was that winning the war was the best and only way the Allies could help. Moreover, the State Department did nothing to ease the draconian immigration measures and quotas which rendered virtually futile the efforts to enter the United States of those Jews fortunate enough to escape. During the war, barely 10 percent of the very meager immigration quota was met.

While most American Jews had friends or family in Europe and were naturally extremely attuned to any news from there, on the whole, the mainstay of the leadership of the American Jewish community did not act vigorously during the war to pressure the Allies to come to the aid of European Jews. Roosevelt was a revered and beloved leader to the Jewish community, and it was difficult for many to acknowledge the indifference he exhibited to their people's plight. They were reluctant to act *as* Jews *for* Jews in the public sphere, thinking that this would somehow appear to compromise their loyalty to America. They mostly limited their protest to symbolic acts within the community itself.

Hillel and several colleagues from the Irgun—Shmuel Merlin, Yitzhak Ben Ami, Aryeh Ben Eliezer, and Alex Raphaeli—took it upon themselves to establish the Emergency Committee to Save the Jewish People of Europe (or the so-called Bergson Group, as it came to be known in the United States). Hillel quickly identified the importance of public relations in American political culture and the potential of the media to promote political change. Thus, while up to that point Jews had limited their discourse to Jewish media, the Jabotinsky influence pushed Hillel to reach out through the media with a public relations and political campaign on the national level, recruiting leaders of the literary, theatrical, and political elite of the United States—mainly non-Jews—in a massive effort to pressure the Roosevelt administration to establish a rescue agency devoted to saving Jews. The emergency committee published hundreds of full-page newspaper advertisements, written by the novelist and screenwriter Ben Hecht, in major papers across the country, including the *New York Times,* the *Washington Post,* and the *International Herald Tribune;* staged pageants that drew audiences of thousands; held fund-raisers; and created a strong lobby in Washington, D.C. It was a nonsectarian organization from the start, establishing sometimes ad hoc interdenominational and multisectarian coalitions with any group that was sympathetic—the Irish, who were also anti-British; leaders of the National Association for the Advancement of Colored People, whose support was based on a shared history of persecution; ultra-Orthodox and non-Zionist rabbis whose entire communities were perishing in Europe; and others.

The organized Jewish community in America opposed their campaigns and fought them tooth and nail. Its leadership argued that the Bergson Group's press advertisements of Nazi violence in terse, brutal phrases were too provocative. One particularly strong ad read, "For Sale to Humanity 70,000 Jews; Guaranteed Human Beings at $50 a piece." By splashing the word *Jew* all over the press, the committee managed not only to keep awareness of the extermination on the public agenda day by day, month by month, but also to defy the sacred commandment of genteel, assimilated Jewish society at the time—that is, not to be too "Jewish" about being Jewish.

Another accusation leveled against Hillel and his colleagues was that they represented no one but themselves and were acting without a mandate. To the American Jewish leadership, they seemed like greenhorn upstarts, with no legitimate or natural constituency. Nonetheless, and much to the dismay of these leaders, in terms of both public impact and public support they were at least partially and belatedly successful (far more than one might have imagined) and apparently more efficient and effective than the established American Jewish leadership.

As a final point against it, the Bergson Group was identified with the Revisionists and the Irgun. Within the Zionist camp—which was a minority among the American Jewish community—rivalries were strong, and the Revisionist party in particular was much maligned and marginalized. The Jabotinsky plan for the massive evacuation of European Jewry raised much opposition among American Jewish leaders, feeding on their fear of arousing anti-Jewish sentiments and accusations of dual loyalty. The majority of the Zionist leadership was aligned with the labor movement, which portrayed Jabotinsky as a fascist, making him anathema to this group of mostly liberal democrats. In fact, the Revisionists themselves did little to support the emergency committee and by the end had joined the opposition.

Historians credit the efforts of the emergency committee with contributing to Roosevelt's decision to form the War Refugee Board in January 1944. This was the only agency created by the American government during the war that aimed at rescuing Jews. Established very late, and with meager funds, the board focused its activities mainly on Hungary and supported various rescue operations there, including those of Raoul Wallenberg. The board has been attributed with the rescue of approximately two hundred thousand Jews.

A NEW VIEW OF NATIONALISM AND CITIZENSHIP

In America, Hillel discovered that nations were in fact political and civic entities rather than organic cultural communities, as they were understood to be in Eastern Europe and Palestine; one could, for example, be both American and Jewish without the one identity threatening the other. For Hillel, distinguishing between Jewish as religious affiliation and Hebrew as national affiliation both reflected reality and provided a solution to the problem of dual loyalty. The Jews in America were Jewish by religion and American by nationality. In Palestine, they were Jewish by religion and Hebrew by nationality. The tragedy of European Jewry was that they were denied the liberty of choosing their nationality and were frequently not accepted into the body politic. The entire raison d'être of Zionism became clear to Hillel: to grant this freedom of choice to Jews.

A discourse of Hebrew—as opposed to Jewish—nationalism had been circulating for decades in certain Jewish intellectual circles in Europe and Palestine. This discourse linked the Jewish national revival in the nineteenth century with the ancient Hebrew, or Canaanite, nation in Palestine. Hillel, who had close relationships with leading members of what came to be known as the Canaanite movement, drew upon the secular and political elements of the Hebrew idea but saw the Hebrew nation as the natural, historical development of the Jewish nation rather than a *new* nation distinct from the earlier Jewish one. His experience with representatives of other ethnic groups in the United States, including his political cooperation with Greek Americans and Irish Americans, led him to the understanding that one can form subtle distinctions in identity without the need to make dramatic separations. An American Jew can identify with Jews in Palestine or Europe without being part of the same nation or sharing, necessarily, the same political interests. The Hebrew nation does not deny its historical origins, nor does it demand a severing of relations with members of the Jewish religion. It does, however, constitute a new political community. It is the modern, nationalist embodiment of the historic Jewish people. In a prescient article he wrote in 1945 titled "Post Zionism," Hillel stated:

> We are neither anti- nor non-Zionist. We are post-Zionist. We recognize the great merits of that movement in the past—in a free Palestine monuments and highways will be named in its honor—but the Zionist program today is archaic. . . . In view of the fact that more than ten million Jews live outside of Palestine, and are not in displaced persons camps or in danger, but enjoy full citizenship in many lands, the insistence upon a world Jewish nation is bound to ensnare many good Americans, Frenchmen, etc., who are Jews, in a difficult and ugly situation.

IN THE NEW STATE OF ISRAEL

In 1948, with Israel's Declaration of Independence, Hillel returned to Israel. For the first time in his life he became a citizen.

Having managed to maneuver so well in the American political sphere, Hillel internalized the tenets of liberal democracy and the American model of civic national identity, the power of the hyphen. This put him, in the Israeli political landscape, someplace in far left field. He returned to Israel charged and anxious to see his political vision implemented, to establish what he considered the fundamentals of a democratic republic: the separation of religion from nationality, the secularization of the "Jewish" state, the recognition of the Hebrew/Israeli nation that would be able and willing to incorporate both Muslims and Christians as equals. It would be a democratic republic unified by a liberal national identity, pluralistic and inclusive. In Hillel's vision there would be no national minorities, but a singular liberal nation that would treat its citizens equally. Unlike binationalism, another approach that emerged in the Yishuv during Mandatory times, which sought equal rights for the Jewish and Palestinian nations regardless of the relative size of their populations, Hillel's civic understanding viewed religious, cultural, and even national identities as irrelevant to citizenship in the Hebrew Republic.

But the political landscape he encountered upon his arrival had little in common with either the American landscape or the landscape he had left years earlier. Six months after his arrival, Hillel was elected to the Constituent Assembly, along with four colleagues from the emergency committee, on the ticket of the

Revisionist-inspired Herut Party. His return to political life in Israel, however, was short lived and accompanied by growing frustration.

The Constituent Assembly's purpose was to draft a constitution. "Rules of the game" were essential in Hillel's eyes, necessary not only to define basic notions and ideas but to put boundaries on the power of the Mapai political machine. On the eve of the Constituent Assembly's first session, David Ben-Gurion, then the prime minister, declared it to be the first Knesset (parliament), thus indefinitely delaying the writing of a constitution. Hillel stood up and cried "Putsch!," implying that this was an illegal attempt to take over a legitimate government. Years later, when his close friend Shulamit Aloni, the founder of the Israeli Civil Rights Party and one of the few staunch Israeli liberals, searched the minutes of that first historic session, she discovered that his interjection was erased, leaving no official trace of the objection of Knesset member Hillel Kook.

Increasingly marginalized in Herut by Begin and with his outburst against the "putsch" duly ignored, Hillel and his close friend Eri—the only son of Ze'ev Jabotinsky—split from Herut, leaving the Knesset at the end of their first term. Shortly afterward, he returned to the United States, hoping that perhaps in a generation or two, Israelis would be free of the memories of persecution, of what he increasingly referred to as their "ghetto mentality," and would be open to his style of liberal politics. He went back to Israel in the late 1960s, eager to reenter the political arena and implement his ideas. Over the years there were numerous attempts and projects, an independent evening newspaper, and endless conversations with different groups who felt, as he did, disenfranchised and distanced from what was known as the tribal bonfire. But sadly, as time passed, Hillel's vision grew more and more distant, with what he saw as parochial politics gaining the upper hand. The traditional categories that he spent his life eluding failed to fade away. In the many interviews he gave, he continued to baffle his readers: he was neither Left nor Right, hawk nor dove. All he wanted, he would insist, was a discussion of fundamentals, of basic issues.

A follower of Jabotinsky denounced by his own tribe, a leftist to the Right and a right-wing fanatic to the Left, Hillel Kook remained isolated and alienated in the new Israeli political discourse. The growing interest in his life since his passing away in 2001—seen in an off-Broadway play called *The Accomplices,* numerous documentary films, and a number of dissertations and history books—is testimony, perhaps, to the lingering relevance of his ideas but also to the possibilities and paths not taken in Israel's early history.

SUGGESTIONS FOR FURTHER READING

Agassi, Joseph. *Liberal Nationalism for Israel: Towards an Israeli National Identity.* Jerusalem: Gefen Press, 1999.

Rapaport, Louis. *Shake Heaven and Earth: Peter Bergson and the Struggle to Save the Jews of Europe.* Jerusalem: Gefen Press, 1999.

Wyman, David. *The Abandonment of the Jews: America and the Holocaust, 1941–1945.* New York: Pantheon, 1984.

Wyman, David, and Rafael Medoff. *A Race against Death: Peter Bergson, America, and the Holocaust.* New York: New Press, 2002.

PART THREE

A State Is Born; a Nation Is Dispersed

IT IS IMPOSSIBLE TO EXAGGERATE the consequences of the 1948 war in Palestine. For the Palestinian people, it meant utter disaster: the loss of well over 70 percent of the territory of Mandate Palestine, the destruction of more than five hundred villages, the scattering of upward of three-quarters of a million refugees across at least six countries (in fact, the world), and the decimation of their political life. For the newly established State of Israel, it was a veritable miracle: out of the ashes of the Holocaust, against the invading armies of five countries and a Palestinian population that outnumbered them roughly two to one, Jews achieved political sovereignty over a territory that was considerably larger than what they had controlled before the war and almost 40 percent greater than what was allotted to the Jewish state in the 1947 UN Partition Resolution.

As important for Israel, the Palestinian Arab population of the areas encompassed by the state decreased from its prewar level of between 750,000 and 874,000 (depending on the source) to about only 160,000, some 14 percent of Israel's population of 1,730,000 after the war. The percentage would shrink further in the next decade as approximately 600,000 Middle Eastern and North African Jews immigrated to Israel, tipping the demographic balance toward the country's Jewish population.

The first generation born after the 1948 war saw the slow emergence of two new identities, Israeli and Palestinian, whose substance and contours were radically different than what the founders of Zionism or the early Palestinian nationalist leaders could have imagined. The chapters in this section offer individual stories that reflect these changes in Jewish Israeli and Palestinian Arab identity, subjectivity, and political and social life.

The newly created Israeli identity was an amalgam of several distinct components. The dominant group demographically, as well as politically and culturally, comprised several generations of veteran ashkenazi immigrants (largely from the Second through Fifth Aliyot) and their Palestine-born children. Joining them were tens of thousands of European Jewish refugee survivors from the Second World War. Hundreds of thousands of Jewish immigrants from Muslim countries augmented a smaller North African and Yemeni Jewish community in the decade and a half after 1948; as is well known, they found themselves politically, economically, and culturally marginalized in the ashkenazi-dominated state.

Modern Israeli history starts not in Israel but, in significant ways, in Eastern and Central Europe. This is not always evident in Israeli historiography, which sees the restoration of Jewish sovereignty in a nation-state as the inexorable aim of Jewish history. In so doing, it shares the teleological bias of other nationalist histories, all of which provide only partial explanations of what moves people. The chapters by Gershon Shafir, Yaron Tsur, and Aziza Khazzoom reflect the myriad factors that pushed and in some cases pulled Jews to Israel in the wake of the 1948 war. One crucial element of this dynamic was growing anti-Jewish sentiment in Muslim countries where large populations of Jews lived, including Morocco, Algeria, Egypt, Iraq, and Iran, although in many cases this was either exacerbated by the actions of the Israeli government (as in Egypt and Iraq) or was less a factor in the mass migration of Jews to the newly created State of Israel than were arrangement made by the Israeli and local governments that compelled them to leave their homes (particularly in Iraq and Morocco) even when they still felt relatively secure.

In Europe, the Holocaust left little but absolute destruction in its wake. Shafir's narrative of his father's arrival in Israel from Hungary, "Joseph Spronz: From the Holocaust to a Safe Shore" (chapter 11), explores both the rapid deterioration in the socioeconomic conditions of Jews in Hungary, from relatively privileged to outcast, and the need for radical readjustment to the new Israeli social order and its bureaucratic machinery as part of the search for safety. It also diversifies the ashkenazi dimension of the well-known narrative, recounted in Kazzoom's and Tsur's chapters, of cultural and other structural forms of discrimination against Sephardi and mizrachi Jews in Israel, as Hungarian Jews were quickly positioned at the bottom of the ashkenazi ethnic hierarchy. Yoshka's life is a portrait of searching for refuge and struggling to retain human integrity through brutal buffering, from Nazism to Stalinism, only to end up ethnically marginalized in a new-old homeland.

Tsur's "The Brief Career of Prosper Cohen" (chapter 13) explores how members of the rapidly expanding Moroccan Jewish community in Israel struggled with their new lives and environment, which in so many ways was radically different from the society in which their community had lived in relative peace and security for upward of one thousand years. In particular, the life story of Cohen, an attorney who arrived in Israel only months after its creation, presents a complex picture of a Moroccan Jewish community that the literature too often describes in unitary and simplistic ways. Tsur demonstrates through the unfolding of Cohen's life in Israel that the erstwhile Moroccan community consisted of at least three classes: the mass of nonelite Moroccans and two sets of elites, a French-educated and Francophone group that could be described, albeit problematically, as Western and secular, and an Arabic- and Judeo-Arabic-speaking elite which in many respects was equally as modernizing as its French-speaking coreligionists but remained culturally rooted in the local Moroccan environment and culture, including its Islamic component.

Cohen's experience and struggles in Israel reveal how all these subcommunities faced significant obstacles against integration into the ashkenazi-dominated society and remind us of the heterogeneous character of Jewish life and its modernization in Morocco preceding the exodus. More specifically, they help clarify that the power of the ashkenazim often served to blur the reality of the immigrant others, the nonashkenazim—their identities, interests, and strategies as they sought to make their way to membership in the Yishuv and the Jewish state.

Khazzoom's "A Tale of Baghdad and Tel Aviv" (chapter 14) reminds us of the importance of understanding the historical differences between the Jewish communities that emigrated from the Muslim world and of placing the stories of women front and center in any consideration of how Jewish Israeli or Palestinian society emerged. As important, it highlights the ambivalent roots of Jewish modernization in the era leading up to the rise of Zionism, a modernization that was also occurring, in a different but related form, among the mizrachi, or eastern Jews, and among their North African coreligionists. Khazzoom's narrative explores how Iraqi Jews experienced the European, specifically French-led modernization effected through the Alliance Israélite Universelle in Baghdad. Her protagonist, Rachel, grew up in the midst of this process, in which the local Jewish community increasingly saw the education of women as a crucial component.

Moreover, Rachel's experiences growing up in prewar Baghdad deromanticize the complex narrative of relations between the Jewish community and its Muslim and Christian neighbors in favor of a more honest portrayal of their myriad interactions and connections. Despite the attention devoted to these issues by scholars, "Arabs did not loom large" in Rachel's daily life or consciousness, pointing to the fact that the integration of Jews with Arabs in Iraq affected the worlds of adult men more than those of young middle-class girls. This dynamic would help explain the lack of cultural connection between newly arrived immigrants and the remaining Palestinian population in Israel after 1948, even as both were on the periphery of the dominant ashkenazi society and, to varying extents, spatially marginalized and dislocated as well.

The Israeli state's denigration of their Middle Eastern or North African heritage ensured that most mizrachi Jews would distance themselves from Palestinians, with whom many shared a common culture, language, and, at least in theory, class perspective vis-à-vis the country's ashkenazi elite. Indeed, within Israel, at the farthest margins were Palestinians, who until 1966 lived under military law despite being granted official citizenship. Between the poles of Jewish and Palestinian identity were the Bedouins and the Druze, who saw their identities refashioned and concretized in an unprecedented manner in the decades after 1948. Both were forced to conform to the constrained and subordinate position articulated for them by an Israeli state (in whose territory most members of both groups wound up when its borders were drawn) that conferred greater benefits and privileges of citizenship to them in return for their service in the armed forces than the majority of Palestinians under Israeli jurisdiction enjoyed.

Safa Abu-Rabia's story of Bedouin slaves in post-1948 Israel (chapter 15) points to one of the most complex webs of identity, power, and territory in all of Israel/Palestine. Although long a vital part of the political, social, and economic ecologies of Palestine, Bedouins, like the Druze, have always had an ambivalent relationship with Palestinian national identity. The State of Israel tried to capitalize on this by according them greater opportunities for citizenship rights through service in the Israel Defense Forces, in the process formally separating the Arab identity of the Bedouin from the specifically Palestinian identity of the majority of non-Jewish Arabs in the new state. Yet Bedouins did not and still do not exist merely on the geographic and socioeconomic margins of Israel, although a large share of their population to this day lives in unrecognized villages with little or no public service or infrastructure.

Bedouin society is highly complex and conflicted, with a hierarchy based on factors such as landownership, gender, and, as Abu-Rabia's story reveals, racially based de facto slavery that lasted well into the twentieth century. This practice's legacy, it is clear, includes deep discrimination within the community against black Bedouins to this day. Yet their gradual integration into Israeli society, however incomplete, has allowed black and landless "white" Bedouins to become effectively the equals of the "white" landowning Bedouins who traditionally were the dominant group in their community. This process is challenging not only the traditional markers and boundaries of identity within Bedouin society but also, Abu-Rabia's narrative shows, the basic contours of Israeli identity, as poor Bedouin neighborhoods become home to families where the other spouse is Ethiopian, "Russian," or just plain Israeli, "creating a new ethnicity" and offering yet more complexity to the shaping of Israeli and Palestinian identities.

The nuances of Bedouin identities in Israel point to the highly complex and multivalent nature of Palestinian identity and through it, Israeli identity as well. The geographic dispersion of Palestinians—throughout Israel, the West Bank and Gaza, and a newly formed Palestinian Diaspora that runs the gamut from an emergent economic elite based largely in the Gulf countries and Jordan to the largely poor inhabitants of five dozen refugee camps located in all the neighboring states—has only increased this dynamic. Regardless of where they settle, Palestinians attempt to preserve and rebuild their identity while not relinquishing their desire to return—or, for those who remained in Palestine, their steadfastness (*sumud*).

Rochelle Davis's "Matar 'Abdelrahim: From a Palestinian Village to a Syrian Refugee Camp" (chapter 10) offers a quintessential story of refugee existence in the decades after 1948. 'Abdelrahim was born in the village of Nahaf, near Acre, and his youth was shaped by the intensifying conflict not merely between Zionism and Palestinian Arab nationalism but with the British government as well. From watching British police beat his father during the 1936–39 revolt to eking out a bare existence as a refugee in Damascus and finally building his own life, 'Abdelrahim had experiences that, like those of the Bedouins described by Abu-Rabia, reveal how post-1948 Palestinian social life became, as he described it, an unprecedented "social melting pot. . . . The hand of fate had dragged [people] from their previously disparate lives and varied social standings to meld them together in a single crucible." For many young men, including 'Abdelrahim, these experiences ultimately led to joining one of the many resistance groups that regularly infiltrated Israel in the two decades after 1948. His frustration with and betrayal by Arab countries whose territory he traversed to get into and out of Israel point to the reality that however much rhetorical support the Arab world gave their cause, on the ground Palestinians had few friends among their neighbors.

Ramzy Baroud explores the life of his father, another peasant refugee, from the village of Beit Daras, near Gaza, in "The Trees Die Standing" (chapter 12). Mohammed Baroud was born in the final years of the Mandate and became a refugee when his family fled the Jewish conquest of his village in the days leading up to the declaration of the Israeli state. Like tens of thousands of their fellow peasants in southern Palestine, they wound up living in a tent in Gaza.

Baroud's story parallels that of Gazan society as a whole. From the most humble of beginnings he rose to became a soldier in the Egyptian army, a migrant in Saudi Arabia, a *fida'i* fighter, a petty tradesman, and ultimately a modestly successful entrepreneur. Along this journey he faced down another Israeli invasion and lost a child to the occupation and his wife to the First Intifada before slowly dying, along with much of Gaza, in the midst of the Israeli siege during the Al-Aqsa Intifada. As it progresses, Mohammed's story slowly becomes his son's, and we get a unique vision of how two generations of Gazans struggled both to resist occupation and to create a viable life and identity for themselves under what for the entirety of their lives has been foreign rule—British, Egyptian, and Israeli.

10

Matar 'Abdelrahim

From a Palestinian Village to a Syrian Refugee Camp

Rochelle Davis

This chapter consists of selections from two autobiographical volumes written by Matar 'Abdelrahim, a Palestinian refugee from the village of Nahaf, in the district of Acre, and selections from a short interview I conducted with him in 2005. 'Abdelrahim's autobiographies were published under the titles *Udfununi hunaka: sira filastiniya yahlum bil-watan* (Bury me there: the story of a Palestinian dreaming of the homeland; Damascus: Dar al-Shajara, 1995, 361 pp.) and *Shadhaya min 'omri* (Shards of my life; Damascus: Dar al-Shajara, 2004, 206 pp.). The covers of the books describe them as novels, likely to avoid the censors as well as any potential embarrassment to his family and colleagues. When I interviewed him, he clarified that these were autobiographical volumes about his life, reflecting his experiences and musings on them.

These translated selections attempt to capture some of his experiences between 1936 and 1978 and include his memories of village life, his time serving in the Palestine Police Force, the trauma of becoming a refugee and living in refugee camps, and his and others' stories of love, family pressures, being Palestinian, joining the Palestinian resistance, and spending time in jail. While in Syria, 'Abdelrahim was arrested for his political beliefs and activities a number of times, and thus some of the details in the stories are missing or vague, likely due to a need to protect himself and his family. I have provided historical background for the selected passages for the English reader.

> Our village of Nahaf was located near Acre, on the absolute edge of what my young mind believed to be an eternal sea. When I would look out to the horizons, I would think there was nothing beyond. It was as if I were standing on the shore of death

itself. But looking back landward, I now realize that I spent the brightest times of life in my village, the time of a beloved childhood, from which I still recall living images and events as if they come to me in unforgotten dreams. These feelings, that I actually still live in the slopes of the Galilee Mountains or the Jarmaq Mountains, have not left me—that I live in my village of Nahaf, in my house and in my country, on the earth that covers my roots, and the land of my people. I feel now as if I am a passerby in the city of exile here in Damascus.

In 1936 the Palestinians began a general strike against the British Mandate that lasted for six months. It was primarily a rural and popular military insurgency against the British authority and the Zionist settlements and organizations. The revolt that it sparked continued until Britain entered World War II in September of 1939. The British cracked down on Palestinians by confiscating weapons, implementing policies of collective punishment on whole villages, and jailing, exiling, and in some cases executing those involved. The Palestinians saw the revolt as a defiant victory that resulted in the 1939 White Paper, which restricted Jewish immigration to Palestine, among other concessions. But the long-term effect of the revolt was that the British exiled the Palestinians' leadership and restricted their access to weapons and military training while allowing Jews to arm themselves, so the two groups were very differently prepared for the war of 1948.

I was eight years old in 1936, the beginning of the revolt against the British Mandate and Zionist immigration to Palestine. My father was away for a few days (later I found out he was part of the revolt), when one evening forty shadowy figures came to our house in the northern edge of the village that abutted the forest. We watched these tired figures dismount from their horses and realized they were fighters in the revolt. They came to the house and asked my mother if they could see my father, Abu Matar. She told them that he was elsewhere in the village and would return shortly, but in the meantime they should come inside. She sent me into the darkness to inform my uncles, who, along with my mother and the rest of the women and men of the village, speedily provided a meal for the men. After they ate, my mother served them all tea, and she informed them that my father was away on an errand and would be back in three days. When I got older and matured more, I understood why my mother had not told them from the outset that my father was not there—our traditions of hospitality and making the guest feel at ease were one of many things I learned from her.

It was during this same year that the British Army surrounded our village, ordered all of the inhabitants out of their houses, and gathered them on the threshing grounds to the west of the village. I was there with my mother and grandparents when we heard explosions and saw smoke rising into the sky; we immediately understood that they were blowing up some of the houses. When the British left we headed home, but some of the village children met us on the path, telling us that our house was one of the ones destroyed. I ran back to our house because I wanted to see my father's reaction. He had escaped outside of the military cordon when they encircled the village, but I knew he would be there. Would he cry, shout, or curse? I saw him standing quietly surrounded by some crying female relatives, and I could tell the depth of the pain he felt, looking at his house, broken into jagged piles, and the remnants of our possessions—furniture, clothing, food stores, even memories—mixed with rubble. I knew, even at that young age, how important homes are to us, how they are part of our being, and I remember shouting at my father that they had destroyed our house. He replied, "We will not leave. We are staying, my son."

While my father usually escaped these military raids and cordons of our village, one time they caught him, and the English officer, a man named Mr. Black, began beating him with a stick and yelling at him in front of the villagers who had, yet again, been herded to the threshing floor. My mother held me tightly in her arms, pressed close against my grandparents, and I could sense their fear. My father remained standing, proud and silent, until they hit him on the head and he fell to the ground. I could see the breath of the villagers in the cold air, the vapor transforming into puffs of anger, and cold, sharp glances at the British. Fearing the rising fury of the villagers, the soldiers stopped their beating and got in their cars and drove away, amid curses and raised fists. It was this generation, these men who began the revolt, who played a crucial role in the creation of our nationalist sentiment. Our teachers in the village were also part of this revolt, but in a different way. Rif'at Ghnaym from Safad, Muhammad al-Salih from Nahaf, and our principal, Shafiq 'Ubayd from Acre, did not arm us with weapons but instead spent their lives combating the deficiencies in our society, setting a higher standard, spreading education and knowledge, and building human potential.

When I was thirteen, I began working as a shepherd in our village. My relatives and some of the other villagers put their sheep and goats in my care, and I would take them out every day to graze, following in the footsteps of those experienced shepherds who knew the land better than I. In exchange for my labor, my family received a portion of the harvested wheat. My problem, however, was that I was ashamed to be a shepherd instead of the educated and cultured person I so desperately wanted to be. I knew that the angels had sent out the shepherds upon the birth of Jesus and that the Prophet David himself was a shepherd, and Jesus too, but that did not assuage my shame. I spent two years as a shepherd, and during that time I did not dare to approach the school because I was too embarrassed to talk to my former classmates. Then I began working on the road-building crew, and that strenuous work developed my physical strength and body. Despite the difficulties, I experienced the height of happiness and satisfaction each week, when I would put the entirety of my salary in my father's hand.

In 1944, I began working at the British Munitions Depot (we called it the Bomb Camp) near Acre. A truck carried us workers from the village in the morning and returned us in the evening. Inside the cavernous warehouse, the workers, covered in dust, made a huge amount of noise as they scurried around with the heavy boxes of munitions on their backs. I had lots of time to think about my family, my life, and my frustrated dreams. I met another young man there, named Ahmad 'Awwad, from Deir Hanna village. He was a peasant with a close connection to his village but was working at the camp to earn money for the hand of a village girl he loved but whom he couldn't marry because her father considered him too poor. Together, we pooled our money and bought books whose stories were small blessings and moments of sheer pleasure. We would talk about what we read and share our life experiences and dreams.

We were both let go from this job in 1945 with the end of World War II, and Ahmad convinced me to take the exam and join the Palestine Police Force. The difficulty was in convincing my family to support such an endeavor that would take me, their eldest son, far away from them. I started with my grandfather, who helped me convince my father. It was my mother, however, who feared my leaving the most, and she cried and did her best to change my mind. But she knew that I would go. I was sent to Jerusalem, and there I passed some of the loneliest days of my life. Terrible pangs of longing for home seeped into my days, amid intensive police training and the easy companionship of my cadet colleagues. When I returned to the village to visit after the training, my father was full of pride and satisfaction, even though I was going to be posted far away from them, in Jerusalem. By the end of the British Mandate, I had not been involved in any fighting, but throughout the first months of 1948 I was burning inside because of what was happening to my people—the battle of Qastal, the massacre of villagers at Deir Yassin. I knew I had to quit out of principle, so that I would change and be a force of change. But they ordered us to report to the police station nearest our home villages, and I was transferred to Acre. Getting there was more difficult, because of fighting and checkpoints, and when I got to Haifa, only fifteen miles south of Acre, I found the road closed. I finally took a boat, full of men, women, and children trying to make the same journey.

Haifa fell to the Zionist forces on April 22, 1948, less than two weeks after I had arrived in Acre. Our immediate job was to receive and provide for the waves of Palestinians fleeing the fighting, mines, shells, and explosions in Haifa in the small boats they used to cross the bay. We would work for twenty-four hours and then return to our villages for the next twenty-four hours. Luckily, I was on my day off back at my village when the city of Acre fell three weeks later to the newly declared Israeli forces, on May 16, 1948. The Israelis began attacking the nearby villages, the ones that hadn't been attacked and evacuated previously. Our resistance at this time was entirely local, uncoordinated with any of the other movements or armies or even the other villages. Each man was supposed to buy a firearm from wherever possible, although the one hundred Palestinian pounds that it cost [approximately $3,800 today] meant that a family had to sell its cow or a mother had to pawn her gold. There were five of us who had served in the Palestine Police Force, and we wanted to train the villagers to fight using the military tactics we had learned in our police training. We succeeded to some extent and attempted to defend the neighboring villages. But the caravans of displaced people passing by our village grew larger and more destitute daily.

My own exile from my beloved homeland began on the evening of October 30, 1948, when we were busy crushing olives in the press. Half of the olives were crushed and pressed, and the oil was packed in jars and boilers. We were about to begin moving the oil to the house and returning the rest of the olives to the press when we

learned that the Arab Army had suddenly withdrawn to Lebanon, without informing anyone of its intentions. The family drew together to discuss what we should do.
My uncle said to me in the tone of a command, "Listen, you need to leave with the
families and take the women and girls to safety. We must protect our honor before
everything else." I responded to him that I had promised that I would not leave our
village and that I would stay and fight and die for my village and my homeland. "Listen," my uncle said, "take them to Lebanon, and then you can return to your suicide
pact." My mother was crying and said, "Listen to him, my son. I've had enough pain,
enough death, enough until the end of my days." My younger siblings hung sobbing
on my clothes. I could no longer see anything around me; I only listened. But I did
not return, and I never saw my grandmother and grandfather again.

While some people stayed in the village, my family and others ended up scattered
in many places and throughout many countries. Some of us went looking for others,
and all of us searched through the remnants of fighters to identify villagers and kin.
We did not meet again until much later. We passed along roads like gypsies, through
villages and cities, leaving behind us the mountains, the sea, and the birds to arrange
their nests in our absence. We were sentenced to dying in the country of exile.

Nahaf village still exists in Israel today, with many of its original inhabitants;
only some became refugees like Matar 'Abdelrahim and his family. In 1948 the village had about twelve hundred residents, while today they number more than ten
thousand Palestinian Arab Israelis. I asked Matar if he had ever returned to visit
his village. He told me no, and that

> my son works in an Internet shop, so he showed me pictures of Nahaf from today.
> I didn't recognize it because of the tall apartment buildings. My village was simple,
> a small house surrounded by a yard, the people that we knew, the places we used to
> sit and talk. . . . All these things have changed. I don't want the village to be like this,
> I want it as it was before. I used to think that if I returned, I would find everything
> still the same. I don't want anything to change, I want the people to be the same, but
> people die and are buried, the village changes.

I asked him what it was it like to write about a place he hadn't seen in almost
sixty years.

> I want to write about loving the village and people and what that love means. What
> is life, and why does it happen in the ways we know it? But I won't write about the
> stones of the village nor record how many families there were or that sort of thing.
> There is someone who wrote a 360-page book about Saffuriya village—he wrote all
> the names of the villagers and about who got degrees and graduated from university
> and who didn't. But this kind of writing is useless. What is useful about saying that
> I had a cousin and he studied at the university, and also we used to have a tract of
> land, and we used to plant this crop or that one? I don't want to write like this. Why
> keep crying over ruins? I must cry over our cause as Palestinians and the world. I
> would like to understand how this world works, about God, and about our feelings as

humans. I don't want to write about stones or about how we used to have a big house and whether we were rich or poor.

IN EXILE

On November 6, 1948, we arrived in Hama, Syria, by train. There were more than fifteen hundred people on the train, and we were all herded off by the Syrian police, who gathered us up and took us to the Grand Mosque. We spent a number of nights there, and the Syrian police brought us bread, canned food, and other things. Poor Syrians came to see us, looks of sympathy on their faces. But a rumor whirled among us that they were going to move us out and distribute us among the nearby villages. I heard my father say that he wondered if they would allow us to go to Damascus, where he thought our prospects for finding a way to survive would be better. I spoke with the officer in charge about transport, and he managed to arrange a bus to get us there the next day.

It was a cold and dreary night that we arrived in this great city. My family and I sat on the pavement of one of the streets, watching cars, people, and animals pass by. We accompanied a passing sheikh [religious leader] from a nearby mosque on his way to evening prayers and spent the night in the mosque. The next day we began looking for someplace to escape from the November cold, when we met someone who took pity on our situation and brought us to the basement of his building. He told us that we could sleep there until we found something better. The basement reeked of the mold and humidity oozing from walls that also sheltered spiders and cockroaches. I gathered a few bags of cement and spread a big pile of sand and rocks over the floor of the basement. The next day we covered the floor with thick sheets of cardboard and sat on top of them.

The responsibility of supporting my family—my father, mother, and four siblings, one of whom was only six months old—weighed upon me. My father was a farmer who tended our olive and fruit trees, grew grain, raised tomatoes, and kept our family fed. My earnings and salary for the past seven years had helped the family with other necessities and allowed us to buy more land. I felt responsible for them, but what was I to do? How was I supposed to make sure they had food, clothing, and warmth? I had always been a strong young man, constantly envisioning my future. I never imagined that we would become refugees with no material possessions.

In Damascus I spent long hours asking for work in stores and every other place. When I tired, I sat on the edge of the sidewalk and stared blankly at the bright shops and restaurants alive with activity.

It occurred to me to ask for some bread or coins from the owner of a restaurant or one of the stores, but immediately I felt as if another person inside me, a man full of pride, stopped me. This man reminded me of my country; he pulled me away from the denigration of being a refugee and he protected me from humiliation and shame. I quickly expelled the thought of begging that had briefly but bitterly passed through my mind. Much later, I came to realize that we cannot be responsible for our dark thoughts, especially when they are born of hunger, oppression, and loss.

I explained my situation and that of my family to everyone that I met in the streets and markets, in front of movie houses and restaurants, and to those I asked for work. They would shake their heads, heads that to me seemed full of ease and happiness and empty of troubles. I don't think that what I said meant anything to them—in their eyes I was capable and strong and in the bloom of youth.

I struggled with what had befallen us, wondering why such a thing had happened to me. I am from a small village on the slopes of the Galilee Mountains; why me of all of the people on the planet to be placed in such a situation of difficulties and troubles? When I would return to our basement at the end of the night, my mother would meet me with tears in her eyes. Our harsh exile ate at her; the strange people all around were so different from the close social circle and frequent visits that had filled her life in our homeland. She wanted to carry with her our entire village: the buildings, streets, trees, and our loved ones. Instead, all at once everything and everyone was so far away, and everything she had touched was now gone. My father, however, was happiest when challenged by difficult circumstances, and at this time he said to me, "We will depend on the sweat of our brow to start again." Fifty years later, these words still guide my life.

The International Committee of the Red Cross first took care of the Palestinian refugees in Syria (as well as Lebanon and Jordan), followed in 1950 by the United Nations Relief and Works Agency for Palestinian Refugees (UNRWA), which took over providing services to the makeshift camps that had been set up for them. UNRWA still runs the schools and health care centers in all of the official camps and provides emergency food and supplies for registered refugees.

The International Committee of the Red Cross provided us refugees with dirt-colored tents on a small bit of land on the edge of the city. For us, it was the end of the world, between the empty sky and this unknown land, where hunger, fear, and depression had settled. We lived amid pools of water and mud, and the rain poured ceaselessly down the sides of the tents. No one was able to leave. The camp was made up of little pockets of people gathered together, forgotten on this vast, empty plot of land, abandoned to their own devices far from the city and any kind of communication with others. We were all lost in the thick darkness of a night that had emerged from the sadness of a cold, heartless daybreak. We feared the guards who monitored and ran the camp, and we passed the things we needed back and forth in silence. These were bitter days for the refugees; we felt subjugated and estranged, dependent upon others for everything. We had to turn to others even for our bread, which had once been the staple of our meals and was baked daily by our families from the wheat we had sown and harvested. Nostalgia dominated our minds, and longing burned in our hearts, but in the end hunger forced us to continue living. We realized that we had to put bread in the mouths of the hungry, no matter the circumstances. Somehow we needed to get beyond this misery and sense of being vanquished and resume our lives, which had been transformed: to get married, have children, and die. In this way, the camps were a theater of the absurd—a drama and a comedy at the same time.

During these days, what concerned me most was finding work, any work, no matter how hard, because I was trying to take care of the family. I was the one who had lived in Jerusalem, knew the ways of the city, had worked in a loading facility and as a policeman. My father was a farmer, and we were here, without land, without any place for him to practice the skills that were part of his very being. Some days I was lucky, other days I was not, and the uncertainty worried my mother. We stood in line, like everyone else, silently waiting. The hours passed slowly until it was our turn. Exhausted from standing, we would stuff our share of the aid rations into bags Mother brought and then haul them home on our shoulders.

In the camp, before the beginning of the organized Palestinian resistance movements, we would relive the happy times of the past through the stories we would tell one another, so distant from the times of troubles and restrictions we were living. One day, my friend Marwan told us a story about the girl he had loved. That story, like so many others, ended in 1948. Marwan farmed his land near the Na'ameen River between Acre and Haifa, planting, watering, harvesting, and sleeping in a small shelter in the warm summer months. The girl's name was Layla, and they would meet on the banks of the river and walk together. Some days Layla was late to visit him, and he would worriedly call out her name to the river, the plain, and the rocks, which echoed it back to him. But in the end, she always came. In the quiet, they could hear the sound of a distant song carried by a warm breeze emerging from the darkness to bounce off them both and disappear again. Marwan remembered the overwhelming emotions he felt the first time he touched her: he placed his hand on her waist, but she pushed it away, her eyes still on the river. Once, twice, and on the third time she didn't object. He held her hand until she felt his warm breath near her face. She turned her head away from him but did not leave, and when he kissed her, she returned his kiss. Marwan knew that he loved her, but with this kiss he felt a happiness, a complete happiness, that he had not known before, and kissed her more. Although she was breathing hard, she remained silent until she blurted out, "I will tell my mother." "Dear Layla," Marwan responded, "don't destroy my happiness with such a threat!" She laughed loudly and placed her head comfortably on his shoulder, saying that she would pray today, tomorrow, and forever for times like this with him. Marwan was sure that he was the only one in this world who loved and was loved like this. But their plans to be together forever were not to be. As they were walking together one day, they heard explosions nearby and saw flames coming from the direction of the village. She ran toward her house and her distressed family, casting a tearful glance at Marwan as she ran from him. Marwan continued on down the street amid the falling artillery shells, but his family was gone and the village almost empty. The few stragglers he found said that his family had headed north out of the village. So he joined up with the exodus from the destroyed and burned village. His heart jumped when he crossed the border into Lebanon and saw his family sitting in the shade of a small tree as waves of refugees streamed around them. He did not know what had happened to Layla and her family—were they in Lebanon or under the rubble of their home? He asked everyone he saw, frantically entreating these scattered people for news. Despair gradually drove him to sit alone in the Red Cross tent, refusing to talk to anyone, convinced that the terrible darkness that enveloped him would last forever. It was this agony that turned him into a man ready to rebel against the power that had wrought unimaginable, terrible destruction upon him and his people. Marwan was later one of the first who joined the ranks of the resistance. Committed to his beloved land and his beloved Layla, he vowed to embrace them both once again, and he honored this promise for the rest of his life.

Memories such as these reminded us of what we did not have, what we were missing. One day, some camp residents held a wedding, commensurate in simplicity and sadness with the situation in which we all found ourselves. The sound of the reed flute [*mijwiz*] kept time to the stamping of the feet of those few people dancing the *dabkeh*, to the songs in the throats of the singers, thick with longing and sorrow, and to the women singing their wedding wishes amid tears. The chaos of the camp made for a social melting pot, because here a Bedouin family was next to a peasant family, which was next to a family from the city. The hand of fate had dragged them from their previously disparate lives and varied social standings to meld them together in a single crucible.

In early 1951, the Syrian General Security [Directorate] approved my petition to join the Syrian police. The president of the Syrian Republic, Shukry al-Quwatli, had decided that the Palestinians could be residents of Syria with most of the rights and responsibilities due to Syrians yet without having to give up their Palestinian citizenship. After I passed all of the exams, I could feel a sense of relief and security wash over my family. My monthly income was 150 Syrian lira, which, when added to the UN rations we received, greatly improved our living situation. With the income from my job, we moved from the tent to live in a house in the Jaramana area.

Palestinians in Syria, from that time until the present, have had the same rights as Syrians to education, health care, and employment. They are not allowed to vote in elections, and they travel on Syrian travel documents, not passports, but they can and do serve in the armed forces and in government positions. The total number of Palestinians in Syria is more than five hundred thousand out of a total population of more than eighteen million, and they are fairly well integrated, living in cities and camps (the refugee camps generally host poor populations). This situation contrasts with that of Jordan, where Palestinians are estimated to be 50 percent of the population and have Jordanian passports, vote in elections, and have the same rights as all citizens of the state. However, since the early 1970s, Jordan has slowly eliminated Palestinians from the armed forces and government jobs, and thus they tend to predominate in commercial, educational, and service sectors. Palestinians in Lebanon, numbering more than four hundred thousand, have neither Lebanese citizenship nor any sort of equal rights. They are prohibited from owning property and working in any occupation that has a union (lawyers, doctors, teachers, engineers, etc.), thus relegating them largely to service jobs. They are treated as foreigners and pay foreign tuition rates for higher education and need permits for legal employment. The UN camps are the one exception where they can be employed in any profession. Over the past sixty years, Palestinians have been part of internal strife and civil war in both Jordan and Lebanon.

MY FATHER'S DECISION

Toward the end of 1951 my father decided to return to Occupied Palestine by slipping across the border. We spent our days anticipating his return to Syria and in constant fear for him as he crossed without papers into Jordan and then into Palestine. All of the worst scenarios crossed our minds. Maybe he wouldn't make it. Even if he did make it, how would he return across those same borders? If he was caught by Israel, they would accuse him of spying for an Arab country. And if he was caught by an Arab country, they would accuse him of spying for Israel. Then one evening, there was a gentle knock on the door, and our minds were at ease. My father told us his story, or at least what he wanted us to know. Torn, dirty, exhausted, he had arrived at his family's house in Nahaf, secretly crossing the same paths he had known so intimately during the revolt. He spent three days in the house with his mother, father, brother, and extended family. At night, he would walk around the village, recalling his memories of his life there. By the time he returned to us, he was no longer the same man. Gone was the optimistic, strong man I had worshiped all my life. His hope for life disappeared with his homeland and home.

After my father returned, he and Mother insisted that I get married. I had always maintained that I would not do so until we returned to Palestine. It was rare that I differed with my father's opinion, and I although I was inwardly adamant about my decision, I trembled with fear as I confronted him. At first he treated me with silence, but then he quietly argued that he was getting old and needed help. I could not resist his plea, and the wedding to my cousin took place on September 18, 1953. I sat alone in a room, then dressed myself and bathed without the traditional party. I was wearing the one shirt and pair of pants I owned that were not my police uniform. What was supposed to be a happy day was a sad one. We were coming to realize, in our own way, in our own time, that our exile was lasting longer than we had imagined it would.

RISING ARAB NATIONALISM

We were all living together, me and my bride and my parents and brothers and sisters, in one house on the Jaramana Road when we heard that Gamal Abdel Nasser, the new president of Egypt, had nationalized the Suez Canal on July 26, 1956. At that moment, I felt a fire in my heart, simultaneously lit in the hearts of Arabs everywhere, because of the defiant actions of this leader who took for Egypt what was rightfully hers, then fought the war of 1956 against the British, French, and Israelis. The joining of Egypt and Syria in 1958 in the United Arab Republic fanned these fires. At this time we were not only Palestinian or Lebanese, Syrian or Egyptian . . . we were Arab. Only a few years later, in 1961, a military coup in Syria brought this dream to an end. Despite the coup, people continued to fill the streets, in demonstrations

and marches, people of all different nationalist stripes, Ba'athists and Arab nationalists, students, professors, workers, farmers, soldiers, and officers. They all brought
about the Ba'athist revolution on March 8, 1963. However, the strength of this revolution began to fall apart, this revolution built on workers and peasants, Arab unity,
and democracy. And then the dismissals and executions began. These increased after
the attempted coup by the Nasserist Jasim 'Alwan in July, which had been supported
by the Palestinian fedayeen [guerrilla] groups. Suddenly, every Palestinian became
a suspect.

In the 1950s and early 1960s, Palestinian political groups re-formed following
the devastation of 1948. After the 1956 war in Egypt and the brief Israeli occupation
of the Gaza Strip (then under Egyptian administration), popular resistance to the
occupation set in motion more organized forms of political organizing and military training. Much of the inspiration for these groups came from people involved
in the newly formed Arab Nationalist Movement (ANM), which was threatening
to the regimes in Egypt, Syria, and Iraq with its pan-Arab rhetoric and push for
action. Matar's account that follows shows the resulting suspicion of Palestinians
in Syria because of their sympathies toward the ANM.

> I was still a traffic policeman in Damascus, and my salary of three hundred Syrian
> lira supported my whole family: my wife; our two sons, Nabil and Marwan; and my
> parents and siblings. My past experiences in life had made me wary, and I worried
> that I could not depend on this job to provide for us. I began to sense that I was
> being watched, partly due to the general animosity toward Palestinians but especially
> because I was known for my enthusiasm for Arab unity, which by now was a suspect
> idea. I received a notice of transfer from Damascus to a reserve division in the city
> of Suwayda, in southwestern Syria, and I was also called in for questioning. In other
> words, my future was limited: perhaps they would just dismiss me from my position,
> but also looming was the threat of prison.
>
> On the morning of one of the days in Suwayda, I was called in to see the head of
> the political unit, who smilingly shook my hand. "Why don't you work with us?" he
> asked. I knew what he meant, but I responded, "I do work and am prepared to go on
> any call, no matter how dangerous." He looked at me and said, "I know you know
> what I mean. I want you to cooperate with us on security matters. You can choose:
> work with us and get an extra salary or refuse and you'll be dismissed this week and
> you and your family will die of starvation." After ten days, on June 21, 1965, decision
> #1322 was recorded in the office of the prime minister, and I was dismissed from my
> position.

The head of the political unit in this story was asking Matar to work for the
intelligence service [*mukhabarat*] as an informant, most likely about fellow Palestinians, as a condition of keeping his job. Hiring people in this way allowed the
state to know what was going on among all of its different communities without
having to maintain a police or state presence in them. Matar does not provide

more details in this story because anyone reading his account in Arabic would understand the implications of being asked such a thing. What he shows, instead, is his refusal to inform on his community.

> My despair at losing my job did not last long, for I soon found work in one of the fancy hotels in Damascus. God saved me during these days because I met up with a teacher from my village, Riyad al-Khateeb, who during the 1936 revolt had been the first to take up arms, gathering the young and old around him, from our village and others, to take part in the revolt against the British Mandate rule over Palestine. At that time, he did not trust the leadership of the elite landowning families nor the traditional leadership nor the Arab Higher Committee. I was full of respect and love for this man, with his history of struggle, his knowledge and wisdom. So when he asked me to meet up with him, I considered it a great honor.
>
> At this time the Palestinian resistance had to meet in secret, which paradoxically meant in public places like restaurants, since the houses of the camp were monitored. I remember that he began with a question: "A long time has passed since we were displaced. Are we going to keep waiting? And exactly who are we waiting for to liberate our land?" I responded to him on that day, in a way that revealed the limits of my awareness, "What should we do? Is there anyone other than the Arab leaders who can do anything? Once they unify, they will fight, God willing." Riyad's answer was that we had to train ourselves now.
>
> Our next meeting was at his house; it was more of a library, actually, with very little furniture and just thousands of books, each with his handwritten annotations in the margins. He didn't care about clothing or how he looked; for him the important things were knowledge and beliefs. He knew that investing in people's minds was more important than physical infrastructure, and he spent his entire life pursuing that goal. He focused on our minds and ideas as part of our development in the resistance, in addition to military training.
>
> These meetings with him and the ideas that came from them changed the course of my life and allowed me to see a path to the future. During this period, politics became an essential part of my being. It was impossible for me to return to my dreams and shut the door on the Arab street, just as it was impossible to close the door on life, happiness, and sadness. I also met a childhood friend from my village who fought with me in 1948 and who had been one of the founders of the Arab Nationalist Movement [Harakat al-Qawmiyyeen al-'Arab].

Students and professors at the American University of Beirut formed the ANM in the 1950s to advocate for the establishment of an independent Arab nation and the liberation of Palestine. By 1967, due to internal disagreements, it had dissolved into a number of smaller, more focused movements, such as the Popular Front for the Liberation of Palestine (PFLP), which adopted a Marxist stance, and the Palestine Liberation Front (PLF), and in 1969, the Democratic Front for the Liberation of Palestine (DFLP) was formed. Matar likely joined one of these groups.

'Abdelkarim Hamad Qays Abu 'Adnan had fought together with Riyad in 1948, but they had not seen each other since, so when we all met it was an amazing reunion. We stayed up late that night, talking and dreaming of the coming victory and return. Abdelkarim and I pledged to be at the forefront of the resistance, and soon after we began recruiting members. Our work had to be conducted in total secrecy, so in houses far from the eyes of the regime and its police we conducted military training (without weapons) for groups of young men. To be doing something had an amazing effect. Action for the sake of the homeland lifted our sagging hearts, which had been dragged down by displacement, the misery of the camps, and the handouts we accepted from the international charitable organizations.

We were forced to forge travel documents and eventually were able to get fake identity cards and passports to travel in and to the surrounding countries. I cannot tell you how many nights my mother did not sleep, her maternal instinct alert that her son was in danger. She showed strength and bravery when the security services showed up at our house looking for me; they broke everything and tossed it all on the ground. Other times they waited patiently, and secretly, for me to return.

When I joined the resistance, I was still a young man. It was there that I witnessed people die and for the first time noticed how the body responds to pain, fear, and horror. I observed the black lines that despair carves into faces and was amazed by the bravery and strength these men displayed. I saw courage pushing people to meet death with a sardonic joke, their pride not allowing them to reveal the fear engulfing their soul.

The Palestinian resistance movements grew from popular movements, but they took over the structures put in place by the Arab League and the various Arab states. The Arab League established the Palestinian National Council (PNC), a legislative body, which first met in Jerusalem in 1964. The PNC founded the Palestinian Liberation Organization (PLO) to serve as its executive arm. At the same time, various popular resistance groups had formed over the years—groups such as the ANM but also Fatah (*Harakat al-Tahrir al-Watani al-Filastini*), whose agenda was purely nationalist and lacked the ideological center that many of the others had. These groups were secretive and radical and called for Palestinians to liberate Palestine through individual and collective armed struggle. Their members were known as fedayeen, and they were called the resistance (*al-muqawama*) or the revolution (*al-thawra*). This struggle—and its growth, support, and strategies—grew from and also influenced other third world and liberation struggles of the time, such as those in Cuba, Algeria, South Africa, and Vietnam, which were seen as successful models of guerrilla tactics and popular resistance. Between 1964 and 1968, the PLO and the resistance movements competed with one another. But the 1967 war and the loss of the remainder of Palestinian land to Israeli control, the bankrupt rhetoric of the Arab states, the momentous battle of Karameh in Jordan in 1968, and the rising popularity of the resistance movements allowed the fedayeen to take over the PLO. They decided to make it the representative of all of the Palestinian groups and movements, which it was, with the exception of a few small splinter groups, until the rise of Hamas during the First Intifada, in 1987. The resistance movements formed political bodies and military wings, and the fedayeen engaged in armed struggle with Israel. In Jordan, this lasted from the 1960s until 1970, when the fedayeen were killed or escaped during Black September, which were the battles of King Hussein and the Jordanian forces against the Palestinian resistance. The 1969 Cairo Accord allowed the PLO jurisdiction over the Palestinian refugee camps in Lebanon, so the PLO and the fedayeen based their organizing and military bases there until exiled to Tunisia as a result of the Israeli invasion in 1982. This event ended the resistance, and the cadres of fedayeen split up. Palestinians (and others) referred to Israel as Occupied Palestine for many years, particularly prior to 1967, when the West Bank and Gaza were occupied. People started using the term *Israel* more consistently in the 1990s.

OUR RESISTANCE

Along with my comrades Marwan, Walid, and Khalid, I would cross the borders of the Arab countries to connect with the other branches of the movement and to check out possible areas to cross borders into Occupied Palestine. These were not casual journeys, and we faced much danger as we moved secretly in the crevices of mountains and down the canyons, over barren hilltops and through thick forests of oak and pine. These were paths that many had walked on before us, different peoples throughout history, uncounted. The first of us to go was Khalid, who led one group of comrades off to enter Occupied Palestine. The moments of good-byes and our hugs carried both pain and hope. I listened as their footsteps grew more distant, the footsteps of our people, and their shadowy figures disappeared in the night. Would we one day meet again, reminisce, and write it down as we had lived it?

Khalid left for Palestine, and I was captured going in the other direction that night while returning the same way that I had come. I was furious with this Arab country [most likely Jordan] that I had to pass through to get to Palestine. The border guards who caught me saw my detention as a great thing, but I wondered how had they found me out. They led me to an isolation cell, where I stayed for weeks. Isolation is the one thing that a person cannot learn from, and I witnessed myself going crazy. During this period my small "tomb" was two and a half meters by one and a half meters, with a low roof that I would hit my head on when I stood up. The walls were covered with writings, drawings, strange shapes, and names mixing together and erasing one another. Every prisoner had wanted to leave some mark behind, here at the very least, letters in pen, chalk, and charcoal, black, white, and gray, and some fading brown ones that must have been blood. I learned that the act of remembering in this situation is tantamount to death and that memory and thought were my enemies.

One day, miraculously, they let us out of our cells, into the prison yard, where the sun was shining. We began getting an hour of this once a week. When they would return me to my cell, I paced back and forth, dreaming of some way to see the sun again—by scratching a hole in the wall with my nails or teeth even, any way to allow just one ray in.

It was a total surprise when I found in the prison courtyard my comrades Marwan and Walid, who had been captured days before and also tossed into this horrid desert prison. We sat in the shade of a eucalyptus tree with our arms around one another's shoulders, staring at each other without saying anything at first, and then we talked about what had happened and about our other comrades who were still on the outside. Walid introduced me to some of the other prisoners, amazing men who were full of respect and love for one another, ready to sacrifice themselves for their beliefs. Because of these unique people who enriched my spirit, I considered my time in prison, and even my torture, a victory. Despite or perhaps because of the calamities of my eviction from my homeland and my presence in the darkness of prison, these life experiences made me hold tightly to the idea of Palestine. Exploding inside me was a love for my homeland, like the pouring rush of a mountain spring, driving my actions and interactions, born of a fierce yearning.

Walid told us what had happened to him. We knew that he had fled his village as a boy in 1948 amid the chaos and fear and found himself alone in Lebanon. He thought his family had preceded him there, but instead they had hidden in the mountains and returned to their village after the fighting stopped, becoming citizens of the Israeli state. He too eagerly joined the first fedayeen, with the goal of sneaking back to his village in Occupied Palestine and seeing his family. Twenty years after he left, he crossed the border, and on one jet-black night he returned to his village. He left as a boy and was returning a man, but he wanted to return as that child into the embrace of his mother and father. He found the house in the darkness of the night and knocked quietly on the door. His brother Mahmoud, who was only three years old when he had last seen him, opened the door. They stared at each other, silently taking in the years of absence, and then suddenly fell into each other's arms. When they finally separated, scarcely a moment had passed before they embraced again. Mahmoud took Walid in to see his aged father, who asked Mahmoud for water, and Mahmoud raised a spoon to his father's mouth so he could drink. "Walid has returned," he told him. His father reached out and touched Walid's face, searching its contours for a lost child and finding instead a man. Walid grabbed his father's hand, kissed it several times, hugged him tightly, and then kissed his chest over his heart. His mother, he learned, had died three years earlier. Walid spent seven days in his father's room, the room of his dearest childhood memories, with the windows shuttered in case the bright sunlight and cool breeze came to sweep away his recollections. He left on the seventh night, walking, crying, laughing back to his exile, carrying with him renewed faith and the conviction that he would continue to struggle for his people so that they would not dissolve into the darkness of history.

In these dark days, I could not prevent my mind from taking me back to the smell of my homeland, that place that we were part of and that was part of us. During the

1936 revolt, we were a group of eight- and nine-year-olds playing war games, fashioning swords from sticks and defending the tops of the rocks as if they were castle towers. When we tired of this, we turned our sticks into rifles, attacking and falling like fighters among the orchards and rocky outcrops and around the springs. Then we would lie on our bellies, between the tree roots, watching the village girls collecting water at the spring. The girls were like statues in the distance, except for their dresses rustling in the breeze. When they lifted their jugs onto their heads, exposing their beautiful arms, they lifted our innocent young hearts with them.

One day in the jail, they released us into the courtyard and began reading the names of the people to be set free the next morning, and ours were there . . . Matar, Marwan, and Walid. In the morning they called me to the office and made me sign my name and put my left thumbprint on a statement swearing that I would not step foot in this country again. The real test was outside: my legs were not used to walking, and the sun that I longed for was so bright. And there were leaves on the trees, and people, cars, and dogs. They took me in a Jeep with two guards to the border of their country and put me in another car to cross the border. I explained to the driver that I didn't have any money. When he learned my story he insisted on driving me to the door of my house in the camp in Damascus and would not take a single lira in return.

I entered the house, unexpected by my wife, sons, and daughters. The littlest ones hung on to my neck and arms, kissing me. The neighbors heard the commotion and came over to participate in the celebration. Then my comrades and friends found out, and soon the house turned into a giant celebration of love, goodwill, and warm wishes.

From my comrades, I heard the news of the resistance, which was made up of men who had no experience in the art of war. My family, friends, and comrades all pushed me to relax and stay out of the field of struggle, for my own health and for the sake of my family. Yet despite the fact that I understood their fears, their discussions shocked and saddened me. How was I to rest when the camps of our people in Lebanon were being bombed by the Israelis?

Few have written about their experiences as Palestinians living in Syria, and Matar 'Abdelrahim's novels/autobiographies allow us a glimpse into that history. In keeping with his greater life philosophy, his struggle for him as a Palestinian was about positive change, redemption, and humanity. In my interview with Matar, I asked him why he chose to write about his life.

I want people to understand the essence of my ideas. The reason I wrote and the reason we worked so hard to educate people and to make our people learn about the world is to show people that the resistance is not about stealing and having a job, but it is a revolution. That revolution is that people in the third world need education and knowledge, to fill our minds with ideas, not just depend only on the gun. I want them to fill their minds so they act like human beings, not just to be overexcited and thus impotent. The problem with the Arab nation is that they do not think for themselves;

instead, they distract themselves with religion, they go to the mosque and pray, when instead they should understand their role, their duty, how the world is run. Civilization is not inventing a weapon to kill people; civilization is to invent something that makes people happy, thrive, and love. All of us are human beings; all of us must be one family in this small village.

11

Joseph Spronz

From the Holocaust to a Safe Shore

Gershon Shafir

As the sun rose high over Óbuda, Budapest's oldest and poorest neighborhood, on June 28, 1914, the Spronz family sat down for its lunch. Besides the father and the mother there were their five children—a sister and four brothers—as well as an additional boy and girl who had been taken in from poorer relatives in the Hungarian countryside. Joseph, known by his nickname Yoshka, then nine years old, was the fourth youngest of the siblings. The father, even as he said the blessing over the bread, trained his ears to the store that adjoined the two-bedroom apartment, in case a customer came to shop. He sold groceries, flour, caustic soda for laundry, spirits. The store's sole objects of value were a great icebox and an industrial-size poppy-seed grinder. Its basement held coal, petroleum, and kindling.

That Sunday an extremist Serbian nationalist assassinated Archduke Franz Ferdinand, heir to the throne of the Austro-Hungarian (or Habsburg) Empire during his visit to Sarajevo, the capital of the province of Bosnia-Herzegovina. This incident activated a system of alliances among the great European powers and precipitated a worldwide conflict that sealed the fate of the tottering Habsburg and Ottoman Empires. The shots, the four-year-long war that followed, and the subsequent end of the age of multiethnic empires all resulted from the rise of nationalist sentiments and separatist movements and the authoritarian attempts to contain them. The sheer length of the war, the massive casualties it produced, the mobilization of all aspects of life for the war effort, and the dismemberment of empires into successor states and mandated territories generated great hopes for a better future. Most of them were dashed within a short time. The Great War, as it was then known, promised to be the war to end all wars, but its course and flawed resolution precipitated the even more horrific Second World War. Joseph Spronz's life led him from one successor state to another, each shaped by the force of nationalism: from an independent Hungary, carved from the Austro-Hungarian Empire after the First World War, to Israel, cleaved by a British mandate from a portion of the Ottoman Empire and established after the Second World War as a national home for the Jewish people and especially the Jewish refugees of the Holocaust.

The grocery store provided a unique vantage point for observing the four-year-long war. It became a distribution center, a node in the rationing of the ever-dwindling supplies of basic necessities. By 1916, the misery was so pervasive that people would line up at 2 A.M. for flour distribution, and police on horseback kept order in the mile-long lines. The crowd's murmur would wake Yoshka and his younger brother, Károly, who slept in the same bed. The beginning of the school year was postponed, and Yoshka worked in the store; by evening the flour had turned his hair white and covered his vocal chords, making his voice hoarse. At 8 P.M., when the store closed, the family members spent long hours gluing thousands of ration coupons onto forms that they turned in the next morning at the rationing center in return for new supplies.

Many of the customers could not pay cash. Yoshka's father insisted on charging the same for cash and credit and would write down the customers' debt in two notebooks, one which they carried and the other which he kept, to ensure mutual trust. He was painstakingly scrupulous in handling money. Yoshka, when five years old, found a shiny coin just below the three steps that led to the store. As he was about to savor the small red cornel berries he had bought from a vendor with this money, a hand, his father's, reached out over his head and knocked the newspaper cone that held them out of his hand. The money did not belong to you, nor did the fruit, he was admonished. He learned this lesson and others like it well; when his bunkmate died in Auschwitz in 1945, Yoshka could not touch his small hoard of stale bread, though by the camp's rules it belonged to him.

HUNGARY AND ITS JEWS

Hungary's Jewry enjoyed a very hospitable environment, comparable only to that of Western Europe, until the First World War. The Jews of Budapest were especially, as it were, in a hothouse of opportunities, and even the poor and the less well-off benefited from access to the country's modernizing cultural life and economy. The country served as a magnet for Jewish immigrants: while Hungary's population grew by about 100 percent in the nineteenth century, its Jewish population surged by 1,000 percent during that period. Hungary, in fact, had one of the highest percentages of Jews of any country: in 1910, 923,000 Jews made up about 4.5 percent of its population. Their share in the urban population was 12.4 percent, and in Budapest, Hungary's capital, it was as high as 23 percent. The reasons for their relatively privileged position was that Jews compensated for two fundamental weaknesses of the Hungarian state: occupational and demographic. At the same time, in a society based not on rights but on the dichotomy of aristocratic privilege and the oppression of peasants, servants, and industrial workers, those allied with privilege could not but be trapped too; Jews' lifestyles, and later lives, depended on their services as a middle-class minority to the Hungarian nobility and were to last only as long as the power of the nobility did.

The endurance of Hungarian feudalism, serfdom, and guilds into the mid-nineteenth century and the exceptionally large percentage of its nobility and gentry, who made up about 5 percent of the population, thwarted the formation of a Hungarian middle class. Modernization increasingly impoverished the gentry, who scorned the modern professions, which were not compatible with their gentlemanly ambitions, in favor of pubic administration. When sections of the Hungarian nobility undertook to modernize the agricultural economy, industrialize, construct railroads, and establish banks, they relied on Jewish (and German) entrepreneurs, bankers, and manufacturers. As part of this accommodation, Jews attained civil equality in 1867, and in 1895, Judaism was raised to the status of a legally recognized faith. Jews in Hungary responded enthusiastically to their emancipation and social mobility by seeking integration and, in many cases, assimilation. They sent their children to Hungarian-speaking schools, adopted Hungarian first names, and Magyarized their last names (*Magyar* is the term by which Hungarians refer to themselves in their native tongue). They took to Hungarian culture: a significant number of well-known Hungarian writers, poets, and artists were of Jewish origin. Jews bought about a fifth of the major landed estates, and about 350 Jewish families even attained titles of nobility. A growing portion also converted to Christianity; by 1941, about one hundred thousand had done so.

Hungary attracted Jewish immigrants from other Habsburg domains. Yoshka's father was an immigrant from Slovakia, where most of his family members were teachers, craftsmen, barbers, or small traders. Yoshka's maternal uncle Joseph Weiss, who was born in Hungary and Magyarized his last name to Vágó, exemplified some aspects of the new Jewish social mobility. The recipient of a Ph.D. in economics, he edited the economic section of the prestigious German-language daily *Pester Lloyd,* wrote a multivolume history of the Hungarian economy, was elected secretary of the Chamber of Commerce and Industry, was put in charge of calculating the national price index, and during the First World War was appointed coal tsar, but when offered the chance to stand as a liberal candidate for Parliament if he converted to Christianity, refused to do so.

Jews also played a crucial role with regard to the nationalities question. Within the historical Kingdom of Hungary, a part of the Habsburg Empire for several centuries, Hungarians were only a plurality. In 1867, they constituted 40 percent of the population, whereas Romanians and South Slavs were 14 percent each, Germans 9.8, Slovaks 9.4, Ruthenes 2.3 percent, and so on. That year the

Austro-Hungarian Compromise transformed the unitary Habsburg Empire into the Dual Monarchy of Austro-Hungary, giving Hungary its own Parliament, prime minister, government, territorial army, and institutions. Though the agreement recognized essential Hungarian national demands, the Hungarian nobility continued ignoring and repressing the desires of other minorities for national autonomy. The rural population of mostly Slavs and Romanians resisted forced assimilation and Magyarization.

A unique aspect of Hungary was that it could not assume a common history, language, ethnic descent, or even religion as the glue of solidarity among the country's peoples. The Magyar claim of the right to rule over other nationalities was based on a presumed cultural superiority and a view of Hungary as a "historical nation" or of "Hungarianness" as a moral and cultural category broader than any marker of nationality. The sociological demonstration of such a cultural superiority complex was found in the willing assimilation of two urban groups, Jews and Germans, into Hungarian culture, a process which gave hope to making Hungarians the majority of the population.

After the First World War, the Dual Monarchy came to an end, though its beneficial effects for Hungary's Jews lingered on as long as the nobility retained the reins of power. With the dismemberment of the Austro-Hungarian Empire, the Hungarian part was also subdivided into multiple successor states. Of these, Hungary itself had 28.6 percent of its erstwhile territory and 36.5 percent of its former population. But in truncated Hungary, Hungarians were the demographic majority. The population of Hungarian Jewry fell to 473,000 but rose to 6.6 percent of the much smaller population of 7.2 million Hungarians. Jews were no longer needed to enhance the demographic share of the Hungarian population and were viewed as an obstacle to the employment of the declassé and repatriated gentry. They turned from a protected and privileged minority into a tolerated minority and eventually into an enemy.

In a Hungary consumed by the desire for revenge and the restoration of lost territories and the peoples therein, national sentiment turned rigid and ugly. Hungarian nationalism took on an organic, Christian coloration. Its adherents viewed Hungary as a mutilated torso whose limbs had been severed, and they made the prewar border into a sacred object of worship. Every day at school, children chanted in unison the Magyar Creed: "I believe in one God, I believe in one Fatherland, I believe in one divine, eternal Truth, I believe in the resurrection of Hungary. Hungary dismembered is no country, Hungary united is heaven. Amen." These aggressive revisionist aims were closely bound up with chauvinistic and, later, racist slogans. Though nationalists insisted on a continued Hungarian mission to spread its superior culture, they turned on the country's Jews—the group whose assimilation in the past seemed to confirm the value of their culture—by proclaiming them to have remained foreigners. Jewish economic and cultural integration were rolled back, at first slowly and after the mid-1930s more rapidly, in phases of alternating spontaneous and state-mandated exclusion.

Hungary's defeat in the First World War, as in many places in Eastern Europe, discredited the nobility for a while and led to the formation of a radical middle-class and social-democratic government and subsequently a communist government. The latter was followed by the seizure of power by the gentry-led military, headed by Admiral Miklós Horthy, and the onslaught of a White Terror: a campaign of murder and beatings carried out by military commando units which specifically targeted Jews. The excuse of this terror was the purported identification of Jews with communists, based on the high percentage of Jews in the short-lived communist regime, conveniently ignoring that the majority of Hungarian Jews, a mainstay of the middle class and its capitalist enterprises, would have been the chief losers of a communist society. But Jews were particularly closely scrutinized. The teachers in Yoshka's commercial high school stigmatized him for expressing radical views in the school's literary and debating society, while his older brother Gyula had to move to a new high school merely for serving as school librarian during the revolutionary months. Anti-Semitism was widespread: during a hike to the hills of Buda, three members of a soccer team assaulted Yoshka and his younger brother, Károly, and tied them to a tree. The brothers, embarrassed and confused, swore to each other not to let their parents know, but Károly's sobbing in his sleep revealed the incident.

After the war, the Hungarian gentry sought to replace Jews in the professions that its members had disdained until the defeat in the war, and university students regularly roughed up their Jewish classmates. Yoshka's oldest brother, Dezső, who resumed his studies at a technical college on returning from his wartime service as a decorated lieutenant in the Austro-Hungarian army, barely managed to escape through an open window when attacked by such a mob. In September 1920, the Hungarian Parliament passed the Numerus Clausus law, which limited the percentage of university students by group to their share of the population. This quota system, which was expressly directed against the highly educated Jewish population, was the first step in curtailing more than fifty years of legal equality. That special incubator of talent, namely the uniquely favorable conditions of Hungarian Jewry, was shattered, and many Jewish professionals emigrated. In addition, thousands of Jewish students from Budapest elected to study and then stay abroad. Among these Hungarian-born Jewish émigrés were scientists such as Leo Szilard and Edward Teller, who played a crucial role in the development of the American nuclear bomb program, while others—Dennis Gabor, George de Hevesey, and Eugene Wigner—became Nobel laureates. There were also famous musicians, such as Eugene Ormandy and Georg Solti (who lived in Yoshka's neighborhood), the mathematician John von Neumann, the photographer Robert Capa, social scientists such as Karl Mannheim and Karl and Michael Polanyi, and many more in other disciplines and arts.

BETWEEN FAMILY AND BUSINESS

The economic crisis that followed the war thrust the grocery store into a slump and made the simultaneous schooling of Yoshka and his siblings prohibitively expensive. At the end of tenth grade, Yoshka told his father that he wished to start working, not revealing that the decision was prompted by his desire to help out the family financially. By putting his family first, Yoshka gave up the opportunity to get the higher education that his siblings did. His sense of responsibility to and for family was deep and lifelong. In his world, the first and the last thought (and many in between) went to family.

Yoshka discovered in himself a business talent that stood him in good stead during the economically uncertain interwar years and for the rest of his life. Though his first job was as an apprentice in the ribbon-weaving mill of a distant relative, when the enterprise was about to go bankrupt and its owner conveniently left for a sanatorium, Yoshka stepped in and salvaged the business by proposing a barter system to three of the mill's main suppliers. Subsequently, one offered him employment, and while working as a traveling salesman throughout Hungary, Yoshka transformed the supplier's retail business into a wholesale enterprise. Another important moment arrived more than a decade later, when he borrowed a small amount for a month from his maternal uncle and opened his own suspender business. "Success multiplied my energy," Yoshka said. His rural network of buyers came in handy, and as orders streamed in, his mother and his sister came to work with him.

In Yoshka's milieu, family members did not just work for themselves, and family ties did not dissolve or diminish when the younger generation became self-sufficient. Some of the best times were spent with family: even as adults, Yoshka and two of his siblings would play classical music at home with their father as a string quartet. Family was where the pieces became whole—but the whole was only as strong as its parts. The family provided the boundary of significant obligations, and these were raised to the level of moral principle. Since so much was expected from family, sometimes family members disappointed one another or fell short, were unwilling to come to help, or even took advantage of one another, and these members were judged harshly. But family always remained a safety net, the place to go home to.

Family was Yoshka's source of strength, what he defended and was protected by, the place where he could take repose, and at times it was the only heart in a heartless world. "Love was so palpable in that home," an aunt recalled decades later, that it "could almost be cut with a knife." Such warmth and mutual care served as a magnet, and the family was complemented with a circle of friends—and friends could make moral claims on one another that were almost as strong as claims by family.

In these interwar years the two younger brothers, and sometimes Gyula, saved up their pennies and with a group of mountaineers from the Third District of the Budapest Tourist Association went on hikes every Sunday. Eventually they organized a hiking and climbing excursion to the Austrian Alps and another to the Italian Alps. During these excursions the brothers had a fixed daily budget, but by sleeping in schools and tourist hostels they stretched their money. By 1930, with six additional families of friends, Yoshka was able to borrow enough to commission a small weekend home—the Not a Care—in Horány, a forested resort area on the Danube. Each of the rooms held a bunk bed, a cabinet, and a table with two chairs. On weekends the families rowed on the river and played ball, table tennis, and, when it rained, cards. There he met Erzsi, from an adjacent weekend house, whom he married in 1938, after which she also came to work with him. The weekends in Horány lasted until 1941. "They equipped me with warm memories which sustained me during the subsequent terrible years," Yoshka recalled.

THE GATHERING STORM OF ANTI-SEMITISM

After the Great Depression of 1929 hit Hungary, the country's stream of right-wing sentiment became a flood. Under pressure from radical nationalists and native fascists, Hungary increasingly fell under the influence of Nazi Germany, allying itself with Adolf Hitler and becoming part of the Axis during the Second World War. Hitler's plan to redraw the map of Europe paid handsomely for Hungary: as his forces occupied Czechoslovakia, Romania, and Yugoslavia, Hungary received parts of their territory and population. But this time the Hungarian elites did not worry about being a minority and needing the Jewish population to enhance their demographic share in the population. In March 1938, even before Hungary became a full-fledged ally of Germany, its Parliament gave a freer rein to anti-Semitism by adopting a so-called Jewish Law—in fact an anti-Jewish law—to be followed in quick succession by two even more radical Jewish laws. The first two laws limited Jewish participation in government and the economy, in some cases, such as the civil service, eliminating it altogether, while the third one restricted social interaction, such as intermarriage between Jews and Christians. Government officials claimed that legal restrictions placed on Jews were a way of protecting them from the masses' spontaneous outbursts and assaults, but, of course, anti-Semitism could never be an effective means of protecting Jews.

As the Second World War approached, the Hungarian military barred Jews from serving in the armed forces, and by 1940, all able-bodied Jewish males were made to serve in labor battalions. These were nothing more than mobile concentration camps: of the forced laborers who were deployed to war zones to do construction work, unload munitions trains, sweep mines, and the like without adequate shelter or food and while suffering brutal treatment from the commanding officers, tens of thousands perished. Yoshka was sent with a unit to the rugged mountains on the Hungarian-Ukrainian border. To his considerable luck, the unit's commanding officer had served with his brother in the First World War and protected Yoshka.

As a Nazi ally, Hungary maintained a measure of domestic independence, and Miklós Kállay, the prime minister, refused Nazi demands to deport Hungary's Jewish citizens. As the defeat in Stalingrad in early 1943 turned the tide of the war against Germany, the Hungarian leadership tried to disengage from their losing ally, only to discover that it was too late. On March 19, 1944, German forces occupied Hungary to forestall Admiral Horthy's attempt to reach a separate armistice with the Allies, and the fate of the country's Jews was sealed with startling rapidity. Together with the Wehrmacht divisions, the special deportation unit of SS Obersturmbannführer Adolf Eichmann had also arrived. The Hungarian Interior Ministry cooperated in issuing a dizzying succession of regulations aimed at isolating Jews: they must hand in phones, radios, and privately owned vehicles; wear the yellow star in public on pain of death; register all mobile and immobile property; and on and on—the list was as endless as it was diabolic. Jews were dismissed from social, cultural, and economic positions, their businesses were expropriated, their stores were closed, and they were concentrated in ghettoes.

SURVIVAL IN AUSCHWITZ

Yoshka was called up again for labor battalion service and, with another sixty yellow star–wearing Jews, set out by train on June 12, 1944. In the city of Hatvan, they were surrounded by Hungarian gendarmes with feather-capped helmets, headed by a Hungarian colonel, Márton Zöldi, dressed in a black German SS uniform. Hungarian police and officials later joined them. The gendarmes beat their victims with sadistic relish and forced them into the overcrowded local ghetto. Next morning, Yoshka and the others were loaded into cattle cars sealed with lead, on which they traveled for three days without water or latrines. They disembarked in the death camp Birkenau, which was part of the Auschwitz complex. The next five minutes were crucial: as part of a selection process, the vast majority were sent to the left, to the gas chambers. Yoshka was pointed to the right, given a paper-thin striped uniform, and tattooed on the left arm with the number A-14588. Three days later he was transported to Auschwitz, where for the next eight and half months he slaved in various work units.

He survived in Auschwitz for eight and half months due to help from friends, the growing disorganization of the Nazis toward the end of the war, considerable luck, and his gumption, probably in that order. Early on, he defied an SS guard and three kapos who demanded that he hand over his hiking boots, knowing too well that lacking proper shoes would condemn him to death. At first he was assigned to a backbreaking earthworks project, where his health almost failed him within the first week, but a Jewish clerk who was attempting to assemble reliable inmates for resistance reassigned him to a leather factory. Later he sneaked into another unit to be with two of his friends by telling the kapo that he had been transferred, a falsehood punishable by death if noticed. The biggest danger was being chosen for the gas chambers in one of the Nazi guards' regular selections. But where Jewish life was of no value, every small incident or random aggression by a guard also posed grave danger.

Friendships old and new were crucial for survival. Sometimes this meant sharing food stolen—*organized,* in the inmates' parlance—from Nazi warehouses. And then there were deeper exchanges. One of Yoshka's friends would recite poetry, and Yoshka, blessed with an exceptional musical memory, would whistle melodies to him from Bach's St. Matthew Passion. One day an inmate from the Netherlands asked to join and recited poems by the German Jewish romantic poet Heinrich Heine. His name was Otto Frank, Margot and Anne Frank's father, and that meeting begat a lifelong friendship between him and Yoshka. Thus, these bald and emaciated inmates kept alive German high culture in Auschwitz while keeping themselves alive.

As winter approached, it became vital for the thinly clad inmates to find indoor employment. With several friends, Yoshka showed up at the kitchen, claiming to be unassigned, and was made a cook. On his tenth day there, another inmate slipped in his wooden clogs, and as a result a one-hundred-liter tub of steaming soup was spilled on Yoshka's hand. On October 19, he was sent to Auschwitz's so-called hospital, a virtual death sentence.

But the handful of Jewish physicians at the hospital, who of necessity practiced their profession without the benefit of medications, noticed Yoshka's strength of character and made him an unofficial orderly, and he cleaned and fed a group of sicker inmates. By this time, the Nazis' deteriorating military situation had forced them to suspend the weekly selections, but Yoshka's only hope of survival remained the victory of the Allies. On January 12, 1945, the long-stalled Soviet troops broke through the German lines, and from January 18 to 22 the Germans sought to evacuate the camp by marching inmates toward Germany. They instructed the hospital to burn the card index of the sick and the staff, a clear sign of their intended fate. Yoshka was given a cartload of cards of 150,000 Polish Jews killed in 1942, some of which he managed to hide under ashes. The inmates were convinced that the Germans would destroy the camp and its inhabitants to erase their crimes, and Yoshka encouraged his friends to leave the camp on the marches. After long soul-searching, he realized that he could not leave the sick in his charge behind, and stayed. A few days later many of the frightened Germans disappeared, but the situation remained precarious. On January 27, 1945, the first Soviet soldiers appeared and liberated the camp. They found thirty-eight hundred survivors from twenty-two countries in the sick bay.

A BROKEN WORLD

The following day Yoshka, eager for news of his loved ones, left on an arduous trek back to Budapest. He walked in the snow, rode on trucks, trains, and a locomotive, along the way receiving help from soldiers and civilians of many nations. Still, twice he came close to falling victim to the liberators. Soviet units rounded up military and civilian opponents and deported 250,000 Nazi collaborators from Hungary alone to forced labor camps in the USSR, where they languished for years. When the soldiers didn't meet their quotas, they hustled innocent passersby into the lines and detention camps. On the trek back to Budapest, Yoshka and two of his companions found themselves behind Soviet barbed wire. They scrounged a stretcher, and two of them carried the third to the gate, where Yoshka pointed to the armband with a red cross that he had worn in Auschwitz. The guard waved them on. More than a month later he reached Budapest but could not cross over to Buda since all the bridges had been destroyed by the retreating Nazis. While he was walking through town, a Soviet officer leading a group under armed guard signaled him to fall in. Yoshka pointed to the striped Auschwitz uniform he still wore and said he was Jewish. "If so," replied the officer, "recite me the prayer preceding the reading of a Torah portion." Yoshka did, and the officer let him go. Even after the liberation of Budapest, survival still could depend on such extraordinary twists of fate as a Soviet officer being a Jew himself.

In Budapest, Yoshka's worst fears were confirmed. In two months, between May 15 and July 9, 1944, 437,402 Jews, almost the whole provincial Jewish population of Hungary, had been deported in more than 145 trains, mostly to Birkenau-Auschwitz. With the exception of several thousand, including Yoshka himself, they were gassed and their remains burned in crematoria. About two hundred thousand Jews herded into a ghetto in Budapest had been temporarily spared by Horthy's refusal to deport the rest. But on October 15, 1944, when Horthy again tried to end Hungarian participation in the war, the native fascist Arrow Cross Party took over the government. Notwithstanding the impending Allied victory, the Arrow Cross remained Nazi Germany's steadfast partner and turned its terror on the remaining Jews, murdering more than eighty thousand in the ghetto. Of all his family, Yoshka found alive only his brother Gyula, who at first did not recognize him. His wife died in Bergen-Belsen; his oldest brother, Dezső, was starved and worked to death in a labor camp; his sister, Regine, was killed on a death march; and his youngest brother, Károly, was shot at the very end of the war.

The swift demise of Hungary's Jews was particularly tragic since President Roosevelt, who knew of the Nazi destruction policy and its extent as early as 1941, had tried belatedly to come to the help of this last intact Jewish community. These efforts by and large were ineffective. The War Refugee Board's Raoul Wallenberg, Jewish emissaries such as Chana Szenes and Joel Palgi from Palestine, and other diplomatic representatives raced to save Jewish lives through protective letters, safe houses, and ransom payments. Yet the Arrow Cross's brutal determination to destroy them meant that only about one hundred thousand survived the war.

Yoshka's endeavors to rebuild, indeed to start a new life, after the Holocaust took many forms. First, he was a witness: Turning to an unfamiliar task, he wrote a memoir of the eight and half months he was an inmate at Auschwitz, the first to be published in Hungarian about the Holocaust and this camp. He also dictated the protocol of his Auschwitz days to Franziska Pollak at the Jewish Agency's Documentation Department in Budapest, which later served as the basis for Yad Vashem, the Israeli institution for the commemoration of Holocaust victims. Second, he sought justice: he served as a state witness against Colonel Zöldi, who had deported his forced labor unit to Auschwitz. But he also looked forward. And so, thirdly, Yoshka started a new family. He and Franziska found each other through his testimony, and they married in 1946. When their son—me—was born in August 1947, many friends and strangers came on a virtual pilgrimage: a newborn Jewish baby at the time was an unusual sight. Fourth, Yoshka and Franziska determined to leave Hungary, where they had been mistreated and betrayed. This would not be easy.

At the end of the Second World War, the cold war between the victors, the United States and the Soviet Union, cast a dark shadow over the attempts of those in Eastern Europe to forge a new life from the remnants of the old one. Hungary's alliance with the defeated Nazi Germany discredited its aristocratic elite, and an internal opposition, sometimes reluctantly, heeded the USSR in the hope of creating a freer and more egalitarian Hungary. The USSR had different ideas. It became an international master that imposed a new regime of terror. During the three years following the war, Hungary retained the semblance of a parliamentary democracy but by spring 1948 was run by the Hungarian Communist Party at the behest of the USSR. As part of its radical transformation, first large and then smaller firms were nationalized; estates were first subdivided among the peasants and later collectivized; and many of the former owners were resettled in the countryside. Yoshka, who had opened a small suspender workshop, had to close it down and work for a state agency. The Social-Democratic Party was obligated to merge with the Hungarian Communist Party, and middle-class parties were disbanded. The economy was centrally planned, censorship was established over the media, legal rights were trampled upon, the judicial system was politicized, a semi-independent secret political police—the dreaded AVO—kept the population under surveillance, waves of purges led to show trials, and the political practice and history of the USSR and its Communist Party became sacred dogma and its leader, Stalin, the object of a personality cult. Even corresponding with relatives in Israel or with Otto Frank, who now lived in Basel, Switzerland, was dangerous, so one night Yoshka burned all his foreign correspondence. In the new Hungary, Jews could easily be accused of being "hirelings of Zionism." The bitter pill was that the label attached to them had changed but not their precarious position: under the Nazis they were enemies of the race, under the Communist regime unreliable middle-class enemies.

THE PROMISE OF SAFETY

Both Yoshka's and Franziska's families harbored deep Jewish feelings, and although these were neither exclusive nor obligatory in their families, now the Jewish identity assumed new and more pronounced meaning. Yoshka's father had regularly taken his children to the synagogue. Yet when he discovered during a service that Gyula was reading a novel by Goethe, which he kept inside the pages of the prayer book, he told his son that if he was not a believer he did not have to attend. Yoshka said mourner's kaddish for his father for one year. Though after his father's death he no longer went praying, even during the Stalinist years he would take his son to the magnificent Dohány Street synagogue for Simchat Torah. The Spronz and Pollak families also had sentimental and deep ties to the historical Jewish homeland. Yoshka's maternal grandfather had been the president of the Óbuda synagogue's Bikur Holim (the association tending to the sick and infirm), and in the first decade of the nineteenth century he had gone on a pilgrimage to the Holy Land, riding a donkey from Jaffa to Jerusalem. Yoshka's father was a gabbai (dues collector) in the synagogue for fifteen years but was too poor to keep his store closed on Saturdays. Franziska's father was a free thinker, though a Jewish one, and her mother, a coloratura opera singer born in Vienna, sang in several concerts there honoring Theodor Herzl, the founder of the Zionist movement.

On the eve of the Second World War, Yoshka had made unsuccessful efforts to emigrate, when his first destination would have been New Zealand. After the Holocaust and with the establishment and successful defense of Israel as a state in the 1948 war, he never wavered in his aim to join the new country. When, during the 1956 Hungarian Revolution, one of the friends Yoshka made in Auschwitz sent an emissary with the promise of an affidavit to bring him and Franziska to Canada, they were not interested. Franziska joined the Communist Party after the war with the hope of trying to create a better Hungary. But when she discovered that the Engineers' Association, where she worked, was not intent on denazification and she was passed over for promotion, she quit. On her way out she ran into a friend who invited her to come and work at the Jewish Agency for the Zionists. After the Holocaust, it seemed that there was one movement and one place that would offer security, a place were Jews could not be excluded. Yoshka and Franziska's feelings for Zion, in short, were of the traditional kind, not exclusive but deep, kindled by the search for refuge. Their best and, it seemed, last hope was Israel. But even once they were there, their Zionism was a coat worn lightly.

The Stalinist regime closed Hungary's borders, and the Spronz family invested prodigious efforts and ingenuity in seeking a way out of the country. The key to receiving a passport with an exit visa lay with the Ministry of the Interior, which rejected their application seven times over as many years. Yoshka offered a high-ranking official a considerable amount of money for a passport so his family could exercise the right of free movement. Just when it was to be delivered, the Minister of the Interior was arrested in one of the purges. Then in the summer of 1953, the family was on vacation near Hungary's Balaton Lake when Franziska found out that one of their fellow vacationers, an avid fisherman, was in the employ of the Ministry of the Interior. Next morning, Yoshka showed up on the shore with his new rod, though he was angling for something far more important than fish. But this went nowhere. It was only in the wake of the Hungarian Revolution of October 1956, when boarders were opened briefly and thousands fled the country, that they were able to leave.

IN THE ISRAELI IMMIGRATION MACHINERY

Yoshka and his family left Budapest by train and a few days later embarked on a boat in Genoa, Italy, with about 150 other Jewish families from Poland and Hungary. On February 17, 1957, they arrived at the port in Haifa. From there they were transported to Sha'ar Ha'aliya (Gate of Immigration, an Israeli Ellis Island), a central classification camp that operated near Haifa, and housed in a tent city. Here, under the Law of Return, Yoshka and his family, like all Jewish immigrants, became Israeli citizens instantaneously, without any waiting period.

Israeli society offered its immigrants a utopia and a refuge. It was different from other immigration countries in seeking to transform the new arrivals. The ideology of the Zionist institutional framework did not expect to meet immigrants halfway but to absorb them—that is, to digest them and reshape them in its own collectivist image. The labor settlement movement championed the subordination of the individual to the collective, his or her transformation into a tool in the service of Zionist state building. From the perspective of Israeli sociologists in the 1950s, accordingly, immigrants experienced the disintegration of their individual role set and the loss of their former social identity, which was to be followed by desocialization and resocialization, leading to rebirth as a *Homo zionismus*. Immigrants were frequently referred to as *chomer enoshi* (human material) to be molded, and those who did not fall in with these expectations were denominated by sundry Israeli leaders as *avak adam* (human dust) which had failed to be converted into a more noble, national substance. In fact, only a portion of the Jewish immigrants came to Palestine as self-conscious or ideologically motivated Zionists, and even fewer lived up to the collectivist values.

Though Israel always remained a refuge for Yoshka, its utopian glimmer never served as a magnet for him. Among the immigrants, like him, mutual help and sympathy were as common as consternation with sabra gruffness and official indifference. Though the immigrants, among them Holocaust survivors, were widely and frequently portrayed as psychologically cast down and hardened (*anashim kshei yom*), they made Israel more tolerant, understanding, and neighborly, more diverse and less ideological than its nationalist historiography would lead one to believe. Nor did Yoshka lose himself in Israel to find himself anew; rather, like most immigrants, he sought to place his already-formed self in new circumstances. This was in part because he was already fifty-two on arrival but mostly because he believed in the individual's moral strength and in his family's evident fortitude.

In most countries new arrivals are on their own to make their way and build their lives. Not in Israel. Sha'ar Ha'aliya was only the tip of a massive and all-encompassing institutional apparatus set up to transport and register new immigrants, administer, find them employment and housing, care for their health, provide them with social services, and, if necessary, rehabilitate them. In short start the process of absorbing the immigrants. Their fate was inexorably tied to the Jewish Agency's Immigration Department until their arrival in Israel, and from then to the decisions of its Absorption Department. The Jewish Agency for Palestine (Sochnut) was established in 1929 to represent Zionist and non-Zionist Jews who supported the creation of a Jewish national home in cooperation with the British Mandate, but instead of being abolished upon the realization of this goal, it was given a new purpose. While the Sochnut cared for only immigrants, a dense network of public bodies catered to both newcomers and old-timers: the political parties; that most unique of Zionist institutions, the Histadrut (General Federation of Jewish Workers in Palestine)—part settlement body, part trade union, part entrepreneur and employer, part health insurer and social service provider and until 1948 the Israeli state-in-the-making; and last but not least, the new state's own parallel agencies. As Yoshka learned, the Sochnut had disproportionate power to sort, select, and regiment immigrants, while the Histadrut's remit covered all residents. Given their ubiquitous presence in the lives of Israelis, the Sochnut and the Histadrut were referred to in everyday speech by their monikers, the Agency and the Federation.

The hundreds of employees detailed to absorption were a source of daily assistance as well as irritation. A contemporary survey conducted at Amidar, the state-owned public housing agency which Yoshka and most immigrants came to know intimately, found that close to two-thirds of its officials who served the public did not believe in greeting their customers or answering their greeting and would let them stand rather than offer them a chair. As Yoshka learned, the officials did not think of themselves as civil servants, let alone servants of the new citizens, but as their benefactors. Immigration was welcome, immigrants rarely.

By the time Yoshka, Franziska, and their eight-year-old son arrived, immigration had already dramatically transformed Israel. The state's Jewish population of 650,000 in May 1948 was augmented by 687,000 Jews who arrived from 1948 to 1951, in effect doubling the Jewish population in three and half years. This was followed by a lull which lasted until 1954, but Yoshka and his family were part of a new immigration wave of more than seventy-one thousand people in 1957, a peak that was not matched until 1990. Two distinct stages in immigration absorption policy preceded their arrival. At first, a monthly average of fifteen thousand immigrants was housed in old British army camps and emptied Arab towns, villages, and neighborhoods of previously mixed cities. When these were filled to capacity by the spring of 1950, the government, fearful of unrest and rebelliousness among the cramped immigrants, decided to erect the canvas houses, tin shacks, barracks, and wooden huts of the notorious *ma'abarot* (transit camps) adjacent to existing municipalities and agricultural settlements, which were expected to provide services and sources of employment. Like other temporary arrangements, the ma'abarot endured far longer than expected: tens of thousands of people still inhabited them well into the 1960s, living off relief work. In the early 1950s, the government also built development towns and agricultural villages in the outlying Galilee and the Negev, to people Israel's long borders and disperse its population from the narrow and densely inhabited coastal strip. Immigrants were sent directly to their destination after disembarking from the ship. Not surprisingly, on seeing the desolation surrounding their new town or village, some refused to get off the trucks that delivered them.

Successfully navigating the pathways of the immigration and absorption institutions, working with and, when necessary, standing up to the Agency without becoming its charge, determined an immigrant's chances of successful long-term absorption. Yoshka felt that retaining a measure of independence was the key; self-employed for most of his life, he was not about to let a stranger make the crucial decisions for him and his family and vigorously opposed friendly offers to send him to development towns at unknown destinations. He wished to be near relatives, his oldest brother's widow or sons in the center of the country. Yoshka recoiled at the primitive conditions of Sha'ar Ha'aliya, where his family was initially sent, and with boundless energy went in search of alternatives. In one week he moved his family away, but it took them more than a year to find a permanent home.

At first, the family moved from place to place as friends and relatives took them in. In a few weeks' time they signed a one-year lease for a basement converted into a one-room living quarter, in Ramat Gan's Arlosoroff Street, the main thoroughfare of a town southeast of Tel Aviv. Their apartment was so tiny that when they unfolded the beds at night there was no space to walk between them, and the future was cloudy. Yet Yoshka remained optimistic, although their living standard had fallen drastically. He felt that nothing could be worse than the Hungary his family had left and was satisfied to be among his own. He liked to say that he had been deprived of all he possessed twice—the first time by the Nazis, the second by the Communists—and now he was ready to start for a third time. He never looked back; in fact, he was now able to look forward.

The main question was where to live permanently and how to get the Agency to approve their choice. In the Israeli bureaucratic universe, the reliance on personal favors, or on "pulling strings," that is, on *protektzia*—a word used with different suffixes and present in all Eastern European countries—was widespread. Though its methods were no different from the more neutrally viewed networking in the United States or from the so-called cronyism of East Asia, *protektzia* was used in Israel not to gain especially coveted jobs or lucrative investment opportunities, namely privilege, but frequently to access the most mundane benefits each citizen was entitled to. Additional factors compounded the inequality produced by *protektzia*. Few Arab citizens had access, and mizrachim (Jews from North Africa and the Middle East) only limited access to pull. Members of the labor settlement movement and affiliated political parties had ready-made networks, old-timers usually had large networks, but immigrants had to begin from scratch. The prevalence of *protektzia* in Israel was not an expression of particularistic normative traditions that survived under a modern bureaucratic order but the child of the central role political parties played in Israel's creation. Privatized access, consequently, was heavily partisan. The officials with whom individuals and families, especially immigrants, came into contact were usually also party officials, playing a dual role as purveyors of services and recruiters of party supporters. An Israeli urban myth had it that the most powerful tool to move a bureaucracy was a tiny *petek*, or chit, on which, above a key signature, appeared the acronym: *hanal mianash*, "the abovementioned person is one of ours." Such pull was not easy to come by, but it seemed that there were other doors.

Yoshka's solution was being included in a category of immigrants rewarded for their contribution to the Zionist movement. Franziska's work in the Jewish Agency's Documentation Department after the Second World War was a borderline case, but she successfully secured the signatures of two elder Hungarian Zionist leaders, which she needed to be recognized as a Zionist activist (*askan*) in her country of origin. As a result, the Spronz family was offered two locations: Bat Yam, south of Tel Aviv, or Ramat Aviv, in the northern part of the city. When

Yoshka discovered that Tel Aviv University was to be built in Ramat Aviv, his mind was made up: this is the university his son would attend, and this is where they should live. They moved into a ground-floor one-and-a-half-bedroom apartment of fifty-seven square meters, and after a few years they left it for a third-floor seventy-two-square-meter apartment with two and half bedrooms, kitty-corner from the future location of the social science building of Tel Aviv University.

THE NEW SOCIAL ORDER

Ramat Aviv was a neighborhood of mostly Polish immigrants, consisting of two- and three-story row houses separated by communal lawns and gardens, divided from Tel Aviv by the Yarkon River. With time, as Tel Aviv expanded northward, even a tiny apartment at a Ramat Aviv address became one of the more desirable in Israel.

The inhabitants of Ramat Aviv were exposed to only scant hints of the area's history. They lived downhill from the scattered houses of the Arab village of al-Shaykh Muwannis, many of which the burgeoning Tel Aviv University would later swallow up or replace. They knew it as Sheikh Mounis but did not know that in 1945 it had held a population of 1,930 Palestinian Arabs living in more than 250 houses; that it had had two elementary schools, one for boys and one for girls; that of its 16,000 dunams (a dunam is about one-tenth of an acre), close to 4,000 had been devoted to citrus and bananas and more than 7,000 to rain-fed cereals; and that Arabs had owned 11,456 dunams and Jews 3,545 and 971 had been public. Nor did they know that an agreement between the Haganah (the paramilitary associated with the labor settlement movement) and the elders of the village to observe a truce during the 1948 war had been violated by the Irgun Zvai Leumi (the National Military Organization, a right-wing paramilitary group, acronymized in Hebrew as *Etzel*), which at the end of March of that year kidnapped five village leaders, prompting a massive population flight. The single "Arab house" on the border between Ramat Aviv and Sheikh Mounis served as the home of the Histadrut's Hapo'el Ramat Aviv sport club and was silent testimony to this unknown history. Its squat structure, flat roof, thick whitewashed walls, and mosaic tiles set it apart from the red-tiled houses of Ramat Aviv.

On Saturday morning walks toward the undeveloped north in the early years of Ramat Aviv, Yoshka and his family would sometimes chance on a Bedouin encampment, where they were offered strong black coffee when they visited. By the time Ramat Aviv's third phase, the building of the upscale Ramat Aviv Gimel, began, the Bedouins were gone. Rarely would Yoshka and most Israeli Jews come across the Arab citizens of the state. From 1948 until 1965, Palestinians in the Galilee and the Negev lived under an Israeli military government which regulated their movements in Jewish areas. Even in the few remaining towns with mixed populations, the Palestinians lived in separate neighborhoods. This partition was particularly pronounced in Tel Aviv–Jaffa. Jaffa, once a flourishing town in its own right, had only several thousand Palestinians by the end of the 1948 war and was incorporated as a neighborhood into Tel Aviv. Only the names of some of the pre-1948 Arab neighborhoods—for instance, Mamila, Ajami, Jabalyye, Abu-Kabir—survived, notwithstanding their attempted Hebraization, and the name of a major road preserved the memory of the adjacent village of Salame. Mizrachim populated the majority of the southern Tel Aviv neighborhoods, some adjoining Jaffa. Many of these areas came to be designated as *shchunot metzuka* (distressed neighborhoods). In short, Israel was segregated by national and ethnic groups: the ashkenazim (Jews from Eastern Europe) of north Tel Aviv rarely, if ever, came into contact with the Palestinian Arabs in the southern part of the city, since they were shielded by a buffer of Jewish immigrants from North Africa and the Middle East and the rest of ashkenazi central Tel Aviv. Nor would new immigrants encounter Arabs in the corridors of the institutions they frequented; the prestate Zionist institutions which were held over after 1948 remained Jewish-only bodies, and for all practical purposes, many of the new state institutions mostly served Jews. Geographical segregation and institutional apartheid mirrored each other.

Most new immigrants did not comprehend and many certainly did not reciprocate the hostility of Palestinian and broader Arab opposition to Israel. When they learned about a joint summer beach and hiking camp for Jewish and Arab children north of Haifa Bay in 1963, Yoshka and Franziska sent their son, who came back surprised and sobered by what he had learned about the military government under which his Arab counterparts lived. Yoshka and his family began to awaken to the nature of the Israeli-Palestinian conflict only when they came into contact with Palestinians under Israeli occupation in the wake of the Six Day War.

Their new society's subdivision of Jews into two ethnic groups, ashkenazim and mizrachim, was another great surprise for Yoshka and Franziska. These categories originally carried only religious and cultural significance, corresponding to two liturgies and styles of worship, but in Israel they transmuted into ethnic groups. Yet ashkenazim and mizrachim were far from homogenous. The mizrachim, Middle Eastern Jews, mostly from Iraq, among whom organized Zionism had already made headway, arrived in the early 1950s and settled in the central areas of the country. On the other hand, North African Jews, less exposed to the Zionist movement and whose largest group came from Morocco, were sent to development towns. The former became the owners or protected tenants of high-value real estate, while the latter found housing in areas of low demand and little value. For Yoshka and especially for Franziska, Jews from afar—whether from Poland, Iraq, or Morocco—were brothers and sisters. A part of the Zionist ideology that they easily made their own—besides *kibbutz galuyot,* the ingathering of the Diasporas—was *mizug galuyot,* the merging of Jews from many lands. And yet, many in their circle of friends were Hungarian speakers from Hungary or the Jewish Hungarian minorities of Yugoslavia or Romania. Though many of their get-togethers focused on the discussion of their new life circumstances and the current events that they followed with close attention, a good portion were devoted to the culture of the Europe left behind. Close friends and a few nephews shared Yoshka's passion for classical music, and he would use his carefully selected LP collection to hold weekly concerts (affectionately named *Spronzerts* by one friend) in his apartment. Books in Hungarian and German, sometimes in Hebrew, would be exchanged.

Those who knew Yoshka then remember him as well built and muscular, of medium height, even-tempered, patient, and a good listener. They describe him as fiercely inner-directed, animated by a sense of justice and responsibility, seeking others with these qualities and these qualities in others. Energetic and decisive, he would never procrastinate and stood out by his ability to translate his decisions immediately into action. With a keen understanding of human nature and an appreciation of the impact of circumstances, he gave great latitude to those who went through the ups and downs of life, but he remained intolerant of irresponsibility. Yoshka was surprisingly modern in encouraging friends to listen to and learn from their children, and he liked to repeat that children do not owe their parents compliance but, rather, parents have to earn their children's trust. When things did not work out, he always counseled not to give in to despair or give up hope.

Ashkenazim also effected an ethnic hierarchy among their ranks. Jews from Hungary were ashkenazim but found themselves toward the bottom of this hierarchy. In the Zionist pantheon, Hungarian Jews were less Zionist than Jews from Russia or Poland, maybe even from Romania, since they had assimilated into Hungarian culture and their Jewish traditions were considered weak (or they were Orthodox and opposed to Zionism altogether). Though two famed founders of Zionism, Theodor Herzl and Max Nordau, were born in Budapest, the one lived in Vienna and the other in Paris, and there were few Hungarian Zionists. Jews from Hungary, favoring integration into Hungarian society, rarely chose to emigrate to Palestine during Mandatory times, when only 10,342 did so. From Israel's establishment in 1948 to 2000, only 30,778 Hungarian-born Jews chose to make their home in Israel, and the number of immigrants from practically any other Eastern European country dwarfed the 14,324 who did so during the state's first three years. Though about 15 percent of all the Hungarian immigrants to Israel settled in kibbutzim and moshavim, a surprisingly high share even in comparison with Jews from the heartland of the Zionist movement, their absolute numbers were small, and collective settlements established by Hungarian Jews or in which they were a majority were few and far between. Nor did most Hungarian Jews partake in the collective ethos of socialist-Zionism, since they tended to be middle or lower-middle class, according them low esteem on the carefully measured hierarchy of contributions to Zionism (which was even harder on mizrachim). Consequently, Jews from Hungary had neither numeric nor political influence within Israel.

The social status of Hungarian Jews in Israel remained contradictory. Educational level and occupational prestige placed Jewish immigrants from Hungary above the large groups of Polish, Russian, and Romanian ashkenazi immigrants, though below the smaller groups of immigrants from Austria, Yugoslavia, Western Europe, and the United States. They were also more likely to be self-employed than other Eastern Europeans. Nevertheless, on the scale of Zionist prestige they were close to the bottom of the ashkenazi hierarchy, and this status discrepancy led to a feeling of being discriminated against.

The one area in which Jews from Hungary stood out was satire—typical of those who are close enough to the center to see its workings but cannot be part of it. Two of the most popular Israeli cartoonists, Dosh and Ze'ev, and the best-known satirist in the 1960s, Ephraim Kishon, were of Hungarian origin. Kishon's weekly column in *Ma'ariv* and his movies (*The Blaumilch Canal* and *Salah Shabati*) offered a counterpoint to the mythical, heroic image of the young state. Kishon presented the immigrant's perspective on the overly bureaucratized state, becoming one of the first writers to legitimate the self-deprecating humor of Eastern European Jews in Israel itself. The characters Kishon created became national icons, from Schtuks, the plumber who never showed up on time and never completed the job, through Ervinka and Kunstetter, who forever chased economic security and dignity in their struggle with both family members and the Histadrut, to the Gingi, the generic, indifferent Israeli whose slovenly, slipshod, and slapdash efforts at improvisation, while charming at times, could easily lead to catastrophe. In Kishon's most hilarious story, "Ze ma sheyesh" (That's what there is), he savagely lampooned doing things in a *partatch*, or half-assed, fashion, an Israeli phenomenon unfortunately all too real for immigrants. Yoshka subscribed to the Hungarian-language daily paper *Új Kelet* (New East), which faithfully reproduced Kishon's column and provided immigrants with a window onto their new country.

Being an immigrant, paradoxically, became a permanent status in Israel, where institutions ask citizens to fill out their year of immigration on every official questionnaire and document, regardless of how long ago it happened. Another, and crucial, hierarchy stratified Israelis along a time line. New immigrants were treated to the *vatik*'s (old-timer's) ritualized litany of *"kesheanu banu artza"* (when we arrived), detailed stories of hardships they had endured before independence—often delivered with a heavy helping of condescension.

Yoshka arrived after the *tzena* (austerity regime) that characterized the era of mass immigration, when basic foods were rationed, though some—such as fillet of cod—were still available only with ration tickets, and most sugar in use was brown. Israel in the late 1950s was a relatively poor country. Besides a radio, a four-burner stove, and a refrigerator, which was in the process of replacing the icebox, families had few appliances. It took at least one year and sometimes several to get phone service. Since not more than one family in twenty owned a phone, most immigrants would use the phones of those few neighbors who had them. In the absence of phones, instead of setting times for get-togethers in advance, Yoshka and his friends habitually visited one another unannounced. Laundry was collected by laundrymen at homes, taken away, washed, delivered again, and paid for by weight. The milkman delivered milk to the door in glass bottles. Horse-driven carriages would roll down the street with vendors yelling in Yiddish, "*Alte zachen*" (old stuff), seeking to buy and sell used goods. Vendors hawked water-melons out of carts, as were, to kids' delight, seedy but sweet sabra fruits and chewy sugarcane sticks. In 1960, only 4 percent of families owned private cars. Television was not introduced until 1965, long after other countries already had it.

The most pressing task for the Spronz family in 1957 was finding a way to earn a living. This laid heavily on Yoshka's and Franziska's minds. Franziska found work first, with a lawyer who processed restitution applications from Holocaust survivors. The topic of reparation and restitution (*pitzuyim*) was a major bone of contention in Israel. Many opposed it on the grounds that Israel should maintain no ties whatsoever with the German state and that accepting restitution would cleanse the Germans of their heinous crimes. As the Israeli Knesset (parliament) debated and adopted the Reparations Agreement, demonstrators battled the police outside. Under this agreement, which the Israeli government signed in September 1952, West Germany paid the Israeli government a fixed sum in German goods over several years and sent restitution to individual victims in lump-sum cash and pensions. Yoshka and Franziska had no misgivings: they saw no reason to let Germany enjoy stolen and looted Jewish property, and having arrived with so little from Communist Hungary, they were in need of resources to rebuild their lives.

Yoshka's search for a livelihood took the better part of a year. After examining various options, he bought from a retired owner a small workshop for manufacturing leather belts for men. Though he had never worked with leather, Yoshka welcomed the opportunity to be independent and get by on his wits. The workshop contained an industrial-quality sawing machine and some other tools and implements, to which he later added a table-long cutting machine. It was in a dark basement. Only its ceiling-level windows looked out to the street, but it was near Tel Aviv's famed Dizengoff Square. Yoshka purchased leather in rolls, bought buckles, later had some cast manually, and imported others. After cutting the leather, gluing smaller pieces, sawing, and attaching the buckles to the belts in the workshop until late afternoon, he would work on the balcony of his apartment until late evening and during the weekend. Since some aspects of the work required little concentration, the family—Yoshka, Franziska, and their son—would sit around and converse while wrapping and packaging each belt. Yoshka's hands were busy. He kept busy. There was so much to forget, and work was the best elixir.

He marketed his belts under the brand name Tikvah—"hope" in Hebrew. The name was symbolic but also a rendering of *esperanza*, the Spanish word for hope and the origin of the family name *Spronz*, whose erstwhile bearers, as tradition had it, left Spain during the expulsion of the Jews in 1492. Franziska had continued working at the law office, but once Yoshka became adept at manufacturing the belts, she quit her job and became a traveling saleslady. She went by bus to Haifa, Jerusalem, Tiberias, and other towns, lugging a collection of belt and leather samples. She encountered the whole gamut of Israeli ethnicities and would report to Yoshka proudly every time she made a new Arab client in Jaffa or Haifa. This was now a family business, and its success depended on the strength of the family's ties. Working together at home in the afternoons, evenings, and weekends, the Spronzes, sometimes including their son, combined family time and work, each enhancing the other. When the Tikvah belts were sold to larger buyers—for example the department stores of the Histadrut's Hamashbir and some of the glitzy stores on Dizengoff Street—the struggling firm reached a safe haven. It always remained a small family business, later with the addition of two older relatives as employees, but provided a secure existence and allowed self-reliance. The fortunes of the Tikvah belts reflected the steady expansion of the Israeli economy, which grew at an impressive annual average rate of 10.6 percent during the 1950s and 1960s.

The economic system Yoshka and Franziska encountered in Israel was very different from the prewar and the postwar ones of the Hungary they had left behind. Yoshka spent many months learning the ropes of the new system. He discovered that the state was powerful, though not as much as in Communist Hungary, and while there was a private sector, it was weaker than prewar Hungary's and depended on and was guided by state institutions and policies. Industrial and commercial companies were usually small, their business volumes paltry, skill levels fairly low, and credit at a premium. The larger firms were owned by the state and engaged in infrastructure, and another 20 percent, producer cooperatives and corporations, belonged to the Histadrut and covered a wide range of economic activities, from the Egged bus company though Bank Hapoalim to the industrial concern Koor. These bodies, like the kibbutz, enjoyed the advantage of shared resources and an internal market. During the 1950s, the government maintained direct control over the economy, for example by selectively issuing import licenses, pegging the Israeli lira (or pound) to the US dollar at a fixed rate, and laying its hands on desperately needed foreign currency. The heaviest and bluntest economic artillery deployed by the government was the periodic devaluation of the Israeli lira relative to the US dollar. Its goal was to make Israeli exports more competitive, but its effect was a price hike that burdened all domestic consumers.

Though in Israel's small economy Yoshka remained a small manufacturer—or, better, artisan—his keen understanding of the economy and business shone through again: relatives, friends, and acquaintances repeatedly asked him for advice and sometimes loans. Others regularly sought his opinion on family matters, marriage, child rearing, and the like. He provided thoughtful advice in a blunt fashion, reaffirming values of old-fashioned integrity while asserting individuals' (especially children's) freedom of choice. Like Candide, the famed protagonist of Voltaire's philosophical romance by that name, Yoshka had sought to re-create in the East a small and vital family and community from the ruins and ravages of Europe (though his Israel itself was never safe from threat).

In 1959, Yoshka's name was read on the national radio service Kol Israel's *Searching for Relatives* program, which ran before the twelve o'clock news for years after the Holocaust. Otto Frank, his companion from his barrack in Auschwitz, had sought him out, and the two were finally able to resume their friendship. Otto visited Israel; Yoshka learned about Anne Frank's diary, and Otto read Yoshka's memoir of the camp. Yoshka also had great satisfaction in reestablishing contact with other friends and some distant relatives in Canada and the United States.

Yoshka's immigration to Israel was the result of several push factors—the outrage at the tragedies that befell him and the continued feeling of insecurity he and Franziska experienced in Hungary—but it also had pull factors. He would not experiment with building a life anywhere else and sought the quiet dignity of being at home. In Israel, this sentiment contributed to a spirit of unity, born in part from the pride of being the generation that had witnessed and achieved the birth of Jewish statehood, in part from the common struggle against austerity and deprivation, and for new immigrants from Europe, in part from the enormity of the turn their lives had taken since the Holocaust.

Yoshka and Franziska proudly identified with the State of Israel and became solid, though passive, supporters of the dominant Mapai (the political party of the labor settlement movement) as a way of expressing that identification. For them, the leaders of Mapai were foremost the leaders of the state, but Yoshka always scoffed at the heavily partisan nature of Israeli public life. Mapai and Histadrut members claimed the status and prestige of pioneers solely on the basis of belonging to the party rather than by setting a personal example; in fact, Mapai decorated with the *pioneering* label any facet of life or group of individuals that it wished to promote. Yoshka questioned Mapai's attempts to fully identify with the State of Israel, which it helped to create and which reflected many of its practices, especially after the late 1960s, when the party came to be viewed as a fountainhead of corruption and the Histadrut as institutionalized selfishness.

Immigrants adopt various strategies to become natives of their new land. Yoshka's identification was in great measure based on the safety Israel provided to Jews.

Though it did not have mountains comparable to those of Central Europe where he used to climb and hike, Yoshka would take his family on several tours each year to get to know the country. The year after their arrival, he went to watch the Yom Ha'atzmaut (Independence Day) military parade in Tel Aviv, which included a display of Soviet weapons captured from Egypt in the 1956 war. In June 1967, he sat with Franziska on the bleachers in Haifa watching the annual Independence Day parade, during which Yitzhak Rabin received the famous message about Syrian troop concentrations on the Israeli border. The response to this and subsequent Egyptian troop movements, the removal of UN buffer forces, and the closing of the Straits of Tiran by the Egyptian leader Gamal Abdel Nasser led to the Six-Day War, which began on June 5. When his son returned from that war, Yoshka felt that now his family had also won. The victory in the war seemed a vindication of the decision to immigrate to Israel.

Yoshka's bond with the Israeli state had already been powerfully enhanced when Israeli agents in Argentina captured Adolf Eichmann, who was the architect of Jewish deportations to the death camps during the Holocaust, and secretly transported him to Israel, where he was put on trial in 1961–62. The daily radio broadcasts of the trial—the Israeli state visiting justice on one of the most brutal victimizers of Jews—were a cathartic experience for Yoshka. Though the trial brought the tragic past back to life, it also served as a way to make manifest the bond between Israel and the Jewish past. Even so, he did not relinquish his hope for a universal lesson to be drawn from the Holocaust. The sentiment Yoshka expressed in the concluding sentence of the preface to his Auschwitz memoir in August 1945, though with premature optimism, still rings true: "Let this book serve as an assurance that humanity acknowledges its errors and will not again, by rights laid claim to by the strong, fling some group as defenseless prey to hatred and cruel instincts."

A NOTE ON SOURCES

This biography is based on the typewritten autobiographies of Joseph Spronz and Franziska Spronz; a published memoir, József Spronz, *Fogoly Voltam Auschwitzban* (I was held captive in Auschwitz; Budapest: Gergely, 1946); the protocol of the testimony of Joseph Spronz, who was deposed at the headquarters of the Hungarian State Police's Political Security Department in Budapest, in the war crimes trial of Col. Márton Zöldi, from October 24, 1945 (file #19868); and interviews of family members, letters, photographs, and documents.

I also relied on data from the 1961 Israeli census on Jewish immigrants from Hungary versus other immigrant groups that was prepared by my colleague Aziza Khazzoom.

SUGGESTION FOR FURTHER READING

For an overview of Jewish life in Austro-Hungary and Hungary, see Raphael Patai, *The Jews of Hungary: History, Culture, Psychology* (Detroit: Wayne State University, 1996); Nathaniel Katzburg, *Hungary and the Jews: Policy and Legislation, 1920–1943* (Ramat Gan, Israel: Bar Ilan University Press, 1981); Vera Ranki, *The Politics of Inclusion and Exclusion: Jews and Nationalism in Hungary* (New York: Holmes and Meier, 1999); and William O. McCagg, *Jewish Nobles and Geniuses in Modern Hungary* (New York: Columbia University Press, 1972). For the history of Hungary, see Jörg K. Hoensch, *A History of Modern Hungary, 1867–1986* (London: Longman, 1988).

Of the vast literature on Israel, I recommend Yonathan Shapiro, *The Formative Years of the Israeli Labor Party: The Organization of Power, 1919–1930* (London: Sage, 1976); Baruch Kimmerling, *The Invention and Decline of Israeliness: State, Society, and the Military* (Berkeley: University of California Press, 2001); and Gershon Shafir and Yoav Peled, *Being Israeli: The Dynamics of Multiple Citizenship* (Cambridge: Cambridge University Press, 2002).

12

The Trees Die Standing

A Story of a Palestinian Refugee

Ramzy Baroud

BEIT DARAS

For most historians of Palestine, Palestinians as well as Israelis, the village of Beit Daras warrants at best modest mention in the larger narrative of 1948. For Palestinians, its fall and destruction in May 1948 were not unique; the town was one of nearly five hundred Palestinian villages that were evacuated and then completely flattened during the war years of 1947–49, leaving some eight hundred thousand Palestinian Arabs as refugees. For Zionist Jews, Beit Daras was just another hill, known by the battle code name Operation Barak, to be conquered and re-created as an Israeli space, free of its former inhabitants and their history.

Beit Daras's inconsequential existence would raise little notice, save two concrete pillars that once upon a time served as an entrance to a small mosque. Like its walls, those faithful to its walls are long gone. Yet somehow they still insist on identifying with that serene place and that simple existence. On that very spot, on the shoulder of that small hill, huddled between numerous meadows and fences of blooming cactus, there once rested that lovely little village. And also there, somewhere in the vicinity of the two pillars, in a tiny mud-brick home with a small extension used for storing crops and a dove tower on the roof, my father, Mohammed Baroud, was born.

1948

The narrative of the conquest of Beit Daras, although reflective of the overall subjugation of Palestine, was as unique as it was tragic for the village's residents.

Beginning in the early part of 1948, the town was under bombardment and surrounded in all directions. There seemed to be no way out. The Beit Daras fighters who were armed said they were going to see if the road was open. They moved forward and shot a few times to see if anyone would return fire. No one did.

Umm (an honorific meaning "mother of," usually followed by the name of her eldest son) Adel, one of the former residents of Beit Daras who now lives in a Gaza refugee camp, remembers that the fighters came back and said, "The road is open; evacuate the people." So the people went out, including those who were gathered at my family house. (If a bomb had hit the house, it would have killed everyone there.) They were mostly women and children. But the Zionist forces were hiding and waiting to ambush them. As Umm Adel recalls,

> The Jews let the people get out, and then they whipped them with bombs and machine guns. More people fell than those who were able to run. My sister and I . . . started running through the fields; we'd fall and get up. My sister and I escaped together holding each other's hand. The people who took the main road were either killed or injured, as were those who went through the fields. The firing was falling on the people like sand, the bombs from one side and the machine guns from the other. The Jews were on the hill, where there was a school and a water reservoir for people and the vegetables. They showered the people with machine-gun fire. A lot of the people died and got injured.

After months of sporadic bombardment, Mohammed (my grandfather) and his family, along with many of the villagers of Beit Daras, finally and frantically scoured their little mud-brick homes, demarcating those items they would have to part with and those that would be of use on the mysterious journey on which they would soon embark. A few old blankets, tea, sugar, rice, cheese, olives . . . and the scant necessities with which they could afford to burden their one faithful donkey. Mohammed sharpened the kitchen knife, the only implement he would have to protect his family from Jewish militia ambushes. His wife Zeinab gazed around her modest kitchen, with its soft earthen floor and a simple wooden table in the center of the room. Bundles of garlic, peppers, dried mint, thyme, and chamomile adorned the smooth mud walls. At that moment, she felt that the peace and simplicity of life in Beit Daras were something to be coveted by kings and that she wouldn't trade her home for a palace. With their own hands, Mohammed and Zeinab had built this house, the place where their first five children were born, where they had escaped poverty and gained prominence and merit in the community.

Spring was one of the most beautiful times of the year in Palestine's countryside. With everything in full bloom, the wind carried the perfume of apricots, almonds, oranges, and lemons for miles. As the villagers embarked on their journey, a rite of passage for generations of Palestinians, many took a long moment to breathe in the fragrance of the fields and orchards, to snatch a large handful of the earth of Beit Daras, wrap it in a small piece of cloth, and tuck it away for safekeeping. They stored their deeds and keys safely, in preparation for their return.

Mohammed, Zeinab, and their children headed south. That was all they knew. First to Isdud, then to Hamameh, then to Gaza. Everywhere they stopped to rest, they were chased with mortars and airplanes and bombs. As the bombardments progressed and more villages were razed, the roads became more and more populated, with some people who carried on with a great sense of urgency and others who wandered aimlessly and in a daze.

Trotting behind his mother, Mohammed and Zeinab's son Mohammed grew hungry and tired. The sun was oppressive and beat down on the back of his neck, so he stopped under the shade of a tree for just a few moments. It didn't take long for the boy to regain his strength, after which he ran to catch up with his family. Meanwhile, Zeinab couldn't remember the last time she had seen him and discovered that he was no longer behind her. She became hysterical, calling his name and running directionless; a deep-seated pain in her belly warned that she might have lost her boy forever. She asked everyone that passed, "Peace be upon you; have you seen my boy Mohammed?" or "For God's sake, have you seen my son? He is ten years old, and he went missing this morning." But she was only one of many who had become separated from their children. Mothers and fathers would express their commiseration, others would say nothing, but for a short moment they would share a knowing gaze, then sadly move on.

After an eternity had passed that afternoon, Zeinab spotted her son, gently tugging on the sleeve of another mother, repeating a supplication similar to Zeinab's, "Peace be upon you; have you seen my mother?" In a mix of rage and relief, she swept Mohammed up in her arms, chastising him while smothering him with kisses. For the rest of the journey, she never let anyone fall behind.

Back in Beit Daras, the houses were blown up, the fields burned. The great mosque was razed with dynamite. It was all gone: The diwans where the mukhtars met to drink coffee with the elders of the village. The elementary school. The al-Massriyyen neighborhood. The small mud-brick home with the dove tower. The citrus orchard that perfumed the village every spring. There would be no going home.

THE WORLD OUTSIDE THE TENT

When Mohammed Baroud, a ten-year-old boy from the now distant and destroyed village of Beit Daras, moved the dirtied blanket that served as a door to his family's tent in Gaza, the world outside was entirely different from what he had once called home. There was little promise here, no lush farms in the distance, and no green meadows to serve as playgrounds. Instead, an awesome and terrifying sight greeted him: tents scattered as far as the eye could see; thousands of unknown, anxious faces; neighbors he had never met; and a whole new reality with which he was hardly familiar. He was overwhelmed with fear and indecision and quickly snuck back to lie down by his parents' side.

The Gaza Strip then was home to a population of eighty thousand—mostly Muslims, plus a small Christian community—largely in urban centers: Gaza City, Khan Yunis, Deir al-Balah, and a few others. It also had nomadic tribes scattered all about. The arrival of well over two hundred thousand people all at once disturbed the established demographics of the Strip and opened the door wide for hostility toward the vulnerable refugees. Some stood in endless lines to receive rations and handouts from the Quakers, the first international group that arrived on the scene to help them. Others offered their services to the relatively wealthy families in the cities or worked as maids or cheap laborers for the nomadic tribes, allowing themselves to be exploited to the highest degree imaginable. They often received a small meal as pay for their long hours on the Gaza farms, one that a mother or father would split with their children. Although they were used to three meals a day, eating just one was no longer frowned upon, for some families were hardly so lucky as to have even that.

It was not until December 8, 1949, roughly a year and a half after the start of the *Nakba,* that the United Nations General Assembly created the UN Relief and Works Agency for Palestine Refugees in the Near East (UNRWA) as a temporary organization to provide aid for the refugees who were soon, supposedly, to return home. UNRWA replaced an ad hoc agency, the United Nations Relief for Palestine Refugees, a group that had operated with no staff or budget, only volunteers from the Red Cross and various religious organizations.

Mohammed would awaken each day at dawn. He would watch his father conclude his morning prayer, and together, with empty stomachs, they would head to one Egyptian army encampment or another, extend their arms well beyond the fence, and beg. His mother, Zeinab, joined thousands of mothers working as cheap laborers in Gaza's farms, toiling all day for a few tomatoes or, if they were lucky, enough money to purchase some tea and sugar. Ahmad, the Barouds' oldest son, found a job at a quarry. His muscular build was more than suitable for such rigorous labor. Unlike the rest, Ahmad returned not with crumbs but with cash—not much, but enough to buy some food and milk for baby Ibrahim.

The years passed, and soon Mohammed was a teenager. He spent much of his time in the streets of Gaza, which were rife with the most interesting and exciting stories and activities. He listened for hours to heated debates and quarrels in coffee shops, as refugees argued about their fate and who would be their likely rulers. Both Egypt and Transjordan labored to ensure that they would manage the only Palestinian leadership that would enjoy any sense of legitimacy within their domains, so the countries quarreled between themselves and also with unruly Palestinians, those who insisted on representing themselves.

THE FREEDOM FIGHTERS

What most impressed Mohammed were the fedayeen—guerrilla commandos—and their daring strikes deep inside Israel. They were mostly young Palestinian refugees but also included some Egyptians who operated outside the scope of their government, Islamic fighters, and others. Their operations grew bolder by the day. They snuck into Israel like ghosts in the night, with primitive weapons and homemade bombs. They killed Israeli soldiers, stole their weapons, and returned with these weapons the following night. Some snuck back into their villages in Palestine, from which they took food, blankets, and whatever money they had saved but failed to retrieve in the rush of war. Those who never returned received martyrs' funerals, with thousands of refugees marching alongside the ones who carried a symbolic coffin into a graveyard. Indeed, hundreds never returned, and few of their bodies were ever recovered. Following every fedayeen strike, the Israeli army would retaliate against Gaza's refugees, inspiring yet more support and recruits for the growing commando movement.

Mohammed was on the threshold of manhood when freedom fighting became his calling. The fedayeen were the antithesis to his humiliation and submissiveness and a manifestation of all the anger and frustration he felt. He offered his services as a watchman for them as they made their initial and most dangerous crossovers into Israel.

As the fedayeen's attacks inside Israel intensified, so did Israeli reprisals, which targeted the Egyptian army (which Israel believed was supporting the fedayeen) as well as Palestinian civilians. Israel justified its actions as a natural response to protect its borders. But Palestinians disputed these borders and this assertion, knowing that some of their villages still stood where they had for hundreds of years in areas that Israel now claimed. Mohammed strongly believed that the path back to Beit Daras began with the fedayeen's bold incursions into Israel, to his homeland. Neither Alexander the Great's bloody conquest of 332 B.C.E. nor Alexander Jannaeus's brutal attack of 96 B.C.E. broke Gaza's spirit or took away from its eternal grandeur. It always rose again to reach a degree of civilization unheard of, as in the fifth century C.E., when it first attained major regional importance. The Crusaders surrendered their strategic control of the city to Saladin in 1170, opening up yet another era of prosperity and growth, which was only occasionally interrupted by conquerors and outsiders with unavailing colonial designs. Neglected ruins of past civilizations were reminders that Gaza's enemies would never prevail and would at best merely register their presence with another disregarded structure of mortar and stone.

Mohammed watched the events of 1948–54 unfolding in awe: the retreat of the Egyptian army, the quick reappearance of Israel, the remarkable actions of the fedayeen, and finally the massive demonstrations that represented a people's power, *his* people's power. Two goals occupied his every fiber at the time, self-education and joining the army, wishes that were duly granted, but at a heavy price.

During an evening that seemed like any other, Mohammed told his family with poise, coolness, and a solemn voice that he would be joining a Palestinian unit in the Egyptian army. Strangely, no member of his family chuckled upon hearing his statement. His father looked him in the eyes and cautioned him about the kind of life he was choosing for himself.

Joining the army is one thing, but joining an ill-prepared army unit in the Gaza Strip facing formidable Israeli forces during the very tense years of the late 1950s was an act of insanity. Mohammed enlisted when he was around nineteen years old, and within a year he was ranked a corporal, the youngest in his unit. He also taught in training programs held for fresh recruits. He often bragged about being the fastest in his unit to assemble and disassemble an automatic rifle.

THE FIG TREE

Mohammed's unit was stationed in the central Gaza Strip. After the end of his shift every day, he would sit and read in a quiet corner for hours, late into the night. His love for Russian literature was clear from the start: *Anna Karenina* and *The Mother* were among his favorites. He was particularly fond of reading under one old fig tree. It was pleasant looking and shady.

The tree had another great significance. Sitting in its shadow one day, he noticed a girl. While very beautiful, her face carried an innate sadness and loss. She reminded him of himself. The moment she walked past him, he would drop his book and gaze, accompanying her with his eyes until she disappeared behind a corner or into an alley. She avoided his attentions and looked the other way. He respected her modesty but was determined to know her name. "I knew from the first moment that we were soul mates," he once said. Mohammed was in his early twenties when he fell in love for the first time, with Zarefah Tayeh.

One morning Mohammed spotted Zarefah and offered her a smile. The young man went as far as walking by her side on her way home and asking her name, audacious moves by the standards of the time. Almost arrogantly but with poise, Zarefah turned to him, saying, "My name is Zarefah, and I come from a respectable family. My father may be dead, but I have a mother, a family, and a home. If you were a noble man, you wouldn't approach me in the street, for we have a respected home and an address." Mohammed was equally taken aback and impressed by the girl's forthright answer, and within a few days, Zeinab, joined by her daughter and a few other relatives, was sipping sweet mint tea at Zarefah's house, negotiating the terms of Mohammed's marriage proposal.

To mark their engagement, Mohammed told Zarefah he loved her, placed on her finger a cheap copper ring, and vowed to replace it with gold one day. Zarefah agreed to this plan and told him that she loved him too, a claim that Mohammed lightheartedly repeated endlessly during their twenty-four years of marriage and Zarefah vehemently denied.

Mohammed heard of many people seeking their fortunes in the deserts of Saudi Arabia, and that's where he resolved to go to earn enough to provide a dowry for his wife and a home for his future family.

THE SAUDI ADVENTURE

Mohammed sat behind a small cart that he had borrowed for the day. It had two large wheels, two handles, and his goods stacked ever so neatly on top. Becoming a street merchant was his first winning move in Saudi Arabia. He was handsome, with a polite demeanor, and he did not hesitate to exploit these valuable traits. The young peddler to Ethiopian expats in Mecca was the darling of the ladies, who bought his knickknacks with little bargaining, to his utter delight. The next day he returned with twice as many goods, and this time the cart was his own. The lucky streak continued, for days and weeks, and his cart was one of the most loaded with everything that a poor woman dwelling in a tent would ever need: towels, undergarments, creams and lotions, and a few "genuine" Egyptian perfumes.

One day, a large lady probably in her forties approached Mohammed, complaining of her many ailments as if he were a learned physician. She had a terrible headache, nightly fevers, and unbearable joint pain. "I would do anything to feel better," she said. Amazingly, Mohammed knew of the poor lady's exact sickness, and equally astounding, he had the very cure. To assure her that he was not a quack, he repeated the exact symptoms she had just detailed. She nodded her head in admiration. "I swear by Allah that you speak truth," she said with broken voice and equally broken Arabic. Of course, Mohammed's magic cure was nothing but a cheap ointment. He instructed the woman, in a solemn voice, to go home, slather herself with the ointment, wrap herself up in two thick blankets, and go to sleep. "In the morning, you shall be healed," he promised. She ran home, anxious to follow the instructions to the letter, not minding the fact that swaddling oneself with two blankets all night in Saudi Arabia's scorching heat was a most foolish prescription, to say the least.

Mohammed brushed this off as a silly encounter, and the next day he had completely forgotten about the woman, until she showed up at the market frantically looking for him. "When I saw her, I though I was dead," he once said. But she didn't tear him to pieces, as he thought she would. When she located him, she showered him with kisses, hugs, and tears. "Last night I thought I was going to die, but I woke up this morning feeling as strong as a horse," she proclaimed. She gave him more money and promised to direct her friends to his cart, for he was not just a salesman but a learned man of wisdom, a holy man.

Mohammed, of course, didn't mind the new title and learned to live with it. His magic potion became the primary item on his cart, displacing the Egyptian perfume. He prescribed it for nearly every ailment, ranging from headache, cold, and diarrhea to, yes, even problems conceiving.

During Mohammed's nearly three years in Mecca and Jeddah, he had no way to communicate with his family or his fiancée. Therefore it was a great surprise when he finally showed up at Zarefah's family's doorstep in the Buraij refugee camp, wearing a silky white shirt and white pants. Just when Zarefah was ready to give in to her mother's demands that she marry a different man, Mohammed arrived, as handsome as ever, loaded with exotic presents—most importantly a golden ring, the genuine kind, not a cheap imitation.

Soon Mohammed had yet another reason to defend Gaza, not only for its own sake, nor his and Zarefah's, but also for that of Suma, his firstborn, who came into the world in 1964. Suma's birth brought both joy and dread to her parents; Zarefah's first meal after delivering the baby in her rented room was a bowl of garlic soup, contributed by a kindly but equally poor neighbor lady.

Other women took shifts looking after the pale mother and spared some of their food to feed her. Zarefah could hardly produce any milk, but Suma blossomed nonetheless, and her happy chatter often distracted the young couple from their many worries. Mohammed had reenlisted in the army on his return to Gaza, and on his first day of duty, on a cold Gaza dawn, he held his wife and softly kissed a sleeping Suma, then reported to his unit somewhere in the southern Gaza Strip.

Mohammed went to sleep every night to the sound of Egyptian president Gamal Abdel Nasser's speeches and spent most of his days between training camps and the trenches of Gaza. Recruits would repeat after him, as they jumped through hoops, climbed walls, and hopped through tires, "*Awda, awda, awda,*" "Return, return, return." Oh, how they all longed to return to their homes and land in Palestine.

In the early months of 1967, Soviet intelligence confirmed Syria's and Egypt's estimation that Israel was preparing for a major attack on Syria. On May 25, Nasser declared his country's intent to block the Straits of Tiran, which lead to the Gulf of Aqaba. Soon enough, on June 5, Israel launched a massive "preemptive" aerial attack against Egypt and moved in force against the West Bank, Jordan, and Syria. Israeli warplanes attacked all of Egypt's seventeen air bases and within hours obliterated most of the country's air force. In a moment, a generation's hope for freedom, return, and victory was completely dashed, preemptively pulverized.

The bitter fighting on the outskirts of Gaza soon concluded with utter defeat. Palestinians there continued their tradition of facing tanks with bare chests and worthless pistols, civilians running away from falling shells and whizzing bullets, all to no avail. The air smelled of blood and salt. The haggard army truck that carried Mohammed across the desert was now an all-purpose-vehicle, transporting living and wounded but mostly dead soldiers. Those killed, Palestinian and Egyptian, were piled atop one another in no specific order. Some of the wounded were quietly uttering Qur'anic verses, those that one would recite before a final breath.

During the Israeli attack, in defiance of Mohammed's orders, Zarefah left Suma with her mother and began running south in search of Mohammed's camp, but the intense fighting forced her to take shelter in a lemon tree orchard. She waited there for hours and hours, finally submitting to her exhaustion and sleeping. She woke up to a violent commotion, including talk in a foreign language with which she was not familiar. The voices drew near; they were abrasive and commanding, interrupted or joined by screams, followed by submissive words pleading in Arabic, "For God's sake, don't take him, he is only a child," "Please spare him, and may you return safe and sound to your own mother."

Such exchanges soon ended with a hail of bullets and shouts in the unfamiliar language. But not long after, the commands were loud and in clear Arabic: "To all of those hiding in the orchard, come out with your hands on your heads. Those who violate the army's order will be shot at once." For the first time, Zarefah came face to face with Israeli soldiers.

Men were shackled, women and children were ordered to run, and Israeli troops shot at their feet. With all her might, Zarefah raced until she reached her home. She flew past her mother and clutched her daughter like a rag doll. Zarefah felt the weight of the world coming down on her shoulders. "I think Mohammed is dead," she wailed before falling into her mother's arms.

To Zarefah's great relief and everyone's surprise, Mohammed returned by foot from Sinai many months later, physically and spiritually battered. He returned to a place where refugees lives remained unchanged: politically marginalized and economically devastated.

THE AGITATOR

Weeks after his return, Mohammed and others who served in the army were summoned to the local police station, where they were asked to join a police force under the command of the Israeli army. Their job would be to coordinate with the Israeli army in "security matters" and to guard the coastal areas from "terrorist infiltration."

The army's spokesman said, "Israel has nothing against Gaza, and we want your help in keeping peace in this area, by apprehending those who force Israel to act in ways that bring harm to your families."

Mohammed turned his back to the Israeli entourage, faced his former comrades, and avidly countered. He delivered his own speech, which went something like this:

> My brothers and my comrades, we are all joined by a common sorrow and fate. We all fondly remember the rolling hills and valleys of our homeland, its villages, towns, its farms, and its humble yet dignified way of life. We long for the days of quiet and peaceful coexistence that Palestine offered, and we grieve the loss of life, the assault on our dignity, the destruction of our schools, mosques, homes in hundreds of villages that are now a fleeting memory. Our struggle has been an honorable and worthy cause, and it is by far more precious than the trivial salaries and extraneous police uniforms the invader offers. I would rather starve, along with my family, as a free man than live rich in slavery with badges of dishonor.

Soon after, the Israeli military intelligence desk in Gaza had an exhaustive and detailed file on him. Mohammed Baroud was officially an agitator. Such a stance, while sustaining his respect for himself and his people's history, was horrendous economically. He was forced to find the most eccentric ways to feed his family, which had grown again, with the birth of his son Anwar, meaning "a brighter light," in 1967.

The one-and-a-half-year-old Anwar's looks and behavior promised a smart, handsome boy. Zarefah and Mohammed couldn't wait for him to grow up. But in Gaza, there were no guarantees, even with simple expectations. Anwar woke up one morning with a high fever. Zarefah rushed him to the UNRWA clinic, which had nothing to offer but aspirin. She sat on the floor of the clinic for hours, until her son died in her arms. She swaddled him in her scarf and walked home. That night, Mohammed returned home to a dreadful look on Zarefah's face: "Anwar is dead."

They buried Anwar in a little plot in the refugee camp's main graveyard. Mohammed understood that poverty had killed his son and spent the rest of his life fearing the revisitation of that injustice. He spent his days at his son's grave, placing coins and candy in the dirt, telling Anwar of all the grand things that awaited him in paradise.

But life continued. A year later, in 1968, Mohammed and Zarefah had another son. They also named him Anwar. I was born on July 22, 1972. The midwife who helped bring me into the world was an old refugee woman, the same one who had helped deliver my older siblings, Suma, Anwar, the new Anwar, and Thaer, meaning "revolutionary."

STRIKING GOLD?

As Mohammed's family grew, so did its financial demands and expectations. After years of resistance, he decided that he had no choice but to brave work in Israel. He insisted that his decision was not a compromise of his principles. He was not a cheap laborer but a businessman. Mohammed toiled to find any dignified interpretation of his new work. But in fact what he did was travel through Israel looking for scrap metal, factory defects, and such to sell back in Gaza. He confined his early trips to areas close to the Strip, such as Ashkelon and Kiryat Gat, but eventually expanded his reach to Tel Aviv, Rishon Letzion, and so on. It pained him to see Palestinian ruins of the Nakba; he tried to relate the Hebrew names of some of the Israeli towns and villages to their Arabic origins. His taxi repeatedly passed by the town of Ashdod, once Isdud, where his brother Ahmad had gone to school. The ruins of the school, riddled with bullets, still occupied a hill that greeted him every time. But Mohammed needed to focus on the task at hand.

One day Mohammed struck gold, or rather a shipment of tomato sauce and lemon juice. An Israeli food company was about to discard two enormous containers of food products, when he stepped in. The items were edible, but the cans had been exposed to moisture and became corroded with rust, hence unmarketable, according to Israeli standards. Mohammed offered a small price for both containers; his proposal was immediately accepted. He then faced the challenge of coming up with the money to purchase the containers and transport them back to Nuseirat. He rushed to Gaza to prepare for what would be the deal of a lifetime. Zarefah readily offered a golden necklace, which Mohammed had bought for her in Ramallah, to offset some of the costs. They gathered whatever little savings they had, and Mohammed rushed back to Israel, but not before making two important stops, one at a Gaza goldsmith's and another to hire a large truck.

Just before the Nuseirat market was ready to close, Mohammed stood atop the back of a truck and with a handheld megaphone called out, "Oh people of Nuseirat, gather around for the deal of a lifetime: imported lemon juice and tomato sauce at unbeatable prices. Ten cans for one lira!" The dead market quickly revived, not because of his deafening shouts but because such a price was unheard-of. Within an hour, Mohammed had sold all of the rusty cans to shopkeepers and individual customers, reserving the nicest few for his devoted wife, who sat at home not knowing the nature or outcome of his latest undertaking.

Before returning home, Mohammed made one last stop, to buy Zarefah's necklace back for the same price that a kindly goldsmith had paid for it earlier the same day. When Mohammed arrived at his house, he spoke not a word to Zarefah, and typical of his playful manner, he pulled out a cigarette and sat down, puffing and shaking his head as if his venture had been an utter failure. It was his classic trick before delivering any good news. But Zarefah was too naïve to decode his many ploys. She sat down by him and consoled, "May all the money in the world be damned as long as you have your health. So what, you lost the money and the necklace? Who cares? Just remember, we will always have each other."

Mohammed, still playing his absurd game, took the necklace from his pocket. "Oh, are you talking about this necklace?" he inquired with a crafty smile. Zarefah was befuddled. What could possibly be the meaning of this? "And are you referring to this money?" he asked as he pulled a large roll of bills out of his pocket, much more than she had ever seen. Zarefah was dumbfounded. She hugged her husband and cried. Mohammed hugged her back triumphantly. His little charade had achieved the maximum intended results, and his successful business call generated enough money for him to return to Israel for more such adventures.

INTIFADA: AND ALL HELL BROKE LOOSE

For me and my siblings, being born, growing up, and coming of age in the refugee camp was all we knew. Perhaps in some merciful way, it was a much easier existence for us than for our parents, for we had never tasted the sweetness of dignity and a life free of Israeli occupation. We all had a very strange and ironic dependence on our enemies, for they determined daily what our fate was to be: whether we would have electricity, whether there would be water, if we would be allowed to go to school or even step outside our front door. We hated them, and yet we needed them and their approval for every step we made.

As a young boy, I endured the open-air prison of the refugee camp by writing poetry. My writings were bold and revolutionary, and signing my name to them would have certainly brought a lengthy prison sentence. So I created them underground, and a very sophisticated network at my school smuggled them to masked men. The following morning you would find my poetry spray-painted on the decaying walls of buildings throughout the Gaza Strip.

I had always aspired to be like my dad, to take a stand for my people and their freedom, and that day arrived in December 1987, after an Israeli truck ran over and killed four Palestinian workers, sparking the intifada. The following morning, Israeli soldiers killed a young man from my school. The school was closed to mourn the falling of our fellow student, but everyone arrived anyway, determined to hold our occupiers to account. Our numbers grew as Jeeps and tanks arrived. I was terrified as I picked up a stone, but stood still. Others ran away, but a few with rocks and flags moved toward the soldiers. The soldiers likewise drew nearer. They looked frightening and foreign. But when the kids ran in the direction of the soldiers and rocks began flying everywhere, I was no longer anxious. I belonged there. I ran into the inferno with my schoolbag in one hand and a stone in the other. "Allahu Akbar!" I cried, and I threw my stone. I hit no target, for the rock fell just a short distance ahead of me, but I felt liberated, no longer a negligible refugee standing in a long line before an UNRWA feeding center for a dry falafel sandwich.

Engulfed by my rebellious feelings, I picked up another stone, and a third. I moved forward, even as bullets flew, even as my friends began falling all around me. I could finally articulate who I was, and for the first time on my own terms. My name was Ramzy, and I was the son of Mohammed, a freedom fighter from Nuseirat, who was driven out of his village of Beit Daras, and the grandson of a peasant who died with a broken heart and was buried beside the grave of my brother, a little boy who died because there was no medicine in the refugee camp's UN clinic. My mother was Zarefah, a refugee who couldn't spell her name, whose illiteracy was compensated by a heart overflowing with love for her children and her people, a woman who had the patience of a prophet. I was a free boy; in fact, I was a free man. In the following years, my father's example would continue to have a profound impact on my life and the road I chose to travel.

TOLSTOY TO THE RESCUE

Living under Israeli occupation posed several challenges for a family with many sons. In the Israeli way of thinking, young men were a great threat to their nation's sovereignty, and thus these families had to be at the top of their hit list. My father was one of the most creative men I've known in finding ways to deter Israeli wrath from his sons. His brain was constantly spinning, whether to soup up a cocka-mamie business deal that only he could pull off (which is how he survived and ultimately prospered, however modestly, under Egyptian and then Israeli rule) or, even more important, to find a new way to keep the ever-present Israeli forces at bay.

My father had a challenging task, for he had five sons all entering or in the midst of their teen years, and he lived in close proximity to swaths of soldiers, who often seemed to torment us for sheer pleasure, or for no other reason than boredom. His antics started with a large basket of spectacles in an array of styles, many of them taped together and missing lenses. Beside the basket sat a large stack of books, all classics, from Homer to Hugo, Aristotle to Zola, ready for an impromptu read at a moment's notice. It was customary when soldiers pounded on our door for us all to dart into the sitting room, grab one of Homer's or Hugo's beloved volumes, adorn ourselves with one of the many pairs of spectacles, and pose as studious intellectuals before they entered the house.

I particularly remember an episode on a sunny curfew afternoon when we had little time to set the stage before the door was kicked in. I grabbed a copy of Maxim Gorky's *Mother* and buried my face in its pages, afraid to look up or make eye contact with those who broke the door down and announced themselves as Jews when they stormed into our home. On such occasions, my father put on the most amazing performances. He would grab the old cane that leaned against the wall beside the door for these very instances and limp so convincingly to the sitting room, where he would explain in Hebrew that his sons were not troublemakers but scholars. That day, as my father pointed out that we all were enthusiasts of "higher literature," I braved a glance from the pages of my book to find that my younger brother Muneer, who sat across the room from me, wore a pair of glasses with no lenses and was reflectively taking in Hugo's *Les Misérables* without noticing that he was holding the book upside down. Although these moments were terrifying, I had to bite down on my tongue to keep myself from bursting into laughter. God knows what might have happened if Muneer or I had blown our cover.

THE BROKEN BONES POLICY CLAIMS
ANOTHER VICTIM

The morning came when my father's ingenuity could no longer protect his family. I was awakened by a large boot pressing against my face. A swarm of soldiers were standing over me.

My mother came running from the kitchen to find an Israeli army unit hand-cuffing her children and dragging them into the street. The event was customary. Soldiers often stormed into people's homes and broke the arms and legs of men and boys so as to send a stern message to the rest of the neighborhood that they would receive the same fate if they continued with their intifada.

My father spoke good Hebrew, which he had learned during his years of business dealings in Israel. My mother spoke none, but even if she had, she would not have been able to articulate one legible sentence. After a brief pause, she let out a howl and cried out to one of them, "I beg you soldier. My sons were sleeping. They have done nothing wrong. I kiss your hand; don't break their arms. I beg you, may Allah return you safe and sound to your family. How would your mother feel if someone came to break her children's arms? Oh Allah, come to my rescue. My children are the only thing I have in this life. Oh Allah, I was raised poor and orphaned, and I don't deserve this."

At first, the soldiers paid no heed to my mothers' pleas and merely responded with "Shut up and go inside," but her crying alerted the other women in the neighborhood, who served as a first line of defense under such circumstances. Local women gathered outside their homes, screaming and shouting, as soldiers lined us against the wall and took out their clubs. The custom was for a soldier to ask a person singled out for a beating, "Which hand do you write with?" before the club would break it, followed by the other arm, and then the legs.

When a soldier asked one of my brothers the same ominous question, my mother's pleas turned into unintelligible cries as she dropped to the ground and held on to one of the soldier's legs with a death grip. He tried to free himself as two others came to his rescue, pounding the frail woman over and over again in the chest with the butts of their machine guns, and as my father forced his body between the angry solider and the desperate mother.

Made more courageous by the violent scene, especially as my mother seemed to be drowning in the gush of blood flowing from her mouth, the neighborhood women drew closer, throwing rocks and sand at the soldiers. What was meant to be an orderly beating of several boys turned into a chaotic scene where women braved guns, tear gas, and verbal abuse from Israeli soldiers, who eventually retreated into their military vehicles and out of the area.

Thanks to my mother, our bones were left intact that day, but at a price. She was bruised and bleeding. Her chest was battered, and several ribs were broken. She was rushed to a local hospital and was incapacitated for days. Her health deteriorated, to the bewilderment of the Ahli hospital doctors, who had hoped for an eventual recovery. Days later, they discovered that my mother had multiple myeloma. Apparently she had been sick for some time, but her illness was exacerbated by the violent encounter, which made her prognosis bleak.

ODYSSEY

Nuseirat was under a curfew, and the Israeli army agreed to allow my mother's burial on the condition that only the immediate family was to be present, monitored by Israeli soldiers. We arrived at the graveyard carrying the coffin and were soon joined by Mariam, Zarefah's mother, who came running in, calling out her daughter's name. We began digging, and neighbors peeking through their windows quickly concluded that Zarefah had died and was being buried. My mother was a beloved neighbor. She was particularly adored among the older women of the camp, whom she treated with untold kindness. "Allahu akbar," resonated a voice from one of the refugee homes. "Umm Anwar has died," cried another. Within minutes, shouts of "God is great" echoed throughout the camp. People appeared from everywhere, carrying Palestinian flags: men and women, children, old people, and youths, all descending on the graveyard. The refugees were outraged that the poor woman was to be buried based on military instruction and was being followed, even to her grave, by the watchful eyes of the occupiers, their guns, their tanks, and a hovering army helicopter. Youths began throwing stones, and soldiers responded with bullets and tear gas. But the people were not to disperse easily this time.

Thousands of them ensured that Zarefah would depart the earth and enter paradise in the company of friends, treated as a martyr should be treated. As an ambulance hauled some of the wounded to the local clinic, Zarefah was lowered into the ground amid chants and Qur'anic verses, recited en masse. Shouts of "Allahu akbar" intermingled with the whimpers and prayers of the crowd, the sound bombs, the tear gas, and the noise of the hovering helicopter. Zarefah's burial represented everything pure about the intifada: the unity of purpose, the courage, the sheer rage at and resentment of the occupation, the sense of community, the resolve and determination of the refugees. My mother died in 1988. She was forty-two years old.

GAZA, OUR REFUGE

As our subjugation continued, my neighbors still spent much of their days queuing up in charity lines where my mother once stood, lines for flour, rice, milk, or maybe used clothes from some European country. They must have pondered many things as they waited for so many hours in those lines. Perhaps they thought it strange that the same insignia from the United States imprinted on the two-liter can of cooking oil or the twenty-five-kilogram bag of flour that was rationed to each family each month was also on the random tear gas grenade canisters littering the streets of Gaza. Such were the ironies that we pondered as Yitzhak Shamir and his like deliberated the "humanitarian problem of the Arab refugees." I often thought of the afterlife and hoped that my mother could sense the gratitude I felt in retrospect for the boredom and embarrassment she had endured for so many years in those lines in her children's stead.

As the late 1980s brought swelling tensions that would soon provoke the First Intifada, Mohammad's joyless life lingered in Gaza. His daily chores were few, with one main highlight, consisting of sitting at the top of the six stone stairs of his housefront, trying to lure passersby or equally bored neighbors to join him in mulling over the day's news over a cup of black tea. The stairs brought him a semblance of pleasure, being where he, along with older neighbors, reminisced about the good old days.

The staircase directly faced the famed Martyrs Graveyard. Zarefah, Anwar, and both of his parents were all buried around the same location there, at the center, surrounded by cactuses and hundreds of soundless refugees. Strangely, Mohammed both feared death and wished for it often, a contradiction that was not unique to him but shared by most Gazans. He often concerned himself with the fact that "all the good spots were quickly taken" in the graveyard and that when he died he might be buried elsewhere, forever separated from his beloved wife, a notion that he dreaded.

Two of his sons were in Jerusalem, less than an hour's drive by car but a world away, thanks to Israeli roadblocks that prevented the family from reuniting for what would be more than a decade. Two other sons, myself included, were studying in the United States. Even though Suma was in southern Gaza, a checkpoint separated her from her father, making their infrequent visits nearly impossible. Gaza's and Mohammed's isolation were complete when his sons could no longer send him money as the boycott of the Hamas government after the 2006 elections extended to reach all financial institutions.

Desperate, Mohammed sold his house, the last tangible connection he had to his beloved Zarefah. That beautiful and battered place that had stood the test of time and bullets was sold for rare medicine, smuggled through Gaza's tunnels, which Mohammed depended on to breathe. He couldn't have imagined the day that he would have to bring Zarefah's photo down from its rusty nail on the living room wall. He left the house and rented a tiny apartment on the outskirts of Nuseirat. As the Hamas government battled to maintain control and order, as the United States insisted on Israel's right to defend itself, as the Arabs stayed silent, as the world watched, as Gazans fell in droves, Mohammed filled a few boxes with his remaining possessions and left.

"Son, I am dying," he softly mumbled on the phone.

"I am sorry, Dad. I am so sorry. I wish I could be there with you. I wish I could do something. I wish it was me and not you, Dad."

"Son, I love you. May Allah bless you and your children."

Mohammed was incapacitated for a few weeks. There wasn't a hospital bed to be found in Gaza, for nearly all the hospitals had been converted to function as massive emergency wards. His neighbors and friends in Gaza took care of him and desperately tried to persuade the Israelis to grant him a permit to enter the West Bank for treatment or at least to die in the company of his sons. Alas, it was determined that this was too great a risk for the security and the well-being of the State of Israel, which sentenced him to die at home with no treatment.

In the last a few days of his life, he would make an occasional groan, an unexpected cry, "I am in pain." There was little to be done.

The last time I spoke to him, I asked a neighbor to hold the handset to my father's ear so I could talk to him, although he was unconscious. I said,

Dad, I know you cannot speak, but I am sure you can hear me. I just want to tell you, thank you very much for all that you have done for us. Although you haven't seen my children, they know you very well. I have spent so many hours telling them stories about you, your antics, and what a wonderful father you have been. Zarefah, your granddaughter, loves you and send her kisses and hugs; so do Iman and Sammy. Sammy is only two, but it is likely that he will grow up to be a troublemaker. Iman has a heart of gold, just like you, and Zarefah looks just like Mom. Isn't that marvelous?

I told them so much about you, about Beit Daras, and about my mother. I also told them that "Grandpa Mohammed is a freedom fighter." They are so proud of you, and proud to be your grandkids.

A few hours later, I called again and spoke with a neighbor. His extra kind voice and the sound of women crying in the background were enough to let me know that my father had died.

Thousands of people came to his funeral from throughout Gaza, oppressed people who shared his plight, hopes, and struggles, accompanying him to the graveyard where he was laid to rest. He didn't even have the money to buy his own coffin. I have often thought it a great mercy that Palestinians must endure Israel's occupation only for one lifetime. The resilient fighter had finished the battle for a badly deserved moment of peace.

DYING, AGAIN

The night my father died, I had a dream.

There we both were, face to face in the middle of one of our family's fields in Beit Daras. We were sitting in the glory of what once was ours. I was a young man; my father was wrinkled and withered. His battle scars were clear, his breathing labored. He looked to me and said, "I'm going to die again tonight."

A dream so vivid—it was springtime, a warm and peaceful afternoon. The trees were in bloom, and the wind carried the perfume of the almond, lemon, and orange blossoms. Farmers were busy in their fields, and children lay flat on their backs, basking in the afternoon sun, without shoes, without a care in the world. I felt a sense of belonging that I have never felt in my life, and I remember thinking to myself, "So this is what it feels like to be home." It was as if the dream were meant to give me just a short glimpse of the beauty and purity of those lovely years before the Israeli settlers came. Until that moment, I don't think I was ever able to fully comprehend the overflowing love my father had for his homeland, for his freedom, and with this understanding came the almost incomprehensible sense of loss of the Catastrophe. The sun poured its light on us. Then I shifted my attention from my father's tired eyes to the menacing band of soldiers on the horizon, whence our nightmare started.

And once more he caught my gaze and said, "I'm going to die again tonight."

13

The Brief Career of Prosper Cohen

A Would-Be Leader of Moroccan Immigrants

Yaron Tsur

In November 1948, about half a year after the establishment of the State of Israel, a thirty-eight-year-old attorney landed at Haifa's airport: Prosper Cohen, a
former secretary of the Zionist Federation in Morocco. Married and the father
of a young girl, he nevertheless arrived alone—the plan being that his wife and
daughter would join him within months. In time, he described his arrival as follows: "It was the Sabbath. I was choked with emotion. Around me, I heard Hebrew,
police, porters, women, children, everyone was turning to one another, shouting
in a language I did not understand, though I was overwhelmed by merely hearing
it. I thought of Renan [the renowned French biblical scholar and philosopher] as
he defined the language of the Bible: 'A quiver of steel, a hawser made of mighty
twine, a trombone of bronze rending the air with two-three sharp notes—that's
Hebrew.'"

No kneeling to kiss the sacred soil; no remembered prayers for the Jewish return. Instead, Cohen recalls his excitement at the sound of Hebrew, a language
incomprehensible to him, whose impact he could define only by reference to his
French cultural identity. Far different is the account of another Moroccan immigrant, Shmuel Ben-Harosh, who had arrived on the very day that the State of Israel
was established, on May 14, 1948. Ben-Harosh had headed the Em Habanim yeshiva in Sefrou, a small town renowned both for its rabbinical Jewish elite and as
a moderate-religious local center of the Hebrew Enlightenment (Haskalah). Ben-
Harosh and his family, nine people in all, reached the port of Tel Aviv by ship amid
Egypt's bombing of the city and were whisked off to an immigrant camp in Netanya
before they were able to perform the ceremony of kissing the ground. But when
one of the rabbi's sons later reminded him, the omission was quickly rectified.

These two initial encounters with the Jewish state rest on the different profiles of the two Moroccan newcomers. Beyond their personal sagas, their stories tell us much about the characteristics of the Jewish elites that developed in colonial Morocco and reveal how much more varied were the experiences of Moroccan immigrants to the new state than is allowed for in the overly simplified and in many respects biased narrative that still dominates public consciousness in Israel.

Cohen and Ben-Harosh represent two types of Moroccan elites that developed under French colonial rule in Morocco (1912–56). Cohen's elite included an intellectual circle that transferred the focus of its high culture to the French sphere, the language of the Western conquerors. In contrast, Ben-Harosh's elite was firmly grounded in Morocco's indigenous cultures: Arabic for the Muslim majority, Judeo-Arabic and Hebrew for the Jewish minority. For purposes of clarity, the members of this second elite—both Muslim and Jews—can be referred to as *maskilim*. Many maskilim were also able to communicate in French, but their command of the language did not approach that of westernized individuals, such as Cohen, who had attended a French high school and French institutions of higher learning.

Some of those who were fluent in French were the intermediaries par excellence between the local populations and the French administration and settlers. The latter new group was a kind of overseas extension of European economy and culture and needed such intermediation: just as Arabic-Berber or Judeo-Arabic speakers lacking Western education were not mobile within the European sector, so too the exclusively French speakers were not mobile in the Arab or Jewish markets and social networks. Moroccan colonial society was thus roughly divided into three economic and cultural systems, or sectors: the distinct French/European and Arabic/Berber-native ones, plus a third, of westernized Moroccans who enjoyed mobility in the first two sectors. The maskilim served as the main modern elite of the native sector, but the westernized elite often claimed this role as well.

The different cultural profile of each group impacted how Moroccan Jews were incorporated into Israeli society, as the experiences of Cohen and Ben-Harosh demonstrate. Our story focuses on Cohen (though Ben-Harosh will make another appearance toward the conclusion), recounting his brief, unsuccessful foray into Israeli politics and his subsequent career during the first years of Israeli statehood.

FROM COLONIAL TO NATIONAL SOCIETY

Our time frame is the first year and a half of Moroccan immigration to Israel, beginning with the declaration of statehood in May 1948. This short period includes only the very beginning of mass Moroccan immigration to the Jewish state, which lasted more than fifteen years and brought in a total of about a quarter of a million people. The Moroccan immigrants arrived mainly in three waves: thirty-three thousand people in 1948–51, some seventy thousand in 1954–56, and about one hundred thousand in 1961–64.

In his memoirs, Cohen speaks of Zionist fervor sweeping through the whole of Moroccan Jewry in 1948. But in discussing the first immigrant wave, he mentions the difficulty of obtaining exit permits and the distinctive social profile of those who chose to emigrate at all costs, illegally crossing the border into Algiers en route to the Jewish state. Cohen pinpoints the two main groups of immigrants: (a) large families from the community's lower socioeconomic strata, who, according to Cohen's memoirs, were encouraged to immigrate by community leaders who did not join them but shared the hope that immigration, or aliya, would solve their social problems, mainly housing and educational distress; and (b) impassioned youths who were eager to enlist in the Israel Defense Forces (IDF) immediately upon arrival.

While the large poor families stemmed from the native sector of Moroccan colonial society and were fluent only in Arabic, some of the youths came from the westernized sector and many from the seam between the two groups, and they used French as their main language. Most of the immigrants stole across the border to Algeria and required the services of passport forgers and smugglers, who were apt to blackmail them. Once across this border, the immigrants were processed by envoys from the Yishuv (and eventually by the government or the Jewish Agency), upon whom they were utterly dependent. They were held in temporary camps in Oran and Algiers, then transferred to Marseilles for embarkation to Israel. In Israel, they were sent off to immigrant camps or else made their way to abandoned Palestinian Arab neighborhoods in the big cities (Jerusalem, Jaffa, and Haifa), where they struggled to find their place along with other groups of new *olim*.

The Moroccans quickly acquired a reputation as bad immigrants, troublemakers who were prone to violence. Those who were mobilized also came into conflict with their commanders more often than their fellow soldiers did, but this was ameliorated by their reputation for bravery in combat. During this period, there were only a few large families from the Judeo-Arab sector whose breadwinners were maskilim, such as Shmuel Ben-Harosh, and they had no impact on the Moroccan image.

In short, within months of their arrival, Moroccan immigrants became associated with a turn for the worse in Israel's societal development—adding, as it were, a group with prominent negative characteristics to the Yishuv's poorest strata. In the context of social relations within the evolving national Jewish society, they constituted a blow to the non-European, "Oriental" or "Sephardic" section, being largely identified with Arab origin and culture as well as backwardness and primitiveness. North African immigrants, most of whom were from Morocco in 1948, were placed at the bottom of Israel's new social prestige rankings.

The status of the Moroccan newcomers was new, unlike the unequal relations between European and non-European Jews. This "ethnic" problem plagued the Zionist Yishuv from its inception. The first to sense it were immigrants from Yemen who had been recruited during the Second Aliya as agricultural workers in the moshavot in place of cheap Arab Muslim labor. Meanwhile, the veteran nonashkenazi inhabitants of the pre-Yishuv period, who were called *Sephardim* and were often financially better off than the ashkenazi *halutzim* (pioneers), also sensed the feelings of superiority and patronization on the part of the European olim, who were gradually replacing them as leaders of the Yishuv. As a nationalist movement that defined all Jews as members of the same *ethnos*, or people, Zionism called for total equality between them, whatever their origins might be. However, in the age of imperialism and colonialism, Europeans looked down on non-Europeans and assigned them statuses and roles that matched their inferior stereotype. Which hand would be upper in the developing emigrant society—that of egalitarian ethnonationalism or that of discriminative colonialism? And to what extent would the real profile of the immigrants from Asia and Africa—in contrast to their stereotypes—determine their absorption and integration into a society ruled by veteran East European Jews? The power of the ashkenazim often served to blur, in both popular opinion and academic historiography, the reality of the immigrant others—the nonashkenazim—their identities, their interests, and their strategies as they sought membership in the Yishuv and the Jewish state. Prosper Cohen's experiences in his first year and a half in Israel, in 1948–49, help shed light on this somewhat obscured aspect of the building of Israeli society.

FROM THE HERUT PARTY TO THE JEWISH AGENCY

As Cohen began to make his arrangements for aliya, news of the unsavory reputation his countrymen were acquiring in Israel was reaching Morocco, along with accounts of the negative treatment the new immigrants were receiving. Feeling a great sense of responsibility not only for the Jewish state but also for his fellow Moroccan Jews, Cohen set his sights on a position in Israel's emergent establishment, as the director of a special Jewish Agency department for the absorption of North African immigrants. Such a job, of course, was also meant to ensure him an income and a position in his new society and thus help him continue the process of upward social mobility he had begun in Morocco. He wrote to an acquaintance, a senior Jewish Agency official named Samuel U. Nahon, telling him of his plans and requesting assistance. However, he left for Israel with no promising news from Nahon.

Upon his arrival, he traveled from Haifa to Tel Aviv and took a hotel room near the beach. "That evening," he wrote, "I beheld the merriest, noisiest, youngest, motliest crowd, clad in the most disparate uniforms, graced by the wildest hairdos.

The gaiety, the smiles that burst out like firecrackers, the unselfconscious carriage, the total absence of snobbism and formality—here was a world, an atmosphere, I had never before encountered." Yet the festive feeling soon gave way to disappointment. The next day, as the first step toward securing the senior position he coveted, Cohen traveled to Jerusalem to meet with the director of the Jewish Agency's absorption department, Giora Yoseftal. He could not get to see him. Instead, he was ultimately furnished with a note to the department's regional director in Haifa, Kalman Levine.

In Cohen's memoirs, Levine comes across as the embodiment of inflexibility and obtuseness, treating the newcomer discourteously before finally offering him the post of a functionary in an immigrant camp, where he would be expected to live. Between one meeting and another, Cohen managed to spend several days at a camp, gaining an idea of the conditions and type of work he would be doing, as a result of which he angrily rejected the offer. He, the only member of the Moroccan Jewish leadership to arrive in the first wave of immigrants, had not expected this sort of integration. He had come to lead the immigrants, not to share a hut with them and ply away at a monotonous bureaucratic job. Levine's suggestion was an attempt to "exile" him, he wrote.

Following his unpleasant experience with the Jewish Agency and the ruling establishment, Cohen sought a curative experience in the rival political camp, the Herut party, the successor to the militant *Etzel* organization and the precursor to today's Likud Party. This was not a sudden development; by Cohen's own testimony, he had had initial contacts with representatives of the Zionist Revisionist movement while still in Morocco, though he had not thrown in his lot with them before arriving in Israel. His path to the establishment blocked, he was welcomed with open arms by the main opposition party. From his first days at Herut's offices, while still acquainting himself with the various departments, he began to fill a role commensurate with his aspirations, receiving North African immigrants, listening to their problems, and directing them to the relevant party officials. As elections to the first Knesset approached, Herut used his French oratory talents, sending him to spread the party word in immigrant camps that had many North Africans. He also accompanied the party leader Menachem Begin to rallies in Jaffa and Jerusalem.

Cohen thus entered Israeli public life very swiftly. Within weeks of his arrival, he had landed a relatively senior position in Herut. In addition to dealing directly with North African immigrants and helping out with party propaganda, he soon became the secretary of a new Herut-affiliated organization, the International League for the Rescue of Arab Jewry. The league's main aim was enlisting public opinion to improve the deteriorating situation of the Jewish communities in Arab lands, and it organized assemblies and protests to that end. Its temporary chairman, Yirmiyahu Halperin, earned high praise from Cohen. In his memoirs,

Cohen juxtaposes the warmth showered on him by Halperin in particular and Herut members generally with the "unconcealed hostility and gruff, brutal cynicism I found among all the Jewish Agency's petty officials."

For all the differences between his traumatic Jewish Agency experience and the restorative experience of Herut, Cohen's primary social reference group was the same in both: the European sector's elite, with its ashkenazi stamp. In his endeavors to be admitted to this elite, one circle rejected him, while another accepted him.

Soon after joining Herut, Cohen published an article in the party's French-language newsletter, *Liberté*, urging immigrants not to allow absorption difficulties to cloud their motives for aliya—mainly, the desire to live freely in their ancestral land—and stigmatizing the surrounding Arab society as the major factor in the oppression of Moroccan Jewry. Elsewhere, however, he was quick to express a more critical view of what was happening in the Jewish state. For instance, among the league's documents is a memo he undoubtedly authored titled "The Situation of the New Immigrants from North Africa." It opens by citing a letter from four hundred immigrants in the Haifa region decrying their substandard housing and sanitary conditions. Following this, the memo summarizes an investigation the league undertook in immigrant camps in Pardes Hannah, Netanya, Binyamina, Atlit, and Raanana, as well as in selected city neighborhoods, in particular Jabeliya (in Jaffa).

Clearly, Cohen saw his two positions—at the league, and as a Herut party official dealing with North African immigrants—as complementary. In fact, he came up with an apt formula that combined them: along with rescuing Jews who had not yet immigrated from Muslim countries, it was necessary to rescue those who had already done so and were suffering from serious problems such as hunger, appalling housing, and no educational opportunities. Cohen could not, of course, make this internal social slogan the main message of the Diaspora-oriented International League for the Rescue of Arab Jewry. But he could add it to the league's original mandate.

While Cohen was busy crafting his rhetorical explanation of his route to Herut—and, in the process, blackening Jewish Agency personalities—individuals connected with the establishment, whose identities he did not reveal, set out to defame him. He was accused of having "betrayed" his mission of playing his part within the administrative bodies dealing with the North African immigrants in the camps, opting instead for a cushy city job for reasons of personal convenience, and in the lap of the opposition to boot. These charges made their way to Morocco, and in February 1949, two of Cohen's colleagues from the Moroccan Zionist Federation, Ayouche Cohen and Maurice Timsit, came to his office while on a visit to Israel and demanded that he part company with the opposition and try his luck once again at the Jewish Agency. Together with them, Cohen returned to the offices of the absorption department, and what had been denied him as an immigrant—a meeting with the director, Giora Yoseftal—was readily granted to the two honored tourists. According to Cohen, they even managed to get a promise that he would receive the appointment he desired: head of a new department for the absorption of North African immigrants.

Thus it was that Cohen entered the ranks of the Jewish Agency in early March 1949. His first project was to prepare a memo with a blueprint for his new department and proposed measures to improve immigrant conditions. He wrote the memo in French, then circulated it among his friends in Morocco and Israel for their comments prior to its translation. It began by listing a number of basic facts. First, it charged, Israeli envoys had mismanaged Moroccan immigration and were thus responsible for the quality of the arrivals, perhaps having received "instructions to bring immigrants at any price." The obvious conclusion was that one should not rely on emissaries who had not proved themselves and had created problems for the state. At the very least, the management of aliya from North Africa should not be left solely in their hands. Turning to Israel, Cohen suggested that there were twenty to thirty thousand North African immigrants in the country (in fact, the correct figure was about twelve thousand), most of them from Morocco. His assessment of them was as follows: "The human material that came to settle here does not represent the healthy mass of the Jewish population in North Africa. This is what earned the immigrants from this area a bad name. Further explaining the quality of this material is that, in all countries, people with a rather high average standard of living—culture, financial means, etc.—generally do not venture or do not want to give up their relative comfort." This paragraph appears in the French original (now in the personal archive of a veteran Zionist leader in Morocco, J. R. Benazeraf), where it is crossed out; it is absent from the Hebrew translation that circulated in Jewish Agency and government offices. Although an uncomplimentary assessment of North African immigrants, particularly Moroccans, was widespread and even shared by the local Moroccan Zionist leaders, the latter were not interested in reinforcing such negative stereotyping of the immigrants.

In fact, the North African leaders' sensitivity about the new immigrants' image in Israel rested on solid ground, as toward the end of Israel's first year of independence the anti-Moroccan sentiments reached their climax. This happened not only because of the actual profile of the new immigrants but because they represented a threat to the veteran ashkenazim, namely that the demographic balance between the latter group and the newcomers from Asia and Africa was turning to the ashkenazim's disfavor and changing the European and Western profile of the Jewish state. Morocco's Jewish community was the largest in the Islamic world and as such represented best the new threat of "bad" Jewish immigration. Haaretz published a nineteen-part series on the general flow of immigrants in April 1949 echoing the new turn of the ethnic problem. In these pieces, written by the prominent journalist Arie Gelblum, the Moroccans—whose ranks, according to him, were overly populated by "idlers," "boors," "lawbreakers," and "knife-wielders"—symbolized all the evils of the "Arab-African bloc" of Jews. Gelblum's radical anti-Moroccan stand, which included a proposal to exclude them from the immigration project of the Jewish state, provoked a general outcry in the Sephardic camp and many objections among ashkenazim who found it contrary to the Zionist ideology.

Himself not overly impressed by the collective profile of North African immigrants, Cohen was nevertheless able to appreciate that misgivings about them did not derive solely from objective facts. In the months since his arrival and his initial Zionist fervor, he had learned a thing or two about prejudice toward Asian and North African immigrants. Although he had no interest in voicing radical criticism in the context of his attempt to return to the Jewish Agency, his memo did not duck the issue of discrimination, especially with regard to employment. He noted, "In the concentrations of North Africans, most are unemployed. One dare not suppose that this is intentional, but even if it is due to mere chance, the distortion must be fully or partially rectified and as quickly as possible. 'An empty belly has no ears,' an old folk saying rightfully declares. This is true sevenfold and especially dangerous when it is not one hungry belly but many at one and the same time." Cohen also took aim at the arrogance and hypocrisy of bureaucrats: "The staff at the employment office does not always take into account how sensitive their job is. To tell someone looking for work, 'I have nothing for you,' or 'Come back in 4 or 5 days,' is to sentence him to death by starvation. . . . That person's reaction becomes even more hostile when he sees—unfortunately this happens too often—that behind him, the *very same slot* is given to someone else."

Critics of the Moroccans sometimes took their likeness to Arabs to the extreme, denigrating the North African Jews as being, in the main, "only a cut above the general level of the Arab black and Berber inhabitants at home; in any case, this is even a lower level than we encountered in the Arabs of former Palestine," as Gelblum put it. Since Israel in early 1949 was at war against Arab states perceived as the ultimate enemy, it is understandable that Cohen, the would-be leader of North African immigrants, was quick to obscure the Arab element in the Moroccan identity by going to the extreme of highlighting its French element. Doing so, moreover, required no change or innovation in his own identity, since he, like other westernized Moroccan Jews, had long since distanced himself from his original Judeo-Arabic cultural milieu.

Read between the lines, the memo reveals that Cohen and his colleagues sensed a design to discriminate educationally and vocationally against North African youths, based on a stereotype that attributed inferior intellectual abilities to them. Soon thereafter, Gelblum confirmed the existence of such stereotypes: "We have before us a people of unparalleled primitiveness. Their level of education borders on utter ignorance and, graver still, intellectual inaptitude. . . . The special tragedy of this [group], in contrast with the worst human material from Europe, is that their children are also without hope. To raise their general level at the depths of their ethnic being will take generations."

THE ASSOCIATION OF NORTH AFRICAN IMMIGRANTS

After completing his memo, Cohen spent all of March 1949 trying unsuccessfully to realize his plan. At the end of the month, the absorption director for the Tel Aviv area, Dr. Haikes, summoned him to request that since Cohen was drawing a salary without doing anything, he should at least help out with his knowledge of French. "Within three weeks," Cohen wrote, "my name had made the rounds of Turkish, Bulgarian, Iraqi, Syrian, Egyptian, English, and Indian immigrants, as a result of which I inadvertently became a multilingual interpreter [for] Spanish, Arabic, English, and sometimes even French. Only for Yiddish did the immigrants rely on assistance from another quarter."

At about the same time, Cohen was notified that his appointment as the director of North African immigrants countrywide had been downsized to the Tel Aviv area and that the senior position was to go to Ephraim Friedman. Friedman, a member of Achdut Ha'avoda, had formerly been the chief Zionist emissary in North Africa. During his stint in Morocco, Friedman and Cohen had occasionally collaborated; indeed, Cohen writes that when he arrived in Israel, the socialist Friedman had promised to support his candidacy for department director. Now, however, following Cohen's association with Herut, the two men found themselves on opposite sides with regard to politics, ethnic affiliation, and the contest for administrative appointments and power. As it happened, however, Friedman's appointment did not materialize. According to Cohen, Friedman's kibbutz refused to authorize his move, and the job went to Dina Werth, another veteran of the ashkenazi Yishuv. Cohen once again felt slighted. Just as he was unqualified to head the department responsible for Hungarian or Polish immigrants, he argued, so too neither Friedman nor Werth was qualified to direct the absorption of North Africans.

At this point, frustrated at every turn, Cohen began a new chapter in his political career as he turned his energies to the formation of the immigrant organization he had proposed in his memo. Originally envisioned as part of the Jewish Agency framework, the organization was now conceived as an independent body. Known as the Association of Immigrants from North African and French-Speaking Countries (Histadrut 'Olei Zefon Afrikah Vehaarazot Dovrot Hazarfatit), the new body began its work in June 1949, with Cohen as its president.

In Cohen's view, the association was to play a role in planning immigration, absorption, and integration. Apart from reorganizing the patterns of reception, it would advocate special camps for North Africans, "to grant them suitable living conditions and prevent the daily clashes and frictions in existing camps," and would serve as a watchdog against discrimination in housing, employment, and education. In addition, it would organize Hebrew classes, clubs, and activities marked by "the characteristic warmth and emotion of our social gatherings." The greatest innovation referred to immigration. Cohen wanted the organization to have an active role in directing the Zionist federations in North Africa regarding the extent and rate of immigration.

In a report addressed to the association's committee, he cited statements by David Ben-Gurion and others to the effect that the aliya from Muslim countries was absolutely vital on demographic grounds. Therefore, if the olim themselves were to curtail it, that might be disturbing enough to force the authorities to act. "The deliberate, desired inertia of the authorities," Cohen wrote, "should be countered clearly: either they stop the discrimination, in which case North African Jewry will continue to be Israel's population reservoir, or, if they do not stop, the responsible organizations of North African Jewry will have to rethink the issue of aliya." Meanwhile, until serious steps were taken, the flow of immigrants should be stemmed. In short, Cohen proposed neutralizing the power of the Jewish Agency and the government to manage aliya—an idea that could be interpreted as a call to revolt against the veteran Zionist and new Israeli establishment and was also prone to be viewed as the product of the subversive influence of the Revisionist opposition.

Another of the report's antiestablishment aspects was Cohen's interpretation of the problems of North African immigrants in Israel. By this point, he had formed the opinion that a form of racism—not altogether unlike anti-Semitism—was involved:

> What is happening in Israel vis-à-vis North Africans or, more precisely, against Francophones, who are referred to by what has become an ominous word, "Moroccans," is not unlike what is to be seen in a number of anti-Semitic countries. From the highest official to the lowliest gatekeeper, from the factory foreman to the simplest laborer, you will most likely [not] hear a bad word against North Africans, yet from the first moment, you are asked where you're from. Hanging in the balance is your employment, your life, and the lives of your children, your future in Israel. You may mask your true character as a North African under the more complimentary "French" label, but you will not avoid the lurking disaster: "French" is equivalent to "Moroccan," and the label draws another in its wake: "knife." Thus, should you be walking on the street and speaking Voltaire's language, you are apt to hear around you, often [in a tone of] blatant fear, "Moroccan."

The colonial conception of European superiority prevailed within the ashkenazi public but clashed with the unifying egalitarian national conception, which made it necessary to conceal reservations about immigrants from Africa, just as an anti-Semite committed to act in accordance with a liberal ethos is not permitted to vent his rejection of Jews. But however apt the comparison between the attitude toward Moroccans and anti-Semitism, the reality was that Cohen himself shared the conception of European superiority, and neither here nor in other public documents did he give expression to the most sensitive aspects of Moroccan aliya—namely, the lowly social origins of most of these immigrants and their Judeo-Arabic culture. He himself always ignored the "native" Arabic side of his community of origin and tried to emphasize its French side.

THE WESTERNIZED'S WAY TO THE MIDDLE CLASS

Cohen's appointment at the Jewish Agency officially ended in August 1949 (effectively, his work had ceased several months earlier). Following his second unsuccessful encounter with the establishment, he took action to put his public activities on the right track: he now concentrated on the Association of Immigrants from North African and French-Speaking Countries, which he sought to strengthen by means of ties with his former colleagues in the Moroccan Zionist Federation, creating a closer bond between Diaspora and Israeli organizations.

The contradictory interests of Cohen and the association, on the one hand, and the distant Moroccan Zionist Federation, on the other, soon became apparent. The latter sought to make the association its Israeli collaborator, albeit without assisting it with funds raised in Morocco or granting it a foothold in the inter-Diaspora Zionist arena. The association, for its part, was reluctant to give its colleagues in Morocco full and free access to the data it had gathered concerning the problems facing their compatriots in Israel, or to accept the right of the federation alone to represent the olim in national forums abroad.

Over and above the conflicting interests of the two organizations, the federation members had serious misgivings about Cohen's leadership of the association. At the end of October 1949, prior to receiving a letter from his Moroccan colleagues demanding that he resign from the leadership of the North African community in Israel, Cohen quit of his own accord. He clearly regarded his image in the eyes of his Zionist colleagues in Morocco as of ultimate importance; when he realized that they had turned their backs on him, he gave up hope, retiring not only from the association but from all public activity. Neither did he go back to work for Herut, though he claimed that he could have. Instead he was unemployed and became destitute:

> The Via Dolorosa lasted seven months, seven long months. We, my wife, my daughter, and myself, bore our cross with courage, with dignity. When our meager means gave out, we fell on poverty. It is easy to say this. But it was not at all pleasant. The days and hours of unemployment, the vain wandering in search of work, the belly that knew only bread and margarine, the lodging bare as only the room of a jobless pauper can be, the inability to meet the fees for the education of our daughter, who was under constant threat of expulsion—all this was what may be tersely called a life of hardship. . . . Seven months, as long as the Exile.

At this point, the Cohen family had seemingly fallen near to the bottom of Israel's socioeconomic ladder. Following its upward mobility in Morocco, the crisis of immigration had brought the family down—almost to the level of the majority of large, poor Moroccan families now crowded together in appalling living conditions in Israel's new centers of poverty in Haifa, Jaffa, and Jerusalem. Once again, however, the differences among those from the various classes and sectors of Morocco were soon manifest. During the early period of his employment, Cohen's income enabled the family to rent a room or two in apartments in Tel Aviv and Holon and thus avoid moving to a disadvantaged neighborhood. Later, during his term at the Jewish Agency, Cohen's name was placed on a list of Zionist leaders from abroad who were entitled to housing after their aliya. In 1949, he received a refurbished two-room apartment, with a small garden, in Tel Giborim (near Holon). In 1952, the family moved from there to Tel Aviv.

If Cohen's privilege or status sufficed in obtaining the Tel Giborim home, his cultural capital was what prevented him from descending to poverty and what enabled him to locate himself relatively quickly within the middle class. After being unemployed for seven months, he found work at an elementary school near his home, where, of all things, he was expected to teach Hebrew.

No doubt Cohen regarded his return to teaching as a step backward in his professional-social career. After all, he had already filled such positions in Morocco, and he had used them as a springboard toward law and public life. In Israel, he had already been hurt by public life, but his future professional plans included a return to the practice of law. Already during his period of unemployment, he had begun to prepare for the Israeli bar exam, which he passed. He then began to work as a lawyer, but after a short time closed his office. According to his daughter, he did so because of economic difficulties, though she ascribes even greater importance to other causes. She writes in her memoir: "Father is not happy. He does not at all like this legal system, which he regards as 'bastard,' for it is made up of Hebrew, Ottoman, British, and Israeli laws. It cannot be compared at all with the Cartesian spirit of French law!"

Cohen's French cultural identity, which had had so strong an impact on his public activities in his first year in Israel, thus continued to leave its mark on his life in later years. He again returned to teaching, this time to the sphere in which he truly excelled: he became a French teacher in a Tel Aviv high school and held this position until his retirement in 1974. His wife, Laurette, also returned to her profession as a French teacher. The couple thus remained devoted in Israel to the high culture that they had brought with them and in which they had been brought up. This was manifest not only in their work but also in other activities, such as giving lectures at the French Cultural Institute, and in their reading and leisure patterns, overseas studies, vacations, and so forth. Cohen may have withdrawn from public life, but his writing abilities, which found an outlet in newspaper articles in 1949, did not disappear, and neither did his love of writing in French. More than material assets, the cultural capital he had brought with him profoundly influenced his professional and socioeconomic trajectory in Israel.

THE RELIGIOUS MASKIL'S WAY TO THE MIDDLE CLASS

For comparative purposes, it is worth recalling the other figure mentioned at the beginning of this chapter, Shmuel Ben-Harosh of Sefrou. As noted, Ben-Harosh was not a member of the westernized sector in Morocco but rather a religious Jewish maskil more closely aligned with indigenous Judeo-Arabic-speaking Moroccan Jews than with the Francophone Jewish elite. Culturally and socially, he was thus closer than Cohen to the broad mass of Moroccan olim. His large family reflected this, having grown from nine to eleven in the State of Israel. So too, the path he traversed in getting to Israel and the trials and tribulations he encountered on the way were characteristic of those of the vast majority of immigrants from North Africa. The Ben-Harosh family's journey included stealing across the border to Algeria, enduring hunger and hardship prior to their transfer to Marseilles, attempting illegal immigration via a clandestine sea voyage, and being captured and detained in Cyprus until they were sent to the Jewish state after its creation.

In Israel, they stayed briefly in an immigrant camp before being directed, in June 1948, to housing in the abandoned Palestinian Arab neighborhood of Salame, now called Kfar Shalem, southeast of Tel Aviv. Formerly a yeshiva teacher, Ben-Harosh first found work as an unskilled laborer and then was assigned to the military industry, where he was injured in an accident and thereafter restricted to light work. At this stage, however, his situation relative to that of other immigrant members of his sector began to improve. He sat for and passed ordination exams and was appointed the local rabbi of his community.

According to the memoirs published by his eldest son, Eliyahu, his meager salary could not support his family, so the Ben-Haroshes sought to increase their income by raising goats, setting up a poultry coop in their backyard, and trading in vegetables in Jaffa. However, within two years, Ben-Harosh went up another rung both in the rabbinical hierarchy and on the social ladder by passing further exams and being appointed a marriage registrar for the religious council of Tel Aviv–Jaffa. Though it was modest, a public service salary signified the Ben-Harosh family's entry into Israel's middle class. While the family continued to live in Kfar Shalem (which became a typical, economically depressed neighborhood settled by olim from Arab countries), its head fulfilled a leadership role. He ran the local North African synagogue, participated in the political system of the religious

Zionist current, and wrote and published essays on rabbinical topics. Eliyahu became a battalion commander in the IDF, helped train the army of Zaire, and in
time served in the senior command of the Israeli police force.

The key to the family's quick exit from the crisis of immigration and the cycle
of poverty was the connection that formed between the rabbi and the religious
Zionist party, Hapo'el Hamizrachi. Culturally, this connection was based on the
common links of Ben-Harosh and ashkenazi party functionaries to religious literature and the Hebrew language. The rabbi possessed Torah and Hebrew-maskilic
cultural capital at a level that was rare among the Moroccan immigrants. Without
the religious similarities, this specific connection would not have been made, yet
it was his mastery of the national language, above all, that advanced Ben-Harosh
at this stage. Unlike his peers who spoke Judeo-Arabic (and perhaps some broken
French), he was fluent in Hebrew, enabling him to navigate within the Zionist
European sector.

In Hapo'el Hamizrachi, the rabbi filled a role similar to that of the westernized
in Morocco, as a mediator and a link between the local European sector and immigrants from the Arab sector who were likely to increase the religious party's
electoral support. Knowledge of the language and his connection with the Yishuv
Zionist party guaranteed Ben-Harosh an entry point into the Zionist sector's social networks. Just as such a mediating role gave the westernized a good starting
point for upward social mobility in Morocco, so in Zionist society it favored the
Hebrew-speaking maskil and community leader. Of course, there were also notable differences between a maskilic "Arab Jew" in Morocco and one living in Israel.
Ben-Harosh's original "native" high culture—Jewish religious culture—which all
members of the French sector in the colonial territory considered inferior, now
enjoyed a higher status, at least in certain European Jewish circles. Another difference was the absence of rigid legal and judicial boundaries between Jews on
opposite sides of the colonial fence. What is more, the demands (and sentiments)
of the national ethos weakened what boundaries like these there were, making
them diffuse and unclear. Consequently, Moroccan immigrant maskilim, like their
westernized counterparts, were able to move up the political, class, and social lad-
ders and integrate into the European sector to an extent impossible in French Morocco. "Native" maskilim, like the "Frenchified" immigrants of the westernized
sector, quickly joined the middle class in their new national society.

THE MOROCCAN OLIM AND THE DEVELOPING
LOWER CLASS

In spite of their immigration and absorption difficulties, Cohen and Ben-Harosh
could pursue their social advancement in the Jewish state and enter the middle
class. This was not true of the average Moroccan immigrant from the Arab sector

or from the Arab-westernized seam. Most North African immigrants were not endowed with Western cultural capital or solid Hebrew education, and their sectorial origins made them prime candidates, alongside Israel's Arabs, for direction to the bottom rungs of the evolving society. Since most of the immigrants from the Arab sector arrived with no or only a low level of modern education, a deficient Hebrew education in Israel was destined to perpetuate the economic mobility gaps they faced. Already in 1949, Cohen and his colleagues blamed discriminatory policy for what they saw as inordinate neglect in the modern Hebrew education of North African immigrant children. They warned that discrimination in education would place the immigrants in an inferior class situation, with disastrous social consequences. They, the maskilim, and the westernized Moroccans had learned from experience that the roots of social advancement lay in the cultural capital acquired through modern education, which facilitated access to the dominant networks of the local society. Only a clear policy of cultural change toward high-level modernity could put this population on the path of upward social and economic mobility.

One future development that Cohen and his friends did not foresee in 1949 was the joining up of North African olim with the ashkenazi Haredim, another minority Jewish group. For most immigrants of the Judeo-Arab sector, religion remained at the core of their identity. Thus they viewed their aliya and the status of the land of Israel in religious, not necessarily modern nationalist, terms. Even when they had been exposed to secular European conceptual and behavioral patterns in Moroccan and Tunisian urban centers, these patterns were largely alien to them. Secular nationalism still had a long way to go before it could capture the minds of most North Africans, and so long as this did not occur, the way was open for other currents. In Morocco, several Haredi networks at that time had penetrated large Jewish population centers, and one of them, Chabad, later branched out to southern villages and the Atlas Mountains.

The Moroccan newcomers shared a similar fate with other immigrants from the lands of Islam. Ben-Harosh's Israeli biography reflects a process that took place in his poor neighborhood, Kfar Shalem: the exit of European Jewish immigrants and the entry of various groups of Jews from Asia and North Africa, who, over time, seemed to crystallize into a single mizrachi (Oriental) "ethnic" unit and lower class. While Ben-Harosh accomplished his social rise entirely within such a mizrachi enclave, Cohen's immigration and integration took place from the outset in spheres dominated by the European Jewish majority: the Jewish Agency, Herut, the educational system, the Israeli bar association, and Tel Aviv's ashkenazi neighborhoods. The different social and geographic spheres within which they moved also reflected the continuation of their original divide, with Cohen remaining loyal to French culture and Ben-Harosh to Moroccan Jews' religious culture.

In investigating the influence of Asian and North African Jews' identity on their absorption in Israel, two schools of thought have predominated: functionalism and critical sociology. During Israel's first years of statehood, the functionalist school held sway, arguing that the decisive stratification factor was the immigrants' cultural capital. That is, those who arrived with a modern education were suitably equipped to integrate into the modern Zionist economy and found appropriate places without encountering discrimination. Arguing against this notion, Shlomo Swirsky, a pioneer of Israeli critical sociology, claimed that the functionalists essentially compared Israeli society to a bookcase that was passively waiting for immigrants to fill its shelves, ordered according to their cultural level. In fact, he argued, the powerful in society placed the weak where they wanted them; thus the ashkenazim put Asian and North African immigrants (or *mizrachim*, in his terminology) on the bottom shelves, actively discriminating against them and benefiting from the cheap labor they provided.

There are substantial grains of truth in both the functionalist and the critical perspectives. Conceptions deriving from colonial heritage did influence public opinion and thinking and did encourage the channeling of Asian and North African immigrants to less-choice niches and areas in the emergent society. Yet the importance of capital, particularly cultural capital, as a factor that molded their fate cannot be dismissed. Not all immigrants from Asia or North Africa lent themselves to manipulation: even if placed on the bottom shelf, the westernized and maskilim of various types were often able to quickly find a way up. Furthermore, if they had their fill of the treatment they received in Israel, they were able to emigrate from the Jewish state. The absence of legal discriminatory barriers, resulting from the dominance of the egalitarian national principle that regarded Jews as equal regardless of where they came from, made it easier for those suffering from a stigmatizing label to advance themselves. Suitable cultural capital had the potential to facilitate the entry of the Jewish immigrant from Asia or North Africa into the middle class and even quite rapidly into leadership positions in Israel, as is evident from Cohen's early days in the country. As noted, there were not many like him in the first wave of Moroccan immigration, although among Iraqi immigrants, for example, who arrived in 1950–51, there were more, including many maskilim in the realm of modern Arabic culture (a type of Jewish maskil that was extremely rare in Morocco). Thus, sticking to stereotypical, overgeneralized conceptions, such as "the Arab-African bloc" or even "the mizrachim," distorts the complex and varied character of the immigrants from Muslim countries and hinders investigation of their histories and paths in the development of Israeli society's class system.

A NOTE ON SOURCES

This story of Cohen's life rests considerably on his memoirs, which he wrote in the 1970s and his daughter, Matilde Tagger, published (with some cuts) after his death: Prosper Cohen, *La grande aventure: fragments autobiographiques* (Jerusalem: self-published, 1993). The part relating to 1948–49 in the memoirs is based almost completely on documents he wrote during the events, in the summer of 1949. I have relied on these documents and correspondence from this period that remained in Cohen's personal archive and was eventually deposited at the Ben-Zvi Institute in Jerusalem. I would like to thank Ms. Tagger for kindly allowing me to peruse the original manuscript of the memoirs and for placing at my disposal two short biographical texts she wrote ("Papa," "La famille en Israël").

Our main source for Shmuel Ben-Harosh's story is his eldest son's book: Eliyahu Ben-Harosh, *Shorashim: toledot mishpahat Ben-Harosh* (n.p., 1987). It contains, among other things, a long poem written by the father that relates the family's story of aliya and absorption into the Jewish state.

Research in the Israeli press and at the Zionist Central Archives (Jerusalem) and the Zabotinsky Institute (Tel Aviv) completed the study.

Books and articles in English on the North African and other mizrachi immigrations may be found in the next section, but the vast majority of this research remains in Hebrew.

SUGGESTIONS FOR FURTHER READING

Bernstein, Deborah, and Shlomo Swirsky. "The Rapid Economic Development of Israel and the Emergence of the Ethnic Division of Labour." *British Journal of Sociology,* Vol. 33, No. 1 (1982), pp. 64–85.

Khazzoom, Aziza. *Shifting Ethnic Boundaries and Inequality in Israel: Or, How the Polish Peddler Became a German Intellectual.* Stanford, CA: Stanford University Press, 2008.

Medding, Peter Y., ed. *Sephardic Jewry and Mizrahi Jews.* Oxford: Oxford University Press, 2008.

Peled, Yoav, and Gershon Shafir. *Being Israeli: The Dynamics of Multiple Citizenship.* Cambridge: Cambridge University Press, 2002.

Tsur, Yaron, "Carnival Fears—Moroccan Immigrants and the Ethnic Problem in the Young State of Israel." *Journal of Israeli History,* Vol. 18, No. 1 (1997), pp. 73–103.

14

A Tale of Baghdad and Tel Aviv

Aziza Khazzoom

A project of cultural westernization is built deep into modern Jewish history. During the Enlightenment, in framing the "Jewish question," western European Christians presented western European Jews as Oriental, and as backward because they were Oriental (Voltaire called ancient Jews "vagrant Arabs with leprosy"). In response to this stigma, western European Jews sought to westernize, modernize, and become more similar to western European bourgeois Christians. As they westernized, French and German Jews turned to other Jewish populations that had not undergone the cultural changes, and tried to help them "progress." Such help ranged from Yiddish literature written by westernized German Jews that poked fun at shtetl life to the more institutionalized, extensive, and resource-rich system of Alliance schools, set up by French Jews to teach Middle Eastern Jews French language, literature, dress, and customs and to provide them with modern occupations.

CHILDHOOD IN BAGHDAD

This was the type of school that Rachel, a woman who grew up in Iraq in the 1930s and 1940s, attended. The Alliance was efficient and highly influential. By 1939, it was operating 127 schools, in Iraq, Syria, Morocco, Egypt, Tunisia, and other countries. These included vocational schools that taught manual occupations, primarily to children of the working class, and academic schools that supplied students with a French *brevet* (diploma following a matriculation exam). Middle Eastern Jews, for their part, encouraged the Alliance and other links with western Europe. As minorities in the Arab world, they had little investment in traditional Muslim rule in the Middle East, and they saw in these links with Europe an opportunity to improve their position in their home societies. In Baghdad, leaders of the Jewish community began their own program of modernization, then invited the Alliance to establish a boys' academic school in 1865. By World War I there were fifteen Alliance schools in Iraq, and the Alliance was the most prestigious French education available to Jews there. Its graduates were community leaders and zealous proponents of French culture and westernization, and as a result, by World War II the project of westernization had become hegemonic among urban Jews (70 percent of Iraq's Jewish population), particularly in the middle and upper classes.

In the Alliance world view, educating women was an integral part of modernization and communal development, and the first generation of Baghdad's Alliance graduates established a girls' academic school in 1893. Though community members initially debated the value of educating women, by the time Rachel was born, educated and wealthy Jews largely saw women's education as a marker of the community's cultural progress, and support was widespread.

In Rachel's life, this cultural legacy translated into a familial emphasis on education, which imbued her studies with importance and even joy. When I asked her about her life in Iraq, she talked about the Alliance. She loved "the studies and the teachers. . . . At the end of the day, we would come home and do homework. My father helped us a lot. In math and languages . . . we enjoyed learning." Rachel's father initiated sending his two girls to school. He was an educated man, Rachel said, well traveled, and spoke French and English at near-native levels, and it was important to him that his children be well educated. Rachel's mother had never been to school, because her father had not viewed women's schooling as important, but she was delighted to see her daughters get a top education. "My mother encouraged us to learn," Rachel said. "She would prepare [food] for us and tried not to give us work to do in the house, but here and there we helped out anyway."

Like other women I interviewed from her Alliance class, Rachel discussed her school experiences in great detail, more than other aspects of her childhood. Classes began at eight in the morning and lasted until one in the afternoon. Rachel walked alone or with her sister, since the school was in a Jewish neighborhood and they lived close by. The girls usually took lunch from home, but it was also fun to buy lunch at school. Classes were conducted in French and lasted forty-five minutes. Although the vocational schools taught girls and boys different occupations, the academic Alliance gave them the same education (though in separate buildings). Rachel's favorite subjects were math, physics, and chemistry. According to students' recollections, the Alliance pushed them hard. To continue to the last years of high school, they had to take two sets of exams, one for the French brevet and another for Iraq's Arabic system. "Our base was better [than at Israeli schools]," Rachel said. "This I want to tell you." The connection with France was strong. Many of the teachers had studied there, and at the end of the year French officials arrived to administer the *brevet élémentaire* exam. They brought the tests and proctored while the students took them.

After school, Rachel and her sister would walk home together and do homework at their desks in their bedroom. The family lived in an older house, inherited from Rachel's grandparents. Her father had split it vertically, into two three-story apartments. In Rachel's half the ground floor contained an entrance hall, a large kitchen, and a room in which an uncle lived. The second floor had six rooms. One bedroom went to Rachel and her sister, another to Rachel's two brothers, and another to her parents; then there were a dining room, a "telephone room," and a large pantry. Each room had a separate coal stove. The telephone room was a sitting room, where the family would gather in the evenings. The third floor had walls but no roof and was used on summer nights. The house had three full bathrooms. Rachel's mother did the cooking herself—it was considered an art and was not left to hired help—but a maid did all the cleaning, and a laundress came once a week. Compared to her friends from school, Rachel sees herself as having been neither poor nor rich.

The Alliance education lasted ten years, and a common next step was to transfer to the Shamash British high school for two more years and obtain a British matriculation certificate. Rachel's sister took this option, but by the time Rachel finished the Alliance, the immigration to Israel had started, and she decided to continue her studies there. Shamash initially admitted only boys but beginning in the mid-1940s began enrolling high-achieving girls as well. By the time Rachel's sister went to Shamash, it was accepting about ten women a year (and eighty men), and the number of women approximately doubled each year. Shamash was a co-educational experience, but it existed in a society where separation of the sexes was important. This separation, combined with the commitment to the education of girls, led to a classroom setup in which the girls sat in the first rows of each class, apart from the boys, and boys and girls had recess in separate yards.

Rachel, like many I interviewed, stressed that teachers were careful that boys and girls didn't mix. Still, the coeducation bothered some parents, who required convincing to allow their daughters to enroll. In the late 1940s, it was rare for upper-middle-class women to have careers, and marriage was their best access to a comfortable life. As in the West at that time, women who were considered loose had limited marriage options, so parents made sure their daughters didn't get such a reputation. In Iraq, women entered the "loose" category if they were known to have been alone with a man. As a result, even the most liberal parents were careful about maintaining their daughters' physical separation from men.

Despite the Alliance's academic rigor, its French founders did not expect middle-class women to have careers but rather provided them top educations so they would make better mothers and wives. It was continuing to Shamash, as Rachel's sister did, that marked women as uniquely intelligent (as one graduate put it, with some glee, "Not everyone got to go to Shamash, just the girls who were good"). This move was likely to have lifelong consequences. The Iraqi Jewish community was undergoing radical changes with regard to the position of women, as about 10 percent of young women with ten years of education entered the formal labor force (the same as for similar Polish Jewish women). Moreover, rumor had it that some had obtained university educations and worked as doctors or lawyers. As a result, Shamash women developed aspirations for university educations and careers. Rachel—who expected to go to Shamash because of her sister's experience and her own attainments at the Alliance and therefore included herself in this category even though she never enrolled—and her sister were in this group, with the latter already expressing the opinion, well before the immigration to Israel, that women should be financially independent from men.

However, Rachel is uncertain whether their expectations would have been met had they stayed in Iraq, and herein lies some of the complexity of assessing the effect of immigrating on their lives. On the one hand, Rachel says, her sister was extremely good. On the other, there was a quota on the number of Jews who could attend university. Historically, the Jewish community had reacted to this limit by sending its boys to France or England for university. Women had already established a tradition of leaving for France to prepare to become teachers at the Alliance, funded by community scholarships, and it may well have become the norm for Shamash's female graduates to attend French and English universities as well. However, the Jews did not stay in Iraq long enough for such a pattern to develop, in part because Israel seemed like a better option. Middle-class Iraqis often report that the difficulty of obtaining education in Iraq was one aspect of their decision to immigrate to Israel; the belief was that without anti-Semitism, Israel would offer easier access to universities.

But to what extent were Jews really discriminated against in Iraq? The above makes it seem like anti-Semitism was a central feature of life there, but scholars—and Rachel—are still debating this question. Some scholars point to long-standing laws that placed special burdens on Jews, like a tax (jizya), restrictions on building, occupational stereotyping, and occasional forced residential segregation, to argue that life in Iraq and other Muslim societies was shaped by anti-Jewish sentiment. Others point to the rarity of pogroms, to Jews' independence and economic success, and to the contributions they made to Arabic literature, music, and politics, to argue that Muslims were relatively accepting of Jews. There is general agreement on two points. First, Jews usually fared better in Muslim than Christian countries. Second, relations between Jews and Arabs deteriorated with modern European colonialism. Middle Eastern Jews had connections with Europe that improved their competitive position vis-à-vis Muslims, who, in turn, perceived them as consorting with the enemy. But Jews were initially receptive to colonial powers precisely because they were already disadvantaged in Muslim societies.

Arabs did not loom large in Rachel's childhood consciousness. She knew that her father was in business with an Arab and that he had other Arab friends. However, scholars tell us that contact between Jews and Arabs largely occurred in the economic arena, not the social, and this meant that Rachel never met her father's Arab friends. In part, this distance was built into the multicultural structure of Muslim societies, in which religious/ethnic/national communities had their own living spaces and social institutions but markets were mixed. The extended family dominated home life in bourgeois Jewish Iraq, and even friends from the Alliance did not usually visit one another's houses. As such, it would be unexpected for Rachel to meet any of her father's friends, regardless of their religion. And research tells us that there was an additional tendency to "protect" girls from contact with Arabs. These factors meant that the integration of Jews with Arabs in Iraq, which many scholars argue was significant, largely happened in the world of adult men, not middle-class girls. The identification of bourgeois Iraqi Jews with the West enhanced this tendency to retain separate communities and is part of the explanation for why those who arrived in Israel appeared to disconnect easily from their Arab origins.

Though Rachel did not have much contact with Arabs, we can use her experience to support both sides of the scholarly debate on the severity of discrimination against Jews in Iraq. Her father and his Arab business associates were full partners. They were wholesalers who imported goods from India and other countries and sold them to shopkeepers in Iraq. Rachel's father brought the international connections and the necessary language skills for communicating outside the Arab world, indicating again how Jewish links with other countries helped the community in Iraq. (Jews there were also prevalent in trade, banking, money changing, and the management of the railroads and the post office). However, he and many other Jews were not able to obtain import licenses, and thus the business, including all its stored property, had to be in an Arab partner's name. This became significant when it was time to immigrate to Israel and Rachel's father was not able to get his money out of the business. It is not entirely clear to Rachel why this happened, but she is pretty certain that her father asked for his share and was not given it.

Scholars have noted the deterioration in Jewish-Arab relations with the emergence of Zionism and the establishment of the State of Israel. Rachel's recollections demonstrate the tight spot this deterioration generated for Iraq's Jews: "I will tell you, the aliya to Israel and the Zionist movement seem to have caused some kind of hatred. But in actually my father was a businessman who worked with Arabs!" Rachel sees a feedback loop in which the availability of aliya generated Arab animosity, which left the Jews little option but to make aliya. "Before the aliya and everything associated with it . . . I didn't feel anything [anti-Semitic]. . . . But after that . . . the reason we wanted to make aliya was the violence. There was a major change when they knew that Jews were making aliya. . . . Many fired Jews who were working for them. The attitude changed." Indeed, 1948 was a period of great unrest in Baghdad, during which, in addition to other events, a highly assimilated and even anti-Zionist businessman with connections to the government was executed. More generally, during this period different sectors of Iraqi power took different stances vis-à-vis Jews, with the cash-strapped and somewhat weak government simultaneously taking steps to physically protect them and arresting them often while demanding large bribes for their release. In addition, a government offensive against the Zionist underground led to the arrests and probably torture of activists. Iraqi Jews report that any sense of security they had disappeared as a result of these events, providing an additional reason for their decision to immigrate to Israel.

IMMIGRATION AND LIFE IN THE *MA'ABARA*

Among the well-informed and multilingual Jewish community of Baghdad, there were a mix of stances on Israel and therefore a mix of reactions to the establishment of the state in 1948. The community had a large and active communist movement, which imagined an Iraq where Jews were integrated as full-fledged Iraqis, and a Zionist movement, which saw the proper place of Jews as being with other Jews in Israel. The Alliance supported neither project; instead, in line with maskilic (Jewish Enlightenment) projects in western Europe, it sought the "cultural regeneration" of Jewish communities (predating similar Zionist goals) and their eventual integration—as Westerners, not Arabs—into their native, non-Jewish societies. Though the Alliance did not support Zionism, it and Shamash were, unbeknown to the teachers and administration, recruiting sites for the Zionist movement.

Most Alliance graduates knew about the movement and were familiar with the basic tenets of Zionist ideology, and many had participated in at least one clandestine meeting. Zionism's goal was to move Jews to Israel, and this idea excited many Alliance students. Many women I interviewed (including Polish Jews) asserted that the Zionists targeted youths, who were idealistic and could be convinced to uproot comfortable lives and immigrate. Their parents tended to take stances more similar to those of western European Jews, supporting the idea of a Jewish state but, aware of the poverty of Palestine, uninterested in starting over there themselves.

Two factors got these parents to Israel anyway. First, once most of their children left, they tended to follow. The second is a set of hotly debated historical events. In March 1950, the Iraqi government announced that whereas previously immigration to Israel had been illegal, Jews who wanted to go could now do so, provided they registered by March 1951, immediately forfeited their citizenship, left all their assets in Iraq (to be managed in absentia by Iraqi representatives), took out only twenty to fifty dinars per person (depending on age), and then left within fifteen days of registering. The Iraqi prime minister did not want the Jews to go. He did not want to help populate Israel with Jews or lose a group that comprised around 20 percent of Baghdad's population and played a central role in the city's economy. Jews held a great deal of Baghdad's wealth, and their occupational skills and international contacts were not matched among the Muslim population, so their mass exodus could spell economic disaster. However, the general population's anti-Jewish agitation was also creating social unrest, which the government feared would be turned upon itself. In addition, Jews were already immigrating illegally, taking their money with them or spending it on smugglers and bribes to get out of the country. The prime minister took a gamble; he did not expect many Jews to leave and hoped that making the process legal would keep their assets in Iraq while getting rid of those who most wanted to go.

As noted, my interviews suggest that most wealthy Jewish parents did not intend to leave for Israel. In addition, Jews reacted with suspicion to the government's sudden announcement that they could immigrate. Thus at first only very few signed up, and those who did tended to be poorer. Collective memory has it that Jews suddenly signed up en masse when several bombs went off within a short period. Over the years there have been loud debates about who set off the bombs, with some accusing Iraqi Muslim groups and others accusing the Zionist movement. Moshe Gat even argues that the massive sign-up would have occurred without the bombs. Whatever the cause, the result was that by the registration's closing, most of Iraq's Jews had signed up to leave.

Then, on the day after the registration ended, the government passed a law "freezing" (actually expropriating) the property of all Jews who had signed up to leave, including those who had already left and were administering their property from abroad. Wealthy Jews became paupers overnight. The Zionists were caught off guard as well, and Jews who had lost everything crowded into the synagogues while awaiting transport to Israel, causing a humanitarian crisis. In the end, most of Iraq's Jews—about 130,000 people—were airlifted to Israel during a period of about a year, the vast majority in the first half of 1951.

In Rachel's family, she and her sister made the decision to immigrate. In 1950, a year before they left, her fourteen-year-old brother had wanted to join a female cousin who was immigrating to Israel illegally. Rachel's father objected that the trip would be dangerous, but her brother "stood his ground," and her father finally gave in. Rachel remembers ironing her brother's clothes and helping him pack for the journey. A Zionist emissary arranged the trip. A group of Bedouins took him out of the country—"On camels!" Rachel exclaimed—and to Iran, from which he traveled to Israel. On the way, "they stole his money and his clothes, and when he got to Israel he had nothing." He still doesn't know who "they" were; he simply woke up one day to find everything gone. Upon arrival in Israel, Rachel's brother was taken to a kibbutz, as was common for young immigrants who arrived alone. When legal immigration became a possibility, Rachel and her sister began to agitate to leave as well. Her parents did not want to leave Iraq but allowed the girls to go.

Rachel and her sister joined the massive airlift to Israel. Upon arrival, they declined to go to a kibbutz. It was a waste of time, Rachel said, because it did not help one obtain a university education. The girls were therefore placed in Sha'ar Aliya, a way station composed of large multifamily barracks with cots. Later, when their parents arrived, the family went to a ma'abara. Ma'abarot were temporary tent cities, with about one (extended) family per tent. Scholars have argued that they were overcrowded because the Israeli government either was taken by surprise at the number of immigrants or let in too many since it was more concerned with populating the country than with the welfare of those who arrived. There was no electricity in the ma'abarot or floors in the tents. The winter of 1951 was unusually cold and wet, and the camps often flooded. The ma'abarot have been the subject of films (e.g., *Salah Shabati*) and collective memory for decades, and for Iraqis, who took for granted indoor plumbing, electricity, and heat—not to mention floors— the ma'abarot still stand out. Rachel recalls her arrival at the airport and the camp: "The flight was three hours, the change in our lives from sky to earth. From sky to earth. They gave us some simple plate and told us to stand in line, instead of the care of the home, instead of the food of the home."

Rachel's parents decided to move to Israel after the girls left, and they arrived two weeks later. Rachel does not know why they changed their minds but presumes it had something to do with wanting to join their children. Communicating their decision was difficult. There were no phones in Sha'ar Aliya, and Iraqi Jews who tried to write to Israel could be labeled Zionists and imprisoned or killed. Rachel's parents contacted relatives in London, who contacted relatives who had arrived in Israel earlier and already had a home, who contacted Rachel and her sister in the encampment. When they learned that their parents were arriving, Rachel and her sister went to their parents' assigned ma'abara and requested family reunification.

Most Iraqi Jews spent at least their first weeks in Israel in a ma'abara, and how long they stayed usually depended on what assets they had managed to get into the country. In Israel, rules and procedures changed often during this chaotic period, and this probably explains the range of assertions I got from immigrants on how they moved money out of Iraq and into Israel. Many say that whatever they had of value was taken at one of two points in time: on their way out of Iraq, when Iraqi officials searched them, or upon their arrival in Israel, when Israeli officials took whatever money they had, saying that it was the cost of taking care of them.

Iraqi Jews used a variety of ways to move their money past both groups of officials. One put diamonds in the hollow handle of a suitcase. Others gave their money to friends who traveled though France, England, or the United States. One even claimed that she wore her jewelry openly through both checkpoints. But according to the immigrants, most moved their money through British banks. Many

Jews worked in British banks in Iraq—a legacy of the Alliance's preparation for modern occupations—and they passed money through England to an office in Israel. Jews who got assets into Israel could buy an apartment—most chose one in Ramat Gan, a new suburb near Tel Aviv—and stayed in the ma'abarot only briefly. Others spent years there.

Rachel's parents lost most of their assets, including stored goods from her father's business, their house, and furniture. Her father did sell the home, but the buyer found out that he had registered to leave Iraq and came by and obtained the deposit back with threats (Rachel does not know the details). The furniture's value is also not to be ignored: household objects included Persian rugs and precious metals, and some Iraqi Jews bought apartments in Israel largely by selling such items. The only cash Rachel's family was able to get out was from the sale of her mother's jewelry. It had been kept in a safe place outside the home (probably a bank), and once Rachel's parents signed up to leave it became illegal for them to reclaim it. However, a Christian Arab friend obtained it and fortunately was willing to buy it for a fair price. Because they took out so little, Rachel's family did not have enough money for an apartment in Israel, and one of their first tasks was to save some.

Like many immigrants, Rachel reports that the ma'abara was less tolerable for the parents than for the youths, who saw some adventure in the spartan lifestyle, made friends, and learned Hebrew. In Iraq, the parents' "expectation was that we would go on [to Shamash and the university]. And then it became possible to go to Israel, and we decided. They agreed. But when they got there and saw the situation, they didn't know how to take it. . . . They were very disappointed, upset to see us working. My father was a successful businessman, an intelligent man, and we had everything. To go and sit in a ma'abara? There were those who literally became sick." Two wholesalers like her father, Rachel said, committed suicide in the ma'abara. For employment, the fathers were often offered *sponga*—that is, janitorial work—but the children I interviewed reported that they could not allow their fathers to do such jobs, and set out to work themselves.

Rachel and her sister similarly set out to support their parents. Academic work on Middle Eastern Jews in Israel often casts large families as a disadvantage, because resources are spread out among many people. However, large families also had their benefits, as tasks and emotional burdens could also be spread among many people. Rachel and her siblings responded to their parents' paralysis with a coordinated effort to obtain an apartment, education, and professional employment. University, Rachel said, was not possible, given the financial situation, but she and her sister, and later her younger brothers, traded off working and studying until they had bought an apartment, learned Hebrew, and gotten bookkeeping certificates. During their first two years in the ma'abara, Rachel and her sister earned money while their brothers, fifteen and thirteen years old, were in a kibbutz and a boarding school, respectively.

The only available work was manual labor, which weighed hard on Rachel. Asked what she had expected, Rachel said that in Iraq they had been led to believe that the situation would be much better, "so we were disappointed. Because we were also at a hard age, seventeen or eighteen, neither here nor there. At first there was a crisis . . . a person coming from warmth and studies . . . [suddenly] working in a factory, and in fields, packing oranges. . . . That was a very hard period, because one felt like one had gone down in status." The family and its cooperation were her solace at this time. "It was hard on us. . . . What was I doing in a factory? . . . But there wasn't a choice, and I knew that when my sister had finished [studying Hebrew at the kibbutz], then I would leave. Maybe that's what gave me the stamina to continue."

Despite her difficulty, Rachel had an advantage vis-à-vis other female immigrants: she came with her parents rather than a guardian. This is probably the reason she was able to work. As can be seen from her description, taking the sorts of jobs that were available to Iraqi immigrants meant downward mobility. For a population just beginning to allow middle-class women into the labor force, such "degrading" work was unlikely to have been approved. Rachel, like all middle-class Iraqis who arrived with their parents, does not report parental objections to her working, but immigrants who arrived with guardians—usually uncles or grandfathers—did experience disapproval. As Rachel and others stress, no one in Iraq anticipated the chaos in Israel, which made working in a factory, unthinkable in Iraq, a necessity. Parents could assess the situation and allow violations of norms, which guardians—who had promised to take care of these teenagers—were reluctant to do. This is important—although Rachel found the work degrading and was worried about her parents and her future, her description of the siblings' cooperation has a sense of purpose and even excitement. For all the hardships, when their parents were immobilized, it felt good for young immigrants like Rachel to contribute. This was only possible when gender and class norms lifted enough to allow them to take whatever work was available.

With the move to Israel, and particularly the Tel Aviv area, all interaction with Arabs ceased, and they moved further away from Rachel's consciousness (as noted, even in Iraq they had only been on the margins of her reality). They returned, however, with the first Israeli-Arab war she experienced—the Suez War of 1956—when, as she says, soldiers started to die. When I asked Rachel what should be done about the conflict now, she said, "Negotiation. Not war. . . . I think we need to talk to them, and to give something up. . . . Also for them it's not easy. Look, after all, after all they have a part here. Also their lives are not easy. But the problem is that there is a lot of hatred in their camp. And that's hard to deal with."

Rachel's ma'abara period ended abruptly, when the facility was closed. With some governmental help, money they had saved from working, and money they had taken from Iraq, her family bought a two-room apartment in Kfar Saba, a ma'abara that had become a permanent settlement. Two rooms was small for six people, but it was "a real home." At this point, Rachel's father decided that the younger of her brothers should leave the kibbutz and study, though he loved the kibbutz. He began preparing for the high school matriculation exam (*bagrut*), while Rachel's sister went to Naharia to study Hebrew, and Rachel continued to work in a factory. When her sister returned, Rachel went to Kibbutz Hatzor to learn Hebrew.

Early descriptions of the immigration say that Israeli state agents avoided placing mizrachim in kibbutzim to avoid violating mizrachi traditionalism (the understanding of this period changed over time). This traditionalism was believed to make them attached to family life and unable to comprehend such modern movements as collectivist living. Rachel and her family were certainly family oriented and, with the exception of one brother, uninterested in the kibbutzim, but the reasons she cites for this have little to do with tradition. On arrival, as noted, she and her sister saw the kibbutz as insufficiently achievement-oriented for the educational trajectories they had begun in Iraq. Later, they went to kibbutzim because they were good places to learn Hebrew. Rachel reports that kibbutz members asked her to stay on, but she did not, and here she references not time wasted but the rather modern concept of individualism. "I like independence. And the kibbutz is, you know, collective life, where you can't do what you want."

So Rachel left the kibbutz and studied bookkeeping. After obtaining her certificate, she worked at a variety of jobs, then found her first position "at a respectable place" and, as she put it, finally started her life. Rachel got this job through her sister, who was already working as a bookkeeper and heard of an opening. In the meantime, her brother finished his matriculation, but again, they didn't have the resources for a university education. So he got a job at a bank and took courses at Tel Aviv university through his job, as did Rachel herself. She, like many bourgeois Iraqi immigrants, mourns her and her siblings' inability to get a university education. "Today, everyone knows, most people go to university after the bagrut. But then there weren't the conditions. One like my sister, everyone says that it's a shame that she was wasted, didn't finish university." It is important to note the extent to which this family valued women's education. When immigration made resources scarce, the siblings divided them so they could all obtain the same degrees; the brothers did not get more than the sisters (and the older sister was the only one who had started at university). In fact, Rachel's primary regrets pertain to her sister's truncated education, not her brothers'.

In this story about a Middle Eastern Jewish immigrant to Israel, some may miss a discussion of discrimination. Two points are relevant. First, Rachel's experience confirms what my quantitative work has found: while it is true that overall mizrachi immigrants obtained low-status jobs regardless of their education, this was not true for those who could show cultural westernization. (Indeed, the pronunciation of *mizrachi* itself reflects this issue. Many Middle Eastern Jews say it with an aspirated *H*. However, Rachel does not use this pronunciation, as is common for those mizrachim who assimilated.) Clearly, Rachel, with an English- and French-speaking father, a sister with a British matriculation certificate, and her own French brevet and knowledge of French language, literature, and dress codes, was in a position to show Westernness, and thus it is not expected that ethnic discrimination would be central to her experiences. One might suggest that because mizrachim like Rachel didn't experience labor market discrimination, it is incorrect to think of their lives as having been shaped by their ethnicity, but in fact they were. The desire to make Israel a Western state was an ethnic concern, born of the maskilic belief that the East was backward and that Jews needed to become Western. To the extent that the criteria of perceived Westernness and Easternness shaped how individuals were treated, ethnicity was operating at all times, even when this led veteran immigrants *not* to discriminate against westernized mizrachim.

Second, it is worth looking carefully at Rachel's description of state agents in the ma'abara as helpful because they told her where to study to be a nurse, teacher, or bookkeeper. She and other Iraqis whose families arrived with little money gave up early on attending university. Immigration officials were then happy to help them obtain these reduced goals. However, Iraqi women who arrived in a better financial position and therefore pursued university expectations with more vigor expressed frustration at the agents' unwillingness to explain how one could study anything *other* than nursing, teaching, or bookkeeping. To the extent that immigrants from other groups received better descriptions of the road to university, the state discriminated. However, it is unclear which other groups might have gotten better information: ashkenazim, or men? My interviews with middle-class Polish women suggest that they arrived in Israel with similar backgrounds and educational goals and also found themselves with certificates instead of university degrees. The overall impression one gets is that both groups of achievement-oriented female immigrants found themselves able to break out of traditional women's roles only to a limited degree. In comparing the experiences of both groups, it seems that Rachel suffered *gender* discrimination but did not realize it because the vagaries of immigration adjusted her goals such that they did not encounter institutional resistance.

A SETTLED LIFE IN ISRAEL

Rachel's father died soon after she obtained her first regular job, and her mother not long after. Rachel says that her father eventually settled into Israel, especially when he saw that his children had found their ways. While working at her first regular job, Rachel met and married her husband, who was studying law. They were introduced by a colleague of her sister's who had married his brother, and when they met there was instant chemistry. They dated for about eight months and married when Rachel was twenty-six. Rachel says that she admired the man who would become her husband because he was educated, and over the years she enjoyed talking to him about decisions that had to be made either together—such as how to handle the children—or alone, such as whether she would leave work when the children were born, and whether she would go back later on.

Through Rachel's work, she and her husband were able to take out a loan to buy an apartment in the new township of Ramat Aviv, across the street from what would eventually become Tel Aviv University (but at the time was the abandoned Palestinian village of Shaykh Muwannis, resettled by Jewish immigrants). Rachel decided to leave work when her second son was born. She was uncertain about the decision, because she liked to be active, but that was a time when there was little help for women who wanted to work and have families, and since her parents were no longer alive and she lived far from her siblings, it was difficult to care for her children and work simultaneously. As it turned out, Rachel said, she really enjoyed being at home with the children, at least for the first four or five years. Then she began to get antsy and started thinking about returning to the formal labor force.

Rachel was out of the labor market for six years and returned half-time when her youngest son started kindergarten. Her husband, who was working at Tel Aviv University, helped her find a job in the university library. She enjoyed this work, she said, because it was at a cultured place. Rachel also liked the general routine of her occupation; she liked keeping the books orderly and reimbursing professors for their trips abroad "according to the rules." However, the salary was low, and she was not given tenure or social benefits (in Israel, which has a socialist tradition, one can get tenure in a variety of clerical occupations), so she left to work at the Tel Aviv Museum. The university then suggested that she come back with full benefits. She did, and stayed until her retirement. Rachel thought about returning to school to get a degree as an accountant (the occupation of her daughter-in-law and two of her three sons; the other is a lawyer). But she found it hard to work, take care of a family, and go back to school.

Rachel's husband died young, when her sons were still in the army, and in retrospect she is grateful that she had a career. This, together with her husband's pension, kept her protected against the financial crises often associated with the early death of a spouse. Today, Rachel enjoys playing bridge, which requires some thought and strategy, and spending time with her grandchildren and friends. Speaking of her immigration and its aftermath, Rachel believes that the hardship was good for her, in that it made her a more independent and self-reliant person.

The loss associated with the immigration, for her, is that she didn't live up to her educational and occupational potential as a graduate of one of the better educational systems available to women in the 1950s. I asked her if she missed Iraq, and she returned to her defining experience in the Jewish Alliance: "No, but every once in a while I think about, for example, people from Bulgaria who go back to Bulgaria. I would love once to see at least the Alliance, where it is. But I don't have any sentiments of my own about Iraq. Because, after all, we left in a different environment—hatred. Some also really suffered, some were killed, during the war. But I'd like to see the school. They say it's all changed, they've added roads, but I'd really like to see it."

In thinking about her attainments and about women's roles in general, Rachel compares herself to two groups: younger Israeli women, who take for granted that they can study, work, and raise children simultaneously, and Iraqi women of the 1940s, whose place was in the home. In Rachel's view, the tight-knit family and community of Iraq are in direct contrast with the gender-egalitarian lifestyle of Israel, because the family-oriented lifestyle requires that people have more time on their hands, something that women staying in the home enables. Rachel's thinking is in line with modernization theory, which says that the movement of women out of the home is part and parcel of a series of changes that come together, including a faster pace of life and longer working hours for all. Within these constraints, Rachel is not sure if the gains are worth the losses, and she misses the socializing she used to do with family members. Still, many scholars attack modernization theory as being too simplistic, and for this stance too one can find affirmation in Rachel's experience. Her very Middle Eastern family structure proved to be highly adaptive in Israel's modern Western environment, as family cooperation increased her attainment in tangible ways, and she articulates social advantages to extended families that would have made her feel less lonely as an older woman. Israel tended to reject any behaviors that were considered Eastern, including forming these large "hamula-type" families (hamula is a word used in Israel to refer to large Palestinian families), and Rachel's experience focuses us on what may have been lost through this cultural preference.

SUGGESTIONS FOR FURTHER READING

Iraqi history, Alliance history, and the immigration to Israel
Babylonian Jewry Heritage Center (Or Yehuda, Israel). www.babylonjewry.org.il.
Gat, Moshe. *The Jewish Exodus from Iraq, 1948–1951.* London: Frank Cass Publishers, 1997.
Laskier, Michael. *Alliance Israélite Universelle and the Jewish Communities of Morocco, 1862–1962.* Albany: State University of New York Press, 1983
Rodrigue, Aron. *Images of Sephardi and Eastern Jewries in Transition: The Teachers of the Alliance Israelite Universelle, 1860–1939.* Seattle: University of Washington Press, 1993.

Israel's ethnic structure

Eyal, Gil. *The Disenchantment of the Orient: Expertise in Arab Affairs and the Israeli State.* Stanford: Stanford University Press, 2006.

Khazzoom, Aziza. *Shifting Ethnic Boundaries and Inequality in Israel: Or, How the Polish Peddler Became a German Intellectual.* Stanford: Stanford University Press, 2008.

Shenhav, Yehouda. *The Arab Jews: A Postcolonial Reading of Nationalism, Religion, and Ethnicity.* Stanford: Stanford University Press, 2006.

Interviews with Iraqi female immigrants

Khazzoom, Aziza. "Orientalism at the Gates." *Signs,* Vol. 32, No. 1 (2006), pp. 197–220.

15

Is Slavery Over?

Black and White Arab Bedouin Women in the Naqab (Negev)

Safa Abu-Rabia

"The whites would buy the 'abed, let me tell you."

"They wouldn't buy him, it wasn't a purchase... they would steal him, bring him by stealing, not buy him, steal him, yes."

Thus begins the argument between the mother, a woman in her late sixties, and her daughter, in their house in Rahat, the Bedouin city in the northern Naqab (Negev). Both women are black, both are engaged in constructing their past identity, and each asserts something different about their origin. The second-generation women of the *Nakba* (the Palestinian Catastrophe of 1948) emphasize that they were the victims of the greed and rule of the white Bedouin, while the first generation of the Nakba, those who lived before 1948, claim a worse fate: "We were bought by the whites." The argument was very much a matter of principle between them.

THE DAUGHTER: Allow me tell you how it was in the past... they [the white Bedouin] would steal and take them [the black Bedouin], they would reach the sea, in Egypt... they would reach Egypt, yes, they would meet up with the whites, and these would kidnap the children, run away with them, call out to them, "Come, children," and take them with them. In other words, our great-great-grandfather was not bought, we were not sold, we were stolen, simply stolen, the grandfather of our grandfather, yes... you know, a long time ago... from the very first [ancestor of ours who was brought here], he lived among them, we were treated like livestock, and that is how he became a slave.

THE MOTHER: They [the white Bedouin] would steal them [the black Bedouin], one, two, three of them, bring them to a *khirbeh* [ruin] and sell them for a shekel, that's how he became a slave. They would bring him a woman to be his wife, he would *yaward* [herd the sheep], serve them, serve them drinks. Inside, his wife would be serving him drinks, and they would call out to him, "Hey darky, get up and bring me some water to drink, get up and grind [the wheat]." . . . They would steal them and take them, meaning they bought them, purchased them, "*ya weli*" [expression of grief]. They would kidnap them in a blanket, and people would come to take them, like thieves, they just kidnapped them, from Sinai, from the sea. . . . First from Sudan, they would come to Egypt.

The way Bedouin women recount the past is based on stories passed orally from generation to generation. But there is not just one version; it depends on which generation is telling, or more precisely, constructing, the story. The essence of the argument—was the slave bought or stolen?—is of the most fundamental sort. It is of great importance in the construction of their identity today: Is the identity of the slave a social construction linked with his arrival in Palestine? Or was he a slave already in the country of origin, in Africa?

It is important to understand the context of this argument, namely that it takes place within a tribal society wherein individuals' futures are determined by their pre-1948 origin—social status, attitudes toward them, marriage (whom they are allowed and, primarily, not allowed to marry), residence (segregated by tribe and/or by race), and more. One's past identity is the direct and uncontested source of one's present-day social identity, for black and white alike. Thus, all are engaged in the debate over the original identity of the blacks—on the one hand, the white owner (of the past), and on the other hand the (former) slave.

All of them live in the Naqab region, inhabited today by approximately 170,000 Bedouin. Half are concentrated in recognized towns, and the other half live in forty-five unrecognized villages, eight of which are undergoing the formal recognition process. The reality of their lives, whether in the recognized or the unrecognized villages, is complex: they reside within the borders of the State of Israel but are not acknowledged as a population deserving of equal civil rights. The exclusion of the Bedouin and their invisibility in the eyes of the law have a direct influence on their unstable way of life and miserable socioeconomic reality. Poverty, unemployment, and social distress wrack the permanent settlements to which they were transferred in the 1970s after two decades of Israeli military government; they lack urban and economic infrastructure, industrial zones, and a reasonable level of urban services. Some of the Bedouin in unrecognized villages live on the very lands they owned before Israel's establishment, while the rest were expelled to other places, where they have remained to this day. These villages' inhabitants live without electricity or water services, education, medicine, welfare services, or the basic infrastructure for their development, and under the constant threat of home demolition and land expropriation. They are struggling for recognition of the ownership of their lands and are driven by the aspiration to continue living on them in a way suitable to their cultural and social needs. The struggle over the land is central to the struggle over social and gender identity, class hierarchies, and intracommunal tribal borders, as revealed through the narratives of Bedouin women from around the Naqab: white and black, of the generation of the Nakba and their daughters.

IN A BEDOUIN TOWN

The entrance to the Bedouin settlement seems as far as could be from the Jewish city from which I came. Only a five-minute drive from the big city, already at the right turn into the town I feel myself entering a different world, a world of distant deserts, somewhere in that other, invisible part of the geographical sphere of Bedouin life.

Entering the settlement takes twice the time it took to drive from the adjacent Jewish city, as if its borders were contained somewhere inside of it, far from the immediate surroundings. The wide, desert-bound streets, with no indication whatsoever that this is the entrance to a settlement inhabited by people, strengthen the feeling of disorientation as I drive inward. Neglect and misery can be seen on all sides—from the unfinished houses visible from the entrance to the tin-structure stores along the edge of the street where few people pass by.

Although this is a recognized town, it feels like the antithesis of someplace inhabited. All are here by chance, and their existence revolves around their transience—they belong not here but to their historical lands. The desert landscape is marked by flatness and primarily by what it lacks; the movement of people, urban structures, and automobile traffic are almost nonexistent within this small and isolated settlement. The distance from Beersheba, the biggest city in the Naqab, seems to be a distance of time, of years; my feeling that this settlement is established yet not established, left untouched, timeless, is palpable. You must drive long minutes to connect to it, and when you arrive you encounter a kind of emptiness, an absence.

Once there, I found the house of my interviewee with great ease; it is hard to get lost in a place like this. The second neighborhood on the left, "three houses down in the first row, stop on the right side": I followed her instructions and arrived immediately. My car was one of the few parked on what could hardly be described as a street, on this gray winter day. I walked inside, and she greeted me warmly, then led me into her house. And there she began to recount her life story for me.

The two of us sat in the *liwan*, a large room filled with colorful, thin mattresses laid out across its length and breadth. The cold seeped into the marrow of my bones. I could hardly feel my exposed limbs—my wrists and my face, peeking out from under the long black coat that covered my thin body, bent forward toward her as a sign of respect and listening. I sat on one of the outer mattresses, and next to me sat Umm Hikmat. She was an elderly woman, more than seventy years old, short and thin, wrapped in a black *'abaya*—the covering that Bedouin women customarily wear on top of the traditional dress, the *thobe*. The wide thobe is cinched with an embroidered belt that connects and divides the chest and the stomach. The traditional dress characterizes the women of this generation, who carry years of gender identity manifested in the varying styles of embroidery decorating its upper part.

The feeling between us is hierarchical. Umm Hikmat is a domineering woman, and she makes her presence felt; her voice is clear, sharp, accompanied by hand gestures. Strong words, full of meaning, come out of her mouth, directed at me. And I sit across from her, my back bent, leaning toward her, trying to capture her every word, every piece of information that might help me piece the puzzle together. I am a researcher just starting out, looking for answers to questions about my identity as a Bedouin woman in the Judaized Naqab. She is an elderly woman from a former landowning tribe who lives in a permanent Bedouin settlement far from the lands of her ancestors. In my possession is a small voice recorder, set down next to the elderly woman to help document the experiences from her past as she tells them to me today.

THE WAY IT WAS

Her tone begins to change. It takes on a faster pace, a higher pitch; her hand motions begin to speak, something inside reawakens, her back becomes straight once again, and her gaze takes on a new sharpness, somewhat angry. I am embarrassed, she is angry, and it is because of me. Here the transition was sharp, from the description of the pre-1948 past to a description of the hierarchy that existed between white and black in the past, of those same people who make her angry, her neighbors: "They live next to me, we go to their weddings, attend their celebrations." For a few moments it seems that she can speak about them in a more egalitarian way. But the difference, the inequality, can be felt in her words and in particular in her tone of voice. She is angry.

Up to this moment she was not so angry. She was busy recounting to me, in the tiniest of details, her life in the not-distant past, that same past that defines her life today, that refuses to disappear and becomes stronger as she speaks. Her description of her pre-1948 life, in which she and her tribe lived on their original lands, is idyllic: "There was a tranquil atmosphere," "we were few people . . . not many." "Things were better," she sums up from time to time. She speaks in short and very decisive sentences, with no question marks. Her descriptions, but more than that, her facial expressions, convey the inner calm, simplicity, and great clarity that marked her life then.

The story of the past begins in a very focused way: "We are from the Abu Amara tribe, from al-Shawahi, next to Ofakim, those are our lands." The place is significant: it marks the tribal status of the Bedouin today, as in the past, in the Naqab.

These details are critical for the definition of their identity as pre-1948 landowners. They were forcefully removed from this land, which was occupied and expropriated during the war. Today, sixty-four years later, it survives in the consciousness of the people and continues to define them, as they say: "We are of the place, and we remain of the place"—despite the physical distance and the distance of many years. In their consciousness, their belonging continues to stem from the place:

> We would grind, we would bring wheat and barley, we mixed them together and ground them on the grindstone, kneaded and baked them, do you know that oven? Yes, and we would cook, all the while threshing and doing *falha* [cultivating the land] . . . a lot of work . . . sitting with the flocks and milking them, stirring the milk and preparing *'afig* [dried butter], which we stored along with the goat *samna* [melted butter] in the winter . . . when summer comes we eat from it, the goat kids aren't . . . today [i.e., in those days] we don't fatten them, we separated the kids from their mothers so that they wouldn't suckle and overfeed, we milk them, mix, prepare *'afig* and *labeneh* [a type of cheese], and that is their life [meaning, that was the life of our tribe]. In the winter we would transfer our belongings and go live in the hills, in the center of the mountain we put up the house to protect them from the winds . . . and in the summer, we would go to an open place—the winter tent is made of goats' hair, while the summer tent is made from sacks sewn together, since it wasn't cold. They would bring the wood on donkeyback, cut from special bushes that only grow in the desert, called *ser, muthnan, 'adher,* and that was our life . . . herding the sheep.

In Umm Hikmat's descriptions, the clear functions she filled in the past were also connected to the place: her duties and identity, in terms of both gender and social status, stemmed from and revolved around the land, on which she relied for survival as it relied on her. Agriculture and livestock were the center of her world: "The women would load the donkeys up with jugs and go out to the well, fill them with water, and return home, and the livestock was herded by the young women [seventeen to nineteen years old], they would take them out to where there was water and pasture, water their sheep, rest in the shade, and in the afternoon return to their house, and this was their life, and they would harvest, take the harvest to the threshing floor, and trample the crop in order to separate the wheat from the chaff."

Life in the past had an obvious organizational structure, in which the borders of gender, class, personal, and social-collective identities were known. These borders are palpable in Umm Hikmat's descriptions, especially that of the separation between women and men and their household functions. Her place was clear: "The woman does not expose herself to the man, always covers her face, and doesn't, doesn't converse with the man." Her description of this separation reflects the borders of her status, and the gender-based functions are a consequence of that, as she sums up decisively, "I wear a thobe," as if to say: I wear tradition, history, gender status, and in particular, a clear-cut identity that defines my role and position in this world.

The inviolable tribal and class boundaries were entirely determined according to land ownership. The landowning (*sumran*) Bedouin employed the peasant fellahin (known as *humran* Bedouin), from those tribes that did not own land before 1948, in exchange for half of their crops. They did not intermingle in the past, and they avoid intermarriage to this day. "If she [a white Bedouin] falls in love with someone [a fellah] and she wants him, they [her family] refuse to marry her [off], because she is a Bedouin and he is a fellah. . . . They [didn't] let them marry, [but] today they can marry, they [the Bedouin young men] bring [marry] fellah women, but they don't let [the Bedouin women] marry fellah men."

BEING BLACK AND BEDOUIN

"That one [the black Bedouin] is completely whitewashed." The elderly woman's tone of voice begins to change, as do her facial features. Each of her glances emphasizes the wrinkles and creases on her face more and more. These tell an entire history, a past that mingles with present and future, all in the eyes of this woman, but more than anything in her words. Her back is straight and her finger outstretched toward me in a sort of blame mixed with warning; this can also be heard in her harsh tone of voice: "That one is . . . whitewashed." The color of the *'abed*—literally "slave," a term still used to refer to the black Bedouin—was washed out; it mixed with white and became lighter, she claims in a sharp voice.

She is angry, very angry: "So many foreigners have come in . . . nowadays the foreigners are Ethiopian girls, they [the Bedouin] take [marry] Russian girls, al-'Arab [i.e., the Bedouin] take them, al-'Arab have started taking Russian girls, meaning in our midst we have Bedouin going with Jewish girls, it's all mixed up, the result is that we've all become one *sha'b* [lit. "nation/people," a term for a tribe], it's not okay, it's not right, that one takes a Jewish wife, an Ethiopian, ruining the *zaria'h* [lit. "the root," meaning the purity of the race, upon which the continuity of the tribal dynasty is built], it's ruined, in another twenty years you won't be able to tell who is an *'abed* and who is a *khur* [a free white man]. Now her [black Bedouin women's] children are like our children, they are all *gamah* [the color of brown wheat, meaning not white and not black], he [the mixed children] will grow up, marry someone, and then he [the mixed children's children] will be completely whitewashed," Umm Hikmat laments. Once, black Bedouin could be identified by their color, which was a symbol of their status, but today their children's brown skin, which is identical in color to that of the white Bedouin, cannot tell you the color of their mother.

Cultural parameters of stratification in Bedouin tribal society established the status of the blacks, who were bought or stolen on the African continent and brought to landowning Bedouin tribes as servants. They were positioned outside the hierarchy between landowning and landless tribes, and the functions—largely agricultural—that they filled as servants of their masters determined their social status. Their color and small numbers also contributed to their inferior status in a society where the size of a collective determined its strength. The laws of Bedouin society codified this status and the appellation 'abed.

The present-day meaning of the epithet is thus in reference to the past, but it continues to be the source of the blacks' low status in relation to that of the pre-1948 landowners. The racial stratification persists to this day, despite the blacks' growing numbers since 1948 and the fact that they no longer serve the white Bedouin or work on their lands.

Although an absolute separation of these groups existed in the past, preventing them from intermingling, today things are different. Umm Hikmat is afraid of the black Bedouin's complete assimilation though marrying white Bedouin. She laments, "The 'abed has disappeared, nothing remains, and in the coming years not one of them will remain. After the death of today's generation of 'abed, everyone will become a khur, free, liberated, not a single 'abed will remain."

She dislikes this idea for another reason: "The slave taking [marrying] a khur?!" The khur is free, independent of any other class or tribe for the definition of his identity and status, while the identity and entire being of the 'abed were dependent on the whites—working for them, being their servant, and fulfilling their needs, all of which invalidated his personal identity and erased his selfhood: "The servant, what does he do? Herds and plows and harvests, and what else?" His roles are confined to maintaining the white man's way of life. Therefore the 'abed cannot marry the daughter of his masters: "To take [marry] a khur like us, like you?! But he is a black slave!" The slave is a servant and is intended, as far as his masters are concerned, only for that: "The slave serves, but the slave is makruh [despised, excluded, scorned]!"

Then, religion enters Umm Hikmat's speech: "But in religion there is no 'abed or khur"; "We are all God's servants, his servants, yes, his servants, we are all servants, we are all God's creations, Ham, Sam w-Khiwan [Ham, Shem, and Japheth—the sons of Noah]." But reality is different, reality distinguishes, clearly differentiates between slave and free and their respective natures: "He is makruh. . . . In Mecca, when I was in Saudi Arabia, I saw an 'abed and a khura [a black man and a white woman], I asked, 'What is this? How did the white woman take a black man?' They told me that such a statement invalidates my hajj duty." But in the reality of the Naqab Bedouin, the black is a slave, inhuman, and not worthy of any contact whatsoever; therefore, separation must be observed, "since the black slave is tanet [pitch black], brother of the donkey—what happened to you?" This question is her way of expressing anger: she is upset once again. I am also angry, at the contradictions in her speech, at the racist notions that spew from her mouth, in particular her apologetics for the segregation. She cannot relate to blacks as human beings, cannot consider her neighbors as humans—they are so different, they are not worthy of living next to her. "The black, we don't want him, despised, simply despised: makruh, I don't know why. He is truly hated, he is not considered a human being." His status is inferior, she adds: "And even when someone from a tribe is killed, the black slave cannot offer himself to be killed in exchange for the murdered one from the other tribe . . . they say to you there is no way the slave can take someone's place or be a guarantor"—the slave is a traitor, absolutely, he cannot be trusted. Even if you throw him in place of the murdered, he cannot stand in for him; *al 'abed baieg, ma lo thinaa*—the slave has no race or values.

Between her harsh words, Umm Hikmat speaks about the positive characteristics of the 'abed: "All of the *zultan* [black offspring of the black goats, as opposed to the white offspring of the white sheep], the children of the blacks, always know how to dance, the 'abed dance well, they are always laughing, even when they are walking they are pleasant." The 'abed have a good temperament; they know how to laugh; they have nice qualities that are not found among the whites. To a certain extent she manages to characterize them as human. Through positive attributes that are visible in them today she can see them in a positive light, different than in the past: "Life with them is good, the 'abed, always laughing, even if he has nothing he will be happy, always laughing, it is nice living with them," she admits.

AND THE WAY IT IS

The present-day situation in which white and black Bedouin live side by side in the same settlement and with a shared fate has contributed to melting some of the boundaries between them. This is visible in the way in which whites are desired guests at the weddings of blacks, and it accentuates the outward differences between them, making the white Bedouin examine their customs in comparison to those of the blacks: "Yes, we khurs are very prudish, they are better, the black [bride] wears hair extensions, even if she doesn't have hair they bring her hair . . . they hang it on her [head], and in the morning at the end of the party you find her bald, they decorate the hair with shiny beads, which the children collect the next morning, and after the party she is bald." Umm Hikmat smiles. "Their celebrations, their weddings are better than ours, they laugh more and are happier than we are." These intentional encounters, in particular at communal events, succeed in introducing the whites to the world of the blacks, beyond the role of the "slave" that was constructed in the past. Their willingness to take some part in the blacks' celebrations, and their description of their richer and more joyful customs, succeeds to a large extent in bridging the constructed and palpable historical boundaries between them.

But even as these interactions increase, the obvious rise in the number of blacks today in comparison to their small number in the past is a threat to white hegemony in Bedouin society: "They were not many, there were not many 'abed, you would find one in an entire tribe, all of one." Once the blacks were a few individuals working under the rule and patronage of other tribes, but now their ubiquity can be felt within Bedouin-Arab society in the Naqab: "Today they fill the entire world. . . . You haven't seen neighborhood B, the one in the west, neighborhood C or is it B? Everyone there is pure black."

Although there is no precise statistical data about the black Bedouin in the Naqab, they constitute a small minority and live in separate neighborhoods in the permanent Bedouin settlements. As opposed to the Bedouin who chose to stay on the lands they had owned uninterrupted before 1948, landless tribes and blacks saw these settlements as an opportunity. The permanent settlements preserved the division of tribes, with each living in a separate neighborhood. This also applied to the blacks, who settled together in separate neighborhoods despite the fact that they had not constituted a single tribe before 1948, having "belonged" to different landowning tribes. It is reasonable to assume that their shared skin color was a criterion for emotional and tribal affinity, and it serves to this day to demarcate the borders of their neighborhoods.

The process of their "liberation" from "slavery" is a complex question with implications for Naqab Bedouin society on the whole and to which I found no clear or straightforward answers during my research. White Bedouin whom I interviewed claimed that this slavery was not de jure; rather, it was an intrasocietal construction connected to the landownership-based tribal hierarchy, with the blacks counting among the landless. The trauma of 1948 turned the social order of the Bedouin in the south of Israel on its head. The expulsion of most of them beyond the borders of the new state and the forced concentration of the remaining Bedouin in the enclosed military area, on the lands of six tribes for almost two decades, have had a great influence on the fabric of Bedouin-Arab life to this day. With the end of the military government in 1967 and the beginning of contact with Jewish-Israeli society, the blacks started working in Jewish society, and their dependence on the landowning Bedouin as a primary source of income weakened. Thus began a process of equalization in all that concerns employment opportunities, living, and even the realization of leadership opportunities within the settlements, which also benefited the landless fellahin.

BEDOUIN DISPOSSESSION AND RESETTLEMENT

The new, mixed reality undermines the absolute hegemony of the whites. Because they defined their status by the invalidation of the other, it challenges the essence of their identity, rule, and mastery: "This neighborhood has two free [white] families, and the blacks grew to become a million [many] . . . those who were our slaves and were called 'abed have filled the world [multiplied], erupted, and brought [married] khuras, and we have became a *khabisa* [a mixture in which the parts collide], but we don't give and don't take [we don't marry our girls to them, and they don't marry their girls to us], we only participate in their celebrations." When there is a mixed marriage between black and white, the disapproval among the tribes is great and often forces the couple to run away to realize their forbidden wish: "Today he loves a slave woman, and he flees, the khur flees with her, in our family black girls ran away [with two of our sons]."

For Umm Hikmat, the crisis is immense; it embodies an entire life story that she has trouble recounting in detail, that same personal, family, and social trauma that the whites refuse to get over—the loss of the land and with it, mastery over the slave; the blurring of her social and gender identity and status. With great sadness and in a slow, somewhat desperate and frustrated tone, she describes her life as divided into two: before we were expelled and after. Before—the life on the land; after—the life off the land. Two diametrically opposed and irreconcilable worlds.

Her alienation, and that of the Bedouin in general, from their new space, which they did not choose and which did not choose them, is palpable, visible, and well known. It is from this space of unbelonging that their day-to-day distress derives: "We left [and were sent by force] to these lands . . . we arrived here . . . we wandered and settled here on this land, this land, this, this is the land of al-Azazme, all of it was the land of Abu Mu'amar with the long history, and we lived in their place, and now they [the Israeli authorities] started selling it off from the sides, dunam after dunam, and we took a loan and built a tent at first, and after that a shack, after that buildings, and that is life." Their rich, proud world crumbled, and they were thrown into another, completely different world, to which they have difficulty connecting. From this stem their feelings of transience and arbitrariness toward the places where they were settled after 1948.

The resettlement and massive transition to an urban way of life took their toll among the Bedouin and manifested in the loss of the traditional sources of income based on agriculture, herding, and the internal economy on their lands and in their homes. For the Bedouin woman, who had filled a central role before 1948, the transition to the permanent settlements solidified her inferior status with respect to men while eliminating her agricultural functions and leaving her with no economic alternative. This upheaval in identity (personal and functional) was the effect of moving from an agricultural life—in which women took an active part as shepherdesses, producers, and managers of home economies—to an urban existence in which they are passive consumers, completely dependent, economically and socially, on men, and structurally and educationally prevented from making a living and contributing to the income of their families. Almost an absolute majority of women, particularly in the unrecognized villages, are unemployed and illiterate, with high rates of school dropouts and polygamy.

BLACK IDENTITIES

Thirty kilometers away, not so far from Umm Hikmat but at a significant distance from her world, a few months later, at the beginning of summer, I met black women in the neighborhood designated for blacks only in the largest Bedouin city in the Naqab. All such neighborhoods are identified by a number, but the locals also know this one as Haret al-'abed (Neighborhood of the slaves).

The same feeling I had when visiting Umm Hikmat accompanies me as I enter it, that feeling of stopping in time. There is no real movement in the neighborhood; the half-built houses line up alongside one another, with people holed up inside, hiding from the heat, and the encircling desert cries out all around. The street is one straight line, with house after unfinished house. In this, the only Bedouin city in the Naqab, the sights and emptiness are not much different from those of the town I had visited just a few months earlier.

In listening to the black women I come to sense how they have dealt with their identity as black women and their 'abed past. I sit between them; it is hot, very hot. Our conversation takes place in my interviewee's courtyard. From her I glean the most significant things I have heard thus far. We sit with a small group of five other women. Two walk in and out, but the others stay for the entire conversation. These three represent three generations of the same family: the first is a very elderly woman, whose face tells an entire lifetime and whose age can be seen in the holes and cracks of her bare feet, upon which she stood while preparing a traditional remedy for a woman who wanted to become pregnant. She is a healer whose traditional wisdom, intelligence, and expertise have cured many people in the region. Each passing minute brings more words of wisdom from her mouth. I make sure that the recorder is taping all the while. This is a vibrant conversation between the grandmother—the healer—her daughter, who sits next to her, and her granddaughter, who contributes her views on the subjects based on her experience today.

Generally, when I interview black women in the Naqab, the beginning is quite clear: despite their pre-1948 landlessness, their linkage to the place where they lived—which is as strong as that of the landowners—is a central factor in the construction of their present consciousness and still clearly defines their gender and social identities. Some even apologize for their situation: "We, we didn't have lands there, as you know, we don't have lands, excuse us, *la tuwakhidhni* [forgive me]. They gave us lands here to rent."

They begin their narrative in the same way that the white Bedouin women do. Through their position on the (white people's) land, they define their selfhood and their character: "We all lived in the Wadi Umm Hitat, on the Dome [name of a place]. Do you know where Wadi al-Imhitat is, where it's located? Next to al-Muhadhara, al-Muhadhara, and north from there is Wadi al-Hitan, after Wadi al-Hitan is Wadi Ghawayn, they also lived in Wadi Umm Hitan." Their lives revolved around the land, which defined their daily routine: "We reap and thresh and herd . . . and you can see the boys and girls planting and reaping, threshing and eating." There was also a yearly routine: "Here you have a *balad* ["land"; meaning, you are given the right to work on the land], we take *baladik* [your land], plant it, cultivate it, and divide it fifty-fifty." They knew who they were and what their role was according to the space in which they lived:

> We had the largest plot of land in all the tribe, we had cattle, herds, donkeys, and we had camels, and we had horses, none of the al-'Arab have livestock like we did. We could always herd our flocks in the center of the Bedouin['s lands], on the edge of the Bedouin['s lands], everyone [the blacks, who usually didn't have their own herds] stays on the side, [but] my father, who owned livestock and herds, could herd wherever he wanted. Now, during the harvest time we would plant all of the ground, and we would wait for the end of the distribution [of the harvest by the whites, their payment to the blacks], it was so good, there was such a good crop that al-Kamalat, al-Balalat [other black tribes], and al-Awarban [a Bedouin tribe] would come, they all would come to us, all the way to us, at al-Hamaysa's place, they would all come to us, all twenty or thirty families would come to us, we would go together to plant. Three days, four days would go by, would fly by, everyone who harvests prepares *ghamawar* [a pile of straw]. Later they would collect them in a big pile, one next to the other, whatever you harvested you laid on the camels and collected it in *jirwan* [pitchers] at the place designated for threshing, called *qawabir*. Yes, everyone brought their crops and laid them in a pile, and this continues the second day and so on every day until the crop that you planted for the al-Hazaylaym [a landowning Bedouin tribe] was harvested.

In addition to their societal identity, status, and work functions, the space also defined their gender identity, primarily the boundaries of their behavior as women:

> When a woman walked in the desert, she left no tracks, there would be no tracks behind her, her dress would sweep away her tracks behind her . . . meaning it was forbidden, forbidden for her tracks to be seen, her thobe dragged behind her like this, she didn't leave any tracks behind her when she walked, no tracks whatsoever . . . you had *tatriz* [a kind of embroidery], today you don't have that anymore, we made from it [used it to attach], it's called, we say *qawa* [a piece of material sewn to the thobe] . . . about this wide [she spreads her hand as far apart as they will go], hanging from the thobe, from the lower back part, dragging behind her and erasing her tracks, it dragged behind her, you would not find any tracks after her, it dragged, she left no tracks, the tracks were covered, the thobe was so long.

These women's conservativeness, conveyed so well in these words, is no different from that of the white Bedouin women; the same behavioral codes apply to
all the women, regardless of color, race, or class. The description of the thobe—
longer than the legs of the woman—erasing her tracks in the desert to prevent
any undesired contact reveals a lot about the way in which women used the their
clothes and the desert to help them keep a separate position, isolated from men. It
is that same space from which they were forcibly removed and whose absence they
mourn: "Yes . . . the state gave it [the land where they are now] to us to rent, to this
very day we are renting, we herd during pasture time, go out with the herd in the
hush [the place where the herds live], pay money, and return to here, now *baladna*
[our land] has become this place, they gave us this place, what can we do [she
expresses helplessness in her tone of voice], as you see now, this is our life, what is
left of it, it comes and goes, crumbles. *La blad wa-la 'ibad*"—"we have no land and
no faith," their expression conveying absolute helplessness—"the story is over, we
have no land and we have no people, it's a dunam [the land the state sold them],
everyone buys, dunam, dunam, dunam, and here we are, living here." The lack of
belonging to the place in which they live can be felt in the tone of voice and in the
words: "This we bought, and when they gave it to us, we lived on it, and when you
work you leave [because this land is not for agriculture], you go and then come
back, and that's it."

FROM GENERATION TO GENERATION

In the later stages of the interview, the argument arises between the women sitting
in the courtyard. Each one has a different version of their past and their origin.
They begin to argue among themselves. The grandmother gets angry, the mother
agrees with her, and the daughter claims something different. The daughter insists
on telling a different narrative than what the others know. She knows something
else—this knowledge which she discovered of late and wants to pass on.

The description of the past differs from generation to generation. While the
grandmothers and the mothers are preoccupied with their changing roles as
women and the space that defined and constructed their position, the daughters
are preoccupied with something else. They talk specifically about being black
women, speaking of the way in which their present-day "slave" construction is a
result of an unresolved story in the past which they are eager to discover. The argument revolves around their origin: Did parents sell their children into slavery to
the whites? Or were the children stolen from their parents in Africa and smuggled
into Palestine to be slaves?

The daughter says, "From Egypt . . . they would sell them, outside, after living
in Sudan, and from there they would bring them to Abu Rabia [a landowning

tribe], four, four blacks, *sumr*, just like us, and they were taken, someone would take one for himself, take two, three, because it's all money, meaning . . . it was like commerce, trade, now, they would search for him [a black slave], maybe he fell into the sea, was eaten by a wolf, maybe he was [hiding] in the *thur'a* [the open space between two tents]."

During and after the 1948 war, many blacks were removed along with the Bedouin who were expelled from their lands, while those who remained were put under the patronage of the tribes that stayed in place (primarily in the closed military area). According to the daughter,

> Now, thirty, forty years later, they discover that he [the black Bedouin who was taken as a child to be a slave] came from this or that family—who would have known? That's how it was for my father, there was a war, a war, they [the blacks] knew one another [because they registered after the war under the name of their patron tribe], they would say, "I'm from such and such family [the white tribe they were attached to], yes, it's official"; he would say, "I'm from Aburabia"; they would say, "That one is from Aburabia" [meaning he didn't have a surname, so he would adopt that of the tribe that owned him]; [a member of the] Aburabia would say, "That is my slave, I bought him." The 'abed were marked, meaning they were marked with signs on their faces. Everyone, for example, [an] Aburabia, would say, "That one is named after such and such," they didn't know who their ancestors, their original families, were.

The women's identity as blacks has contradictory and interconnected dimensions. On the one hand, they have little or no knowledge about their past, as this subject was not dealt with, out of shame and denial. On the other hand, they, in particular the younger generation, are engaged in a reconstruction of the past as a narrative of empowerment. This is how the daughter tells about the lives of the slaves:

> This one comes, people take him, and the al-Hazaylaym take him. They would live with them, he was their slave, and they would say to him, "But your parents sold you," and his poor parents would be looking for him, they can't find him, one day he disappears, doesn't return to his parents. . . . They search for him, but he is already far away from them. Who will find him? . . . They took money for him when he was a small boy, that is how they would bring him, when he was a small boy, *jahel* [innocent boy], he doesn't know where he was taken, where he's from. He gets down and walks next to the herds, and so that he doesn't run away and so they can locate him if he does run away, they mark his face with a *wasem* [every tribe's distinctive mark for its slaves] . . . there are people, for example, who belong to the al-Hazaylaym, or who belong to al-Assad. Today, for example, in Sudan [there are people who] have a mark on their face belonging to a specific tribe, such and such a tribe, and the guy with the mark on his face, on his forehead right here [they demonstrate where], and

that is how they know to what tribe the person belongs, and some have marks on their hands.

The preoccupation with these markings is an important part of their engagement with the past:

When my [white] girlfriends would ask me why were they marked like that on their faces, I would tell them that these were the marks of their tribal belonging, these were from such and such tribe, and this is from such and such tribe, marked with the mark of a camel, that was in the days of the bu'aran [camels], there was a mark like this . . . and this was the mark on the slave's face that marks him as belonging to a certain tribe from his country of origin, they would also mark [brand them with] six or eight numbers, they would also number their herds, the camels, and there are people who were marked with names, the mark was like a line, the second mark from his ears, the third on his forehead, there are people [marked] on their side, here, there are people [who are marked] on their backs, the main thing is that every family has its own mark.

The daughter continues: "For example, al-Hazayal [a landowning tribe], let's say, they would bring a boy, people would bring him when he was small, meaning they took him out and sold him to Aburabia, his parents didn't sell him, but he was stolen, someone stole him and sold him." She is insistent. "It was for the money, a white person, for some money, sells him, he's a small child, twelve or fifteen years old, he was out herding the sheep. . . . He would go bring water, they would train him how to herd the sheep, the flocks. Go there, do this, go to the mountain, go herd the herds far away, pasture them in the field. . . . He doesn't know where he will be when he grows up, he doesn't know who his parents are, he doesn't know anyone in the world, meaning he was brought to Aburabia, and then he grew up there, they find him a wife, build a husha [a small improvised hut] for him far away from them, like a shepherd, the black is the shepherd . . . no one goes near him, the black man, he stays to live there, his wife stays in the husha, and he continues to work outside, goes and comes, and returns to her."

She says that the treatment of the slave depended on which white tribe he served: "Maybe he was a shepherd for Aburabia, and if they have a conscience and heart and religion . . . the tribe wouldn't discriminate between the blacks and their [the tribe's] children [that is, the tribe's members would treat their children and the blacks in the same way], some of them treated them well, and some didn't." "He [a slave] would have children and raise them and marry them [off], and then al-Hazayl [another landowning tribe] would notice that he [the slave] was getting stronger, growing, and then they would say, the slave has grown, he is bigger than us, now the slave has established a family, established a society and established, meaning established himself, he is the big man."

Living in the shadow of their past identities as slaves influences the way these women cope today. The reasons for their engagement with their past are very clear to them. For one thing, their children must know who they are in terms of the land-based tribal boundaries accepted in Bedouin society:

> My son wants to know which land was his, he sits in the *shig* [the men's meeting place, which each tribe, including the black ones, has] and hears people talking, he sits with the small and big children, he hears the young people, he asks who his relatives are, where each family came from, how did this family became important when they are black like us? How do these tribes think, Abu Shareb, Aburabia, al-Hazayl, al-Asad? How do they tell the difference between the tribes? Everyone has an origin, especially when there are tribal rivalries, he wants to know whom he belongs to. And why does this tribe not come to protect that tribe? And who does come?

The black Bedouin's origin is critical for the construction of their future lives. The answer to the question "Who am I, and where do I belong?" is directly linked with where they came from. Their attempt to broach the past necessarily shapes their future identity vis-à-vis the whites but primarily vis-à-vis themselves. The renewed construction of their identity through the revelation of difficult and painful details pertaining to how they became the whites' slaves teaches us about how they are trying to transgress the borders of their social identity as the white landowners constructed it for years. While they have been physically freed from slavery, the painful journey toward the liberation of their consciousness from their slave identity raises questions about large parts of the past that for years were pushed aside. They have opened these wounds today to discover more about themselves, to fill in the blanks in distant parts of the past, as part of the construction of their complete and equal (vis-à-vis the whites) identity.

ENDS AND BEGINNINGS

The end takes us back to the beginning: borders, separation, clearly demarcated tribal belonging. The black Bedouin's renewed construction of their tribal belonging in reference to their past as slaves associates them with the white tribes whom they served. However, while in the past they were only individuals, today they are part of a tribe in its own right, trying to construct its status in relation to but not beneath the white tribes, applying the same rules and laws of status that structure all of Bedouin society—that is, tribal belonging based on the land.

Visibly, the loss of land—which not only was a geographical space but symbolized a social space comprising a way of life, customs, and their cultural corollaries that defined social, class, and gender identities—fundamentally undermined the physical borders on which the tribes were based but did not entirely challenge class, tribal, social, and particularly, racial differences.

Different groups in the Judaized Naqab are engaged in an investigation of their social and gender identities and their histories. While white Bedouin women are preoccupied with the loss of their status as the "lords of the slaves" and the threat this poses to their identity and hegemony, black Bedouin women are engaged in a fundamental inquiry into the conditions of their existence—whom am I, from where did I come, and how were my people constructed as slaves under the white master?

The essential questions that derive from this are: Can their preoccupation with the past free the blacks from mental slavery? And can the whites free themselves from their master complex, which defines their strength through the dismissal of the identity of the blacks?

PART FOUR

A Land Occupied and Liberated

THE SIX DAY WAR OF 1967 SAW THE REUNITING of Palestine under one jurisdiction, only now it was the Israeli state, rather than the British Mandatory government or the Ottoman Empire, that was in control. For Israelis the victory was almost as miraculous as that of 1948: not only were its main frontline enemies decisively defeated, but the territory under its control—including the biblical heartland of Judaism—increased severalfold. The situation was radically different for West Bank and Gaza Palestinians, for whom the Israeli conquest meant direct occupation and soon thereafter systematic expropriation, creeping annexation, and increasing colonization.

While the uniting of Mandate Palestine under Israeli control opened new and more lucrative opportunities for Palestinians to work inside Israel, the restrictions on many aspects of their lives frequently outweighed the benefits. Both politically and economically, Palestinians were incorporated into the Israeli system at the bottom rung; they were denied political rights and, when suspected of violence against Israelis, subject to arbitrary arrest, imprisonment, torture, and extrajudicial execution. Territorially, the Israeli government also asserted its control of—or at the very least, denied Palestinians access to—well over 50 percent of the West Bank and the Gaza Strip through various means.

Palestinian fedayeen, or guerrillas, had been infiltrating Israel regularly since 1948 and were a source of constant tension and sometimes violence between Israel and its neighbors. The defeat of the frontline Arab states in 1967—the same year that Yasser Arafat's Fatah movement took over the Palestinian Liberation Organization—militarized Palestinian society further, as Palestinians understood that no one besides them would be able to liberate their territory. Thus were born the PLO's two decades of high-profile violence and terrorism, in and outside Israel.

With the outbreak of the First Intifada at the end of 1987, new types of resistance emerged that combined a much more active civil society with locally grounded strategies of resistance incorporating a variety of types of violence. Lætitia Bucaille's portrait of Majed al-Masri's experiences as part of the grassroots resistance of two intifadas (chapter 19) underscores both the limited life choices available to young Palestinians in this period and their attempts to exercise a measure of agency against an overwhelming military and political force.

Several factors stand out as shaping the new political and social dynamic in Palestine. The first is the time spent in prison by young Palestinians, who emerged as hardened activists with knowledge, experience, and ties to other activists and militants inside and outside the Occupied Territories. This new leadership, a good share of which comprised the children of refugees living in the Balata Camp next to Nablus, challenged the existing power structures in that city, which had operated in the region for generations. Other crucial elements of the narrative unfolding here were the power of the Israeli military and intelligence services to disrupt even the most sophisticated resistance networks, and the reality of exile for those militants who, like Majed and his friends Yasser and Nasser, were unable to avoid capture. Perhaps the most unique element of the life trajectories of these protagonists was their problematic reintegration into Palestinian society after their return during the Oslo years, and how the realities of continued occupation slowly vanquished their dream of independence.

The role of colonization in both the post-1967 relationship between Israelis and Palestinians and the larger Arab-Israeli conflict is widely understood. From 1967 to 1989, the number of settlements increased from less than a dozen with fewer than two thousand total residents to several hundred with a combined hundreds of thousands of residents by the time the Oslo process began. The presence of these settlers and their control of a huge swatch of the West Bank (either directly, through the built-up area of settlements, or through the many layers of "security" controls that block Palestinians from accessing their lands in the vicinity of settlements or bypass roads) are perhaps the most important factors contributing to the failure of the Oslo peace process.

Moriel Ram and Mark LeVine's "The Village against the Settlement: Two Generations of Conflict in the Nablus Region" (chapter 18), reveals just how profoundly different the process of settlement is for those on opposite sides of a bypass road. It tells the life stories of two twentysomethings, Youssef Najjar from the village of Burin, just outside Nablus, and David Ariel, born and raised in the settlement of Yitzhar, one of the most militant settlements in the West Bank and an unending source of conflict between Israelis and Palestinians.

Najjar and Ariel grew up literally within shouting distance of each other, but they have never met. Ariel's family is at the forefront of a radical redefinition of Jewish and Zionist identities, combining ultra-Orthodox theology and religious practice normally associated with the Haredim with the hardcore Zionism of Gush Emunim and the nationalist right. Ariel's view of his neighbors at once holds to and challenges the negative stereotypes that most strongly Zionist Israelis harbor about Palestinians. His experiences growing up in Yitzhar/Burin, among the most beautiful landscapes in all the West Bank, tell of a freedom of movement, thought, and identity that few if any Palestinians could even imagine, let alone enjoy.

For his part, Najjar has known nothing but conflict with the settlers of Yitzhar. To this day they attempt to gain control of his family's land, going so far as to steal chickens and goats and cut down thousands-of-years-old olive trees to achieve their goal. His inability to move freely even in the immediate environs of his home and land and his ultimate exile to the United States stand in sharp contrast to the continued freedom of movement, and of identity, enjoyed by David Ariel. Their radically different perspectives on the past, present, and future of this small part of the West Bank speak to the extreme difficulty of reconciling the Israeli and Palestinian visions for the country.

Israel's expropriation of territory and attempts to control and even curtail Palestinian education have from the beginning accompanied an equally important, if normally overlooked, expropriation of other arenas, including material culture. A few scholars and occasionally the media have written about the "war" over who invented or has the right to claim as their own such indigenous Palestinian foods as hummus, which has become a staple of Israeli cuisine as well. But the appropriation of Palestinian material culture after 1967 was in fact much broader, including not just the homes formerly occupied by Palestinians but also their architectural motifs, works of artistic and craft production, and clothing. Rebecca L. Stein's "Of Possessions and Dispossessions: A Story of Palestinian Property in Jewish Israeli Lives" (chapter 16), about Ruth Shapira, a Jewish American immigrant living in post-1967 Jerusalem, reveals the conflicted nature of cultural consumption in an occupation setting, where aesthetic beauty is often tied to the appropriation of the native population's material culture.

An archaeologist by training, with a keen interest in Palestinian embroidery and architecture, and a devoted Israeli peace activist, Shapira has a unique perspective on the ethical and political implications of the many cultural products she has collected. Her narrative of living in several mixed Palestinian-Jewish neighborhoods in Jerusalem, the artifacts she collected during her time there, and her realization that some items, such as a delicately embroidered Bedouin dress that became fashionable among bohemian ashkenazi Jews, remind us that even when Palestinians were absent, their material culture continued to shape Israeli Jewish experiences of the landscape around them.

Adding fuel to the settlement fire was the arrival, beginning in the mid-1980s, of what was ultimately one hundred thousand Jews from Ethiopia and, more dramatically, upward of one million immigrants from the Soviet Union since 1989. Not only did the Russians tend toward a right-wing nationalist political outlook, but the Israeli government attempted, though unsuccessfully, to use their arrival and the related urgent need for inexpensive housing as a reason to increase the number of settlements and settlers in the territories. Nelly Elias and Julia Lerner's "The Rise and Fall of the Russian-Speaking Journalist in Israel" (chapter 17) offers a fascinating portrait of one early-1990s immigrant, a journalist named Alexandra.

The economic and political instability associated with the breakup of the Soviet Union pushed Alexandra's wave of emigrants toward Israel. They were among the most highly educated ever to immigrate to Israel yet also among the least religious; their Judaism was largely ethnic. This, along with the zero-sum ethnic conflicts then plaguing the former Soviet Union, facilitated their socialization into Israel's secular and political right.

At the same time, however, this immigration wave had a healthy distrust of political authority, reflected in the robust state of Russian-language journalism in the years after Alexandra's arrival in the country, the result of an unprecedented official tolerance for an immigrant group's maintaining its galuth, or Diaspora, identity. During this period, Alexandra established herself as a political reporter who, at least as she saw it, was willing to challenge official government claims and narratives whenever they contradicted her view of what the realities on the ground were. The Russian-language press consolidated and downsized, however, as the Russian community Israelified. As this process unfolded, Alexandra's life prospects and sense of her place in her new society narrowed significantly. Yet as Elias and Lerner's narrative reveals, neither Alexandra nor most of the hundreds of thousands of other Jews from the former Soviet Union have questioned the fundamental dynamics of the society into which they have been incorporated; the challenges they have faced have largely been absorbed, if not deflected, by the ongoing Israeli-Palestinian conflict.

16

Of Possessions and Dispossessions

A Story of Palestinian Property
in Jewish Israeli Lives

Rebecca L. Stein

The dispossession in 1948 of nearly half of Palestine's Arab population, placed a massive body of Palestinian property into circulation within Jewish-Israeli economies. While vast tracts of agricultural land represented the bulk of Palestinian material losses, such losses also extended to a wide array of goods at smaller scales that had been left by the populations that fled in haste: tools and livestock, furniture, jewelry and children's toys. Property that remained in the wake of looting by Israeli soldiers and civilians was seized by the state under the legal rubric of "absentee property" and was eventually redistributed within Israel or sold at public auction. Israel's victory in the 1967 war would place another body of Palestinian property into circulation, primarily as a result of the country's expropriation and settlement polices in the newly occupied territories. But Palestinian property also moved into Israeli possession in less violent and more quotidian ways in the aftermath of this war. The Israeli victory and subsequent military occupation catalyzed what was called an Israeli shopping invasion into the Palestinian territories—a wave of mass consumption that set its sights on souvenirs, artistic goods, and inexpensive household wares alike.

In the broadest terms, this chapter chronicles the movement of Palestinian property into Israeli private lives following the wars of 1948 and 1967. More narrowly, it follows the story of one Israeli Jewish woman, focusing on snapshots of her complex relationship to Palestinian cultural objects and formerly Palestinian houses in the decades after her immigration from America in 1973. The individual in question, Ruth Shapira of West Jerusalem, is perhaps best known for her work within the Israeli peace movement—activism that began in the late 1980s and continues to the present. When considered alongside this political history, the story of her relationship to Palestinian material culture helps to illustrate the polyvalent ways in which Israeli Jews across the political spectrum have encountered and contended with Palestinian people, communities, and histories through the medium of objects. Stories of consumption and property ownership, seemingly peripheral to an account of the Israeli political landscape, thus provide an important lens on the most intimate and personal, everyday ways that Israeli Jews have lived with Palestinian history and the legacy of the 1948 dispossession.

AFTER 1967: RUBBLE, OCCUPATION, CONSUMPTION

In 1968, while living in Greece to conduct research toward her PhD in archeology, Ruth Shapira paid her first visit to Israel. She arrived during a moment of postwar euphoria—or so most American Jews perceived it. Israel and American Jewry deemed Israel's victory against the neighboring countries of Egypt, Jordan, and Syria in the 1967 war—which mainstream Israeli historiography long heralded as a defensive battle and which resulted in the military occupation of Arab territories conquered during the course of the war—a triumph of almost mystical proportions, one thought to powerfully rewrite a history of Jewish powerlessness. What resulted was a seismic shift in American Jewry's relationship to Israel, a shift toward a popular culture of Zionism. Yet for Ruth, the visible signs of the war and subsequent military occupation evident on the ground produced a set of markedly different political feelings—ones that set her apart from the majority of her Jewish American conationals and presaged the political direction she would take in subsequent decades:

> I first came to the Old City of Jerusalem in the spring of 1968, before I came on aliya to Israel. I was living in Greece that year doing archeological research and taking a lot of trips in the region, including to Egypt. I just came to Israel out of curiosity. I didn't know much about what was going on politically, and I don't think I had a formulated political opinion. It was not that long after the 1967 war, and there was still a huge amount of rubble in the Old City. We found ourselves walking over all this destroyed material—the remains of the Mughrabi [Moroccan] Quarter, although I didn't know it at the time. You literally had to pick your way over these piles of things, and all around there were Israeli soldiers standing and guarding. What's now the plaza in front of the Western Wall was just full of rubble, topped with flags. The impression that it left on me was one of arrogance and destruction. I left Israel at the time not feeling very Zionist, not really wanting to come back.

Despite the tenor of her first encounter with Israel, Ruth and her husband Aaron formally migrated in 1973. They settled in West Jerusalem, first renting in the neighborhood of Talpiot and then buying in the Greek Colony, a formerly Palestinian neighborhood on the Israeli side of the Green Line (the 1949 armistice

line). The house in which they lived, one built in the early decades of the twentieth century, had been owned by a family of Palestinian Christians who had left
Palestine before 1948, moving to South America. Ruth and Aaron renovated it
painstakingly, seeking out appropriate tiles and interior design. As an archeologist
by training—one attentive to aesthetics, architecture, and the history of the built
environment—Ruth sought furniture and decorative items befitting the house's
age and history. This search led her to Jerusalem's Old City.

"By the mid-1970s, after I was living here, I was doing a lot of shopping in the
Old City. Everyone was." She gestures around her living room:

> That table we were just sitting at is from there. So is that tray. We bought two of these
> tables with metal trays on top—Syrian style, I believe—from the Old City. We bought
> two beautiful Hebron wedding embroideries on silk, for wedding pillows, and I still
> have them hanging up. For me, the textiles were particularly interesting. There was a
> fabric store in the Christian Quarter—not an antiquity store, not a tourist store, but
> a real fabric store, run by a Palestinian Christian family. And since I was into textiles
> and weaving, I was interested in this store. On the upstairs floor they had these really
> beautiful cottons and brocades and interesting weaves from Syria. I went mad over
> them, really loved them. So I bought lots of that and made curtains, pillows, and
> those chair covers [she points to her right]. I went there lots of times, and I got to
> know the owners. Other people were buying Palestinian pottery and antiquities. The
> Old City was definitely a treasure trove for people trying to furnish their houses or
> bring back souvenirs.

While Ruth's studied interest in Arab material culture was unusual among Israeli Jews of this period, her history as a consumer in Jerusalem's Old City was
not. Indeed, the Israeli victory in 1967 catalyzed a tremendous explosion in Israeli
and international tourism and consumption in the newly occupied territories.
East Jerusalem was the locus of this explosion. It housed not only the city's most
important religious and historic sites but also its most celebrated markets. Israelis
had been unable to visit these territories in the years between the wars (1948–67),
when they were under Jordanian sovereignty. In the immediate wake of the Israeli
victory, they came en masse. Many Jewish Israelis went as secular pilgrims to sites
of biblical importance. Many Israelis of an older generation returned to routes
and sites they had enjoyed in the prestate period. But large numbers, Ruth among
them, also traveled into the territories as shoppers, seeking both "authentic" Arab
wares and household goods that were available at a fraction of their Israeli prices.
Initially, Jerusalem's Old City was the locus of the shopping frenzy, as (according to the Israeli press of this period) "mass[es] of sightseers and bargain hunters
surg[ed] through the narrow alleys." Mass consumption gradually spread to other
West Bank locales, as Israeli visitors "descended" on "statues, soap and the rest."
Articles spoke of a "shopping invasion." Indeed, this was an invasion in which

the press colluded. Food critics documented the best place to drink European-style coffee in the Old City, where to buy "Indian dates" and Italian shoes, and recommended restaurants in Hebron and Bethlehem, most of which were already mobbed with Israelis. "When we got to Bethlehem," one reporter noted on June 22, "we saw all of Dizengoff eating hummus and pickles."

Consumption took two forms, primarily. The early days of the consumer frenzy saw a run on souvenirs, culinary delights, and luxury goods. Next came the demand for inexpensive household goods and appliances. "First we bought transistors, cosmetics, straw baskets, and mens' shirts," one Israeli journalist wrote, "and even English salt at a pharmacy. Today, the prices have already gone up a little, but you still won't find your friends at Israeli stores. The West Bank stores are still tens of percentages away from the Israeli prices." Although prices rose rapidly, and despite the Israeli taxes levied on goods purchased in the territories, the rush to consume was not tempered. In mid-July, the "scope of Israeli shopping in the West Bank" was valued at approximately ten million dollars per month. Jewish merchants and sellers complained that the magnitude of Israeli purchases in the territories was devastating their profits. When Gaza City opened to Israeli visitors on July 21, headlines announced, "Thirty-Five Thousand Israelis Spent a 'Shopping Shabbat' in Gaza."

In Ruth's telling, her own history as a tourist-consumer in Jerusalem's Old City was also an experience of social and political exploration, grounded by the consumer goods in question. It was in the context of her shopping trips in the early 1970s that she had some of her first intimate encounters with Jerusalem's Palestinian population. Many of the cultural objects and folk wares she purchased on those trips continue to decorate her West Jerusalem home. Most bear happy memories, summoning up histories of both the period and their Palestinian vendors. Others are the objects of more political ambivalence:

> I remember buying a long Bedouin dress with embroidery on it, an old white Bedouin dress, and owning that dress since that time. When I first bought it, I was a weaver with an interest in embroidery and textiles, and for me it was simply an artistic object—period, end of story. And there was a period of time when I would actually wear it, like to a party, or on Purim. It was very special, with beautiful embroidery on the bottom and on the sleeves. The longer that I lived here and kept this dress, the more my attitude toward it changed. I stopped wearing it after a while, as it became more popular. I mean, everyone started buying Bedouin dresses after a while.

As Ruth noted, both the purchase and the occasional wearing of such a dress were not unusual practices in the Israel of the late 1970s and 1980s. Indeed, this garment acquired popularity among a certain cadre of middle-class ashkenazi Jews, adopted as part of a bohemian lifestyle with roots in the progressive, alternative movements in the United States and Europe. After her politicization in the late 1980s, the adaptation of such ethnic markers by Israelis seemed distasteful to Ruth—a stylistic choice that she could not separate from the broader political landscape: "To see people, Jewish people—still now or in the 1980s or 1990s—wearing Arab embroideries is difficult. It doesn't seem right, somehow. Why should an American Israeli, an ashkenazi, walk around in a Bedouin dress? It's like a costume, and given the tensions of the political situation, it didn't seem right to wear that kind of costume. I haven't seen [mine] now for years. It's buried someplace."

LEGACIES OF 1948: HOUSES AND HOMELANDS

In 1983, Ruth and Aaron moved from the Greek Colony to the western side of the neighborhood of Abu Tur. Abu Tur had been a predominantly Palestinian village prior to 1948, although it had housed a small population of Jews (Martin Buber among them), some of whom had been in residence in the area since the nineteenth century. After the war of 1948, its fate was that of all Palestinian neighborhoods in West Jerusalem occupied by Israel: it was resettled with Jewish families. New immigrants were the primary recipients of formerly Palestinian houses in West Jerusalem, as in all urban areas, with preference given to former residents of displaced persons camps in Europe, who received their pick of Arab homes and apartments. Jews from the Middle East (mizrachim) numbered heavily among the populations resettled in neighborhoods immediately proximate to Jordanian-controlled East Jerusalem, Abu Tur among them, which most veteran Israeli Jews of European origin deemed dangerous and undesirable. In virtually all cases of state confiscation in West Jerusalem, the legal Palestinian owners neither received compensation nor gave permission. Also in virtually all cases, the new Jewish owners knew nothing of the former inhabitants, their histories, or their claims on the properties in question.

Ruth and Aaron came to Abu Tur for primarily logistical reasons—seeking a larger house at lower costs. But their move into a formerly Palestinian neighborhood in West Jerusalem can be historicized as part of the general shifts in the Jerusalem landscape that followed the 1967 war and subsequent Israeli occupation. In Israeli-occupied East Jerusalem, the previous decade had witnessed both the beginnings of politically inflected Jewish settlement and the movement of bohemian Israelis into Palestinian neighborhoods—places valued for their "character" and "flavor":

> We moved to this house in Abu Tur in 1983 from the Greek Colony in Jerusalem. At the time we were simply looking for a larger house. I had a preference for older houses because I think they're built better then newer houses and they're more interesting, and I like the materials—but in a totally neutral way, let's say. In the 1970s,

there were actually left-wing Jewish people who rented and lived in all kinds of places, including in the Arab sector of Abu Tur—and in Sheikh Jarrah, the Mount of Olives, Mount Zion. It was inexpensive, it was fun, and the places were interesting. This was before the First Intifada [uprising], in the 1970s and 1980s, and the Arabs in East Jerusalem were happy to rent to people like that. They were bohemian types, mostly in their thirties, and of course it was cheap. But I think these people were actually interested in living in an Arab sector in Jerusalem. They certainly weren't settler types—it wasn't anything like that. It was sort of romantic.

For both political and social reasons, neither Ruth nor Aaron had contemplated a move to East Jerusalem. Yet their purchase of the home in Abu Tur provided them with a new understanding of life in the newly occupied Palestinian city— an understanding born largely of the house's physical location, directly on the summit of the Green Line and affording unobstructed views of the Palestinian villages below. The legacy of their neighborhood and of the house itself inspired both Aaron and Ruth to embark on informal studies of their histories (Aaron, for his part, conducted interviews with the neighborhood's residents—both Jews and Palestinians—on both sides of the Green Line, collecting stories about life in the interwar period). Because of the historical moment in which they purchased the house, and because of their dealings with its then-owners, both Ruth and Aaron have a deep association with its mizrachi history:

When we went to see the house in 1982, it seemed quite isolated. It was right on the edge of the Jewish part of the neighborhood and directly on the Green Line. At that point, the Green Line was very disorganized, not the way it is today. It was just a very badly paved street, full of eroded dirt and pieces of barbed wire. It had been the narrowest point in the no-man's-land that existed between 1948 and 1967 dividing Jordan and Israel. It was only three meters wide, and it was right behind our house. Two of the houses directly across from ours that had been Jordanian headquarters had been bombed during the war. The Israeli army had been stationed upstairs in our house, or in what became our house, and it was surveyed by the British Mandate headquarters with telescopes as they were overseeing cease-fire lines.

It was an interesting neighborhood between the wars—something we learned later. There was a lot of contact between Arabs and Jews, mainly in the lower strata of society. It was a dangerous border area, but people managed to smuggle things back and forth and to engage in joint criminal activities. The Jews that were moved here in the early 1950s, that were moved into the houses that the Arab population left in 1948, were largely mizrachi immigrant groups from Libya, Kurdistan, Morocco. In 1949 or 1950, a large Kurdish family had been moved into the building that subse- quently became our house—that is, an extended family, the two halves of which were not on speaking terms. The house was divided into two parts, and when we bought the house we had to deal with each part of the family separately. When we came to look at the house with the real estate agent, it was really a wreck. The family had no money to do renovation. The kitchen and bathroom were outside in a kind of hut, as in the Ottoman period. So obviously the price was not so high, even though it had a big piece of land that went with it. The negotiations went well for us, though we're not very talented at that kind of thing. And we bought it, even though our parents though we were totally insane.

Ruth and Aaron were attracted to the house's architectural attributes: its stone-work, its domed roofs and arches, its tiled floor. In renovation, they endeavored to preserve these characteristics, laboring to find Palestinian workers with knowl-edge of its architectural details, all in an attempt to remain true to its historical form:

When we started the renovations we found some very beautiful things, like stone arched interior doorways that had been plastered over. Being the kind of people we are, we cared a lot and hired an architect. The renovations were extensive. The arched doorways that are in that room [she points to what is now the living room] and those connecting to our bedroom had been built over, and we reopened them. We didn't do anything with the domed ceilings—the fact that they are very uneven is actually very typical of a nineteenth-century Jerusalem house. Eventually it became possible to find construction engineers that knew how to deal with Arab buildings, but they weren't available at that time. We hired a whole series of Arab workmen for the reno-vations. It took a very long time, also because of the intifada.

She pauses. "I'm pretty sensitive to interior decoration and architecture, so this house isn't just a space, to me. It has a certain presence and a style, and I believe that the architectural features should be appropriate to that presence."

At the time when Ruth and Aaron purchased their home in western Abu Tur, most middle-class ashkenazi Israelis still considered the neighborhood a danger-ous and undesirable place, its architectural charms not withstanding. Tensions between its Jewish and Palestinian residents were particularly high at the time of the first Palestinian uprising (1987–91), when clashes between young Palestinian activists and the occupying Israeli army were frequent in eastern Abu Tur, as was the torching of neighborhood cars as acts of political protest. In Ruth's backyard during these years, the smell of Israeli army tear gas was frequently in the air—wafting up from eastern Abu Tur or the adjacent village of Silwan, known as a center of Palestinian resistance.

The Israeli perception of Abu Tur changed considerably in the 1990s, during the Oslo peace process. In this decade, the neighborhood drew increasing numbers of Jewish families as buyers and renters, eager to take advantage of its spectacu-lar views of the Old City and its charming "Arab houses." Indeed, as a perusal of

Israeli real estate copy makes evident, Israeli advertisements for homes in Abu Tur and other formerly Palestinian neighborhoods of West Jerusalem henceforth employed this term as a means of identifying the value of the property in question: "authentic Arab-style house in Baka ... with original tiled floors and high ceilings"; "superb Arab house completely refurbished in the heart of Neve Tzedek"; "Arab house for sale in the Jewish Quarter of the Old City of Jerusalem ... with lots of arches." In these commercial invocations, the term *Arab* is shorthand for a set of distinct architectural features: stone walls, tiled floors, arched doorways, towering ceilings and windows.

The prevalence of this real estate nomenclature suggests something about the complex ways in which aesthetics and politics are disarticulated in dominant Israeli imaginations where formerly Palestinian houses are concerned. As with similar items in the long history of Israeli orientalism, in which this architectural term is situated, the increasing embrace of the Arab house by Israeli consumers in the 1990s did not necessarily imply an acknowledgement of the history to which *Arab* refers (Ruth and Aaron were exceptions in this regard). Rather, the perceived value of the property rested precisely on the evacuation of (Palestinian) history, or ethnonational particulars, from the house in question. In most cases, the Jewish buyers neither knew nor sought these histories, even in their most local sense, as they threatened to undercut the value of the property with the specters they would have raised.

OF DRESSES, HOUSES, AND ZIONISM

Ruth's involvement with the Israeli left, beginning in the late 1980s, owed its genesis to larger trends in the political landscape of that decade. The Israeli invasion of Lebanon in 1982 catalyzed and strengthened what had been, heretofore, a relatively marginalized protest community. Its size and vitality grew further following the outbreak of first Palestinian uprising in 1987—particularly in response to the intifada's demand for an end to occupation. Feminist and women's groups were at the forefront of this new left-wing political environment, and conscientious objection to army service was on the rise. Ruth's political activity began in earnest in the context of this changing landscape. In addition to working within the Orthodox feminist community in West Jerusalem, she and other West Jerusalem activists became involved in dialogues with Palestinians under occupation—in Abu Tur, Nablus, and Beit Sahur—meeting in one another's homes to foster conversation about the conflict and united behind the slogan "Palestine and Israel: Two States, Free and Secure." In the late 1980s and 1990s, when such dialogue groups were particularly popular and well attended, Ruth often dedicated weeks at a time to these endeavors—encountering, in the process, the most violent days of the intifada, security closures in the territories, and the possibility of punitive responses from Israeli soldiers and Palestinian detractors alike. Like other members of the Israeli peace camp, she considerably muted her political activism following the dissolution of the Oslo process and the outbreak of the second intifada in 2000, both of which fueled her pessimism about the political yield of grassroots dialogue and activism.

How does one connect this political history with Ruth's relationship with Palestinian material culture—that is, with her history as a consumer in the Occupied Territories and as resident of a formerly Palestinian home? I asked her this question directly: as someone who has long struggled with her Israeli identity in the midst of a military occupation she actively opposes, what was her political relationship to the Arab cultural objects and architectural details with which she has intimately lived for three decades?

She responded: "Some of those things remain politically neutral to me. Because I collect fabrics from all different places, I think there's no reason not to collect fabrics from Palestine. But the Bedouin dress is different somehow. Maybe if I hung it up I wouldn't feel so conflicted about it. It's something else to actually wear it." She paused, looking around her room. "For me, it's interesting to think about which objects remain neutral and which have some kind of a political or human content to them."

Ruth's relationship to the Bedouin dress is unusual. Her discomfort can be read as an index of her involvement in left-wing political culture, reflecting a concern about the meanings associated with the appropriation of Palestinian cultural wares by Israelis in the context of the military occupation. Interestingly, this discomfort is less evident in her discussion of the house itself. For while both she and Aaron were committed to the house's architectural history, striving to conduct renovations in a manner true to its original aesthetic terms and to its mizrachi social history in the post-1948 period, they were less preoccupied by its pre-1948 Palestinian history—a history with which they were well acquainted through both scholarly and activist contexts. At issue was not a refusal to acknowledge this history but a contention that it failed to haunt her. Unlike the dress, an article of clothing whose former human imprint was perhaps easier to discern, the house's Palestinian memories existed at something of a distance from her lived experience as its resident:

I just want to make a Zionist statement before I go on, in terms of living in an Arabic house. This did not bother me in the slightest. I mean, if it had bothered me, I wouldn't have made aliya. And because we had contact with the Kurdish family who lived here before us, I actually associate the house more with their period than with the previous Arab owners, none of whom I had any contact with. This isn't to say that I'm not interested in the history of this house, the question of why there was a cistern underneath the property, and so on. As an archeologist and ancient historian, I'm very interested. But politically speaking, it's not a problem for me.

My attitude is that all houses, wherever you're living, have very long histories. People come, people go, and nobody really owns a house. The house is there, the land is there, and people come and go. Soon we'll be gone too. . . . And since I am and remain in favor of the State of Israel—I mean the founding of the State of Israel—and made aliya because I wanted to live there, I don't think I have the right, sort of, to turn around and say, "But I'm not going to live in this house or that house." I *can* say I wouldn't live over the Green Line, in the Occupied Territories. But I accept the founding of the State of Israel as a fact, as part of the history of Palestine.

Despite her political affiliations as an activist, despite her knowledge of the history of the Palestinian dispossession in 1948, Ruth lives in her house without regrets—that is, without a discomforting sense of the specters of the Palestinian past. To the contrary, questions about this house not only fail to illicit political discomfort but incite a narrative of Zionist identity, one unusual for this former activist (a narrative that might be understood as a by-product of the post-Oslo shift in the political affiliations of the Israeli left).

Taken together, these snapshots illustrate something more than just the particularities of Ruth's biography. Her stories of shopping in the Occupied Territories in the aftermath of the 1967 war, when read in the broader context of the Israeli postwar period, draw attention to the ways that the Israeli military occupation implicated and spawned Israeli consumer practices, desires, and imaginations. In Ruth's case, shopping for Arab cultural wares in Jerusalem's Old City in the early 1970s provided access to Palestinian stories and lives that complicated the dominant Israeli mythologies in which new immigrants were schooled. Yet at the same time, her experiences in the Old City are instances of the ordinary ways that Israeli civilians reaped the benefits of the occupation, therein helping to sustain it, in this case through acts of consumption. For Ruth, the cultural objects garnered during these shopping trips—objects with which she lived in the intimate and personal spaces of her home for the next three decades—were not souvenirs of conquest. Neither their presence in her living room nor their histories disquieted her. The Bedouin dress, deliberately stashed away in her home, was perhaps the exception in this regard—a garment whose circulation within ashkenazi bohemian culture makes visible the ways that an elite cadre of Israeli leftists could perpetuate the Orientalist logic of the occupation through the seemingly apolitical domain of style.

These snapshots of one Israeli life spent in formerly Palestinian houses also tell another story. They suggest the ease with which, as part of the Israeli nation-building project, the formerly Palestinian landscape was stripped of its ethno-historical markers—even in the face of visible and audible signs ("Arab house") that belie this act of historical erasure. They also point to the willingness of most Israeli Jews to collaborate in the state-sponsored project of collective forgetting. Ruth's story draws attention to the highly intimate and personal ways in which

Israeli Jews, even those on the political left, have cohabitated with the history of the Palestinian dispossession through the medium of material culture and largely without political discomfort. The fact of this intimate relationship between Israeli Jews and Palestinian things complicates the nearly consensual Israeli refusal to acknowledge the lasting imprint of prior Palestinian histories. Houses, dresses, and cultural wares tell another story—about the ways that Palestinian lives haunt and enable the Israeli present.

17

The Rise and Fall of the Russian-Speaking Journalist in Israel

Nelly Elias and Julia Lerner

ALEXANDRA'S LIFE STORY: MAIN LANDMARKS

Alexandra was born in western Ukraine in the 1950s, in Chernovtsy, a town known for its large educated Jewish population. Like many Jewish girls there, she went to university, taking general arts subjects—philology and foreign languages—and was directed to the familiar career offered to graduates, to be a literature teacher or a translator. Neither option was tempting for Alexandra. It was only when she moved to Georgia with her mother a year after finishing university that she decided upon a clear career path.

Alexandra lived in Georgia for the next fifteen years, a period she defines as formative in her personality and professional career. It was there that she began to work as a journalist, despite having no prior professional education in this field. Alexandra's first job was investigating and reporting for the *Vecherni Tbilisi* (Night Tbilisi) newspaper. Contrary to her life in Ukraine, which she mentions only in passing, she speaks profusely about her life in Georgia, expanding on her love both for its people, whom she calls proud, talented, and brave, and for the state itself, which she describes as the only republic of the USSR that was, de facto, free of the Soviet regime's restrictions. In Alexandra's words, "there was no fear whatsoever" there. She would adopt these qualities—courage and pride—as her personal and professional guiding lights.

When she was thirty-six, Alexandra left for Israel along with her mother and her only son, then fourteen. They were part of the mass immigration wave from the former Soviet Union (FSU) to Israel that began in 1989 with the falling of the iron curtain. Mostly motivated by push factors (e.g., the political and economic instability of the USSR), the majority of this group lacked any substantive Zionist motivation for their emigration; the lack of other options, by and large, explained their choice of Israel. Today, immigration from the FSU has almost stopped, but the Russian-speaking immigrants are still the largest ethnolinguistic group, constituting 12 percent of the Israeli population.

Alongside their demographic significance, high cultural capital characterized the Russian-speaking immigrants from the start: more than half had higher education, and the USSR had employed two-thirds in white-collar occupations. Acquiring higher education was a dominant strategy of social and geographical mobility for the Jews as an ethnic minority both during the latter stages of the Russian Empire and throughout the Soviet regime. Concomitantly with their rapid secularization and modernization, Jews in Russia came to be identified with the most educated groups, and they appropriated the lifestyle and practices of the Soviet intelligentsia. As such, most were irreligious and defined their Jewishness in ethnic terms. Furthermore, about 80 percent of the Russian-speaking Israeli immigrants had lived in European areas of the USSR, including the largest Soviet cities, such as Moscow, St. Petersburg, Minsk, and Kiev, as well as other scientific and cultural centers. This cultural background resulted in their perception of Russian language and culture as key aspects of their self-definition, which they wished to preserve after immigrating to Israel.

The immigrants' cultural demands went hand in hand with changes in Israel's integration policy that inevitably occurred with the massive Russian aliya of the late 1980s and early 1990s. Until then, the dominant policy had been to assimilate immigrants so they shed Diaspora cultural identities and languages in favor of Hebrew language and culture. However, with the post-Soviet Russian aliya, Israel adopted cultural pluralism as its main integration policy; because of this, the FSU immigrants were treated with greater tolerance than their predecessors of the 1950s and 1970s had been. Their cultural and organizational demands were granted public resources, and many institutions were established that supported Russian-language culture—including the bilingual Gesher (Bridge) Theater, the Mofet network of Russian-speaking high school teachers, and the rich map of Russianlanguage media—several even funded by various government agencies.

Despite the FSU immigrants' tendency toward cultural preservation, they didn't isolate themselves from Israeli society. "Cultural dialogue" would be a better description of their interactions, which have included the selective adoption of Israeli norms while they themselves influenced Israel's social, political, and cultural landscape.

It was to this milieu, specifically the Russian-language press, that Alexandra acclimated upon her arrival. During the 1990s, around 130 periodicals in Russian were published in Israel, four of which were daily newspapers. This was significantly more than the number of publications targeted at other minorities, including the Arab citizens of Israel, and is considerable even when compared to the

Hebrew-language press. These immigrant newspapers have not only aimed to preserve their audience's culture of origin but also facilitated immigrants' adaptation to Israeli society. Along with community organizations, immigrant journalists are perceived as cultural brokers, providing their newly arrived compatriots with information about the host environment.

The centrality of the Russian-language press as an "interpreting" institute for the Russian-speaking community in Israel cannot be emphasized enough, partially due to the special authority attributed to the written word in the Russian-Soviet tradition, which assigns to ideological, publicistic, and literary writing the role of an active agent in constructing the immediate sociocultural reality. The scope and diversity of the Russian-language press in Israel are a product of that tradition, as well as the arrival of hundreds of thousands of new immigrants in the early 1990s.

Alexandra sought to become part of the cultural leadership of her community upon her arrival. Thanks to her English proficiency, she could communicate with her Israeli neighbors in Tel Aviv, who suggested that she apply at a Russian-language newspaper they knew. And so, a month after arriving, Alexandra found her first job, as a journalist for Israel's oldest Russian-language newspaper, *Nasha Strana* (Our country). This paper had been in existence from the late 1960s, but prior to the mass immigration of the 1990s it was on the verge of extinction. The new immigrants revived it, with both their demand for publications in their mother tongue and the injection of new professional energy.

In search of better payment, Alexandra soon moved to *Hadashot* (News), a Hebrew-language tabloid that had recently began to publish a version in Russian, and after five months in Israel, she had already landed at *Vremya* (Time), established as an extension of the Hebrew-language daily *Ma'ariv*. *Vremya* had been founded by the media tycoon Robert Maxwell and was still in its pilot stage. She worked for this newspaper, which eventually became *Vesti* (News), Israel's leading Russian-language daily, for ten years, becoming one of its most prominent and valued journalists and enjoying generous conditions, including tenure and a monthly salary that matched the going rates in the Hebrew press. During her employment there, Alexandra worked on a wide variety of journalistic assignments, but the most important was her job as an investigative reporter, which held special appeal for her ever since her early days in Georgia. This was a period of "euphoria" for her, when she enjoyed both complete professional fulfillment and economic affluence.

The editor-in-chief of *Vremya* at the time was Eduard Kuznetzov, a colorful and well-known figure in and outside Russian circles in Israel because of his refusenik past, who arrived in Israel in the 1980s following a long history of subversive activities against the Soviet regime. Kuznetzov enjoyed broad support and the high esteem of his journalist staff, so following his dismissal in 2000 a number of journalists, Alexandra among them, tendered their resignation in an unprecedented show of protest. However laudable, her resignation marked the end of Alexandra's professional ascent and began a new phase: a time of professional and economic deterioration.

In 2001, having been unemployed for several months, Alexandra joined *Vesti*'s competitor *Novosti Nedeli* (News of the week), which was owned by an Israeli businessman, a former sports reporter who found in the emerging Russian-language press a lucrative business opportunity. Unlike *Vesti*, which offered extremely generous terms of employment, *Novosti* paid journalists the minimum wage, without giving them basic social benefits or proper conditions to pursue their professional preferences. In Alexandra's case, she could not continue working as an investigator and instead was relegated to a host of reporting assignments with the condition that she meet a highly demanding weekly quota, which eventually amounted to six full pages (the quota for the Hebrew press is around two pages on average).

Her professional demotion brought a severe economic downgrade as well, forcing her to look for complementary income: a minimal wage for translating Russian subtitles for the cable channels. Despite all her hard work, six years later, as part of a general downsizing, Alexandra was fired from *Novosti* and had to find new employment, this time as a translator and language editor for a news website in Russian. The job is, in Alexandra's eyes, little more than slave labor, as she is forced to do ten- to twelve-hour shifts of what is a far cry from the professional journalism that is so important to her. Her life has become one of "despair [and] failure," yet her age (midfifties at the time of this writing) makes it difficult to imagine finding another occupation.

LEARNING A PROFESSION, LEARNING HOW TO BE ISRAELI

A main feature of Alexandra's life story as an immigrant-journalist is that her professional learning took place concurrently with the process of learning her new culture. Through mastering the journalistic terrain, she got to know life in Israel. "Little by little, you begin to comprehend deeper stuff; you learn everything empirically. Whatever you encounter, whatever you experience, that is what you learn." The actual contact, the hands-on, unmediated experience that Alexandra found in her fieldwork as a journalist, became for her a source of learning about Israeliness as an identity, a culture, and a political sphere. "Now I am a journalist. I am a professional. I am a Western journalist! Free!" she declared, broadening her identity beyond Israel and into the larger Euro-American cultural ecumene to which she had long aspired.

Alexandra attributes her growth into such a journalist to her Israeli colleagues at the beginning of her career: "Who taught me? That guy, Roy, from *Ma'ariv*, who said to me, 'You're a journalist. Where they won't let you in through the door, you'll get in through the window.' For Alexandra, "getting in through the window" began on her first assignment at the *Hadashot* tabloid—when she was asked to prepare an item about a sex shop:

> Right away he [the editor] sent me to do a story about a sex shop, and I didn't even know what it was. . . . I was wearing a white shirt and a knee-length skirt, and I said to the guy, "I am a journalist and I want to interview you." I remember it clearly—there were red curtains there, and there was this dark-skinned guy. He nearly fainted. . . . So this man began to walk me around the shop, showing me everything, and he would stop and say, "This is a . . . ," and then fall silent. There was not much communication between us, so I thought to myself, "OK, I'll have to look it up later in an encyclopedia and see what it means."

Her first assignment as a full-time journalist for *Vremya* was to report from the court:

> The supervisor, Roy, said to me, "You have to go to the court in Tel Aviv and to sit there from 8:30 until 13:00 and bring your report here." It took me a while to find the court. I could hardly understand the basic Hebrew, but this was court Hebrew. . . . I brought the protocols home. I was hysterical. There were seven pages there. I bought every dictionary I could get my hands on. I sat and translated and wept; it was a disaster. A few months later I realized that I knew legal Hebrew, legal terms. . . . I knew it all—I knew that a *hashud* [suspect] is not *ne'esham* [guilty], and when you sit there, inside, you learn things like you'd never dream. I didn't know the words for a cucumber or a tomato, but I knew everything about legal procedure, legal details that only a law graduate would know. And when later I began to do serious investigations, I knew how to avoid any pitfalls. It was hugely important at the time.

Professional style is inseparable from cultural style, which posed personal as well as professional challenges for Alexandra, who had to adopt an Israeli cultural style that was far more pushy than her natural disposition.

> I am by nature very shy and delicate. I never push. But paradoxically, when I work in my profession, then I do have it in me, if I am in the field. . . . I didn't used to be like that. Once I was with a tape recorder in the field, and there were lots of Israelis [reporters], and immediately someone pushed me aside, simply pushed me out, and I was deeply insulted; it really hurt me. It was in court, and Ayala Hasson [a prominent TV reporter] was there, and I asked her, "What is going on? How should I react? What should I do?" and she said, "How?! If you don't use your elbows, you will always end up without an interview, without a recording, and you will return to the desk empty-handed." I said to her, "But that's not nice." And she said, "There's no such thing as 'nice.' You're a pro, you're in the free world, that's how you're supposed to do your job." And it's true; I've learned to do it.

Essentially, Alexandra learned to accept the brusque nature of the Israeli "person-ality" by wrapping it within an understanding of "Western professionalism."

Not long after arriving in Israel, Alexandra experienced several dramatic events that intensified this dynamic and reinforced her understanding of the sabra per-sonality as reflective of an uncompromising nature that is understood to be neces-sary to stand up against perceived internal and external enemies. The first such event was the First Gulf War, in 1991, when she was already working for *Vremya:*

> That was an extraordinary experience. We were sitting there in some sealed room. We used to run with our gas masks in hand and hear every [bomb] drop; it was re-ally nearby. I had just begun to understand Hebrew, because the radio was never turned off—it was on twenty-four hours a day. . . . One time we were sitting in the sealed room at work . . . and Nachman Shay [an Israel Defense Forces spokesman at the time] comes on the air: "Residents of Rishon Letzion, you can take off your gas masks." So the Israeli guy sitting opposite from me, someone from *Ma'ariv*, takes off his mask, and everyone says, "What are you doing?" and he says, "What's the prob-lem? I am a resident of Rishon Letzion." It was amazing! It was then that I understood this nation has balls. I still didn't know how to say that in Hebrew, but I realized that I had come to the right place.

LEARNING POLITICS IN THE FIELD

One of the most prominent signs of the FSU immigrants' influence in Israel can be found in the political arena, where they have played a major role since the be-ginning of the 1990s. They expressed their demographic power, combined with their prominent educational and cultural capital, almost immediately in extensive political activity, especially in establishing the ethnic party Israel Be'Aliyah (Israel on the Rise), seven members of which were elected to the Knesset in 1996. This party was replaced by another (and much more right-wing) list targeting Russian-speaking immigrants, Israel Beiteinu (Israel Is Our Home), with fifteen members in the Israeli parliament at the time of writing.

Indeed, one of the interesting questions concerning this community is the pos-sible factors which shape their political outlook and predominant right-wing lean-ing. These views could be explained as a legacy of Soviet orientalism and the Soviet policy regarding national minorities. They also could stem from the Russian-speaking immigrants' need to reaffirm their Jewish identity to demonstrate their allegiance to the host society. But all possible explanations should also point out the role of the Russian-language media as active agents of formation and articula-tion of immigrants' political consciousness. Although she had already realized that Israel was the "right place" for her to live (as she put it) and fully identified with her new home, Alexandra took some time to form her own political opinions as a citizen and as a journalist. She remembers of her first years in Israel, "I didn't understand anything. I didn't understand what kind of government we had here. What I did understand, and that was an iron-clad rule for me, was that I had no right to write about the big things, about politics. . . . God forbid, it didn't even cross my mind to write about politics."

Thus, in 1992, two years after her arrival, Alexandra did not vote in the Yitzhak Rabin–Yitzhak Shamir premiership elections, because she had not yet understood the political situation. The shift in her position of "staying away from politics" took place in late 1994, when she happened to be present at the epicenter of a terrorist attack in central Tel Aviv, during a wave of mass terrorism in the wake of the Oslo Accords:

> You have to understand, as a journalist I got into politics completely by chance, only from the field. . . . In 1993–94, buses began to explode. There were terrorist attacks in Afula and in Hadera, and for me it was like watching a movie—you watch and you realize that something is wrong, but you don't understand what it is. And then on October 19, 1994, . . . I was in the car with my boyfriend, who had a clinic in central Tel Aviv, and the car radio was always on, and then they announced that a bomb had just exploded in Dizengoff Plaza. And we left the car and ran like crazy [to the explosion site]. . . . I was among the first reporters to arrive on the scene. And then, when you are stepping on the asphalt, all covered in blood, and the worst is when you find out what burned human flesh smells like—it haunted me for years . . . then your political views, which you may or may not have had before, they just spring into being, all by themselves. . . . Since then, wherever there was a terrorist attack in Israel, I went there. . . . I just knew, I felt that I had to be there right then, I had to listen to what the people were saying, I had to witness it and write about it.

It appears that Alexandra's insights about life in Israel and her political position mostly came to her "from the field." In this respect, the course she describes differs from the prevailing interpretation in the research literature, which regards the right-wing attitudes of FSU immigrants as a product of the cultural baggage they brought with them. Despite the formative effect Israeli journalists had on Alexandra's professional development, that did not include what she perceived to be their "leftist political views."

Yet it would be wrong to conclude that Alexandra's political attitudes developed without the influence of local Israelis. She was frequently sent to interview right-wing intellectuals, who played a major role in her socialization into the right-wing camp:

> I keep in touch with right-wing Israeli intellectuals. They are people on such a high level, no one can even imagine. I've been in touch with them since the 1990s. . . . When you sit down to interview those people, that is when you realize that Israel does have pluralism, and that there are people who think clearly, who understand what's happening, and who realize that it's not set in stone that this country will

continue to exist. Because it's only been in existence for a short time, and the current formula "land for peace" is a flawed one, and . . . however much land you give, they [the Palestinians] will want more.

This ability to "think clearly"—that is, in an independent, nonaligned, and unflinching way—Alexandra finds in right-wing intellectuals, who deeply impress her and whom she regards as deserving partners for dialogue. This ability, in her opinion, is also characteristic of her generation of Jewish intelligentsia brought up in the USSR:

> My generation, those who came here in the early 1990s, they are all rightists. . . . The Russians who came here were already mature people, like me. We were schooled [in the USSR] in independent thinking. The [Soviet] press may write anything and try to persuade you about anything, but you knew how to read between the lines, you knew how to analyze what is happening, independently, based on the facts. So when in the USSR we would be told, "We have a democracy," while you see that it's a totalitarian regime, then you realize that you are being lied to. And then you must either shut your mouth or you must shout and fight.

In this analogy, Alexandra decides not to shut her mouth, and she begins to write profusely, criticizing the Oslo Accords, the withdrawal from Lebanon in 2000, the evacuation of the Gaza Strip in 2005, the management of the Second Lebanon War in 2006, and many other political decisions. This is where she combines the meaning of a journalist as someone who confronts the establishment, which she has brought along from Georgia, with the meaning of fieldwork that she has learned in Israel: "Nowadays I already know what to ask [in a political interview]; I have a clear knowledge. But then [in her first years in Israel], I didn't. . . . Today, when I hear that a Kassam rocket fell in Sderot, and there have been two thousand already, I know exactly why it is happening—according to my view, of course. And if my view is not accepted by the current government, then I am willing to defend it to the bitter end. Why? Because I am sure of it, because I already know this stuff, I've touched it, I've grasped it, I just know."

Paradoxically, while Alexandra's professional socialization brought her closer to Israeli journalists, whom she has characterized as professional, free, and Western, her political socialization ultimately drew her away from them and led her to develop a critical view of the local media as a whole, which she sees as politically mobilized, and therefore unprofessional: "I have lots of stories about the total lack of objectivity of the Hebrew media . . . because the Hebrew media remind me of the USSR in the 1970s. It clearly reminds me of Brezhnev, of that era when the press was a vehicle of propaganda, not a source of information. . . . Here it's just the same, exactly the same, the entire Hebrew media."

Alexandra also does not align herself with other Russian-speaking journalists, from whom she feels deeply alienated due to what she perceives as their reluctance to adopt new professional standards. In search of a political ally, she clings to the views which she believes are prevalent among her readers, who have learned to think in a dual-consciousness pattern by always doubting the truths of Soviet ideology: "The Russians were trained to do it. They were firmly in the habit of doubting and questioning everything and trying to figure out everything on their own. They know how to think independently, how to analyze. A Russian does not need others to analyze things for him. So ultimately, these views [the right-wing positions of the Russian-speaking community in Israel] are largely not derived from the [Russian-language] media; it's simply their own analysis of the reality. In this sense, now when I think about it, it's actually the Russian-language press that followed its readers' views."

Contrary to the common perception of the Russian-language press as shaping the immigrants' political views, Alexandra offers us the converse interpretation: the press responded to their inclinations and preference for "independent" thinking. However, in other "learning areas" of life in Israel, Alexandra attributes a tremendous influence to the Russian-language press, and as shown below, she sees its role as a "guide" for the readers.

LEARNING WITH THE READERS

Like many immigrants, Alexandra describes her first months in Israel as a period of disorientation, confusion, and even cultural disability. "The key word here is *incomprehensible*," she says, "because everything was incomprehensible." And because she soon began to work for a press that addressed an immigrant audience, she understood that "everything was incomprehensible" for her readers as well: "I suddenly realized, *Oy vey*, my readers have no idea what the police are like here, what the court is like. . . . So I always, from the beginning, wherever I managed to catch a chunk of reliable information, [would] pass it on to my readers. . . . We were the only address new immigrants could turn to for help and advice. We were a guide for those who still did not know Hebrew."

And so she began to write for them, starting from the description of the assortment in that sex shop—"I knew my readers, just like me, knew nothing about it, so like me, they would be rolling on the floor laughing"—continuing with shedding light on the legal, financial, and consumerist aspects so vital for newly arrived immigrants, and through to offering them interpretations of political processes. All this she did while herself a newly arrived immigrant. She learned and passed her insights on to her readers but displayed an ambiguous relationship with them: "We were learning together. There are no differences. We [journalists] didn't think

we were better or knew more than our readers; we never felt we were above them."
At other times she sounds more patronizing toward her readers, who were supposedly less experienced and knowledgeable than she was and to whom she tried
to impart her own world view and integration strategy: "We [journalists] thought
that to begin with, people must have their eyes opened for them, so that they understand where they are and love this country, yes, love it. And then, when they
have a certain basic knowledge, they will figure things out. . . . It was important for
me that the readers love the country, because I fell in love with it madly."

Alexandra discovered that the combination of love and knowledge was a good
basis for figuring things out in Israel, and she tried to pass this on to her readers.
In her ongoing dialogue with them, she articulated her emotional connection to
Israel and her place in its society, especially in a letters column that she edited
and named "Repatriation or Immigration?" The title reflects the official ideological position of the State of Israel, which regards the Jewish immigration to Israel as
homecoming, or repatriation, in contrast with that of "regular" immigrants, who
have no primordial connection with their country of destination. Realizing that
many of her readers did not feel that they had "come home," Alexandra undertook
the role of educator, encouraging them to bond emotionally with the country, as
she had done. She saw this bond as a crucial basis for their sense of belonging: "I
used to tell them, 'We are repatriates, we are citizens, we have all the rights.' And
my readers would try to argue with me, saying things like, 'You say we have rights,
but I work as a guard, and what rights are you talking about?'"

Based on her view of her journalistic duty as a socialization agent for newly
arrived readers, Alexandra interprets the decline of the Israeli Russian-language
press in recent years as part of the inevitable process of immigrants' successfully
settling down. It was therefore during those years in which they suffered the "throes
of absorption" that the Russian-language press thrived, whereas today, when the
vast majority of readers have found their place in Israel, or at least learned to "figure it out" on their own, they tend to desert their "guide." "Nowadays the Russian-
language press is dying out," Alexandra says.

> It's about time, because there are no new immigrants, there are no questions. They
> [the readers] already know everything. And it's not because of the Hebrew; that's a
> lie, because not so many immigrants have mastered Hebrew to a level that enables
> them to read Hebrew newspapers and turn to information sources in Hebrew. . . . So
> it raises the question, why is the Russian-language press dying? Because we taught
> them how to survive here. So when our readers had learned, for instance, what to do
> when your employer cheats you—that you should apply to the trade union, or the
> Workers' Hotline, go here, go there—it was us who taught them all of it! So when the
> huge Russian community graduated from that "school," that was it. We've done our
> bit; now we're no longer needed.

NOT BY WORDS ALONE

A salient theme in Alexandra's life story links her personal decline as a journalist and the general deterioration of the Russian-language newspapers with the state of economic and social marginality of the immigrant press in Israel, which its readers abandoned. Alexandra explains: "Ten years ago, a pensioner like my mother could afford to pay eight shekels [two dollars] and bring home the *Vesti* weekend edition. Since then, the benefit payments have not been increased, not even updated; there is a total erosion of social benefit payments to all kinds of needy populations, old people, social groups—prices went up maybe four times, but the pensions remained the same."

Alexandra's professional trajectory, in fact, is different in many ways from those of most other Russian-speaking immigrants. Customarily, in the first years after arrival in their new home, most immigrants have difficulty finding proper employment and are thus forced to begin their career at the bottom of the ladder, progressing gradually as they get better at adapting themselves to new professional standards.

Due to the high demand for Russian-speaking journalists in the early 1990s, which kept increasing as hundreds of thousands of new immigrants from the former USSR flocked to Israel, Alexandra found a job in a Russian-language newspaper within a month of her arrival. Moreover, in her first year in Israel, while she was still trying to find her way around, she managed to navigate among the mushrooming new newspapers until she found permanent high-paying employment at *Vremya*, where she was professionally coached by senior Israeli journalists and quickly acquired the local professional secrets.

But her thorough professional transformation paid off only as long as she worked for *Vremya* and later *Vesti,* where the work practices and terms of employment were closer to those of the Hebrew press. As part of Yediot Tikshoret (one of Israel's leading and richest media corporations), *Vesti* was exceptional compared to other Russian-language publications, in terms of both wages and working conditions. It is no surprise, therefore, as Alexandra emphasized in the interviews, that in her early years in Israel she did not feel herself an immigrant at all, since she was enjoying the working conditions of the Hebrew-language media, enabling her to position herself in the local middle class.

The majority of Russian-language newspapers published in Israel were based on an extremely poor financial infrastructure, which dictated their practices, human resources, and terms of employment. Hence, the majority were small businesses, with a staff of three to ten producing the periodical. Their small size resulted in low division of labor and the unification of diverse functions in a single position. Financial considerations also made it difficult for these newspapers to establish their own information-gathering sources. So in the coverage of the social and political

agenda, there was a clear preference for recycling existing information—from Hebrew press and news agencies—even at the expense of timeliness. *Novosti Nedeli*
crushed Alexandra under the load of a weekly six-page quota, which did not leave
her time for the investigative reporting that she loved so much, and paid her a
paltry salary that was not enough to live on and forced her to find complementary
income by translating subtitles for the cable channels:

> I worked at *Novosti* for six years. During these years, my poverty level got to the point
> where I could no longer pay the mortgage, and on top of the six pages I had to write
> every week, I had to look for another job. I finally found one, translating subtitles
> for nine shekels [$2.50] an hour. That was real slavery. I hit rock bottom. . . . When
> you find yourself with such low pay, without benefits, not even life insurance, then it
> dawns on you—you begin to look at things differently. I went through two phases in
> Israel. The first one was middle class. . . . In the 1990s I did not have an "absorption";
> *absorption* was a foreign word to me. But it made the fall even more painful.

Alexandra's story is also that of an immigrant who was successfully socialized in
new professional norms, and yet she ultimately failed because she remained within
the boundaries of the Russian-language press, which was mostly built on the harsh
exploitation of immigrant journalists by native owners who saw in these newspapers a quick way to financial prosperity. Her professional career in Israel indeed
reflects the general decline of Russian-language print media since the beginning
of the 2000s. This decline is also closely connected with the swift development
of the Russian broadcast media and especially channel 9 (the Russian-language
Israeli TV channel), together with the rapid growth of Russian-language websites
originating in Israel.

With the dwindling of the Russian-language newspapers, the ongoing political debate has moved to Russian-language cyberspace. In publicistic websites and
numerous blogs and discussion groups, Russian-speaking immigrants articulate
their views on the public agenda in Israel. In most cases this is not professional
journalism but community discourse, typified by the clear dominance of right-
wing world views, sometimes radical and militant. One cannot equate this virtual
discourse with the voice of the entire immigrant community, but it is possible
to discern a complex interaction between writers and readers, as in the Russian-
speaking journalist's story presented above. Such interaction creates and preserves
the immigrants' distinct identity as people deeply involved in figuring things out
while combining their Russian-Soviet cultural heritage with the immigration
experience.

18

The Village against the Settlement

Two Generations of Conflict
in the Nablus Region

Moriel Ram and Mark LeVine

For years, if not the majority of their lives, Youssef Najjar and David Ariel, plus their families, lived only a few hundred meters apart; their locations at different altitudes relative to the same mountain represent the vastly different levels of power and freedom enjoyed by each. Yitzhar, David's settlement, sits atop the hill; the village of Burin, where Youssef's farm is located, is in the valley. There was a time, in the late 1980s and early to mid-1990s, when the two might have passed each other roaming through the fields and olive groves that lie between their two communities, although David would certainly have been accompanied by someone heavily armed, who likely would have looked at Youssef and his companions as a nuisance, if not a threat. Since 2000, however, it's become even harder for the Najjar family to reach its fields up the mountain, while David has spent the better part of his adult life attempting to colonize other hilltops in Samaria.

Yitzhar sits on one of the most beautiful spots in the Samarian mountains of the north-central West Bank, about six kilometers from Nablus, on top of a steep mountain overlooking Palestinian farms and hamlets. The region around Nablus remains as famous today for its olive oil as it no doubt was during biblical times, and the settlement of Yitzhar takes its name from a biblical Hebrew word describing very-high-quality olive oil. The western side of the settlement provides a panoramic gaze to the entire coastal plain of Israel, from Ashqelon to Hadera; the eastern side faces down over the Palestinian towns of Madma and Burin, although it's difficult to see the houses from below, as they are largely on the eastern slope. Standing at the summit of the settlement, one can also see the various small outposts scattered around. Most consist of a few trailers, and a couple are built up with concrete houses; none are within the settlement perimeter.

Only road signs give evidence of Yitzhar's presence, towering above its Palestinian neighbors. It is a steep climb, even for cars, although it's only about a three-minute drive from the Huwara checkpoint, one of the most important of the Nablus region. A small electronic gate stops any visitors, ensuring that no Palestinians, even those with Israeli identity cards, enter the settlement. Modest cottages are spread neatly throughout the settlement, giving Yitzhar's roughly nine hundred residents a Western suburban atmosphere. Close to the entrance is a small number of caravans, or mobile homes. They are a relatively new addition, provided to accommodate about fifty to seventy yeshiva students and other youths who live there. The caravans have no electricity or running water, and in order to wash up in the morning, the students stroll to public toilets specially constructed for them.

Despite its importance in the larger geography of Israeli settlement in the West Bank, Yitzhar gives the impression of being a rather small, even humble settlement—a fitting landscape for the conspicuously pious population. Walking through the settlement, one cannot be blamed for assuming that it is the quiet suburbia of a larger city. Narrow streets crisscross the main road, children play on the streets, and a kindergarten, a large synagogue, a basic grocery store, a cultural center, and a sport center with field goals and basketball poles are all found within the settlement.

The men of Yitzhar are extremely religious. They have long beards and long hair, with lengthy *paos,* or curled locks, on the sides of their heads; their demeanor is not unfriendly, but they are alert to outsiders, especially if they appear to be non-ultra-Orthodox.

Yisrael, David's father, was known as an independent soul and a nonconformist. He studied at the Yashlatz (Yeshivat Yerushalayim L'Tzeirim, or Jerusalem Yeshiva for Teenagers, a yeshiva high school affiliated with Merkaz Harav), which combined the religious and secular curricula of the followers of Rabbi Tzvi Yehuda Hacohen Kook, whose political philosophy greatly influenced many religious Jews and had a crucial part in the creation of Gush Emunim. Although Yisrael looked up to Rabbi Kook's intellect and intense character, he developed an independent stance that was influenced by other theological and social trends, especially Hassidic ones. He also had a keen interest in European philosophy. When he graduated from the Yashlatz in 1982, he decided to join the Yamit settlement block in the Sinai, taking part in activities against the expected Israeli withdraw from the peninsula and becoming a member of the Yamit Yeshiva, where he met David's mother, Noa.

Noa was from a secular moshav (a cooperative agricultural community) called Nir Tzvi, next to the city of Lod. Her family was secular, but she developed a religiously Orthodox and politically hard-right posture regarding Israel's future that led her to join the struggle at Yamit when she was eighteen. It was there that she embraced Orthodox Judaism and became a born-again Jew. When Noa had completed her personal transition and become a practicing Jew, she and Yisrael married.

Their early married life was marred by disappointment as the struggle against the pullout from the Sinai failed and Yamit was demolished in preparation for the return of the territory to Egypt. Yisrael, who was strongly opposed to any idea of territorial withdrawal from the historical land of Israel, was bitterly disappointed. He became even more dismayed when he returned to the Merkaz Harav yeshiva and saw how quickly things got back to normal without any acknowledgment of the dangerous precedent Yamit had presented.

Just as Yisrael was becoming estranged from his fellow students, a man named Romam Aldubi encouraged him and several of his hard-core comrades to create a new and activist yeshiva fully supportive of the settlement project. They established the Od Yosef Chay (Joseph Yet Lives) Yeshiva, a national-ultra-Orthodox rabbinical school, at Joseph's tomb inside Nablus. Until then the national Orthodox had been the only religious group allied with the Zionist movement—after 1967 they started many of the settlements in the West Bank. But it was the ultra-Orthodox, or Haredi, community—which strictly observes the rules of the Halacha (Jewish laws and regulations) and was (and mostly still is) theologically anti-Zionist—that initiated the new yeshiva. Od Yosef Chay signaled the public emergence of a nationalist ultra-Orthodox tendency that combines religious fundamentalism with radical right-wing nationalism.

This particular subset of Judaism is crucial to understanding David's life story and political and social views, as the nationalist ultra-Orthodox living in the Occupied Territories have in many ways renounced Israeli state control or sovereignty over these lands, declaring that no human government has the right to relinquish control of land whose title God has given the Jewish people. If forced to choose between the Israeli state and society and fighting for the land, there is no question where their loyalties will lie. It is not surprising in this regard that one of the main Yitzhar rabbis, Yosef Paley, was arrested for "sedition and incitement" in 2006.

As a national-Orthodox center, Od Yosef Chay from the beginning clearly was going to diverge from Rabbi Kook's more traditional religious Zionist orientation. The new yeshiva quickly became a focal point of radical activism, preaching an aggressive approach toward the Palestinians and a robust settlement policy even at the price of confrontation with the authorities. Theologically, it combined messianic and mystical orientations, epitomized by the appointment of a Chabad (a subset of the Hassidic movement) rabbi, Yitzhak Ginsburg, as its headmaster. Yisrael became one of the more popular teachers in Od Yosef Chay. He and Noa (with little David) resided in Elkana, near the old border separating Israel and the West Bank, one of the major settlements of mainstream Gush Emunim. Yisrael found it difficult to teach and study in Nablus while his family was so far away, so in 1987 they moved to Yitzhar. Yisrael now is one of the most well-known and radical rabbis of the settlement movement.

COMING OF AGE ON THE HILLTOPS

With its mystical Hassidic orientation, Yitzhar is a unique community even within the spectrum of West Bank settlements. The Halacha is carefully observed: women and men are strictly separated in public activities, both sexes dress modestly, and day-to-day life is lived according to the most strict interpretation of Jewish religious law. David doesn't know much about the early history of Yitzhar, "just that it was army outpost that was civilianized. Only one of the original families stayed at that point; the rest moved on." He and his family arrived several months before the outbreak of the First Intifada, when it was still possible to go into Nablus and buy candy at a Palestinian store.

According to David, the first settlers were a heterogeneous group of both more secular and religiously grounded people. At the time, Yitzhar was still relatively small, with only a few families, maybe twenty-five in all. David went to kindergarten and elementary school there until the third grade and afterward was sent to the regional school in Itamar, a nearby settlement.

The story of David Ariel and the story of the settlement of Yitzhar are inextricably linked. "I was three years old when we came to Yitzhar. It was established the year I was born, in July 1984," he explains. He remembers his childhood there with a lot of affection. He and the other boys were free to roam wherever they pleased. He attributes his resistance to extreme cold weather to those years, when he and his friends ran all around the mountain regardless of the weather. "It gave me a natural immunity. Today even if it's freezing I don't really mind."

Although his father had separated himself from Rabi Kook's mainstream ideology, David decided to attend the Yashlatz as Yisrael had. He enrolled when he was fifteen. It was a boarding school, and he saw his family only every other weekend. He soon became more bored than exhilarated. He had gone to the Yashlatz to follow in his father's footsteps, but he eventually dropped out. His parents tried to dissuade him and were unhappy with his decision but respected it. Soon thereafter, David went to live in a secluded civilian outpost and became a "hilltop youth"; he was only sixteen.

The "hilltop youth" phenomenon began in the 1990s after Ariel Sharon, then the national infrastructure minister and later the prime minister, urged committed young settlers to "run and grab as many hilltops as possible." The goal was to replace the suburban culture of the established settlements with a renewed frontier ethos that would make it impossible to adopt any territorial compromise.

Most hilltop youths are in their teens or early twenties; they include youngsters who seek alternatives to their conventional religious Zionist upbringing and also delinquent youths looking for a way out of their troubles. They reside in un-recognized locations on hills (hence the name), where they set up illegal civilian outposts. They are infamous for attacking neighboring Palestinian villages and equally celebrated for their "natural" and somewhat hippie appearance. Most stay until they are married. Some even return after starting a family, and thus several of the hills have become minisuburbs or de facto neighborhoods of known settlements like Yitzhar. There are currently four illegal outposts surrounding Yitzhar, most of which have been manned at some time by hilltop youths.

David stayed at first in Ronen's Hill, a secluded outpost overlooking the Judean desert that was established by Ronen Arusi, one of the dominant and charismatic figures of the hilltop youths. Arusi became estranged from the settlers' mainstream leadership and followed a more eccentric path. Joining the hill and its community was relatively easy for David, as he was already familiar with several existing hill-top youth communities in the vicinity of Yitzhar.

He doesn't see his move to the hills as a soul-searching experience. "I was not like those IDF [Israel Defense Forces] soldiers who after their military service go to India to find themselves—nothing like that. I was a bit childish perhaps, but I looked at it as a real experience and as an important cause in the service of settling the land of Israel. I didn't go there to learn who I was or what to do with my life." Life on Ronen's Hill was simple. "We did some agriculture, like sowing wheat; we also had a small herd of goats which we milked. It was a lot of fun—living on the hill is a real joy." He and his comrades would wake up every day around 4 A.M., go to Od Yosef Chay, study until noon, and then return to the hill, where they performed various chores including cultivating their small fields.

David enjoyed this time in the yeshiva, for the curriculum here was not as demanding as it was in Jerusalem—at least not to him. He also could come and go as he pleased. "I was a free spirit there," he explains. He did not stay at the school for long, however. A month after he showed up, overall security severely worsened. This was the heyday of the al-Aqsa Intifada, and in October 2000, Palestinian militiamen along with regular protesters surrounded Joseph's tomb and forced an Is-raeli withdrawal. Od Yosef Chay moved to Nablus, and David stopped attending it.

Life on the hilltops is a transient one. After six months David decided to leave Ronen's Hill to raise a new outpost near Yitzhar. This was done as a secret operation during one night. Many students of Od Yosef Chay came to help. Amanah—the logistical branch of Gush Emunim—assisted with material, technical help, and support. It also provided a regular supply of gas to the generator that was the sole source of electricity. Most of those who took part in the establishment of the outpost left soon afterward. David and a few other teenagers remained. They lived in wooden cabins that they built themselves with some assistance. David has very warm memories from that time. He recalls that this group resembled the Zion-ist pioneers of the beginning of the twentieth century, only more New Agey and relaxed: "We didn't need to dry any swamps. We used to sit by the campfire in the evenings, and in the day we did a bit of agriculture. The important thing was manning the outpost."

The yeshiva students of Od Yosef Chay participated in sentry duties at night. Yitzhar had an armory that provided firearms, and they used to walk over there, receive a weapon, and then patrol the outpost. Although David and his friends were manning an illegal outpost, the army gave them a short training course. Officially they might have been portrayed as a liability, but each new conquest was seen as a semimilitary stronghold that should be defended.

The army did not send a detachment to guard David and his friends in their outpost, yet a company was regularly assigned to secure the perimeter alongside the settlers themselves. This was standard procedure everywhere in the West Bank. The army is directed to provide security to all Jews who reside in the Occupied Territories, whether in "legalized" settlements or self-declared civilian strongholds. A security perimeter around a Jewish outpost is a proximity circle of a few kilometers. Palestinian entrance into such areas is banned, even to visit privately owned plots.

Despite its active role, however, David saw the army as little more than a United Nations–type presence, there "simply to maintain the peace" between settlers and Palestinians. Some soldiers, especially reservists, used to taunt him and declare their hope that he'd be kicked off the hill. At first he became "crazy" from these remarks, but he eventually developed some empathy for their views. "If you had been pulled from your home, taken away from your wife and children, just to look over a bunch of psychos for thirty days, wouldn't you hate it and them?"

From time to time the Civilian Administration—the Israeli governing body that operates in the West Bank—paid David and his friends a visit to issue a demolition warrant. This could have led to forced removal by the military, but that never happened. Although David had participated in numerous protests against demolitions in many illegal outposts, he never had to face bulldozers coming to destroy his own.

After several months he and his friends decided to build a house to establish more permanent facts on the ground. Although there was a danger that the house might be demolished, they decided it was worth the risk. David and three others chipped in their savings and hired several handymen who were experts in the blitzkrieg building of outposts. In one night and with the help of fifteen other people, they built a small hut which was later plastered, insulated, and connected to electricity. Eventually David bought the others' shares. Today the house is registered in his name and rented to other people. There are now six more houses on the hill. Although there is no direct link between it and Yitzhar, it is considered a natural part of the settlement because "all who live there are actually settlers from Yitzhar."

People chose their own lifestyle on the hill. Some were busy all day, working or praying. Others would just lie back and pass the time in the usually serene and quiet (or more accurately, pacified) landscape by doing nothing. David usually belonged to the latter group. It was a period in his life when he felt stuck. He had a lot of fun but also a sensation of going astray. He enjoyed the feeling that he had contributed to settling the land by erecting a new place, but he was also bored, wondering if there were some higher calling he should be following. In particular, he had no sense of spiritual contentment. In 2003, when he turned eighteen, he decided to join the IDF. "I saw I was doing nothing, so I figured, 'What the hell—let's enlist.'"

STATE AND ARMY

Contrary to the views of most non-ultra-Orthodox Israeli Jews, David did not see joining the IDF as an honor or a crucial rite of passage into adulthood. Many settler youths do enlist, and they can be found in all of the military units, with exceptionally high numbers in special commando units—but David came from the Haredim, who do not value the state or its institutions. David signed up because he had nothing better to do and because living in dangerous surroundings, he needed to know how to defend himself, and the IDF was the only institution that could fight the Arabs. As he explains: "Our [the hilltop youths'] view of the military was always unclear. It was unclear whether they were with us or against us. Their mandate is only for keeping the quiet. If I make a mess, they will screw me; if they [the Arabs] make a mess, it will screw them."

Nor was the army especially interested in hilltop youths like him, given their reputation for wanton violence and hatred of Palestinians. "If a hilltop youth wants to evade conscription, he can just walk up to the recruitment officer and confess that he wants to kill Arabs. It's not like when somebody from Tel Aviv says it and everybody thinks he's just making it up—they will believe *you*." In the end, the military discharged David after refusing to allow him to join one of the special units for Orthodox soldiers and a special mental health committee found him unfit for service on the grounds that he is paranoid.

He was "a little hurt but greatly relieved," since most of his friends did not join up and he didn't attach any special importance to doing so. "The army today has forsaken most of its Jewish values. Today they are even talking about burying gentile soldiers [David refers to Russian immigrants who are not Jewish according to Halacha] in Jewish cemeteries—this mocks the basic notions of Jewish entombment. . . . The army wants to enable non-Jews—Druze, Bedouin, and Christians—to enlist and to swear allegiance on the Qur'an or the New Testament instead of our Holy Bible."

CHANCE ENCOUNTERS DEFINED BY CONFLICT

Despite never being evicted, David was no stranger to army crackdowns on outposts or settlements and got a record of being a troublemaker when he joined a group of teenagers in throwing rocks at the cars of several police who had entered Yitzhar in a provocative manner and aggressively questioned them about their activities. He was also summoned for questioning when a Palestinian filed a complaint against him after an altercation in the well-known Wadi al-Qult in the Judean desert, which is home to the oldest synagogue in Israel/Palestine, dating to the time of the Hasmonean kings, in the first century B.C.E.

The altercation was unremarkable, but David's awareness of its implications are telling. He and a group of friends were bathing in one of the pools. As practicing Jews they followed an austere separation of women and men. Then a Palestinian man came and wanted to enter with his all family where the Jewish women bathed. "Now I know that technically speaking this is not a provocation. From one side you can say that he is a citizen and has every right to go where he pleases. But only a fool," David explained, would disregard the ingrained hostility between "Arabs and settlers. I don't say, 'Don't come to the stream,' but what do you expect? Settlers don't like Arabs—we don't like it when you want to enter our pool. I mean, it was, like, 'What are you, an idiot'? Don't you know that there is hostility between settlers and Arabs? Don't you know that to us it's not cool if you try to swim in our pool?'"

For David, the idea of a Palestinian entering "our" pool is the same as if he were to enter Birzeit University and raise a huge poster that said "Operation Cast Lead [Israel's incursion into Gaza in January 2009 that claimed more than a thousand Palestinians lives] was a good operation." David tried to reason with the Palestinian, but others were not so restrained. One of David's friends physically attacked the man. The Palestinian lodged a complaint blaming David, and police questioned him, eventually releasing him for lack of evidence. He had an alibi—witnesses testified that he had not touched the man at all.

KNOW THY NEIGHBOR

Although he is practically their neighbor, David has never really talked to any of the Palestinians who live near him. There has always been hostility between his community and theirs. Yitzhar in particular, unlike most settlements, has almost since its creation prohibited Palestinians from working in it, for security reasons. And over the years individual Palestinians have attacked the settlement at least twice.

According to David, the reason for the small number of attacks is that Yitzhar settlers "always made sure to present a very tough image to the outside world. If a

Palestinian comes close to our perimeter, even by mistake, he will get roughed up. He will not be shown mercy, not at all, though he will remain alive." And indeed, Yitzhar has a reputation as one of the most extreme settlements, with its residents committing routine acts of violence against Palestinians, particularly when they try to work their lands on the slope below the settlement's built-up area.

Ultimately, David's experience with Palestinians resembles the turf battles of rival gangs in Los Angeles or New York, with the difference that in the West Bank, one gang has the full weight of a state behind it, even if it sees that state as a neighborhood cop at best. As he describes the animosity: "If I were to stand at a bus stop and a Palestinian were there, then there'd be immediate tension. If only two of us were there, I could growl at him or just order him to move one hundred meters away from me. If there are three against me, then I will go away—there aren't many other options." When he was little he hoped they would all die. When he grew up he wanted them just to go away, but when he matured he understood that this would not happen.

The Palestinians are there to stay, David understands, just like him. Until recently he did not particularly care about their lives, ideas, or wishes. "I really didn't give too much thought to it. They were my enemies, and that's that—you don't try to explore any shades or nuances in how you feel about them." Today, on the other hand, he is much more interested in their story and reasoning. Though still regarding them as the enemy, he thinks he understands their nature more clearly. He sees Palestinians as an "inflammatory" audience, susceptible to radical preaching that awakens violent emotions slumbering within them. The popular election of Hamas in the Gaza Strip in 2006, consequently, was not a big surprise for him. It was what he expected.

He believes that Islam tells Muslims to "rule the nation by sword and fist and enslave all the non-Muslims." The riots in 1929, when eighty-nine Jews were killed in Hebron, provide the historical grounding for this conviction, which was reinforced by the lynching of two Israeli soldiers in Ramallah at the start of the al-Aqsa Intifada and by his experience of witnessing rage in Palestinian faces when he dared to drive through Burin with his friends one day when he was around eighteen, just to see what would happen.

Although David believes that a messiah will eventually come and redeem the nation of Israel, he views himself as a realist. "The Palestinians are here to stay, yet it's clear that wolves [e.g., David himself] will never share their homes with sheep." When he looks at the Kingdom of Jordan, he sees a failed state with a failing economy and huge social problems, but he doesn't really care because Jordan is not his country. In his land, as a "sovereign," he is in charge of all of his subjects' well-being. His vision endows Palestinians with what he calls "unequal citizenship," without the same political, economic, or territorial rights as Jews but with the right to live their lives quietly, "with honor, happiness, and joy," for that is what ensures his own quiet. "If a family of ten lives in a small house in a village, it must be given a building permit so they can expand their home. It is inhuman otherwise."

David thinks that most Israelis treated the Palestinians as subhumans, herded around in slave markets for their cheap labor. But in the same breath he claims that they are well off because of the Israelis. "They might get spit on at work, but they are able to build enormous castles in their villages, bigger than any I ever saw in my place."

Following the master narrative of Zionism, David believes that until Zionism arrived, Palestinians were living miserably, unable to manage their political or economic lives. He holds that they "adore strength and power. The way to keep the status quo is to be tough and act tough, so you will be admired and feared. One must never forget that their religion rules that the Jews should die. . . . This is why they should be under strict supervision. They should be able to run their own lives but be treated like little children: nourished, educated, disciplined, and if they transgress, severely punished, as the old Hebrew proverb suggests, 'Respect him but suspect him.'"

For David, Palestinians should never be eligible to vote or carry weapons and should always be suspected of irredentism. "Ruling over them calls for a delicate mixture of harshness and softness," he believes, but he seriously questions whether Israel can achieve such a balance. Even so, he suggests that such a scenario will only be possible in a distant and hypothetical future, not in the current daily conflict over what remains of the hilltops of Samaria.

THE OTHER SIDE OF THE MOUNTAIN: CONFINEMENT AND EXILE

Ground zero for David's notion of a delicate balance in controlling Palestinians is the village of Burin, located down the mountain slope from Yitzhar. Like its neighbor higher up, Burin is in one of the most beautiful spots in the West Bank, but it has a different character. The settlers focus almost entirely on the hilltops for their settlements, which are windier, colder, and a bit removed from water sources. With the exception of some nineteenth-century "throne villages" that served as seats of local power in the latter Ottoman era, Palestinians have tended to build in valleys or on slopes, where the fields and water are closer. Olive trees alternating with golden wheat fields cover Burin's hills, which have little of the rockiness that defines the landscape of much of the West Bank. In the spring there is an explosion of flora; summers are hot but not oppressive, while winters are similar to those of Southern California.

The Najjar family farm lies right in the middle of this beautiful yet tortured landscape, above Burin proper and below Yitzhar and Har Bracha. From the farm, one cannot see Yitzhar, which mostly lies beyond the crest of the hill. Har Bracha is more visible from below. On a hill next to Har Bracha is a single structure, a mobile home, the beginning of another settlement, and once one starts looking for them, it seems that the majority of seemingly empty hilltops in the area have at least one or two structures built by hilltop youths.

Below Har Bracha is a fairly large mosque, completed and paid for by residents of the village and their relatives in the Palestinian Diaspora. Despite lying within the built area of the village (which over the past several decades has clearly expanded beyond its traditional limits as the population increased greatly), the mosque is on land that the Israeli government considers Area C (per the Oslo Accords) and thus under its control. It declared the mosque to have been built illegally and therefore ordered it to be torn down. Residents appealed this decision, and the case was making its way through the Israeli court system as of 2011, although people from Burin fear that settlers might try to burn down the mosque before a judgment is rendered, as happened in the nearby town of Yasuf in 2009.

Indeed, as Yitzhar and Har Bracha have expanded, the Israeli government has become more reluctant to allow Palestinian residents to build in Area C. Though the middle and high school just down the block from the mosque, which the Najjar children all attended, has not been threatened with demolition, the settlers regularly attack residents attempting to work the surrounding fields and have largely prevented them from harvesting crops or grazing their flocks.

All told, Yitzhar, Har Bracha, and neighboring settlements have expropriated something like eighteen thousand acres from Burin and adjacent villages. This includes much of the most valuable agricultural land in the region, some of which is now part of the security perimeters of the settlements and thus fenced off to prevent Palestinian from accessing it. According to local Palestinian leaders, the area controlled by Yitzhar has grown fivefold in the 2000s alone, while closed military zones have enveloped entire Palestinian towns to make it even harder for them to expand organically.

Burin is a very old and poor village, with a population of around three thousand. It is home to farmers and shop owners, not overly religious—it has two mosques—and more supportive of Fatah than Hamas. The streets are dirty, although it is clear that residents do their best to keep the town relatively clean. Little girls walk down the street dragging makeshift dollies loaded with water bottles because the village has little potable water. It does have a Roman-era fountain, which residents proudly show to visitors, but it is covered with garbage. Preserving their ancient history is a luxury that villagers cannot afford.

Mahmoud Najjar, the family patriarch, was born in 1933 in the Haifa region and died in 2006 at seventy-three. He and his family wound up in Burin after a stint in a refugee camp in the wake of the 1948 war. They were farmers and shepherds, but they couldn't afford land of their own, so Mahmoud moved to Kuwait to work in the construction industry, which he did for five or six years in the late 1950s and early 1960s. Land was inexpensive when he returned, so he and his brother bought a parcel, immediately planted trees, and got the farm that still sits there up and running. They planted about thirty trees around the house and about one hundred more on their land heading up the mountain toward Yitzhar. For the next four decades the Najjar family devoted most of its energy to farming. In 1973, Mahmoud married Khitma, a traditional, devout woman born in 1955. They had a typical division of labor, meaning that she did most of the chores around the house and helped where possible with feeding animals, while the men did the heavy work.

Mahmoud built his home to house his four sons and their families, but only twenty-four-year-old Abed and nineteen-year-old Ahmad still live there; both work on the farm. The oldest brother, Mansour, thirty-eight, lives in the Gulf, where he works as a civil engineer, while Youssef, twenty-two, was forced into exile in the United States after too many run-ins with settlers and the Israeli security services. Mahmoud died one month after Youssef left to attend college in the United States in 2006; neither he nor Mansour has been able to return home to visit their father's grave. As the primary farmer in the family, Abed has a big and strong physique, a consequence of working from seven every morning till at least two or three in the afternoon. He has eighty trees to tend to, plus the wheat field and the animals. Yet despite these responsibilities, he sports a funky haircut and wears cut-up jeans and shirts rather than more traditional clothing.

Today the Najjar farm is a bit dilapidated but pretty. To enter it you drive under an awning with grape vines, past chickens running free and tied-up goats and a horse. A rusty bicycle sits on the roof of a shed next to the awning. The house is a 1960s concrete structure. It is decently sized and comfortably furnished, as cool inside in the midday sun as it is hot outside.

But constant reminders of the unremitting conflict puncture the pastoralness of the setting. A bypass road—No. 60, also known as Yitzhar Road—one of the main conduits through the West Bank, runs only meters behind the house on land that once belonged to the Najjar family. To the left, perhaps thirty meters up the hill at the edge of the property, sits an Israeli Jeep with a few soldiers watching the scene. It's hard to know whom they are there to protect, the settlers above or the Palestinians below. The settlers have attacked the house many times, trying to burn it down and stealing goats and sheep—they even stole the horse when he was only a month old, but the soldiers managed to have him returned. "It has no name," Abed replies when asked about the horse. "Why bother? They can take it again at any time."

Some of the family's olives trees date back to Roman times. One can tell the really old ones by how big and distorted their trunks are. Most are between forty and sixty years old, with about half planted when Najjar père bought the farm. A large percentage of the olive trees are small because settlers cut them down at some point. Yet despite the assaults on the trees, Burin continues to produce some of the best olives in all of Israel/Palestine. Their oil is incredibly green, cloudy, and even "dirty"—it would likely not be considered refined enough to sell in an American supermarket or specialty store, but it is among the strongest yet most delicious olive oil one is likely ever to taste, the fruit equivalent of fresh, raw milk.

A CHILD OF THE INTIFADA

Youssef Najjar was born the year the First Intifada broke out, in 1987. He has never known a life without conflict or settlements. "My favorite thing to do when I was a kid was to play basketball with my cousins in the afternoon. But it wasn't always safe to do that, because settlers could at any moment start shooting into the air and sometimes at people. My uncle died after being shot at by settlers, who claimed that he attacked one of their cars." Settlers also shot his cousin Hamdam to death in 1988.

Settlers from Yitzhar as well as soldiers have routinely harassed Youssef's family and other villagers since the start of the First Intifada. His earliest memory of direct conflict is as a five-year-old in 1992, when soldiers came to his house and arrested his oldest brother for being an intifada activist. According to Youssef, the reality was that Mansour had thrown stones at settlers to keep them from harming his house. "He spent eighteen months in jail for protecting his house. This was a typical thing—settlers provoked, we defended, and soldiers arrested us for defending our homes."

The head of the village council, Abd al-Rahim Kadus, described the dynamic slightly differently, explaining that almost "every Saturday, settlers come to the village, attack the locals, and destroy property, leading to clashes with the Palestinians. Israeli troops usually intervene to break up the fighting, which then turns into a confrontation between young villagers and the soldiers." The regular violence also resulted in the imposition of repeated closures—internally, between cities and towns in the West Bank, as much as externally, between the West Bank and Gaza, Israel, or Jordan.

This situation grew worse over time. Checkpoints were larger and more restrictive, the neighboring settlements continued to expand, and it became almost impossible to get to nearby Nablus, never mind Ramallah or the southern West Bank, which could take two to four hours, four times the normal time. Sometimes up to five hundred people might be stuck at a checkpoint for hours on end. "It was insane," Abed explained.

By the mid-1990s, settlers also became violent. Youssef's middle school faced his house from across a road that leads to one of the nearby settlements, and frequently settlers would stop the cars traveling on it and start shooting into the air with their automatic weapons to scare the children on their way to school. Sometimes they would shoot into the air near the school, creating even more heightened panic. Yet despite these constant negative interactions, Israel was absent from the school's curriculum. "We studied English, math, geography, and other subjects, but they never taught us about the settlements. They never even talked about them. It was a fact—there was no need to put it in a book. In any case, our books were written by Jordanians, who didn't know anything about our land."

SIGNPOSTS ON THE WAY TO ISOLATION: OSLO AND AL-AQSA

The launching of the Oslo peace process in 1993 and the threat it posed to their enterprise led settlers, with the support of key sectors of the military and political establishments, to try to seize as much land as possible in advance of continued negotiations. Ironically, the very terms of the Oslo process, negotiated by a weak and inexperienced Palestinian side, made the grabbing of the hilltops so effective, for rather than acknowledging the settlement enterprise as illegal on its face, Oslo declared it subject to negotiation during final-status talks.

But if the settlement infrastructure, or matrix of control, was strengthened during the Oslo years, the outbreak of the al-Aqsa Intifada in 2000 led settlers to become particularly violent. As Youssef and Abed describe it, attacks in the 1990s often involved stone throwing by both settlers and villagers, but after the outbreak of the al-Aqsa Intifada, settlers began attacking in groups, sometimes one hundred strong, while Israeli soldiers looked on. "First it was the fields and the trees that were the object of attack; soon it was our house that became the principal target," Youssef explains. One such attack in 2003 left their car and their mother's hand burned, youngest brother Ahmad with a serious head injury, and many sheep missing. "We could not resist or leave the house till the entire village and an Israeli police patrol came to rescue us," Youssef recalls. "I suffered smoke inhalation, and it took me days to be able to breathe normally again."

At the height of the violence, settlers attacked almost weekly. During one stone-throwing assault, Youssef was hit in the head and knocked unconscious and required several stitches. *Haaretz* dubbed the Yitzhar-Burin area "the land of unchecked settler harassment." In November 2005, Youssef and his cousin Mohammad were feeding their sheep in the fields below Yitzhar when seven armed settlers approached and punched him in the face, declaring that "you are not allowed to feed the sheep here, because this land is for us, not for you." Youssef replied, "This is our land; it belongs to my father. I live down in that house over there," but the settlers said that he could only feed his sheep in the village: "You can't come here anymore." Then, grabbing Youssef by the shirt, one put his rifle by Youssef's head and began shooting right above it. "After that, I didn't take the sheep there anymore, even thought it actually is our land." Youssef's conflicts were not only with settlers. The Israeli military is a constant presence in his family's farm and the surrounding region. He was routinely questioned and occasionally beaten whenever there was a stone-throwing incident nearby. The situation became worse after the outbreak of the al-Aqsa Intifada, as on one occasion soldiers commandeered his home, held the family in one room throughout the night, and used the remainder of the house as a post to look out for stone throwers. When a woman from one of the nearby settlements was shot in 2004, soldiers interrogated and beat Youssef inside one of their cars for the length of a night before letting him go at 7 A.M. The next year, after a settler's car was stoned, the army again took him temporarily into custody but this time offered him money if he would work with them and inform on anyone who attacked settlers or was hiding weapons.

Notwithstanding the ongoing violence, Youssef has fond memories of his childhood. "During school [days], we would get home in the early afternoon, sit for couple of hours, then go out to the fields to feed the sheep. Then I'd come home, have dinner, and do my homework. In the summers, we'd work the fields most of the day, as there are a lot of trees and other things to take care of."

In spite of the constant conflict with both settlers and soldiers, the Najjar family has never been politically active. "No one in our family is especially political," Youssef explains. "We do not agree with Hamas or Fatah or any group that advocates violence. I see that most of the time Hamas and Fatah kill civilians, and I don't think they care about people. My family doesn't even vote." This desire to avoid politics is characteristic of the people of Burin, but it's not easy to remain aloof: "Once Hamas tried to recruit me, offering me money. Fatah did the same thing." With few means of gainful employment, residents who don't own a decent-sized farm have a harder time resisting such offers.

THE ROAD TO EXILE

As the situation in Burin continued to deteriorate, Youssef decided to attend college at the University of Houston. His intention was to return home after his studies: "I hoped to work for a large grocery store in my village."

At the end of his first semester, he received the news that his father had died. "He had been supporting me and acting as my sponsor at school. After he died, I had no money, so I had to leave the university." The college would not allow him to take a leave of absence without providing a copy of his father's death certificate, but that proved impossible because Hamas had just won the 2006 elections and Israel was refusing to cooperate with the Palestinian Authority. Without the certificate and unable to return to the school, Youssef moved to California, where his cousin Muamar was a PhD student at UC Davis. Muamar agreed to sponsor him at Sierra College, where he was accepted and began to study.

But before starting at Sierra, Youssef had to engage in a lengthy battle to obtain political asylum in the United States, having become technically illegal after dropping out of the University of Houston. He felt he had no choice: "Things have gotten so bad that I'm afraid to go back home. I'm afraid I'll be hurt or killed or arrested." The judge presiding in his case agreed that the situation in his hometown was so dire that Youssef would face persecution and likely death should he be forced to return. In 2010, he won his asylum.

THE UNREMITTING OCCUPATION

With Youssef and Mansour permanently out of the country, the responsibility for taking care of and protecting the farm, their mother, and their youngest brother fell squarely on Abed's shoulders. It's a job that becomes more difficult all the time, as the Palestinian police almost never come to the village; even if they did, they would be of no help against attacks by settlers or Israeli soldiers. "The only law is the IDF, and the problem is that the soldiers are even more religious now. We know this because they refuse to demolish settlers' homes, and it seems that most of them are settlers themselves, and a few even live in Yitzhar or Bracha," Abed says.

When settlers began to believe that peace negotiations might move toward final-status talk and lead to the abandonment of major settlements, they adopted what has become know as the price tag policy, meaning that they would make Palestinians who lived near a settlement pay for any anti-settlement act—by committing violence against them. As Abed explains it, "Any tension that happens in the West Bank, the Yitzhar settlers attack our house in revenge."

The situation became so bad that the IDF set up a new unit specifically to deal with the settler violence in the area, although even then local commanders admitted to "turn[ing] a blind eye on settler violence." The Israeli government's lack of control over the situation led the normally neutral political officer of the U.S. consulate to visit the Najjar home and, quite literally, stand with Khitma in support of the family's plight. He had no illusions about the long-term prognosis and suggested that she consider either building a fence around the farm or moving away. "He asked the Israelis on our behalf if we could build a fence, but they refused. And there's no way to move even if we wanted to, because of the harm and mistreatment that most likely we would receive from our village. And moreover," Youssef sighed, "we have no other place to move to."

ESTRANGEMENT, EXILE, AND THE IMPOSSIBILITY
OF LOSING ONE'S ROOTS

David Ariel and Youssef Najjar have, to the best of their knowledge, never met. According to David, he has never taken part in the physical attacks on Palestinian people or property in Burin of which Youssef and his family have been among the primary victims. And Youssef and his brothers are too wary of the consequences of being perceived of as a threat by settlers to share any public space, such as bus stops, with Israelis, even if they were to outnumbered them.

The constant conflict between the settlers of Yitzhar and the families of Burin has driven two of the four Najjar children out of Palestine, quite possibly for good. Mansour has a family and career in the United Arab Emirates, having settled into the well-established Palestinian Diaspora in the Gulf, where so many of his colleagues and friends have stories remarkably similar to his. Youssef has taken a different road, in good measure because he didn't have time to plan a future that would have kept him closer to home.

Where once he wanted to be an accountant at the local grocery store (where his younger brother Ahmad works part-time after school), he now hopes, after completing his accounting degree at Sierra College in Northern California, to make a life for himself in the United States, once upon a time heralded as the New Jerusalem for millions of people who fled persecution in their ancient homelands. In the meantime, he works with his cousin in a local gift shop. He thinks constantly of home, guilty yet in many ways relieved to be safely outside. "I miss my village. I miss the land, the school. It's home, so I miss it and think about my family often."

David has not left Israel, nor does he plan to. Yet in many ways he too is living a form of exile, however self-imposed it may be. He no longer roams the hilltops that defined him, conquering new territories. He no longer lives in Yitzhar, which despite his nostalgia and its ideological importance, he seems to have outgrown. After marrying a woman more observant than him, he became a student at a yeshiva in Shaalvim, close to Ramla, not related to any settler-movement institution. "You just sit there and learn Torah all day long," he explained. He even took acting lessons—theater has become a "life calling," he explains—although he made sure that he was not doing so in a way that would violate Orthodox norms. Ultimately the couple moved to the Maale Levonah settlement, which is closer to Jerusalem. But David now declares that he no longer wishes to be part of any distinct ideological niche.

Most interestingly, David doesn't define himself as Israeli. Unlike most ultra-Orthodox Jews—whether Haredim or Zionist—he feels that the question of whether Israel is the promised kingdom and whether Jews should live there before the coming of the Messiah is "redundant and petty." The State of Israel for him is a given, but he has no particular allegiance to it and in fact has never voted. "I'm used to living outside conventions, so I see it as a kind of outsider—if it does good I'm with it, and if not then I oppose it."

In fact, David believes that Israelis are trapped in an identity in which they "want to stay Jews but reject all of the divine commands." Israel is almost "like all the other nations"—precisely, it should be recalled, what Zionism's father, Theodor Herzl, hoped it would become. This identity is a far cry from the mystical, almost cosmological one with which David was imbued while growing up in Yitzhar. For him, Israel's half-secular-half-sacred identity is a trap that will likely cause the state to "vanish as history continues." His way out is to focus on his direct relationship with God, even at the price of letting go of the Zionist national mythology and identity that shaped him and his parents before him.

Increasing numbers of Haredim have become more Zionized in the past decade as their population has moved further to the right. David, starting from the other end, has moved toward a traditional Haredi attitude of ambivalence toward the Zionist state even as he, like they, benefits in innumerable ways from its policies and ideological favoritism toward Jews.

For their part, Youssef and his brothers, whether in Burin or the Diaspora, cannot conceive of abandoning their Palestinian identity. Yet however strong their attachment to their land and identity, none of them can imagine how that identity can be realized on the ground. What David takes for granted—the freedom to roam the hills and indeed the whole country at will and to pick and choose what kind of Israeli, if at all, he wants to be—Youssef has never experienced. Just being able to leave the chickens outside at night without fear of losing one or two before the morning comes would be a marked improvement in his family's quality of life. As he sits in the college library studying for his CPA exam, Youssef wonders, "Will I ever go home again?"

POSTSCRIPT

In September 2011, villagers in Burin organized their yearly olive harvest. Together with a group of other international volunteers, three senior female members of the Israeli nongovernmental organization Machsom Watch, which focuses on the expansion of the Separation Wall in the Occupied Territories, helped with the harvest that year. This was particularly important because most Palestinian villagers depend on olive trees as their main source of livelihood, and in recent years the harvest season has become a tense time in the West Bank. Settlers and Palestinians clash daily, many times with significant injuries on both sides, while a large share of local Palestinian property has been destroyed, otherwise ruined, or confiscated.

Many of Burin's olive trees date back to Roman times, but the trees under Yitzhar have not been groomed in any way in recent years, as no heavy machinery is allowed in the area. Nor are Palestinian residents allowed to irrigate these trees. The difference between these and Jewish-controlled groves, which are well kept, cultivated, and maintained, is striking, but so is the difference between Burin's groves and other patches cultivated by Palestinians, which share less-specific arrangements but can be tended to.

The labor of harvesting the olives was as pleasant as it was tiring, but the Yitzhar settlers rebuffed all the villagers' attempts to or reach a modus vivendi with them, and the local military commander declared that the Palestinians would have only three days to harvest all of their trees, after which he could not guarantee their safety. As of early 2012, the basic dynamics of life in Burin and Yitzhar, and the alienation of David and Youssef from each other and from their neighbors, remain intact.

A NOTE ON SOURCES

Besides interviews with members of the Najjar and Ariel families, we relied on these articles:

Blau, Uri. "Behind Closed Doors, Police Admit 'Turning a Blind Eye' to Settler Violence." *Haaretz*, August 15, 2008. Available online at www.haaretz.com/hasen/spages/1011977. html.
Issacharoff, Avi. "The Land of Unchecked Settler Harassment." *Haaretz*, August 7, 2008. Available online at www.haaretz.com/hasen/spages/1009375.html.

SUGGESTIONS FOR FURTHER READING

Updated information on Israeli settlements in the West Bank, including around Burin, is available from Peace Now Settlement Watch, at http://peacenow.org.il/eng/content/settlements, and the Israeli Committee against Home Demolitions, at http://icahd.org/.

19

Majed al-Masri in Two Intifadas in Nablus

Lætitia Bucaille

Majed al-Masri was born in 1971 in the Balata refugee camp, next to Nablus. His grandparents were peasants in the village of Fajja, near Jaffa, who left their homes during the 1948 war. The family settled down in the camp and established a new life in the West Bank, working for the notable families of Nablus at their factories or in their homes.

The relations between the refugees and the townspeople were not easy. Nablusis felt invaded by the flow of refugees; for their part, the refugees felt the disdain directed against them and in return complained of being exploited by the local elites. The Balata camp, which in fact is a prolongation of the town of Nablus, is only a few minutes from the urban center. Yet it's quite clear where the town ends and the camp begins; the camp remains a place apart despite the improvements its inhabitants have made—the houses are built one against another, thus condemning their inmates to perpetual half-light, if not total darkness.

The leading extended families (or *hamulas*) of Nablus built their economic and social power as landowners under the Ottoman Empire. During the nineteenth century, they adapted to the transformation of economy, set up textile and soap-making factories, and developed commercial relations in the region. They preserved strong ties with families in Amman, and some are close to the royal family of Jordan. Members of the prominent Shaka and al-Masri hamulas served as Nablus's mayors. As employers and landowners and through a network of charities, the hamulas had a strong social importance and position. But whereas the poor families of the old city of Nablus were dependent on and felt obligated to them, Balata residents were weary of their prestige and contested their authority.

After the war of June 1967 and the occupation of the West Bank and the Gaza Strip by Israel, many refugees crossed the Green Line and worked in Tel Aviv or Netanya in the construction, textile, and agricultural sectors. By 1993, at the start of the Oslo period, the Israeli job market had absorbed between 25 and 30 percent of the West Bank's workforce. This policy created a Palestinian economic dependence on Israel but also contributed to raising living standards among the inhabitants of the Occupied Territories. The wages were higher in Tel Aviv than in Nablus, so educated residents of the Balata camp would go and work in Israel. Sometimes teenage boys would join their fathers at work during school holidays. That was the case in al-Masri's family until his father died, when Majed was eight years old. From then on, his mother and older brothers struggled to take care of seven sons and three daughters. Despite their name, they were not related to the powerful al-Masri family of Nablus.

Already as a child Majed was rebellious. When he was seven, his nascent nationalist consciousness drove him to sew a Palestinian flag and to join with Yasser, his best friend, in a demonstration against the occupation that was marching by the camp. When he returned home his parents thrashed him.

Before becoming politically active, Majed and Yasser were troublemakers at school. When they were thirteen, they physically threatened a teacher who had suspended one of them from school for a few days. A year later, in 1985, they and some other boys cobbled together a homemade gun and let it off in the general direction of an Israeli settlement. But Majed and Yasser were not yet integrated into political structures such as Fatah's Shabiba (the common name for the Youth Committee for Social Action), whose militants controlled the camp. Unrest had been brewing in Balata since 1982, which finally convinced Israeli soldiers to avoid its inner parts.

Because of his participation in the amateurish gun attack, Majed, who wasn't yet fourteen, was arrested and sentenced to five years in prison by an Israeli military court. The sentence was a shock to him, but this tough experience was a turning point in his life, and the time he served in jail transformed him from a rebellious teenager into a political activist. Indeed, in trying to neutralize adolescents like Majed by repressing them harshly, the Israeli military administration failed spectacularly. Behind bars, Majed and thousands like him met older militants, who had created the first resistance networks affiliated with the Palestinian Liberation Organization (PLO) in the Occupied Territories and provided a solid political and nationalist education to the young detainees. Majed learned about history, global politics, and Fatah's goals and strategies. In prison, he became a fully integrated member of the organization. Hussam Khader, a Fatah leader of the Balata camp, organized discipline, learning, and discussion in the cells. He tried to prevent the youngest from smoking, but Majed refused to accept this regulation.

THE FIRST INTIFADA (1987-1993)

The First Intifada started while Majed was behind bars. After a car accident with an Israeli military Jeep killed four workers from the Jabalya camp in the Gaza Strip, Jabalya residents attacked Israeli forces with stones and Molotov cocktails. In a few days, the rebellion spread, and factions in the West Bank and Gaza used the outburst to structure a political movement of resistance. Representatives of Fatah, the Popular Front for the Liberation of Palestine (PFLP), the Democratic Front for the Liberation of Palestine (DFLP), and the Communist Party formed the Unified National Leadership of the Uprising (UNLU). This organization planned actions and transmitted instructions to the popular committees that operated in each neighborhood. The committees distributed leaflets and indicated to the population which civil disobedience actions would be conducted on the following days. Towns and villages paid their tribute to the resistance, but the refugee camps often appeared to be on the front line. Camp youths were particularly active, and many of them formed the cadres of the uprising. As important, the intifada changed the social status of camp residents. Previously considered the lowest layer of the social edifice, they gained power and prestige through their political involvement and exposure to repression. Militants became proud of their refugee camp identity.

During the first year of the intifada, most groups in society joined the uprising and followed the UNLU's instructions. Merchants agreed to go on tax strike, police employed by the Israeli administration resigned, families boycotted Israeli products, and teachers organized home lessons when the army shut down schools and universities. But by the time Majed got out of prison, the intifada was not the popular movement it had been. Political leaders had been jailed or banned, and younger and less experienced militants had imposed themselves on the resistance movement, sometimes using violence against their own society. The middle class was reluctant to obey their slogans or to accept their authority; its members refused to accept the reality of the occupation but disagreed with some of the young militants' strategies. The unity of Palestinian society had vanished.

In particular, the killing of collaborators was affecting social cohesion. Many Palestinians who became agents for Israel disrupted the nationalist struggle and exposed militants to capture and repression. At some point, the UNLU decided to punish collaborators: sometimes a bullet in the knee would be used to sideline them. With the radicalization of the intifada, certain groups took the initiative to eliminate them entirely. The problem was that sometimes there was no evidence against the suspected collaborators. In addition, gangs became more efficient at erasing members of their own society than at attacking occupation forces. In the Occupied Territories, the number of suspected collaborators killed by intifada activists overcame that of Palestinians killed by the Israeli army. The PLO called for a halt to executions, but some of the gangs carried on.

Yasser al-Badawi and Nasser Uways were Majed's childhood friends from Balata, companions in battle and detention. In 1990, as soon as Majed was released from prison, he formed a group with Yasser and Nasser, which they connected to the UNLU. They turned quickly to military activities, which became prominent after the Gulf War in 1991, accelerating the failure of the social movement that the intifada had once embodied. Majed took action on two occasions. As he describes it:

> I shot one collaborator near the Nablus town hall. He was a well-known intelligence agent, and he openly consorted with the [Israeli] army. I went up to him and asked if his name was such and such. He said yes, and I shot him dead. You mustn't think it's an easy thing, to kill somebody. I was shaking like a leaf, and I had nightmares all the following night. But the second time wasn't so bad. The target was a Palestinian policeman who went on working for the Israeli government even though he'd been told to resign several times. He was at the wheel of his car. I climbed in beside him. I verified his identity in the same way; he realized what was up, and there was a struggle. That really annoyed me, and I let him have it—six bullets in the body. Yasser came and pulled me out of the car.

The intifada also shook up the relations between the refugee camp residents and the traditional elite of Nablus. Majed and his gang had a bone to pick with some of these powerful families. The gang of Balata wanted to impose its authority and make the notables abide by it. One reason for Majed and his friends' negative feelings was their suspicion about the elite's views and actions concerning the intifada and relations with Israel. They also expressed class resentments. Majed, Yasser, and Nasser even challenged Ghassan Shaka, a representative of one of the prominent Nablus hamulas and a member of Fatah who served as a courier moving PLO funds into the hands of intifada activists, trying to control him or at least limit his power. Without giving further explanation, Majed says, "I got on very well indeed with Ghassan Shaka—after I torched his car." Ultimately, Shaka negotiated informal arrangements with some leaders and militants of the uprising, finding a modus vivendi with them.

Toward the end of the intifada, Fatah and Hamas competed to impose their authority over the population. Hamas refused to be integrated into the UNLU and sometimes developed its own agenda. Strike days were a matter of particular friction. On the ground, there were clashes between some militants who were more concerned with consolidating their power in a certain territory than confronting the Israeli army. According to the place and the period, tension or cooperation would prevail between the two movements. For their part, Majed explains, he and his friends avoided clashes with Hamas and other groups of activists.

Within a few months of the start of their activity, Majed's group became wanted by the Israeli army. Forced to live underground, they made contact with the PLO in Amman and Tunis to obtain material support and formed a secret armed cell. They maintained links with the local resistance command structures while preserving complete freedom of action. Armed with a few light weapons, they concentrated their attacks on army patrols and Israeli settlers. Most of the time they hid alongside roads, waiting for targets to pass by—then they briefly opened fire and ran. A few times, they were successful. They hid in caves, never slept in the same place two nights in a row, and relied on other militants for food and to move around without being caught.

The Israeli Defense Forces (IDF) finally managed to suppress them. In July 1992, Majed, Yasser, and Nasser went to al-Najah University, in the hills of Nablus, to meet one of their contacts. An agent informed the Israeli army, which sealed the campus. Majed and his friends had no intention of giving themselves up, and consequently the army laid siege to the university. After seventy-two hours, the cafeteria ran out of water and provisions and some of the students took ill. Most of the students supported Majed's group, whose existence was proof of their society's resistance to the Israeli occupation. The siege lasted four days. Outside, negotiations were under way between the Israeli military, the International Committee of the Red Cross, and Palestinian political representatives. The compromise they reached averted prison for the activists, who were instead banished from the West Bank on the spot. A vehicle supplied by the Red Cross transported them over the border to the capital of Jordan.

Majed, Yasser, and Nasser began a completely different life in exile. After Amman, the PLO leadership sent them to Baghdad, where they studied and developed a social life. The solidarity among exiles was strong, and they made new connections. Majed became close to Marwan Barghouti, one of the leaders of Shabiba expelled from Ramallah at the beginning of the intifada. On one of their trips back to Amman, Majed, Yasser, and Nasser were introduced to Yasser Arafat as "the heroes of Nablus." Majed couldn't believe it. He kept saying to Barghouti beside him, "Did I really just meet Abu Ammar [Arafat's nom de guerre]? His hand is so tiny!"

THE OSLO ERA AND PALESTINIAN AUTONOMY
(1994–2000)

Israel allowed Majed, Yasser, and Nasser to return in 1995, when the Palestinian Authority (PA) extended its control to Nablus. The three friends supported the peace agreement that gave them the opportunity to end their exile. They trusted their leaders and accepted the two-state solution. Arafat had set up a dozen security services to absorb as many militants and cadres as possible, many of whom wanted to carry on serving their people by joining the police and the armed forces.

Intifada militants were integrated into the lowest ranks of the security forces. In the Gaza Strip, where the PA was first established, Fatah activists joined en masse, using the opportunity to get a secure job and a promising career.

As Hamas and the Palestinian Islamic Jihad, which opposed the peace agreement, perpetrated suicide bombings in Israel, the new Palestinian police were given the task of dismantling the Islamist armed cells and stopping the terror attacks. As part of the Oslo Accords, Israel in essence had subcontracted its security to the PA, and Fatah recruits started arresting and interrogating Hamas militants to protect Israeli citizens.

The General Intelligence bureau recruited Nasser and the Preventive Security Service Majed. Yasser refused to follow his friends, arguing that he couldn't deal with discipline and early mornings. However, he managed to get a not particularly demanding job within Fatah which paid his salary.

At first Majed had to neutralize Palestinian collaborators. But soon the Preventive Security Service was at the forefront of repressing the opposition, and Islamist activists came under his surveillance. When one of them accused him of working for the Israelis, Majed could not cope with this allegation and resigned. He moved to the civil police, which kept him away from politics.

With a steady job and, seemingly, a secure future, he decided it was time to get married. He was looking for a woman with an education and went to al-Najah University to find one. He eventually met Leila, a Nablusi studying for an accounting diploma. It was a personal challenge for a young man from the Balata refugee camp to choose a woman who belonged to a good family of Nablus and had a higher level of education than he did. Leila was aware of their class and social differences, but she admired Majed's nationalist commitment and believed in his promise to start a new life. Both decided to ignore their relatives' qualms. With his guns, Majed intimidated Leila's uncles who opposed their union. His mother considered girls from the middle and upper classes to be fussy and difficult to satisfy, but he didn't listen to his family's warnings about the trouble that bourgeois women could cause.

He covered his new wife with gold, showing everybody that he was able to give her a good life. The couple decided to settle in Ramallah, where life was easier and freer. There they escaped from the austere and conservative atmosphere of Nablus, its strong social stratification, and their families. In Ramallah, Majed had no matters in dispute with the leading families and could enjoy the benefits of his friendship with Marwan Barghouti, who was also living there. In addition, the de facto capital of the PA, Ramallah was more westernized than Nablus—Palestinian immigrants who lived in the United States visited regularly. This economic, political, and intellectual center also attracted migrants from the interior, giving it a mixed population. The PA and a number of other civil servants had settled down in Ramallah as well; Arafat made the Muqata (his compound of buildings which contained the governmental headquarters) his central office instead of Gaza. Leila and Majed were happy in Ramallah, but after a year Yasser and Nasser put pressure on Majed to come back. Yasser had gotten into a fight and needed some support. Friends like Majed's were hard to get away from. Despite Leila's objections, he resolved to return to Nablus. He was going back to the tough place.

Majed focuses on the class conflict in Nablus. As he explains it, "From the British Mandate onward, Nablus was run by its leading families. All that changed with the intifada: children ruled the streets, and we had direct access to Abu Ammar by phone. When the [Palestinian] Authority took over, everything was like before, and the leading families got their power back. Ordinary people had done the fighting, while the bourgeois reaped all the benefits."

Unlike in Gaza or Ramallah, where the PA relied on the Fatah militants massively integrated into the security forces, in Nablus and Hebron Arafat had to take into consideration the powerful families and their alliances with Jordan. As a policeman and an ex-activist of the intifada, Majed believed he had certain rights. He was quick to use his gun to threaten people he argued with. He shot in the air in the office of one of his senior colleagues and was aggressive with a local businessman. Twice Majed's own security apparatus sent him to prison. These were only warnings, though, and Majed resumed his position and his uniform a few days or a few weeks later. Although he was a headache to his superiors, the best way of neutralizing him was to keep him in his job.

But Majed and his friends were disappointed by the treatment they got from the PA, and Majed decided to compensate himself for the injustice. His monthly salary was the equivalent of only $270, which was not sufficient to provide his family with material comforts. Still, he rented a place in a residential part of Nablus and wanted to give the best to his wife and their two young daughters. Even if he spent most of his time in Balata, he derived satisfaction from the fact that his family was used to a certain standard. "I wouldn't go back to live in the camp," he says. "Once you've made progress, there's no looking back. And my daughters get sick when I take them down there."

To support his family's lifestyle, Majed got involved in the car-stealing business: he ensured protection for young men who organized the smuggling with Israeli counterparts and made sure the Palestinian police would not disrupt the thieves' traffic. Later, when the peace process was about to collapse, he got into arms deals. He also helped some businessmen recover their debts from difficult clients, for a share.

The Balata militants tried to reassure themselves that despite appearances, Abu Ammar was on their side. However, gradually they lost patience with Arafat and the returnee-dominated leadership. First, they did not get the recognition they expected for their involvement in the intifada. Second, they were disappointed that Arafat treated the local notables so considerately and favored Palestinians from the outside to locally rooted people. "The people from Tunis" is the name given to the returnees from Arab countries to the territories when Palestinian autonomy was established. Their political and military experience differed from Majed's, as they were active in Jordan and Lebanon during the 1970s and 1980s. The generation of the intifada's leaders felt that this group supplanted them in the first circle of power. Moreover, Majed's cohort thought that the PA was not able to properly negotiate the fate of their people. In the beginning Majed supported the peace agreement. He participated in meetings with Israelis to discuss the issue. But after coming back to Nablus, like all Palestinians he needed an Israeli permit to go to Israel, the Gaza Strip, or anywhere else in the outside world. And the Israeli security services took the view that his activist past was just too heavy. But on several occasions Majed and his friends ignored the regulations, managing to reach Tel Aviv at night and have some fun. He was excited to break the law and felt satisfied that his money allowed him to access entertainment among Jews. Except for these risky trips, he was confined to the area between Hebron in the south and Jenin in the north.

He thought that Oslo would lead to a Palestinian state and freedom of movement for him. New fenced settlements surrounding Nablus in the late 1990s made Israel closer every day but more and more unreachable. In July 2000, when Arafat was participating in the Camp David Summit in the United States, Majed feared that Abu Ammar would not cope with international pressure and would give up on Jerusalem and on the settlements issue. He was relieved when the negotiations were suspended. He was excited as well, thinking that an opportunity for him to return to center stage might be close. In the fall of 2000, Ariel Sharon's provocative visit to the Haram as-Sharif and the Israeli repression of Palestinian demonstrations diverted Majed's anger from the PA.

THE AL-AQSA INTIFADA

By 1999 Majed had changed his mind about the Israelis and Palestinian autonomy. Apparently, Israelis were not credible partners, and there was no way they would let Arafat build a state in the West Bank, East Jerusalem, and Gaza. Since Majed was convinced that Israelis understood only the language of force, he was ready again to kill IDF soldiers and settlers.

The earliest confrontations with the Israelis in this period took place around the tomb of Joseph in Nablus, which was kept under guard by soldiers because a few Jews came there regularly to pray. Majed was immediately active on the spot. Soon his pictures were posted on the Israeli intelligence website: he appeared with teenagers he was training to shoot. After an Israeli soldier got trapped and killed at the tomb of Joseph, the IDF withdrew from the zone. But other military checkpoints surrounded the town and checkered the West Bank. Each Israeli spot was a source of confrontation. Majed, Yasser, and Nasser operated together, trying to reach Israeli soldiers with their bullets. Their chances of success were limited: the lack of territorial depth on the Palestinian side hampered guerrilla tactics. However, the gang of Balata could not simply go back to civilian life. They were wanted by the Israeli army, and because of this they kept constantly on the move, within an area of several square kilometers. By day they avoided the high ground around Nablus, where they might be arrested at army checkpoints or recognized by soldiers watching from the hilltops.

Majed's clandestine life drove him away from his family. He stopped sleeping at home. Several times, Leila was upset and went back to her parents, but she always returned to Majed. He felt that he was unable to be a good husband and father. Loving his wife and daughters to him meant that he had to provide for all their material needs. "They would be better if I leave them with money and die," he said. Sometimes he was too tired to be on the run and wished that everything were finished.

Death appeared as the only escape. Trapped by the IDF, stuck with old friends he could not live without, Majed had lost his chance to change his destiny. Before he met Leila, he had fallen in love with a Canadian woman he could barely communicate with. Despite their differences and their difficulties of exchange, they spent a lot of time together. After a few months, she offered to help him emigrate to Canada. Majed thought about starting a new existence, but he felt he could not shun his fate as a "guy from Balata," from occupied Palestine. He had never worked in a civil environment. Would he be able to have a normal job in a peaceful country? Would he be someone outside Palestine? Escaping from his destiny was both a dream and a nightmare.

By the end of 2000, Majed, Yasser, and Nasser had launched a new armed organization affiliated with Fatah to give direction to the current intifada. They published a leaflet announcing the creation of the al-Aqsa Martyrs Brigades. As militants of the first uprising, the Balata group felt they had a responsibility to carry out, and because they were disappointed with the Palestinian leadership during the Oslo period, they thought they had to take back the initiative.

They now felt strong again in Nablus and decided that during the intifada people should stop having fun. Majed, Yasser, and Nasser went downtown together and burned shops selling alcohol. It was time for fighting: Majed stopped drinking and demanded that everybody respect their nationalist duty and show solidarity with the martyrs killed by Israeli bullets or missiles. Nablus restaurants lost their clients. But if tables stayed empty, it was not because people could not afford to go out. Rich families knew it would be more cautious to stay at home. Majed was not particularly religious or puritan, but in most militants' minds, patriotic duties and recreation were irreconcilable. In addition, his initiative made him feel that he ruled the town again, like in the old days of the First Intifada.

He was especially annoyed with the Nablusi elite, who he believed were trying to stop the intifada to preserve their businesses and to keep intifada militants like Majed under control. "They don't support the intifada, because they have money and they are the ones who can go to Tel Aviv anyway. There is not a single son of these families who participates in the struggle. We never saw one in prison. Ghassan Shaka's son has been in the United States since the intifada started."

Majed was wrong about at least one thing: during a demonstration in 2001, Israeli bullets wounded the son of General Mahmoud al-Aloul, a member of a power family in Nablus and the governor of the town. The treatment the governor's son received, though, was special: an Israeli helicopter evacuated him to a hospital in Tel Aviv. But despite this intervention, Mahmoud al-Aloul lost his child.

Even during violent clashes, contacts remained between a few Palestinian officials and Israeli officers. The Nablus governor and mayor spoke regularly to the commander of the northern region of the West Bank. The aim of the talks was to relieve the tension on the ground. Once Ghassan Shaka and Mahmoud al-Aloul tried to convince Majed, Yasser, and Nasser to stop shooting at the IDF from the center of town. Majed said of the meeting, "They invited us to come and meet them. Ghassan Shaka told me, 'You know, you frighten me because you act and then you think.' I told him he was right. I would be happy to follow his commands in order to fight, but I knew he would never give me any." Pressure was also coming from the inhabitants of Nablus, who refused to be caught by cross fire. In many places in the West Bank, Palestinian residents opposed confrontations and tried to stop armed militants.

Nasser, Yasser, and Majed consented to halt their assaults, but the agreement was fragile. Taking into account moves by the IDF and the actions of Nablusi notables, they could again start their offensive. The PA took other steps to control them. In December 2000, the police confiscated cars stolen in Israel. Officially, the reason was to prevent some gangs of thieves from driving around madly in Nablus and disturbing the town's tranquillity. In fact, the police were trying to reduce the militants' mobility. They burned Majed's car, and Yasser sold his vehicle before the security services could intervene. Majed argued with his superiors and left his job. A few months later, he came back to work and negotiated an arrangement. He was allowed to keep a small car stolen in Israel and to paint it as a police car. But he remained a problem for people among the PA, who made an official decision to arrest him.

He did not worry about this: "Let them try, and we'll see what happens. Anyway, they can't even enter Balata!" With the return of Israeli repression, the PA could not afford to upset armed militants involved in the national struggle. Moreover, the Balata refugee camp offered protection for its people. If Palestinian security forces were to enter the camp to catch one of them, the inhabitants would physically oppose the intervention. Even though many of the people in it supported Fatah and worked for the authority, they presented a united front against attempts to use force against them. Just as the refugees had squeezed out the Israelis, they now refused the Palestinian police admittance to a territory in which they had become a law unto themselves. Indeed, none of the security services took the initiative to come and arrest Majed or his friends. The three even gave protection to a wanted man from Jenin: he stayed in Balata to escape Israeli and Palestinian forces.

Majed was so sure the police would not dare to touch him that he bragged and passed by the police station. As a provocation, he even went into his superior's office and sat down comfortably in his armchair. His boss felt helpless sometimes. He tried to control Majed and to negotiate some limits to his conduct. But because of the strong Israeli repression, the police could not stop their employees who became leaders or militants of the al-Aqsa Intifada. Police forces tried to maintain security and order, but between the PA and the armed activists, the situation on the ground was complex, and it fluctuated according to international pressure. Arafat tried to remain a credible negotiating partner and to use the intifada as a political tool at the same time. Majed believed the road of negotiation was a deadlock. He comments, "I used to support the [Oslo] agreement. I thought the autonomy would become a state. But . . . people who want to shoot at Israelis get arrested by our leadership. I can't cope with that—that's why I left Preventive Security. Abu Ammar is surrounded by people who pressure him."

Majed, Nasser, and Yasser continually discussed the best strategy for fighting the occupation. They had long realized that such methods as shooting at Israeli outposts or Jewish settlers were far from efficient. This risked their lives and endangered the lives of their fellow citizens, usually without hitting the enemy. Demonstrations where teenagers threw stones at Israeli soldiers were a failure; the stones hardly ever reached their intended targets, who were too far away or equipped with sophisticated protective gear. Besides being ineffective, this tactic also proved to be counterproductive, since the IDF killed dozens of young people armed with projectiles. Some Palestinian intellectuals called for the organization of nonviolent forms of struggle, but they were hard put to specify how this could be achieved. Aside from the question of whether or not such tactics were possible, Majed and his friends had no intention of participating in civil resistance campaigns. The idea that became more and more popular was that Israelis understood only the language of force. Among the armed militants of Fatah, some thought Hamas and the Palestinian Islamic Jihad had found a way to invert the balance of force. Should Fatah also carry out suicide attacks? Even if Majed thought Islamist leaders behaved as cowards when they sent young men as kamikazes rather than going themselves, he considered imitating them.

The turning point came only in 2002: the al-Aqsa Martyrs Brigades perpetrated suicide attacks against Israeli civilians. They thus distanced themselves from the policies of their leaders, who had designated the soldiers and the settlers in the

West Bank and the Gaza Strip as the only legitimate targets. Whether Majed's group was behind the shift remains unknown. The fact that the territories were dispersed and the militants isolated contributed to the multiplication of separate groups cut off from one another. Their organization was based on neighborhood connections and affective ties. The loss of one member of the group could sometimes set off a violent reaction. Additionally, in the context of the growing Israeli repression, Fatah militants did not want to be eclipsed by Hamas members who struck at the enemy. Even if the Islamist movement had not achieved a political victory in the territories at the time, Hamas leaders managed to spread their rhetoric, which permeated Palestinian society: negotiating with the Israelis was a mistake, and the Palestinians' moral and religious superiority could overcome their material inferiority; Israelis were afraid to die, while Palestinians were ready to be martyrs.

The IDF carried out a methodical policy of eliminating Palestinian activists. The approaches varied. A booby trap exploded in the office of Jamal Mansur, the Islamist leader in Nablus. It killed six people: four Hamas members, including Mansur, and two journalists who had come for an interview. Majed discovered a man trying to put a bomb under his car. Israeli forces also raided the offices of the Palestinian security services.

In August 2001, as Yasser and Majed were strolling down a narrow street in the old city of Nablus, they were struck by a missile. Some children nearby were slightly hurt. Majed was hit in the leg, Yasser in the head. A doctor rushed out from Jerusalem, but nothing could be done to save Yasser, who died soon after.

Majed, Yasser, and Nasser had made a vow to one another at the beginning of the al-Aqsa Intifada. If one of them was killed, Ghassan Shaka, the mayor of Nablus, would have to pay for it. They firmly believed that some people in Nablus were trying to ruin their political and military strategy and therefore would help the Israelis to get rid of them.

In the meantime, their situation remained precarious. The PA put pressure on its militants to halt their violence. Majed and Nasser had the feeling that Arafat was giving up because of Israeli and American demands. Again the security services tried to neutralize the two. Nasser worked out a compromise and was placed under house arrest by the Palestinian police.

In April 2002, in the course of Operation Road Closed, the Israeli army finally caught Nasser and sent him to a prison in Israel. Majed found himself the last free survivor of the original Balata group. He refused to submit himself and went underground yet again, and even when the Israeli army finally lifted the curfew it had imposed, in early October, he never showed himself in the open, unless it was to move to a safer hideout. To avoid Israeli electronic traps, he juggled mobile phones, through which he issued his instructions to the remaining cells of the al-Aqsa Martyrs Brigades in the West Bank. But the IDF wanted him badly.

In November 2002, they located him in a middle-class area of Nablus where he had been hiding for a few days. The soldiers closed down the town and entered every house of the neighborhood to find him. A military court sentenced Majed al-Masri to ten life sentences.

In April 2004, Ghassan Shaka, the mayor of Nablus affiliated with Fatah, resigned as a sign of protest against the deliquescence of the state of law in the territories. He had escaped an attempt on his life in November 2003, when his brother was killed instead of him. Five months later, nothing had been done to investigate this death: none of the security services had looked into the case or tried to catch the authors of the attack. Among Fatah and the PA, had confusion developed: the al-Aqsa Martyrs Brigades demanded reforms inside the PA and the dismissal of controversial personalities; Arafat condemned their attacks against Israeli civilians and tried to hold together the edifice of power.

Both the strength and the weakness of Majed's group lay in the class dimension of their struggle. Their strong social identification and solidarity enhanced their determination and bravery, but their wariness toward the notables bred intra-Palestinian tensions. The divisions among Palestinians have long weakened the national project. The al-Aqsa Intifada fell apart and Israeli repression and the "security fence" rose, damaging Palestinian society even more. Majed, Yasser, and Nasser are dead or imprisoned. They belong to a generation who chose to fight; however, they had some knowledge about Israel and Israelis and were ready to compromise. The younger generation socialized during the Second Intifada supported and used strong acts of violence. Deprived of any contact with the enemy except for Jewish soldiers and settlers, these youths are condemned to live in a shrunken world, and their almost total ignorance of the other side has nurtured radicalism. Many have developed a quasi-fantasized vision of the Israelis and have difficulties imagining them in human terms. Thus, the martyr approach allows them to entertain the prospect of sending Israelis to death while escaping from their own collective and individual impotence.

PART FIVE

An Impossible Peace, a Shared Future?

THE OSLO PEACE PROCESS, which began officially with the signing of the interim accords on Palestinian self-government in September 1993, was supposed to bring an end to the century-long conflict between Palestinian Arabs and Jews. Seven years later almost to the day, what remained of the negotiating process ground to a standstill with the eruption of the al-Aqsa Intifada. Many factors contributed to the failure of the peace process, including those highlighted in the introductions to the previous sections of this volume. The core of the problem lay in a simple calculus that was already recognized by the settlement movement as a strategic principle in the 1970s: create a system of occupation that is so deeply embedded in the West Bank and involves so many sectors of Israeli society that the costs of uprooting it are far higher than the costs of letting it continue.

This strategy was at the heart of Likud policies in the Occupied Territories after the party came to power for the first time, in 1977. And it has continued in one form or another, regardless of who runs Israel, to the present day. The biggest challenge to the ideological and political focus of the state on settlement was the emergence of globalization in Israel, which produced economic and cultural changes that offered true alternatives to the status quo across the board. A "new Middle East" was how Shimon Peres famously described it, to be achieved through the liberalization of the economy; the incorporation of Israel, and through it the "Palestinian Territories," into a globalized Middle Eastern system; and the gradual fading away of territorially grounded, ethnonational identities and politics that would result from such a process.

Michal Frenkel's portrait, "Benni Gaon: From Socialist to Capitalist Tycoon" (chapter 20), explores how neoliberalism impacted one of the most important forces in the Israeli economy, Koor Ltd., the country's largest industrial conglomerate, which under Gaon's leadership transformed from the epitome of a state-coordinated socioeconomic regime into a privatized, foreign-owned multinational corporation. Gaon's insider-outsider status as a religious Sephardi Israeli who grew up marginalized from the secular and ashkenazi centers of political, cultural, and economic power well placed him to lead this broad institutional transformation. He presented the new Koor as a model for the postsocialist Israeli economy and with other leaders of the Israeli business community tied the new economy to the peace process, offering a vision of mutual Israeli-Palestinian and indeed Israeli-Arab economic development. And in fact, the peace process led to the erosion of the Arab economic boycott of Israel. But rapid economic growth gave the average Israeli a standard of living found in the lower tier of European countries while contributing to growing inequality and poverty. As the Israeli and Palestinian economies became ever more separated, by the intifadas and the building of the separation wall, Palestinians have not benefited from this growth; on the contrary, until recently, their standard of living has plummeted.

The Israeli elite adapted to globalization quite successfully, but other sectors of society became even more marginalized. Yigael Amir, the assassin of Prime Minister Yitzhak Rabin, is one extreme example; the anarchist activist Jonathan Pollak is another. As Michael Feige makes clear in his portrait of the former (chapter 22), before his murder of Rabin, Amir exhibited all the signs of being a normal Israeli. But with that fateful act he was forever embedded in the Israeli, Palestinian, and Middle Eastern psyches, for most as a hate-filled psychopath but for a significant minority as a hero who fulfilled the prophesy, embodied in his name, of bringing redemption to the people of Israel by assassinating an internal enemy of the Jewish people.

Feige's retelling of Amir's life reveals how youth, religiosity, ethnicity, and gender all intersected to produce both Amir's personality and the situation which allowed him to act on his impulse to save the nation by assassinating its leader. In particular, his Haredi education and his unusual exposure to secular society, which shaped his politics, link his experiences to those of David Ariel (see chapter 18).

Bader Araj's portrait of two Hamas suicide bombers, Na'el Abu Hilayel and Maher Hubashi, who killed themselves and twenty-nine Israelis in separate attacks, enters into one of the darkest manifestations of resistance against both the Oslo process and the occupation that continued throughout it (see chapter 21). It reveals them to have been motivated by a potent mixture of religiosity and revenge, with—surprisingly—the thought of concretely aiding in the liberation of their homeland a tertiary consideration, if that. The lives of the two young men included experiences that, however suffused with the everyday violence and indignities of the occupation, did not differ significantly from those of the vast majority of their peers, who either remained on the margins of extreme violence or engaged in more traditional forms of resistance. This narrative also points both to the violent synergy between Palestinian and Israeli violence, and to the importance of Hamas's penetration into so many facets of the daily lives of Palestinians in the Occupied Territories by creating the social networks that provide emotional solidarity and tactical support (but far less economic aid than is generally assumed).

Jonathan Pollak's politics couldn't be more different from those of Hilayel and Hubashi or, indeed, Yigael Amir (see chapter 24). But this twentysomething, like Amir, is a product of the increasing globalization of Israeli-Palestinian politics and identities. One of the leaders of the small but determined anarchist peace movement in Israel, he comes from a long line of rabble-rousers: his grandfather was one of the first workers to take on the Histadrut, in 1951, and his mother took him to his first protest. Thus it was that at three months old, he saw masses of Israelis demand an investigation into the extent of their country's responsibility for the massacre by Israel's Lebanese allies of Palestinian refugees in Sabra and Shatila.

Pollak's activism is a unique combination of animal rights, punk, anarchism, and a concerted focus against the occupation and militarism more broadly in Israeli society. After coming of age as part of the antiglobalization movement in Europe in the early 2000s, he returned home and opposed the intensified occupation in the West Bank, where he quickly became both an activist and, to the extent that it is possible within anarchism, an ideologue, radically critiquing the liberal Zionist peace camp and Israeli society more broadly. In so many ways the antithesis of David Ariel or Yigael Amir, Pollak represents an important if still little-understood point on the continuum of Israeli political culture.

It is clear that the discourses of globalization that circulated in Israel/Palestine in the past several decades have significantly reshaped the contours and extremes of Israeli politics. But Palestinians have not been mere objects in this process, even if it did strengthen rather than mitigate or challenge the occupation. Ala Alazzeh's history of a small refugee camp community center in the West Bank and its founder, "Abu Ahmad and His Handalas" (chapter 25), reveals the challenges and opportunities brought about by the globalization of the Israeli-Palestinian conflict. Abu Ahmad lives in the Beit Jibrin refugee camp in Bethlehem, came of age during the First Intifada, and has spent the past decade working with the children of the al-Aqsa Intifada. Several of them have grown up in and through the center, named Handala after a famous Palestinian cartoon character, and are now putting their own stamp on its goals and programs. Abu Ahmad's evolution from factionalized activist to teacher, educator, and community center organizer reveals how important culture and education have been within the larger context of *sumud,* or steadfastness, in Palestinian society. It also reminds us that while attention is often paid only to members of the Palestinian intellectual and political elites, the grassroots activists on the front lines of the struggle have played an equally important role in sustaining and even developing their society during the four decades of occupation.

Erin F. Olsen offers a fascinating discussion on the life of a young Palestinian woman in "Mais in the War of the Words" (chapter 23), through the prism of language, in particular the language of peace. As Olsen describes it, Mais's story represents the peculiar melting pot of the Holy Land, whose effects become even more interesting when young Israelis and Palestinians meet one another abroad, as students, where they inevitably find themselves flung into the role of representative of their people at round-table discussions, forums, and other settings. In Mais we can see how the "peace industry" and innumerable Track II negotiations have shaped the daily life of a child, then teenager, then young woman who has taken up the role of a Palestinian while recognizing that she must be a global citizen who knows the stories, cultures, and languages of both sides. As important, we come to understand how the malleability of her identity, the product of her relatively privileged position as a citizen of Israel and a Jerusalem Palestinian who moves more or less seamlessly between Arabic, Hebrew, and English, ultimately has given way to an attempt to more narrowly define herself within the realm of one identity, Palestinian. As she concludes, "I have [the] blood running through me or have lived in parts of all of Palestine." How she reconciles her "blood" heritage with her proclivity for a cosmopolitan, postnationalist identity offers many insights for anyone imagining a gradual transition by the younger generation of Israelis and Palestinians away from the ethnonationalist and religious circumscriptions that have defined their communal histories and toward a more open system of representation as a way of achieving the peace and justice that have for so long eluded the Holy Land.

20

Benni Gaon

From Socialist to Capitalist Tycoon

Michal Frenkel

From the final years of Ottoman rule through the 1970s, the socialist Labor movement was the dominant social, political, and economic force within Zionism, the
Jewish community of Palestine, and the Israeli state. Cracks in its hegemony began
to appear in the 1970s, and the 1977 victory of the Likud Party, heir to Labor's
historic nemeses, the Revisionists, shattered the movement's historic dominance.
The arrival in power of Likud accelerated a long-term process that—somewhat
similarly to events in the United Kingdom—by the mid-1980s saw the replacement
of the state-coordinated socioeconomic regime with a neoliberal, market-oriented
ideology and policy.

The socialist and statist ideology of the Labor movement served the political
elite's need to secure its long-lasting hegemony by justifying its policies as the singular expression of a pioneering and state-building ethos. Elected representatives
of the Labor Party (Mapai and its various reincarnations) sought to construct and
maintain an economic system that was largely dependent on the state or owned
by either the state or the General Federation of Jewish Workers in Palestine (the
Histadrut), established in 1920, which was itself affiliated with the Labor movement. As part of this regime, even before the state was founded, the Histadrut
used national capital to establish or acquire industrial and commercial enterprises
that could secure Jewish control over the country's economic infrastructure and
provide a large number of relatively good jobs for party and Histadrut members.
These workers, in turn, supported the Labor Party and were committed to the
reinforcement of the party's political domination.

The archetype of this state-Histadrut-coordinated economy and the flagship of
the Histadrut's economic arm, also known as the Workers' Society, was Koor Ltd.,

Israel's largest industrial conglomerate throughout most of the state-coordinated era. Owing to the financial and political umbrella provided by the Histadrut, and later the state itself, Koor flourished, acquiring and establishing more and more firms in different industrial sectors. Indeed, in 1987 it employed between twenty-five and thirty-four thousand workers in about one hundred different plants, constituting approximately 12 percent of the Israeli industrial sector. However, the transformation of the socioeconomic regime in the mid-1980s shook the ground beneath even Koor's supposedly solid foundations. The underlying principles that had guided both the state-coordinated regime and the management of Koor for more than forty years could no longer secure the corporation's future. In 1987, Israel's largest corporation found itself on the verge of bankruptcy.

The huge bailout program that turned Koor from the epitome of a state-coordinated socioeconomic regime into a privatized multinational corporation—owned by the United States–based Shamrock Holdings—is the most visible sign of the transformation of Israel's socioeconomic regime. The architect of this bailout, and the man whose public biography best represents this transformation, is Benni Gaon (1935–2008), Koor's oft-celebrated CEO and the founder of Gaon Holdings, one of Israel's most prominent private holding groups of the neoliberal era.

AN OUTSIDER-INSIDER

Israel's economy could not have been transformed by the traditional economic elite, whose vision and life experiences could not allow them to turn their back on the well-established institutions they had created. At the same time, lacking political experience and networks, purely professional managers could not have rescued Koor either. It took an insider-outsider, someone like Gaon, to change the direction of such a heavy ship.

Much like its eventual rescue, Koor's crisis was a manifestation of the socioeconomic transition with which it overlapped. While during the state-coordinated economic era, Koor could rely on state and Histadrut resources to secure its steady growth, when the winds of globalization and internationalization started blowing and the state was increasingly reluctant to maintain its generous support, the corporation's prosperity became dependent on foreign investments and loans provided first and foremost by U.S. banks. Drawing on past experience, the foreign bankers, who kept seeing Koor as an arm of the Israeli state, assumed that the government would come to the rescue if a corporate crisis were to emerge. However, when Koor faced difficulties in paying its debts and Israel refused to bail it out, the bankers soon initiated a liquidation process, aimed primarily at putting pressure on the state to pay Koor's debts. In such circumstances, the rescue process was just as dependent on Koor's ability to convince its foreign creditors that it would turn its back on its old, "irrational" ways of conduct and start to act like a "regular," "market-oriented" business firm as it was on the corporation's capacity to persuade state and Histadrut politicians that they should maintain their support and keep bailing it out as if the state-coordinated era had never ended.

Gaon's distinct background and life experiences, in comparison to those of most managers in Koor and in Israel in general at the time, at least partially explain his ability to act against the grain and to contribute to the far-reaching transformation of the Israeli socioeconomic regime. While his meteoric career at Koor and his role as a close campaign advisor to some of the Labor Party's top leaders granted him much-needed political access, his childhood in a self-conceptualized marginalized Sephardi family allowed him to turn his back on some of the sacred norms of managing Histadrut-owned enterprises. This insider-outsider quality, which characterized his biography, personality, and managerial conduct, also defined many of his fellow leaders of the transition era and helps to explain some of the features that are unique to today's market-oriented Israeli economy.

A HINT OF OTHERNESS

The son of Moshe David Gaon, the general secretary of the Sephardic Community Committee of Jerusalem and a marginalized scholar of the history of the Sephardi Jews and their Language (Ladino), Benni Gaon did not share his fellow managers' upbringing in the traditional strongholds of the Labor Party. Instead, he grew up in British Mandatory Jerusalem in a family that valued its historical and religious heritage as much as the new aspirations of Zionism.

The place of the Sephardic Jewish community in the Zionist project, its role in the establishment of Israel, and the demarcation of Sephardic (descendants of Jews who were deported from Spain in the fifteenth century but maintained their traditions in separate communities around the world) and mizrachi Jews (those of Asian and African origin who arrived in Israel after statehood as part of the extensive wave of immigration in the 1950s) have all been highly politicized issues in the history of Israel's identity politics and, as a result, in Gaon's biography. While for religious purposes the term *Sephardim* means all Jews who use a Sephardic style of liturgy, in Israel's history the term *Sephardic* has come to describe the nonashkenazi (non-European) Jews who arrived in Palestine before or during Ottoman Empire rule and developed their community's institutions prior to or in parallel with the first waves of Zionist immigrations from Europe. After statehood, members of the veteran Sephardic community in Israel were sometime considered part of the broader mizrachi ethnic group but in other times and social contexts were seen as a separate, much more prestigious group. Gaon, much like others of the veteran Sephardic community, moved between embracing a mizrachi identity and highlighting the differences between Sephardic and mizrachi identities.

Coming from well-known dynasties in the Jewish world and building on their commercial skills and connections within the Ottoman regime, many Sephardi families were considered the elite of the pre-Zionist Jewish settlement in Palestine. Yet the religious characteristics of this community, which stood at odds with the secularization that characterized the Zionist leadership; their lack of political aspirations and organizations; and especially the different Jewish tradition to which they proudly adhered made this group the ultimate Jewish "other" in the eyes of the European Jews of the prestate years.

The sense of belonging to this ancient and glorified community on the one hand and the rejection it experienced in its encounter with the European Zionists on the other became the engine that drove Moshe David Gaon to dive into his life project: writing the history of the Sephardic Jews, their intellectual heritage in their Diaspora communities, and their contribution to the Zionist project. According to Benni Gaon's autobiography, this project, together with the preparation of full a Ladino dictionary, came to occupy his father's every waking hour. Moshe David's inability to convince scholars at the Hebrew University of the importance of his project or to sell the books in which he invested all his free time and resources left him with strong feelings of bitterness, marginalization, and ethnic discrimination. Yet according to his son, he never ceased to believe in the glorification of the culture he represented or to instill this sense of pride in all four of his children.

His father's ongoing longing for public recognition pervades Gaon's childhood recollections, which are reinforced in the memoirs of his brother, the famous Israeli singer and actor Yehoram Gaon. In his autobiography, Benni Gaon affectionately describes his father's insistence on creating a small Sephardic quorum during the Jewish High Holidays so as to avoid joining the majority of the neighborhood's Jews, who followed ashkenazi traditions. He lauds his father's decision to move him out of the secular but prestigious elementary school in Beit Hakerem, Jerusalem, to a traditional Talmud Torah school in the Sephardic tradition, where he learned to appreciate Jewish religion and heritage. Nostalgia colors his depiction of his school years, such as when he describes physical punishment as a legitimate way to discipline unruly pupils. He attributes his memorization skills, which later helped him in his preparations for business meetings, to his years at the Talmud Torah. He describes his family's home as humble but happy: his father's modest income as a municipality clerk—an inferior position that he attributes to his father's inability to compete with better-networked ashkenazi clerks—provided for a family of seven, including Gaon's grandmother. Gaon also underlines their positive feelings toward Arab culture, represented by his brother's tendency to dress up as an Arab for Purim. He mentions this to distance his family, or his community, from European Zionism, which distinguished itself by the rejection of any sign of

Arab affiliation and therefore forced later Jewish immigrants from the Arab world to turn their backs on their cultural origins.

In Gaon's telling, his Sephardi origins and the ethnic-based marginalization that his father experienced shaped his life experience and constructed his idiosyncratic world view, despite his long-term affiliation with the old economic elite. This unique vantage point, he argued, allowed him to understand what his fellow businesspeople and political leaders failed to see. For instance, Gaon claimed that his understanding of the political development of the 1990s was better than that of his colleagues since he could juxtapose the Sephardic world of traditionalism and spiritualism that had characterized his childhood environment with the business circles within which he built his career: "It was clear to me in September 2002 that the cultural gap between the social circle of Shas [a mizrachi-religious party aiming at improving mizrachim social and economic status] voters and the social circle within which the Israeli business world operates remained wide and complicated. I realized that these are two parallel universes: one in which biblical law is valued, and another in which it is considered as questionable mysticism." His take on this gap reflects his experience in bridging it. As he presents it: "[I am] the son of Moshe David Gaon, the great documenter of oriental Judaism, a Ladino poet who passed away with a bitter taste of ethnic discrimination in his mouth grounded in his unaccidental and sequential failures to be promoted in his workplace at the Jerusalem municipality, yet I am also a businessman, a son of a 'Frank' [a derogatory nickname for Sephardi Jews] who learned that in the business world, color is not everything."

Gaon mentions one incident in which his Sephardi origins were used to humiliate him. An Israeli newspaper article describing his meeting with Bankers Trust, a $25 million creditor of Koor at the time, said that the U.S. bankers did not trust him, owing to his "Oriental table manners." "It seems as if the reporter wanted to describe the gap in mentality between me, the uncivilized Oriental from Jerusalem, and the polite, well-perfumed Americans," Gaon writes. "Was I angry? Yes. Was I insulted? Yes. Yes, because it was rubbish. Bankers Trust simply wanted their money back. . . . They did not care if they got it from an ashkenazi [European] Jew, a mizrachi, an Ethiopian, or a Circassian."

His ultimate revenge for such humiliating events (which he describes as sporadic) was the establishment of the Moshe David Gaon Center for Ladino Culture at Ben-Gurion University, which celebrates his father's accomplishments. He also tells fellow mizrachi businesspeople that they should stop feeling tormented: "You are who you are, and you deserve to be envied more than you envy others. Try not to hate others but love yourself. Remember that even I, Benni Gaon, was mentioned once as someone who has Arab table manners." To this he adds a list of successful Sephardi Israeli businessmen whose fame, he argues, is grounded in hard work rather than opportunities based on affirmative action. The business heritage these people leave behind them, Gaon stresses, is nonetheless their own. It belongs to successful individuals and not to any ethnic collective.

It is important to recall, however, that while in recent years distinctions between the Sephardic elite and the poststatehood immigrants from Asian and African countries (mizrachim) have blurred, neither Gaon nor his family suffered the discrimination that characterized the treatment of later waves of immigration by the Zionist establishment. In fact, Gaon mentions that his fellow managers at Koor, all of whom were ashkenazim, often told him that he was not a real mizrachi but rather part of the veteran Sephardic elite. Furthermore, while he treats mizrachim as a homogenous group facing ethnic discrimination, his examples of successful mizrachi businessmen are mostly from elite Sephardic families. And at times, like most members of the Sephardic elite, he protests against the overrepresentation of the experience of Moroccan Jews in the general struggle of mizrachim to gain recognition, claiming that this marginalizes the experience of stronger mizrachi groups, such as the veteran Sephardic establishment and immigrants from Iraq.

The juxtaposition of marginalization and pride, of being part of an elite group that is also an "ethnic other," and of belonging to and being rejected by the Zionist elite prepared Gaon well for his future mission as the leader of one of the Zionist elite's greatest projects—namely, Koor—which he led in an entirely new direction.

KOOR'S FAVORITE SON

Gaon started his career as an air-conditioning technician, a trade he acquired during his military service. He joined Electra Air Conditioning Ltd. before taking up his first marketing job in a Koor-owned company, Ramla Engines Industry. When Ramla merged with Tadiran Ltd., another of Koor's corporations, Gaon took over the air-conditioning unit and turned it into a larger division focusing on consumer goods. Between 1971 and 1977, he was the CEO of that division. In 1975, he moved to Europe for the first of his two six-month periods of advanced business education at the International Management Institute (IMI), now the highly regarded International Institute for Management Development (IMD) in Lausanne, Switzerland. Unlike other business schools, IMI was not part of any university. It was founded by Alcan Ltd., Canada's largest aluminum company, and today IMD still prides itself on its practical orientation.

After Gaon completed his studies, Meir Amit (a onetime general in the Israeli military and one of Gaon's predecessors at Koor) asked him to launch another Koor company, Koor Sachar, Europe (Koor Trading Europe Ltd.). Gaon located it in the Netherlands and within five years turned it into a $200 million company with ten offices across the continent. Koor Sachar in Europe enjoyed its success during Koor's heyday, when, riding on the success of its arms industry, Koor prospered and strengthened its leading position in the Israeli economy despite growing criticism of its "irrational" management.

Gaon's success at Koor Sachar, together with his international experience, paved the way for his nomination in 1982 as CEO of the Co-Op. Owned by the Workers' Society, the economic arm of the Histadrut, the Co-Op was an old-fashioned cooperative supermarket chain. A large but low-profile firm, it provided Gaon with excellent experience of top-level management unhindered by opposition, and he transformed it into a successful corporation that was traded on Wall Street. A key component of his strategy was sending store managers abroad for educational tours, then asking them to duplicate the models they had seen. His experience in marketing, plus the fact that this grand transformation did not require much turnover of personnel, smoothed the change, contributing to Gaon's reputation as a successful manager who was able to salvage and modernize companies he worked at. Yeshayahu Gavish, a renowned Israel Defense Forces commander in the Six-Day War and Koor's CEO at the time, took note of Gaon's success and asked him to head Koor's food division but refused to nominate him as one of Koor's deputy CEOs. Gaon preferred to stay at the Co-Op.

In 1987, when Koor's deficits of $250 million and its general debt of $1.2 billion were exposed and its bankruptcy was seen as almost inevitable, Gavish resigned. Gaon's self-publicized perfect managerial record led Israel Keisar, the general secretary of the Histadrut, to ask him to take on Koor's rescue as a personal mission, as CEO.

In support of the purely professional image he endeavored to establish during his years at Koor, Gaon mentions his political relations within the Histadrut, the Labor Party, and the state in his pre-Koor era only rarely and in passing. The media archives documenting his career, however, tell a different story. He was in fact part of a closely knit political network within the Labor Party. In 1986, for example, he was credited as one of the leading figures behind the Labor Party Convention. He later successfully led Keisar's campaign for Histadrut general secretary, thus tightening his bond with the sponsor and close friend who would make him Koor's general manager. He was also close to Uzi Baram, the general secretary of the Labor Party, who considered Gaon a personal friend and a brilliant marketer, and he worked hand in hand with Shimon Peres during the 1987–88 election campaign. Beyond the professional services he provided as a highly committed marketing consultant to his friends and allies in the party, Gaon, along with Yossi Beilin and others, was one of the founders of the younger generation's Mashov Circle within the Labor Party. Between 1982 and 1992, this group promoted the semi privatization of the Workers' Society, the adoption of a progressive but less socialist "new Labor" agenda, and efforts to break the impasse in the peace process. Gaon, then, was as much a political leader as a professional manager.

Thus while he projected a professional managerial identity, Gaon's political position was undoubtedly a critical ingredient of his managerial career. His identity as a complete insider (the favorite son) but not a member of Koor's "native-born" managerial elite makes him the ultimate representative of the in-between generation in Israel's business leadership, a group that could capitalize on the political, cultural, and social assets of the old Labor Party and transform it from within.

A TRANSFORMATIONAL LEADER

In Gaon's view, the rescue of Koor consisted of combining three separate but interdependent projects: (1) the transformation of the corporation's different units from labor- to business-oriented firms; (2) the engagement of Israel's economic leadership, both right and left wing, and bankers in the rescue mission; and (3) the mobilization of foreign support for the process that would eventually make Koor an international corporation. While the combination of Gaon's in-between Israeli position and his international experience should have enabled him to succeed on all fronts, his account suggests that his skills at that point were not sufficient to win the fight on the third front and that what he learned during the struggle changed his business manners and helped him become a leading figure in Israel's postsocialist globalized economy.

When he accepted Keisar's request that he become Koor's CEO, Gaon knew that the Workers' Society's economic flagship was sinking rapidly. Indeed, a secret report that an independent consultancy firm prepared for his predecessor described Koor as a huge aircraft flying at full speed in a cloudy sky with broken navigational instruments. Gaon's job was to provide it with new navigational tools and put it back on course.

Today there is wide agreement that to rescue Koor, Gaon had to close or sell unprofitable enterprises, cut wage and other labor benefits, weaken the company's very strong workers' committees, and reorganize the entire corporation. At the time, though, he faced extreme opposition from his predecessors, who claimed that he was to blame for the situation; from right-wing commentators, who thought that there should be no attempt to rescue Koor, especially not under the auspices of the Histadrut, and that bankruptcy was the only solution; and from workers and left-wing commentators, who saw his moves as the last nail in the coffin of Israel's humane, semisocialist economy.

The Koor whose reins Gaon took up was an insolvent corporation. In 1988, it could no longer pay its debts to international or Israeli creditors. Given the long history of Histadrut and state guarantees of its debts and its central part in the Israeli economy, the international creditors expected the Israeli government to cover Koor's liabilities. They also thought that since 1988 was an election year, the Labor

Party would not allow its flagship to collapse and, furthermore, given Gaon's close affiliation with party and state leadership, he could convince it to pay Koor's loans. It was on this front that Gaon failed.

After firing Shevach Offir, Koor's highly influential financial manager who was also the middleman between the corporation and the foreign banks, Gaon soon lost the international creditors' trust. Offir, whom he held responsible for Koor's collapse, became a bitter enemy. In his autobiography, Gaon blames Offir for feeding the new management inaccurate data concerning the corporation's financial situation and for giving the international creditors false internal information, which reduced their trust in Koor and Gaon. For his part, Offir argued that Gaon chose to present an overly optimistic picture aimed at deceiving the bankers. There is no disputing the painful outcome of this loss of trust, which for three long years overshadowed Koor's rescue efforts. The foreign banks threatened and eventually attempted to dismantle Koor and requested that Israeli courts declare it bankrupt.

Yigal Arnon, one of Israel's most esteemed lawyers, a well-known negotiator, and the then-chairman of the Israeli First International Bank (one of Koor's creditors), eventually restored a degree of trust between Koor and its foreign creditors. It was under his leadership, and with Finance Minister Shimon Peres's personal intervention, that the foreign bankers agreed to forgo part of Koor's debt and thus paved the way for a general settlement that allowed for the company's survival. It took until September 1991 for the Israeli state to provide the guarantees needed to close the deal, and only then could Koor embark on a new path, one that involved detaching itself from the Histadrut. Gaon's main contribution to this agreement lay at the Israeli end. His political connections allowed him to harness the state, the Histadrut, and the Israeli banks in rescuing Koor, and he left his most fundamental mark as the man behind the company's reorganization. His phenomenal success during the previous three years in turning Koor into a lean and profitable corporation—signaling its vitality and right to exist—made it much easier for the creditors to decide to support it. Gaon's long-term experience with Koor and the Workers' Society on the one hand and his complex affiliations with the organization's old elite on the other facilitated the corporation's transformation.

It is important to note, however, that improving efficiency meant the loss of thousands of quality jobs that had offered relatively high income and fringe benefits to workers in Israel's social periphery. Attempting to break workers' resistance to the massive layoffs, Koor took measures that, until then, even privately held firms had considered unacceptable. The fact that a Histadrut-owned firm hired armed strikebreakers, who used dogs to suppress the striking workers, led to extremely strong condemnations of Koor and Gaon. In his book he argues that he was not aware of those actions at the time, but this became a stain on his otherwise quite clean career.

GAON AS MANAGER

While the common wisdom in Israeli history describes Koor's management before the crisis as driven by political aspirations rather than business orientations, Gaon was by no means its first professionally oriented manager. Nor was the reorganization he led the first such process that the corporation undertook. As an amalgam of dozens of firms, established or acquired for different reasons from different local and international sources, Koor had long been characterized by diverse corporate cultures, managerial systems, and attitudes toward the Histadrut and the Workers' Society's political aims. While some of its firms were created with the intention of providing jobs for new immigrants in development towns, others, like Tadiran, had been previously owned by international corporations and seemed to be run on a purely professional basis.

Throughout its forty-four years of operations before Gaon became CEO, Koor had been a pioneer in the introduction of advanced human resources models of management, from scientific management and human relations to sociotechnical systems and quality circles. However, the introduction of these systems was always partial and implemented through negotiations with unions and workers' committees at the plant and Histadrut levels. Because of Koor's affiliation with the Histadrut and its high level of unionization, the dependence of the Histadrut leadership on the electoral support of the chairs of the plant-level workers' committees, the Labor Party's quest for industrial peace in the firms affiliated with it, and the fact that many of the firms were security related, which, in the context of Israel at the time, secured high and steady income, the working conditions in most of Koor's units, regardless of their efficiency or profitability, were far better than the Israeli average.

Another of Koor's features was the financial system known in Hebrew as *mislaka*. This system subsidized failing firms with the profits from successful ones, making it unnecessary for Koor's less-successful firms to reorganize but difficult to depict the company's real financial situation. By 1988, though, its corporate losses were so severe that successful firms could no longer cover for the failing ones. Significantly, since by then the Labor Party had lost its predominance to Likud, which made it less likely that the state would come to Koor's rescue, Gaon's many opponents and potential rivals clearly understood that his failure could lead to the total collapse of Koor and the loss of their own jobs. This helped Gaon to implement the moves that his predecessors had been unable to carry out. In his first three years as CEO, he fired two-thirds of Koor's employees and closed or sold fifty of its eighty plants. During that time, productivity rose from 190,000 to about 285,000 new Israeli shekels per person per annum. In 1991, after five years of continual losses, Koor declared itself profitable.

It is difficult to estimate Gaon's personal contribution to Koor's rescue. His supporters attribute the corporation's resurgence to many of his real and supposed features. His superb human relations allowed him to win the workers' trust above the heads of their militant leaders. His close acquaintance with the Histadrut system enabled him to navigate the stormy waters of labor relations within the union-owned industrial giant, and his experience as a manager in several of Koor's corporations facilitated his understanding and manipulation of the power structure in both organizations. His well-marketed success at the Co-Op gave him some credit among the workers who had not been dismissed, while his political ties secured backing for even extremely unpopular and brutal layoffs. From his own point of view, the skills behind his unquestionable success were, above all, directly communicating with workers at different levels of the corporate hierarchy—but primarily manual workers—and presenting himself as a role model by working long hours and cutting his own salary. Gaon attributes his ability to establish direct communication to his modest upbringing away from the Israeli elite. He certainly milked his success for all it was worth and became an iconic figure of the managerial class of Israel's new globalized, private-oriented economy in the early 1990s.

MANAGING KOOR AS A TRANSFORMING EVENT

Koor's detachment from the Histadrut's Workers' Society and its privatization were transforming events for Gaon, his partners in the Mashov Circle, and many other members of his generation in the Israeli social and economic elite, leading them to conclude that despite its former contribution to the Labor Party's domination, the economic establishment associated with the Histadrut and the party had become a liability.

Writing in retrospect, Gaon tends to conceal his faith in the importance of a Histadrut-owned economic sector in his first years at Koor. Here and there, though, he writes about how he was the last "socially" rather than business-oriented CEO and how he struggled to hold on to Koor as a Workers' Society–owned corporation. However, he reports that after 1991 he reconsidered this position and came to believe that Koor should be privatized and sold to a larger, international company. During Koor's recuperation, it seems that he concluded that the corporation's affiliation with the Histadrut, however minor that might have remained, would only hinder its progress. In 1995, when the Workers' Society was forced to sell its stake in Koor, Gaon acted as the engine of the transaction, which was considered the largest in Israel's history. The Workers' Society sold its 22 percent ownership for $252 million to the United States–based holding company Shamrock, which in 1988 had been willing to pay only $70–100 million for 50 percent of Koor. Gaon remained the company's manager until 1998, leading it to a $400 million Wall Street stock issue in November 1995.

In 1997, Koor changed hands again when the Bronfman family bought it. The background for this transaction was Shamrock's dissatisfaction with the share value and the refusal of Bank Hapoalim, one of Koor's major Israeli shareholders, to dismantle the firm and sell it off in parts. For his part, Gaon did not like the idea of spinning off different parts of Koor and preferred to expand its investments abroad as a way of increasing share value. At first the Bronfmans seemed to accord with this general view, and their investment secured Koor's place as the flagship of the Israeli economy, but disagreements between them and Gaon emerged a few months later, and they forced him to leave the company.

Gaon's experiences at Koor, turning it from a sinking boat owned by the Workers' Society to a corporation traded on Wall Street and reporting first and foremost to international stakeholders, transformed his understanding of business conduct and management. Drawing on his golden parachute, his international relations and experience, and his reputation, he wasted no time in setting up Gaon Holdings. Not surprisingly, despite his many successful years at Koor, his insider-outsider position affected the capital structure of Gaon Holdings. To his surprise, people who had sought his acquaintance when he was Koor's CEO refused to invest with him, so in addition to his own wealth, his new company was backed by international businessmen of Sephardic origin, who tended to see his success as proof of his personal rather than political skills. It is interesting to note, however, that even as a private businessman representing private capital with no official political aim, Gaon could not adapt to the new Israeli spirit of neoliberal capitalism altogether. He had become one of the tycoons of Israel's new economy, but his national sentiments and old-economy instincts remained in place. Unlike most post-transformation Israeli business leaders, Gaon did not distinguish between his business and socially oriented activities. He combined a strong business orientation with a twist of old-school Zionism in building his company's portfolio. Ignoring the conventional wisdom of investing in the fast-growing Israeli high-tech industry, Gaon favored the retail sector (which brought his experience at the Co-Op and his marketing skills into play), old-economy businesses, and the agriculture and water industries (considered areas of Israeli expertise and important aspects of sustainability in Israel and the Middle East in general).

In his autobiography, Gaon hardly mentions his active political engagement. His second book, *Benni Gaon,* follows the example of American management legends, such as Lee Iacocca or Jack Welch. In this work, addressed to an imaginary young businessman, he offers advice and even presents his experiences in fighting cancer as an example of good management. Gaon took much pride in his involvement in Israel's Management Center (known by its Hebrew acronym, MIL), a previously semigovernmental professional association that he privatized and strengthened. He also became active in philanthropy, chairing the Israel Cancer Association before he fell sick with the disease. Yet his political aspirations never disappeared completely. While he claims to have refused several attempts to include him in the Labor Party's list of candidates for parliament, he openly admits his desire to have been the minister of finance or to have taken some other executive position in Yitzhak Rabin's administration. He was passionately involved in the attempt to implement Shimon Peres's vision of "a new Middle East," through both his business and public initiatives. Gaon got involved in Israeli-Egyptian projects when at Koor and later on in Israeli-Jordanian business initiatives, and he was the chairman of the Israeli-Jordanian Chamber of Commerce. He was one of the first investors in an Israeli-Arab venture capital fund aimed at investing in joint business initiatives. On the public-political front, Prime Minister Rabin sent him to meet the Palestinian leader Yasser Arafat before the Israeli-Palestinian peace process had been made official, and he was an active supporter of Arab-Israeli social collaboration.

Gaon personalizes the argument that the new economic and business elite, driven by their interest to open up global markets and increase international investments in Israeli firms, supported the Israeli-Palestinian peace process and helped to reconceptualize the conflict in economic terms rather as a purely political issue of national security. However, while this is often presented as a critique of Israel's peace process and its self-interested promoters, the capitalist elite, Gaon seems to have been a most ardent supporter of the thesis, claiming that mutual business interests constituted the strongest guarantee of the survival of the otherwise fragile peace agreement.

In 2008, Gaon died of cancer, a disease against which he fought twice: personally, and in his capacity as the long-term president of the Israel Cancer Association.

SUGGESTIONS FOR FURTHER READING

Murphy, Emma. "Structural Inhibitions to Economic Liberalization in Israel." *Middle East Journal,* Vol. 48, No. 1 (Winter 1994), pp. 65–88.

Shafir, Gershon, and Yoav Peled. *Being Israeli: The Dynamics of Multiple Citizenship.* Cambridge: Cambridge University Press, 2002.

Shalev, Michael. "Zionism and Liberalization: Change and Continuity in Israel's Political Economy." *Humboldt Journal of Social Relations,* Vol. 23, Nos. 1–2 (1997), pp. 219–59.

21

From Religion to Revenge

Becoming a Hamas Suicide Bomber

Bader Araj

The second Palestinian intifada, or "uprising," triggered by the visit of Ariel Sharon to the Temple Mount, or Haram as-Sharif, on 28 September 2000 and lasting until 2005, was far deadlier than any other confrontation between Israelis and Palestinians in the West Bank and the Gaza Strip since 1967. It started two months after the failure of a serious attempt to find a solution to the Israeli-Palestinian conflict at Camp David, where the Israeli government had been willing to make the biggest concessions ever, so from the Israeli perspective it presumably showed that the Palestinians were trying to force them to offer more concessions. The timing was challenging for Israel in several ways. Since the uprising erupted four months after the Israeli withdrawal from Lebanon, the Israeli military could not let another challenge to its power pass without proving it still retained its once-vaunted deterrent capability. In addition, the first months of the intifada coincided with the Israeli electoral campaign, and Prime Minster Ehud Barak wanted to show the Israeli public that his policies toward the Palestinians were no softer than those of his rival, Ariel Sharon. The confluence of these factors may explain why the Israeli army adopted a harsh and repressive policy from the very beginning of the uprising despite the fact that the levels and kinds of violence of the Palestinian protest, at least during its first three months, were roughly similar to the demonstrations, marches, and stone throwing of the First Intifada (1987–93). Harsh Israeli repression, in turn, partially explains why the second uprising witnessed an unprecedented number of suicide attacks: of the approximately 200 Palestinian suicide bombings since they first employed this tactic, in 1993, 173 were conducted during the Second Intifada.

This chapter explores the lives of two Hamas suicide bombers, Naʾel Abu Hilayel and Maher Hubashi, who killed themselves and twenty-nine Israelis in separate attacks during the height of the Second Intifada, in December 2001 and November 2002, respectively. Both were members of Hamas, though their motivations for becoming suicide bombers differed.

Hamas, the first Palestinian and Sunni religious organization to employ suicide bombing, in 1993, was established in December 1987, a few days after the eruption of the first Palestinian intifada. Until the 1980s, Muslim fundamentalists in the West Bank and Gaza were affiliated with the Muslim Brotherhood and little involved in direct confrontation with Israel. The 1979 Iranian Revolution shook the political quiescence of brotherhood members in Palestine by demonstrating that radical Muslims could mobilize to overthrow a powerful, United States–backed regime. This assertiveness became the hallmark of the First Intifada, which gave young Palestinian activists an opportunity to become politically involved and revolt against the reform-minded older generation. Misperceiving Islamism as a conservative counterforce to the nationalist Palestine Liberation Organization, the Israeli government permitted the founding of Hamas in 1987 and the funneling of money from Saudi Arabia to the new organization. It even allowed Hamas activists to speak publicly, organize, publish, and demonstrate while punishing the PLO for similar actions.

Unlike the PLO, which explicitly recognized Israel in 1988 and then again with the Oslo Accords, Hamas has never officially assented to recognize Israel, at least not in advance of a permanent agreement that would satisfy core Palestinian demands regarding territory and refugees. Believing that Israel's influence over U.S. policy made any American-sponsored negotiating process futile, Hamas leaders concluded that "we must depend on the nation's options of jihad and resistance rather than American or other mediations." Within this paradigm, large-scale violence, and suicide bombings in particular, were understood as a way to exact a high enough price from Israel to force it to make desired concessions. As the Gaza-based leader Khalil abu Laila explained, "Martyrdom operations enabled us to get rid of the unjust Oslo Accords, put the Palestinian cause back on the right path, mobilize the Palestinians around the choice of resistance, and attract Arabic and Islamic attention and support. . . . They also put an end to the Zionist dream of expanding Israel to include the area between the Nile River and the Furat [Euphrates] River. Instead, and for the first time, martyrdom operations forced the Israelis to separate themselves from the West Bank by building a wall and hiding behind it." This was the strategic aspect of Hamas's rationale. Equally important were the retaliatory considerations. As the Hamas leader Abd al-Fattah Dukhan (who many people believe wrote Hamas's first communiqué) argued, "They [the Israelis] target our civilians all the time, [so] martyrdom operations treat them the same way. . . . Our first suicide attacks came to avenge the killing of twenty-nine Palestinians in the al-Harem al-Ibrahim [in 1993] as well as the massacre that took place earlier in the al-Aqsa Mosque [in 1991]." Given both considerations, it's not surprising that Hamas also believed that it was legitimate to strike Israel inside its 1948 borders, where both of the suicide bombings discussed in this chapter occurred, rather than limiting them to the Occupied Territories.

NA'EL ABU HILAYEL AND THE ROLE OF RELIGION

"I do not want to marry a woman from this life but women from the afterlife [the seventy-two virgins that the Qur'an promises to martyrs]." These were the words of Na'el Abu Hilayel, a twenty-two-year-old Palestinian suicide bomber, to his uncle three days before he blew himself up, on 21 November 2002. Many Palestinian men of Na'el's age, especially those who, like him, did not pursue a university education, get married. But his words did not surprise people who knew him well.

According to his parents and brother, Na'el had been religious since his childhood. As young as eight, he prayed regularly in the mosque. Later he used to fast not only for the month of Ramadan, not eating or drinking anything from sunrise to sunset, but also on many "extra days," as the most religious Muslims often do throughout the year. He also used to lead people in prayer (a task that sheikhs usually undertake). Na'el memorized the entire Qur'an and always carried a small copy of the holy book in his pocket. Even while working with his father in Bethlehem's vegetable market, when fewer customers approached the stall, he would steal some moments to read verses from the Qur'an.

Na'el's father, Azmi, was fifty-three years old when I interviewed him in 2006. He had a long black beard peppered with white hairs and often uttered Islamic religious citations when speaking to indicate to listeners his deeply held religious beliefs. Na'el was also influenced, but probably to a lesser degree, by his mother, a homemaker, who was forty-five when I met her in the family's house that summer. She was wearing a full dress and a *hijab* (head covering), whose end she used to wipe the tears that formed in her eyes when talking about her late son despite the three and a half years that had passed since his death.

Spending most of his life in the Governorate of Hebron, well known as a conservative region of the West Bank and a base for religious Palestinian organizations, especially Hamas, also likely influenced Na'el's strongly religious sensibility. Indeed, he made a tour of the mosques where he regularly prayed in the last month of his life in preparation for his suicide bombing. He only shaved his beard two days before his death. His mother, surprised, did not know that the shaving was part of his preparation to carry out a suicide attack—religious Palestinian suicide bombers typically shave their beards right before participating in a suicide mission to be able to enter Israeli towns and crowds without raising any suspicion. Hours before his death, Na'el, who was fasting, was seen praying in the Khalifa Umar bin al-Khattab Mosque, built near the Church of Nativity about fourteen centuries ago when Muslims first came to spread Islam in the Holy Land.

Na'el's father recalled his last meeting with his son with mixed feelings of pride and sadness:

> He came back from the mosque with a glowing face and apologized for not being able to replace me so I can have my turn to pray. He pointed to the other side of the [open] marketplace and said, "Some of my friends are waiting for me." I did not know that was the last time I would see him. He left and never came back. He called me from his mobile phone after half an hour, telling me he had to go to the northern area [of the West Bank] to take care of some important matters. The next morning, I learned from Israeli media that the Palestinian who blew himself up on bus number 20 in Jerusalem was my son. . . . May God have mercy upon him. He always cared about the afterlife, not this life. . . . He realized his wish to die as a martyr.

Na'el carried out his attack at seven in the morning on 21 November 2002. He wore an explosive belt packed with five kilograms of explosives and shrapnel, boarded a crowded public bus at Mexico Street in Jerusalem, and detonated the explosives while in the suburban neighborhood of Kiryat Menachem on the way to the next stop. Before boarding, Na'el dropped his personal identification—which the Israelis found soon after the attack and which noted his place of residence—a move his father, citing some analysts who commented on the event, thinks was intentional, to send a message to Israel's prime minister that Israeli military operations in Bethlehem in the preceding months had failed to prevent Palestinian suicide bombers from reaching their targets in Israeli cities and towns.

The attack killed eleven Israelis, including five children who had boarded the bus to go to their schools on that cold morning, and injured more than fifty people, some seriously. Hamas claimed responsibility and described the attack as "revenge."

Despite Na'el's religiousness, many of those who knew him were astonished that this quiet and somewhat shy young man would carry out a suicide attack, but close friends and family members were less surprised, as they were aware of his involvement in Palestinian resistance in the past. As a child and a teenager, he had participated in some of the First Intifada's activities, such as throwing stones at Israeli soldiers. A local newspaper, in fact, published a picture of him throwing stones during that period.

Na'el's father thinks his son was influenced by the massacre that the Israeli settler Baruch Goldstein carried out in Hebron in 1994. Goldstein opened fire inside the Cave of the Patriarchs mosque, killing twenty-nine Palestinians, an event Palestinians often link to their first suicide bombing campaign, which preceded the Second Intifada. It is likely that Na'el was also affected by his father's arrest and torture by Israeli occupation forces in 1973 for allegedly throwing a grenade at an Israeli military facility in Bethlehem. (He was released after eighteen days due to the lack of evidence and the absence of a confession.)

In the years that followed Goldstein's attack, the Oslo peace process continued, and with it an intensification of both settlement activity and conflict between Palestinians and Jews in the Hebron region. During this period Na'el was heard saying several times that Palestinians should take revenge for the Goldstein massacre. His mother recalled seeing him one day "sharpening a knife at both edges." She did not know at the time that her seventeen-year-old son was planning on stabbing an Israeli soldier. He changed his mind at the last minute to avoid hurting a Palestinian mother and her daughter, who were passing by when he was about to approach the soldier. One of his friends heard him talking one day about that event: "I was a coward in the last moments. . . . It was difficult. . . . I was worried about that mother and her daughter who came from nowhere. I was afraid that the soldiers might start shooting in all directions if I attacked one of them."

The Second Intifada, which erupted when Na'el was almost twenty years old, provided him with the opportunity he was looking for to achieve his dream of becoming a martyr and inflicting maximum damage on the enemy. He published a telling short article in a local newspaper during the first year of the Second Intifada. Here is its full text:

> On a calm summer night, I sat as I usually do, reading and thinking about God's Book [the Qur'an]. It was late. . . . I fell asleep while the book was still in my hand and heart. [Suddenly] I woke up because of the noises made by the atrocious feet, the feet of the rapist [Israeli] soldiers hitting everything and in every direction. They took me while I was unconscious to the interrogation room. I saw many questions in the eyes of their frenzied dogs and heard too many voices: *Confess . . . confess.* I agreed: *I will confess, I will tell everything.* I will tell about the mourning [Palestinian] mothers and the whimpers of the injured. I will tell about the demolished homes and ripped olive trees which they pulled from their roots, our roots. I will confess that I ate bread dipped in blood and drank glasses of bitterness, the last of which was the massacre in the al-Aqsa Mosque [referring to the Palestinians killed on 28 September 2000 and the following days when Ariel Sharon, then the leader of the Israeli opposition, visited the mosque] and what has followed it and what will follow if we remain silent. I will keep confessing and confessing and confessing.

Na'el's story references examples of the Israeli repression of the Palestinians which he thought would only grow in intensity if the Palestinians did not react. This text also shows his deep religious feelings and the effect of his father's 1973 experience on him. Its themes confirm that Na'el was motivated primarily by religious inspiration and secondarily by the desire for revenge. Unlike many Palestinians, he was never arrested or injured by the Israelis. However, his deep religious commitment and strong sense of national belonging made him feel that Israeli attacks on his people were personal attacks on him.

Muslims use the terms *martyr* and *martyrdom* in a religious context to refer to individuals who give their lives for the sake of Muslims and Islam. There is a debate among Muslim clerics whether suicide bombers are martyrs. However, most clerics consider Palestinian bombers to be martyrs since they die in the context of liberating their occupied land and attack civilians only as a reaction to the killing of Palestinian civilians by the Israeli army. The renowned French sociologist Émile Durkheim would call this reaction an "altruistic suicide," a rare—in his time—form of suicide which, he argued, tends to be most frequent among tightly integrated groups.

My talks with the Abu Hilayel family were part of eighty-seven interviews that I conducted in 2006 to understand this type of suicide: forty-five with senior leaders of the six most influential Palestinian organizations, such as Hamas and Fatah (about seven leaders from each organization), and forty-two with close relatives and friends of suicide bombers in the year that followed the Second Intifada. The interviews' aim was to examine the veracity of the five main motivations of suicide terrorists suggested by social scientists: psychopathology, culture (religion), rational choice, harsh state repression, and deprivation. The last can be either absolute—longstanding poverty and unemployment—or relative, the growth of an intolerable gap between expectations and rewards.

MOTIVATIONS FROM LIFE UNDER OCCUPATION

Na'el's motivations for becoming a suicide bomber fit in with the complex set that influenced the majority of suicide bombers I have studied, for the vast majority of whom revenge for Israeli violence was the principle motivation. Religion, which plays a primary or secondary role in motivating at least two-thirds of suicide bombers, also clearly shaped his actions. What is most interesting is that for Na'el, as for the majority of suicide bombers I have studied, "liberating the homeland" was not among the most important rationales.

One thing that seems certain is that Na'el was not suffering from any form of mental illness, a factor that some analysts have described as motivating the bombers. During the two interviews with Na'el's family and one of his close friends that my research assistant and I conducted separately but concurrently in one big room because of space limitations, we asked about his mental and psychological status in his last year. They stressed that he was mentally and physically healthy and that he did not suffer any personal crisis in the last year of his life that might have prompted him to conduct a suicide attack. We were told that he used to love and practice wrestling. He was social and popular among his friends. His father, for example, described to me how a Palestinian Christian woman from Bethlehem who knew Na'el from the market burst into tears when she came to buy vegetables and he told her, "Your friend is gone." Na'el also enjoyed a strong relationship with his parents, three brothers, and nine sisters. "We give our kids whatever they need. . . . We spoil them," said his mother, who was trying to hide her tears under pressure from her husband, who urged her to be patient and accept God's will. When M.N., the close friend, heard me questioning Na'el's mental status in the interview, he declared in a firm tone, "Since Na'el was very religious, he would not commit suicide for personal reasons, because that is against the Islamic religion . . . It will prevent him from going to heaven." He also explained that the same applies to material incentives.

The family received financial support from some Palestinian and Lebanese institutions established to aid the relatives of suicide bombers, but this did not come close to covering its losses, including one of its main providers and its home, which the Israeli army destroyed right after the suicide attack. Na'el, who obtained a certificate in welding from a community college, used to sell vegetables from a car with his father in nearby villages before they moved their business to the town's vegetable market. Like 95 percent of the suicide bombers in my sample, he was employed. His father stressed that his family's economic situation has become much worse because of his son's involvement in a suicide attack.

There is another indication of the limited impact of socioeconomic motivation on suicide bombers. Forty-six percent of those in my sample came from cities, 34 percent from villages, and 20 percent from refugee camps. Palestinians consider refugees a low-status group, but only 31 percent of suicide bombers are from refugee camps or are refugees who live outside the camps.

One day after the attack, the Israeli army surrounded the family's home, gave them twenty minutes to remove their personal belongings, and then destroyed the house. "They did not give us enough time to remove any of our furniture or other belongings. I was only able to take some important identification documents, such as our birth certificates, and the Qur'an. . . . Also, several of the neighbors' houses were damaged during the destruction process," Na'el's father recalled.

The large family now lives in a rented, old, decrepit, small house of only two rooms. Na'el's father told me that "when a guest or a relative comes to sleep over, I sleep outside in the open yard." He and one of his sons also described the difficulties the family faced in its attempts to find a place to live after the destruction of their house. Homeowners in Bethlehem refused to provide the Abu Hilayel family with a place to live because they were afraid that might put their houses at risk of expected visits by the Israeli army. "I even thought of putting up the tent given to us by the International Red Cross in the Nativity Square to protest against homeowners. I have not executed this idea, because finally a good man agreed to rent us this old place [their current home]," the father said in a tone of bitterness and disappointment. Right after the attack, the Israeli army arrested him, two of Na'el's brothers, and two of Na'el's uncles, to take DNA samples, collect information about Na'el, and make sure that family members had not helped him. It also imposed a curfew on the whole town of Bethlehem, which suffered from harsh Israeli actions in the following months.

Na'el's body, like the majority of the bodies of suicide bombers in my sample, was interred in a special military cemetery inside Israel. According to his father and many other relatives of suicide bombers that I have interviewed, a family has to hire a lawyer and pay thousands of dollars to the lawyer and the Israeli government to obtain such a body for burial in the West Bank. Most of the bombers' bodies are still in the hands of the Israelis because their families cannot afford to recover them.

The harsh Israeli actions against the families of suicide bombers, including banning them from traveling outside the West Bank, are aimed at deterring other Palestinians from becoming suicide bombers by making them think about what will happen to their families after they die. Israel adopted the policy of destroying the homes of suicide bombers in July 2002 after the significant increase in Palestinian suicide attacks starting in 2001. That policy was also intended to make meaningless the financial support that families of suicide bombers received from Saddam Hussein from 2000 to March 2003. However, the collapse of Saddam's regime in April 2003, less than five months after Na'el's attack, prevented his family from receiving any Iraqi financial support, which had increased since February 2002 from the equivalent of $10,000 to $25,000 for each family, still barely enough to build a modest house in Palestine.

Na'el's action provoked international condemnation and different reactions from local and regional leaders. Hamas, which he had been a member of since he was seventeen years old and which was responsible for about 44 percent of the suicide attacks during the Second Intifada, declared that very day that Na'el Abu Hilayel's suicide attack came as part of a "bill" the Israelis "must pay for assassinating Salah Shehade, the general leader of Hamas's military wing, Izz ad-Din al-Qassam." Shehade was killed along with his wife, his daughter, and fifteen Palestinian civilians, including seven children, when an Israeli F-16 aircraft dropped a one-ton bomb on a building in a crowded residential neighborhood in Gaza where he lived. Hamas's now-late leader Dr. Abdel Aziz al-Rantissi, whose picture Na'el kept in his room, declared on the Arab TV station Al Jazeera on the day of Na'el's attack that "such attacks have forced some Israeli leaders to urge their government to withdraw its forces from the West Bank and the Gaza Strip."

A spokesperson of the Israeli government declared that its response was going to be quick. However, this was a sensitive time for Prime Minister Sharon, who was preparing to participate in the Likud Party's internal elections. Na'el's attack showed the limited effects of the large-scale Israeli military operation Defensive

Shield on 29 March 2002, which Sharon and his ministers had masterminded and which led to the reoccupation of major Palestinian towns in the West Bank to prevent Palestinian bombers from attacking targets inside Israel. This operation had been triggered by a major Palestinian suicide attack in Netanya that killed more than thirty-five Israeli civilians, including many elderly people, some of them Holocaust survivors.

MAHER HUBASHI'S MIXED MOTIVATIONS

Three Palestinian young men, twenty-three-year-old Maher Hubashi and his close friends Ashraf al-Saeed and Imad Zubaidee, decided to conduct suicide attacks in March 2001 against Israeli targets, to revenge the hundreds of Palestinian activists and civilians, including tens of children, the Israeli army killed in the West Bank and the Gaza Strip during the first period of the uprising. However, the friends had a dispute over who would conduct the first suicide attack. Each one expressed his willingness to take the first turn. To solve this unusual conflict, one of them suggested drawing lots. Imad picked up the first number and Ashraf the second; Maher, the subject of this section, probably felt unhappy when he drew the number 3. Muhieealdien Hubashi, Maher's father, who told me this story when I interviewed him in the family's house in the summer of 2006, believes that the turning point in his son's life which made him fulfill the promise he gave to his two friends, who blew themselves up a few months before Maher's attack, came in the summer of that year.

On the morning of 31 July 2001, the phone rang in Hamas's media office, in a sixth-floor building in the city of Nablus, Maher's home city. "Who is calling?" asked Jamal Mansour, one of Hamas's senior political leaders in the West Bank, who had come to the office a short time earlier accompanied by Jamal Saleem, another Hamas senior leader in the West Bank. The person on the line explained that he worked for the BBC and was calling to arrange an interview with the two leaders about their perspectives regarding the Palestinian uprising which had erupted ten months earlier.

About one minute after that phone call, an Israeli Apache helicopter, seen flying in the area by some of the city's residents, fired several missiles on Hamas's office. The two leaders died instantly, in addition to four other Palestinians killed as "collateral damage" during the Israeli attack: the brothers Bilal and Ashraf Abdelmun'em, eight and ten years old, respectively, who were playing on the street near the targeted building, and two Palestinian journalists. Hours after the incident, the BBC issued a statement stressing that none of its journalists or employees had called the Hamas media office that day.

It turned out that the phone call was arranged by the Shabak, Israel's internal security service, to verify the presence of the two leaders inside the office. The assassination provoked furious Palestinian condemnation and triggered an intense debate among Israeli politicians, who were split over this significant change in Israeli policy during the intifada, since for the first time the state was targeting Palestinian political leaders rather than field leaders and activists.

Maher, as a Hamas member and field activist in Nablus, had long known the two leaders and had an appointment with them on that day. He arrived a few minutes after the attack and saw the body parts of the six Palestinians scattered in the office and the street. He was in shock, lost consciousness, and was taken to a nearby hospital. Some of what he wrote in his will verifies the connection his father made between Maher's willingness to conduct a suicide attack and the attack on the Hamas media office. Maher mentioned the two leaders by name:

> It is better for someone who has been beaten up to hit back rather than do nothing. Those [the Israelis] who watch us will increase their attacks on us if we stop our jihad [religious struggle and, in this context, military operations]. Yes, there is no solution but jihad. Anyone who thinks that the blood of our leaders Jamal Mansour, Jamal Saleem, Ahmed Marshoud, and the engineer Ayman Halaweh [the last two were also assassinated by the Israelis] and the blood of all our martyrs will go for nothing is delusional, delusional, delusional. As the Izz ad-Din al-Qassam Brigades has taught us through its strong retaliations, [Prime Minister] Sharon will, God willing, taste the bitterness we have tasted. God is witness to our words.

After the three friends delivered their promises to one another, Imad, the winner of the first turn, killed two Israeli civilians and injured about fifty others, some seriously, when he blew himself up in a bus station in the Israeli city of Kfar Saba in April 2001. This was about three months before the assassination incident, which strongly affected Ashraf, the second to carry out a suicide mission. When one of his friends came to the store where worked and told him about the assassination of the two leaders, whom he also knew personally, he left in tears and went to see the targeted building. Nine days later, he drove a white car and blew himself up at an Israeli military checkpoint in the Jordan Valley, killing two Israeli soldiers and seriously injuring a third.

Maher's attack, which took place eight and four months after the attacks of each of his two friends, was far deadlier. Two days before his death, he told his mother after he kissed and hugged her before going to work that "I do not know how I am going to leave you, Mother." Unaware of the exact meaning of his words, she replied, "What are you talking about? You are just going to work, and you will be back in the evening."

When he left his house for the last time, he told his mother that he was going to sleep in the house of one of his married sisters. According to his mother, "We [family members] were surprised when I called his sister the next morning and she said that he did not come. . . . He is not the type of a person that would lie . . .

We went to his workplace, but he was not there. We asked his friends from the [an-Najah] University, but nobody had seen him. We kept calling his mobile phone, but it was [off]. . . . Several days after his death we found his mobile phone hidden in a locker in his room."

Maher's bombing occurred on 2 December 2001, in the Israeli coastal city of Haifa. According to Israeli newspaper accounts, after Maher boarded a bus, he approached a woman who looked like an Arab and asked her to leave immediately because something terrible was going to happen. He paid the driver with a large bill and went to the middle of the vehicle, then blew himself up as the driver asked him to collect his change. The bombing killed more than eighteen Israeli civilians and injured about forty, some seriously.

In addition to the deaths of the two Hamas leaders, Maher had wanted to revenge the killing of young Palestinians by the Israeli army. According to his mother, Maher, who was known for his love of children—especially his youngest brother, Kareem, who was six years old at the time of Maher's attack—used to hang the pictures of Palestinian children whom Israeli soldiers had killed on the walls of his room. These included, for example, the picture of Mohammed al-Darra, the twelve-year-old Palestinian boy who was killed in the second day of the uprising as he hid with his father behind a barrel in Gaza and whose death the correspondent of the French TV station France 2 videotaped. Maher also kept the picture of the four-month-old Palestinian Iman Hijou, whom an Israeli bullet killed while she was in her mother's lap.

Maher was also eager to revenge the deaths and injuries of some of his neighbors, friends, and relatives, such as his aunt who was seriously harmed by an Israeli action. He was also affected by the assassination of his friend Mahmoud abu-Hunoud, who was killed by an Israeli missile that targeted his car ten days before Maher's suicide attack. Abu-Hunoud, a local Hamas military leader, had been a political prisoner in a Palestinian Authority prison but was released after he survived an assassination attempt by Israeli aircraft that bombed the prison, killing several inmates and guards. Maher, who mentioned his friend by name in his will, used to visit Abu-Hunoud in prison. Eyewitnesses told the family after Maher's death that he also used to visit his friend's grave and cry there. These and other incidents explain the deep hatred Maher felt toward the Israelis and some of the strong words he used in his will: "I wish I had many souls [lives] so that I could revenge, time after another, too many massacres and humiliations [committed by the Israelis]."

A suicide attack is typically a collective action, requiring the involvement of several individuals to carry out various tasks, including collecting detailed information about the target and the best time and way for the attacker to enter Israel, driving the bomber to the target, making a suicide belt, videotaping the bomber reading his or her last will, and declaring responsibility. A letter to the family from the incarcerated individual who helped Maher install the suicide belt around his body said that Maher pressured this person to add as many explosives as he could: "I told him that he could not carry this huge amount of explosive materials around his body, but he kept insisting, 'Put more. Put more.' He carried tens of kilograms of explosives." This may explain the high number of Israeli casualties from his attack and the huge explosion that Israeli eyewitnesses described, which blew apart the Egged (Israeli bus company) number 16 bus. The bus was traveling from the Neveh Sha'anan area in Haifa to Hadar, passing through the mixed Jewish-Arab Halissa area.

If revenge was Maher's primary motivation, religious inspiration also drove him. According to his family members and close friends, Maher was a religious person who prayed daily in nearby mosques and fasted the whole month of Ramadan. He even made a pilgrimage to Mecca, a religious duty that Muslims normally try to fulfill when they are older. He had also memorized seventeen parts of the Qur'an, which he used to teach to some of the children who came to the mosque where he often prayed. "The sheikh in the mosque told us that Maher used to read the Qur'an better than him," Maher's mother said proudly.

In a move that expressed his strong belief that Muslim martyrs go to heaven after their death, Maher visited the father of his friend Ashraf one day before he conducted his attack and asked if he needed anything from his dead son. "I was sitting in my store when Maher came to visit me. He greeted me, asked me how I was doing, and left. Then, after he walked about fifty meters, he turned back and asked me with a smile on his face, 'Uncle, do you want anything from Ashraf?' I did not take his weird question seriously. I thought he was joking." This is what Ashraf's father told Maher's family when he came to express his condolences after hearing that Maher had been killed in a suicide attack. In the two paragraphs that Maher devoted to his two friends in his will, he also expressed his deep belief that martyrs go to heaven and meet with the prophet Muhammad: "Dear friend Imad, I am coming soon. I'm so happy and excited to see you and meet and hug the master of humanity Muhammad, peace be upon him. I miss you. . . . I have been waiting a long time, Imad. Since you went to heaven on 22/04/2001, I have been awaiting my turn in the [military] operation right after you, but God's will was that I will be late this time. God has honored and rewarded me because I allowed you to achieve your wish for martyrdom before me."

Finally, in a mixed religious and retaliatory motivational logic, Maher refers in his will to what he saw as a humiliating cartoon of the prophet Muhammad made by some Israeli settlers and to what Israeli soldiers did to him when he visited the al-Aqsa Mosque in Jerusalem:

I have [also] chosen to revenge God and his Prophet, whom they [Israeli settlers] humiliated through bad words and by drawing a picture of a pig [probably the most unpopular animal in the eyes of most Muslims] and writing on it, "This is Muhammad, the prophet of Muslims." I also sacrifice myself and [my] soul to the al-Aqsa Mosque, this mosque which they stopped us from visiting [several years earlier, Israeli soldiers took his personal identification documents and kept him for hours when he tried to visit the mosque]. I say to them [Israelis] loudly: . . . "If you were able to prevent us from visiting the al-Aqsa Mosque physically, you cannot prevent our souls from visiting it. Here I am, giving my blood as a gift to light its lamps instead of oil. Can you prevent me from doing that?"

According to something Maher wrote that his family found after his death, his desire was to blow himself up in Jerusalem, but it seems that for operational considerations (i.e., stricter Israeli security measures because of frequent attacks in the holy city), Hamas chose Haifa for him as a target. This choice expresses part of the organization's ideology, political vision, and tactics. It seems that Maher shared the feeling of many Palestinians that despite the Israeli withdrawal from Palestinian towns, the whole West Bank and, before Maher's death, the Gaza Strip were under Israeli occupation.

RELIGION, REVENGE, AND LIBERATION?

Like Na'el Abu Hilayel and most of the other dozens of suicide bombers whose lives I have examined, Maher could not be characterized as suffering from any form of mental illness or psychopathology or from deprivation. Instead, religious inspiration and revenge primarily motivated him and Na'el. But Maher had an additional motivation, as he believed that suicide bombing was an effective means to liberate his homeland. And so in his will he asked the Palestinian negotiators to stop the Israeli-Palestinian peace process, which he saw as humiliating:

To the negotiator: enough humiliation. . . . Enough shaking hands with [an Israeli] hand that is dripping with the blood of our people. . . . We have achieved nothing except that the Jews have recruited thousands of collaborators and are planning to kill our mujahideen [fighters]. They [Israelis] meet you and wear a mask called "peace," but in fact it is "disgrace." . . . You should know that peace has become an old brittle fashion. Jihad [in this context, military struggle] is the option toward victory and the liberation of Jerusalem. . . . No more fallacies and cease-fires.

Neither Na'el nor Maher was unemployed. Indeed, Maher was one of the two main providers for his family, who suffered financially after his bombing, also losing their home in much the same manner as did Na'el's family. After obtaining his high school diploma, Maher started at an-Najah University in the city of Nablus. However, after several months he decided to enroll in a community college to study cooling and heating systems, which enabled him to have a good job in the last two years of his life. His father recalled how Maher used to help financially, offering his savings (about $3,000) to his father to cover the last payment for a piece of land that the family had bought. "When I told him that I would register part of the land under his name, he refused. . . . He also used to fully cover Kareem's expenses."

According to his family, Maher was physically and mentally healthy. He was a member of a soccer team called Solidarity and used to participate in competitions. He was described as social, calm, polite, generous, and energetic. He clearly had good relations with his retired father, homemaker mother, four married sisters, and two young brothers, to each of whom he devoted a paragraph in his will. He urged his mother to be "patient" when hearing about his death, his father to be "proud of him," and his two young brothers to take care of their parents and be good Muslims.

ACKNOWLEDGMENTS

The author thanks Robert J. Brym, Jack Veugelers, and Fida Jiryis for their comments, his research assistant Nida' Shuhbour for her work, and the families and close friends of the two suicide bombers analyzed in this chapter for their cooperation during interviews.

SUGGESTIONS FOR FURTHER READING

Araj, Bader. "The Motivations of Palestinian Suicide Bombers in the Second Intifada (2000–05)." *Canadian Review of Sociology,* forthcoming.

Araj, Bader, and Robert Brym. "Opportunity, Culture, and Agency: Influences on Fatah and Hamas Strategy during the Second Intifada." *International Sociology,* Vol. 25 (2010), pp. 842–68.

Durkheim, Émile. *Suicide: A Study in Sociology.* Edited by George Simpson and translated by John A. Spaulding and Simpson. New York: Free Press, 1951 [1897].

22

Yigael Amir

The Making of a Political Assassin

Michael Feige

Yigael Amir was born to Shlomo and Geula, Israelis of Yemenite origin living in the town of Herzliya, ten miles north of Tel Aviv along the coast. His parents were not merely religious but believers in the Kabalistically inspired mystical popular religion. They thus chose a name for their son with extra care and earnest serious- ness. Geula wanted to name the boy *Ehud*, after a biblical judge. Shlomo insisted on *Yehuda*, the name of a son of Jacob. Each relied on biblical verses, believing that the choice would predetermine, or at least influence, the future of their son. In the berith ceremony, when the name has to be declared, an uncle suggested *Yigael*, meaning "shall bring salvation," and the parents concurred. Geula later said, "I thought that by his virtue the people of Israel shall be redeemed. Afterward it was pointed out to us that the family names formed a holy trinity. The name of the baby, Shlomo's name, and my name together give the phrase 'Yigael geula shlema' [Shall bring forth full redemption]. That is proof, isn't it?"

Until November 4, 1995, Yigael Amir was what one would regard as an ordinary Israeli, and the promise of his name seemed to have no consequence. But on that night, when he shot and killed Prime Minister Yitzhak Rabin in a peace rally in Tel Aviv, he became anything but ordinary. To most Israelis he is now a horrific killer and a demonic figure who has changed Israeli, Palestinian, and even Middle East- ern history for the worse. His admirers from the Jewish radical right would claim that he has fulfilled the prophesy embodied in his name of bringing redemption to the people of Israel.

WHO IS YIGAEL AMIR?

One of the questions raised in the horror and outcry of that night was how Amir penetrated the so-called sterile security area, where the prime minister was assumed to be well guarded. This failure was a breach of security and a tragic mistake of horrendous consequences. However, the reason that the guards overlooked Amir was so evident as to escape most viewers: to all involved, Amir seemed an ordinary Israeli and thereby, in a metaphorical sense, an integral part of the sterile area. Minutes before he pulled out his gun, he talked freely with passersby and guards, exchanging racial jokes on the composition of the rally. None of his interlocutors suspected that the sympathetic-looking young man was about to shoot the prime minister and shatter Israel's confidence in its democratic institutions.

But why him? The question "Who is Yigael Amir?" holds great import for Israeli society: the Israeli right claims that he is an act-alone killer, nonrepresentative of the law-abiding members of the nationalist camp, while the Israeli left holds that there is a direct link from the right's world view to Amir's criminal act. The debate that raged after the assassinations focused on the attribution of blame, yet it did not touch upon biographical intricacies and stopped short of explaining how a seemingly regular Israeli becomes a political assassin. In Amir's case, youth, religiosity, ethnicity, and gender, all embroiled in the context of the Israeli-Palestinian conflict, came together to produce a political assassin with radical opinions and low inhibitions.

Yigael Amir was born in 1970 as one of eight children of an ultra-Orthodox (Haredi) family of Yemenite origin in Neve Amal, an eastern suburb of Herzliya. Shlomo, his father, was a Torah scroll writer (*sofer stam*), and his mother, Geula, was a kindergarten teacher. Shlomo Amir was a short, polite man and seemed not to have much influence over the education of his children. The newspapers portrayed Geula as a know-it-all, very involved mother. Like other ultra-Orthodox women, she wore a wig, which she could move, to the fascination of the secular children in her kindergarten. This school, in the yard at the back of her house, was known, respected, and praised in the neighborhood. Starting in the 1970s as an ethnic Yemenite kindergarten, it expanded and catered to many Jewish neighbors of all ethnic origins. Yigael Amir grew up as an ultra-Orthodox Yemenite boy in an ethnically and religiously diverse neighborhood, and his mixed encounters and hybrid identity became main characteristics of his biography.

The Amirs lived modestly but gradually enlarged their home. They sent their children to the ultra-Orthodox school nearby, though other options existed. The Israeli government decided in the early years of statehood to unify the different school systems and create a single national system, but it left out religious schools, among them the strict ultra-Orthodox ones, called independent schools in Israeli bureaucratic terminology. They offer mainly religious studies, segregate the genders, and observe few, if any, Israeli national holidays.

After Amir became notorious, the Israeli ultra-Orthodox community denounced any connection to him and his act for reasons of substance and ideology. Notwithstanding the fact that thousands of Haredim participated in violent demonstrations against Rabin, they claimed that since the state is not sacred to them, the question of who leads it is therefore not consequential and certainly does not warrant illegal actions to remove an elected prime minister. Furthermore, they insisted that their community is peace loving—their men do not go to the army but study Torah in yeshivas—and therefore they do not understand or accept solving problems through violence. Using firearms to eliminate opponents is, so they claim, a modern nationalist invention, far from the Haredim's traditional way of thinking. Furthermore, they like to point out that they were the ones who warned other Jews of the dangers of the secular Zionist–nationalist path. There is some credence to these claims, yet it should be taken into account that the Haredim community is undergoing great changes that are endangering its closed-enclave nature and pulling it into the mainstream of Israeli politics and society.

Amir went to Yeshivat Hayishuv Hachadash (the Yeshiva of the New Community), an ultra-Orthodox high school in northern Tel Aviv. For children coming from afar it was a boarding school, while those living in the vicinity, such as Amir, returned home at about 8 P.M. Amir studied some eight hours of Torah and Gemara (part of the Talmud) daily and in the evening had four hours of secular studies, enabling him to receive an Israeli matriculation certificate and opening his path to university education.

The "little yeshiva" (high school) the Amir family chose for Yigael was unique among ultra-Orthodox educational institutions, as it offered its graduates a certificate that enabled them to integrate into the general secular Israeli society. Established in 1939, this school and its hybrid concept were highly contested in the Haredi world. Most Haredim live in enclaves, in what the sociologist Menachem Friedman called "a society of scholars," and do not send their children to institutions that teach secular subjects. Even the Hayishuv Hachadash's own teachers, headed by the legendary Rabbi Yehuda Kolodzki, pressured their students to enter the Haredi community and join the more ultra-Orthodox (*black*, in the religious community lingo) higher-level yeshivas. However, because of both its ethnic background (Yemenite, not ashkenazi) and its place of residence (a mixed neighborhood), the Amir family was not part of the hard-core Haredi community. Following a milder, softer Haredism, they regarded Yeshivat Hayishuv Hachadash as the best educational option and the perfect solution for their version of religiosity.

The Hayishuv Hachadash yeshiva prides itself on having produced some famous figures in Israeli society, among them esteemed rabbis but also politicians, lawyers, and artists (needless to say, it never mentions its most famous gradu-ate, Yigael Amir). The facts that many of its graduates prefer not to go to higher Haredi yeshivas and some do not even stay religious are major sources of criticism against the institution within Haredi circles. More important for our story, Hare-dim also expressed apprehension when the number of mizrachi children in the school began increasing. Amir was one of the mizrachim seeking upward mobility through a school that was considered a bastion of elite ashkenazi students. While Hayishuv Hachadash students claim that mizrachim are not subjected to discrimi-nation and that all students are treated equal, they do mention that mizrachim are called by the derogatory term *Frankim*. In fact, the school has a problematic repu-tation of maltreating mizrachi students, an issue common to many institutions in the ultra-Orthodox community.

Religious affiliation has a somewhat different meaning for mizrachi Jews than for ashkenazi Jews. Because of historical circumstances, including the late arrival of European Enlightenment values there, being religious and being secular did not evolve into clear antinomies in some of the Jewish communities in Islamic states, as has happened among European Jews. Consequently, for a Yemenite Jew like Amir, studying in an ultra-Orthodox school did not mean that he also had to become part of the ultra-Orthodox community.

Furthermore, the ultra-Orthodox community is partly anti-Zionist and sees nationalism as one of the vices of modern times. Amir, on the other hand, em-braced nationalism in its most extreme form. His zealotry may have had its roots in the ultra-Orthodox-fostered hate and disgust toward gentiles, however. The dis-dain that Jews reserved in the past for Christians has transformed, in the specific context of Israeli society and the Israeli-Palestinian/Arab conflict, into hatred of Muslims. Amir's nationalist sentiments and hatred for "the other" were not mit-igated by a more universalistic organized ideology, which is what children and youths receive in secular and national-religious schools in Israel. These schools bring non-Haredi children together with members of other Israeli social groups, teach them to respect the state and its laws, and expect them to internalize univer-salistic values. This does not mean that they are immune to bigotry and racism, however. Thus, going to an ultra-Orthodox school can be seen, maybe ironically, as Amir's first step toward national radicalism and uninhibited racism. The ultra-Orthodox community also fosters extremism through its emphasis on purity as a way of life, and even if Amir chose a different path, the lessons he received at his little yeshiva were not lost on him.

At the age of eighteen Amir went to study at Yeshivat Kerem Beyavne (the Orchids in Yavne Yeshiva), a *yeshivat hesder* where he was able to express both his religious orthodoxy and his nationalist fervor. A yeshivat hesder is a unique national-religious institutional synthesis which combines religious study with army service. The students are required to study in the yeshiva for a year or two, then join the army for a similar period, and afterward return to the yeshiva to finish their studies. In 1965, Kerem Beyavne was the first to initiate this arrangement, which has since then proliferated through yeshivas in Israel. It was, and still is, considered an elitist educational institution of the national-religious camp. When Amir arrived at this mainly ashkenazi bastion, it was growing more Haredi than before, though its dedication to nationalist and right-wing ideology remained unquestionable. In the 1996 elections, less than a year after one of its graduates had killed the prime minister, 100 percent of the yeshiva's students voted for the right-wing Benjamin Netanyahu over Rabin's successor, Shimon Peres. Immediately after the assassination, the head of the yeshiva disavowed any connection to Amir's act, claiming that the yeshiva educates and teaches Torah, not murder.

Amir enlisted in the army in August 1990, as part of the yeshivat hesder arrangement. He served for a year and a half in the Golani Brigade, in a company mainly consisting of religious soldiers, before returning to finish his studies at the yeshiva. His army buddies remember his religious zeal: he stood out even within a company of religious soldiers, waking his friends early in the morning for prayers and nudging them to stay awake. While he did not discuss politics with his friends, one recalled, "In Golani everyone beats [Arabs]. Even I was not clean of this, but Yigael was something special. I remember that in searches we conducted in Jabalya [a refugee camp in the Gaza Strip], when the officer said to take care of them, Yigael was the one to do it. He would go strong, beat them up, destroy equipment, and enjoy bothering them just for the fun of it."

Right after he finished his studies, Amir went on an educational mission to the USSR to teach Hebrew and was assigned to the local Jewish community of Riga, Latvia. The national-religious camp had great influence on these missions' recruits, mostly former members of the Bnei Akiva religious youth movement. Amir has explained that secular students are not sent on these missions because they lack knowledge of Jewish law and therefore cannot answer the questions of Jews who are planning to emigrate to Israel.

In 2002 Amir started at Bar Ilan University in Ramat Gan. For religious youths, the choice is quite obvious: Bar Ilan defines itself as a religious Jewish university, based on the American model of Christian universities and colleges. It developed during the 1950s as a national-religious answer to the "promiscuous" campuses of other universities, which religious teachers and students claimed discriminated against them. Later it started attracting local secular students, and by the time Amir arrived, about half of the teachers and students were secular. Nevertheless, religious life on this campus is much richer than on other Israeli campuses, and that, combined with the campus's central location in the city of Ramat Gan, a fifteen-minute drive from Amir's home, made it his choice.

Amir went on to study law (which, in Israel, is an undergraduate program), a glaring irony in light of what was to follow. His grades were well below average, probably due to his lack of interest in secular studies. His friends don't remember him as a distinguished student, although a picture of him studying appeared in one of Bar Ilan's publications: a young mizrachi law student, toiling over books in the serene atmosphere of the campus library, was the kind of publicity the university cherished. Later, the picture would come back to haunt the school.

In his career to that point, Amir could be seen as a mobile mizrachi, moving up the social ladder of the national-religious community. Though he kept his Haredi solid-black skullcap rather than wearing the colored knitted skullcap preferred by and symbolizing national-religious Jews, going to Bar Ilan and studying law were indicators of an attempt to integrate into the general Israeli society. In that sense, Amir was part of a wider phenomenon: the rise of the lower-class mizrachim into the Israeli middle class. It is probable that he has encountered discrimination and rejection because of his ethnic background, but if he did, he never once mentioned it. However, this story of upward mobility and integration into the Israeli middle class was about to take a fateful twist.

On the Bar Ilan campus, Amir participated enthusiastically in the university *kollel's* evening religious studies. There he excelled, and his teachers had nothing but praise for his industriousness and motivation. Of even higher importance to Amir was his political involvement. In 1992, the moderate Rabin government had just come to power, and the national-religious university students were agitated and active, participating in and initiating demonstrations against the government. Amir took part and found his favorite extracurricular activity in joining and leading groups to the West Bank and Gaza Strip settlements. He claimed that he just wanted Bar Ilan students to see for themselves both the beauty of the places and the dangers encountered by the settlers in the wake of the Oslo Accords between the Rabin government and the Palestine Liberation Organization that was signed on September 13, 1993. For him, the truth of his convictions was self-evident, and he restrained himself from expressing his opinions, so not to alienate his fellow students. He even shied away from the more extreme right-wing factions, worried that if he became connected to them, regular students would refuse to join his group's tours. So while the head of the extreme Eyal group, Avishai Raviv, was ousted from the university and not invited on these trips, Amir was considered a respected young leader who enriched the social life of university students.

ON THE ETHNIC FRINGE

Amir attributed his radicalization to one particular event: the funeral of Baruch Goldstein. In November 1993, on the Jewish holiday of Purim, Goldstein, a physician living in Kiryat Arba, donned his army uniform with his officer's marks, took his rifle, entered the Cave of the Patriarchs (Cave of Machpela) in Hebron, and shot dead twenty-nine Muslim Arabs while they were praying. Once his rifle stopped firing, he was beaten to death. In the riots that followed, more Palestinians were killed. These events, which occurred several months after the signing of the Oslo Accords, came as a shock to the Israeli public. Public and political outcries arose demanding the evacuation of Jews from Hebron. In Kiryat Arba, Hebron, and the rest of the settlements, most of the settlers, especially their leaders, expressed horror at the massacre.

Amir went to Goldstein's funeral and was impressed by what he perceived as the suffering of the settlers, threatened by Palestinian terror and misunderstood by their Israeli compatriots, and he expressed no remorse for the massacre. He later explained to the Shamgar committee investigating Rabin's assassination:

> I went to the funeral. I wanted first of all to learn. I never met this public, so I wanted to go and see. I said to myself that if a man gets up and sacrifices his life, then probably this public is under stress, anxious about something. So I went there and watched all the thousands who were there in the funeral. I saw the love they had for him, and I understood that the issue is not simple. I talked to people and started to realize that what we have here is not just an extremist fanatical public. It is a public that fights for the people. Values are very important to them . . . but they are ostracized and radicalized.

Goldstein's and Amir's biographies exhibit some resemblances. Both belonged to the wide ethnic fringes of the ideological settlements. Goldstein had immigrated from the United States and was therefore in a sense an outsider among his veteran Israeli friends. Amir, being a mizrachi of an ultra-Orthodox family, was also an outsider. A careful examination of all Jewish ideological killers—of either Arabs or Jews—to emerge from the Israeli right shows that most share the same characteristic: they are not part of the core ashkenazi group that created Gush Emunim, and they are not motivated by the teachings of Rabbi Abraham Isaac Hacohen Kook, his son Rabbi Tzvi Yehuda Hacohen Kook, or the yeshiva these rabbis created and headed for many years, Merkaz Harav in Jerusalem.

This is a point of utmost importance for two reasons. One is that the ideology/theology that informed Gush Emunim was the engine behind and legitimated the settlement project yet also set limits to what was morally acceptable. This ideology claimed that messianic salvation is apparent and visible in our time and that discrepancies between the glorious future and the disappointing present are only a temporal delay in the divine process. Furthermore, the ideology of the rabbis Kook, father and son, portrayed the State of Israel, its secular institutions and leaders, as nevertheless sacred, since they serve as the vehicles through which God brings about redemption. Followers of these ideas can sustain tensions and discrepancies, believing them to be only temporal, and possess built-in inhibitions against exercising violence against the State of Israel and its representatives. This ideology does not extend to relations with Palestinians but in a more limited fashion acts to inhibit violence even against them, because it regards Israeli-Palestinians relations as an affair of state, and consequently, acting violently would signal that they are skeptical about the chances of divine national salvation.

The second reason for the importance of the Kookist world view is that while it invited all Jews to join in the sacred project of redeeming the people and the land, it marginalized those who were not familiar with its intricacies. The ideology/theology supplied a language with which to discuss issues of Zionism, settlements, Palestinians, and evacuations. Those who learned the sacred teachings and understood their complex meaning were privileged in being able to comprehend the salvation process in its entirety and to connect to the primary logic that motivated the settlement project. The ashkenazi national-religious group that studied the Kookist books in schools, youth movements, and yeshivas used this knowledge as its main symbolic capital in marginalizing those who, like them, believed in maximalist Zionist expansion and an exclusive Jewish state but based this on other logics and motivations.

The project enthusiastically welcomed mizrachi such as Amir, who did not belong to the traditional national-religious elite, as they were seen as living proof that the ideology held appeal for Jews regardless of ethnic background. At the same time, the same ideology marginalized them, kept them away from leadership positions, and restricted their social networks. They often did what marginal groups in other times, places, and contexts do: they tried to excel and prove their worth in what they felt was the pivotal mission confronting the hegemonic camp. Turning to radicalism, Amir tried to be a better religious Zionist than his friends.

In his struggle for the settlements and against the Oslo Accords, Amir did not share the inhibitions of his friends, because he did not feel that the Kookist ideological system applied to him. For him, the idea that salvation was predetermined regardless of setbacks was unacceptable—during his interrogation he expressed a Haredi position contrary to the teachings of the rabbis Kook, claiming that he cannot know if and when redemption will arrive. He saw Rabin as a mortal threat to the future of the Jewish people and an urgent danger to Israelis on both sides of the Green Line. The concept that Rabin and his government were in any sense sacred and should not be physically harmed was, for Amir, just an expression of weakness. While he admired the leadership of Gush Emunim and the ideological settlers for their suffering and bravery, he also despised them for what he interpreted as an unwillingness to follow through on their convictions. In his interrogation he stated that he felt they could not do what he had done, because they were still restrained by their desire to be liked by the rest of the Israelis.

Being of Yemenite parentage and having an ultra-Orthodox upbringing probably also influenced Amir's world view. The Yemenite community in Israel was extremely critical of the treatment its members received during their immigration in the early state years—expressing its bitterness through stories, never substantiated yet deeply believed, of stolen children given to ashkenazi families to raise—which left scars that have still not healed. The ultra-Orthodox, for their part, are critical and suspicious of the state, which has sought to enforce secular education on children and abandoned the age-old teachings of Jewish tradition. Amir belonged to two identity communities that hold bitter memories of the way they were treated in the past and are critical of the way they are treated today. Upon joining a third community, he took the national-religious deference toward the state and its leaders with more than a grain of salt.

SEEKING TO BELONG

The tension between wanting to belong, being rejected, and turning more radical can be observed in Amir's romantic choices during his time at the university. He was attracted to young ashkenazi women, dated some, and was in special, deep relations with two in particular.

Amir's first girlfriend was Nava Holzman, a student from Bar Ilan University. Later, when the media focused on their relationship, onlookers shamelessly mentioned the socioeconomic and ethnic divide, verging on racist contempt: "He who watched the two knew in his heart that this match is doomed to failure. In the campus people did not understand what exactly Nava—the twenty-two-year-old daughter of Yitzhak and Puah Holzman, a beautiful and smart blond from a rich, good home, considered a very desirable match in the longing eyes of the young men in the campus—found in a guy who did not seem very impressive." He brought her to visit his home and meet his parents, yet she preferred that he stay away from her home. While his parents hoped that the relationship would lead to marriage, her parents tried to separate the two. Eventually, Nava followed her parents' advice and left Amir after a six-month-long relationship. Soon afterward she married one of his friends, an ashkenazi student of her socioeconomic background. Amir's acquaintances suggested that this failed romance, colored with ethnic and class undertones, drove him farther down the road to radical extremism. Nava downplayed the entire affair: "Usually people in the university are looking for a match, but you are not going to marry the first one you happen to meet. Leaving Yigael had no special meaning for me, regardless of what everyone assumes."

Amir's next attempt at romance was even more consequential. Margalit Har-Shefi was a twenty-year-old law student at Bar Ilan who had grown up in the settlement of Beir El. She belonged to one of the more "aristocratic," or pedigreed, families of the national-religious camp, since her uncle and aunt, Benni and Emuna Elon, were influential figures among the settlers. This time Amir was aiming very high on the national-religious social ladder.

Later, when discussing with police investigators the way they met, Amir revealed his pick-up line: "I don't start with a girl easily. First we talk ideology. I am a great admirer of Goldstein, so to get to know a girl I would ask a single question: what do you think of Goldstein? Her answer revealed to me if the girl is shallow or deep, meaning attractive to me." At first, Har-Shefi confronted Amir, especially when he claimed that Rabin should be eliminated, telling him that he was insane and she would inform the authorities. Her answer presented Amir with a challenge he appreciated, of justifying his positions. This unlikely beginning brought about a deep friendship.

He was in all probability romantically attracted to Har-Shefi. While she appreciated him for his knowledge, zealotry, and ability to move between worlds (Haredi, national religious, secular, rabbinic, academic), she claimed never to have considered him as a romantic partner. After a few months of friendship they parted ways, and Amir's second attempt at being accepted by the national-religious aristocracy ended in another failure.

THE PLOT

At this point, Amir started planning in earnest how to carry out his plan to kill Rabin. During his years as an activist, he had developed a few connections which assumed public import after he was apprehended. His brother Haggai shared his views and helped him, along with a friend, Dror Adani. Both were later convicted as accomplices and sent to jail. Another friend in the clandestine groups, Avishai Raviv, posed as a right-wing radical but was working for the Israeli secret service under the nickname Champagne. Amir confided his plan to Raviv, who was later tried for failing to alert authorities but acquitted. This friendship became the hinge for numerous conspiracy theories that accused the Israeli security forces of putting the gun in Amir's hands in an elaborate plan to boost Rabin's failing popularity that went horribly wrong. Amir was ambivalent toward Raviv, saw him as an infantile provocateur, and mentioned that while Raviv's flamboyance brought attention, no one suspected the shy and reserved yet much more focused and dangerous Amir.

According to Amir, he decided to follow Goldstein's example when he realized that bringing groups to tour the settlements and observe the settlers' plight following the Oslo Accords failed to bring about a wide movement. To his dismay, his fellow students came to visit the settlements as no more than tourists wishing for the opportunity, difficult to come by in the gender-segregated national-religious camp, to meet members of the opposite sex. Amir claimed that most Israelis were against the Oslo Accords, and therefore Rabin's policy, which Arab Knesset members and some defectors from right-wing parties also supported, was illegitimate. He further added that he did not want to kill the prime minister and revenge was not one of his motives: all he wanted to do was neutralize Rabin and thereby avert the dangers he assumed faced Israel. He decided to trust no one and, like his hero Goldstein, take upon himself the salvation of the nation.

On a few occasions he came close to Rabin but either backed down or failed at the last moment—once in Yad Vashem (the Holocaust Memorial and Museum in Jerusalem), from which Rabin was called away by a terrorist attack elsewhere, and again at the ceremonial opening of an intersection near Amir's home. Amir stalked Rabin's house and considered the use of ingenious killing devices. Even on the evening when he executed his plan, he carried a bag filled with his university material, just in case he had to back off again at the last minute, and will need to explain his whereabouts.

On the evening of November 4, 1995, Yigael Amir took his gun and went to the plaza in Tel Aviv now named Rabin Square, to the rally in support of Rabin's peace policies. He waited patiently near the steps of the stand on which Rabin was to speak to the public, trying not to attract attention and allowing government ministers, including Shimon Peres, to pass him by. After the rally, as Rabin was approaching his car, Amir sneaked behind him and shot him in the back three times. He mortally wounded Rabin and injured a bodyguard. He was immediately apprehended.

Two days later, Amir said in his interrogation, "I have been thinking about this for two years. I was always afraid that the gun would not fire. I was afraid that I would shoot, nothing would happen, and I'd get caught and spend the rest of my life in jail like an idiot. . . . I also thought that they would kill me, but I was ready for that."

The events of that evening were a traumatic watershed in Israeli memory, on par with the sudden coordinated Arab attack in October 1973 (the Yom Kippur War) and, in comparative terms, with the assassinations of the American presidents Abraham Lincoln and John F. Kennedy. Rabin's election, for the first time since the 1970s, gave the Labor Party a clear mandate to implement its moderate program, and Rabin did so with dramatic policy changes culminating in the Oslo Accords. His assassination marked the decline of hope for implementing a two-state solution, even though it is not clear to what extent can that failure be attributed to Rabin's death. As he became an Israeli and international hero of peace, an elaborate cult, including a national day of remembrance with Amir positioned as the demonic villain, developed around his image.

THE TRIAL AND ISRAELI SOUL-SEARCHING

Amir's murder trial lasted from January 23 to March 27, 1996. When his figure and biography were first revealed, Israeli audiences, media, and the judges were critical of, even shocked by, his demeanor, his smile, and his lack of remorse or regret.

In his defense he used traditional Jewish religious reasoning, claiming that he had carried out the proper response to a *din rodef,* namely acted to stop a criminal before he could commit further crimes. Amir stressed that his motivation was not vengeance but an attempt to avert future disaster that would follow necessarily from Rabin's policies. He was found guilty and sentenced to life imprisonment. His appeals were rejected, and the Knesset passed a law barring pardon for any assassin of a prime minister.

Amir's friends were also placed on trial, and some were convicted. The trial of Margalit Har-Shefi as an accomplice to murder is of special interest. As the judges deliberated the case, a public argument raged, especially between the so-called peace camp, which claimed that she carried clear responsibility, and the settlers from Beit El and elsewhere, who argued that she was being victimized by settler-hating left-wing supporters and could not be blamed for the radicalism of her friend. Since practically no one in Israel claimed that Amir was innocent (though struggles to cut his sentence started soon after he was convicted), the loaded question of the broader social and ideological responsibility for the murder was laid at the foot of Har-Shefi's trial. As a typical settler girl, she represented the entire settlement project in its claim of not being accomplice to Amir's murderous act.

In 2001, five years after Rabin's assassination, Har-Shefi was found guilty, and her appeals all the way up to the Israeli High Court were denied. She was sentenced to nine months' imprisonment. Upon her early release, she was greeted in her home settlement with a joyous party that was jarring to the eyes of Israelis who were hurting from the death of Rabin and felt that through celebrating her return home, the settlers were actually celebrating Amir's act. The opposite seems closer to the truth: by accepting Har-Shefi back into their ranks, the settlers were making a statement that she, and by implication their entire camp, was not guilty of the most notorious crime in Israeli history.

Amir, serving a life sentence, did not receive the support he wished from the settler rabbis, the settler establishment, or even the young woman settler he considered his friend. One can only conjecture what direction Israeli history would have taken had Har-Shefi not declined Amir's advances, adding a further insult to his career of marginalization. The settlers, through their celebration, have redrawn the boundaries between themselves—those who, owing to their refined education, can differentiate between talking about redemption, treason, and revenge and actually taking the law into their own hands—and those in the ethnic margins, people like Amir, who lack such education and refinement. Making a distinction between Har-Shefi and Amir was, for the settlers, a way of not dealing with one of their deepest anxieties: that their ideology, while giving meaning to their lives and showing the way to bring salvation for the entire people of Israel, is a major cause of distress, discrimination, and division, even endangering the fabric of the society they so cherish. Furthermore, by symbolically ousting Amir, the settlers shrug their responsibility for the acts of those who try to join their camp and choose what parts of the theology and ideology fit them best. The denial of responsibility by ashkenazi leadership is by no means new to mizrachim in Israel.

While in prison, Amir never stopped fascinating the Israeli public, and he captured the attention of the media with his demands and complaints. The bizarre story that most occupied Israeli imaginations and was subject of numerous jokes was his relations with an older woman, Larisa Trembovler, a university professor and an immigrant from the former Soviet Union. She left her husband and an academic career to marry Amir, a man she had never met, who faces a future of life imprisonment, plus public shame and hatred. Their attempts to marry and have conjugal visits were publicly debated. Amir applied to the prison authorities to allow him and his new wife to conceive a child through artificial insemination. After a long struggle that included a hunger strike and subsequent denial of his prisoner rights, he was allowed a ten-hour-long conjugal visit with Larisa, who in October 2007 gave birth to a son, named Yinon Eliya Shalom. Public argument ensued regarding the proper upbringing of the child, often seen as a Rosemary's baby-type creature carrying the genes of a monster.

Larisa Trembovler is a far cry from the young, ambitious, national-religious, well-connected ashkenazi women Amir used to date in his university days. Since his story did not end with Rabin's assassination—he was not shot on the spot—he has had to reinvent himself in light of his fame and in the solitary confinement of his cell, with little connection to the outside world. Those he sought to salvage have betrayed him, and his family, though fighting on his behalf, was devastated by his act. To the dismay of many, Amir is using the new celebrity culture, attraction of reality programs, and fascination with the strange and bizarre to formulate an image that remains relevant in Israel's rapidly changing society.

His biography holds important lessons in the development of the Israeli-Palestinian conflict, as well as conflicts internal to each of these societies, and especially in the rise of radicalism in fringe groups and individuals. Most of the research regarding the broader conflict sees ideological opinions and diplomatic deliberations as determining political decisions. The inner social divisions of the conflicting sides, as expressed in individual and collective biographies, however, are also significant factors in reaching a fuller understanding of the tangled history of the Middle East. The importance of this examination lies in deciphering the complex ethnic tensions and frustrations that fuel explosive dynamics and foil diplomatic opportunities.

Amir's admirers returned to the mystical Kabalistic logic that guided Shlomo and Geula years before and examined the name of the one who, according to their version of history, saved Israel from further catastrophe. They noticed that when you subtract the first and last letters from Yigael Amir's name—Y and R, which are the initials of Yitzhak Rabin—you are left with Ga'al Ami, meaning "saved my people." These Jewish fanatics thus procured proof that Yigael Amir, by removing Yitzhak Rabin, saved Israel, and that his very name foretold the deed. Ideology and superstition, death and kitsch, all combined in the story of the political earthquake that changed the history of Israel and set the Israeli-Palestinian conflict on a new course.

ACKNOWLEDGMENTS

In formulating the ideas presented in this paper, I have benefited greatly from long discussion with Malka Katz and Nissim Leon and from the industrious work of research assistant Moriel Ram.

A NOTE ON SOURCES

The sources for this article are mainly Amir's investigation and trial transcripts and the media coverage of the events.

SUGGESTIONS FOR FURTHER READING

The literature on Rabin's assassination is growing, especially in Israel. Among the most important contributions are Yoram Peri, ed., *The Assassination of Yitzhak Rabin* (Stanford: Stanford University Press, 2000); and Vered Vinitzki-Saroussi, "Commemorating a Difficult Past: Yitzhak Rabin's Memorials," *American Sociological Review*, Vol. 67 (2002), pp. 30–51. On the assassination and its context, including a biographical sketch of Amir, see Michael Karpin and Ina Friedman, *Murder in the Name of God: The Plot to Kill Yitzhak Rabin* (New York: Metropolitan Books, 1998).

On Israel's extreme right and especially Gush Emunim, see Ehud Sprinzak, *The Ascendance of Israel's Radical Right* (New York: Oxford University Press, 1991); Ian Lustick, *For the Land and the Lord: Jewish Fundamentalism in Israel* (New York: Council on Foreign Relations, 2001); Gideon Aran, "Jewish Zionist Fundamentalism: The Bloc of the Faithful in Israel, in Martin E. Marty and R. Scott Appleby, eds., *Fundamentalisms Observed* (Chicago: University of Chicago Press, 1991), pp. 265–344; Avi Ravitzki, *Messianism, Zionism, and Jewish Religious Radicalism* (Chicago: University of Chicago Press, 1996); and Michael Feige, *Settling in the Hearts* (Detroit: Wayne State University Press, 2009). For an inner history of Gush Emunim concentrated on the Jewish Underground and the discussion following its acts of violence, see Haggai Segal, *Dear Brothers: The West Bank Jewish Underground* (New York: Beit Shamai, 1988).

On the status of mizrachim in Israel, see Yoav Peled, "Ethnic Exclusionism in the Periphery: The Case of Oriental Jews in Israel's Development Towns," *Ethnic and Racial Studies*, Vol. 13, No. 3 (1990), pp. 432–43; and Oren Yiftachel, *Ethnocracy: Land and Identity Politics in Israel/Palestine* (Philadelphia: University of Pennsylvania Press, 2006). On the Haredim in Israel, see Samuel C. Heilman and Menachem Friedman, "Religious Fundamentalism and Religious Jews: The Case of the Haredim," in *Fundamentalisms Observed*.

23

Mais in the War of the Words

Erin F. Olsen

Mais is a beautiful young woman in scarves—not a veil but wisps of fabric that catch the wind and the attention of her college co-eds, as if her penetrating black eyes were not enough. She is at the end of her studies in the United States and at a point of thrill and despair. How will she use her education, which has taken her from her people and her family, to benefit the common good of a region in struggle? Will she be more than a statistic, more than another Arab caught in the vacuum of Palestine—never able to leave because of inner pulls, yet never able to accomplish dreams because of the hostile environment?

I first met Mais as I was searching for Hebrew-speaking natives for my Modern Hebrew classes. Being at a private Christian university ensures a low enrollment of Israelis, but there are typically a few who can fill the demand for a native speaker. Mais was student-teaching in the Arabic courses, also in my department, and caught wind of my search. When she came in and offered herself as a native Hebrew speaker, I was confused. Her Hebrew was good and her accent convincing, but I couldn't help feeling a little like an Israeli contractor in one of the settlements hiring day-laboring Palestinians who can't find a better job thanks to checkpoints—men who pour concrete and lay foundations for communities that illegally sit on their own ancestral lands. Why would she want to teach the language of the enemy? Other members of my Hebrew section wondered if her willingness to help me was agenda based—that is, based on a desire to declare Palestinian rights or unjust Jewish domination.

This was clearly not the case, however. At our first meeting she noticed S. Yizhar's *Khirbet Khiz'e,* an Israeli novel that details the destruction of a fictional Palestinian village and demands that Israelis consider the suffering inflicted on

Palestinians, on my desk. It was a book my Israeli literature class was reading. She borrowed it and a few days later returned shocked to know it was part of the Israeli curriculum required reading; she was frustrated that no such work representing the plight of early chalutzim had been part of her own curriculum growing up. We spoke of Mahmoud Darwish and the desire to find parallel works in Hebrew and Arabic on similar topics with different, even opposing, perspectives. Thrilled to find a student with similar interests, I hired her. We continued working together in gathering films from the region to show for film nights in the department. I offered her my Israeli film library, and she was my gatherer of bootlegged copies whenever she had the chance to fly home, often returning with parallel films by Arabs.

Mais's story represents the peculiar melting pot of the peoples, especially the youths, of the Holy Land. Although there is today a security fence—or Great Wall of Israel, or occupation barrier, or whatever other names it is known by—dividing Israelis and Palestinians, there are now fewer walls between the youths of Israel and Palestine. Interestingly, as Palestinians and Israelis go abroad for education, they often find themselves flung into the role of representative of their people at round-table discussions, forums, and other settings. In addition to these foreign opportunities for interaction, organizations promoting peace have covered the Holy Land seeking to mediate discussions between youngsters as a form of reconciliation. Track II diplomacy, the informal efforts at mediation that retired officials, policymakers, and activists lead, often focuses on youths. Numerous schools advertise themselves as promoting peace with curricula designed for their students to achieve a deep understanding of one another. Such efforts and good intentions are sometimes exploited, and the "peace industry" has its own flourishing corner of the market. These have all been parts of Mais's childhood and present experiences.

She has grown up with the stories of many of the figures represented in this book, or of people like them. Their tales served as bedtime stories, spawned the pop music she sang to, and were the subject of debates she had while attending a multitude of peace camps. Through her life we can see how these historical contexts have shaped the daily life of a child, then teenager, then young woman taking up the role of a Palestinian while recognizing that she must be a global citizen who knows the stories, cultures, and languages of the Israeli side too. And through these languages, Arabic, Hebrew, and English, we see a young woman who is forced to have a malleable identity—perhaps too malleable over the years: now she seeks to narrowly define herself within the realm of one identity, Palestinian, although she is fluent in the identities of daughter of an immigrant/refugee, Arab-Israeli, American university student, and peacemaker.

Through Mais's retelling of her life experiences we see that there are many more fragmented identities in the Holy Land than those that she lists above. Linguistic choices have also colored her interactions with Bedouin, Christians, and

Jordanians. The languages that these groups use aid in unfolding Mais's perspective on where their loyalties lie. Throughout her narrative we see words as forces that unite and divide people in the Holy Land.

When it comes to the Holy Land, the war of the words is perpetuated far beyond its borders. In fact, in typing this chapter I am very aware that it is easier to write *the Holy Land* than *Israel/Palestine*, which I would then have to rotate into *Palestine/Israel* for equal representation. The terms *Arab-Israeli* and *Palestinian* represent very different realities for Mais. I never write *Israeli-Arab*, as this was a term that my interviewee cringed to hear. As scholars and journalists, we choose words that color the reality of the conflict for millions of onlookers. Was he a freedom fighter, martyr, or terrorist? Are the bulldozed houses of Palestinians breeding grounds of covert terrorist activity or family homes filled with the innocent? Are those posters propaganda or advertisements? Should the Israeli Defense Force be called the Israeli Occupation Force? And is it a conflict or a war? All of the writers in this book have painstakingly framed their perspectives with the right words to contribute to an image that they are aiming toward. Mais's story allows us to see that a person can be fluent in multiple languages, fluent in the global view of the conflict, fluent in broad history and narrow personal drama, and still be without words for the next action that she will take.

THE LANGUAGE OF A SIGN

Mais's family is a mixture of many varieties of the Palestinian Arab experience. In her words:

> There are four main divisions of Palestinians: Those who were forced into exile and became refugees—this is my mother; she and her family fled to Jordan. There are the '48 Arab-Israelis who were forced into citizenship in Israel if they did not flee and were not killed during the declaration of Israel and subsequent takeover of Arab lands—this is my father, the "Arab-Israeli" who gives me an unwanted passport. Then there are Palestinians who live in Jerusalem—this is me; I was born in Jerusalem and spent all but four years of my life there. West Bankers remain—my family moved to Ramallah for those four years out of Jerusalem, and so this is part of my experience as well. In this way I consider myself a part of all of Palestine. I have [the] blood running through me or have lived in parts of all of Palestine.

Her mother, a schoolteacher in Jerusalem who completed her education in Jordan while in exile from Palestine, was able to return to the Holy Land through marriage. Mais's father was never forced to leave Palestine, although he had to leave his original village near Tel Aviv. He began his education in Nazareth and then completed his bachelor's, master's, and international law degrees in Russia. Because of his status as an Israeli citizen, Mais carries an Israeli passport, which she often regards as a "document forced on people like me so they can stay in their homeland." Her family lives relatively comfortably on account of the education that both of her parents pursued and now require of their children. She is following in the footsteps of three sisters as she completes a graduate degree in the United States. Education and shunning ignorance, including ignorant hate in the Palestinian-Israeli conflict, is a common theme of her speech.

As a child growing up in Jerusalem, Mais was surrounded by signs in a foreign tongue. "I used to see Hebrew, and it didn't make me feel comfortable—I knew that it was the language of another people, a people that hurt my own, that made my mother a refugee." In her school in Jerusalem she learned Hebrew, but most of her ability came from the necessity of interacting with others on the streets or in official settings, such as when obtaining passports or crossing borders:

> It took a long time to get good at Hebrew. Of course we didn't practice it in my home—that would be ridiculous. My father is fluent in Hebrew—it might have even been his first language along with Arabic—but my mother refuses to speak it, as she was forced out of Palestine by speakers of Hebrew. And there was a huge part of me that didn't want to get good at it, that inserted mistakes and a heavy Arab accent into my conversations with checkpoint guards. I think that all of us do this, try to show that we are only speaking it because we have to.

But as Mais came of age she realized that she did not want to be quasi-fluent in the language. She had met Israelis who had fluent skills in Arabic. She would tell herself that this was not owing to their scholastic vigor or craving of interaction with Palestinians but solely on account of military training, yet their fluency inspired her own attempts to perfect her Hebrew.

> When I was a little girl I remembered that this was the language of the enemy. I kept it marked in my mind as the dirty language I had to touch to be safe. But then I realized that I didn't want to be a part of the ignorance. So many of my relatives and friends refused to learn Hebrew because they hated Israelis. I thought to myself, Ignorant hatred is stupid. I will not be ignorant. I did not learn Hebrew because I wanted to be friends with Israelis. But I have never met an Israeli that learned Arabic because they wanted to be friends with Palestinians—maybe there are some. They learn it to yell at us. But at least they learn it—and learning is always good. I respect parents who encourage their children to learn Hebrew, as their children will not be the stupid ones who fall to radical speech. Their children will be able to knowledgeably choose their path—not be forced into a path of allegiance out of lack of higher education.

The traffic signs that caused early discomfort in Mais and encouraged her to learn Hebrew were in Hebrew, Arabic, and English, identifying place-names in all three languages. In July 2009, Israel Katz, the transport minister, announced that signs on all major roads in Israel, East Jerusalem, and possibly parts of the West Bank would be "standardized," with the English and Arabic place-names converted into straight transliterations of the Hebrew name. *Jerusalem* in English, *Al Quds* in Arabic, and *Yerushalayim* in Hebrew, which are now on the signs, are to be replaced with only *Yerushalayim*. Some reports said the decision was in response to the Palestinians' refusal to use Hebrew names for Israeli towns, while others claimed only simpler signage. Arab members of Israel's Knesset say the government is manipulating signs to erase the place-names of the Palestinian people and in doing so erase the existence of Arab people. They identify this as one of many attempts to eliminate the two-state solution from rhetoric by requiring Palestinians to formally recognize Israel as a Jewish State.

Mais sees the change in signage as a nominal act, since for many years the writing in the Arabic versions had already held the Hebrew names of towns—names that were changed when the land was taken from the Palestinians.

My mom is from Sobareen, a Palestinian village evicted in 1948. I don't even know what Sobareen is called today, the homeland of my mother; even the name has been erased. This is typical. The town Bissan was changed to the Hebrew Beit Shean, and many others. Who cares if the sign has Arabic characters on it if they are announcing the usurpation of a village and refusing to remember the history of the location by eliminating its name?

I think that Israeli government members get excited when they hear of groups that want to destroy the signs with Arabic on them. In the news stories they always include that there are parallel radicals, also Israelis, who are going around and repairing the signs for the poor Arabs. It shows to the world that Israel is a democracy—it has inhabitants with varied passionate opinions that it allows to be reported on in its media. Americans shake their heads and say, "What a mess in Jerusalem this week—they are ruining the signs, but at least there are some noble Jews who will fix the problem." In the next news story they hear about some ridiculous happening in Egypt where the government injured its citizens, and Americans go to bed knowing that their country supports the "only democracy" in the Middle East. These stories that affect Palestinians very little become powerful evidence that Americans rely on when they question if they should continue the support of Israel.

WARS OF WORDS

Language war is no new form of aggression, especially in a region where each ethnicity has celebrated its language as the official language of a deity. There is an almost supernatural quality to possessing the power of language policy. In Israel, ideology drives language policy. Hebrew is seen as an instrument of cohesion, a symbol that Zionist ideology was strong enough to bind diverse peoples from diverse lands into one nation. Not only is the use of Arabic in constant struggle, but all the Jewish immigrant languages—Russian, Ladino, Yiddish, and Amharic—are discouraged and seen as being in opposition to the state language of authority.

> Of course Israel wants to encourage the use of Hebrew. The immigrants need to feel that they belong to Israel and not to some other national identity, so speaking Hebrew is a quick way to make them feel this powerful identity. It doesn't bother me that they are trying to force Yemeni Jews to speak Hebrew instead of Arabic. But it does feel like attempting to weaken the power of the Arabic language for Palestinians would be motivated by erasing the Palestinian culture. If enough Arab-Israelis are willing to become fluent Hebrew speakers and use Hebrew at work—we already have to take entrance exams into college in Hebrew—then eventually the more wealthy Arab-Israelis will be a symbol for the erasing of our language throughout the land. It would be another reason we did not need our own state if we did not have a definitively separate culture and language.

Official language policies in Israel are minimal; in fact, there is no language requirement to gain full citizenship: the only requirement is that you be Jewish. English, which has no official position in Israel, has a very high status—it is used in academia, government, and business interactions. However, Arabic, which is an official language (along with Hebrew), has a very low status; it is never used in government situations and has a much lower visibility than that of English, the exception being in homogenous Arab neighborhoods. Mais's number one conversation for using Hebrew was in negotiating passports and other travel documents. She never did this in Arabic, and the interaction with the government official determined what language she would use. She spoke to rude officials in English and would feign stupidity if they spoke Hebrew.

The most visible language policy in Israel is the Language Education Policy (LEP), by which politicians are able to adapt the school systems of both Israelis and Palestinians in ways that increase or diminish the prestige of Hebrew, Arabic, and the languages of migrant populations. In 2006, Israel's Ministry of Education released a consolidated plan for language instruction. The plan was called the 3+ plan, and its stated goal was to graduate students proficient in three or more languages, following the reality of Israel's linguistically diverse society. Hebrew is the primary language of all Jewish schools. At fourth grade English is added, and at seventh grade Modern Standard Arabic (MSA) or French begins, continuing for three years. For Arab schools Arabic remains the principle language of instruction, but at third grade Hebrew is included in formal education, followed by the addition of English in seventh grade.

Opponents of the plan have stated that the language policy only appeared like a move in the direction of a pluralistic society, because it strengthened the prestige of Hebrew in a way that suppressed all other languages in the country. The LEP said that all Jewish students were to be tested in their national language (Hebrew), and consequently it removed the opportunity for immigrant students to engage in literature studies in their mother tongue because of the great demand on them to become highly proficient in Hebrew to be competitive in entrance exams for college. The difficulty for Palestinian students lies in the lack of English instruction until seventh grade, as proficiency in English often correlates with better scholastic and professional opportunities.

Despite the criticism that the LEP has received, for Mais the language policy of Israel concerning schools is not controversial. She says that all of her cousins are enthusiastic to learn Hebrew since they wish to enter one of the universities that demand proficiency in that language. For Arabs, learning Hebrew is like learning calculus: it is a system that must be memorized so that students can pass an entrance exam into college. It is not a mode of communication. It is the language of the signs. And the reciprocation of Israeli Jews learning Arabic usually owed not to their desire for communication and understanding but rather to their military training. In this way Mais's mother tongue transformed into a weapon in its own right.

LANGUAGE WAR AT CHECKPOINTS

Mais had learned Hebrew for entrance into higher education but also for safety— that she might be able to communicate in Hebrew during official business and at checkpoints. Taking the theoretical knowledge of a language into the streets is where the story should get interesting, but the reality is that Mais does not share a harrowing story of speaking with Israelis through Hebrew when I ask her to describe her experiences with checkpoints when crossing into Ramallah. Rather she mentions a time when she was terrified by fluent, sometimes native speakers of Arabic. Mais describes the checkpoints as the places where the soldiers with the most hate toward Arabs are assigned.

> I don't know that they teach them to hate. I think they simply capitalize on the ones that already hate us, and they put them there knowing that they will use their negative feelings and treat us [Palestinians] in a way to discourage our crossing. Why else would the hardest areas have Bedouin right there staring at us, fluent in our language, looking down at us? How demeaning to take your own people and turn them against you, to use them and their fluency in our language as a weapon against us—the Bedouin are always at the most dangerous checkpoints.

The topic of Palestinians and Bedouin—both Arab and many sharing the heritage of Islam—changes the entire atmosphere of the room as I am interviewing Mais. The Bedouin are unquestionably enemies in her eyes. Worse than plain enemies, they are enemies who ought to be allies but have been duped by the Israelis. They were and are evidence of the danger of ignorance. As Mais describes them,

"Maybe they are not forced, but they are promised things and money if they join the military. I have heard stories of the wells of Bedouin villages being dumped with scrap metal to make the water dangerous to drink from all of the rust—this is what they do to villages that do not send their sons into military duty. And the Bedu [Bedouin] become so mean. They must use psychological training on them to convince them they can hurt and kill their own. The Bedouin are the ones you don't want to meet at the checkpoints."

Mais's interaction with Bedouin is minimal by her own admission; however, her description of this sector of society is fascinating in that it is such a powerful description, not allowing room for exception or alternate interpretations. She eagerly qualifies her stories of negative and positive interactions with Israelis, stating that she knows her experience is not common to all Palestinians. But in speaking of the Bedouin she allows no other explanations for the choices that they have made and says that they are uniformly distrusted by Palestinians.

Truly the Bedouin, a once-nomadic people relying on open borders for raising flocks, are one of the many groups stuck between the proverbial rock and the hard place in the Holy Land. They, unlike the Druze and Circassians (two other minorities in Israel), are not subject to mandatory conscription. By law the defense minister has the discretion to grant an exemption to any Israeli citizen from the three years for men and two for women of military service. There is a long-standing government policy of exempting the Bedouin; however, they have been "encouraged" to "volunteer." Some of the encouragements were significant social benefits, such as specialized training associated with military service and a promise of future employment with the attained security clearance. Bedouin come from the poorest and least-educated portions of Israel. Many of their lands have "unrecognized village" status and are not supported with buildings or supplies for education, health care, or even water. Their complaints run the gamut of courtrooms, with judges saying that discrimination against Bedouin is obvious and unacceptable, but the Bedouin's refusal to follow landownership laws cannot be excused by courts—illegal Bedouin settlements cannot be condoned (a difficult argument for anyone of Arab descent to hear, given the numerous illegal Israeli West Bank settlements). Human rights groups in and out of Israel have called these violations of basic needs and refusal of human dignity, citing the complete absence of pediatricians, gynecologists, and pharmacists in Bedouin villages as having a direct correlation with their incredibly high sickness and child death rates.

With their living conditions so far below those of other Arabs or Israelis, it does not take a creative mind to see why young Bedouin consent to volunteer to join the military, seeing it as an escape from eternal poverty—military service as a ticket into Israeli society and prosperity. But the picture within the military is not so rosy, as they experience deep resentment from the Arabs whom they police, often as "trackers" searching for border violations and arms smuggling. Bedouin frequently feel shunned by fellow military personnel, who question their complete devotion to Israel. According to Mais, such service and effort rarely pay off. It should be noted that there are examples of Bedouin who return from military duty serving Israel to find their homes destroyed by Israeli machinery or their water cut off by recent court decisions.

THE CLOAKED LANGUAGE OF EQUALITY

As we speak of the Bedouin attempting to assimilate into Israeli society, I realize that Mais has the right to vote in Israel as she is officially an Arab-Israeli with an Israeli passport. She quickly corrects me to be sure I write that she is a Palestinian—this is her true identity no matter what form of identification card she is required to carry. About her voting options she states unequivocally, "I would never vote in Israel. My parents, they vote. They vote for the few runners for office who are Arab-Israeli, who will never get a seat, but they vote because they feel it is their obligation to try and make Israel a better place so that one day Israel will have enough loving leaders to allow the Palestinians to return. I will not do this. I will never do this. To vote would be accepting Israel as a state and giving up on a dream for our own state."

In this conversation the real strength behind the word *Palestinians,* as opposed to *Arab-Israelis,* unfolds. Mais sees Arab-Israelis, those who identify themselves as such, as luxury advocates. When deep moral issues are in question they will write an article to the newspaper or post a criticism on an Internet blog, but they don't get their hands dirty with the refugee issue or other mundane, constant struggles. They are willing to talk at length about problems, but they will not go and take significant action for change. She gives the example of a restaurant in Tel Aviv that had a waiter who wore a particularly offensive T-shirt.

> The Arab-Israelis were offended! What does that mean? They are upset, and so they will go and get their tea and biscuits at another restaurant? They created a site on the [Internet], and they all became friends of the site and signed their name to a boycott of the restaurant. I had family members who invited me to protest this crime and asked me to join them in being a mediator for the Palestinians. I was disgusted. The problem here is not the T-shirt. The problem is that we live in a society that doesn't mind the T-shirt. Do you think that was the first day he wore the thing? Do you really think a boycott of a restaurant is going to change anything? I don't want to sympathize or be a mediator. I want to work on the real problems. If someone wore that T-shirt in a Starbucks in the U.S., it would be on the news. In Israel, there are fifty people walking around with the same shirt on all over the city.

Mais sees those who take on the name of *Arab-Israeli* as missing the mark, in that they are still pursuing equality within the framework that is given—a framework that is inherently unequal. They are not bold enough to search for broader solutions. Many are willing to stop asking questions concerning the right to return if it means they can live a comfortable life. They are willing to take on a name, *Arab-Israeli*, that gives them a title of assurance. "It is all a name game. They are confused; they are fooled by the words and a passport." In describing Arab-Israelis, Mais points out that they are much more willing to speak Hebrew. They seek out jobs that require the language. They change their dress to be less conservative in an attempt to look Israeli and "cool." Mais considers these people to be living without a cause.

> Usually to live without a cause is easier. You can choose to wear clothing that will make you more accepted by the Israelis around you. Maybe you can go to a café and show your ability in speaking Hebrew and get a nice-paying job, but I wonder what these Arab-Israelis do when real disasters happen, like the war with Gaza a few months ago. I picture them standing at their closet trying to decide what clothes they will wear. Will they choose to continue down their path of comfort and stand side by side with the server in the restaurant wearing the offensive T-shirt? Or will they put on Palestinian clothes and go and surround themselves with Palestinians and grieve and talk about something they can do to help those in Gaza? If they would go and have this conversation with Palestinians, it would be in Arabic; maybe they would remember who they were.

THE LANGUAGE OF PEACE

Mais has attended many peace camps during her short life. She has had positive and negative experiences. Many camps have felt like unique efforts to bring about reconciliation, but a like number have had the tenor of the "peace industry," where the intentions of the organizers were questionable and at times she and others wondered if all of the effort was made simply to get a good photograph of youths with varied hair and skin color smiling. She has worked with organizations that she felt were covert attempts at laundering money under the guise of being nonprofit, and she has considered founding organizations of her own (not the money-laundering sort) to counter the damage some of these groups have done in stripping the trust of both peoples of the land of conflict. Mais was a counselor, and her sister has been a director of numerous camps.

Her earliest recollections of religious intolerance come from these days, when she remembers having an uncle who worked at a Jewish company in Haifa. Her parents could not fathom working with Jews on a daily basis and helping Israel build an economy through such businesses, while her uncle could not accept the decision that her parents made to send her to a Christian elementary school. Mais began her experiences negotiating differences among peers as a child in that school, where she saw no great difference between the students who were

Christian or Muslim, as they were united in being Arabs. It was at this early age that she formed her perspectives on the value of teaching acceptance, which she would take with her to peace camps in her teenage years.

> As a young adult I was a counselor at a peace camp for smaller children. We would spend the day teaching little Israelis to speak Arabic and the little Palestinians to speak Hebrew. They were very good at their lessons. Then right after they were successfully showing friendship by laughing at one another's new languages, I would hear one of them say, "Don't play with that kid, he's a Christian," and I would go to the children and tell them that they were at this camp to learn to understand one another, not to make labels for one another. At home my mom would laugh about the fake religious tolerance that we are all asked to show to one another. Really it is not religious tolerance. My uncles were not appreciative of the Jewish faith, just as I didn't hold close to Christian theology—I didn't even know what they believed, they were simply my friends. At the end of the day it is not what is right or wrong . . . it is simply what you are used to. If you are used to people who are Jewish or Muslim or Christian, if you have lasting relationships and good interactions with them, you will be "tolerant." But this is something the peace camps will never create in a week at a time. We all have to create it through our lifetimes.

In addition to her own "peace-talk" experiences, Mais has been influenced by the conferences and schools attended by her siblings, including a younger brother who was sent to a school where Israeli and Palestinian children learned side by side.

> It has all been a very important thing to my parents, but many of these are peaceful only on the outside. Many of them are just bad ideas. At my brother's school they would celebrate Israeli Independence Day and commemorate the *Nakba* ["catastrophe," referring to the loss of Palestine] on the same day. He was very confused. He came home singing "Hatikvah" [Israel's national anthem], and when we told him what it was he was crying. He told us the stories of Palestinians they had learned at school, and we all sat wanting to cry and hearing the anthem music in our minds. He was just a child. We all felt sick and confused. It would be like celebrating September 11 in the United States and calling it a holiday celebration and not a day of mourning.

One of the many summer peace camps that Mais attended was the Seeds of Peace camp in Vermont. Begun in 1993 to gather Palestinian, Egyptian, and Israeli youths, Seeds of Peace now includes summer camps for other regions of conflict. Part of Mais's experience was to visit Washington, D.C. After a day full of intense debates on sensitive topics of the conflict, the counselors took the group of Israelis and Arabs to the Holocaust Museum. The Arab counselors were opposed to this because there was no equivalent beautiful museum where the Israeli campers could experience the hurt of the Palestinians, but it was part of the established schedule, and so the visit took place. Mais says, "I am an observer. I remember the faces of all of the campers. I remember the Israelis who were filled with compassion and emotion. I also remember the Israelis who were stronger and held back emotion. It seemed to me that instead of being overwhelmed by the pictures, shoes, documents, they were more interested in seeing how the Palestinians would respond." She describes the visit as filled with a heavy and dark feeling. The students had just spent a day in intense conversations and were not feeling amiable even before entering the museum. It was a dangerous, even explosive atmosphere for such a trip. "One of the Palestinian girls began weeping, and an Israeli boy said, 'So now you understand a little bit of what we feel like.' She responded by saying, 'No, this picture reminds me of my own people. I am weeping for them.' It began a whole war within our group. We felt as though we were being forced into peace, we were being forced to show compassion as though that is something you can make in a factory." As Mais says, "Ignorant hate is stupid," but informed anger can be a similar burden.

> I recognize the Holocaust to be devastating. I understand the sheer numbers of it. It was a huge destruction of human life. I want to say to the Israelis that we may not have a six-million-member Holocaust, but that woman who stands at the checkpoint, in the midst of losing her unborn child, who is not let through to go to the hospital—when she lost that child, that was a holocaust for her. When each of us lose members of our family to war crimes, it is a holocaust. Numbers do matter. No one should destroy, marginalize, or ignore the suffering of the loss of so many, but I believe that to kill your first human is the hardest step. If you can kill one human life, you can kill a million. If Israel has created a society where it is okay to kill a single Palestinian in the name of Jewish survival, they are perpetuating a holocaust. That's what we all need to consider this conflict on—a personal level. It should not be about if my group of people is worse or better than another group of people, but ask if I myself continue destruction or find a path to good. And could we stop using the word *Holocaust*? It is such a powerful word. It is language that makes people required to agree with you. I guess it is why I just used it.

The Seeds of Peace experience was particularly strange to Mais in that the campers were removed from their reality and brought to picturesque American countryside. She recalls sitting under trees with quiet sounds of nature in the background, playing Monopoly with an Israeli boy, when she started feeling angry at the entire situation.

> What did they think this was accomplishing? We are playing games in a safe place, and in a week we are going to return to or own land, and will the Monopoly experience magically change us when he has entered the military and I am at a checkpoint and he has to choose to let me through? Will he laugh and remember that he lost all of his money at my Boardwalk and there will be a break in the conflict? How stupid this is. He has to play a role. He must be a violent figure against my people. He won't

treat me differently because of a false security we felt in Maine, and I won't treat him any differently than any other soldier.

The most interesting thing to a linguist about the Seeds of Peace camp is that these are all young adults. They have all gone through school and know quite a bit of the Hebrew and Arabic languages, yet Mais says that there was only one moment when something other than English was spoken to her. It was at the first meeting, when one of the Israeli girls came up to her and said, "I know some Arabic—let me see if I can say it right." She proceeded to say to Mais, "Give me your ID card and park on the side." The entire group laughed hysterically, as they all knew how ridiculously accurate it was that an Israeli would only know a soldier's command in Arabic, even after years of language instruction.

Mais does not consider Seeds of Peace beneficial, because it sought to normalize all of the attendees. She thinks that instead of all of them thinking the same thing and formulating a united opinion, they should have been seeking to better their own communities. In recent years she has acted on this model by attending conferences of Arabs and Israelis that discuss possibilities for microfinancing and building businesses for indigent women. Israelis gather and discuss solutions for other Israelis, while Palestinians come together to help find solutions for Palestinians. She has found this version of peacemaking to be superior and hopes to create her own organizations that will focus on such work.

It is obvious that the efforts of family and community to expose Mais to Hebrew, academic opportunities for debate and discussion, and summer camps have shaped the person that she is today. That person is filled not with hate but very much with passion. Her passion includes compassion for the plight of Israelis, shaped by a knowledgeable perspective on them from personal interaction through camps and debates. This perspective nonetheless refuses to accept the lack of a Palestinian state. Mais has traveled much and lived out of her homeland for many years to ensure a proper education. She has spoken with many about the plight of her people:

I have heard my entire life how hard it is to be a Palestinian. I have heard in the U.S. when I am interviewing students in Arabic for their weekly assignments that I deserve pity for the suffering of my people. Personally, I have not experienced this. I have a homeland, and it is beautiful. It is filled with people I love who have conversations I love, who eat food I love. I love the air. I love that it is the center of the world. I would never consider having or raising my children elsewhere. I have never seen it as a land that I am getting a respite from while I live here in the U.S. Instead I have found in the U.S. a land filled with people my age who are lacking purpose. Belonging to an occupied country has not been a heavy responsibility for me to carry that I cannot get away from, it has been a purpose. It has given meaning to life. Other college students are trying to build their lives around their studies so they can spend their life devoted to a career. Others are busy falling in love so they will have something to breathe for. I already have a love. I already have meaning.

SUGGESTIONS FOR FURTHER READING

Language policy

Shohamy, Elana. *Language Policy.* New York: Routledge, 2006.

Shohamy, Elana, and Bernard Spolsky. "An Emerging Language Policy for Israel: From Monolingualism to Multilingualism." *Plurilingua,* Vol. 21 (1999), pp. 169–84.

Bedouin of Israel

Falah, Ghazi. "How Israel Controls the Bedouin in Israel," *Journal of Palestine Studies,* Vol. 14, No. 2 , (Winter 1985), p. 35–51.

Kanaaneh, Rhoda. "Embattled Identities: Palestinian Soldiers in the Israeli Military." *Journal of Palestine Studies,* Vol. 32, No. 3, (Spring 2003), pp. 5–20.

Seeds of Peace

Feller, Leslie Chess. "In Search of Peace on Common Ground." *New York Times,* 29 August 1999.

www.seedsofpeace.org

24

Jonathan Pollak

An Anarchist "Traitor" in His Own Society

Neve Gordon

FROM BEIT SURIK TO BIDU

On a chilly February day in 2004, military bulldozers began destroying the agricultural lands of Beit Surik to prepare the terrain for the annexation barrier. Hundreds of Palestinian villagers from the town, along with a few Israelis and international activists, tried to reach the bulldozers in a hopeless attempt to stop the destruction. Armed soldiers and border police stood in a column pushing the demonstrators back. Tear gas filled the air, and the explosions of stun grenades diffused the whistling sound of rubber bullets.

Jonathan Pollak, one of the few Israelis in the demonstration, heard his cell phone ring. The voice on the other end screamed that one of the protesters in the adjacent village Bidu had been shot in the stomach and killed; "He did not make it to the clinic," the person on the other end continued. Meanwhile, Anna, another Israeli activist, had inhaled too much tear gas and began vomiting on the hillside. As Jonathan ran toward her, his phone rang again. Even though the gas was suffocating, he managed to answer. The same voice cried, "They've killed another protester."

Together with Anna, Jonathan decided to go to Bidu. Before they reached the village, however, the military had succeeded in forcing the protesting Palestinians off their agricultural lands and onto the main street. By this time, the casualty count had risen to three: an older man died from a heart attack after inhaling tear gas from a canister that had been shot into his house.

Thick black smoke from burning tires filled the air. Palestinian teenagers and young adults began building barricades to delay, if only for a short while, the military takeover of their village. Jonathan joined them, helping several teenagers to move a run-down white van into the middle of the road. Some of the protestors used the van as cover, throwing stones at the soldiers, who responded with rubber bullets. As the bullets hit the toppled van, more and more light appeared through the punctured holes. From behind one of the buildings, Anna yelled at Jonathan, "Don't be stupid—come back here!" Reluctantly, he ran back a few meters. In the midst of the commotion someone began shouting that there were snipers on the rooftops. Suddenly, one of the teenagers who had been standing behind the van fell, blood trickling from his forehead. He was the fourth fatality.

The demonstration ended. Scores of people rushed to the medical clinic to find out what had happened to the injured protesters. Jonathan and Anna headed back to Tel Aviv, which, though only a forty-five-minute car ride distant, seemed light-years away. On the way home they listened to the radio. During a news flash, a military spokesperson announced that the "incident in Bidu was under investigation." Later the military declared that live ammunition had not been used to disperse the demonstration, only rubber bullets.

THE MEETING

On a warm autumn morning more than four and a half years after this incident, I met with twenty-six-year-old Jonathan Pollak. I traveled from Beersheba to his apartment in Jaffa, which he shares with a few other activists. Having reached the dilapidated building, I reread the email with the directions to his home to make sure that I had gotten the address right. It was then that I noticed, for the first time, the lines below his name: "Brothers and Sisters, what are your real desires? Sit in the drugstore, look distant, empty, bored, drinking some tasteless coffee? Or perhaps BLOW IT UP OR BURN IT DOWN. . . . You can't reform profit capitalism and inhumanity. Just kick it till it breaks. Angry Brigades, Communiqué 8."

After climbing two flights of stairs, I entered the apartment, whose two-room suite Jonathan occupies. A black bicycle hanging from the ceiling, four bookcases full of books, mostly of a political nature, a computer, a bed, a small coffee table, a few chairs, and a worn carpet adorned his rooms. Jonathan was wearing black pants and a sleeveless shirt, leaving his tattoos visible for all to see. Every five to ten minutes his cell phone vibrated as he received calls and SMS messages from other activists about an olive harvest scheduled for the following Tuesday. He switched from Hebrew to Arabic and then to English, depending on who was on the other end. While I have known Jonathan for many years, this was the first time that we sat down to talk.

POLITICAL ROOTS

Jonathan is the grandson of the sailor Nimrod Eshel, who in 1951 led the sailors' revolt against the all-powerful Prime Minister David Ben-Gurion and the

Histadrut, which had been founded in 1920 as a federation of Jewish trade unions. By securing the rights of its members and offering them an array of social services, the Histadrut not only managed to enlist about 75 percent of the Jewish workforce within less than a decade of its creation but rapidly became one of the most powerful institutions in prestate Israel, a position that it was able to sustain for many years after the state's establishment. The Histadrut has always been a peculiar institution, because this union body not only was the largest employer in Israel for years but also perceived its primary role as advancing national rather than class interests.

Thus, when Eshel and his fellow sailors felt that the Histadrut was not representing their interests, they decided to create an independent workers' union. Fearing, however, that this would diminish its powers, the Histadrut refused to allow it. Ben-Gurion joined the fray and labeled the sailors "traitors" and "enemies of the state." Police and hired scabs were sent to storm the ships and violently remove the workers from the vessels, while the Histadrut attempted to enlist other sailors to replace the existing workforce. These strategies have been used elsewhere to split and crush workers' organizations, but when Ben-Gurion understood that the sailors would not give up on the idea of creating their own union, he adopted an unusual approach. He instructed the Israeli military to call up many of the sailor activists for reserve duty in an effort to undermine the workers and their organizers. Thus, he used the military, an ostensibly apolitical institution, to advance his political agenda. But even this strategy did not break the sailors, and they continued their strike. Finally, following a violent police attack against one of the ships, they gave in. Despite the failure to achieve their goals, Eshel became a mythological figure, a laborer who managed, against all odds, to stand up to Ben-Gurion.

POLITICAL INTERPOLATION

Not surprisingly, Jonathan's mother, Tami, was a red-diaper baby and grew up in an intensely political household. She, however, chose not to dedicate her life to politics, and after marrying the Israeli actor Yossi Pollak, she studied psychology and currently has a practice in Tel Aviv. Politics, though, was always an important part of the Pollak household, and in 1982, when Jonathan was a few months old, Tami took him to his first protest. It occurred three months after Israel's June 1982 invasion of Lebanon and a few days following the Sabra and Shatila massacre.

The war in Lebanon is remembered for its many intrigues, among them the pact between Israel and the Lebanese president-elect Bashir Gemayel, the leader of the Kataeb Party, which had a military arm called the Phalange. The Phalangists were Maronite Christian militiamen. They played a central role in the Lebanese Civil War, which erupted in 1975 and was characterized by sectarian violence.

Over the years the major opponents and leading targets of Phalangist attacks were the Palestinians in Lebanon, led by the Palestine Liberation Organization (PLO). The deep-rooted animosity between the Phalange and the PLO was well know to Israeli officials, a fact that did not sway the Israeli military from permitting Phalangists to enter the Palestinian refugee camps Sabra and Shatila a day after the assassination of Gemayel. While it eventually turned out that a member of the Syrian Social Nationalist Party had murdered him, at the time the Phalange thought a PLO gunman had carried out the political assassination. Under the command of Elie Hobeika, the militiamen murdered somewhere between eight hundred and thirty-five hundred Palestinian children, adults, and elderly in a bloodbath that lasted between thirty-six and forty-eight hours.

The two camps are on the outskirts of Beirut in an area that was under Israeli control in September 1982. Outrage erupted in Israel when it became clear that Israeli soldiers camping nearby had watched the massacre of the Palestinian refugees without stopping it. According to police estimates, four hundred thousand people filled the streets of Tel Aviv in the biggest protest in Israel's history. Obviously, Jonathan does not remember the demonstration, but he knows and values the fact that he was there.

Jonathan does recollect a demonstration that took place a few years later. A couple of weeks after the eruption of the Palestinian uprising in December 1987, known as the First Intifada, Tami took five-year-old Jonathan and his baby brother to a march on the boardwalk from Tel Aviv to Jaffa. Yesh Gvul, the Israeli movement of soldiers who refuse to serve in Lebanon and the Occupied Palestinian Territories, had organized the march to protest the ruthless measures that the Israeli military was deploying against the Palestinians' uprising. No one expected the event to become violent, least of all Tami, but at one point police on horses clashed with the demonstrators. The image of his mother running for cover with a stroller in one hand and himself in the other is still engraved in Jonathan's memory.

ANIMAL RIGHTS, PUNK, AND ANARCHISM

Initially, Jonathan's political development and activism were unrelated to the occupation of Palestinian territories or Israel's relations with its Arab neighbors. One day, at the ripe age of seven, he asked his mom what they were eating for dinner, and when she answered that it was a cow, he decided that he would never eat animals again. It was an instinctive decision, based, as he tells it today, on empathy toward living creatures.

A few years later, when he was in seventh grade, his class went on a day trip to the amusement park in Tel Aviv where trained dolphins performed for large audiences. As the children were entering the building, he stopped by a group of people who were distributing flyers that protested the cruelty of holding the dolphins in captivity. Twelve-year-old Jonathan was struck by what they were saying and immediately joined the fledgling animal rights group Anonymous.

At the time, Anonymous was made up mostly of anarchists who had created the animal rights organization following the breakup of the Israeli anarchist movement two years earlier. The members were much older than Jonathan, but they were friendly and inclusive. Quickly, they became his social community and the organization a central part of his life. The group campaigned against numerous corporations that were particularly cruel to animals, including McDonald's; it distributed flyers, sprayed graffiti, and obstructed traffic to influence public opinion. Around this time, members of the Animal Liberation Front and some people from Anonymous carried out a number of sabotage operations, such as entering laboratories to free animals.

As his commitment to animal rights deepened, Jonathan showed up less and less for school. The studies bored him, and he did not really understand why he needed to sit in a classroom for so many hours. He rapidly developed an aversion toward regimented activities, particularly studies which are in some way policed. By ninth grade he decided to drop out. Animal rights, anarchism, and the Israeli punk scene filled his time. He adopted the straight-edge lifestyle, which had emerged in the United States in the 1980s punk scene to counter the dominant radical individualism and live-for-the-moment ideals. Straight edgers refrained from alcohol, tobacco, and drug use, and the movement later also adopted vegetarianism and a commitment to animal rights. Although Jonathan may not have been able to articulate it at the time, he now understands that he became a straight edger to distance himself from the pervasive cultural obsession with money and the commodification of leisure. Today, through the filter of his years of activism and ability to translate straight edge into clear political terms, it is clear that neither asceticism nor an attraction toward some kind of purity motivated his decision, but rather a desire to take part in the creation of an antihegemonic culture.

The hardcore punk scene in Israel was tiny during the 1990s, but it was intricately tied to anarchist activism and politics. The atmosphere at shows by bands like Dir Yassin was political in a very deep and in-your-face way. Pollak, who is not a musician, helped design some of the posters for these shows. In the mid-1990s, in the midst of the Oslo years, when most people in Israel were euphoric about the possibility of reaching a settlement with the Palestinians and the Israeli peace camp was supporting the Israeli government and its policies, Jonathan helped prepare fanzines (noncorporatized pamphlets or magazines produced by fans or activists who wish to share their cultural, political, and economic interests with others) calling on soldiers to refuse to serve in the military. He was twelve going on thirteen at the time.

His anarchist friends also organized weekly protests against the military. During Independence Day in 1995, Jonathan went to distribute flyers against the military in Tel Aviv's central celebration area. People who came to attend the festivities got angry, a commotion erupted, and just before several individuals attacked Jonathan and his fellow distributers, the police arrested the anarchists for sedition and for disturbing the public order. Jonathan was thirteen years old. He remained silent throughout the interrogation, taking, as it were, the Fifth. At this early age, he already knew how to follow the anarchist activists' culture of arrest. When the police released the offenders late at night, he and his fellow detainees decided to celebrate—happy at what they had achieved on Independence Day.

Jonathan's conception of anarchism at the time was primarily instinctive. Currently, he understands it as the *aspiration* to abolish hierarchy, knowing full well that this is an impossible task and that anarchism is consequently, by definition, a never-ending struggle. "People who are against rape," he explains today,

> are against rape absolutely, but they also realize that they cannot do away with rape altogether. We are absolutely against hierarchy and exploitation, but we are also aware that overcoming hierarchy is impossible. It is, however, possible to create a better society, and this is our objective. I do not mean a better society in the sense of offering a prescription of how society needs to be organized, since anarchism is not an ideology of *after the revolution*. . . . It is the struggle to expand the boundaries of ethics that interests me. . . . I am not a utopian. I do not believe in the fulfillment of the good society, but I do believe we should struggle to improve society and to provide people with more and better opportunities.

At the age of sixteen, Jonathan began working as a graphic designer in one of the mainstream city papers—Tel Aviv's equivalent of the *Village Voice*. A year later he left home. While military service is mandatory for Jewish Israelis, conscription was simply not an option for him. The Israeli military was not particularly eager to draft him either, and at the age of seventeen he received a letter notifying him that he had been released from duty thanks to a regulation that involved "a surplus of manpower." "I had quit school a couple of years earlier," he explains. "I already had a police record for a few arrests, and when I arrived at the conscription station, I refused to cooperate and told them that I did not intend to be drafted. . . . The personnel there seemed to agree that it might be a better idea not to draft me."

EUROPE AND THE ANTIGLOBALIZATION MOVEMENT

Several months later, in September 2000, Jonathan traveled to Prague to help with the preparations for the demonstrations against the World Bank and International Monetary Fund summit. The protests drew a considerable amount of attention, with the international media continuously covering the thousands of activists who had traveled to the Czech Republic from all over the world to demonstrate against the policies of these two global financial institutions. Ultimately, they led to the cancellation of all of the meetings scheduled for the last day.

Following the summit, Jonathan decided to stay in Europe and settled in Amsterdam as a squatter, living during his entire two-year sojourn there on $2,500 that he had saved while working as a graphic designer in Israel. He continued his activities in the antiglobalization movement and for animal rights, but he also began working on issues relating to migration and squatting rights. Much of his time he spent in front of computers, as part of a collective providing free Internet access through recycled computers with open-source software and wi-fi antennas.

It is not coincidental that Jonathan did not join any local or international nongovernmental organizations during his stay in Europe. "I do not like NGOs," he says, "since they represent the professionalization of resistance in its worse sense. They have introduced and helped perpetuate an extremely destructive political culture. The nine-to-five struggle, the struggle that is policed by the NGO itself, ends up circumscribing political goals and consequently restricts rather than empowers activism and activists."

In July 2001, he traveled with friends to Genoa, Italy, to join the protests against the G8, a governmental forum of eight of the most prosperous industrial democracies in the world. This was the heyday of the antiglobalization movement. The Italian police tried to prevent activists from entering the country, while in Genoa the government suspended the freedom of movement for the duration of the G8 summit in an attempt to monitor protesters arriving from across Europe. A Red Zone, surrounded by barricades and declared off-limits for nonresidents, was also designated for protesters who managed to reach the city. Notwithstanding these restrictions, the summit drew an estimated two hundred thousand demonstrators. Jonathan took part in the protests, many of which developed into clashes with the Italian police. The police killed one demonstrator, and dozens were hospitalized; there were a number of documented cases of activists being abused in custody.

When the summit ended, Jonathan returned to Amsterdam, but after a little less than a year he was deported to Israel. Undercover agents arrested him during a protest, and after a week in an isolated cell, he was taken in handcuffs to the airport and put on a plane. He landed in late March 2002, perhaps the bloodiest month in Israel's history in terms of civilian deaths, with eighty-one Israelis killed in suicide attacks by Hamas and Palestinian Islamic Jihad. On March 27, thirty people were killed and 140 injured in the Park Hotel in the coastal city of Netanya during a Passover celebration. Jonathan arrived in Tel Aviv right before this massacre, which prompted Ariel Sharon's government to launch the military operation dubbed Defensive Shield. Call-up notices for twenty thousand reserve soldiers had been issued a few days before the operation, the largest draft since the 1982 Lebanon War.

THE SECOND INTIFADA

On March 29, 2002, Defensive Shield began. Tanks rolled into Palestinian cities and towns throughout the West Bank, and population centers were placed under prolonged curfews, confining residents to their homes for weeks on end. In March and April, close to five hundred Palestinians were killed. The most lethal raids were the ones in Nablus and the Jenin refugee camp, where Israel made use of aerial shelling, tanks, armored bulldozers, and infantry to quell Palestinian resistance. The blanket curfew in several cities, towns, villages, and refugee camps drastically restricted basic movement, entailed the denial of access to medical treatment, and caused a severe shortage of food, water, and medical supplies. The violence was directed toward not only Palestinians, as it had been in the past, but also the civilian infrastructure. The operation severely damaged or destroyed roads, electricity grids, water pipelines, and buildings throughout the West Bank, thus erasing the few signs of the Palestinian Authority's achievements during the Oslo years. According to assessments by the World Bank, Defensive Shield resulted in damages of $361 million to Palestinian infrastructure and institutions. The United Nations Economic and Social Council calculated that from the eruption of the Second Intifada to May 2002, a total of 385,808 fruit and olive trees had been uprooted, while several wells had been destroyed. This type of violence was unheard of before Oslo—primarily because Israel considered itself responsible for Palestinian infrastructure—and its magnitude shocked Jonathan and his fellow activists.

On April 14, 2002, in the midst of the massive military operation, the Israeli cabinet decided to establish a permanent barrier, to "improve and reinforce the readiness and operational capability in coping with terrorism." The idea of creating a wall between Israel and its Arab neighbors is by no means new and can be traced back not only to the writings of the Zionist leader Ze'ev Jabotinsky and his right-wing Revisionist camp but also to the ideologues of mainstream Zionism. And there was a precedent: in the middle of the Oslo peace process, Prime Minister Yitzhak Rabin had decided to build a fence around the Gaza Strip. Within a relatively short period, a patrol road and a series of fences fifty-four kilometers long closed off the border between the strip and Israel, leaving only four passageways to connect the two regions. The Palestinians did not oppose the construction of this fence, since it was erected on the Green Line, the border that differentiated Israel proper from the area it occupied in the 1967 war, as determined by the 1949 armistice agreement. Not long after the construction of Gaza's fence, military officials introduced the idea of creating a barrier to separate the West Bank from Israel. The discussions concerning the erection of this barrier did not, however, reach the highest echelons within Israel's ruling establishment until November 2000, about a month after the outbreak of the Second Intifada. A public outcry within Israel for the creation of some kind of fence that would stop Palestinian suicide bombers seemed to have had an impact. Prime Minister Ariel Sharon entered office a few months later, and although he initially opposed the construction of a physical barrier between Israel and the West Bank, he quickly recognized that an overwhelming majority of Israeli citizens supported it.

Sharon's ambivalence toward this project stemmed primarily from the fear that such a barrier would reestablish the Green Line and thus undermine attempts to actualize the dream of a greater Israel, undoing years of intense political labor in one fell swoop. Yet the barrier had become a byword for security at a time when suicide bombers were exploding themselves on public buses and in shopping malls, killing dozens and injuring hundreds of Israeli citizens. It was considered a mechanism for achieving complete separation between Israelis and Palestinians, and since the Likud in general and Sharon in particular had run on the national-security ticket, it was very difficult for them to ignore the public's wishes in this matter.

Even though the government used security language to formulate its decision, it had no intention of building the entire barrier on the Green Line. Accordingly, Israel began erecting the barrier deep inside Palestinian territory, severely shrinking and regulating Palestinian space. The barrier leveled hills while restricting inhabitants' mobility and otherwise egregiously violating their basic human rights. The fact that it has not been constructed on the internationally recognized border underscores that one of its major objectives is to redraw the border between Israel and the West Bank. The barrier, at the time of writing, surrounds fifty-six Jewish settlements, legitimizing them and incorporating their land and 171,000 inhabitants into Israel. The building of the wall in East Jerusalem is meant to reinforce the 1967 annexation of this part of the city and to further legitimize the 183,800 Jewish settlers living there. Thus, if the barrier does become the new border, it will solve the problem of about 87 percent of Israel's illegal settlers. The remaining 13 percent, or 52,500 settlers, will have to evacuate, as the Jewish settlers in the Gaza Strip were forced to do. It is unclear what Israel intends to do about the 30,500 Palestinians who are now living between the barrier and the Green Line, but even if it does not evacuate them, it is still likely that they will be unable to stay in this area, since in many respects their infrastructure is being drastically undermined.

Since Sharon's fateful decision to build the annexation barrier, Palestinian land continues to be confiscated to allow it to encircle Jewish settlement blocs from the east and in this way incorporate them into Israel proper. Instead of separating Israelis from Palestinians, in many areas the barrier separates Palestinians from Palestinians. While it is presented as a temporary security mechanism, it has been deployed as a political means of confiscating land and redrawing Israel's internationally recognized border.

Jonathan and his anarchist friends were among the first to conclude that this was the barrier's objective, and they undertook an energetic campaign in opposition to its construction. They began by creating a camp with a few tents on lands owned by Palestinian farmers from the small West Bank village of Mas'ha, which is home to thirty-two families. For months Jonathan and a group of young Israelis and internationals lived in the camp, which enabled them to join the villagers in their struggle to stop the building of the barrier, which would eventually leave 96 percent of the town's agricultural land on the eastern side and consequently out of reach of its rightful owners. They managed to hold off the bulldozers for four months. During this period the camp became a kind of experiment in direct-democracy decision making, with long discussions into the night followed by direct actions in Mas'ha and a few neighboring villages. Even though the land was ultimately confiscated and the bulldozers destroyed the camp, the adjacent olive groves, and part of a Palestinian house, Jonathan believes that the activists who tried to save the land emerged from the struggle empowered. It inspired him and his friends to create the movement Anarchists against the Wall (AATW).

FROM PEACE TALKS TO ANTICOLONIALISM

The campaign against the annexation barrier commenced several months after Jonathan had returned to Israel and after his first reencounter with the police, during a Peace Now protest staged in front of Israel's military headquarters. Neither the Peace Now organizers nor the police approved of the sign Jonathan was holding, which read, "The Knesset [Israeli parliament] is the Infrastructure of Terrorism," and underneath, "Profile 21 Now." The military classifies the physical and mental health of each potential soldier with standard profiles; those who have Profile 21 are considered mentally ill or unstable and therefore unfit to serve, and some people try to avoid conscription by being so designated. Thus, Jonathan was calling on Israelis to refuse to serve in the military, which is antithetical to Peace Now's position, since it officially opposes the Israeli refusenik movement. Peace Now, after all, had been founded in the late 1970s by a number of reserve military officers who were concerned that the Menachem Begin government would not respond favorably to Anwar Sadat's peace initiative. In due course, it turned into a mass-based grassroots organization whose aim was to pressure Israel to reach peace with Egypt and other Arab countries and to withdraw from the territories occupied in 1967, and it was able to get tens of thousands of demonstrators to turn out in support of its goals.

Jonathan is critical of Peace Now and other members of the Israeli Zionist peace camp. These groups want to sustain the Jewish character of the state, and anyone who does so cannot be a leftist, since such a state would be racist, in Jonathan and his anarchist friends' opinion. This is not to say that Peace Now is not part of the Israeli peace camp—it is—but rather that the anarchists do not conceive of themselves as part of this camp; they are members of the anticolonial camp. The fact that their struggle is all encompassing has led many of them to seek to change the terms of the debate. In the context of the Israeli-Palestinian conflict, the term *peace*, for example, has become, in Jonathan's opinion, a form of Newspeak: translated into English, it means that Israel will continue the occupation. He is equally critical of the language of human rights. Instead of "peace" and "human rights," he insists that the tradition of resistance needs to be accentuated and strengthened. Therefore, when people ask him to situate himself on the Israeli political map, he answers that he is an anticolonialist and not a peacenik.

Zionism, in this view, is a colonial movement that gained the support of the international community partly as a result of the catastrophe of the Holocaust and partly because the members of the movement were European and white and their demands suited Western interests. The Zionists ended up forming, in Jonathan's eyes, a racist state where Jews have more rights than others. Hence he also identifies himself as an anti-Zionist.

This manifests itself in the political strategy and way of life that Jonathan has adopted. It is unclear whether Peace Now activists have ever spent the night in a Palestinian village or joined a preplanned Palestinian protest and followed the lead of the Palestinians. Jonathan, by contrast, has often been a guest in Palestinian villagers and on principle will not lead a protest but rather will join it in the most organic way possible while constantly trying to remain aware of his privileges as an occupier. He does not want to be a "colonial liberator" coming to free "the natives," since he considers it vital that the oppressed lead their own struggle, that the Palestinians liberate themselves. It is his responsibility to struggle with them but not to control or lead their struggle. That being said, his life revolves around the struggle, so his community is made up of activists—Jews, Palestinians, and internationals—and his job is a side gig that supports the activities he considers important.

Jonathan believes in duty and lives a life of duty. The duty of all Israeli citizens, he tells me, is to resist immoral policies and actions carried out in their name. "Israeli apartheid and occupation," AATW's website notes, "isn't going to end by itself—it will end when it becomes ungovernable and unmanageable. It is time to physically oppose the bulldozers, the army and the occupation." Jonathan might very well have written these lines.

Popular committees in the Occupied Palestinian Territories often coordinate AATW's activities in their villages. In 2004, Jonathan, together with AATW, joined the village of Budrus in its struggle against the barrier. The village's popular committee mobilized the community, and through a persistent struggle and continuous resistance, the villagers forced the Israeli government to change the barrier's route so that most of it was built on land not owned by the farmers. The mere presence of Jonathan and other Israeli anarchists at the Palestinians' demonstrations offers the latter some degree of protection against military violence, since the Israeli rules of engagement that regulate the opening of fire are significantly different when Jewish Israelis are present. Budrus's success inspired many other villages to mobilize popular resistance and also helped change many Palestinians' position regarding contact with Israelis. Though some of the villages were initially hesitant to cooperate with Israelis, over the past years not a single one has rejected AATW's participation in efforts to stop the annexation barrier. Consequently, AATW has played a crucial role in almost all the struggles against the barrier, not least in Bil'in, which has gained international recognition for its unwillingness to yield.

Jonathan tries to be respectful of the local culture, and even though there are irreconcilable tensions between his anarchist world view and traditional Palestinian society, he is willing to overlook them within the context of the occupation. Anarchism, in his eyes, is first and foremost the struggle of the here and now; it is the ongoing struggle against oppression. Therefore he believes that the people with whom AATW struggles do not need to be anarchists or socialists; they do not need to rally behind a libertarian cause to be worthy of his support: "What is happening there is definitely a struggle against oppression, and that is enough for me. There is no perfect society, and if one waits for a perfect society and perfect allies in order to join the struggle, then he or she will never struggle."

VIOLENCE VERSUS NONVIOLENCE

Nonviolent movements reject the deployment of violence under any circumstances for three major reasons. First, violence usually begets violence, and therefore the use of violence will only exacerbate an already bad situation. Second, in deploying violence, one carries out an act that is in essence unethical, and therefore he or she becomes unethical. Finally, by deploying violence, one often loses the moral high ground. For Jonathan, by contrast, violence is not unethical a priori. Circumstances determine the ethics of violence. Not every form of violence is acceptable, but there are acts of violence that are at times necessary, and carrying them out is the moral thing to do. One example is the stone throwing that has characterized the First Intifada and the current protests in Palestinian villages. In Jonathan's view, this violence has proven to be extremely efficient and is also ethical. The ongoing confrontations with the military during the Second Intifada are also very powerful, he maintains, since they attract the international media and draw attention to Israel's violence. In his view, the Palestinians could not have reached similar objectives using only nonviolent methods.

Whereas those who espouse nonviolence think that violence ultimately destroys the soul, in Jonathan's view violence can be empowering. People, he maintains, do not like to be victims. It is difficult to ask people to join a struggle in order to become punching bags. To create a popular movement, one needs to be able to mobilize people, and according to Jonathan, in some cases stone throwing is necessary for that. "Stones," he says, "create symbols, stones allow people to present and channel rage, and stones are something that people can connect with. Stone throwing can be extremely empowering, since people [who do it] do not feel victimized." The claim that violence can be liberating and can help create a more moral society is, to be sure, a provocative argument but one that Jonathan takes very seriously. He justifies his claim by noting that even systems of criminal law organized by the state recognize and acknowledge the right to self-defense. In his view the Israeli military is the direct aggressor against the Palestinians, so they have a right and at times an obligation to defend themselves using violence. "I think violence should be minimized. I do not like violence, I do not enjoy it, and I do not take pleasure when anyone is hurt, including soldiers, but at times it is the moral thing to do."

STRUGGLE AS A DESIRE

Jonathan has taken part in hundreds of demonstrations and has been arrested and beaten on numerous occasions. At the time we met in Jaffa, he had forty-one entries in his police record, had four pending indictments, and had already been tried three times. He was found not guilty twice, and in the third trial he was held responsible for an illegal assembly and threatened with three months' imprisonment if caught protesting illegally again. When asked about the driving force behind his activism, he mentions the importance of a political ethos based on political commitment, devotion, and desire. "People often relate to political activism as a sacrifice," he says, "yet I cannot live without it. Often those who are not activists cannot understand this. They fail to see that living a life of resistance is empowering."

Paradoxically, because the horrors are in their backyard, Jonathan and other Israeli anarchists have both an opportunity and, in Jonathan's opinion, a responsibility that is in many respects unique. He believes that in Israel he has more freedom than he would in the United States, where a person like him would most likely have been imprisoned a long time ago. The cruel irony is that his freedom is in many respects due to the privileges that Jews enjoy in Israel. By allowing Jews like Jonathan to resist the occupation, Israel can portray itself as a liberal democracy even as it oppresses millions of non-Jews and denies them their most basic political and civil rights. Jonathan is not a liberal and suspects those who adopt the liberal perspective. He notes, for example, that a trace of liberalism can be detected in the different people-to-people groups. The underlying assumption of such groups is that the conflict is the result of a lack of contact between Israelis and Palestinians. If only the two sides would meet and get to know each other, the conflict would be solved. But anyone who visits the Occupied Territories and talks with Palestinians knows that the attempt to normalize the occupier-occupied relationship by drinking tea and talking as if the two sides are equal has traumatized them. Personal encounters are important, indeed vital, in Jonathan's view, but the idea that the occupation will end by people getting to know one another is absurd. To him, the real problem has little to do with ignorance regarding the other side, even though this ignorance is widespread. The major problem, he says, is the occupation.

Jonathan has accordingly adopted the pervasive Palestinian view that at this moment in history any personal relationship between Israelis and Palestinians needs to be based on resisting the occupation. All his relationships with Palestinians began with resistance and are based on resistance. As I begin packing my tape recorder before returning to Beersheba, he reminds me of the Arabic saying "You can always forget someone you laughed with, but you can never forget someone you cried with." From Budrus and Bil'in to Hebron and Ni'lin, Jonathan has witnessed a fair amount of suffering, and it is, I suspect, precisely his willingness to acknowledge this suffering and his decision to resist it that connects him with the Palestinians.

25

Abu Ahmad and His Handalas

Ala Alazzeh

The tradition of the oppressed teaches us that the "state of emergency" in which we live is not the exception but the rule.
—WALTER BENJAMIN, "THESES ON THE PHILOSOPHY OF HISTORY"

Abu Ahmad, forty-one years old, is a political activist and the founder of a small grassroots community center. He lives in the Beit Jibrin refugee camp in the Occupied Palestinian Territories (OPT) with his wife and two children. The Beit Jibrin camp is the smallest West Bank camp in terms of population (1,700) and covers only .02 square kilometers. Its original residents came from the destroyed village of Beit Jibrin. Forty-one percent of the camp population is under the age of fourteen and 59 percent under twenty-five years old. Almost a quarter of the camp's people live below the poverty line, with 15 percent characterized as hardship cases, according to the United Nations Relief and Works Agency for Palestine Refugees (UNRWA). Despite their generational differences and different experiences, Abu Ahmad's life has overlapped with the lives of many youths in the camp. His experiences have informed his work with them, mainly those who came into adolescence amid the breakout of the al-Aqsa Intifada in 2000, making him an important mentor. Issa and Maher, two of the first members of the community center, joined when they were twelve and in a few years were running daily programs and overseeing the younger generation. The center was named after Handala, a political cartoon character of a ten-year-old boy, which became one of the most popular symbols of Palestinian nationalism. Abu Ahmad takes pleasure in calling the youths "my Handalas."

LIFE AND POLITICS

Abu Ahmad was born in 1968, one year after the Israeli army occupied the West Bank and the Gaza Strip. His parents were residing in the Beit Jibrin refugee camp, having fled their ancestral village of Beit Jibrin in the western hills of Hebron, an area that was ethnically cleansed in the 1948 war. On the very day of his birth, the camp was placed under curfew by the Israeli occupying forces after Palestinian communist activists called for demonstrations, preventing his mother from going to the hospital. She screamed at her husband to do something. According to Abu Ahmad's mother, her husband left the house barefoot and approached an Israeli army Jeep, telling the officer that he needed to get a midwife. The officer ordered the soldiers to stop pointing their guns at him and offered him a ride to the midwife's house. Despite the humaneness of this gesture, Abu Ahmad's father refused the offer and insisted that he would walk. He did not want people to think he was a collaborator, as collaboration with the occupation army was—and still is—a social disgrace in Palestine.

At the time of Abu Ahmad's birth, support for the Palestine Liberation Organization (PLO) was sweeping through refugee camps in Jordan, Lebanon, and Syria, and a parallel underground process was taking place in the West Bank and Gaza. PLO supporters and other activists, including pan-Arabists and communists, started organizing armed and unarmed resistance activities. A massive campaign of arrests, corporal punishment, and curfew confronted their efforts toward popular mobilization. The Beit Jibrin camp was subject to a curfew and constant search and arrest campaigns, part of Israel's attempt to prevent the emergence of a movement of popular resistance in the OPT. One such campaign resulted in dozens of deportations and hundreds of arrests, including that of Abu Ahmad's father. He was incarcerated for five months and tortured to forcibly acknowledge that he was a member of Fatah, the central faction of the PLO. Despite these repressive measures, support for the PLO did not diminish, and acts of resistance continued.

Abu Ahmad and his seven siblings grew up in two rooms, each measuring eighty square feet. They were built by UNRWA, which was established one year after the *Nakba* began in 1948, to provide humanitarian aid, education, and basic medical care for Palestinian refugees. Like all kids from the camp, Abu Ahmad studied at UNRWA-run schools. He received a decent education, although he didn't like school, because of the overcrowded classes and the teachers' use of physical punishment to enforce discipline. At the age of twelve, he joined the tourist industry, working after school in a small olive-wood workshop carving sculptures of Christian iconic symbols. This local handicraft, which can be traced back to the influx of religious tourists to Bethlehem in the seventeenth century, came to serve a central role in the town's economy. As a young teenager, Abu Ahmad, who loved to play soccer, joined the camp team and a camp voluntary work committee.

The committee, comprising youths led by political activists, focused on building in the community, cleaning the camp streets, planting trees in nearby villages, and organizing cultural events from time to time. Abu Ahmad's early exposure to politics on a larger scale came in 1982, when the Israeli army invaded Lebanon. He remembers watching PLO fighters leaving Beirut on a TV that was bought only a few years before. That scene nurtured a daily habit of listening to the news, mostly on the radio and from his favorite station, Radio Monte Carlo, an Arabic-language station owned by the French government.

Higher education in Palestinian culture is a main source of cultural pride, as well as an assertion of social status and a means of social mobility. However, like most of the youths who grew up in the Beit Jibrin camp in the early 1980s, Abu Ahmad started construction work in Israel after finishing high school. Although he achieved college-qualifying grades, his family was supporting three other children in college at that time and was not able to finance another college education. The UNRWA Teachers' College in Ramallah was another option closed to him, because of a policy restricting the opportunity to only one member per family. This policy was a result not only of UNRWA's aim of providing services to as wide a social base as possible but also of the agency's larger procedure of treating Palestinian refugee needs on a household rather than individual basis.

Abu Ahmad was forced to take a nonunionized labor job in Israel and hope for enrollment in college a year later. He worked mostly in settlements around Jerusalem, leaving the house at six in the morning to go to work or to meet *al-ma'lem*. The Arabic *al-ma'lem* generally refers to a teacher or a work chief, but in this context it meant the contractor of the construction company, an Iraqi Jew who came to the refugee camps in search of Palestinian laborers. It is worth noting that some form of relationship developed between the ma'lem and the workers from the camp, as the ma'lem would visit their houses as a guest. However, the interaction was one-sided, for the workers would never enter al-ma'lem's house unless for a specific job. The construction work continued for the first few months of the 1987 intifada, a period marked by *shabab* (youths) in the camp throwing stones at Israeli cars, identified by their yellow plates, although not at the cars of al-ma'lemeen, or construction bosses. Abu Ahmad recalls the day when al-ma'lem told all the workers that he wouldn't have jobs for them for a few months because the Israeli army reserve had drafted him to militarily confront the intifada.

While direct resistance to the occupation had been persistent during the first two decades of Israeli rule, it was generally intermittent and locally based; periods of more widespread unified struggle did not last long. With the outbreak of the First Intifada in December 1987, however, another political landscape took form. Abu Ahmad was nearly twenty years old at the time. In addition to the stone-throwing protests, popular demonstrations and large movements of civil disobedience against the military occupation characterized the intifada. Resistance throughout the OPT was now daily, coordinated, and resilient—a veritable uprising. Israeli responses included massive arrest campaigns, house demolitions, deportations of key activists, and long-term curfew policies. During this time, there was hardly a family in the Beit Jibrin camp without members who had been either imprisoned or injured.

Human rights organizations estimate that since 1967, Israel has imprisoned 650,000 Palestinians, nearly 20 percent of the entire population of the OPT. Most of the Beit Jibrin camp's youths participated in some aspect of the First Intifada's activities, Abu Ahmad included. He joined one of the leftist PLO factions and started organizing activities like graffitiing walls, producing Palestinian flags, distributing leaflets, and throwing stones at soldiers. He was arrested only a few months after the start of the intifada and placed in administrative detention, a practice in which the Israeli military holds a prisoner without charge or trial for indefinitely renewable six-month terms, often based on what Israeli intelligence calls "secret evidence," which does not need to be substantiated in court or revealed to the accused. His arrest was not exceptional, as a majority of the youths in the West Bank and Gaza experienced incarceration.

Abu Ahmad spent his first imprisonment in Ketziot Prison in the Negev Desert, which its inmates renamed Ansar 3, referencing an Israeli detention camp for PLO members in the Israel-occupied sections of southern Lebanon. Though the 1987 intifada began as a grassroots popular movement led by West Bank and Gaza residents, the renaming of Ketziot was part of a larger effort to emphasize the connection between the intifada in the West Bank and Gaza and the PLO-led liberation project in exile. For Abu Ahmad and his comrades, there was a continuity of struggle and unity of political experience among Palestinians in the OPT and the Diaspora, illustrated by naming children after PLO leaders and refusing legitimacy to any leadership unless the PLO approved it.

Abu Ahmad describes his detention experience in Ansar 3 as "fortunate" and "fruitful," because he encountered several older prisoners of diverse ideological backgrounds there. "In the middle of the night, a freezing one," he recalls, "soldiers knocked on the door. I knew they were coming to arrest me. I had fear but also a hidden feeling of pride. It took me a month to get used to the prison. For sure having many friends from the camp with me was helpful, but more important was having the older guys, who played the role of fathers and mentors." Many of them had been imprisoned in the early days of the 1967 occupation, and all were keen to pass on their stories, knowledge, and politics to Abu Ahmad and his generation. Abu Ahamd's understanding of the different factions and their political and ideological distinctions crystallized in Ansar 3. The older generation he met there came from four PLO factions: Fatah, the main faction; the Marxist-Leninist and pan-Arab Popular Front for the Liberation of Palestine (PFLP); the pro-Soviet Palestinian Communist Party (PCP); and finally, the Democratic Front for the

Liberation of Palestine (DFLP), which had split from the PFLP in 1969 over ideological disagreements. A much smaller number of prisoners came from a politicized Islamic ideological basis.

Prison taught Abu Ahmad about the "logic of colonialism and the logic of being colonized." But more important, it taught him the "persistence, devotion, and determination" that helped shape him into "a political being." As he described it, the experience in Ansar 3 was a form of national initiation, a traumatic yet productive rite of passage and an inspirational encounter that shaped his future political, ethical, and intellectual commitment to national liberation and questions of social justice.

The outbreak of the 1987 intifada and Abu Ahmad's multiple imprisonments delayed his higher education for five years, until 1992, when Israel closed the Gaza Strip off from the West Bank. This made it impossible for Gaza students to reach Ramallah and attend the Teachers' College, therefore opening space for Abu Ahmad. By the time he finished two years of teacher training in 1993, the PLO and the State of Israel had signed the Oslo Accords.

The PLO leadership envisioned the creation of the Palestinian Authority (PA) as the first step toward the establishment of a state, so it built statelike institutions, supported by a relatively large bureaucracy. Higher education in Palestinian society was now not only symbolic capital but also a necessary qualification for social advancement and economic stability. Abu Ahmad found a job in the PA bureaucracy, but although he had a degree in education, his work there shifted between clerking, accounting, and food inspection. Yet because he believed that neither his two-year diploma nor his political opposition to the Oslo Accords would enable him to advance beyond a low-ranking bureaucratic job, he decided to continue pursuing his higher education.

He enrolled in Al-Quds Open University, a PA-supported school designed as a continuing-education institute to serve those with day jobs or who were not able to go to conventional colleges because of the First Intifada, when universities were closed for long periods and a whole generation was not able to pursue its education. Although higher education has long been a central component of social recognition in Palestine, it began gaining more practical relevance among West Bankers in the 1990s owing to large structural transformations in the political and economical spheres, both globally and in Palestine/Israel.

The Oslo peace process coincided with and to a large degree enabled the spread and institutionalization of a neoliberal economic system within the space of Israel/Palestine that closed Israel off to an unprecedented degree from Palestinian workers, who were replaced by lower-cost laborers from Eastern Europe and Southeast Asia and at best could hope to work in tax-free industrial zones along the seam lines separating the OPT from Israel and Israeli settlements. The development of a semi-independent market within the West Bank, where private sector jobs became more available and nongovernmental organizations (NGOs) began to flourish, should have offset this process, yet it contributed to an internal neoliberal structure that resulted in a deeper dependency on the Israeli economy. But while Abu Ahmad's life might have seemed satisfactory, with a job and the opportunity to continue his education, that is not the way he experienced it:

> I wasn't happy with my job, where corruption was the norm. But neither my political beliefs nor the new reality after Oslo permitted me to work in the '48 areas [Israel proper], even if I wanted to. Israeli security forces would not allow it. I can't leave the country. I tried in 1998, but the Jordanian government didn't allow me to cross the border, for security reasons as well. So I needed to think of a way out of this reality. I turned to private work, where I failed miserably, and to education, where I succeeded.

In his last year at Al-Quds Open University, Abu Ahmad resigned from his "mundane and brainless bureaucratic job." With the help of a small loan from a local bank, he opened a small auto parts store. The work at the shop was in fact no less mundane than that of his government job, but at least he was free from bureaucracy. Unfortunately, Abu Ahmad's shop was at the entrance of the Beit Jibrin camp on one of Bethlehem's main roads into Jerusalem, which became a no-man's-land, a site of frequent military clashes, when the al-Aqsa Intifada broke out in 2000. As a result, his business collapsed, costing him most of his investment and savings.

However, the failure of Abu Ahmad's experiment should be attributed not only to the intifada's eruption but also to a vision of himself that was not compatible with the kind of work he was doing. Indeed, his efforts to combine his political activism with a business pursuit became a source of humor among his friends and family. They joked about whether he was opening a car parts shop or a library, speaking to the number of books in the shop, which exceeded the number of car parts.

In 2001, Abu Ahmad graduated with a degree in history and geography. He then started work as a history teacher in the public school system, obtaining a stable source of income and "an intellectually challenging profession."

NEW IDEAS: COMMUNITY YOUTH WORK

Before the start of the Oslo peace process, anti-occupation political activism was mostly action oriented, but this changed as opponents of Oslo struggled to devise effective ways of opposing the peace process and the power of the Fatah-dominated PA.

With the lack of clarity regarding how to resist the emerging Oslo process, many activists found themselves outside the political landscape, whether willingly or reluctantly. One was Abu Ahmad, who had decided to abandon disciplined factional activism and started thinking about new forms of action, imagining new norms of politics in Palestine. One of the ideas he shared with other activists in the Beit Jibrin camp was to found a community center, to help the camp's children overcome the hardship of camp life and to create a development model that would challenge the PA and the "fashionable" NGOs operating in the OPT.

Abu Ahmad recalls being approached by a Palestinian ex-leftist in the late 1990s about NGO work. The ex-leftist, who had just started a well-paying job in one of the new foreign-funded NGOs, approached him "to organize a meeting with people in the community to talk about tolerance and peace in Palestine." Abu Ahmad refused to be a part of such a meeting in the refugee camp because it would result in the camp being the focus of a "nice" report by the NGO that would neither refer to refugee rights nor to the source of the refugee population. For him, not acknowledging and addressing the impact of the past was the most effective way to ensure that another generation would grow up dispossessed of its homeland and in wretched conditions.

Instead, he and his cofounders viewed the community center as a response to both the burgeoning Western-funded NGO network, which draws its sustenance from the peace process, and the inability of political factions to appeal to national liberation as an inspiration for continued struggle against the weight of the PA and its United States–backed development paradigm. Abu Ahmad, like other activists, had particular distaste for the NGOs, which put hardly any effort into grassroots activism and organizing, preferring instead to speak a "fashionable liberal discourse of human rights, democracy, and good governance, and were trapped in the illusions of civil society, as if Palestinians were living in Sweden and not under military occupation."

He and his comrades were equally disdainful of the PA. For Abu Ahmad, the PA political paradigm was essentially a failure, representing nothing more than "the beautification of the ugly face of the occupation," and he argued that the Oslo Accords were a "one-sided 'peace' that enabled Israel to take more land and maintain its colonial project." As he would point out, all one has to do to understand where his view comes from would be to look toward the horizon in almost any direction from his house, which is increasingly surrounded by Israeli military bases and settlements.

Abu Ahmad believed that community development was the only way out of the dominant framework of politics and political practices in the OPT. He also understood that refugee camps were last on the PA's list of priorities and that the PA elite would compromise the refugees' right of return. With these beliefs in mind and with the support of other activists from the Beit Jibrin camp, he began mobilizing resources and organizing around the idea of a community center that would target the younger generation in the camp and advocate for the centrality of the right of return for Palestinian refugees. One of the project's main impediments was finding a suitable place for the center in the very crowded camp, most of whose families barely had adequate living spaces.

Throughout its sixty years of history, there were major transformations and improvements in the camp's living conditions. For the first ten years, Beit Jibrin camp refugees lived in tents. The Red Cross provided each family of fewer than five members with one tent. The winter season was the most horrendous experience for those who lived it. Families used to dig small channels around their tents to prevent the rainwater from turning their floor soil to mud. One year in the early 1950s, remembered as *sanat eth thaljeh el kbeereh,* "the year of the grand snow," saw the devastation of camp residences, with many children and old people killed. In 1958, UNRWA started to build shelters, eighty-square-foot rooms, to replace the tents, one room for each family of fewer than six people. By mid-1970, refugees had started to build new rooms, improving those built by UNRWA. Also around that time, the camp was connected to the city of Bethlehem's municipal water grid. By the late 1970s, electricity was provided to the camp. By the mid-1990s one finds hardly any UNRWA shelters standing, as almost all were replaced by new buildings. Meanwhile, the sewage system had been insulated, and most of the camp roads and alleys were paved.

As his family had demolished its UNRWA-built rooms and constructed a two-story house in the early 1990s, Abu Ahmad suggested using his living quarters there as a starting point for the community center until a more suitable location could be found. And indeed, his rooms became the site for language lessons and meetings for the center's founding committee.

THE HANDALA CULTURAL CENTER
AND THE NEW GENERATION

A few months after these initial meetings, a family moved out of its house in the camp to live in Bethlehem. The owner, a former activist, donated his property, free of rent for two years, for the use of a youth center in the camp. The house, below ground level and in a state of disrepair, consisted of three rooms, each representing a different era of the Beit Jibrin camp's history. The first room had thick stone walls covered with a mixture of dirt and straw. Because the camp initially only comprised tents donated by the Red Cross, some families started building these dirt-straw rooms as winter shelters in the 1950s. This form of construction, which was common among Palestinian villagers, was used mostly for the storage of crops and supplies. The second room was an eighty-square-foot UNRWA room, made of hollow cinderblock walls and a thin cement roof. The third room, built by the previous resident in the late 1970s, was made of cement plus surplus materials of a generally meager quality that he collected from an Israeli construction site where he worked. The disheveled nature of the place, however, did not prevent Abu Ahmad and his friends from pursuing their idea of establishing a community center, a place that would profoundly shape Abu Ahmad's life and more directly intertwine his story with that of the camp, bringing to life Mahmoud Darwish's famous lines about the power of art, and culture more broadly, to preserve a people under constant siege: "And we love life if we find a way to it. We dance in between martyrs and raise a minaret for violets or palm trees."

After a few months of intensive repairs by twenty volunteers, the site was child friendly, and it soon housed the Handala Cultural Center (HCC).

The center was named after Handala, a simple character designed and drawn by the famous Palestinian political cartoonist Naji al-Ali. Al-Ali introduced Handala in 1969 in *Al-Siyassa*, a newspaper published in Kuwait. Handala was a ten-year-old refugee boy, shown with his back to the reader and the world as he watched the farcical and often tragic charade of Palestinian political life. Al-Ali explained:

> The child Handala is my signature, everyone asks me about him wherever I go. I gave birth to this child in the Gulf and I presented him to the people. His name is Handala and he has promised the people that he will remain true to himself. I drew him as a child who is not beautiful; his hair is like the hair of a hedgehog who uses his thorns as a weapon. Handala is not a fat, happy, relaxed, or pampered child. He is barefoot like the refugee camp children, and he is an icon that protects me from making mistakes. Even though he is rough, he smells of amber. His hands are clasped behind his back as a sign of rejection at a time when solutions are presented to us the American way.

Al-Ali further explained:

> I presented him to the poor and named him Handala as a symbol of bitterness [the Arabic *handal* means "bitter"]. At first, he was a Palestinian child, but his consciousness developed to have a national and then a global and human horizon. He is a simple yet tough child, and this is why people adopted him and felt that he represents their consciousness.

Al-Ali had been a refugee in the Ein al-Hilwa refugee camp in Lebanon and learned to draw on the walls of the camp shelters. Following his assassination in 1987, Handala became a Palestinian national icon and a symbol of persistence, critique, and creativity.

The HCC is on the only street inside the camp that is wide enough for a car to pass. A painting by youths covers its facade. The cultural signs in the mural encapsulate the HCC's vision: education, art, and politics. The mural presents several images: an old woman in traditional dress carries and leads young children; Handala holds a pen that writes the words *Beit Jibrin;* a boy and a girl hold hands and dance the *dabkeh,* a traditional folk dance and a form of cultural heritage in

Palestine that symbolizes and reinforces national identity; and two other children have their arms on each other's shoulders. When entering the center, one encounters a large world map painted on fabric and a hand-drawn map of the camp's narrow alleyways that includes the name of each household. On the wall of the library are portraits of al-Ali, the Palestinian intellectual Edward Said, and the Palestinian novelist Ghassan Kanafani.

The HCC was formally established in 2000. Its founding committee elected Abu Ahmad as the center's director and set the modest goal of having the center's first project be the establishment of a children's library. Without money for the HCC, the founders decided to give some of their own books to build the library and to ask for book donations from individuals, local NGOs, and universities. In a few months, the HCC had gathered dozens of random titles, none of which were suitable for children but books nonetheless. It took anther year for the HCC to have a functioning library dedicated to youths and children.

The day the center opened, more than 180 children aged six to fourteen years arrived to register. The HCC was the first community center to open in the Beit Jibrin camp in its then fifty-year history, and the children and most families in the camp were enthusiastic about the initiative. The families saw the HCC as a place that could supplement their children's education and provide them an alternative to the streets where most of them spent their days. With the help of local and international volunteers, the HCC began providing painting classes, chess training, homework assistance, and remedial education.

Things were not as easy as the founders had imagined they would be. In the first years, the HCC lacked skilled volunteers to run programs including theater and computer training. Meanwhile, the available financial resources were not adequate to maintain the operational costs of the center, which was forced to close down for a few months. One year after the official establishment of the HCC, the al-Aqsa Intifada broke out. The camp's location on the seam line between Bethlehem's Area A (the designation for PA-controlled areas under the Oslo Accords) and Area C (the designation for areas under the control of Israeli occupation forces) made it an ideal starting location for the daily demonstrations that headed toward Rachel's Tomb, the site of a nearby Israeli military base. Most camp children threw stones at the Israeli military position, and many were injured.

Abu Ahmad and other HCC founders increasingly felt pressure from the community to reopen the center. Parents would question them: Why is it closed? When will it reopen? How can we help? Many families relied on the HCC as a place where the children could play rather than demonstrate, and other families thought of it as a site for education and release in an era of extreme violence. One father of an HCC child described the time as follows: "I used to ask about the reopening of the center because one of my children had suffered severe psychological trauma because of the daily military attacks and shooting of the camp. He suffered sleep disturbances, bed-wetting, and he isolated himself. The only thing that made him feel better was when he was participating in dabkeh dancing. The center became essential for my child's mental health. That is why I wanted the center to be open."

The HCC's founding committee attempted to meet the challenge and began a fund-raising campaign, proposing an emergency plan to foreign donors. The idea was to reach out to international NGOs and international pro-Palestinian philanthropists to collect funds for building a new center and implementing education programs. The fund drive was productive, and the HCC began a new phase, demolishing the old structure and laying the foundation for a new facility. The new HCC was stronger than the original. It introduced new emergency programs in response to the reality that the al-Aqsa Intifada brought. For four years, the camp was under nearly nightly military attacks, shelling, and shooting. Several people from the camp were killed, dozens were injured, and the majority of houses suffered some form of direct shelling.

Most Beit Jibrin children exhibited signs of trauma, anxiety, and other psychological disorders. Abu Ahmad believed that "it [2001–4] was the moment of *sumud* [steadfastness], and the HCC needed to provide the means for it." The center's approach to sumud was a trauma-reduction program that focused on cultural entertainment activities such as music festivals and art workshops. With the support of UNRWA and local NGOs, it also provided psychosocial counseling for the children and their families in the camp.

Despite the devastating aggression of the occupation in the West Bank and the unbearable violence inflicted on the people in the camp, the HCC founders and youths insisted on an international spirit in their work. They constantly compared Palestinian resistance with different struggle traditions in apartheid South Africa, Ireland, and Algeria and with the civil rights movement in the United States. They felt it was important to make these comparisons because many people in the camp did not know that other regions had similar trials. For certain founders of the HCC, it was important to get these politics and ideas out there, for "people to make connections." HCC activists saw these examples as educational tools for better understanding Palestinian conditions. For instance, Ireland was a case where the partition of the country did not bring peace but rather radicalized more people to fight back. Algeria represented an example of the defeat of colonial powers. South Africa and the U.S. civil rights movement were used to evoke the discrimination policies of the State of Israel and to think about possible solutions, such as a state of equal rights for all its citizens, Palestinian and Jewish. The HCC also organized musical and artistic activities about experiences of human suffering around the world. Abu Ahmad points out how "our common humanity necessitated informing our community about injustices worldwide and protesting them. It forced us to make a performance about victims of the nuclear bombs in Japan, to organize lectures and to show documentaries about Martin Luther King, Gandhi, and Malcolm X."

Among the many children who joined the HCC were Issa and Maher. Both were born in 1988, when Abu Ahmad was in Ansar 3. Issa was the first of five children, and Maher the third, also of five. Their lives resembled that of any other child in the Beit Jibrin camp. They divided their time between attending school for half of the day and playing games with their peers in the camp's streets. The camp's lack of facilities meant sports were not an option, with the exception of informal soccer games played in the narrow alleyways. Neither Issa nor Maher developed any particular hobby or interest, but they did obtain survival skills by playing and fighting with other kids in the community.

They were in the sixth grade when the al-Aqsa Intifada broke out. The uprising impacted all sectors of society in the OPT. Economically, the least affected was the professional sector, including employees of NGOs and PA public employees. Palestinian workers in Israel, such as Issa's father, were the most affected, for since the mid-1990s opportunities in Israel had decreased significantly for them. With the eruption of the al-Aqsa Intifada, Palestinians in the OPT were subjected to long-term curfew policies, the strict policing of their movements, and the banning of travel to work inside Israel. Issa's father was forced to find a job within the West Bank. Lacking higher education, he could not get employment other than low-paying construction work in Bethlehem. To save money, the family transferred Issa from his private school to an UNRWA school. Unlike Issa, Maher moved from an UNRWA school to a private school, counter to the general pattern in Bethlehem. His family was concerned that because of the political instability, Maher would get into dangerous situations. Students from the Beit Jibrin camp used to walk to their UNRWA schools in the nearby Aida refugee camp, a journey that became increasingly dangerous with the new reality of the intifada. Furthermore, Maher's family was keen on removing him from the context of the refugee camp, worrying that if he stayed in the UNRWA system with other youths from the camp, he was more likely to get involved in politics, especially on reaching early adolescence, the traditional age when youths become politically active.

Maher's family was very supportive of his joining the HCC, which it saw as a good place for him to learn new skills, develop a hobby, and reduce the time he spent in the streets. In contrast to Maher, Issa describes his family as "conservative and not encouraging" of his becoming a member. In fact, at first they prevented him from doing so, insisting that the HCC would cause him to disregard his religious duties. So in his enthusiasm to join, Issa lied to his family, telling them that he was heading to the mosque when in reality he was going to the HCC.

Issa and Maher joined the dabkeh dance troupe, one of the center's first projects. As Abu Ahmad notes, the troupe aimed "to combine art and politics, individual creativity and collective commitment." It consisted of fifteen twelve-year-old dancers, eight males and seven females. Since the HCC building lacked sufficient space, the troupe began their training in homes and sometimes in the streets. After a few months, the dancers mastered the essential steps and began preparations for staging a full-length performance.

When Issa and Maher turned fifteen, both began taking more central roles in leading the HCC's activities, particularly those of its dabkeh troupe. Issa, together with another youth, started training the fifteen-year-olds' dance troupe, and Maher began teaching the younger children basic dabkeh steps. "It was the moment we [the HCC founders] felt the success of the center. The fruitfulness of the center was to see a new generation capable of taking initiative," Abu Ahmad explains. Issa and Maher were two of many teenagers to take on responsibilities in the HCC, whose daily activities began to be run in large part by them and their peers—the first generation of dabkeh dancers.

The new generation of volunteers wanted to leave their mark on HCC activities and programs and thus took the initiative to organize the first performance of the dabkeh troupe, which was held in the camp's only wide street. A majority of camp residents attended the event, which included a dance by both dabkeh groups, the boys wearing Palestinian flags on their chests and the girls wearing traditional embroidered dresses. Issa and his cotrainer chose two songs for the performance: "Romanna" (Hand grenade) and "Nasheed al-Intifada" (The intifada song). Their justification for their choices was that "it was impossible to use anything other than patriotic and revolutionary lyrics. Everything around is death, resistance, and violence," Issa commented.

The HCC is open every day for all the youths and children of the camp. One of the youths described it as the only public place in the camp, with the exception of the mosque, "but unlike the mosque," he said, "it is a place to have fun." On a daily basis, approximately fifty to seventy youths and children visit the HCC. Some of them use the library, comprising a few hundred books, while others frequent the computer room, a small room housing seven old computers that are constantly in use. Since these machines are not always connected to the Internet, most of the kids use them to play games and on occasion to write school reports. The HCC administration has expressed concern about the games, as a lot of them include shooting, killing, and graphic military attacks. All violent games were uninstalled several times, but the youths would always reinstall them or install new ones. In the end the administration decided to let the children play these games but for a limited time per day.

Violent computer games are popular among youths worldwide. Nonetheless, in Palestine their prevalence is due in part to the violent political context. The seven computers at the HCC connect to one network, so several boys and girls between the ages of seven and fourteen can play together in one game, fighting against one another or as part of one team. One of the games popular in the summer of

2008 was clearly an American production. It has a team of solders attacking a hypothetically terrorist military base in a desert landscape. What is surprising is that it has been dubbed into Arabic from English, and players now hear the words *Allahu akbar* when one of the enemy fighters is shot down. What is interesting is the fact that the soldiers, despite their U.S. army uniforms, are shouting "Allahu akbar" and the enemy, who are supposed to represent Arab or Muslim terrorists, are speaking incomprehensible English. The role reversal shows how new technology facilitates new imaginings, new perceptions, and perhaps new identifications. These games differ from those that older generations used to play, such as marbles, hide-and-seek, and one called (Israeli) Army vs. Arabs. Army vs. Arabs consists of two groups of children simulating a war, with the former group armed with pieces of wood shaped like guns while the other group is armed with stones. Most kids preferred to be an Arab despite the predetermined results of the game, which usually ends with the Army taking the Arabs into custody. Yet it continues when the Arabs break out of jail. One of the HCC kids commented on the game, "It was impossible [for me] to imagine an Arab-Palestinian army."

For the youths, the HCC was not merely a space to play games but primarily an educational center containing a library, computers, chess training, and a Ping-Pong table. The HCC also schedules educational programs, such as remedial-math instruction and Arabic and English language classes, as well as academic support for children during the school year. In addition, nonmember children come to the HCC to engage in artistic activities on the occasions when it holds art workshops and art therapy classes. The HCC sponsors those who demonstrate artistic talent to take art classes in Bethlehem.

Music and dance have a special place in the HCC's vision. Nineteen children are enrolled in classes for violin or oud, one of the main Arabic stringed instruments. Music classes usually take place at the HCC, while some students also go to advanced music schools in Bethlehem and Ramallah. Dabkeh dancing training takes place three times a week, with approximately forty children participating, divided into two age groups. Each group has its own training, the younger dancers concentrating on basic movements and the older ones developing performances, or *lauhaat,* a form of dancing that combines thematic, theatrical, and expressive dancing with traditional dabkeh movements.

Abu Ahmad's community activism and political opinions made him a target of the occupation army. He was arrested again in 2006, charged with organizing youths for "terrorism," and served a year and a half behind bars. He spent most of it reading, reflecting about his past, and thinking about the future of his fellow prisoners, who were predominantly in their teenage years and early twenties. This period in prison reaffirmed for him the "accuracy of [his] political vision" and solidified his views about the nature of occupation, which was a policy "essentially not to give [Palestinians] the right to be humans." The right to humanity, for Abu

Ahmad, transcends the demand for statehood and political independence. It is a fundamental demand to be seen as an equal:

> My last imprisonment opened my eyes to the fact that I was less than a human in their [the Israelis'] eyes. I am a thing they hate. I only want to be seen as a human with life and dreams.... My anxiety comes from how I perceive them versus how they perceive me. I know a lot about the Jew [Israeli] who is living five minutes from me in Jerusalem, [whom] I might not like but never hate.... I hate the soldiers, the prison guards, and the occupation apparatus. I constantly think of what is the way out of this [conflict]. I become more anxious when I see [Palestinian] society heading toward political radicalism and religious conservatism.... I understand why that is. People see only destruction and oppression.

Then he added, "Could the solution be like what happened in South Africa? Maybe ... but seeing reality [the situation on the ground], it seems it is closer to the example of the Native Americans.... This usually wakes me up from the utopia of beautiful intellectual daydreams [*ahlam elyaqatha*], because I sense that our people want political independence, which has almost become like a nightmare these days.... I don't know the way out, and I don't want to answer that. Why should I answer it? They [Israelis] have all the power; the question should be directed to them."

Alongside the HCC's political framework, education continues to be a key issue in Abu Ahmad's community development plans, because, as he argues, "our human resources are the only resource in the refugee camps." After his release from jail, he went back to education, enrolling in a masters program in development focusing on community initiatives like the HCC. He sharpened the center's primary goal—providing quality education to the camp's youths—and launched several education-oriented initiatives, including scholarships to local and international universities. Issa was one of almost forty youths to get a scholarship from the HCC. It enabled him to earn an international baccalaureate diploma from the United World College of the Atlantic, a prestigious preparatory high school in Wales, and later to be admitted to the University of Essex in England to study philosophy and political science. He believes his future is to go back to the Beit Jibrin camp and continue his work at the HCC.

The Israeli military invasion of Area A in the spring of 2002 made the occupation more visible to the younger generation of Palestinians. Army tanks were constantly patrolling Bethlehem. The children and the youths of the camp did not miss an opportunity to let the occupation forces know that that they were unwelcome. Youths, according to Maher, "knew that a stone would do nothing to an armed vehicle, but [they] wanted the army to know that we don't want the occupation." Stone-throwing events increased in the Beit Jibrin camp in the following years, and greater numbers of youths got involved in the national struggle.

Political party affiliation began to regain its value among them and in society in general. Dozens of youths from the camp were arrested, including fourteen dancers from the dabkeh troupes, and nine remain in custody, Maher among them. He was arrested in 2008 just before his twentieth birthday. Maher describes his jail time as "eye opening and educational," similar to Abu Ahmad's words about his first prison experience, but he refrains from saying more "for security reasons," which means his personal safety.

Edward Said noted that perhaps the greatest battle Palestinians have waged is the one over the right to a remembered presence. Such presence is not merely represented in a national narrative but rather created by the everyday life of people with aspirations, hopes, and a strong belief in their ability to make change. It is not clear what kind of change the work of Abu Ahmad, Issa, Maher, and other HCC members will bring. Yet their stories remind us that anticolonial nationalism is still the central driving force in Palestine and that the national liberation framework is not an ideology or false consciousness but rather a set of practices embodied in ordinary people's lives.

To what extent has the HCC been successful in achieving its goals? Though its efforts are plagued by obstacles from the occupation, the PA, social conservatism, and cynicism and despite the complex reality of poverty and oppression, its activists still believe in themselves as agents of change. This social biography of Abu Ahmad and his Handalas has aimed to evoke that agency and to shed light on a part of the political, cultural, and sociological context of the OPT.

A NOTE ON SOURCES

This collective-account biography of Abu Ahmad, Issa, and Maher is based on intimate knowledge of their experiences, families' lives, and work at the HCC. It was collected through multiple in-person interviews with Abu Ahmad, Issa, and their families and phone interviews with Maher from prison in the summer of 2008.

SUGGESTIONS FOR FURTHER READING

al-Ali, Naji. *A Child in Palestine: The Cartoons of Naji al-Ali*. London: Verso, 2009.
————. "From Lebanon to Kuwait, the Cartoonist Has So Far Survived Attempts to Stop His Work." *Index on Censorship*, Vol. 13, No. 6 (1984), pp. 12–13.
Farsakh, Leila. "Palestinian Labor Flows to the Israeli Economy: A Finished Story?" *Journal of Palestine Studies*, Vol. 32, No. 1 (2002), pp. 13–27.
Nashif, Esmail. *Palestinian Political Prisoners: Identity and Community*. New York: Routledge, 2008.

Peteet, Julie. "Male Gender and Rituals of Resistance in the Palestinian Intifada: A Cultural Politics of Violence." *American Ethnologist*, Vol. 21, No. 1 (1994), pp. 31–49.

Rosenfeld, Maya. *Confronting the Occupation: Work, Education, and Political Activism of Palestinian Families in a Refugee Camp.* Stanford: Stanford University Press, 2004.

Saʿdi, Ahmad H., and Lila Abu-Lughod, eds. *Nakba: Palestine, 1948, and the Claims of Memory.* New York: Columbia University Press, 2007.

Taraki, Lisa, ed. *Living Palestine: Family Survival, Resistance, and Mobility under Occupation.* Syracuse, NY: Syracuse University Press, 2006.

CONTRIBUTORS

SAFA ABU-RABIA is a PhD student in the Department of Interdisciplinary Studies at the Ben-Gurion University of the Negev and a faculty member in the Mandel Center for Leadership in the Negev. The subject of her dissertation is the construction of historical discourse among Arab-Bedouin women of the 1948 generation in the Negev. She is also a business consultant, a group leader in the field of social and financial empowerment, and a columnist for the *Mizad Sheni* (On the other hand) journal.

ALA ALAZZEH is a PhD candidate in social and cultural anthropology at Rice University and a faculty member in the Department of Sociology and Anthropology at Birzeit University. He is the coauthor of *Toward a New Internationalism: Readings in Globalization, the Global Justice Movement and Palestinian Liberation* (Ramallah: Muwatin, 2006; in Arabic) and has published several academic and journalistic articles on Palestinian society and politics.

BADER ARAJ is an assistant professor at Birzeit University, Palestine. He completed the requirements of his PhD dissertation, titled "Suicide Bombing and Harsh State Repression: The Second Palestinian Uprising, 2000–05," in the Department of Sociology at the University of Toronto. His general areas of interest are political sociology, suicide bombing, revolutions and social movements, and sociological theories. Since 2006, he has authored or coauthored several book chapters and articles on these subjects in leading sociology, political science, and security studies journals, such as *Social Forces, Political Science Quarterly, Studies in Conflict and Terrorism,* and *International Sociology.* Currently, he is studying the ongoing Arab uprisings.

RAMZY BAROUD is an internationally syndicated American Arab columnist and the author and editor of the *Palestine Chronicle.* He is the former head of AlJazeera.net's English Research and Studies Department and taught mass communication at the Malaysia campus of Australia's Curtin University of Technology. He is the author of several books that have been translated into multiple languages. His latest volume is *My Father Was a Freedom Fighter: Gaza's Untold Story* (London: Pluto Press, 2010). For additional information, visit http://ramzybaroud.net.

NITSA BEN-ARI is a professor and the chair of Diploma Studies for Translation and Revision in the School of Cultural Studies at Tel Aviv University. Her major research interest lies in translation and ideology: manipulation, subversion, and censorship. Her 1997 book, *Romance with the Past* (Niemeyer), examined the role of the nineteenth-century German-Jewish historical novel in the emergence of a New Hebrew and a new national Hebrew literature. Her 2006 book, *Suppression of the Erotic in Modern Hebrew Literature* (Ottawa University Press), focused on censorship and self-censorship. Ben-Ari is also an editor and translator. She has translated into Hebrew twenty-seven books from English, French, Italian, and German (including Goethe's *Faust* and *Hermann und Dorothea* and Schiller's *Die Räuber*). She is the chairwoman of the Israeli Institute for the Translation of World Masterpieces.

PHILIPPE BOURMAUD is an assistant professor of contemporary history at the Université Jean Moulin—Lyon 3 (Lyons). His extensive stays in academic institutions of the Palestinian Authority, Jordan, and Lebanon enabled him to complete a PhD at Aix-en-Provence University, with a dissertation under the title "'Ya Doktor!' Devenir médecin et exercer son art en 'Terre sainte': une expérience du pluralisme médical dans l'Empire ottoman finissant (1871–1918)." He also edited *De la Mesure à la Norme: les Indicateurs du Développement* (Bangkok: BSN Press / Institut Français du Proche-Orient, 2011).

LÆTITIA BUCAILLE is an associate professor of sociology at Bordeaux University and associate research fellow at CERI-Sciences-Po (Paris). Between 2003 and 2008, she was a junior member of the Institut universitaire de France. She has studied Palestinian society for many years and also works on postconflict and postcolonial societies in a comparative perspective. Her books include *Growing Up Palestinian: The Israeli Occupation and the Intifada Generation* (Princeton: Princeton University Press, 2004) and, with Amélie Blom and Luis Martinez, *The Enigma of Islamist Violence* (New York: Columbia University Press, 2007). Recently, she has published *Le pardon et la rancœur: Algérie/France, Afrique du Sud—peut-on enterrer la guerre?* (Paris: Payot, 2010), the winner of a 2011 Seligmann Prize, and "Armed Struggle and Self-Esteem: Ex-combatants in Palestine and South Africa" (*International Political Sociology*, Vol. 1, No. 5 [March 2011]).

ROCHELLE DAVIS is an assistant professor of anthropology at the Center for Contemporary Arab Studies, School of Foreign Service, Georgetown University. She is currently a fellow at the Woodrow Wilson International Center for Scholars, working on a project on the U.S. military's conceptions of culture in the wars in Iraq and Afghanistan. Her most recent book, *Palestinian Village Histories: Geographies of the Displaced* (Stanford: Stanford University Press, 2011), won the Albert Hourani Book Award from the Middle East Studies Association in 2011.

DAVID DE VRIES is a professor of history in the Department of Labor Studies at Tel Aviv University. His research interests are modern labor and business history in Palestine and Israel. Among his publications are *Idealism and Bureaucracy in 1920s Palestine: The Origins* of *"Red Haifa"* (Tel Aviv: Ha-Kibbutz Hameuchad, 1999; in Hebrew); *Dock Workers: International Explorations in Labour History, 1790–1970* (Aldershot: Ashgate, 2000), coedited with Sam Davies, Colin Davis, Lex Heerma Van Voss, Ludewij Hesselink, and Klaus Weinhauer; and *Diamonds and War: State, Capital, and Labor in British-Ruled Palestine* (New York: Berghahn Books, 2010). He is currently writing a book on strikes and society in the history of Palestine and Israel.

NELLY ELIAS is a senior lecturer and the chair of the Department of Communication Studies at Ben-Gurion University of the Negev. In her studies, she combines research on media audiences and the sociology of immigration. Her recent projects deal with the role of mass media in the lives of immigrant children and adolescents, media representation of Russian-speaking Jews in different cultural contexts, and the religious transformation of the immigrants from the former Soviet Union to Israel. She is the author of *Coming Home: Media and Returning Diaspora in Israel and Germany* (Albany: State University of New York Press, 2008) and has published extensively in leading academic journals in English, Hebrew, and Russian. For additional information, see www.arikonga.co.il/bgu/nelly_elias/main_en.htm.

MICHAEL FEIGE is a sociologist-anthropologist who teaches at the Ben-Gurion Research Institute at Ben-Gurion University of the Negev. His fields of interest include social movements in Israel, especially Gush Emunim and the West Bank settlers; the history of national archaeology in Israel; and issues of collective memory, such as the commemoration of David Ben-Gurion in Israel society. His latest book, *Settling in the Hearts: Jewish Fundamentalism in the West Bank* (Detroit: Wayne State University Press, 2009), won the Yonathan Shapiro Award for best book in Israel studies.

MICHAL FRENKEL is a senior lecturer of sociology and anthropology at the Hebrew University of Jerusalem. Her research focuses on the transformation of local and transnational social orders in the context of the globalization of management practices and the cross-national transfer and translation of organizational and states' work-family policies. Among her articles are "The Politics of Translation: How State Level Political Relations Affect the Cross-National Travel of Ideas" (*Organization*, Vol. 12, No. 2 [2005]), "The Multinational Corporation as a Third Space: Rethinking International Management Discourse on Knowledge Transfer through Homi Bhabha" (*Academy of Management Review*, Vol. 33, No. 4 [2008]), and, with Yehuda Shenhav, "From Binarism Back to Hybridity: A Postcolonial Reading of Management and Organization Studies" (*Organization Studies*, Vol. 27, No. 6 [2006]).

JOSEPH B. GLASS teaches in the School of Advancement at Centennial College in Toronto. He is a geographer specializing in historical and contemporary issues in Israel, the Middle East, and Canada and has written on the development of modern Jerusalem, biographies in historical-geographical research, Canadian and American Jewish migration to Palestine, and the role of local intermediaries in the development of Israel. His most recent book, coauthored with Ruth Kark, *Sephardi Entrepreneurs in Jerusalem: The Valero Family, 1800–1948* (Jerusalem: Gefen, 2007), received the award for best academic monograph in the fields of Turkish banking, finance, and economic history in 2009. In recognition of his contributions to the development of Canadian studies in Israel and internationally, Glass was award the International Council for Canadian Studies' Certificate of Merit in 2009.

NEVE GORDON is a professor in the Department of Politics and Government at Ben-Gurion University of the Negev and the author of *Israel's Occupation* (Berkeley: University of California Press, 2008).

RUTH KARK is a professor emerita at the Hebrew University of Jerusalem and has written and edited twenty-four books and two hundred articles on the history and historical geography of Palestine/Israel (see http://geography.huji.ac.il/.upload/Kark/prof%20Kark.htm). Her research interests include concepts of land and patterns of landownership in the Middle East and Palestine/Israel; settlement processes; and Western civilizations, ideologies, interests, activities, and interactions with the local populations in the Holy Land. Her recent studies and publications focus on global indigenous and Bedouin land rights; women and gender; and Sephardi and mizrachi (Middle East and North Africa) Jewish entrepreneurship in Palestine/Israel. Her books relevant to this study are *Sephardi Entrepreneurs in Eretz Israel: The Amzalak Family, 1816–1918* (Jerusalem: Magnes Press, Hebrew University, 1991) and *Sephardi Entrepreneurs in Jerusalem: The Valero Family, 1800–1948* (Jerusalem: Gefen, 2007), both written with Joseph B. Glass, and *American Consuls in the Holy Land, 1832–1914* (Jerusalem: Magnes Press, Hebrew University, 1994).

AZIZA KHAZZOOM is a senior lecturer in sociology at Hebrew University. She obtained her BA from Wellesley College and her PhD from the University of California, Berkeley. Her work traces the formation of ethnic inequality among Jews in Israel in the 1950s, combining quantitative and qualitative methods. Her book, *Shifting Ethnic Boundaries and Inequality in Israel, Or: How the Polish Peddler Became a German Intellectual* (Stanford: Stanford University Press, 2008), argues that concerns over producing the state as Western were a central dynamic in determining who was excluded and who included in the developing society. In addition, she has published in the *American Sociological Review, Social Forces,* and *Signs* and has held National Science Foundation and Israeli Science Foundation grants.

REBECCA KOOK is a senior lecturer in the Department of Politics and Government at Ben-Gurion University. She completed her PhD at Columbia University and is interested in questions relating to the constitution of collective national identity and memory as well as the role of collective identity in the stability and governability of states. She is the author of *The Logic of Democratic Exclusion: African Americans in the U.S. and Palestinian Citizens of Israel* (Lanham, MD: Lexington Press, 2002).

JULIA LERNER is a lecturer in the Department of Sociology and Anthropology at Ben-Gurion University of the Negev. Her research interests are the anthropology of knowledge and migration studies. On the crossroads of these fields, she explores the relocation of ideas and people and studies both the cultural changes in post-Soviet Russia and Russian-speaking immigrants in Israel. Among her recent publications are "'Russians' in Israel as a Post-Soviet Subject: Implementing the Civilizational Repertoire" (*Israel Affairs,* Vol. 17, No. 1), "The Managed Soul? Adapting Therapeutic Self at Post-Soviet TV" (*Laboratorium: Russian Review of Social Research,* Vol. 3, No. 1), and the forthcoming coedited anthology "*Russians" in Israel: The Pragmatics of Culture in Migration* (Jerusalem: Van Leer Jerusalem Institute and Hakibbutz Hameuhad).

MARK LEVINE is a professor of history at the University of California, Irvine; distinguished visiting professor at the Center for Middle Eastern Studies at Lund University, Sweden; and senior columnist at Al Jazeera. His books on Israel/Palestine include *Overthrowing Geography: Jaffa, Tel Aviv, and the Struggle for Palestine, 1880–1948* (Berkeley: University of California Press, 2005), *Impossible Peace: Israel/Palestine since 1989* (New York: Zed Books, 2009), and *Reapproaching Borders: New Perspectives on the Study of Israel-Palestine* (Lanham, MD: Rowman and Littlefield, 2007), coedited with Sandy Sufian.

SONIA NIMR is an assistant professor in the Department of Cultural Studies at Birzeit University in Palestine. She received her PhD in history from Exeter University in 1992 and writes books for children and youths in both Arabic and English. Her English books include *A Little Piece of Ground*, which she wrote with Elizabeth Laird (Chicago: Haymarket, 2006), and *Ghaddar the Ghoul and Other Palestinian Stories* (London: Frances Lincoln Children's Books, 2008). She has served as an education officer in the British Museum and as the head of the Museum Department in the Palestinian Ministry of Tourism and Antiquities.

ERIN F. OLSEN is a PhD student in the Department of Sociology at the University of California, San Diego. She has worked as a Hebrew and Arabic instructor, and her interests include immigration, Diaspora literature, language policy and preservation, narrative force during revolutions, the reenchantment of knowledge and religious experience, and religious minorities of the Middle East. She is currently living in Qatar and is researching topics related to the Arab Spring.

TALIA PFEFFERMANN is a postdoctoral scholar in the Department of Sociology and Anthropology at the Hebrew University in Jerusalem. She wrote a PhD dissertation at Tel Aviv University, "Hidden Entrepreneurs: Women's Independent Economic Activity in Israeli Society, 1930–1980" (2011), and published "Women's Silence in 'The Life of a Worker in Her Homeland' (1935) by Henya Pekelman," in *Gender in Israel*, edited by Margalit Shilo and Gideon Kats (Beersheba: Ben-Gurion University, 2011; in Hebrew). Her current research focuses on the history of women's working lives in Palestine and Israel.

MORIEL RAM is a PhD student in the Department of Politics and Government at Ben-Gurion University, where he teaches courses on Israeli geopolitics and the Israeli-Palestinian conflict. His research deals with the normalization process of contested spaces, mainly focusing on a comparative analysis of Israel and Turkey.

GERSHON SHAFIR is a professor of sociology at the University of California, San Diego; the director of its Institute for International, Comparative, and Area Studies (IICAS); and the founding director of its Human Rights Minor. He received his BAs in political science, economics, sociology, and anthropology from Tel Aviv University; his MA in sociology from the University of California, Los Angeles; and his PhD, also in sociology, from the University of California, Berkeley. He is the author or editor of seven books, among them *Land, Labor, and the Origins of the Israeli-Palestinian Conflict, 1882–1914* (Cambridge: Cambridge University Press, 1989); *Being Israeli: The Dynamics of Multiple Citizenship* (Cambridge: Cambridge University Press, 2002), the winner of the Middle Eastern Studies Association's Albert Hourani Book Award in 2002, coauthored with Yoav Peled; and *National Insecurity and Human Rights: Democracies Debate Counterterrorism* (Berkeley: University of California Press, 2007), coedited with Alison Brysk.

REBECCA L. STEIN is an associate professor of cultural anthropology at Duke University, the author of *Itineraries in Conflict: Israelis, Palestinians, and the Political Lives of*

Tourism (Durham: Duke University Press, 2008), and the coeditor, with Ted Swedenburg, of *Palestine, Israel, and the Politics of Popular Culture* (Durham: Duke University Press, 2005) and, with Joel Beinin, of *The Struggle for Sovereignty: Palestine and Israel, 1993–2005* (Stanford: Stanford University Press, 2006).

SALIM TAMARI is an editor of the *Jerusalem Quarterly* and a professor of sociology at Birzeit University. Currently he is a visiting professor at Georgetown University. He authored *Mountain against the Sea* (2009) and *Year of the Locust* (2011), both from University of California Press, and coedited *Family Papers: The Social History of Bilad al Sham* (2009), *Ottoman Jerusalem* (2005), and *Mandate Jerusalem* (2006), all from the Institute for Palestine Studies in Beirut and all in Arabic.

YARON TSUR was among the founders of the Open University of Israel in 1975 and chaired the team that created its texts in modern Jewish history, including the four-volume *Jews in an Era of Transformation: Introduction to Modern Jewish History* (Tel Aviv: Open University Press, 1978–80; Spanish translation, 1981; revised Russian translation, 2002–3). In addition to Jewish history, he is interested in Muslim societies and the ethnic problem in Israel. In 1990 he started at Tel Aviv University, where he founded the Jews of Islamic Countries Archiving Project (http://jic.tau.ac.il) in 1999 and the Historical Jewish Press website (http://jpress.org.il) in 2004. He was also the chair of the Department of Jewish History (2007) and head of the Doctoral School of Jewish Studies (2008–10) at Tel Aviv University. Among his books are *A Torn Community: The Jews of Morocco and Nationalism 1943–1954* (Tel Aviv: Am Oved, 2001; in Hebrew), which won the Shazar and Toledano prizes, and *Jews among Muslims, 1750–1880*, 3 vol. (Tel Aviv: Open University Press, 2003–4; in Hebrew).

MAHMOUD YAZBAK is a senior lecturer and the chair of the Department of Middle Eastern History at the University of Haifa, where he teaches Palestinian history. He studies social history and issues concerning modern Palestinian society. He coedited, with Yfaat Weiss, *Haifa before and after 1948: Narratives of a Mixed City* (Dordrecht: Republic of Letters, 2011) and published *Haifa in the Late Ottoman Period: A Muslim Town in Transition* (Leiden: Brill, 1998) and, most recently, "The Muslim Festival of Nabi Rubin in Palestine: From Religious Festival to Summer Resort" (*Holy Land Studies*, Vol. 10, No. 2 [November 2011]).

INDEX